MEDAL WITHOUT BAR

MEDAL WITHOUT BAR

BY
RICHARD BLAKER

The Naval & Military Press Ltd

Published by

The Naval & Military Press Ltd

Unit 5 Riverside, Brambleside
Bellbrook Industrial Estate
Uckfield, East Sussex
TN22 1QQ England

Tel: +44 (0)1825 749494

www.naval-military-press.com
www.nmarchive.com

IT was not any independence of thought or peculiarity of emotion that had established the Cartwright type (of man or of business) where it stood in the London of 1914, and where it remains to-day.

An individual Cartwright was as likely, while other men were beating ploughshares into swords, to think any un-National thoughts as his scalp was likely to shed its smoothly-brushed covering and miraculously put forth the wool of a Zulu or a Hottentot.

The War, to Charles Cartwright, was a startling and stupendous situation upon which his first silent comment was to thank God for the Old Boy.

He himself was at that time thirty-six, and the Old Boy, his father, sixty-one—good, Charles reflected, for another dozen years. A dozen years from 1914 would make John, the son of Charles, twenty-six. He would have been in the office by then for four or five years, after Oxford. He would thus be a ready and a competent man by the time the Old Boy was dead ; for the Old Boy was hard as nails, and John was a long-headed youngster.

Cartwright therefore, broadly speaking, had nothing to worry about. The War would not mean his leaving Dorothy in the lurch. The Cartwright, Mollison and Cartwright practice in Clement's Inn was itself as sound as a bell ; and besides, the Cartwright nose as inherited by the Old Boy was a nose for investments.

The War for Cartwright was thus convenient.

Any possibility of his having kept out of it was as remote as the possibility of his having, fourteen years earlier, kept out of anything so obvious as the firm of Cartwright, Mollison and Cartwright.

Between himself and Dorothy there was no discussion

of it.   After about seven weeks of War he told her that it
was probably " that Chancery Company—no, not Territorials—but an Officers' Training Corps affair " that he
would join.

Then he suddenly stopped, a little aghast at the relationship of him to his wife wherein he could calmly make such
an announcement to her and she could calmly say, " Oh."

Then he remembered again that the day was the
fifteenth anniversary of their wedding and he produced
from his pocket his fifteenth present to her to commemo-
rate it.   She undid the little package ; a manicure set in
tortoiseshell and silver.   She kissed him.   Her lip
trembled; and she went (but not hurriedly) from the
room.

John's only immediate comment before dinner was,
" I rather expected it would be the Inns of Court that
you'd join ; not this private-school thing."

And yet Cartwright had a feeling of thin ice about it
all ; as though there would have to be more trouble of
some sort than this before he could embark upon the
adventure that was, for all his sombre steadiness (remembering that he was thirty-six), a tremendous one.

After dinner, when John and David had gone upstairs—
John to more home-work, David to bed—and he and
Dorothy were alone, he explained the economic convenience of it all to her : the firm would go on quite well
without him while he was away.   (In saying how sure he
was that the Old Boy would do the work of both and
continue paying over Charles's share, he allowed Dorothy
to see that he had not yet discussed it with his father.)
He went on to say that there was Johnnie.   He reminded
her that Johnnie was not only fourteen now, but a very
solid fourteen.   In a few years, a very few years, he would
be pulling his weight in the firm and a deed could be drawn ;
the Old Boy would agree to it like a shot—and old
Mollison, her father—settling a share of the partnership's
proceeds on Dorothy, so that if . . .

At this point he took her hand and squeezed it.   He
added, " So you see, old girl, you've nothing to be
afraid of."

" That," she said, very slowly, " is not the kind of thing I'd be likely to be afraid of." There was a sting in the words ; and he recognised it as the trouble he had expected—some of the trouble that must be the inevitable price of adventure.

" No," he said. " Of course not, dear. But—you see what I mean. It all—seems to fit in rather neatly."

" Yes," she said. And then, " I can't help wondering, though, if it would all have fitted in so neatly if—if I had been twenty instead of thirty-five ; fifteen years ago——"

All he could think of, and he thought of it with sudden inspiration, was, " my dear, it's fitting in—it's jolly well *having* to fit in—with a good many thousands of people who *are* twenty. . . . Honestly, Dorothy, would you prefer me not to do anything ? "

The question was unanswerable ; for she was a Mollison; and Mollisons and Cartwrights were of the nation's backbone, as indistinguishable as adjacent vertebræ.

She said, dully, " Oh—I quite see you've got to go."

They were playing no more than the part assigned to them by the impulse of the whole body, themselves contributing neither more nor less than vertebræ to this general impulse. Yet she in her contribution was as yet unmoving and wide-eyed, as though stunned ; while through him, now that he had told her and the boys, there ran a tremor.

Her question, that he had so neatly turned with another question, had been, considered strictly, irrelevant. But like so many irrelevancies, it drew sudden attention to a poignant fact : many things had impressed him of late, attracted him and repelled him. They had excited him, puzzled him, thrilled him and saddened him ; but never one of these things had chanced to be the kind of thing indicated by Dorothy's question. He saw, suddenly, the somewhat astonishing fact that he had altogether omitted a thought of the inmost relationship of himself and Dorothy as a possible target for this colossal blow of War. And he looked down upon her fine bosom and shoulders that rose and slowly fell to her breathing, and upon the top of her still head as he stood with an elbow

on the mantelpiece.   A prodigious yearning towards her
filled him.   Its suddenness and its shock caused the fine
shape of her to grow a little blurred and indistinct in his
eyes.   It became, for some moments, a quivering dazzle ;
and he knew that his voice, if he had tried to use it just
then, would have broken or cracked or done something
else equally absurd. . . .

With his two hands upon her further shoulder he pressed
her body against him.   " Oh, God—Dorothy," he said in
a voice low enough to evade any treachery on the part of
his throat, " you—you've been marvellous, marvellous,
darling.   Such a brick."

He was looking back over fifteen years, seeing—now
that an immense moment had revealed to him the
full achievement—all the hundreds of quiet days that
had gone towards its making.

He saw trivialities and absurdities among those days ;
a settlement conference had taken him once to Paris (not
so long ago either) and he had made rather an idiot of
himself there for a few silly hours.   Then, before that—five
years ago, or six or seven—he had tended towards some
drivel with a client, a youngish widow with turquoise ear-
rings ; but that had stopped in time—well, almost in
time. . . .

These items flicked by before his vision.   But what he
saw most steadily in those fifteen years was the way
Dorothy's end had always been kept steadily up.   He
was shaken by the disruption he had announced of such
an achievement, and by the fact that he had never before
this moment recognised the achievement itself.   All the
other disruptions and dislocations he had weighed and
deeply considered ; speaking the words of a wiseacre,
while in fact only absorbing the leaders in his newspaper.

' Moratorium ' was the last big word of the wiseacres,
a word of inspiration ; and Cartwright grasped at it now.

World-credit, like Dorothy's achievement in wifehood,
had become apparent only when the smooth working of it
was threatened—possibly shattered for good and all.
And as he stood looking down upon the coil of her hair
another thought sprang up to startle him : what was he

thinking of, any way, meddling in this damned war?
" Business as usual. . . ." Surely in that robustious
slogan, too, there was something ? But he smiled, knowing that for himself, at any rate, there was nothing ; for
his small share of ' business ' was amply manned by the
Old Boy and old Mollison ; and after the Old Boy and
old Mollison there would be John when he had finished with
Westminster. And following John, David. " Business
as usual " would go on without him.

Dorothy lowered her head a little, allowing her cheek
to lie upon his wrist ; and soon his wrist was wet with her
quiet tears.

" Don't, my dear one. Don't," he said very softly.
What he meant, groping about in the tangled darkness
of his thoughts, was some vague application of the wiseacre's device of ' Moratorium.' Dorothy, in other words,
in so far as she was an affair of himself, must be postponed.

Dorothy saw it, too. " No, my dear," she said ; and
the tears dried upon his wrist and upon her cheek. " I
won't."

The end manned by her was, as ever before, up. He
leaned down and raised her face and kissed her lips.

. . . . . .

With his father Cartwright found no possibility of
' Moratorium.'

" I wondered . . ." the old man said, when Charles
had finished speaking.

It was typical of Cartwright's state of mind during
those days that he had not opened the subject for his
father with a discussion of the rights or wrongs of war
in general or of his own enlistment in particular.
He had opened it with the proposition, and a very
short draft, of a deed of settlement.

" Wondered ? " said Charles.

" H'm," said his father. " Yes. I quite saw that
you'd have to be up and doing—being under forty. Forty
seems to be the age-limit that's somehow established
itself for the team. Why it shouldn't have been thirty-
eight or forty-two, God knows." It sounded a little

cynical, but Cartwright knew that the Old Boy enjoyed sounding cynical.

" Even thirty-eight would have let me in," he suggested.

" The point is," said his father, looking at him over the top of his glasses, " there are a thousand and one perfectly decent reasons for staying out. And you know it. Looking at the thing squarely and quietly, if we'd had conscription—as we ought to have had it years ago and not got caught napping like this—and as we'll *have* to have it yet—your type and age would be the last to go."

" Just as well first as last," said Charles. He was pretty certain that the old fellow was bluffing.

" And then this enlisting business," his father went on. " Line of least resistance. Why don't you go in for a Commission ? You could get one to-morrow."

" Because I don't know a thing about it all," said Charles. " I can't shoot and I can't shout." It was the truth, but not the whole truth. He was of the backbone (only one lusty vertebra) and could not, by his nature, contribute any kind of leadership to the body's movements.

If he had told the whole truth so far as he was himself aware of it he would have said simply, " I don't want to be an officer. I want to be in the crowd." But accurate shooting with a rifle was taken, in those early days, to be the essence of war-winning, with a clear and fluent uttering of words of command as a desirable adjunct and embellishment.

He explained, " It isn't just ordinary enlisting, you know. It's a training corps. All decent fellows—and the efficient ones will get Commissions in time."

" Don't forget," said the old man, " that you're no chicken. Roughing it will come pretty hard at your time of life."

" I'm as fit as a fiddle," said Charles. " Never felt fitter in my life." They were thinking, both of them, of tough men incessantly on the move ; they were assessing the endurance required to leave the eye steady and the trigger-finger untrembling after nights of long and stealthy marching and days of brisk battle.

The old man moved in his chair, and the movement made him appear suddenly older and frailer. He withdrew his eyes from his son's and focused them on the middle of his glasses. He sat forward and folded his hands on his desk. " We must remember, son," he said, " that it isn't only lying down in ditches and shooting off guns that's required. Things have got to be kept going. For every man with a rifle there's got to be a man somewhere with quick brains, and probably a pen. It's just as necessary, and just as decent and honourable—more honourable, if he's more fitted for the job."

The poor old chap, Charles could see at a glance, was talking it over with himself.

" Dad," he said, and smiled. ' Honestly, would *you ?* "

Old Cartwright thought steadily for a few moments. Then he spoke up with the millions of other ancient Cartwrights who were wistfully saying the same thing at the same moment : " My boy, if I were twenty—no, damn it, twenty-five—years younger . . ."

" Very well," said Charles. " Then that's that, isn't it ? "

" H'm," said his father. " That's that, indeed ! What does Dorothy say ? "

" Nothing," said Charles. " I mean, of course, she sees it. She knows there's nothing else to be done. It's sink or swim."

" Have you never wondered," his father said—very detached, so that the question was only an aside, a sort of footnote to the text proper of their conversation, " why some people—and I mean really decent people of our sort—don't just say, ' sink' ? After all, sudden death isn't exactly swimming. Fat lot of swimming we—your mother and Dorothy and the boys and *you*—would get out of it if you went and got shot ? After all, getting shot is a kind of ultimate, isn't it ? "

" And a fat lot of swimming *any one* would get out of it if no one went and got shot ; and we had the Bosche over here, running our show *his* way ! "

There had been the *Punch* cartoon of the little peasant

boy holding the gate of the field that was Belgium against the onslaught of a great snorting bull that was Prussia.

The snouty, slit-eyed, vapidly lecherous face of ' Little Willie ' had been stamped for ever on the British mind ; and millions for whom the science of physiognomy had begun and ended with the ability of recognising acquaintances had become familiar with the approximate shape and implications of the ' Hapsburg mouth.'

Halfpenny newspaper stories of atrocities were confirmed by the penny dailies and behind them all stood the august, oracular utterance of the threepenny.   (This was the kind of fact that David, fourteen years later, was to get hold of.)   Men in Clubs and women in suburbs knew some one who at least knew some one whose friend or son or brother had been killed in action.

The question of old Cartwright, therefore, had been no more than a quite futile speculation ; and the retort of Charles was its irrefutable answer.

" It's rough luck on Dorothy all the same," the old man said.   " And on your mother.   You might as well admit that."

" Don't you think you're perhaps just grousing because you can't be in it, too ? " Charles suggested.

" I dare say.   And I expect the women are really a bit jealous.   All this business of husbands and lovers rushing off and enlisting.   It loosens up their hold."

" Oh, only for a bit," said Charles.   " Moratorium, you know.   They'll get it back afterwards."

" I dare say.   Those for whom there is any afterwards." He stood up and straightened out his waistcoat and re-adjusted his glasses, facing the situation afresh.   " I can tell you one thing, my boy.   Your mother is going to raise merry hell.   Anyhow, I've done my best to stop you."

" Yes," said Charles.   " But what's the use ?   When a place is on fire you've jolly well got to give the fire-brigade a hand, haven't you ? "

" I think you might run down and tell her that yourself. Take it better, you know.   She might think I've encouraged you.   How are you off for cash just now ? "

" Oh, pretty good, thanks," said Charles.   " Plenty to go on with.   If you'll fix this thing up for Dorothy."
" Yes," said his father.   Then he smiled.   " You've suggested five hundred.   Do you think the pound is going on being worth a pound for long ?   Let me tell you, *I don't.*"

A T the time of his enrolment the question " Infantry or Cavalry ? " came to Cartwright as a mild surprise, a little like saying " Piano or Oboe ? " to some one who had asked for music lessons.   Anything but Infantry struck the general run of early volunteers as somewhat of an eccentricity.   He therefore answered, without any hesitation, " Infantry."

His uniform was quickly produced by his city tailor, his boots by his bootmakers in the Strand who also supplied him with a very good imitation of a regulation belt.   A rifle he only touched and handled for a few minutes each day.

In February of 1915 he went into Camp at Wilverley with the ' unit.'

He told Dorothy the truth about this movement—he did not know what it meant ; it might mean anything. Enviable battalions of Territorials were already in the trenches and more were on the point of going.   " At the Front " had quite given way to " In the Trenches " in common speech.   Mud and water were being recognised as the local colour of soldiering instead of the zip of bullets and flash of bayonets and sabres.   The number of British killed, wounded and missing now well exceeded sixty thousand ; the war, as people were saying, was being ' brought home to them.'   Already a new spirit could be sensed in the training camps.   The robustious swashbuckling of the few first months was giving way to something a shade grimmer.   The idea of some kind of patient skill was laying quiet hold upon the minds of

soldiers.   Half a million visualisations of a romping about
in the open with a rifle and a belt of ammunition had been
one thing.   Prowling in viscid mud, working in shallow
holes, sneaking through fences of barbed wire armed not
with a rifle and bayonet but with wire cutters and a home-
made bomb was quite another.   Standards of good
soldiering were shifting from the 'Absent-Minded
Beggar' qualities to the less dramatic but cannier
technique of the 'Better 'Ole.'   Courage, from a matter of
cheering and charging, was already a matter of grinning
and hanging on.

Men, so far, had gone off from Cartwright's Unit,
gazetted to battalions by a process known among the
Cadets as 'sniping.'   All, automatically, had applied for
Commissions when joining, and it was impossible to detect
any system according to which groups or isolated individuals were 'picked off' and gazetted.   It was not
alphabetical; it was not according to age; and it was not
just as obviously, according to physical fitness or general
efficiency.   A suspicion grew till it was almost a certainty,
that the thing was to get "asked for" by some particular
Colonel who was training a new battalion.   Cartwright
did not know any such Colonel so he turned away from
the order-board day after day seeing that his name was
not among the 'sniped.'   The feeling grew upon him
after a very few weeks at Camp that he was getting
absolutely no further.   He was called out, from time to
time, to drill a section and then a platoon.   He lost his
nervousness in the knowledge that others would have to
do it too.   He got through it as audibly and correctly as
most; but he felt no particular urge as yet towards a
Commission.   He liked the ranks and the jostle of a right-
hand man and a left-hand man and a covering-file—but
still, he was getting no further.   A way out of this
occurred to him in the possibility of working a transfer,
enlisting in a territorial battalion among 'decent fellows'
something like the London Scottish or Artists.

While this plan was developing in his mind he was sent
for, one morning, by the Adjutant.

The Adjutant was a Mons veteran some six or eight

years younger than Cartwright. He had lost his left hand, and one eye-socket was empty.

" Your name Cartwright ? " he asked.

" Yes, Sir," said Cartwright. He said " Sir " to boys or old rascals quite automatically now and without the least stiffness, as easily as he went " on the hands down," and then " raised " and " lowered " a dozen times without the least trouble.

" Well—I've got a job for you, Cartwright. Bombing Instructor. You can stand at ease."

Cartwright obeyed ; first properly at ease, and then " easy."

He said nothing, because the information as yet conveyed nothing to him.

" You'll be a Sergeant," the Adjutant explained. " On the permanent staff."

" I—er—as a matter of fact, Sir, I was just going to ask if I might see you. I'm rather keen on enlisting in something. I——"

" That's quite all right," said the Adjutant. " You have *got* to enlist before you can be made a Sergeant."

" But I want—you see, Sir, I'd like to get out."

" I dare say," said the Adjutant. " So would I."

" Oh, but it's very different for you, Sir," Cartwright suggested with some indignation. " You've *been* out."

The Adjutant calmed his indignation by saying very quietly, " The cases are exactly parallel, Cartwright. I would like to go out and can't. You would like to go out—and can't. That's all there is to it. You've got to enlist in something. You'll be promoted Sergeant and attached here for duty. You can enlist in anything you like. We've got the necessary papers here—Blues, Greys, Buffs, A.S.C.—anything you like. I'll get you promoted, and there you are."

Cartwright was beginning, for some reason or other, to like this Adjutant. " Suppose I just waited on here for my Commission, Sir ? " he asked.

" You'd wait," he answered, with a confident twinkle in his surviving eye, " a hell of a long time." He spoke as one who knew what he knew ; for after all, getting this particular job with only one hand and one eye was an achievement to give confidence in the means that had achieved it. Then, in a very friendly tone he continued, " Much better take the stripes, Cartwright, and do your waiting as a Sergeant. You see, we're not entitled to permanent Officer-Instructors on the establishment of this little show ; only N.C.O.s."

" It's rather disappointing," Cartwright said humbly. Then experimentally, to try out the possibilities of revolt, he said : " I don't think there's anything to prevent my just going off and enlisting somewhere—anywhere—off my own bat."

" There's nothing at all to prevent it." The Adjutant smiled. " You're not a real soldier yet. You could quite well leave this lot, by just resigning, and go and enlist— say in Edinburgh. And then I'd have you by the short hairs. This is a first-rate telephone." He stroked the instrument admiringly. " You'd be spotted in no time and sent back here. We could still promote you to sergeant—or not—just as we happened to think fit. You see, Cartwright, you'd better remain a civilian if you want to go on following your own sweet bloody will instead of obeying orders."

It was a jar to be reminded, with the faintest indication of contempt, that he was not even a soldier yet—he who had been impatient at not getting out.

" I don't object to obeying orders, Sir," he said ; " it's just—don't you see——"

" Yes." And the Adjutant was all friendliness again. " I know. It must be rotten. But there's a terrific lot to be done outside the trenches, you know. Licking all this new stuff into shape is a man's job all right, and bombing is going to be the guts of infantry work for the next seven years of the war. We could put in some good stuff here, making sound officers in quick time. It's next best to the real thing."

" Yes," said Cartwright. " Next best."

" I never saw such a fella ! " said the Adjutant. " D'you know how long I'd served before I saw any action ? Eight years. And d'you know how long I'd been training before that ? Most of you will have started and finished with your soldiering well inside of that time. Believe me there's no hurry. Everything in good time."

"But you said this instructing was to be a permanent job," Cartwright reminded him.

"Permanent hell!" was the retort. "We can do what we can but we can't exactly *guarantee* anything just now, can we ? "

Guarantee ? thought Cartwright ; and the word threw a sudden light which became immediately a fog. With no evidence whatever at that moment, and with no proofs thereafter, he knew beyond any doubt that the cunning hand of the Old Boy had been moving somewhere.

The confidential friendliness of the twinkle in the Adjutant's eye seemed to justify the question, "Where did you meet my father, Sir ? "

Cartwright knew at once that he had misjudged his man. " I've never set eyes—eye I should say—on him in my life." The Adjutant's eye was grown cold. "That's all, Cartwright. You can fall out."

Cartwright's heels, with Cartwright from the ankles upwards feeling a distinct fool, clicked together and he saluted and 'fell out.'

"By the way!" the Adjutant recalled him from the door. "You can come and enlist when I've got the Corporal here. He's got the papers and can raise a Bible somewhere, I expect. Better put in the name of my lot— the Worcesters. All right. Carry on."

MEDAL WITHOUT BAR   CHAPTER III

CARTWRIGHT left the orderly-room with a new belief added to the furniture of his mind ; it was in the stories told of the devotion of men to their officers. This was the first real, Regular officer with whom he had had any dealings that even approached to intimacy. The youth, discipline and nonsense quite apart, by dint of what seemed to be sheer assurance and balance had

B

stumped him and altogether wiped the floor with him. Leadership and command were qualities inherent in the fellow, something quite distinct from the mere bounce and swearing that he had often enough encountered before.

Now if he, Cartwright, had been *that* sort of man, he thought, he would have struck out for a Commission right at the very start. . . . But the Adjutant had had eight years of service in which to learn it. . . . So Cartwright marched back to the parade ground with a quite new and very warm and very profound admiration for the regular army.

There had also been revealed to him the existence of that mystery and sinister and beneficent power behind all these new affairs of life, the Power for whose propitiation the only instrument was what was recognised, in after times, by the name of ' wangle.'

So Cartwright thought next of the cunning Old Boy and the strings he must have quietly collected together in his hand ; and after him he thought of Dorothy. Well, Dorothy would be pleased ; and she, he was somehow sure, was not in the Old Boy's sly secret. He wrote to tell her ; and after giving her the bare information he went on to say, " It's this young Adjutant fellow, Capt. Henderson. You never saw such a youth. There's more in what's left of him than in any other six complete men. I suppose he was only a platoon commander last September until all the other men were wiped out, and he commanded the Battalion till he, too, was laid out ; but he's got a grasp of all this soldiering business and a heart for it—if all the men in that first lot of ours were anything like him, no wonder the Bosche was stopped . . ." and then Cartwright wondered what on earth was possessing him to write this testimonial. He wondered what Dorothy would think of it ; and, finally, what comment Henderson himself would make if he could have seen it. He tore up this letter and wrote another one. It contained only the news of the three stripes that were coming to him and of the probability that, on the strength of them, he would soon get a week-end leave.

He did not get the next one, for he did not make his

application for it in the manner of a soldier, but broached it to the Adjutant tentatively, in the manner of a considerate civilian ; he asked him if there would be anything special to be done during Saturday afternoon and Sunday.

Henderson said, " Yes, Cartwright. We've got to win the war between us, during Saturday and Sunday. I was going to see some people for a couple of nights ; but I've scratched, so that we can get really down to it and make some plans. I shall want you here at two-thirty."

" Very good, Sir," said Cartwright, and wrote to tell Dorothy not to expect him for a week or two. He felt now that he was no longer standing quite still but moving, forward.

He reported to the Adjutant punctually on Saturday, and was told, while the Adjutant was writing a letter, to sit down and that he might smoke. When his letter was finished, Henderson said, " Things move damn' slowly, Cartwright ; but I dashed up to see an old Sergeant of mine at Millbank and got him to hand over the stripes and numerals and buttons from his tunic. He won't be needing them again." He handed Cartwright a small parcel from his pocket. " You'll have to stick the stripes on that cadet thing you're wearing till you can get an imitation G.S. one made by your tailor. Put the stripes up ready to start work on Monday."

" Yes, Sir," Cartwright said. He was not only moving, but Henderson produced the feeling that the movement was important.

" First of all," Henderson continued, and the coldly businesslike attitude of him changed into something a little self-conscious and more friendly ; " ——preamble," he mumbled shyly. " I've got to get one or two things off my chest and you've got to treat them as—well, *you* know." He paused, tidying his papers. " This job is a godsend to me. If I hadn't nailed it down—anyhow, the point is I have nailed it down and here we are. You are—well, a gentleman among other things—and I don't mind telling you that I tried like hell to work it that you should stay here as an officer. But they couldn't be certain. You see, the Establishment only allows for one

officer and that's got to be me. We're allowed six Sergeants, though, attached permanently for instructional
purposes. That's why I went in for this other dodge.
See ? "

" Yes," said Cartwright. " I don't mind not being
an officer. I just didn't like—at first—missing my
chance."

" Changed your mind, now, have you ? "

" No. Not exactly that," Cartwright tried to explain.
" But it doesn't seem quite so bad. And I suppose I
will get out—some time ? "

" I dare say you will," said Henderson. " But I'm not
going to hurry it so long as we go ahead with this job as
swimmingly as I hope we shall." Suddenly, after producing a loose cigarette from his table-drawer and lighting
it with a match struck upon a box held between his
knees, he sat up and said, " Good God, man ! If I could
only get you to realise the chance we've got here ! I had
only just about a month to see something of it all—and
then about five in which to think it over. . . . You
might think it's all just because I'm a foot-slogger, and
prejudiced—but I tell you it's a fact ! You can bring
guns, and guns, and more guns and bigger guns—but the
real guts of the whole thing is the foot-slogger. After all
the gunning and sapping and mining it's just hands and
feet that are going to win or lose—the best hands and
the best feet—the best guts. . . . It's Infantry that's
the back-bone of the whole show. It's the section and
the platooon that's the back-bone of the Infantry—and
it's the platoon commander that's the back-bone and the
marrow of the section and the platoon. Put *that* in
your pipe and smoke it. The subaltern—none of your
breezy Generals and brass-hats ; but the muddy-behinded,
one-pip fella—and by God it's up to you and me to
make him—some few hundreds or thousands of him—
and if that isn't a man's work, I'd like to know what is ! "

" Well," said Cartwright, " I'll do my best."

It struck him as a lame and slightly idiotic remark, but
it was the best he could do in such a hurry. For it was a
hurry ; Henderson was bringing a kind of life and move-

ment into the War that were new. The most that Cartwright had felt so far was a kind of thrilling vibration caused by an outside disturbance terrific, but dim and very distant. Henderson brought it within the table's-breadth of him.

" You bet you will ! " he said. " See some of the poor muck we've got to do it with. I mean, you must admit they're not *all* the clean potato. Are they now ? "

" Well——" said Cartwright. " No. Perhaps not all. But they're not bad, you know." He felt a sudden surge of loyalty to himself and his fellow-civilians-turned-soldier in the grim emergency of the moment against the professional swashbuckler. " After all," he said ; " there must be something in every man Jack of them—us. There's no other reason for their being here at all."

" Oh ! " said Henderson coldly. " Isn't there ! My poor innocent Cartwright ! Never heard of jobbery and pot-hunting ? There's a good round dozen loafers among the cadets here at the present moment—I can talk to you like this because you're not a cadet any more but a Sergeant of the Worcesters—a good round dozen who have no more intention of seeing the trenches than I have of becoming Archbishop of Australia, if there is such a bird. Never heard of female relations, Cartwright ? Then how the devil do you suppose I got here ? —with only one eye and one flipper and less than ten years' service ? Oh, we'll get lots floating through here, using it as a rest camp on their way to nice little jobs of one sort or another. But it's up to us to do the best we can with the others."

" But, you know, Sir," said Cartwright, " all this is new to me just now. I'm only just getting the hang of rifle-drill and foot-drill and that sort of thing."

" Oh, blow that ! " said Henderson. " It's the inner inwardnesses of the job that are the most important in quick training. There are far better chaps than you to teach foot-drill and rifle-drill and physical jerks and bayonet work and all that ; long-service birds like Ruggles and Bighe and Foskitt. And I've snaffled a couple more. Throats of brass and eyes that wither and

blast recruits into shape.   You'll do the bombing, as I
said ; and a hell of a lot else besides.   You wait. . . ."

" Bombing ? " asked Cartwright.

" Yes.   I'll tell you more about that.   And there's an
office which is going to grow and grow, *and grow*, as we
settle down into our stride ; and offices were never my
strongest suit.   That—partly—is where you're going to
come in."

" Good God ! " thought Cartwright.   He said, " I'm
not particularly good at office work myself."   He knew
that one must move warily with this Adjutant of his.
" But I could lay my hands on an excellent man for you.
He's not fit for active service, but he'd be just the man. . . ."

" We might want him, in time," said Henderson.
" But not yet.   The way this show of ours is going to
work out is something like this : The Colonel will leave
us alone.   There'll always be one, of course, but he'll
live mostly on paper.   Later on I suppose we'll get a
convalescent.   If he's the right sort so much the better.
If he isn't, he won't bother us ; so that I'll be the C.O. to
all intents and purposes, and you've got to pull up your
socks and be sort of Adjutant."

" But what will I have to *do* ? " asked Cartwright.

" Everything," said Henderson.   " A decent Adjutant
can—and does—do everything.   He's the right-hand man
of the C.O. and the darling of the men."   One of the
things that Henderson had was this ability to toss a joke
into his headlong talk so that you did not know exactly
where the joke began and if it had ended.   " As for the
office *work*," Henderson continued, " don't you worry
about that.   The Corporal is first-rate and writes a
beautiful hand.   What you've got to do in the office—
is *thought*.   And you've not got to be too jolly conspicuous
over it either."

" I'm afraid I still don't quite see——"

" As a matter of fact," Henderson said thoughtfully,
" I don't either—quite—yet.   The fact is I jumped at
this job and went out after it bald-headed, setting one or
two sainted relations to pull strings hell for leather.
There's simply tons to be done.   I saw that at once.

I've been and talked to two or three old fellas about it
—and they didn't see the point ; seemed to think I hadn't
quite steadied down after my knock last September.
One asked if we had got any real rifles as it was no use
talking about anything till you had real rifles.   Another
said the first thing was to lick all these city-bred youths
into marching twenty miles a day.   Good God ! and all
they'll do when they get out there till they get knocked
out, will be sit on their behinds in mud and sneak about
a few hundred yards at night for exercise.   They can't—
not one of those old dug-outs—see that what you've got
to make is the *inside* of a soldier.   No, by Jove ! they
never saw Sandy Morrison holding a couple of tree-stumps
and a dirty little drain of a trench with twenty men
against a dozen acres of Bosches. . . . Then a dozen
men. . . . Then ten. . . . Then three.   And one of
Sandy's legs of no use to God or man.   They never
saw Teddy Kyle, the gunner, squatting beside a chimney
on a roof from two o'clock till dusk, shooting his section
of guns while the tiles were peeled off the roof and finally
poor old Teddy came down in a bundle with the chimney.
. . . No.   They don't understand, these poor old
johnnies.   What use would proper rifles and hefty
calves have been to Sandy and Teddy Kyle and their
men if they'd had nothing inside them ; if they hadn't
been *soldiers ?* "

Cartwright still could not accept that particular feeling
with which Henderson persisted in speaking of ' soldiers.'

" Aren't they ' soldiers ' themselves ?   These old men
you've tried to talk to ? " he asked.

" God knows——" said Henderson sadly.   " They
may have been, once.   But they're dead now and it's a
pity they couldn't have shuffled right out of the road
before this war started.   Because it's *live* soldiers that
are wanted this time and no mistake.   They can talk
themselves black in their ugly old faces about ' war of
attrition ' and ' war of inventions ' and ' scientists ' and
all that drivel ; but it's a personal, hand-to-hand, and
man-against-man show if ever there was one.   Dash it !
The lines are as near together in places now as the base

lines of a tennis-court! And I'd like to know when *they* ever got as close as that—and *stayed* as close as that for more than five seconds—in South Africa or Balaclava or wherever else they wielded their muskets and bows and arrows and gatlings and pom-poms."

" My own idea of soldiering," Cartwright said, " was just no more than joining up and learning the job and getting it done the quickest way, and getting it over." So much at least he felt obliged to state against the snobbery—even though it was inspired snobbery—of a professional soldier's thinking that the salt of the earth was professional soldiers.

" Quite," said Henderson. " That's good enough. The only point of my eloquence is that the first and most important thing to teach people who go to work in banks is honesty. It's important, of course, that they should make four every time they add two and two together—but any silly ass will do that without much bother. It's *quality* that's going to count in soldiers more than anything else and more than ever. I've seen it, Cartwright ; that's why I've got so worked up about it. I've seen something pretty damn' close to it in some of the old Bosches who gave us such a merry time of it. But even the best of 'em seemed to fall short of it somewhere. Too solemn or something. Our fellas seemed a bit cheerier over it all ; as though they weren't making history so much as just playing the game all out and hell for leather. See what I mean ? "

" Yes," said Cartwright. " Of course—but still—I don't quite see what I've got to do."

" You've got to get the *idea*," said Henderson grandly. Then, " Sorry—because you've got it already. You've had it all the time. That's why it struck me that you were the man to back me up. . . . You know how you sometimes come across a fella somewhere and say to yourself at once, ' That chappie's the goods. He's *It* all right—white man and all that sort of thing. . . . It doesn't matter a damn whether he's a silly-ass, pudding-faced youngster or a lantern-jawed father of families like yourself. What I want to do is to send out officers from here so that whenever one of them reports to a Colonel the Colonel will think, ' This blighter's all right,' and when he's taken over a platoon the men will say ' good egg.' "

Cartwright smiled. " You ought to have been a parson, Sir," he said.

" Incidentally," said Henderson ; " I very nearly was —near as a toucher. But what's that got to do with it ? "

" It seems to me it's the moral side that's bothering you all the time," Cartwright explained. " What you want to do is not just turn clerks and schoolboys and business men into efficient soldiers but to turn men of one sort—men of every sort—into men of another. That's a parson's job, surely ; not an Adjutant's and a Sergeant-Instructor's ? "

Henderson's monosyllable was unanswerable. He paused after it and then went on slowly. " I wish you had known our ' old man,' Cartwright. He was among the first to take it in the neck, and every man who went down after that seemed to conk out as happy as a sand-boy just because the ' old man ' had gone before him. You ought to have seen that retreat of ours, the ' old man ' dead and left behind us ; and yet holding the rags of the battalion together—knocking the men up on to their feet from their empty stomachs, sending them from cover to cover as though his cracked old dribble of a voice was still gingering them along. . . . Don't tell me that you've got to be a blinking parson to make different men of fellows. Our old man did it in two shakes of a duck's tail. . . . And he was no parson. . . ."

And thus Henderson struggled to articulate his hazy dream of Samurai ; and Cartwright listened to him.

He reflected that he was eight or nine years older than this youth, and the reflection gave him some kind of vague satisfaction ; but he was thrilled by the dream.

Henderson himself, at the first meeting, had set emotions moving in him of the kind that had been dormant since the days when he had watched his house's famous scrum-half leaving a wake of enemy ' threes ' neatly handed off, and shooting over the line like an arrow.   Thus in Cartwright, too, was born an idea of Samurai ; but he still found himself staring at the puzzle of wondering what it was, exactly, that he was going to *do*.

Henderson threw a very little light by saying, " By the way, you'll have to detail a couple of Cadets to go down to the blacksmith's shop by the post office.   God knows when there'll be any proper dummy grenades for instructional purposes, so I've got the smith to make us fifty or sixty knobs of iron or some muck weighing a pound and thirteen ounces apiece for you to carry on with.   They're paid for.   A couple of suitcases will be best for carrying them."

" Very good, Sir."

" Another thing.   I'm putting the Sergeants in billets instead of that tent.   You can keep that for a Sergeants' Mess just the same, and there's a lot you can learn from the others about the ' two and two are four ' part of the job. . . .   You'd better fall out and go and doctor up that tunic of yours with my old Sergeant Hunter's stripes and numerals."

Cartwright felt that a mere springing to attention and saluting and turning smartly right would be a weak and inappropriate end to this discussion ; what seemed, quite vaguely, to be required was a symbol of friendship, but Cartwright knew of none that fitted the circumstances. He realised that it would be the work of some months to show Henderson that the flame he had sought to kindle was kindled brightly.

MEDAL WITHOUT BAR   CHAPTER IV

IN the tent, when he got back to it from Henderson's billet and orderly-room, Cartwright found it flatly and utterly impossible to unwrap the twist of brown paper in his hand and display his stripes and numerals, and then proceed with the needle and cotton from his suitcase to stitch them upon his tunic.

Bullock, who occupied the cot next his, had appropriated the hurricane-lantern and was reading "Infantry Training." Bullock never talked much to any one ; his greatest anxiety was to attract no attention during the period of waiting for his Commission. It was something of a mystery among those to whom he had talked at all why he had ever appeared in the Chancery Company ; for he had been in his second year at Oxford and it was an accepted fact that any fit man at Oxford or Cambridge could get an immediate Commission for the mere asking. And Bullock was as fit as the animal from whom he had borrowed his name. He had rowed in Junior Fours, the Togger and then the Eight. He could, if he had not been stolidly rowing, have played in the Rugby team, and could equally have filled gaps in the cricket eleven. But there was a dark secret about Bullock of which Cartwright alone knew—either because chance had thrown him into the next cot or else because his greater age and probable seriousness had drawn the confidence. The secret was that Bullock could talk quietly and fluently for minutes on end, sometimes for hours. He could get through days and perhaps weeks— but he never knew. There always lurked the menacing possibility of a fit of stammering. Whenever the threat became a reality Bullock was done. Nothing was left for him but blank, idiotic silence ; for there were no means in the world for untying the syllables that had got knotted up together in his throat. It was his absolute belief that the affliction would never come upon him when once he had got his Commission and all was clear before him for training with his men and getting to the front. A very old friend commanding a Kitchener's battalion was ready to ask for him. He had gone to Oxford on the fifth of August—to find that on the Board inter-viewing candidates for Commissions was the young Don to whom he had, for two terms, been reading essays in Roman History and from whose rooms he had twice retired in defeat at the hands of the enemy in his throat. He had not risked the selective interview. He had not risked a direct application to the War Office supported by his Colonel friend ; for at the War Office too, so he had heard, were interviews. After some months of patient waiting for a letter from a college porter he heard that the young Don whom he feared at Oxford had been posted to a battalion in training ; but by that time Bullock was sure that any interviewer at Oxford, even a deaf mute, would tie his tongue and make a fool of him. The first flood of recruits was over and he felt there would be both leisure and also some vague motive at Oxford for encompassing his defeat. . . . And then he had heard that through membership of the Chancery Company his way would be smooth and fairly easy. Men were gazetted, so he was told, through that select, small Corps, more or less in groups. So that he sat now swatting his drill-book, accepting the necessities that forced him to keep an eye open for the possibility that would let him through under cover of a group, untackled by an interview, to his goal. And he was monopolising the lantern whose light was required by Cartwright for the displaying of tokens that signified his own willingness to stay contented where every one else chafed to be away, further along the road. . . .

Cartwright could, perhaps, have talked to Bullock ; returned confidence for confidence, tried to kindle in him, too, the spark that Henderson had kindled within himself. But Adams also was in the tent, and Adams was no more capable of seeing that sort of thing than he was of flying. Adams had come to the Chancery Company from a farm of some kind that it had taken him four years to exhaust in South Africa ; and he despised every phase of soldiering except actual battle. Any kind of training towards the consummation of battle was so much idiocy or malingering. " Hell ! " was his argument. " Have you forgotten the Boers ? "—though he could not have been more than ten years old while the Boers were teaching whatever lessons they had taught to trained soldiers.

" The Adj. wants a couple of fellows to go down to the blacksmith's shop for some dummy grenades," Cartwright said.

Bullock immediately shut his " Infantry Training "

over the little map-scale that always marked his place in it. Cartwright thought that if Adams could be induced to go with Bullock, the stripes and numerals could tell their story in the lantern-light without explana-tion when they returned ; but Adams merely yawned.

" Oh, Lord ! " he said ; " it looks like their beginning to teach us to shy bricks now. Who hasn't known how to do that since the year one ? "

" It might be a little different when the brick is liable to go off in your hand and blow you to glory if you don't know how to look after it," suggested Bullock. But Adams only mumbled " More eye-wash," and rolled over on his cot from his stomach to his back.

" Well, come on, Cartwright," said Bullock ; and it seemed to be the only thing to do.

A unit like the Chancery Company lacked such a detail of organisation as a wheel-barrow ; so Cartwright and Bullock set out from the tent with two haversacks and a Gladstone-bag.

Cartwright said nothing of the things in his pocket. He felt that it might take longer than the walk to the blacksmith's and back to explain his position clearly—his position, that is, in relation to himself. If any one, a fortnight ago, had told him that all the curious yearnings within him would be satisfied and the unrest stilled by the prospect of sitting down in a Surrey village for some months, doing office work and instructing in the fantastic art of pitching bombs, he would have thought him an idiot. Yet here he was, after less than an hour spent with Henderson, satisfied to the point of being thrilled, at just this prospect. It occurred to him that Bullock, too, might be useful in Henderson's scheme—but he realised that Henderson himself was the only man capable of tackling Bullock on such a point.

When they got back to the tent Adams had not altered his position. " His nibs wants you again at the office, Cartwright," he said.

" What nibs ? " asked Cartwright.

" The Adj. He sent the office Corporal along in a great hurry, just after you had gone. I expect he's anxious

about his toy bombs. You'd better run along and tell
him Bullock and I are counting and polishing them
for him."

No, thought Cartwright, as he hurried to the Adjutant's
billet; it would be useless trying to explain the stripes
and numerals to a youth like Adams. He was an instance
of where Discipline would have to come in.

"Sit down, Cartwright," said Henderson, when
Cartwright had knocked at the office door and entered
and saluted. "I've been thinking. Good——" he had
glanced at Cartwright's still stripeless sleeve. "I'm
glad you haven't put the stripes up yet. You're going
on leave to-morrow. Two or three weeks special—I'll
let you know when you're to come back."

"Leave?" asked Cartwright. "Why?"

"It's better," said the Adjutant. "All this present
lot will be cleared by then—I'll get 'em off quickly and
you can start with a clean slate. It'll save a lot of
worrying that way."

"It's—I shouldn't worry much," said Cartwright.
"Of course there are one or two who might be a little
scathing; but I'd soon settle that. It wouldn't really
bother me."

"No, I dare say it wouldn't," said Henderson. "And
as a matter of fact I wouldn't care two hoots if it did."
His eye began to twinkle again with the twinkle that
Cartwright began to know so well when Henderson said
serious things lightly. "I'm one of those Napoleonic
gents who is willing to sacrifice the feelings of one to the
good of the many. I've pulled it off once to-day already,
haven't I?"

The question was a purely rhetorical one, and he
went on. "In the army—any army, I suppose—the
most poisonous thing is suspicion of favouritism, or
spite—which is the same thing turned inside out. Home-
service just now is either a matter of favouritism or spite.
Whichever way these fellows looked at it in your case
it would be a rotten thing among us, and it would be
handed on from group to group; and we don't want
any muck of that sort. I've got really big, whiskered

ideas about the kind of little factory we're going to build up here."

" Yes," said Cartwright and he smiled at the youth, for he felt that at last he was able to make a response more appropriate than saluting. " Yes—I had almost begun to suspect something of the sort."

" It *would* be something to have accomplished in this show," Henderson went on, almost dreamily. " We'll have it all our own jolly old way, Cartwright. We'll try to feel that every fellow who gets a Commission from here is absolutely the goods. That he'll pull up his socks and do his damnedest, and his damnedest will be something to write home about. And it'll be rather fun sitting here and watching the dispatches and the Gazette for names afterwards, and patting ourselves on the back. . . ."

" Yes," said Cartwright. " And the casualty-lists. . . ."

" God—yes," said Henderson. " They're pretty thick. We'll have to be busy, keeping up the supply. The Inns of Court are turning out over a hundred a week—and that goes nowhere—and things are quiet now, too."

" And yet *I* am going to stick here, looking on. . . ."

" You've just got to cut that out for good and all !" Henderson snapped. " I've thought of it—from your point of view, too. If you were to drift off now you'd be just one platoon commander. By staying here and sticking to the job with me you will be hundreds, possibly thousands, stock—seed—goose with the golden eggs and all that."

Cartwright shrugged his shoulders. " If I'd been out—even for a month—I dare say I'd feel differently. I'd—I just feel a little bit, sort of uneasy. That's all. I'm delighted, of course, for a lot of reasons. But there's something that just sticks, somewhere. If I'd already lost an eye, too——"

" H'm." Henderson made a bitter sound. " There's already some feeling getting cooked up about that, in certain quarters. Certain people are wondering if crocks like me can possibly have enough ginger to do any good—to imbue raw recruits. . . ."

"Good Lord!" said Cartwright. "Had you more ginger before?"

"I dunno," said Henderson. "Like the chappie and the violin, I'd never tried. There hadn't been anything to use it on—not like now. But you really *must* get over those scruple things of yours, Cartwright. They're sheer sentimentality—and we've got to be practical. I thought this leave brain-wave of mine would possibly lighten the cargo for you."

"It does," said Cartwright. "Like anything." He was thinking, most particularly, of Adams and his blunt, absolutely idea-proof mind.

"Good," said Henderson. "And, you know, I'll do anything else I can, as we go along."

"I don't suppose there will be anything else," said Cartwright. This was not ungracious. It merely stated the probable fact. Just as Cartwright was absolutely sure that the Old Boy had somehow got behind all this, so also he knew that Henderson was not deceiving him; however, the scheme had been started in his mind, the truth had developed that he and Cartwright had, in the current phrase, 'clicked.' They would get on together. The pleasantness of understanding would be added to daily life, and the work would prosper.

"By the way," said Henderson. "There'll be a lot of spare time hanging over. I understand you're married. There's no reason why your wife shouldn't join you if she's at a loose end. I dare say you could get a very decent billet."

"Oh . . ." said Cartwright, a little startled; for this was a surprising addition to his ideas of war. "Oh—well. It's a biggish household. It would have to be kept going somehow. I've two boys at Westminster."

"Just as you like." Henderson was very casual. "It cropped up in my mind. You see, I'm contemplating the great step myself. I expect I'll have taken it before your leave is up. I'm taking that little house near the Vicarage—for a year. I think it's safe to assume that the War will last another year."

Cartwright was absolutely innocent of any idea on this point. He said, " Congratulations."

Henderson said, " Thanks."

CARTWRIGHT wrote to his tailor that night, asking him to make and post to him at Chiswick, as soon as he could, two G.S. pattern tunics of heavy gabardine, with Sergeant's stripes, but no buttons or numerals.

On Sunday morning he took the first available train to London Bridge. From there he telephoned to Dorothy that he would be home to lunch and would be staying for two or three weeks.

She opened the front door for him. He had not been able to determine the exact way in which he was going to say the things he had to say. He had only settled on the general mood in which he was going to give the news— a mood of cheery, bland acceptance of fate ; a mcod, in short, that fitted a soldier of good *morale*. But about Dorothy, in the first instant of looking at her standing to the door-knob and in the moments of kissing her, he perceived a new quality. She smiled and her lips moved to his kiss ; but she had changed. "Statuesque" was the kind of word that alone could hint a description of this new quality, and it accorded ill with his selected mood of soldierly cheerfulness.

It was not his nature, however, to evolve lightning plans. He was obliged to stick to the old one. He could vary the detail within easy limits, but not the principle. He put down his suitcase and took her shoulders in his hands.

" I've some news, old girl l " he said. " Let's go into the drawing-room. We'll tell John afterwards."

They went into the drawing-room, Dorothy with the deliberate balance of one walking with confidence over a difficult way. She quietly shut the door.

" John knows already," she said quietly.

o

" It's damned smart of him, then," said Cartwright—gaily, for his plan still held.   " Damned smart of him—since I thought Henderson and I were the only people in the world who knew.   Even his Corporal-clerk didn't see the letter to the War Office."

" But John says it's quite usual," Dorothy said. " Every one gets leave before going out—it's a sure sign." And she didn't tremble as she spoke.   She did not avert her grey eyes from his, but gazed steadily, with the light in them neither hot nor cold. . . .

It was too much for him.   " You old goose ! " he said. " In this case it's a sure sign of something else.   I've been given a job that will keep me sitting here so that I won't go out for—probably never."   He got a ring of triumph into his tone.

Dorothy closed her eyes and fell upon the floor.

" God Almighty ! " Cartwright exclaimed aloud ; for he had never before seen any one fall in precisely that way —by the amazingly direct process of merely ceasing to stand.

He had been quite unable to intervene, but the completeness of her sudden plasticity had saved her from any kind of bump.   He quickly raised her and propped her against the sofa and knelt with her face between his hands, mumbling " Dorothy . . . Darling . . . Old girl . . . I say . . ." till her eyelids flickered and disclosed her eyes again, grey and deep and unflinching ; and a smile flickered to her lips.   She kissed the palm of his hand, a disturbing caress.   " Sorry, dear," she said and rose from the floor to one corner of the sofa with a pressure on his shoulder.   " So sorry.   But when one has been *waiting* for a thing to happen . . ."

" Yes.   One gets sucked in if it doesn't happen."   He sat down beside her and lighted a cigarette.

He had filled his squat little case the night before and the cigarette he now took from it was the last.   By his new forethought, however, there were two unopened yellow packets in his suitcase.   It was astonishing the number of cigarettes one had begun to smoke during these days ; cheap, pungent things. . . .   There was nothing else for it—he would have

to get one of those new, long cases instead of having to fill
up two or three times a day. . . . And there was the
astonishing fact of Dorothy, first standing at the door
looking out from behind a sort of mask and speaking from
a thousand miles away, and then the mask disappearing
and Dorothy crumpling up on the floor as though dropped,
quite soft, out of a spoon ; then the tingling kiss in the
palm of his hand. . . . And his own bluffing in the
poignancy of all this, faithfulness to Dorothy forcing him
into infidelity to something else—into a pretence of sheer
delight in this home-service job.

"Old girl," he said and took her hand in the one whose
palm she had kissed. "We fellows don't seem to have
stopped to think how rotten all this must be for you. But
what's the use ?—you—you've just got to back us up."

"Oh, yes," said Dorothy. "Only—well, it was a little
sudden, wasn't it ? " Her smile now was no mask-smile.
It had the wistfulness that belongs only to life.

"You're a trump," said Cartwright. He considered
Henderson's suggestion of the possibility of finding rooms
at Wilverley. There was the question of some arrangement for John and David—shutting up the house for a
time, perhaps, and sending them as boarders ; or perhaps
Dorothy could find a Mollison or two to come and keep
house for the boys.

Her hand was caressing his.

There would, he supposed, be endless evenings down at
Wilverley. A little of the company of his fellow Sergeants
would go a long way ; he would no longer be the familiar
of any cadet-filled tent and Henderson would have added
to his own lofty rank a bride.

Dorothy's kiss in the palm of his hand tingled again at
her caresses.

"Dear," he said ; "it's pretty dull for you here, isn't
it ? "

"Yes," she said. "I don't think I could stand it any
more. I've arranged to try some—work."

It would be an overstatement to say that he was
offended ; and yet a sense that had never been questioned
before was questioned now, his sense of possession. . . .

He felt consciously decent in that he showed none of his
surprise.   He kept as steady as Dorothy had been when
he came home with his intention of joining the Chancery
Company of Cadets.

" Nursing ? " he asked, because the question was so
obvious.

" No," she said.   " Not exactly.   I couldn't get away
for that without making a lot of changes and difficult
arrangements.   It's at that home for Belgians which
was started in October.   I'm told that a lot of the women
who were helping at the start have gone away—become
V.A.D.s most of them ; and those who are still there are
getting rather sick of it.   It isn't much to do, but it's
something to keep one busy—part of the time.   Just four
hours a day, or night.   It'll leave time to look after
things here."

" I believe you would like to be doing something a bit
more thrilling," said Cartwright.   He laughed and pressed
her hand to his cheek.   " Something with a bit more
D.S.O. and V.C. about it."

She answered very quietly, " I don't mind what it is—
anything at all to get us through it.   It's—it's a little
different now that you are not going out."   She added,
"—at once. . . ."   But that made no difference to his
inability to talk about it.

" When does your new job begin ? " he asked.

" It began yesterday," she said.   " I'm on again to-
night.   Eight to twelve."

Here was another need for mild readjustment.   Cartwright said " Oh . . . Eight to twelve . . ." and she
said, " Of course, I could telephone and ask them to
change it as you've come home suddenly.   But it's a
little soon to be starting that, dear.   It's just what all the
difficulty has been about.   Every one started by feeling
they hadn't enough to do—then they all at once seemed
to get sick of it, and began to find other things."

" Rather not, old girl," said Cartwright.   " Don't think
of shifting it on my account.   You stick to it.   I'll be all
right."

" You could come along, too," she suggested.   " There's

quite a cosy office-room, and you might be amused talking to some of the refugees. They're quite nice, some of them."

" Righto," said Cartwright. " And, I say—let's not say anything yet about this job of mine ; I mean, about my being a sort of refugee myself."

" Charles," said Dorothy ; still there was no mask, but only the wistfulness that touched Cartwright in the new, extraordinary way. " You're not—uncomfortable—about it, dear, are you ? " She took his hand again. " Don't be, Charles. After all, you've offered yourself, dear, altogether—I know you had to. I would, too, if I could. But since you have offered yourself—altogether —the rest is out of your hands. If you're needed more in one place than another, surely it isn't any of your business ? "

Honour was satisfied ; that was what she was driving at. But her wistfulness and her very caress reawakened the discomfort which Henderson had utterly soothed. But he could not talk about it with her. That was clear.

" Every man can't decide for himself what he's going to do," Dorothy elaborated. " Or there wouldn't be any army, would there ? "

" Don't worry. I'm not the least bit uncomfortable," he lied broadly. " I'm taking whatever comes."

For some reason or other—or else for none at all—he omitted to give her any account of Henderson beyond stating that his Adjutant was a good sort ; one of the old crowd of Mons people, and one of the best of them ; with an eye and a hand gone.

H E wore mufti that night when he went with Dorothy to the Belgian Home—flannel trousers and a Norfolk jacket. One reason for this was that people were becoming versed by now in the lore of badges and numerals ; another was a fellow named Hamilton, who (he had gathered from Dorothy) usually

fooled about the Home during the evenings in the capacity
of Honorary Treasurer. He preferred not to appear
before this Hamilton in the same non-regulation, O.T.C.
jacket wherein he had answered his questions in the
District Railway three months before, concerning the
value of the function of the Chancery Company of Cadets.
Hamilton was one of those lions of patriotism—who
flourished and dreamed dreams till their dreams came
true in the bestowal upon them of styles and titles
invented for others. They were ' over military age '
when such a thing as military age did not exist. They
were afflicted with some internal medical mystery while
consumptives unobtrusively spat blood in the trenches.

Cartwright got through that evening peaceably by means
of heartiness and a few evasions, and a withdrawal from
the office to the refugees' general sitting-room as soon as
Hamilton took up his position with his books at the office
desk.

He smoked his pipe with a frail little printer from
Brussels and a conjurer from Antwerp. The other
members of the group round the fire did not distinguish
themselves from the group. They were sombre men ;
whatever anxieties they might have suffered had now
moved on, leaving them weary even beyond bitterness.
After an hour or so of their company Cartwright noticed
two or three incorrigibles among the group looking with
the kind of glance that was now prehistoric in a quality it
possessed of surrender, towards the women at the other
end of the room. And it came upon Cartwright as a
discovery that ' women,' in the old sense of the word with
all its implications, had faded out of the picture in a most
extraordinary manner. The other men with the printer
and the conjurer talked or were silent upon points of
military, geographical and statistical fact ; for these
points and these alone were now the verities. The two
or three sly dogs on the fringe of the group with their
inattention to the talk of the printer and the conjurer and
Cartwright, and their wandering away even from their
own secret thoughts, after women in the peculiar old way,
were survivors from a Lost World.

And Cartwright knew, walking home with Dorothy at twelve o'clock when she had hung up her white overall and cap and washed her hands with carbolic soap, that he had done right in saying nothing of the possibility of rooms in Wilverley. It was best that the moratorium should be observed absolutely—since it had to be, in fact, observed.

The matter of delivering grenades at a given spot from fifteen up to fifty yards away, with the maximum of accuracy and the minimum of fatigue to the sender, was a matter stark and august ; a necessity that left no room, anywhere, for Dorothy. And Dorothy, too, now had a canoe of her own to paddle—with the cap that fitted closely to her shapely head, and her white overall. She had cooked porridge in the last four hours and counted out rashers of bacon. She had counted, likewise, bed-sheets and pillow-cases and pyjamas and night-dresses ; and there was for him, Cartwright perceived, no room whatever in the kitchen and the larder and the basement where these things were done.

Surprisingly, this was not estrangement.

He pottered about from the bathroom to his dressing-room, smoking another of those cigarettes while Dorothy took a bath (after that laundry work at the Home). She came into the glow of the lamp over the bed, warm and fragrant.

He talked to her as he had not talked before, rewarding her with words which had never been a particularly loose change with him before, for her fifteen years of quiet devotion to their daily life. She was magnificent and always had been magnificent and she was lovely ; and he told her so. He had missed her, sleeping in a tent on his iron cot and straw mattress ; and this, too, he told her. It was a peroration to the speeches he had never or seldom made to her ; for somehow, in the old days, one had just expected loveliness and fragrance and magnificence—and there you were.

She did not again make him uncomfortable with allusions to the new and marvellous comfort within herself— the comfort whose revelation had knocked her to the floor

John, with his sardonic outlook, gave away none whatever of the thoughts that might have stirred within his long head. He said " Good egg," but that might have meant anything at all.

" It's home-service," his father explained, to draw him.

" There's one more river to cross," said John, unexcited. " The War is young yet."

The only reflection that Cartwright could get out of this was that John would make a solid enough man, in due course, to take care of the affairs of Cartwright's generally, and of Dorothy.

He put in an odd morning here and there at the office, lunching with the Old Boy and once with him and Mollison ; and all he felt that he was really doing at the office was getting in other people's way. He had climbed out of the water and the water had closed over the space he had occupied.

He was not sorry when a post card arrived from Henderson before his third week at home had ended, telling him the simple fact that he would report for duty next day.

Walking with him to the station Dorothy said, " Don't ever worry about money, dear. I've had a thing from the office saying your share of the business will be paid into a joint account for us. And besides, Father came out the other afternoon and told me that he is going to make me a special allowance while you're gone. I think you ought to have some of it to be really comfortable."

" My good girl ! " said Cartwright. " Don't you realise that I'm going to have a Sergeant's pay—whatever that is—a day—and everything found besides ? The question of money just doesn't exist any more."

After saying this and hearing the slam of the District Railway door, he was impressed by the weight of its truth. . . . That was what War did for one. Cares belonged to the lost world. There was no responsibility of action ; obligation towards women was suspended, and there was no more question of money. . . .

Cartwright opened his paper. There was a fresh colour

in the news now after the winter's weeks of sombre facts. The Canadians had brought it ; and even the dullest imagination was stirred with a vague pride in these adventurers. It would be something to talk to Henderson about, if Henderson had time ; for these Canadians, as soldiers, were more kin with Cartwright himself than with Henderson—emergency fellows, amateurs and not professionals . . . and Cartwright was satisfied by his vicarious pride. He anticipated a zest in the licking of new Cadets into shape ; for zest, he realised, was the key to Henderson's secret and the foundation of the design according to which they were going to produce soldiers. The new stripes on his sleeve and the Worcester numerals and badges on his shoulders and cap were as a sword and breast-plate.

Till Bullock saw them.

Bullock surprised him by coming out of the Wilverley post office.

" Hello, Carters," he said.

" Bullock ! " said Cartwright. " I thought—haven't you gone ? Isn't there a fresh lot in ? "

" Yes," said Bullock. " But I've torn it properly now—the last chance."

" Torn what ? " And they walked up the street towards the camp.

"Same old foozle," said Bullock dismally. " There've been a couple of birds down from the War House. Every son of a gun that was here has been gazetted—on Thursday—except me. Even Adams and that oaf Tredgold. I got through everything first-rate—drilled a section to blazes for a good ten minutes—till one of the brass-hats got it into his head to come out and chat to me and rag me while I was at it."

" What happened then ? "

" What happened ? What else *would* happen ? " Bullock demanded bitterly. " The whole box of tricks came unstuck in my throat. I could no more shout " Section, halt ! " than fly. The blighters would have marched through the recreation-tent if I hadn't pulled out my whistle and let fly on it."

" Then ? " asked Cartwright.

" They halted all right before falling over the tent ropes. But the War Office bloke said, ' What the hell's that performance for ? No one asked you for a tune.' And all I could say was ' pup-pup-pup-pup-pup-pup-pup—' till he said, ' My aunt ! ' . . . and ' good God . . . you'd better fall out. . . .' I don't blame the beggar. I expect my face was blowing up red enough to bust. . . ."

" Bad luck, old boy," said Cartwright.

" Oh—well——" said Bullock. " I suppose there's something in the argument. I expect big shells and muck are more frightening than a gilded staff-bloke . . . and if a gilded staff-bloke can reduce me to a gibbering idiot . . . we'll *see*, though. But what about you ? Every one expected to see your name in the Gazette. The Adj. seems to have taken a fancy to you. But—I say, I hope things aren't as bad as you thought ? "

" What things ? " asked Cartwright.

" It got about somehow that you had been called home suddenly. Private trouble of some rotten sort." Bullock moved his eyes to Cartwright's stripes. From there he looked at the Worcester numerals.

" Good Lord ! " he said. " So it can be done that way —so quickly ? I've been wondering."

" Wondering what ? " Cartwright took out a cigarette and lighted it.

" I can't go on like this for ever, either," said Bullock. " If I can't get a commission, I can't. And that's all there is to it. I'll join up like you and get a stripe or two perhaps, and get out."

" My dear old boy," said Cartwright. " These damned stripes are not going to get me out. The idea is for them to keep me here. I'll tell you just between ourselves ; I joined the Worcesters, Henderson's regiment, and was promoted Sergeant because Henderson wants to keep me here as bombing instructor."

Bullock attended to his pipe for a few moments. He then looked Cartwright straight in the eye and said, " Well, I don't blame you. You're a married man and have got kids and a house and a business, and all that. It's different."

"Different your grandmother!" said Cartwright. "*Blame* me, indeed! My dear chap, d'you think I *want* to hang about here? What's a wife and kids and a business *now?* When a house is on fire can *any* one sit down and say he's got a wife and a business? If he's got a dozen wives, a dozen businesses and any guts at all he just butts in for all he's worth, bald-headed, and gives a hand. And if his wife's got any guts she doesn't cling round his neck while the house is burning. And if his business has got any guts it goes on without him." Very roughly Cartwright had stated some of his present creed. Coldly he said, " Thank you, my wife and my ' business,' as you call it, are both the right sort. They're not keeping me."

"Sorry," said Bullock. " I didn't mean to be objectionable. What I really meant, I suppose, is that it's nothing to do with me, and that whatever *you* do is likely to be pretty decent."

Of the twenty-one sunny years of his life Bullock had devoted very little time to the making of handsome remarks. He stopped short now, not because his throat had played its old treachery, but because he had run out of words. He added, rather quickly, " —and all that——"

Cartwright said : " It's that blighter Henderson. I don't believe I'd have done it for any one else in the world. But he *gets* you—somehow——"

" Yes," agreed Bullock. " He's great stuff. He must have been a great lad in that retreat of theirs."

" And cunning!" said Cartwright. "Cunning as a jackal. He had me by the short hairs. If I'd chucked this lot and gone and joined up somewhere else in the ranks, he would have had me detailed back here. If I'd gone and tried to apply for a commission anywhere else he would have blocked it. He said so quite cheerfully. He's got some sort of a pull at the War Office and admits it."

" So he damned well ought to!" said Bullock. " Didn't

you know he's just married Mollie Sampson ? and what the Sampsons can't do with the War House isn't worth doing."

Cartwright remarked that Bullock knew a hell of a lot for a fellow of twenty-one.

" This is a sheer fluke," said Bullock modestly. " The Governor's parish happens to be in the gift of the Sampson family."

" Couldn't they fix you up, then ? " asked Cartwright.

" Yes," was the sardonic answer ; " in the A.S.C."

" Bullock ! " Cartwright suddenly said, " why don't you see Henderson ? "

" I have. I've told him all about the stammering fits," said Bullock. " He's going to try the Flying Corps, but I might be a bit on the heavy side. It's the last chance, and if I am a hundredweight or so too heavy I'll enlist in something. Gunners, I think. It'll be a bit of a disappointment, I suppose."

" I don't see why it should be," said Cartwright stoutly. " Any soldier's as good as any other—if they're fighting."

" Yes," Bullock agreed. " But an officer is as many soldiers as he commands, according to your friend Henderson."

" H'm," said Cartwright thoughtfully. " I know. And if I go out I'll be just one subaltern ; if I stick here I'll be as many as I help him to train."

" That's sound, isn't it ? " asked Bullock. " By Jove ! Don't you think I'd jump at a chance like yours ? "

" No," said Cartwright. " You rotten old humbug ; I don't."

NOT least, perhaps, of Henderson's triumphs in the matter of dealing with life was his ability to make everything appear normal. The state of marriage, after he had been married for a week, seemed to be the natural state of a soldier with one eye and one hand, in time of war. He referred to his ' wife ' as glibly as though the term had been a conversational one all his life ; and he skipped away from the parade ground or his orderly-room at ten minutes to one each day as though the punctual eating of a domestic lunch had been his habit from the cradle.

By March his time-table for the Cadets and their Instructors was criticised and classified and he was named, after about two months of his Adjutancy, with the nickname of " At the Double." Sergeant Ruggles, the Physical Instructor, could say no more of the curriculum than " Cripes—*what* a curri-culum." He thereafter finished his glass of beer in the Sergeants' tent and said, " I'm going before 'is nibs with this lot." He smacked the two or three sheets of paper on which Henderson had sketched the outline of proposed training. " You best glance your eye over your little lot, Cartwright, and come along with me. You can hand out suggestions to him better than what I can, with your University training and mixing with nobs in the civie days."

Cartwright looked through his sheets. A share of the section—and platoon-drill, lectures on ' discipline ' and ' King's Regulations '—a fact that almost set his hair standing on end—were indicated as his portion together with his major responsibility of bombing instruction.

" Oh, I don't know," he said to Ruggles. " I suppose it's possible. He seems to have got the right number of hours into each day—allowing no time for getting from one place to another. But I wish he'd get me some instructions to go on, for this bombing business."

" Be a sport," Ruggles exhorted. " You can find something to arst 'im all right. Arst 'im to lend you the King's Regs. 'E's sure to've got one, and then ole Bighe here can show you about it. Provo' Sergeant, 'e's been in 'is time."

" Oh, yes. I'll show you all about King's Regs,' said Bighe, and Cartwright did not for a moment doubt his ability. For these Sergeants that Henderson had col-lected were an hourly marvel to him. After ten minutes in their company one realised their belief that they could

have run the War, quite smoothly and without much
effort, between them. After ten days of it one was
staggered by the suspicion that this might have been
true.

They knew, as far as Cartwright was able to see
—everything. They *knew*. . . . That was why, when
any one of them roared, " 'Shun ! " " 'Shun ! " it was
without a tremor or the winking of an eyelid in the
ranks.

They could recite " Infantry Training " from the
first of its pages to the last. They knew rations,
equipment and establishments ; scales and rates of pay
and allowances of every rank to Field-Marshal—including
such nobility and gentry as Farriers, Artificers, Armourers,
and artillery wheelwrights. They could drink beer
round the lantern in the tent till there was no more beer
in the barrel at Bighe's elbow ; and they could wake
thereafter at a given instant in the dawn.

Each of them had been hit. Ruggles and Foskitt had
been given the D.C.M., and old Bighe mentioned in
dispatches. Bighe and Ekins wore the ' rooti ' ribbon
of long service. This ' rooti ' and other words from the
' bat ' acquired in India were ancestors of the common
speech of the army of the coming years : ' Rooti,'
' pinnicky pawnie,' ' dekko,' ' jildi,' and the more ordinary
' buckshee.' Gossip of the Old Contemptibles was as family
chat to them. Present Generals were mutual friends and
idols, or worthless horrors to them. They had known them
as Subalterns and Captains. Equally well they knew
the lesser, but just as shining lights. " That lad Sloper
. . ." one of them would say. " . . . in the Black
Watch. 'Im that was champion man-at-arms at Meerut
in owe-seven. . . ."

" Ar . . ." Another of the five would assent. " I
see 'im. Smart lad. Owe-seven, d'yer say ? . . ."

" Ar . . . " from another. " It was owe-seven. We
sent a lot down from Kasauli. It was owe-seven. . . ."

Two more " Ars " and the matter of Sloper would be
allowed to rest, giving place to speculation as to the
present whereabouts of Atkinson. All were agreed that

the star of Atkinson had been a bright one. Enlisting
from the Military Orphanage at Sanawar he had been
full corporal inside of eighteen months, heavy-weight
champion of the Army in India inside of two years.
Ruggles had seconded him in the Simla Town Hall, a
sad yearning in his heart while his chin rested on the
ring's corner that the lad was too late for a rub at Tiger
Smith of the Third Hussars . . . and this same Ruggles,
in all humility now begged him, Cartwright, to stand
beside him in facing the Adjutant's surviving eye.

"Oh—all right," said Cartwright. "If you really
funk it."

"Funk it my elbow!" snorted Ruggles. "But what's
the use of a bloody lawyer in the Mess if it isn't to hand
out a bit of argument? Come on. We'll catch 'im if
we jildi."

They left the tent and strolled into the lane leading
to the village. Ruggles drew and expelled a deep breath.
He had developed, for demonstration purposes to
successive squads of recruits, a method of audible breathing; the swirling jet of steam that spread from his
moustaches into the still, frosty evening was a whistling
sigh. His manner thereafter changed into something
calmer and more profound and intimate.

"'E's 'ot—'is nibs the Adjutant," he said thoughtfully.
"No flies on 'im, Cartwright. It's a bit of a teaser
trying to get officers like 'im out of these boys—in the
time. They're all *right*, mind you, but——"

"Well—that's the job he wants us to do," said
Cartwright.

"'E's got a funny way of starting on it," said Ruggles.
"In the old days you were given best part of a year
to develop a bloke in. It's what every Instructor had
to watch—physical training to be progressive; nothing
more than the recruit would stand. Slow and steady
does it."

"That's all very well when you've got a year to do
it in," suggested Cartwright. "But these fellows have
got to get out into the firing-line. You haven't time to
make athletes and prize-fighters out of them."

"No, cocky," said Ruggles. "But there is ruddy limits. We can't go making casualties by 'on the 'ands down' and bending and stretching. I'll tell 'is nibs that. You watch me." He threw out his chest with another cubic foot or two of humming oxygen as they entered the orderly-room and saluted Henderson.

Cartwright did watch him as he aired his phrase about not being able to make 'casualities' on the parade-ground during a production of subalterns that should be economic.

Henderson listened thoughtfully. "That's certainly a point of view, Ruggles," he said. "But—why not?"

Ruggles for a few moments could find no answer. "Your curri-culum would bust a lot of 'em up, Sir. Arf of them are schoolboys—under age, properly speaking —and the other arf are older blokes, like Cartwright 'ere. They're not used to it."

"My idea is to get 'em used to it—quick," said Henderson.

"Some of them," said Ruggles doggedly, "will bust up."

"Let 'em," said Henderson. "Better now than later."

Ruggles was driven, as in every crisis, to quotation of the printed word. "Over-straining of the recruit," he almost chanted, "will damp his infusiasm and lower his spirits."

"Yes," said Henderson. "I know. The aim of physical training should be progressive. . . . But don't you see, Ruggles, the enthusiasm you've got to work with now is absolutely red-hot?—and spirits are as high as the moon. It's only the absolute wash-outs, physically, that you're likely to bust up with your physical jerks; and the sooner you find them out, and I throw them out, the better for every one. Let's try it, anyhow. If it doesn't work—if anything doesn't— you'll find me the first to admit it. That's what I want all you chaps to understand. You know what we're up against, out there, as well as I do. Is it any use sending wrecks and wash-outs into the scrap?"

The rhetorical question was magnificently unanswered.

Ruggles, defeated, contributed " Ar——" to the pause.

" What I mean to say, is . . ." and Henderson turned to Cartwright. " It's all a new show this. It's an altogether new kind of war. No one knows more about it than any one else just now. We're only finding out how to do things. The only old rule that still holds good is that we've got to pull together—we who are running this little show."

It was time for the Adjutant to hurry home to dinner. Cartwright and Ruggles, after smart salutes, were out in the frosty air again. They were silent for a time ; Cartwright wondering at the way young Henderson had of terminating meetings with a kind of feeling that hands had been shaken over an honourable pact.

Ruggles at length said, " And as for you in there, sonnie !—just about as much use as a sick eddick. . . . Never said a ruddy word."

" Well," said Cartwright, " I didn't see that there was anything much one could say."

" Ar," said Ruggles.   " That's just it."

MEDAL WITHOUT BAR   CHAPTER VIII

THE remaining months of 1915, considered from Cartwright's point of view, were the preparation of a canvas on which a picture was to be painted. The details of this preparation were not to appear in the finished picture, except subtly, through the quality and depths of certain of the shadows and in the brilliance of the higher lights.

Nothing in particular happened.   The work which he contributed daily became a routine more prosaic than his fifteen years of office-life had ever been. Armies confronted by a situation very like a brick wall had come to the fairly obvious conclusion that the only thing to do was to smash down the wall and stagger over the rubble.

D

Guns were going to do the smashing; and men, loaded like beasts of burden, the staggering. Training was based on the method of bombardment and assault, and Cartwright's work soon became a very simple matter for his mind and a most beneficial one for his body. Henderson's periodic disappearance for a day from Wilverley always resulted in the acquisition of the latest ' sheets,' and appendices to the training manual. Trenches were dug and timber gantries erected. Stuffed sacks were suspended therefrom. Cartwright, instructed privily by Ruggles in the Mess-tent, led forays over the trenches and assaults upon these sacks. He acquired the hair-raising snarls appropriate to these exercises, plying his rifle and bayonet, while his acolytes, plying some a rifle and others a boy-scout's pole cut to the proper length, followed him.

He glowed and sweated in the frosty air of spring; his shoulders broadened and his skin toughened; a pint of beer from the barrel in the tent slid down his throat at noon by the unassisted working of the law of gravitation as smoothly as it slid down the venerable beer-ways that were the throats of Ruggles and Bighe and Ekins and Foskitt.

His earlier manner of speaking that could to-day be described as ' an announcer's accent ' became adapted to the picturesque terms and figures employed by the other four.

Henderson, after appearing round the hedge when he had been addressing a squad prior to dismissing it, said : " So you are also a linguist, Cartwright. . . . That hardly sounded like a legal document."

Cartwright smiled. " It's an extraordinary thing," he said. " I don't intend to say those things, you know. They just come in themselves. . . ."

" That's why I call you a linguist," Henderson explained. " The grammar-rules don't bother you any more. . . ."

But the bombing instruction remained little more than an exasperating dream in the mind of the Adjutant. He looked on at musketry-instruction and at the bayoneting of swinging sacks with an impatient sadness that he confided only to Cartwright.

He too saw the blank brick wall of entanglements and trenches, but was irked to the point of despair by the necessity of accepting ancient weapons for a new game. Beyond that itch of despair, however, his genius could not go. He could not invent a bomb; and Cartwright could not invent a way of handling and throwing an uninvented one. Somewhere, Henderson was told during his absence from Wilverley, there were actual, live bombs. There were going to be more; somewhere, too, a method was being devised for throwing them with the least possible exhaustion and risk to the thrower. But as yet he could bring back nothing for Cartwright and Ruggles and Bighe and Ekins and Foskitt but the last official words on musketry and bayonet-fighting, on the care of the feet, the care of telephones, the disposal of camp refuse.

Yet Henderson remained undaunted and undimmed.

" The next time you go home—and you can go as soon as you like if there's nothing special doing," he said to Cartwright one afternoon in his office, " you might bring back your dinner-jacket. I dare say you'd feel easier in it than your G.S. tunic—among ladies and your superior officer. I'd like you to feed with us one night, if you can tear yourself away from the low company in which I've placed you."

"Thanks," said Cartwright, reverting to the prehistoric manner of speech. " I'd love to."

When he did go home at the end of the week, Bullock travelled with him as far as London Bridge; for Bullock's dream had at last come true. Henderson had achieved the realisation for him; he was going where his tongue could dither and jam all it pleased so long as his hands, and later his gun, did not—to the Flying Corps. There was a vague pulling of some kind inside Cartwright as they shook hands and Bullock said, " Well—cheerio."

" Well—good luck, Bullock," he said.

The hazard with which he himself was immediately faced did not demand any invocation of luck, so Bullock

only said, " Thanks. . . ." He added, grinning, " I
don't suppose I'll ever stammer again, now that it doesn't
matter a d-d-d-damn. And don't you go fidgeting where
you are, Carters. You hang on. It's a great job you're
doing. The fellows think you're just about i-i-it. You
and old At-the-Double. Anyhow, let all of us free-lance
johnnies get out first. . . . Well—so long. . . ."

Thus passed Bullock.

Cartwright heard in November that he had been
killed in August ; but for the present he reflected on
his general excellence ; he reflected, too, that the only
compensation for the pulling and straining of something
inside him at the going of Bullock and the staying
behind of himself, was Henderson. The approval of
the Cadets mentioned by Bullock and already sensed
—now that he had stopped to think about it—by Cartwright himself, was something. But Henderson,
somehow, was a great deal more. Henderson had
beliefs ; he believed in bombs, he believed in Samurai.
(And he believed in Cartwright.)

If his evening-dress had been in its old place in the
tall-boy in his dressing-room he would most probably
have packed it up in his suitcase with socks and shoes
and a couple of shirts and collars during some of his
odd hours of hanging about the house till it should be
time to go to fetch Dorothy from the Belgian home.
Dorothy, however, had apparently stuck the thing away
somewhere—probably with moth-balls ; so he had to
ask her for it. She was delighted, and showed her delight.

Something—and tenderness was not altogether lacking
from it—impelled him to say, " Old girl, you—we—ought
not to count on this sort of thing for ever, you know.
You've got to be prepared."

" Well," said she, " haven't I been ? I mean, I
haven't stood much in your way so far, have I ? "

She was near him, reaching up to a high shelf of the
cupboard in the box-room, and Cartwright stood back
to look at her taut body.

" Free-lance," young Bullock had proudly said of

himself ; and Cartwright realised that he was every whit as free as the freest of them. He had sons and the woman who had borne them ; yet none of them, owing to her own peculiar splendour, exerted upon him any of the pressure of a hostage. He kissed her while she still fumbled for the parcel containing his dinner-jacket, the new symbol to her of his security ; he said, " It's a great lark—having these times with you, Dot. They knock spots off the old first honeymoon."

They did.

The *morale* of the time, it must be remembered, was high. The gloomy spectacle of new battalions training in civilian overcoats dyed dark blue to the point of blackness, in forage-caps which only the wearers' native jauntiness could transmute out of a semblance to prison head-wear—battalions whose marching-songs were broken from time to time and drowned in spasms of bronchitis—this spectacle was presented only to the few who lived apart in villages and provincial towns and University cities ; and it was of the sort that even when presented was not exactly seen. Eyes had a peculiar focus in those days : they would see smart uniform and twinkling buttons and accoutrements but could take no account of the more sordid shifts. Ears were peculiarly adjusted so that they could hear the lilt of ' Tipperary ' on a mouth-organ, and be deaf to the wheezing and coughing, in unison, of a hundred men. They could hear the whine and the challenge in the snarl of anti-aircraft shells ; but the falling and the crash of enemy bombs they heard not at all.

Dorothy, if she heard the bombs while Cartwright listened to the shells, gave no sign. So Cartwright, like another soldier some three centuries before him, had freedom in his love, and in his love was free . . . and for the same reason, his lady looked on and bade him good luck and God-speed while he, with his predecessor's stronger faith, embraced a sword, a horse, a shield. . . . That, at any rate, was approximately the feeling of it. The fact that he was not, in grim reality, embracing any sword or horse or shield, but sitting quietly and for an indefinite length of time on a job, was obscured by the movement of cadets who were not nursing any jobs but were passing swiftly on. While Dorothy slept (or lay as quietly as in sleep) beside him, and he thought for a moment of this job-holding of his, the going of Bullock to the Flying Corps somehow appeared to him consolingly in the light of an exploit of his own.

It was only when he was with the two boys that the thing seemed quite definitely to stick. . . . The beggars said nothing that could be taken up and answered with a complete explanation of one's position and one's function. But they appeared to have friends at Westminster who had brothers—and fathers—who were rapidly making not other men, but themselves, into soldiers. . . .

The packing of the dinner-jacket was not, as it happened, referred to in the presence of the boys.

CARTWRIGHT continued for very nearly a year in that same state to which it had pleased God to call him. It was a year of changes all round him, and of a general psychology wherein every change seemed to be a change for the better.

In the whole year there was only one event. In the autumn of 1915 Henderson had spent one of his days in London and summoned him to his office in the evening and quickly shut the door and said, " Cartwright, my son ! at *last !* "

Cartwright mumbled some sound indicating inquiry.

" Bombs ! " said Henderson. " Bombs, my lad ! Can you come in to-night, and feed ? "

" Yes, rather," said Cartwright. It was about his twentieth dinner with the Hendersons.

" Shove off and change then while I finish up the stuff the Corporal has got for me here. Tell Mollie I shan't be many minutes, if you get there first."

Cartwright did get there first. He said, " It's an

order, Mrs. Henderson ; that's why I'm here in this unforgivably sudden way. I know what *my* wife would say if I fired a man into the house five minutes before dinner—to dine. I really am sorry, but his nibs is full of something rather important."

Mollie Henderson was shaking his hand. " Come in," she said. " If the man you shot into your house meant as much to you as you mean to Jim—and me—she'd be delighted—whenever you shot him in. I'll just go and make sure that there'll be something for you to eat."

She closed the drawing-room door on him and followed the maid towards the kitchen.

What the devil, Cartwright wondered, did she mean ? Her phrase seemed to overload the facts; and Mollie Henderson had never struck him as the sort of person to overload facts. She was about Henderson's age as far as one could judge. It is true she had appeared, from the very first, to be inclined to mother him a little, but Henderson's lack of an eye and an arm would be enough to account for that.

But she seemed solid enough, and level-headed, for all her gaiety and nimble, dark attractiveness ; not at all the kind of person who made embarrassingly sentimental remarks and then vanished towards kitchens. There was an upstanding sort of jolliness about her, and in the young relationship of her and Henderson he had noticed an enviable ingredient that had always been missing from the relationship of himself and Dorothy. In the early days it had been missing because of an insensitive, heavy stupidity of his own ; an illusion that man's estate (when the man in question was the junior partner in an ancient firm of solicitors, and the head, moreover, of a newly-established household in Chiswick) was a solemn affair. The ingredient was still missing, but now inevitably so. Now between him and Dorothy there was the War ; moratorium. Between Henderson and his wife there was no moratorium. For them the War was virtually over. . . .

He heard Henderson coming in at the front door and shouting " Mollie ! " answered by her coming from the kitchen. There was the rustle of his hanging up his coat and cap and pushing his stick into the stand. Then from conversation mingled with the splashing of water he gathered that she assisted at the washing of Henderson's hand ; and then they both came to the door and Mollie Henderson said " Come along, Mr. Cartwright."

Henderson's spirits were still at their height. He was bursting with his news ; and she, because of the peculiar ingredient in their relationship and because there was no moratorium between them, was anxious to hear it.

" Out with it, Jim," she said, as they sat down. " You'll only choke if you try to take your soup without telling us."

" And you'll choke as soon as I *have* told you," said Henderson proudly. " Look at this, my child ! " He drew a fat War-Office envelope from his pocket and handed it to her. While she was taking out of it a couple of letters and some printed forms, Henderson handed a map to Cartwright and said, " You might open that. She *won't* choke, as a matter of fact. You can now observe a soldier's wife facing destiny. Biting on the bullet or chewing a dinner-plate. . . . As a matter of fact, she's known all along that I've been trying to pull it off."

She stuffed the papers back into the envelope and shrugged her shoulders, and said, " Oh—well . . . If it's safe enough for old Freddie to go there, I suppose it's safe enough for you." The fact she was facing was not a particularly startling one ; but the philosophy with which she faced it was a new one.

" Down there, about one o'clock from your left thumb," Henderson said to Cartwright, who was looking at the map. " I've marked it—La Loge. That's where we're going, my lad. What do you think of that ? "

Cartwright was only in a position to say, " Who's going ? I mean . . ."

" *You*," said Henderson, " and I. A specially wangled Cook's tour, to see bombers in their nests. Real bombs at last, young fella. And real bombers. There's a school there. And we're going to have a week of it. We can measure and weigh the stuff—and if we don't bring back at least a *dummy* or two I'm a Dutchman. On the ground of my disabilities old Freddie has allowed me to take an orderly. You're the orderly."

"I say !" said Cartwright. "How *did* you manage it."

"I married strings," said Henderson. "You mightn't think it to look at her, but she's got most of the War House in hand, what with aunts and nieces and one thing and another. It wouldn't surprise me a bit if I ended up Commander-in-Chief of the Orkneys. Anyhow, you are going to get a bit of the real stuff out of it ; and that ought to cheer you up."

MEDAL WITHOUT BAR   CHAPTER X

THE next time he saw his family Cartwright was able to inform it very casually that he had been in the trenches. For a night and a day therein had been the crowning touch to Henderson's miracle-working.

During a week of ' Cook's Touring ' the War had more significance and what artists would call ' impact ' for Cartwright than it had at any other time. He saw it and felt it spread out large before him. And it was not too far away ; for even in those days of the somewhat coy attitude of commands towards the expenditure of ammunition, the isolated snarls of batteries merged, in travelling twenty-five to fifty miles, into a dull, steady boom that was a pulse-like pressure on the ear-drums rather than an articulated sound.

The men on those instructional parades at the bombing-school were like the tired, busy pupils at a night-class— a class to which only those go for whom the work is important. They were weather-beaten, too, beyond the hardest beating of any weather at a training-camp.

Their boots displayed the individualities of the feet inside them; for it was the warmth and movements of those same feet that had dried them at intervals out of shapeless softness. Their putties were faded, their tunics shrunken, their caps (generally the flapped ' Gorblimeys ' as yet not much in evidence at home) had a touch of grim realism added to them by resembling the pictures in the *Bystander* and the *Sphere*, and the photographs in the daily papers.

Artists had ' got ' the men a good deal better than the journalists ; for the journalists were depicting swashbucklers like old Ruggles and Foskitt and Bighe and Ekins or else the cold-tub-and-cricket type of the *Tatler* pages. The five hundred or so undergraduates in the art of bomb-throwing at La Loge, officers and men alike, were neither of these. An obvious but indescribable difference marked them. Perhaps the difference was nought but their doom.

A phrase like " the jaws of death " had a meaning as one stood among the men—watching a body, strained back in its shrunken, weather-beaten khaki, for the exhibition flinging of a grenade—with the dull pressure of distant guns upon the ear-drums.

The twenty-four hours in the trenches, hair-raising and awe-inspiring enough for the first moments of being actually ' there,'—as near, perhaps, as any one to the crouching enemy—made less impression upon Cartwright than the first days at the school itself.

Henderson, after half a dozen words with the company-commander in the line, told Cartwright ostentatiously that he was fixed up for as much of a batman as he was likely to require, and the company commander told his Sergeant-Major to ' take over this sergeant ; and show him everything.'

Thus Cartwright saw the front line of a Company's sector, with its various dumps, communication-trenches and latrines. He went forward along a sap with a corporal who whispered that it might be advisable not to sing much or play the piano. A Sergeant took him out to have a ' dekko ' at the wire ; and he stood still in the ghostly light of Verey rockets. The Sergeant strolled on, his whispering chat uninterrupted by the ping of occasional bullets ; and Cartwright strolled with him. He saw also one of those contraptions that passed, at that time, as dug-outs in the Hooge sector, and he drank therein a good quart of that unique draught—dixie tea. Thereafter, sitting on a petrol-can against the dug-out side, declining a hand at nap for the simple reason that it was a game he had never played, he slept.

At 'stand-to' he was left suddenly alone; and loneliness of this sort was a new sensation—standing in wet boots and socks and putties, peering up a hole in the earth from its clammy bottom, seeing a criss-cross and clods of legs and boots against the pallor of sky; and then the pallid rectangle empty. . . .

At Victoria, he went down the platform to Henderson's first-class carriage and took his suitcase. When their taxi had swung out of the station Henderson said, " Lord ! I thought I'd never be able to manage it. But I *did* get one, Cartwright."

" Good," said Cartwright. " That makes three." He opened his haversack and produced two socks, lumpy like two clumsily rolled pairs.

It was thus that Henderson's command acquired its three dummy Mills grenades.

" By God, you'll make a soldier yet ! " said Henderson. " And didn't those trenches show you ? "

" The school showed me a good deal more," said Cartwright, thinking again of the shabby, intent fellows and the pressure upon his ear-drums of the distant line.

" Yes—but what a change ! " said Henderson, " and scarcely any one saw that it must come—until it *had* come. Thank God they tumbled to the gas business a bit quicker. But you would have thought that the moment both sides had got dug in within spitting distance of each other the brass-hats would have seen that rifles were going to be no good. Golly, *I* saw it, and lost no time in saying so. Perhaps some of the little shindy I kicked up, with those priceless old things of Mollie's, did have something to do with planting the idea. . . . Well, even if it has taken a whole year, I suppose it's something."

" It's a neat little thing," said Cartwright, handling

the grenade removed from the sock. " I take my hat off to Master Mills." He weighed and gripped the thing and imagined himself going through the movements as expounded by a Jock sergeant.

Henderson started out of the pause and suddenly gripped Cartwright's arm. " I'm glad we wangled this show—for your sake, you know. You'll be able to trot round among the lads with your tail up now."

Cartwright saw the idea and how, superficially, it was true enough.

But there was that something about those five hundred men at the school—even more than about his cheery hosts in the trenches—that kept them far aloof from himself. They had lost some vague sort of virginity that he and all the other stay-at-homes still possessed. By a peculiar twisting and readjustment of values virginity had become a secret shame. The proud thing was the matron-like dignity of the grouped five hundred officers and other ranks that had been 'there'; soldiers who had become assassins.

MEDAL WITHOUT BAR   CHAPTER XI

T HAT was the only event personal to Cartwright in that quietly uneventful year. It was completed and rounded off by his subsequent week-end at home.

It was startling that he could have slipped off to the front and come back again so smoothly that he need not, in fact, ever have told her of it . . . but she accepted it, and was quiet. She asked for no details.

It was the boys who wanted these; and the surprising fact emerged for Cartwright as he told them of his twenty-four hours in the line, that there had been no real danger. There had been the song of a bullet here and there—but one heard that song in the butts of a rifle-range. Shelling, for that day and night, had been the exclusive affair of other sectors and of batteries a mile or so behind. Shells had gone sliding through the sky overhead as harmless as geese. Another emerging fact was that he had felt absolutely no fear—a little excitement, perhaps, when pottering about with the Corporal in the wire and standing still in the light of rockets; but not fear. It was therefore with perfect honesty that he was able to represent the front as not, on the whole, 'bad.' To John's question of how so many men were reported killed, wounded and missing he could only answer that he had seen neither a dead nor a wounded man; nor, indeed, a man in any way distressed. For it was not distress that distinguished the five hundred bombing students and separated them from himself and gave him the uneasy feeling that there was something more in all this than met the eye.

That uneasiness is a small ' residue ' as chemists would call it, from the happenings of that whole year. The year can be looked at now as a dull series of blunders, idiocies and fiascos; it can be looked at as a dazzling page of heroic achievements in the history of a warrior nation. Anyhow, it was a year in which things did happen. A mere catalogue of place-names covers half the world— from the half-week's epic and failure of Neuve Chapelle, along a continuous battle-front to the eight months' epic and failure of Gallipoli. There was Hill 60 and the second battle of Ypres with the début of poison gas; Rudolph Binding, adept in the matter of straight, orderly thinking and simple recording, filled a page on the 27th of April. His billet at the moment was five miles from the line (on the wrong side of it). He says, " The effects of the successful gas attack are horrible. . . . A sleeping army lies in front of one of our brigades; they rest in good order, man by man, and will never more wake again—Canadians. . . ."

An astonishing word appeared and was accepted to indicate a fact no less astonishing—' Coalition.'

The *Lusitania* was sunk.

Fromelles and Festubert appeared in the small sketch-maps of the daily papers; ammunition, as financiers would say, was 'tight.' Density of numbers advancing against well-placed and adequately handled machine-guns meant, to a few critical minds, nought but density of corpses. From May to August the Russians had lost 750,000 men in prisoners alone—and the only obvious result to England was a series of jokes about the possible pronunciation of Przemysl. There was the battle of Loos ; Salonika ; the siege of Kut. The Derby scheme grew from a topic to a fact, giving place to the new question of practical politics—Conscription. . . .

And what Cartwright personally got out of that year, sufficiently permanent in memory to stand the passage of a dozen years, was a feeling of sudden awe, or shame or fear—or else no more than mere bewilderment at standing among some five hundred men with the knowledge that he alone among them was in some sense virgin.

With this bewilderment was the slight new difficulty in his mind about Dorothy ; he did not understand her very clearly.

AT the beginning of winter Cartwright had dined two or three times with the Hendersons without changing his sergeant's tunic for his dinner-jacket. This meant that Henderson was becoming more excited and hurried in his issuing of invitations ; it meant, too, that this relationship—which seemed to include the presence or absence of Henderson's wife just as chance had it—was now developed quite beyond the ' man-and-officer ' feeling that had been so miraculously accepted by some millions of men who, little more than two years before, would have been immensely amused by the suggestion of saluting and sir-ing any individual, however dressed up.

Barristers, financiers, and school prefects with an enviable fame for repartee and the retort scathing had become as little sheep in the matter of docile herding. The glance of a sergeant-major could petrify them : the scorn of a subaltern (who need not necessarily have played any football but soccer) could submerge them in a wave of the darkly mounting blood of shame ; a company-commander could loosen their knees with a word and turn their bowels to water . . . and Cartwright had achieved a friendship with his commanding-officer and an understanding with his colleagues, Foskitt, Ruggles, Ekins and Bighe.

He could drink his pint of beer in the Sergeants' tent and hurry off to dine with Henderson, stopping at his billet only to wash his hands and brush his hair, but not bothering to change if the invitation had been a sudden one.

The invitations were becoming, generally, sudden ; for things were not going smoothly with Henderson and the ' Company.' People—to whom even Henderson referred as ' brass-hats ' instead of ' old So-and-so ' or ' old Somebody Else '—had come down to inspect the ' Company ' and to form opinions, and to make reports. They were nice enough to Henderson and charming to Mollie if they stayed to lunch or tea ; but it was a sinister machinery that had caused them to come—twice with not a moment's warning.

There was no antagonism to be detected in the men themselves, but the antagonism of the machine was obvious—towards Henderson and towards the ' Company.'

Henderson's touch, as a result, was losing its sureness. Things had got, for the moment, beyond his powers of wangling. Of seventeen cadets whom he recommended at the end of October as being fit and suitable for commissions, five were turned flatly down after a two- or three-minute interview in a War Office corridor. Henderson had been furious, and Cartwright spent many hours of subsequent evenings in toning down portions of a great many letters he drafted. Henderson bitterly championed the rejected five—two schoolboys, a commercial traveller, a professional soccer-player and a music-

hall artist ; for he was the champion of his own judgment,
and Cartwright's.   It had been a judgment very carefully
and thoughtfully formed.

" We can't mind their h's and g's any more, Cartwright,"
he said ; " and whether their neckties have the right
colours.   Those days are gone.   This War is *eating*
subalterns.   We've got to look lower and deeper now than
neckties—for guts."   And the rejected five had ' guts.'

Heaven only knew what the War Office interviewers
had sought, and expected to find, in the course of a two-
minutes' talk in a corridor.

Of the twelve candidates they passed three had been
very doubtful cases to the minds of Henderson and
Cartwright.   Only the urgent call for ' twenty recommended ' cadets had accounted for their inclusion in
Henderson's list which was still three short, since
nothing would have induced him to include any of
whose unreadiness he was certain. . . . He fought
for his five ; and Mollie fought for the recognition
of his judgment.   By the end of November the five
had been duly gazetted.   And by the end of November
also there was a general order from the War Office that
no more Commissions would be granted.

Here was cause for another dinner without time for
changing into evening-clothes.

A very glum Henderson poured gin into a couple of
glasses when Cartwright arrived at the cottage, and
added vermouth.

" Well—cheerio, old thing," he said gloomily.   Friends
' old-thinged ' one another freely at that time.   " I
suppose it couldn't have gone on for ever."

"But this order may only last a week or two," said
Cartwright.

Henderson shook his head.   " I doubt it, said the
carpenter, and shed a bitter tear. . . .   Besides, even
three weeks would get us into a hell's own mess.   If we
can't get the fellows away every week, to battalions, we
can't take any more in.   There are thousands of the best
chaps in the world who are at last able to come now that
the only alternative is to get conscripted in a few weeks'

time. Take your own case; you're damned lucky.
But if you hadn't had a business that could go on just
as well without you, would you have cleared out and
left a wife and kids to shift for themselves ? "

Cartwright did not immediately answer.

" Damn it ! " said Henderson. " Would you, now ? "

" I don't know," said Cartwright slowly. " I got
rather taken hold of by the thing, somehow. It never
really occurred to me that one could very well do anything
but go. And I don't believe I can continue—just—
hanging on here—for ever."

" Ah, there you are ! " said Henderson. " Why have
you stuck it for a year, then ? "

Cartwright did not for the moment see the point
Henderson had scored ; but Henderson made it clear.
" You have stuck here against your instincts and your
inclinations—and have made a damned fine job of it.
You've wanted to go all the time—and you just haven't
gone."

" Well—I don't quite see——"

" No," Henderson went on. " Nor could thousands
of those poor other beggars *quite* see how they could
dash off, before. Chaps with women round their necks
—I mean old mothers and paralysed sisters and things—
as well as wives. It'd have first meant more or less
killing some one whom they didn't much want to kill.
Now conscription's going to do the killing for them—
and they're free ; as you will be free as soon as those
blasted, fog-bound old gravediggers have shut up this
little shop. And you'll be damned glad of it, just as
those others are. Golly ! There's as good stuff floating
about among the thousands trying to dodge into something before they get conscripted, as ever there was before.
And we'll lose them, because we can't get any more fellows
commissioned to make room for them. Here ! have
another."

They had another.

" It's the thin end of the sanguinary wedge." Henderson
had struck a match for their cigarettes by his old device
of sticking the match-box between the first and second

buttons of his tunic. " This ' Chancery Company ' of mine is the last little show of its kind on the map ; and they're going to shut it down."

Cartwright was beginning to make some protest, but Henderson said, " No . . . straight from the horse's mouth. I've had the tip—anyway, they're going to try. You bet I'm going to put up a fight to hang on to it. Damn it—those letters are *something*. . . ." His mind drifted off from the conversation, and his eye shifted from Cartwright to his glass and from his glass to vague distance. He was referring to half a dozen letters he had had during the year from officers commanding battalions ; letters that congratulated him and thanked him for the subalterns that had joined them after three months in the ' Chancery Company of Cadets.'

" They ought to help," said Cartwright.

Henderson said thoughtfully, " I've got plenty of help. But there's a very ugly old sod getting a lot of rope one way and another. He's outside the War House, but he wants to make a name for himself—a better one than the one I've given him. We can't do anything with him —I and Mollie's lot—and he's too big to be just ' downed.' The odds are he's going to pick on the proper recruiting and training of officers as his life's work for a knighthood. Blast his eyes."

Henderson emptied his glass and sat down. " I've had four of those blighters to your two," he said, nodding at their glasses—" two before you arrived. I'll be glad of a spot of soup, or a bit of bread-and-dripping to steady things up a shade."

He sat down and seemed, Cartwright thought for the first time in all their dealings, tired. One noticed his empty sleeve and his empty eye-socket as one had seldom noticed them before.

Cartwright had always addressed him scrupulously as " you " off parade.

He now said, " Jimmy Henderson, you've taught me a hell of a lot, you know, in a year."

" Same to you," said Henderson. " With knobs on. . . . The girl is out to-night, and Mollie's cooking. What we lose in punctuality we'll gain in quality. By the way, we won't talk too much about this business to-night. It bothers her."

" This stopping of Commissions ? " asked Cartwright.

" No. Shutting down the company. She got the tip in the first place. But I denied the possibility. She's getting quite solemn over things at times. You know, I suppose, that we're expecting a Henderson reinforcement of some sort ? "

" No," said Cartwright. " I didn't. But I'm awfully glad. . . . Congratulations, Jimmy."

" About April," said Henderson. " She wants you to be godfather and godmother at his baptism. . . . Mollie thinks you're no end of a fellow."

At that moment Mollie came in and said, " You poor things ! Starved ? "

MEDAL WITHOUT BAR   CHAPTER XIII

BY February Commissions were being granted again ; but the recruiting for the little Chancery Company which had been run on a system of what Henderson called " private connection and recommendation of old customers " had received too great a set-back from the November stoppage. In February Commissions left only the utterly hopeless cases behind ; and Cartwright, with Ruggles and Foskitt and Ekins and Bighe, was hard put to it to fill in the days with these remnants.

Henderson meanwhile was racking his brains and writing reams of letters to the end that not a sparrow of his should fall on the ground. If only ' they ' had given him time he could have made officers of them— he and Cartwright and the others. There was good stuff in them all, and if he was not careful—careful to the point of inspiration in the aiming of his reams of letters —conscription would sweep them all away into its immense heaps of jumbled material ; and the ' good stuff ' would be lost. . . .

It was in March that the ' Company ' finally went into liquidation.

Henderson had not yet told the five sergeants of the final winding-up notice.

He had only said to Cartwright at lunch-time, " Better come and feed to-night." And Cartwright immediately knew.

He in turn said nothing to the other four, but they too somehow knew that the order must have come. The five sat round their beer-barrel at six o'clock, glum and evasive of each other till Foskitt wiped his moustaches and very softly and sardonically sang :

> ". . . And the Lord knows when
> We'll be all together agen,
> We'll be all together agen.
> Heah, heah. . . ."

" Ar . . . " said Ruggles. " That's right. No mistake."

Now that speech was free again Cartwright's cigarette case went round the group. Four cigarettes were taken therefrom, while Cartwright took an identical one from the packet held out to him by Foskitt.

" Coo—but 'is nibs has made a fight for it ! " said old Bighe, projecting a solid funnel of smoke to the tent door. " The corp. told me two munfs ago our number was up, and what d'you think 'is nibs done ? He said, ' Corp'ral, I'm going up to the War Office. Field-day. If there's any telephoning from there, tell them you haven't seen me since last night and that I haven't yet seen this morning's bumph.' "

" Yers," said Ekins. " It's a miracle. You'd thought a little man-and-a-boy shop like this would of been shut up donkey's years ago. All the others have."

" And if you ask *me*," said Foskitt, the starter, as usual, of fresh lines of thought, " what *I* say is—what's going to become of us ? "

Ruggles said, " Ar . . . that's right."

Cartwright had no lot in this question. It belonged only to the professional adventurers.

" Don't worry," said Ekins. " 'Is nibs will see to that. We'll fall pretty. 'E's not the one to stand by and watch us tinkered abaht by War Offices and that, at this time of day, after the way we've stood by him through this lot. Is 'e, Carters ? "

Cartwright perceived the diplomacy underlying this question, and smiled. " He isn't," he said. " If any one can do anything for us, you bet he will. As you say, we've stuck by him. . . ."

" All damn' well for you, my lad ! " said Foskitt, " coming down to live among the poor for a funny joke or something. If we'd been scholards—us four—there'd of been a Commission for every one of us, and there you are. But we're not—and *there* you are."

" It isn't only scholars that get Commissions nowadays." But Cartwright knew he was only doing what Henderson would have tauntingly called ' passing the compliment.' It would take greater miracles than Henderson could perform to get Commissions for these grand ruffians. (In three cases, incidentally, the miracles were performed— by the extent of the Somme casualties. Old Bighe had died, by that time, of pneumonia at Shoreham.)

Then, tapping the barrel for his second glass, Bighe said, " I dare say, sonnie. But nor 'an 'un' " (this phrase was his masterpiece of thoughtful emphasis), " nor 'an 'un of us knows 'is ears from 'is elbow when it comes to learning—learning like you orficers have got up your sleeves."

" Even if there *is* more ears than elbow in it." Cartwright was again ' passing the compliment.' But there was a sombre wistfulness in Bighe's regret, and in his humility.

" It's the pack ! " Ruggles suddenly exploded—Ruggles the gymnast and pugilist and trainer of pugilists. " Ker—ist ! This picnic's spoilt us for any more pack and equipment 'umping. That's one reason why I wouldn't say ' no ' to a Commission. 'Is nibs is right in those lectures of 'is ; as long as the foot-soldier has got to be a beast of burden, too. . . ! Ancetera. That's what gets me . . . and you can strike me pink if I wouldn't do anythink rather than carry a pack again with all these later trimmings."

(Cartwright saw 2nd Lieut. Ruggles in 1917, coming out of the alleged trenches to the West of Passchendaele as Cartwright and his signallers went up. He was carrying a pack belonging to one of his men who walked very slowly between two others ; in addition to his walking-stick he was also carrying four rifles. There had been a good deal of gas, and officers know that slightly gassed men should be relieved of physical exertion.)

MEDAL WITHOUT BAR   CHAPTER XIV

CARTWRIGHT shaved for the second time that day in a leisurely manner and thoughtfully dressed for dinner with the Hendersons.

They were both in the drawing-room when the maid let him in ; and both glasses on the little brass tray with the three bottles were unused.

Mollie removed the corks and Henderson mixed the gin and vermouths. He handed a glass to Cartwright. " Mollie's on the wagon," he explained. " I'm not sure, by the way, that you oughtn't to be in some sort of training yourself. This godfathering business isn't a thing that should be lightly entered into."

This was the first allusion made in Mollie's presence to her current preoccupation.

Cartwright said, " I'll drink it quickly, then—before you can get the idea into orders. Here's to him—and his ma."

Cartwright's smile at her was answered by a trembling of her lip, a surprising flicker of eyelids and a sudden sparkle of moisture on the long lashes. Mumbling some vague apology or excuse, she shot out of the room.

" It seems to have given her a knock," Henderson said. " It's come at last, you know. We—the Company—

shutting down at once. But all of you seemed to know as soon as I did."

" Every one's felt it coming," said Cartwright.

A cadet was at that moment collecting four shillings apiece from his fellows for the purchase of six silver cigarette-cases. This cadet, the originator of the hurried scheme, had been a humorous journalist. Henderson's case was to be inscribed :

> " PRESENTED
> (' AT THE DOUBLE ')
> TO
> CAPT. J. V. HENDERSON
> BY
> ALL THAT WAS LEFT OF THEM,
> LEFT OF SIX HUNDRED."

The ornamental phrases were to be omitted from the five sergeants' cases. The words on theirs were to be simply, " Presented to Sergt. ———, by the last of the Company."

A second cadet was able to promise that he could get ' his firm ' to push the order through immediately.

" When a number is up, people do seem to know it somehow." This thoughtful generalisation came from Cartwright because his mind had gone back to the day that war was declared.

" H'm," said Henderson. " You must admit it's a bit of a sod, all the same . . . We'll have one more." He took Cartwright's glass.

" I suppose you'll get something else without much trouble," said Cartwright. " In one of those Cadet Battalions or something. . . ."

Henderson shook his head. " No," he said. " I dare say it would be a good thing for Mollie, if I could. I think she'd like it better than—just——" he paused, to savour his drink. Then he slowly admitted what was in his mind, "——just chucking in. Finished."

" Finished ! " said Cartwright. " You ?—finished ! " and he laughed.

" Golly ! I wasn't finished ! " said Henderson ;—" as long as I had this thing to mess about with."

" Couldn't you—mess about, as you call it—in a Cadet Battalion—just the same ? "

" Just the same ? " asked Henderson incredulously. " No, you damned fool, I couldn't. No more could you. Or do you want to ? " He smiled, sardonically. " I can still pull wires enough to wangle that for you—if you like."

" No," said Cartwright ; but he did not rush in with the same indignation that he would have felt a year before. " No. I don't think I do. But if you can wangle a Commission for me—on this new ' Ranker' basis . . . I suppose that's really what I've been waiting for."

" So you're fed up, too ? " said Henderson. " You are sorry that we've been bust at last."

" Yes," said Cartwright. " Of course. But I don't know. I've felt all the time that I've really been waiting —for this ; to get out. It's been different for you—and the others too—old Ruggles and Foskitt, and Ekins and Bighe. I didn't join for anything else, did I ? I suppose the only thing I'm sorry about now is—breaking up the 'appy 'ome."

Dorothy, eighteen months before, had given him a feeling of something tugging at something else inside him —but there had been no regret ; not, that is, if one really aimed at strict accuracy in one's words. The dominant feeling had been confidence and high satisfaction : every-thing was all right, and the road was clear for his adventure and there was no load of care upon his back. It had been shouldered by the Old Boy, who would carry it if ' anything ' should happen to Cartwright's self, till John could take it on. It may have been the general excite-ment of the time that had set him romping off among the others with a light heart ; but whatever the reason for it, the fact remained that his heart had then been light and now was heavy.

" You'll get out fast enough," said Henderson. " I can get the others fixed up nice and ' cushy,' instructing. They're born instructors."

" And me ? "

" We'll chat about that at dinner," said Henderson. " It's rather a cheerful outlook, as a matter of fact. Not a bad topic while Mollie's got such a hump. Look here, I'll see if she'll come in and chat to you. You might cheer her up a bit. Talk about the prospective, if she doesn't choke you off."

He went out and called to her from the hall and then went upstairs. Presently she came in. " I thought I'd leave you to your fond farewells. It wasn't rudeness ; it was delicacy of feeling."

" Yes ! " said Cartwright. " But now that I'm admitted to the intimacy of godfathering future people, I don't mind telling you that it isn't the first time I've seen the same kind of tear—for the same kind of reason. It's a pity this disbanding couldn't have waited a bit longer. Making sudden changes will be a bit of a nuisance."

" Beastly nuisance," she agreed. Then, " Look here, it's no use hedging. I'm just about as disgusted as can be over this break up. The Company seemed to be the one thing in the world for Jim. Didn't you think so ? "

" I can't say I'd thought about it from that point of view," Cartwright admitted. " I did notice that he seemed to be the one fellow in the world for *it*, though."

" I'm worried," said she, " worried to death."

" I don't see why you should be," said Cartwright. " You—of all people, with all the pulls you've got. He's sure to get something just as good as this show."

" H'm . . ." said Mollie, and her smile was very superior and detached. " I dare say . . . but men are so absurdly sentimental."

" What on earth do you mean ? " asked Cartwright.

She shrugged her shoulders. " He's lost his profession," she said slowly. " With him it really was a profession."

" Yes," said Cartwright. " He's a born soldier. About the only one I've ever met—a soldier just like some chaps are born musicians and painters—and solicitors, too, I suppose."

" He lost some of it with his hand and his eye," she

went on slowly. " He's lost the rest now. And he's losing you."

" Me ? " said Cartwright.

" It's difficult for men to lose their profession, and their friend. They're so sentimental. Jim's been just delighted ever since you said you would be godfather to this new person."

" He said, by the way, that it was your idea."

" He would," said she. " I don't mean that I'm not glad, too. But women, at the moment, are not sentimental."

" No," said Cartwright. " I suppose it's logic that sends them off into tears at odd moments. Eh ? "

" That's mean," she said, " and beside the point. He's coming down. Anyhow, let's be as cheerful as we can at dinner."

" I don't think there's going to be any difficulty about that," said Cartwright, and moved towards the door as she rose. " His nibs has got a scheme of some sort for me."

" He's assuming that you still want to go out." She turned at the door and faced him suddenly with the question : " Honestly now—*do* you ? "

Accuracy by means of a single word—or, for that matter, a dozen or a hundred words—was impossible. He answered " Yes," as being immeasurably nearer to the truth than " No " would have been. But he tried to explain. " It's not a matter of really wanting, you know. There's some kind of ' must ' about it. I don't mean the conscription ' must ' ; but a sort of feeling."

" Yes," she said. " Quite. Sentiment."

" Sentiment your grandmother ! " said Cartwright. " The thing is obvious ! " and with that they were in the hall as Henderson came downstairs.

" MY brainy little brain-wave," Henderson
explained when they had settled down to
dinner, " is the Royal Regiment of Artillery
for you, my son."

" Artillery ? " said Cartwright. " Why Artillery ? "
The existence of Artillery had not seriously occurred to
him during the past year.

" Reasons strategic, tactical and personal," said
Henderson. " I met a fellow the other day ; fellow
called ' Sulky ' Sinclair. One of the best ; skipper of
one of the old Lahore field batteries who got shot up a
bit last winter. He went out commanding a new battery
this year and got another shooting up at Loos. He's
one of those natural-born gunners and he's now got
the gunner cadet school at Exeter."

" What's that got to do with me ? " asked Cartwright.

" My son," said Henderson ; " the War has changed.
We wanted bombs a year ago, and bombers instead of
musketeers—and we've got 'em—and are getting more.
So that's all right. The next requirement is guns—
and gunners. Gunner officers ; the proportion of officers
to gunners knocked out is pretty high."

" But," said Cartwright, " wouldn't that mean having
to start everything from the beginning over again ? "

" It would mean that, anyway," said Henderson.
" You'd have to go through a cadet school course for
any sort of a Commission now."

" But I thought perhaps *you*——" Cartwright stopped
when Henderson shook his head.

" Not now," said Henderson. " Our star is set."
He smiled across at Mollie. " There's an anti-wangle
campaign in full swing. Newspaper johnnies on the
war-path. But I've spoken to Sinclair about fixing you
up. It was easy enough—working with the tide. . . .
By Jove ! " he exclaimed suddenly. " You've never
seen a battery dropping into action ! "

"Yes, I have," said Cartwright quietly. "I've seen a ' musical-ride,' I think they call it. . . ."

"So 've I," said Henderson; "when the music was Bosche coal-boxes. I'm an old foot-slogger at heart right enough—but if you had seen a battery the day I got knocked, you wouldn't sit there turning up your nose at the chance of being a gunner."

" I'm not turning up any nose," said Cartwright.

Henderson's sudden outburst—an outburst of the old fiery sort after some months of morose scheming and acrimonious letter-writing—had startled Cartwright back to a vivid recollection of an evening at Olympia or somewhere. . . . Black teams of the Horse Artillery with the sparkling chains of traces taut on gleaming flanks. . . . Men and horses and weapons with the pace of demons and the delicate grace of rapiers. . . . That was the only picture Cartwright had of artillery. It is possible that a quarter of a century before he might have been attracted by it—as by spangles and tights and a hazardous performance upon a tight wire or a trapeze. . . . Still there were some colour and some glamour in it ; and the War, of late, had been losing colour. Casualties now amounted to 300,000.

"Would you go into the Artillery yourself?" he asked.

"I? . . . I'd go into a sanitary battalion," was the answer. Henderson spoke *de profundis ;* it was the first time he had been lugubrious about his wounds. Cartwright was sorry for his question, but saw that the best thing was to go straight on.

"Of course," he said. "But I mean from choice."

"Yes," said Henderson. "If I were starting at the beginning, without any ties like my old regiment, I believe I would."

"*My* old regiment, too, incidentally," Cartwright reminded him with a smile.

"Well—it's gone now," said Henderson. "All that you ever knew of it ; so there you are. But look here—I mean to say——" It was obviously something awkward that he meant to say. "Don't be silly and let me rush you into anything just because I am keen. Wangling isn't perhaps quite as lost an art as I tried to make out a while ago. I dare say I could get you something a bit softer. You ought to think it over. . . ."

" Don't be an ass," said Cartwright.

" I'm not being an ass," said Henderson. And there was a dispassionate seriousness altogether new about the surprising fellow. " It's—it seems to have got a bit late for rushing into things now. You've got to do them gingerly. Like grown-ups instead of kids any more."

It was true. The affair had become sombre. Air raids were no longer exciting in the same old way. They were a bore. One did, in point of fact, do things differently—like grown-ups instead of kids. . . . But could one, did one, on that account, do different things ?

" You mean my responsibilities ? " said Cartwright slowly. " Well, I've got none. You know that. My wife's got a thumping good share in a practice which the Old Man is running. She's a brick ; and I've got a son over fifteen. No one is dependent on me."

Each one of the three looked steadily in front, for some moments, saying nothing.

Henderson was once more trudging down a roadside ditch with a bare score of shambling men behind him. . . . " About time for you to pack up, Major," he was saying; " there's only a bit of a company in front now. . . ." " Yes," said the Major, pausing with an 18-pounder shell under each arm on a track he had worn from a little stack of ammunition under a tarpaulin to the gun in front. One leg of his breeches was flapping in the breeze, split from the pocket to the knee, giving a glimpse of shirt, under-pants, hairy thigh and a strip of bandage with a smear fringed with the blue of iodine and starch. The gun, snarling back and running smoothly up again every few seconds, while Henderson and the Major chatted, was manned by a subaltern, a sergeant, a telephonist with earpieces strapped to his head and an individual obvious at the first glance from the grace of his tunic as the Major's batman. " I'd like to get rid of this stuff first," the Major continued, indicating the stack under the tarpaulin. " Might just as well. We're beginning to get 'em with open sights now and we've got to wait till Sinclair gets back with another team—if he does. . . . I've got the other five away. I'd move on, if I were you. The blighters have got their fuses set to a turn this morning." Henderson moved on. Under the hedge behind the Major's ammunition dump were five huddled forms. Four were still, and one was smoking a pipe ; but Henderson had already left half a dozen such smokers behind him that morning, men of his platoon. . . . Presently there was a jingle on the road ; Sinclair coming with the gun-team and the Major's groom with a couple of horses. . . .

Cartwright, meanwhile, was seeing those miraculous fellows at Olympia with their braided jackets and high bonnets, their dazzling Wellingtons and twinkling spurs, whirling and swerving through the sand, limbers and guns skimming after them. . . .

It was a long time since the War had had a glimmer of adventure in it. . . .

And Mollie Henderson saw two men absorbed in one of their sentimentalities.

" I believe," she said thoughtfully, " that Jim will get almost as much joy out of sending you off into it as he would from going again himself."

" Yes," said Henderson. " Out of the mouths of babes. . . . Oh, damn it ! it's true. But look here, I'm *not* sending him off ! Haven't I just said that he must think it over—quietly ? And that I'll try to do just what he likes ? "

" Since swearing has become general," said Cartwright, and he smiled because of Henderson's dead seriousness, " you know damned well that there *is* only one thing to do." It was the bare fact that he stated. It may have been true that a good deal of the bounce had gone out of it while he had been growing accustomed to his billet and the parade ground at Wilverley and week-ends with Dorothy and the boys at Chiswick, while his mind had been absorbing the detailed geography of little maps in the papers that never changed, while the only news was to be found in casualty lists ; bounce may have gone out of it all, but there was still no alternative.

E XETER, however, brought some of the bounce back again ; for there was a swing and zest about the Cadet School at Exeter.

The portfolio held by Henderson's 'Sulky' Sinclair (now a Lieutenant-Colonel with a D.S.O. ribbon on his chest and a perpetual glove containing two fingers and the thumb of a left hand) was a weighty one, designated by the initials C.I.G.—Chief Instructor in Gunnery. It was partly Sinclair himself that brought a feeling of tradition to this newest of institutions, and the swing and the zest ; and partly that we had got, as the critics of the time said, our second wind.

Winter was gone and the spring of 1916 was perhaps as great as any spring in the history of mankind with Hope and Promise.

The sunshine of Devon and the magnificent snobbery of horsemen as against men who knew not the ways of horses ; the quiet, austere pride of the Colonel (who bared his head in a lecture when he spoke of the biggest and finest regiment in the world in which he and his listeners had the honour of serving—the Royal Regiment of Artillery). . . . Yes, staleness had gone out of the War ; the first glow of the proud adventure had come back to it with the sap rising afresh in the hedgerows.

The glow was brought by men from Africa who had romped through a campaign in German West—horsemen already made. With them were Yeomanry N.C.O.s back from Gallipoli and Egypt ; youngsters picked from the disintegrating cadet units, boys straight from school ; two or three tough old Sergeants and a Territorial Sergeant-Major from batteries in France. They were all fresh volunteers alike in that the immediate and chosen

desire of each was to be an officer in the Artillery. The
Sergeants and the Sergeant-Major from France were less
robustious than the rest, held a little aloof perhaps by
their possession of some of the lore that was as yet a
mystery to the others. But the prevailing spirit of that
first ' Group A ' that formed the cadet part of the 18th
Battery was the spirit of the fresh and innocent ones.

The first and startling revelation to Cartwright was
that of his immaculate ignorance. The simplest of all
orders, " Squad—number " was changed to the strange-
sounding " From the right—number " followed by
" From the right—tell off be fours."

He had thrust up his hand to indicate that he could
ride ; for he had had a pony from as early as he could
remember till he was fourteen, and he had hacked three
or four times each term at Oxford ; but after ten minutes
in the riding-school, when the hand-raisers had been
twice round with stirrups crossed over the horse's withers,
he saw that it would have been more accurate to have
kept his hand down.

He had thought that his muscles were in pretty good
trim ; but the lithe, indistinguishable corporals, each of
whom was known as Nijinski, who glided about the
square in blue slacks, white sweaters and canvas shoes,
convinced him that his muscles, on the contrary, were
soft.   (Old Ruggles had feared that Henderson's cadets
were being put through it ' too 'ot '—cadets who had had
no horses to groom three times and to ride for forty
minutes each day !)

After the first six full days of it Cartwright lay, face-
downwards on his cot, and wondered if the flogged soreness
of his limbs was due to the fact that he was no longer
eighteen or twenty or even twenty-five like the others,
but nearly thirty-eight.

After eleven full days of it he spoke, at the door of the
riding-school, to the Sergeant.

" Don't ask *me*," said the Sergeant.   " You'd best go
sick.   Or I'll take you up to the Major if you like."

" All right," said Cartwright.

This Major was famous, a source of pride and an

adornment to the Cadet School, a special wangle of Sinclair's. He had been, immemorially, riding instructor at the shop at Woolwich when Sinclair was a cadet. His chin was flat from resting upon the railing of riding-school galleries, and enormous moustaches had grown outwards and downwards to rest, in the manner of mahogany props for his genial face, upon these same railings. But with the rich brown moustaches and the tufts of grey sticking out of his ears his capillary achievements abruptly ended. His head was so shinily bald that his cap was kept in position not by the grip of its band but by the pressure of his pate into its top.

"Cadet to speak to you, Sir," said the Sergeant, with the short, snappy salute that Cartwright was learning.

Cartwright stood forward.

The Major, unmoving, gazed ahead into the riding-school. He had seen Cartwright walking behind the Sergeant across the tan to the gallery stairs. He had glanced at him climbing the stairs and knew all there was to know.

"Ever tried pipe-clay, my boy ? " he said.

"Pipe-clay, Sir ? " asked Cartwright.

"Not on your head-ropes," said the Major. "On your behind."

"No, Sir," said Cartwright.

"Well. Do. Plenty of it. He can fall out to-day and to-morrow, Sergeant."

"Thank you, Sir," said Cartwright ; and he could have hugged the old man in his gratitude ; for never before had he had such reason for shrinking from torture.

"But, mind, only to-day and to-morrow," the Major said. "Get it calloused before it goes soft again. . . . Hair of the dog that bit you. All right."

Cartwright saluted and followed the Sergeant down the stairs as the ride filed into the school.

As soon as he had got out from under the gallery, the Major looked down and roared, "Stop that cadet! Stop him ! "

Cartwright looked up. " Yes, that's right, you ! "

F

Cartwright stood to attention

" Don't you ever let me see you with that chin-strap like that again."

Cartwright's hand went up to his chin. Prepared for the very worst the world could offer him—to wit, forty minutes (or as many of them as he could manage) upon a horse—he had pulled down the chin-strap of his cap and tightened it into position on the point of his chin. He stared up at the kind old man, mystified.

" I thought I might have to ride, Sir," he tried to explain.

" Thought you might—but what the hell's that got to do with it ? " The Major was positively gasping for breath. He had actually lifted his chin and his moustache-ends from the railing, whipped off his own cap, giving Cartwright and the ride one glimpse of that indecently bald old head.

He tore the chin-strap over the peak and flung the cap upon his head again, pulling the strap down over the moustaches and the square chin. He proudly set the strap right under his chin, back against his throat, and proudly shouted, " There ! that's where a gunner wears a chin-strap ! . . . Put it right, boy ! "

Cartwright did so.

" That's better." The Major's chin was back again on the gallery railing, and he spoke now peaceably. " Coming into a gunners' riding-school dressed like a blasted Cavalryman. . . . Cavalryman ! I'll tell them what you came and said to me a minute ago if you ever do it again. That'll show them how much you're a Cavalryman. . . . Pipe-clay, don't forget. The Q.M.S. will give it to you—not dubbin."

Cartwright grinned and saluted up to the gallery and turned and marched off with uncomfortably splayed strides, first to the Quartermaster's store and then across the square and up the path to his cot in the hut.   There, in the perfect isolation of a man ' fell out ' during hours of parade, he applied his Spartan salve and lay upon his stomach smoking a cigarette and caring quite passionately, for all his thirty-seven years, for the fact that a

Cavalryman wore his chin-strap on the point of his chin and a gunner against his throat.

One's care and jealousy were for strange matters in those days. Among them arose, in the course of another fortnight (when sores were healed and duly calloused and an entirely new pair of muscles had developed to maturity), the matter of spurs. The three artillerymen from France, Gallipoli yeomen, two or three of the South Africans and the North-west Mounted Policemen had worn spurs from the third or fourth day of their appearance.

On the fourth Saturday the Major, passing into the school, acknowledged the Sergeant's salute with a flick of his fingers and said, "Spurs to-day, Spooner." Sergeant Spooner saluted again and passed out into the sunshine when the ride was assembling to file into the school. "Spurs to-day, soldiers," he said to any of the Cadets that might hear him.

" Soldiers " was the familiar, amiable term of address for the Cadets devised by some one genius among the Regular N.C.O. Instructors to meet the delicacy of the position in which they found themselves. ' Chum ' and ' Sonnie ' and ' Boy ' were applicable only, and then only for the time being, to occasional Cadets of the type of the present three from France. For the others, the natural tendency was towards ' Sir.' ' Cadets ' (or more accurately, ' Kiddets ') was right enough for ceremonial ; but something easier and friendlier had to be found for informal address ; so the genius in the matter of relationships found the half-bantering, cheery ' Soldiers.· " Double up there, sonnie," shouted on a fatigue by a permanent and chronic N.C.O. to an incipient officer would have been as unsuitable as ' my lad,' or ' chum,' or ' cocky.' ' Soldier ' blended irony and bonhomie, patronage and respectful amiability to the degree that justifies the word genius for its discoverer.

It was a godsend to men like Spooner ; for Spooner was a rascal. Starting life as a trumpeter in the regiment while most of the present Cadets were as yet unborn, he had discovered from an adored and an adoring farrier-sergeant

the divers ways in which the horse might be ' coped '
to serve the ends of man.   As a rough-rider corporal he
had retired to the Reserve and a great little horse-coping
business in Berkshire.   He bought wrecks for a song and
sold hunters and cobs—at a price.   During the first year
of the War he had continued his meditative chewing of a
straw among Remounts.   As one of the Sergeant rough-
riders at Exeter he discovered among the Cadets that
horses are not the only vanity of man—vanity for which
man will pay in cash ;   this sly thrusting forward of his
face when speaking, his ability to leave an eye-lid stuck
in the position of winking and his peculiarly caressing use
of the word ' soldier ' indicated that whatever a ' soldier '
most desired could be supplied by him, Spooner,—at a
price.

The desire of some was for rough-exercise on Sundays, of some it was for exemption therefrom.   Late-
passes, week-end leaves, exemption from stable-pickets,
guards and fatigues—Spooner could materialise all these
at Exeter as he had materialised sound hunters and cobs
in Berkshire.   For in addition to being a riding-instructor
he was a nominal Number One of the 18th Battery,
and therefore orderly sergeant in rotation.   The fee,
rigid as though determined by statute, was a flat ten
shillings and the method of transferring it from purchaser
to vendor of the service in question a childishly simple
one.   Spooner walked about the square after a parade,
smacking his boot and his swan-necked spur with his
rough-rider's yard-long quirt, rolling an unlighted cigarette between his lips.   The Cadet desiring a service would
stop the Sergeant and offer him a box of matches.   The
Sergeant would say, " Ta, soldier," and light his cigarette.
But the match-box returned to the Cadet would be
Spooner's own, that he had been carrying in his restless
hand ; for folded into the Cadet's match-box would be a
ten-shilling note.

Even his " Spurs to-day, Soldiers," indicated that
Spooner was standing by his stall.   This, however, was
sheer force of habit ; since his stall was empty, for the
moment, of wares.   Spooner, as every cadet knew, could

sell no spurs while the broad, sad old face of the Major was propped on its square chin upon the gallery railing.

"Fall out the Cadets with spurs, Sergeant," said the Major.

"Cadets with spurs, prove!" the Sergeant shouted. The half-dozen right hands of the spur-wearers shot smartly out to the front.

"On the centre, walk march . . . 'Alt. Eyes right. Dress. 'Old up to the bit.'—Ride, walk, march. From the front, number. As you were. Smartly, now. Ride from the front—number." Heads were again jerked to the left and numbers barked out in the manner of a good hound throwing its tongue. The number that Cartwright flung over his left shoulder to the file behind him was thirteen—the number of his hut . . . (*Adfuisset omen.*) "Four feet from nose to croup. . . ." Sergeant Spooner was chanting in mechanical, sycophantic peevishness. . . . ". . . Four *feet*, number seven, not four inches."

"Stirrups," the Major mumbled down to him. The ride was gently trotting.

"Ride—Wa-a-a-a-a-lk."

The blasé old soldiers carrying the alert new ones steadied to a walk with an eye cocked at the four-foot interval and an ear in the direction of Spooner.

"Ride—quityour—stirrups. Crorse—stirrups."

The irons jangled against boots and then against each other as they were swung over the ambling withers.

"Ride—terrr—*rot.*"

Ears cocked away from the Sergeant, satisfied with the information they required for their next move.

"Number three," the Major said wearily.

"On the centre," Spooner commanded. "Number three."

Number three turned into the centre, halted on the left of the six already there and took up his dressing.

"Seven . . . Eight . . . Eleven . . . Fourteen . . . Seventeen." The numbers turned into the centre.

"Number them again," the Major complained. "God knows where we've got to now. All messed up."

On the second numbering Cartwright was nine—the number of his house in Chiswick. (*Adfuisset omen.*)

"Two . . .   Seven . . .   Four . . .   Five . . . Cruel . . .   Awful. . . .   Poor old ladies on motor-buses . . . Eleven. . . .   Well, there's a war on, I suppose. . . ." And for four days now Cartwright had thought that he had found the one and only secret of the art of riding—to straighten your legs comfortably down and merely adopt the advice that had been roared at you and roared again and monotonously again—to sit back ; to lean your shoulders backwards over a hollowed spine beyond the point that seemed, from every feeling of instinct and reason, to be the point of decency and common safety.   But he knew now that beyond that point lay, not destruction, but the promised land.   He could have jogged on, steady and in harmony with every movement of the popular old " Rajah " under him, till Doom's-day.

And the Major missed him out again, mumbling into his moustaches : " Sixteen . . .   Ten . . .   Eighteen. . . .   Well, I suppose as Gambardier's with those damn' great naval guns and siege stuff . . . ride on lorries ; and when they fall off the lorries, they walk . . . get there in time for the finish, I shouldn't wonder.   Walk them and give them their stirrups, Sergeant, or you'll have them all in the tan. . . .   As you were—that fifth man from the front now, I've forgotten his number—can fall out.   Elderly man who knows that pipe-clay isn't only meant for head-ropes."

"Number nine ! " commanded Spooner, and Cartwright, leaning magnificently back, trotted to the centre and picked up his dressing.

He signed his name on the Quartermaster's sheet as the trumpets sounded ' dinner ' against an entry of ' Spurs, jack, plated, pairs, 1 ' ; and for the pride that went into it he might have been signing his first cheque on the counter of the bank at Oxford.

THE stripe given to one Cadet in each hut in order to set the regular Eighteenth Battery Corporal free to move on to another hut filled by the fortnightly arrival of a fresh draft of recruits was given, in No. 13, to Hall of the Transvaal Police.

Curiously, and pleasingly, Hall was the man that Cartwright would himself have chosen from the eighteen in the hut for this office of acting and unpaid Bombardier-Cadet. It was from riding behind him, incidentally, on the third Sunday morning's rough exercise along the Clyst St. Mary Road, that Cartwright received the revelation of straightening the legs down and sitting back. They changed cots when Hall's preferment was announced in Orders ; for the stumbling up the two steps in alphabetical sequence on the day of their arrival had given Cartwright the first cot by the door and Hall the one next it ; and the orderly-sergeant for the day of Hall's promotion said that the N.C.O. Cadet in charge of the hut must take the first cot on the right of the upper entrance.

Hall, roughly speaking, was one of the very men that Henderson had yearned for and sought to make out of schoolboys, clerks and stockbrokers. The choice of him gave Cartwright a thrill of confidence in the machine that had chosen him (the same kind of thrill that he had found in the impassive old Major's recognition of himself, after a whole fortnight, as the user of pipe-clay). That was about all the two had in common—the fact that Hall was chosen and that Cartwright approved the choice— and it was as sound a basis for companionship as any that existed in the hut.

Couples and groups with white-banded Service caps soon became as much a feature of the evening traffic of Exeter as strolling undergraduates had been at Oxford ; and Hall and he usually made up one such couple.

Hall (like Bullock, who had been killed flying) was the son of a country parson. It was apparently a complex

about what he called, roughly, " brain-work," that had
led to his choice of profession. Nothing short of the
fact that there was a big War on could have braced him
to face again, after four or five years of magnificent
oblivion of them, academic statements printed upon a
page ; and, the War notwithstanding, he admitted to
Cartwright, if he had only known what ' the gunners '
was going to let him in for . . .

This bitter reflection was made by him on a day he and
Cartwright simultaneously wrote down, at a lecture, that
the ballistic coefficient of a projectile is equal to $\frac{W}{nD^2}$.

The bursting of a shell near by, the plunging of a
horse gone for the moment utterly mad, would have
kindled a fire in the eye of Hall ; the crumbling of a house
in which he sat would have drawn back his broad shoulders
and lifted his sandy head in a proud challenge of his
destiny. The equation made of him a wan and helpless
thing, a man defeated and broken. Cartwright, on the
other hand, suffered from no complex of the sort ; for
he had the deep and tranquilising conviction that
things beyond ready understanding were things of slight
importance. He was willing to accept this $\frac{W}{nD^2}$ thing
quietly, and without prejudice. He told Hall, " My
dear fellow, it *doesn't matter*. It doesn't matter a damn."
Even the italics made no immediate impression on Hall.
As well to tell a man with the snake-complex that a fine
effigy of a snake ' doesn't matter.' It might not ' matter ';
but it is enough to produce heaven alone knows what
writhings of nameless horror and utter despair.

" I believe I could show it to you," Cartwright said
quietly, seeing that merely brutal reassurance was not
enough. " I think I can follow it myself—it's only a
fairly neat way of saying a rather long thing. . . ."

" Neat way ! " Hall mumbled in glum irony. " Neat
. . ."

" Well, it is rather neat as a matter of fact ; and if you
want to understand it, I dare say I can . . ."

" You can't," said Hall. " No one can. And if
being a gunner means starting Algebra all over again——"

" Of course it doesn't ! " Cartwright reassured him.

" There are people who like to be told things like that
Whitehead is one of them.   You can see it by the way he
chalks these things up.   He's a schoolmaster, don't
forget.   He likes to get everything into the shape of a
formula.   It's only one way of looking at things ; and
it's not important to people who don't see them that way."

" Well——" the passion of Hall's bitterness was abating.
Anger, at any rate, had gone from it.   He sat down on
the boards of his cot, unbuttoned his tunic and began to
unroll his putties.   " Well—even if this n into W squared
or whatever it is doesn't matter, there must be some things
that do.   There's ' angle of sight.'   Even old Sinclair
said that ' angle of sight ' is important—and he isn't a
schoolmaster."   Hall sat up, his bitterness turned to
truculence as he saw that he could prove his point.
" Let me tell you, I don't understand ' angle of sight.'
I don't know why you've always got to stick it on.   I
don't know—*what—it—means*.   There."

" Then you're just the most pig-headed blighter in
the whole army," said Cartwright.   " Here ! "

The hut broom stood in the corner a yard from the
folded blankets and rolled palliasse at the head of Hall's
cot.   Sympathy with the strong man in his dark hour
and exasperation with the stony, stubborn stupidity
that had landed him there struggled in Cartwright as he
seized the broom and thrust it into Hall's surprised
hands.   " Here ! take this damned thing and aim at the
bottom corner of that window.   Pretend it's a rifle. . . .
Go on.   Do as I tell you. . . . " for Hall was hesitating.

Still a little inclined to resist the possibility of understanding, Hall slowly obeyed.

" Now fire one round at the top corner," Cartwright
commanded, and Hall raised the end of the broom.

" What are you doing that for ? " asked Cartwright.
" Why are you moving ? "

Puzzled and sullen and inclined to be bored, Hall put
down the broom.

" Oh, no, you don't, my lad ! " said Cartwright.   " You're
going to understand what ' angle of sight ' is—and why—
during the next minute, or I'll eat my hat.   Come on.

Bottom corner again." He coaxed the broom back into Hall's hands and Hall obediently aimed it. " Now the top; slowly. Watch what you're doing. Tell me— what do you think you *are* doing ? "

" Aiming at the top corner," said Hall solidly, as though he, too, had a point worth proving, but one that would prove itself by the weight of sheer obviousness without any melodrama from him.

" Yes," said Cartwright. " Even you are not such a damned fool as to think you'd hit the top corner by aiming at the lower one. Both corners are in the same line and in the same range. The only difference is that one is higher up than the other. When you can see them from your rifle or your gun, all you have to do is to point it up. It's no use pointing at the bottom if you want to hit the top. When you can't see the target from your gun there's got to be some way of telling you how much to cock it up. I could tell you to raise the end about a foot, but that wouldn't be accurate enough. The thing you can measure most accurately is the angle through which you've got to raise the axis of the piece from the horizontal. Now do you see why you've got to ' stick on angle of sight ? ' It's just because you can't expect to hit the top of a window by aiming at its bottom."

Hall put down the broom. A smile slowly brought life into the features that his sombre despair had, for the time being, killed. " Well, I'm jiggered ! " he said ; then solemnly, " By God, Cartwheels, you're a ruddy genius ! Look here, can you lend me a quid, till I can get a cheque changed ? "

" Yes," said Cartwright. " Two if you like. I find the easiest and quickest way is to get my wife to change cheques for me."

" Good," said Hall. " We'll have a real blow-out at Dellers to-night—with me. Now that I've got the ' angle of sight ' knocked out, by Golly—will you ? "

" Rather," said Cartwright ; and he set about unrolling his own putties ; for there was a lordly comfort in putting one's legs into slacks and one's feet into canvas shoes for an hour before walking up to the tram for Exeter

BEER was not good enough for Hall that night.
After their second bottle of wine he expressed his
confidence that in due time, with the friendly
hand of Cartwright guiding him he would understand the
angle ' T.O.B.'; parallel lines of fire would be no longer a
mystery ; concentration and distribution would be second
nature. Cartwright, too, was warm with confidence.

Hall leaned, over coffee and a brandy, towards
Cartwright and said, " I say—about marriage . . . "

He paused. There seemed to be something here of the
same enigmatic quality as $\frac{W}{nD^2}$; but the puzzle this
time was alive.

" What about marriage ? " said Cartwright.

" Well—you're married, aren't you ? " But Hall was
very much afraid of appearing to pry into other people's
affairs. " I mean, you said something about a wife
cashing your cheques."

" Yes," said Cartwright. " What about it ? I've been
married for some years."

" Oh," said Hall. " I suppose that's different. It
wouldn't apply." He sat back again, willing to drop the
subject.

" Apply to what ? " Cartwright asked.

" Well—to me," said Hall. " To getting married now.
You see—well, you seem to be a pretty wise old bird,
Cartwheels, and I'm dashed if I know."

" You haven't let *me* know very much yet," Cartwright
suggested.

" But that's all," said Hall. " There isn't any more.
Just a question of whether one ought, or oughtn't. What
do you think ? "

" I don't know," said Cartwright. " The question got
itself answered for me about seventeen years ago." The
seriousness of Hall, however, demanded honest and careful
consideration. Cartwright, moreover, was not in the
superior position where he had found himself when the

question was "angle of sight." He said, thoughtfully:
" I don't believe—quite honestly and on the whole—that
I've ever been sorry."

" Not even now ? " asked Hall.

" N—no," said Cartwright. " I don't think so.
I'm not just leaving a wife and family to shift for themselves."

" Yes," said Hall. " The dibs do make a bit of
difference. . . . I suppose a good round dozen of the chaps
in our group have wives down here. Most of them
war-wives—chaps like Archer and Burnett and Tracey.
Youngsters, I mean. Roughly in my own sort of position
—but they don't seem to have worried much about it."

" But what is your particular worry ? " asked
Cartwright.

" Well——" said Hall. " Partly the dibs. You see
I couldn't afford to get married before. It's no sort of a
life for a girl in Africa till you've got on a bit—in fact it's
a rule of the Service that you mustn't marry for a time.
Not that she would have minded. It's one of those
things that's been on the cards since we were kids. It
seems to me one ought to look a bit farther than these
other fellows do—just intercourse *de luxe* before they
shove off to the front. I mean, suppose we don't come
back ? What's the use of just having made a young widow
—and possibly a kid ? Or suppose we come back
messed-up—eyes and hands gone ; feet missing ; silver
tubes instead of proper innards. . . . And if I do come
back all right we'll be in the soup. See what I mean ? "

" No," said Cartwright. " I don't. Why in the
soup ? "

" Well, I shan't have got much further in my job.
It's at least ten years' service before one can expect to
marry. This show won't have altered that."

" I suppose you *want* to marry ? " Cartwright suggested.
He felt that they really ought to thrash the matter out.

" I did," said Hall. " In fact I intended to as soon as
we'd got settled in here. As far as *she* knows I still do.
It was you who started holding me up. As soon as I
knew that you had a wife and she wasn't down here with

you—although you could obviously afford it—I thought there must be some kind of a wise old reason behind it. You're obviously not one of the refugees from marriage—like Bradshaw. He, poor chap, would have jumped into the Thames to get away from his wife if he couldn't have jumped into this."

" Well, I'm damned ! said Cartwright.

" Sorry," said Hall. " Honestly I didn't mean to pry. . . . Oh, hell ! " He crushed out his cigarette-end, and took another and laughed. " Now you'll think it's because I'm tight that I'm talking like this. But I didn't set out to pump you about your affairs. I wanted you to chat about mine."

" My dear fellow," said Cartwright ; " I assure you I wouldn't mind if you were trying to pump me. The question surprised me. It makes me wonder if it's true."

" I wouldn't have the damned impertinence to ask if you had any special private reason. But there might be a general sort of reason that would apply to me and Sheila."

" It seems to me," Cartwright made his pronouncement after some moments' thought ; " it seems to me that if you two would like to spend some time together, now that you've got the opportunity, there's no reason why you shouldn't take it."

" Then," said Hall, puzzled, " why—— " but he stopped.

" Because," said Cartwright, smiling benignly at his embarrassment. " In my case the opportunity isn't quite the same. A family of nearly seventeen years' standing is somewhat of an organisation. There's a damned great house to be kept going for two boys who go to school. Servants and so on. . . ." He did not go on to say that he had, as a matter of fact, merely omitted to think of it. He did not say that, perhaps, after seventeen years of companionship, hastily snatched company during the late afternoons and early evenings of a few weeks did not seem to be a matter of the utmost urgency. What he did say, quite suddenly, was, " But dash it ! I dare say it could be arranged ! . . . Why not ? . . . Perhaps Dorothy would like it."

" That's another thing that makes a chap think," said Hall. " The way women—all women, are making such a grand do about ' giving themselves '—honestly, I've heard them say it—' giving themselves ' to soldiers. Suppose old Sheila were just bitten by that fly ? That would be nice, wouldn't it ? "

" Oh, rot," said Cartwright. " You say it's been in the wind since you were kids."

" Yes. . . . But you see what I mean," Hall insisted. " Might look like just—hustling because it's nearly closing-time. And there's another point, too, don't forget. We've got a hell of a lot to *do* down here. It's all very well for fellows like you. But these battery angles and things are going to take me all my time. And then, if the girl gets really humpy there's no way of *proving* that everything's going to be all right in the end. We can say that the artillery is safe as houses—safer than the Feet—but there's no getting away from the casualty lists. They always queer the argument. ' R.F.A.,' ' R.F.A.,' ' R.F.A. in a list as long as your arm doesn't look exactly like a picnic."

" No," said Cartwright. " Being married to a clinger wouldn't be exactly a lark at the moment. But the ordinary good sort realises that she can't ask for guarantees. My wife, for instance——"

" But they must *think*," said Hall ; " think like blazes. And I'm not one of these breezy, tactful jokers, don't forget. If I saw Sheila getting the hump and the glassy eye, wondering if her darling was going to come back a hero or get it in the neck, I'd be stumped. I'd probably be wondering the same sort of thing myself. . . . I'd want to hurry out for a stroll or get on with a page or two of the battery angle. I don't know. It's a teaser."

Cartwright thought back to the simple affair that his own marriage had been. . . . At that time, too, now that he came to think of it, there had been a war. But it had not been his war and Dorothy's—as this one was Hall's and the problematical Sheila's with its puzzles of " angle of sight," of $\frac{w}{nD^2}$; its enigmas of human relationship ; his own too, and also Dorothy's. He had had no more thought of identifying himself with that old war in Africa than of demanding a place in the English fifteen against Wales. . . .

"I think, old thing," he said, "I think your Sheila is the party that ought to be consulted. She's probably got ideas of her own. Of course, there's the money end of it."

Cartwright's thumb moved forward along one side of his jaw and his forefinger along the other. "If you get knocked out"—he smiled and looked judicially wise—"the lady will be better off to the extent of a pension, I suppose. If you don't get knocked out, you'll be worse off to the extent of having a wife on your books. But if she was going to be able to live without your support, having married you oughtn't to incapacitate her from that. But the odds are, anyway, that you'll be able to support her. If the Service you were in won't pay you enough you'll be able to get another job. There'll be lots of jobs going after the War. . . . Seems to me there's only one thing that might complicate the economics."

"Kids ?" said Hall.

"Yes," said Cartwright. "Or even just one."

"Suppose she says she wants one ? " was Hall's next anxiety.

"I suppose you'll have to believe it," said Cartwright.

"Oh, damn it ! " said Hall in complete exasperation at last. "A soldier *can't—shouldn't*—go bunging himself up with all these things. You can't use guns and limbers for lugging about perambulators and household junk." (He had not yet seen to what simple and homely uses these same austere engines of destruction might be put ; nor had Cartwright.)

"But the whole world is soldiers now," said Cartwright ; and he felt a certain pride in noting the fact. "And perambulators have got to be kept on the move more than ever."

Pride increased as the argument developed ; and the last sip of Hall's festive cognac gave a fitting flavour to proud words. "We'll look after the guns and limbers while the stout-hearted women take care of the prams and the junk. They won't let us get bunged up if they're the right sort. And if they're not the right sort it's their own look out."

Hall signalled for the bill. "Let's stroll," he said. "We'd tumble into some crowd or other on the tram."

The talk, as talk, might not have amounted to anything very much ; but there was something about the evening that did. Walking, from being a merely unnoticed and unhonoured device for getting from one place to another, had itself been made an art. Ruggles had started it for Cartwright, bringing poise and swing and rhythm. The nimble youths in Exeter with their blue slacks and white sweaters and canvas shoes had elaborated upon the elementary work of Ruggles. Hall was as hard as nails and as lithe on his feet as in the saddle or on a numna. Paces rang clear on the pavement with the clink of spur-chains.

"There's one thing about it," said Hall, as they got away from the last of the pavement-traffic on to the Topsham Road. "We'd be able to save every bean of my gunner pay. The Service is paying me, you know, as long as I'm soldiering, and it's enough for us both to live on." This marked the final disappearance of the last of Hall's immediate problems.

For the rest of the way to Topsham they discussed the technique of their craft.

HALL, in the manner of one to whom has been vouchsafed a revelation, applied himself to the small library in his possession and Cartwright's that dealt with the matter of ballistics. The simplicity required to convert a formula for him into an intelligible device made a great expert of Cartwright. Each day after tea, when putties and boots had been removed, Hall would produce his protractor, scale and dividers, the Ordnance map of Swanage (because of its fantastic contours), and Cartwright would assume the mantle of Pythagoras. Each day he expounded some corollary or other to that first article of the gunners' faith, the Radian Triangle.

When a happy smile had replaced the look of sullen bewilderment and Hall had set feverishly to work upon the problems set by Cartwright, Cartwright would discard the Pythagorean attitude and expand his legs into the easy posture of a reader, his pipe going lustily, his back against his kit-bag and folded blankets. There was a steady piety about his reading as there was a grunting, mumbling excitement in the work of Hall. He read from those pages of Field Artillery Training devoted to " Equitation and Driving " and from the epic " Animal Management."

There was a sense of movement and achievement. Hall could arrive, quickly and fairly accurately, at a line of fire and an angle of elevation for a battery. Cartwright could ride with enough efficiency to be completely inconspicuous in the lead, the centre or the wheel of a gun-team in battery manœuvres. Either of them could get through a quarter of an hour as a battery or section-commander, a layer or a Number One.

Dorothy Cartwright, meanwhile, found a deputy for herself at the Belgian House, and a sister to keep house for the servants and the boys. Cartwright found rooms for her in the Wonford Road. She came down about the middle of April, and Hall was duly married to Sheila.

No one at the School but Cartwright knew of the ceremony. Hall did not state the purpose more specific-ally than " urgent private affairs " on his application for a week-end leave. He sniffed at the suggestion of a honeymoon at Dawlish or Teignmouth with " No, *thank* you. There are plenty of our fellows having—honey-moons—at Dawlish and Teignmouth. And plenty's enough. In town, too, for that matter."

He wanted to be sure that his position was regular in the eyes of his wife's prospective landlady. Hall con-sulted her as to churches. By a stroke of luck she was the widow of an organist, and Hall was married in the

G

church of her late husband. So that, as Hall said, was all right.

Cartwright was best man and the guests at the wedding were Hall's parents and Sheila's, a girl in some sort of khaki and an odd relation or two who got to the church just in time, shook hands heartily with every one after the service and hurried back to the station.

In the retrospect of a dozen years the whole affair, in its almost fierce simplicity, appears in a wan light. Hall standing up to the decision that had been so momentous, striving to make of it the most everyday, normal and casual affair in the world. Sheila, standing beside him, her feet firmly planted in a neat pair of brogues. They were " chancing their arm," as any one at the school would have put it, on some sort of a destiny—any sort of destiny at all, the gamble being only on the matter of permanence. And they lost. (Hall was killed fifteen months later taking up ammunition, somewhere between Brielen and Zonnebeke. Sheila drives a small two-seater about the country in the solitary practice of massage while the eleven-year-old boy shows some aptitude for prep-school cricket.)

They lost ; but their bid was made in a ' kindly, easy manner, but collected '—in a phrase from " Equitation and Driving." Their legs and feet were well under them, she in her brogues and Hall in his smartly polished, square-toed boots and plated jack-spurs.

It was unlike the other religious ceremony attended by Cartwright and Dorothy a fortnight later—the christening of Henderson's son in a West-End fane. His colleague godfather was a staff-officer. There were young Majors and old Generals at the reception at the house lent to the Hendersons for the purpose. Cartwright was introduced to odd ones here and there among them as they moved about in the two rooms and the hall with sandwiches and glasses. He caught few, or none, of their names, and found that their inevitable remark, when Henderson had moved on, was " So you've been with Henderson ? Great fella—young Hendy . . ." or " Stout lad, little Hendy. . . ."

One old man said slyly, " A gunner, eh ?—you *wait !* "

It was all like coming up from a builder's yard to keep holiday with architects.

Cartwright knew that he was cutting something of a figure among them with his Major's face and Cadet's uniform.

Henderson himself was unchanged. " Hang on a bit," he said. " Mollie's upstairs. Still feels a bit indecent. We'll go up when these brass-hats and things have staggered off. Your wife is with her."

" So long, Dickie," he said to the other godfather, " thanks awfully for the kind words and all that. Same for you some day. See you to-morrow." And then to Cartwright, " Now, we'll make off into the conservatory or somewhere. Those old jossers can take care of themselves for a bit. I've promised Mollie to talk to you."

They found a little room with a desk and bookcases in it, and Henderson shut the door.

" Well," he said very seriously, " what about it ? "

" About what ? " asked Cartwright.

" It—generally. The whole show."

" Oh, I like it," said Cartwright. " It's a great place. I'm becoming no end of a gunner."

" Yes," said Henderson. " I mean—the point is, we could still do something, you know."

" How d'you mean ' do something ' ? " asked Cartwright. " You can't stop the War, can you ? "

" I mean—stop it for you." And Henderson was very solemn. " Fact is—Mollie's been getting at me like anything. And I said I'd talk to you." He hesitated and then went on. " You don't know. *I* don't know more than an umpteenth of it all. Nobody does. But the dirty work hasn't started yet, old thing. Of course every one isn't going to get scuppered ; but Mollie says we might as well try to make sure of you instead of just taking a chance." He did not look at Cartwright, but sent the twinkle of his solitary eye drifting about the room. " I believe we've got landed in the only really dry spot in this whole house. There's a bottle and a syphon or so in every other room I've been in."

Cartwright had a slight sense of relief in the feeling that he was talking not to a principal but an agent. " Thanks most awfully for thinking of it," he said.

" The drink ? " asked Henderson, " or the—suggested dug-out ? "

" Both," said Cartwright, " but you don't really think there's much need for either.   Do you ? "

" Oh, I don't know so much about that," said Henderson —the agent, Cartwright perceived, trying to identify himself with his principal.   " I don't know. . . .   You see, old thing—" he looked quite squarely at Cartwright. " The fact is—you're going into this business blind.   You don't know what you're letting yourself in for.   Dash it, *I* don't.   We Mons angels saw nothing—just a few weeks of red-hot slaughter . . . everything merry and bright while it lasted . . . but . . . nothing at all to what it is now—and what it's going to be."

" I know," said Cartwright.

" You don't," said Henderson.   " But there—don't say I didn't warn you."

" You old idiot ! " laughed Cartwright.   " Don't worry —I'll tell Mollie that you've tried your damnedest, but I'm not taking any."

" H'm," said Henderson.   " And what about your wife ?   Mollie's had time to get properly at her by now and tell her that you could work a soft job if you wanted to."

" She thinks I've worked one already," said Cartwright, " by being a gunner."

" Mollie will have corrected that error by now," said Henderson.

They spent some minutes in private thought.

" Jimmy," said Cartwright, " tell me just for curiosity, would Mollie hang on to you if you were fit ? "

" It's impossible to say.   On the whole—no.   But it's different.   I'm a soldier. . . ."

" Oh, to hell with that ! " said Cartwright.   " I'm as much a soldier by now as you were.   I've had as much training, and as good a training."

" Yes ; but I had no other training," said Henderson.

" And I wasn't an old josser like you, with a family and a profession."

" Look here ! " said Cartwright, and he was positively startled. " What are we trying to get at ? "

" I asked a civil question," said Henderson, " and I'd like a civil answer. Will you let me scrounge some sort of a softish job for you ? Count ten before you answer."

It would have been possible, and very easy, to thank Henderson quite amiably and have done with the matter ; but Cartwright felt an uneasiness in badinage at the moment. " There wouldn't be a ghost of an excuse for me," he said. " I'm no more tied than a schoolboy. I've told you before, Dorothy is perfectly provided for."

But coherent argument was quite impossible. " No, Jimmy. You know darned well it's all rot. I've got to go. You would have to, just the same." . . . Funny old Hall, for example, was an illustration of his meaning. He was not messing about at that moment wondering whether he should, or should not, take a big chance—beyond the chance of matrimony. He had ridden his hundreds of miles about Africa with his carbine and his bandolier and his water-bottle, parching his throat and callousing his rump, and was going straight ahead now, with his funny, puzzled look, slogging at ' battery angles ' and the ' buzzer.' . . . And there were all the others with him ; stockbrokers, undergraduates, school prefects, insurance agents, a sculptor. . . . " I'd like to see *you* falling out now ! " he said morosely.

Henderson smiled at the challenge. " Well," he said, " it beats me. Everything they say—the women, I mean—is sound enough. It's just sheer common sense that we ought to try to save you instead of letting you get scuppered. But there you are ! I kidnapped you once rather neatly. I won't again—unless you ask me to."

All that Cartwright now said was " Ta."

IN the room where they joined their wives nothing more was said of the War.

Cartwright smiled, looking out of the window as he and Dorothy sat in the train to Exeter. He was thinking of Henderson's obvious fidgeting about on hot bricks, waiting for the women to indicate what they were going to talk about. When Dorothy had indicated the newly-christened baby, Henderson's relief and gratitude were positively touching.

Dorothy leaned across from her corner and touched his knee. She said, " What do you think of the Hendersons' plan, dear ? "

He grunted. " Those Hendersons ! " he said. " You've got to take everything they say with a goodish grain of salt. What did Mollie have to say ? "

She looked into the far corner to make sure that the sailor seated there was actually asleep and then said : " Only that Captain Henderson was offering you some kind of a safe job."

Cartwright's first thought in his immediate discomfort took the form of a tribute to Henderson's skill in predicting precisely such discomfort. The grunt is its most accurate expression. Once more Cartwright grunted. " *Talk*, my dear," he said. " Sheer talk ! " Then, a little more testily : " There are no jobs floating about in these days. Every one has just got to take what comes, and stick it. Old Henderson can do no more than the man in the moon. He said so to me."

" He kept you back quite effectively before, didn't he ? " Dorothy asked quietly.

" I dare say," said Cartwright. " The War was young then. There was such a thing as influence. But that's all been knocked on the head. Mollie might think they can do all sorts of things—but Jimmy knows better. He could try, of course——"

" And he is going to ? "

Some instinct made Cartwright select the answer that was nearest to the truth. " How can I say what the beggar is going to do ? Incidentally he hasn't got a job of any sort for himself yet."

Dorothy sat slowly back in her corner again. She crossed one leg over the other. " Poor old Charles," she said very thoughtfully. " I suppose it *must* be so. . . . We'll never be able to talk to each other about this War—till after it's over."

The profound sadness of her moved Cartwright forward from his own corner into a position of crouching with his elbows upon his knees, lighting a fresh cigarette from the stump of the old one.

" Don't get humpy, old girl," he said. " We're not as badly off as some—as most, in fact. Gunners are not the Infantry, you know."

He knew at once that he ought to have had more sense than to say anything so lame as that. Dorothy was about to answer ; but she didn't answer. She set her lips again and looked out into the night.

When she did speak it was to say, quite lightly : " Do you know, Charles, you're taking ever so much more interest in people than you ever did before. You always took them for granted ; and now you seem to think about them in some way."

" I *like* the beggars," he said. " Where could you find better fellows than Jimmy Henderson and old Hall, and those old rascals Ruggles and Foskitt and Ekins and Bighe ? "

" Oh, I'm not jealous ! " said she. " I think you're taking more interest in me too."

" Well—" said Cartwright. " Dash it, I am. But——"

" I know, old boy," she said. " I know. But we can't talk just now."

Cartwright saw the great kindliness of her. He was relieved so far as she could give him relief.

" It was fun having yesterday with the boys," he said. " Isn't old John getting on ! It's wonderful how much they grow and develop in two months at his age. And David is going to be a canny little beggar."

" There ! " said Dorothy. " You're more observant of them."

" One would think," said Cartwright, " that I'd always been a complete and perfect cabbage."

" You were never a particularly sensitive creature, were you ? " said she. " I've often chuckled over the calm way you announced that you were going off to the War."

" You've *chuckled !* " he exclaimed.

" Yes, dear." And in her smile there was again that stab of kindness. " What else could one do but—chuckle ? " They both looked away into the scurrying darkness that was now Dorset. . . .

This must have been the kind of thing of which Hall, in his analysis of the married state, had fought shy that night at Deller's over their coffee and brandy. . . . Cartwright was glad, for reasons utterly vague, that Hall's wife and Dorothy seemed to have taken to each other. Their rooms were near enough together in the Wonford Road for them to pick each other up and go into the town together, shopping and having lunch. They even went to the cinema one afternoon, before ' the boys ' should be due from Barracks ; for they referred to their massed husbands as ' the boys.' Friendships, Cartwright reflected, had not, for some reason or other, grown up like this in the old days.

IT must have been about the beginning of June that Hall said one afternoon as they were walking up: " What do you think about doing something with the girls, Cartwheels ? "

" I suppose it is pretty dull for them," Cartwright admitted.

" I don't mean just go to a show, or anything like that," Hall explained. " I mean something a bit organised."

" Go ahead," said Cartwright. " Organise it and let's see."

" 'T seems perfectly marvellous to have been married for seventeen years," Hall went on. " You and your wife, I mean. She's a godsend to Sheila, by the way. Awful good sort. But I mean Sundays seem a bit long, just mooning about in the digs. I can see Sheila beginning to get stodgy at about tea-time—wondering how this show is going to turn out. And—just between ourselves —it gets on my *nerves*. It seems like messing about with one's luck to go asking questions about it. . . . See what I mean ? "

" I don't see that you've done much organising so far," Cartwright suggested.

" Well—we could pack up a nosebag of grub after lunch and float off somewhere, the four of us, and have tea and supper. We might go halves in a car, or a pony and trap. It would prevent Sheila's chewing her spine. I don't want to be butting in on your time, old thing ; just sing out if you don't like the idea. But it just seemed to me that it might be—convenient—to you, too."

" I think it's a good idea," said Cartwright ; " I'll see what Dorothy thinks about it. I think it would be better to sound them out before we fix up anything, don't you ? "

" Oh, I can guarantee Sheila," Hall said. " She's feeding from the hand, poor kid. She'll agree to anything. She's sort of—I don't know what to call it, quite— intimidated, I think. Your missis doesn't seem to be."

" Well—" said Cartwright, " you must remember she—we—are a good deal older than you two."

" I know," said Hall very solemnly. " It's damned sporting of you to turn out the way you've done. Every one thinks that."

" Oh, do they ! " said Cartwright. " Thirty-eight isn't quite being a grandfather, as you ought to have seen. Some of the youngsters have conked out under the training, and—well, I haven't. All I meant was that Dorothy and I have been married a good deal longer than you, and that makes some sort of a difference. . . .'

But it made, as he found a few weeks later, less difference than he thought.

It must have been on about the third or fourth afternoon of the battle of the Somme that something of a sensation was caused in Hut 13. Putties, boots and breeches were being changed along the whole length of the hut for slacks and shoes. Some one, sitting on his cot and unlacing his boots was also reading a paper laid on the floor between his feet. Suddenly he whistled. "Gawd ——" he said, drawing the syllable out sufficiently to impart jocularity and to get some attention. "Gawd !— Look at Gunners ! "

It was the casualty list that he was examining. "And this," he continued, pushing his boots off and pressing his feet down on the boards, "isn't even the beginning. It'll take about a fortnight for the first day's bag to get completely published."

Others in the hut opened their own papers or strolled over to the speaker's bed to glance over his shoulder and get their several impressions from that little slab of type under the heading " Royal Field Artillery. Officers. . . ."

Two mornings later the 18th Battery orderly posted up a special order on the board during early stables :

"The following cadets have been gazetted as from to-day's date and will parade at 9 a.m. in room C."

Cartwright's name was first among the fourteen on the list, but Hall's was missing.

At nine o'clock the Colonel came into room C, one of the schoolrooms of the old barracks and stood the fourteen at ease and told them to sit down. " I'll only keep you about two minutes," he said, " before you pack up and dismiss on leave. And you'd better do it quick—because I don't suppose you'll get very long." He smiled at them and sat on the edge of the schoolmaster's table. " Well —it's like this. As you know, the last fortnight of this course is supposed to be ' practice ' at Okehampton ; but I was told some days ago to put up as many of you as I could for immediate Commissions. I think you'll do all right. I don't suppose you'll go straight out ; probably to new batteries on the Plain or somewhere. But even if you do you've only got to remember that shooting the ' bandooks ' with ammunition in them is just the same as shooting them without. You've done thundering well, you fellows. You might have noticed that not a single one of you here is really a youngster."

The fourteen looked at each other and thirteen pairs of eyes rested, smiling, on Bellingham who was, perhaps, twenty-two ; but he had been a corporal for a year and a half in a Territorial Infantry battalion.

" That's been an eye-opener to me," Sinclair went on. " I expected it would be the kids—the real cadet age—who would be the top lot. I suppose I thought that just because they wouldn't have had time to become proper civilians. It's you civilians that have surprised me. If I had to take a battery of guns into the line now I'd be devilish glad to be taking any three of you with me. If I had a brigade I'd like to take the lot. There you are. That's all." He stepped down from the schoolmaster's platform. " Don't forget to leave your addresses at the office when you go for your warrants, or you'll be shot for desertion." He opened the door and held out his hand to the nearest cadet, who happened to be Cartwright. " Good-bye, Cartwright," he said. " Good luck to you." But Cartwright's was not the only name he knew. He knew them all.

It was when he got to the rooms in Wonford Road at eleven o'clock instead of half-past five that he realised how little difference nearly seventeen years of marriage made.

He ran up the cement steps of the house and into the sitting-room where Dorothy was standing in surprise at his early coming, and made the astounding discovery that he was in love with her again—or still in love with her. The fact of merely looking at her was a delight. He knew that in a moment he would take her in his arms and hold her body to his, and kiss her soft lips and whisper something to her. . . .

God alone knew what he would whisper, but it did not matter.

She wore a short, light skirt of a spurious tartan pattern and a soft, white blouse that fitted to her hips over the skirt. It was open at the throat that held the head up proudly facing him, and curving away to the breasts that had fostered his life in John and David. The coil of hair gleamed against the sunlight of the open window as it had gleamed in pigtails twenty years before. The lips smiled and the eyes, too, smiled—flinching for an instant in a question, but quickly steadying again. . . .

" Darling ! " was what he did whisper to her. " I love you ! "

Her lips answered his kisses, but her eyes were hidden from him.

" Dear," she said, when she did again look at him. " What is it ? Tell me."

The question came as a sudden chill, with the fear of hurting anything so precious and so loved as the questioner.

" Nothing at all, sweetheart," he said. " I mean, nothing to be worried about. Can't you guess ? It's just finished, that's all. This cadeting business, I mean. I'm a full-blown second loot as from to-day's date. I've sent up my other tunic to have the pip and braid put on, and we'll go up presently and get some lunch and a Sam Browne."

" But, Charles," she said ; and there was a sudden depth in the shadows of her eyes that were again for a moment searching him and their destiny, " Charles, does it mean—I thought you said you all had to go to Okehampton first."

" Some of us," said he lightly, " are altogether too bright. We don't need Okehampton. We're efficient."

All she said for a time was " Oh. . . ." She had been darning the socks that Cartwright brought for her on Tuesdays in his pocket. She rolled them up and put them away in the small satchel that had been equipped as a work-basket. " I wonder—this new battle that the papers are so full of."

" Oh, rot ! " said Cartwright. No thought whatever had

gone towards the production of the word. It was sheer blind instinct. " Rot ! " he said again, and then gave himself up to thought. Slowly, as the thought became clear and plausible, he put an arm around her and drew her to him. " Can't you see, you silly old thing ?—It's sheer favouritism, my being gazetted like this ? Henderson——"

He felt a quick movement in her.

" But you're not the only one," she said.

" Practically the only one," he glibly answered. " Even old Hall isn't in it. . . ."

" Oh—dear boy ! " she said and raised her face.

His words may have been lies. His kisses were the truth.

He saw himself, over Dorothy's shoulder, moving away to his place among those mysteriously ravished men with peculiar boots, and tunics with violet sweat-stains at the armpits ; and he saw Dorothy (thinking God alone knew what) as she watched him go. But while he had her there in the sunlight of the sitting-room with its plush, convex sofa, its lace curtains and its potted palm, he kissed her and whispered to her.

Then, when his whispering was done, he said : " Poor old Hall ! He's as sick as mud."

" But I thought his only anxiety was to get out— quickly."

" Oh, well," said Cartwright, "—he wants to get on, too ; who wouldn't ? It's a real pat on the back, you know, being shoved forward like this without even a shoot at Okehampton."

MEDAL WITHOUT BAR   CHAPTER XXII

LUNCHING at Dellers' he was stricken suddenly by the wistful frailty of Dorothy. She had been for him first a hefty flapper with a back-hand drive from the base-line of a tennis-court that was something hard to bite upon in those days when the well-placed, elegantly dispatched " lob " was still an ornament of the game and he, looking over the net at·her or sitting beside her on the warm turf had been moved by the splendour of her fine young body, the straight steadiness of her mind.

Neither of these had ever bothered him since by any hint of failing. She had carried their sons without any particular fuss for the appointed time, and had suckled them thereafter till this function was adequately fulfilled. When they had required her attention during nights or days of the following years they had got it. When their need had been for a caress they had got it ; equally they had got a smack when it was for a smack that the demand had been. She had asked Cartwright's advice without throwing upon him the weight of any of her own responsibilities ; and these had been quietly discharged with a meeting of ends, and a margin. And now, at Dellers', he saw that the splendour of her body was not altogether as the might of an off-horse (while he was the near one) ; but as the loveliness of a flower.

The straightness and steadiness of her mind had become something poignantly gullible.

If only they could somehow steer clear, for the next few hours, of Hall. . . . .

" Dorrie," he said, " let's get away at once and start a sort of holiday."

" We've got the rooms here," she said, " and we ought to give them a couple of days at home to get things ready. Alice has moved into our room, you know ; and I expect that Miss Dawson friend of hers is still there. You never liked Miss Dawson."

" Blow the rooms ! " said Cartwright. " Blow home, and blow Miss Dawson. I meant a *holiday*. Now ; at once. You see——" he hesitated. If he was going to achieve the avoidance of Hall and his genius for the dropping of bricks, it behoved him to choose his words with care. " You see—I don't suppose this leave of mine will be a very long one ; and once I get posted to some job or other, I don't suppose I'll get another in a hurry. I thought we might—— a real holiday. Sort of honeymoon, Dorrie."

All he could do was hope that she did not see through the transparency of it all. " We could run down into Cornwall if you like. Or up to town. Stay *in* town, I mean."

" At the Strand Palace ? " she asked ; and there was a touch of sly knowingness in the question, just enough to hint that she was seeing through it. The awkward factor now was that it had been just some such thing as the Strand Palace that had occurred to him. Then why not the Savoy ?—but he saw that there was no real difference. They were both generally and equally the same kind of escape from the same fix, and it was the fix that he could not admit to her.

" Blow the Strand Palace ! " he said. " We'll nip down to Cornwall. There's sure to be a train. You can get packed up and I can get my kit in a taxi by four. The tunic will be done."

" Dear," she said, after a pause, " I'd prefer London."

There was no slyness now. " Even the Strand Palace. We can see something of the boys."

" Well, you're not going to the Strand Palace," he said magnificently. " You're going to the Savoy. I'll wire for a room."

" To-morrow," she said. " Really—I'd rather go to-morrow." She was not peevish as she spoke, but apparently tired ; for he had seen that she was frail with that frailty which gave him a hurt and a yearning that she should not be frightened.

" Right," he said, and smiled. " Just as you like."

He would take that taxi down to the hut for his kit. And he would get hold of Hall and prime the fellow, rubbing it into the blunt old thing quite frankly that he must interpret this dramatic elevation of him (Cartwright) while forgetting the equally dramatic elevation of the thirteen others, as a sure mark of favouritism and an obvious portent of prolonged and valuable service at home or on the staff. One would have to be as broad and as exact as that with Hall. . . .

It was agreed between him and Hall that they should admit, if pressed for statistics, that *three* others had been

likewise gazetted. The odds were that Dorothy would
never see the Gazette. She never yet had looked at it.

Then Hall twisted up his forehead. " Yes," he said.
" It's all damned fine. Look here ! Why don't you
buzz off, or let us give you a miss to-night ? "

" I can't," said Cartwright. " Dorothy doesn't want
to go till to-morrow and I don't want to push it. Come
along, you can do it."

" I dare say I can," said Hall, very glum and still frowning his twisted frown. " But it gets me into a jolly old
mess."

" You ? " said Cartwright. " What's it got to do
with you ? "

" Haven't I got a wife ? " demanded Hall. " And
hasn't she got the wind up already ? If I spend the evening blowing like hell about your being kept at home
because you've been specially gazetted, doesn't it prove
that all of us others are going to be chased out quick
because we haven't ? "

Cartwright said, thoughtfully, " Damn ! " Then he said :
" Look here, old thing. You know as well as I do that
it's only a matter of days. They're not hurrying people
out of here when there's a battle on for anything except
sending us out pretty quick. You can quietly tell Sheila
anything you damned well please. And as soon as I've
gone it will be proved. See ? "

When Cartwright got back to the rooms with his kit
and the announcement that the Halls were coming to
supper, Dorothy was hurrying down the road from the
pillar-box wherein she had posted a very careful letter
to Mrs. Henderson.

" Oh," she said. " So nice and early ! I've written to
Alice. They'll be expecting to hear from us to-morrow.
We can ring up."

" What about some beer ? " asked Cartwright. " Will
the old girl be able to get us some ? And some whisky ?
Old Hall is very down in the mug."

.   .   .   .   .   .

Hall rose magnificently to the occasion. His congratulation of Dorothy on her stupendous luck was a triumph of astonishing rhetoric. " And as for poor old cannon fodder like *me*——" he concluded, shrugging his shoulders.

It was clear that he had said something private and utterly convincing to Sheila ; for she smiled benevolently, and freely added her own congratulations.

No light was lighted in the sitting-room throughout that farewell party to Hall, for the west was still glowing from the sunset when he and Sheila left them.

In the flicker of matches for cigarettes and pipes, and in the cool twilight, Cartwright looked many times at Dorothy. It seemed to him that she must have come privily to some conclusion or other ; for when she smiled at him her eyes were bright with a laughter which he knew to be beyond the powers of simulation. It seemed, from her talk to Sheila, that she was quite thrilled by the prospect of this jaunt at the Savoy. She was going home first, she said, to collect a rag or two.

" After the way we've been pinching and saving down here," said Cartwright, " we'll *buy* a rag or two, my dear."

There was something positively great in that idea ; the idea of adorning the newly beloved. And the beloved smiled at him with the new smile which had no sadness in it, but only laughter.

She had been successfully bluffed, he thought ; taken in, with her new gullibility, by all those lies of his and the fantastic insinuations in the robustiousness of Hall.

He did not know that her joy sprang from the plausibility of the lies she herself had at last found for the filling of the letter she had written and posted to Mollie Henderson. . . . " Of course Charles will write himself to Captain Henderson asking him as soon as he has a single moment."

But it was not from any lies that laughter had come to her, but from the truth of his kisses and his desire.

H

CARTWRIGHT seemed to lose sight of the more solemn issues during the following days. Dorothy, too, seemed to lose sight of them. Her response to the ' rags ' they bought—and the response of the ' rags ' to Dorothy—as she gaily donned them before the tall mirror in the Savoy bedroom, were something entirely new. Never before had Cartwright seen her so abandoned to the merriment of finery ; and never before had he, smoking a cigarette at the other end of the room, been so magnificently the kindly Sheik or Sultan. And what, he wondered smiling, were they up to, blossoming out in all this cheeriness and frisky extravagance after seventeen years of a steady jog-trot ? Was it all just a seasonal device of Nature driven slightly frantic, Nature trying to wangle the replacement of another casualty ? . . .

He did not care.

Nor, apparently, did she.

She came across the room to him and with her came a fragrance. It was the wonderful new frock perhaps, and the diabolical daintinesses that went with such frocks to keep the dour men of Dept. T.I. so busy upon their high desks at Cox's. Perhaps the fragrance was a minor invention in the device aforesaid, quite as independent of frock and finery as the gleam and lustre of white skin, the glow of lips and the sparkle of eyes. . . .

She kissed him.

" What a difference they make, dear! " she said, standing away from him and looking again, a little shyly, at the mirror. " And what a difference they make to *you*."

He took her cool shoulders in his hands and kissed her.

" Oh, no, you don't ! " he said. " You can't get away with a remark like that. This whole thing was my idea long before you thought of them. I had it while you were wearing those jolly old dungarees, and shoes weighing a pound apiece. So there." Once again it did not matter what he said. . . .

Rendered phonetically, the concluding words to the refrain that came distantly up from the barrel-organ on the Embankment were—

" . . . Wherever yew find a little bit er kar-kee,
Yew're bahnd to find a little bit er fluff. . . ."

In the lobby they found John and David top-hatted and decorously gloved, reading the strips from the tape-machine. David was in Etons, and John's back view demanded a moment's silent criticism owing to the fact that he was wearing, at the beginning of the second week in July, his overcoat and a white muffler.

They turned at the touches of parents on their respective shoulders. The hats were lifted from slickly-brushed heads, gloves pulled from miraculously tended hands, and kisses and handshakes bestowed.

" Hold tight," said John, " —just while I hand this rough tegument to yonder flunkey. And don't go and let me down by sneezing or exploding when said deed is done." He moved away to the coat and hat-shelves followed by David. With an air he handed over his coat and hat and muffler and gloves and turned to face his mother and father, unperturbed, over a magnificent shirt-front defined into a wedge by the lapels of a dinner-jacket.

" Now," he announced, " let no man say that he came to the feast without a wedding-garment."

" But, good Lord ! " said Cartwright. " How on earth . . . No, it isn't new. . . . But where . . . ? "

" Ginger Hargreaves," said John. " He's a perfect sportsman, old Ginger. I put the case before him, that we were bidden to the feast and he saw, like a shot, that no one of my mature years could consume baked meats at the tables of the exalted, otherwise than richly dight. I went home with him and collected the things. The socks and shirt are yours, by the way. Aunt Alice put a couple of neat sutures in the neckband, to adjust it to the collar which I bought. The shoes, incidentally——"

Cartwright and Dorothy looked down at them and smiled ; brogues.

" We'd better go and stick them under a table or chair or something. Ginger said they were not quite Beau Brummel, so we mustn't let some elegant General spot them, or he'll denude you of the hard-earned pip. Concerning the which—congratulations."

They went into dinner, Cartwright wondering at the vague and mild feelings of shock and distrust aroused by the fact that fellows of fifteen wore boiled shirts and dinner-jackets wherein to talk their inexhaustible rubbish, and got away with it.

John remarked, looking about him during the meal, that some one had told him all leaves had been stopped. His gaze examined the soldiers dining. " Staff-people, I suppose," he said. " The light of battle is not in their eye. . . . And convalescents taking a bit of nourishment. Well—all power to them. Old England bids them welcome. And wassail."

" There's a putrid old josser over in that far corner," David remarked, " tucking into some stuff made of boot-laces. Is he a General, Dad ? "

' He's a goormong," said John.

Thoughtfully John said to his father a little later, " I say, I suppose this pip of yours and the festive top-boots I noted before you interred them under the table are prelude to adventure good and proper ? "

Cartwright wanted to smile and say something like " Yes, old man, I suppose it won't be very long now. . . ." But he looked solemn and shook his head. " No . . . doesn't follow a bit. I've been shoved through quick—specially quick. I'm a favoured one."

" Good egg," said John ; and there was a brief silence.

But on the whole the dinner was a success. When they had said good night to the boys and seen them vanish round the bays of screening that tastefully locked all light into the lobby, Dorothy caught her breath for a moment and said :

" Oh, dear, I hope there won't be a raid before they get home."

" Well," said Cartwright, " John confessed to me in the lavatory that he's been hoping, ever since we left them with our invitation last night, that there will.   So it depends which of you has the better standing with G.H.Q."

They seemed to cease their own movements and to drift inert for a few moments in the lobby, looking first towards the lift and then towards a small table by a sofa and an arm-chair.

" We'll wait, old girl," said Cartwright.   " We'll have a smoke and a drink presently over there.   Then I'll ring up the house after they've had time to get home."

There was not much talk between them as they sat for three-quarters of an hour by the clock, listening intently for any distant sound among the immediate ones, and waiting for the boys to get home.

" Both doing well," was John's answer on the telephone when the three-quarters of an hour had gone.

Cartwright, given any kind of a start, could have talked that night in the bedroom.   The boys and the dinner had produced in him a glow.   He could have said something about man's necessity in those grim times for a man's work.   He could have said something of the world's necessity for men capable and solicitous to do that work—men with definable qualities like simple courage and clear, unmuddled minds and the indefinable qualities of the Samurai that placed them in relation to other men where Henderson had stood. . . . But Dorothy, seeing that he was deeply thinking of some distant thing, only smiled at him—and held out her arms.

MEDAL WITHOUT BAR   CHAPTER XXIV

THEIR next guests—and on the following evening —were the Hendersons. Henderson almost flung him, after handing over his stick and glove and cap to the attendant, into the lavatory.

" It's a swindle ! " he exclaimed.   " A damned swindle.   I know it is."

" What ? " asked Cartwright.

" Dining here—in this damned place instead of a decent house."

" Well, you've never been my guest yet, you know," said Cartwright.   " I thought it would be rather jolly."

" Jolly your grandmother ! " said Henderson. " That's not *their* idea of it.   They've fixed it here so that we can't decently get away from them for a dozen minutes."

" Something," observed Cartwright, " seems to have upset you."

" Huh," grunted Henderson.   " Thank God they can't get in *here*, anyhow."   His eye glared at the dark green screen carrying the mirror and hair-brushes before the lavatory door.   " Old thing," he said, and his voice was lowered to a note of gentleness, " *were* you going to write to me ? "

Cartwright understood neither the tone nor the question. " Write ? . . . Why, of course I'll write to you—some time——"

" There ! " said Henderson.   " She's a liar, too ! Didn't I know it ?   Didn't I say so ? "

" I expect you did," said Cartwright, "—whatever it was, and whoever she is."

" ' She ' is your wife," said Henderson.   " She wrote plausible guff to Mollie about your not having the time at that moment—what with buying tunics and field-boots and God knows what—to write for yourself.   But, by Golly, it was damned nearly good enough to suck me in. *Me !*——" then suddenly he became gentle again in that fantastic manner of his.   " But I'd have done it like a shot, old thing—like a blooming shot, if I could.   I'd have put every ounce I've got into having a damned good try— if you yourself had wanted it."

" Wanted what ? " asked Cartwright.

" What she said in the letter," Henderson said evasively. ' Something cushy."

" My hat ! " said Cartwright.   " Dorothy wrote that— from Exeter ? "

" Dorothy did," said Henderson grimly.   " And Mollie's taken it.   The two of them are after us, hell for

leather ; and God help us. Mollie's got twenty times the
pull that I have. What the deuce could I do against that
letter ? She had me by the short hairs. I couldn't go on
saying, in the face of that, that you wouldn't hear of it."

" But," said Cartwright, " dash it, you might have
known——"

" I suppose," Henderson said quietly—" well—I suppose I did know, really." He smiled ; and the act of
smiling that particular kind of smile seemed to embarrass
him. " —Hell of a fix to be in, all the same. . . .
Devilish sauce for me to say such a thing, I know, but it
would have given me a bit of a jar——"

" Oh, shut up ! " said Cartwright. " You're getting a
touch of what Mollie tried to explain to me as sentimentality once. And it is, too—if you take it like that."

" Sentimentality be blowed," said Henderson. " You
do want to go and you might just as well admit it."

" Oh, Lord ! " said Cartwright. " You people who talk
about ' wanting ' make me sick. It's—and poor Dorothy,
I don't believe she'll ever see it—it's just that one can't
help it. And that's all there is about it."

" Good enough," said Henderson. " Same thing."

" It isn't the same thing," snapped Cartwright.

" 'S near enough," insisted Henderson. " And now
that you've told me, we'll join them—and do them in the
eye."

" It's hard to believe," said Cartwright thoughtfully,
" that my destiny is depending on the way an argument
goes between you and Mollie."

" Oh, that's nothing ! " said Henderson. " The harder
anything is to believe, the better women enjoy believing
it. Haven't you found that out—after your thousand
years of marriage ? Mollie might be able to hang you up
altogether ; but it would take time, because she has to
start the ball rolling from the top. Well—we'll just let
her go ahead. Things will have happened before the
word gets through."

" Then you will have to work against her ? " asked
Cartwright.

" No," said Henderson significantly, " no need. I was

talking to a stripling in A.G.6 to-day, and I can just give you a quiet, straight tip to go on with : it's any day now ; so don't go very far away from your address. And it probably won't be any depôt job either—not even for half an hour. It's from factory to consumer with scarcely time on the way to buy your bottle of Eno's and your flannel for next the skin."

There was a tremor inside Cartwright ; it was sheer excitement—and a touch of horror as he thought of the way he would in a moment see Dorothy again, proud and gay in her new dress and in her futile scheming with Mollie Henderson.

Henderson drew a little nearer to him and softly touched his arm. " Old fellow," he said softly, " you can still say the word if you want us to take that long chance. I've left the ghost of an opening for it. You've got things on your mind that I haven't ; and I'll know it's O.K.—whatever you do."

The stammer of Bullock who was already dead came back to him. . . . " . . . of course, anything you do is sure to be pretty decent. . . ."

In the stress of the moment he spoke the only words that he knew to represent the truth. " You know damned well that I can't."

" Keep your shirt on," said Henderson, and his touch on Cartwright's arm became a quick squeeze. " Now we'd better get back to them quick or they'll come bursting even into here. And the easiest thing will be to agree with everything they say."

" As a matter of fact," Cartwright said as they glanced at their hair and neckties in the mirror on the screen and went out to the lobby, " I've been letting Dorothy think that there probably will be some softish job or other for me after the way I've been rushed through."

" Good," said Henderson. " There's nothing to mar a cheery evening then. Mollie's chat will have given her confidence. I've told her I was at A.G.6 to-day. It does seem a bit on the furtive side, when you see them all smiles like that, waiting for you. . . . But what the hell can you do ? They *ask* for it."

Mollie and Dorothy looked up and made room for them on the sofa and indicated the two glasses that awaited them.

.   .   .   .   .

This dinner, too, was a success.

Cartwright and Henderson got only another dozen words—again in the lavatory—when the party was over ; and Cartwright again had that feeling of excitement, and fleeting sense of horror. Henderson said, over his shoulder, " I don't suppose you'll have much time on your hands. Mightn't see you again before you shove off. But good luck ; write us a line when you can."

" You bet I will," said Cartwright.

" And by the way—you know I'd give my boots to be going with you, don't you ? "

" Yes," said Cartwright. " You bet I do.'

MEDAL WITHOUT BAR   CHAPTER XXV

IT was precisely six days after his appearance in the Gazette that Cartwright received his ' *Cinchfor* ' telegram instructing him to report at Waterloo next morning.

More accurately, it was Dorothy who received it.

Cartwright, at the time of its delivery, was talking to his father in the office. He had not been with him for more than ten minutes when the old man frowned at the buzzer on his desk, and picked up the receiver of his telephone.

" Yesyesyes ? I'm *speaking !* " was his usual formula for answering the telephone. He used it, and listened for a few moments with his lips screwed up as though for whistling. Suddenly he relaxed them and said quickly, " Good God ! " then slowly, " Very well—I'll tell him. . . . No, dear girl, I don't think so. . . ." There was a caressing tenderness in his voice which made Cartwright wonder who could be at the other end of the

wire. " Yes . . . No, dear one.   No, I know you won't
—Yes—good-bye—good-bye."

He hung up the receiver and took off his glasses and
blew his nose.   He put on his glasses again and drummed
his finger-nails half a dozen times on the desk.

" Dorrie," he said, nodding at the telephone.   " It's
you—off to-morrow morning.   Poor girl. . . . Damn and
blast. . . .   And I wanted to get you a decent pair of
glasses if you *did* have to go out.   Proper artillery things
that a man was telling me about, and a prismatic compass.
He said it ought to be in oil."

" Never mind, Dad," said Cartwright.   " I can get
them cheaper from Stores, I believe, out there."

" There's a big difference in Ordnance stores, this fellow
said.   You can't be certain of the stuff.   You ought to
get them from a decent old maker.

" Oh, well," said Cartwright, " you can send them out.
Or, look here !—couldn't we go out and get them now,
before lunch ? "

" No," said the father.   " We couldn't."

Cartwright smiled and shrugged his shoulders.

His father said, " Oh, all right. . . .   And I'll come and
eat some lunch with you and Dorothy."

He took his top-hat and umbrella from the wall-
cupboard and ran a clothes-brush over the lapels of his
coat.

" I say, Dad," said Cartwright, " there is something I
wish you *would* get me.   We'll taxi round to that crony
of yours in Harley Street and he'll fix it up for us.   A
bottle of morphia tablets."

" Going to start eating morphia ? "   The old man was
jocular.

" They're rather a handy thing to have," Cartwright
explained ; "—according to a fellow at Exeter who has
been with a battery for a year or so.   Men occasionally
get hit, and if there isn't a doctor near, a suck at a morphia
tablet keeps them cheery as far as the dressing-station."

" Yes," his father said slowly.   " Men do appear to
get hit—occasionally—judging from the casualty lists."
In the corridor he slipped his arm through Cartwright's

for a moment and said, " D'you know, son, I'm inclined to agree with that admirable warrior who is said to have written to his aunt Jane ?   Well, take care of yourself, old man.   John and your mother and I will look after Dorothy."

Cartwright pressed the steady, lean hand to his ribs.

After lunch, at which not a single word was said of the telegram, he and Dorothy went down to Bromley to see his mother.

In the train Dorothy said, " I'm sorry, Charles, about that letter to Mollie Henderson—since nothing has come of it."   She smiled the normal smile of an amiable person saying something of no particular importance ; but her eyes were curiously veiled.   She saw into his eyes clearly enough as she looked at him, but he could not see into hers.

An inspired generosity caused him to say : " Nothing—yet.   But don't be sorry we wrote to them.   It's a long way, old girl, from the base to the firing-line."

From Bromley they went out to Chiswick to spend the evening with the boys and Dorothy's sister-in-law.   They walked over, before going back to the Savoy, to the Belgian Home.   Hamilton was still in the office, steadily laying bricks upon the foundations of his order.

" So they are sending you out after all ? " he said. " But I dare say they'll find something for you on the line of communications, or at the base.   It's only fair for the older men—men with families depending on them."

" My family, thank God," snorted Cartwright, " does not depend on me."

" All the same——" said Hamilton, " I'm on the local tribunal, you know.   We *do* have a time ! "

" I bet you do ! " said Cartwright.   " Well—congratulations."   He felt that anything short of hitting Hamilton over the head with his absurd ledger was as futile as anything else.   He turned to leave him.

" Bong Voyarge," and Hamilton stood up sedately and held out his hand, " and bong shawnce."

Cartwright took the hand and said what John might have said in reply, or David—" Thanks.   Same to you. With knobs on."

He had never yet succeeded in leaving Hamilton with any feeling but that he had made an idiot of himself.

He joined Dorothy in the sitting-room, and as soon as a very old man with a spade of a beard and a Forsyte tweed suit had completed a patriotic farewell speech in Flemish, they walked to the station.

At Charing Cross they found that an air-raid alarm had been given.   With only a moment's pause on the platform and no consultation, they walked up the stairs and slowly up Villiers Street.

It was Cartwright's first raid.

Lying in bed, a little amazed at Dorothy's calm, he reflected that she must have got used to the din and the lashing to and fro of searchlight beams at Chiswick, while he had been peaceably tucked away at Wilverley and Exeter.   He was a trained expert in the science, as F.A.T. had it, of directing a projectile at a given object ; and this was the nearest he had yet been to the practice of gunnery, and some of it seemed devilish near.

The din subsided and the tremor of lights became still.

Dorothy turned to lean over him for a moment.   Slowly and very lightly she ran her fingers over his face and kissed him.   " My poor dear old boy," she said ; and no more.

His arms held her to him.   He wanted to say that he could die a far happier man for those last few days and nights with her, for the dinner with David and John in his fantastic dinner-jacket ; for the evening of brave talk with the Hendersons, . . .   What he did say was " Darling, it's been a great lark. . . ."   And then she was suddenly broken in his arms.

" Charles . . . Charles . . . Charles . . ." was all she said to him between her sobs.   And all that he could say was " My dear . . . dear one . . . dear. . . ."

.   .   .   .   .   .

In the dawn, when he was dressed and she was pouring coffee for him from the pot on the little silver tray, he said, " Look here, old girl !   Promise there's going to be no worrying over letters.   Remember what a marvel it is that there should be any letters delivered at all. So if you don't hear   . ."

" Yes," she said, " I'll remember."

" And keep the kids in hand," he said.   " Young John could easily get uppish, now that his voice is sinking an octave or so. . . . See as much as you can of the Old Boy and Mother.   They'll love it, and it's very good for her. . . ."

So he went on till there was a tap at the door and the voice of an adept said, " Your kit, Sir."

" Come in," said Dorothy.

The adept and his satellite took the neat new valise and haversack and greatcoat.   " The taxi will be ready, Sir," he said.   " Would you mind another gentleman with you, Sir ?   There may be a shortage."

" Not a bit," said Cartwright.   " I'll be down directly."

The door closed.

" Well, dear boy," said Dorothy, " good-bye."

The word staggered him as though it were an entirely new, preposterous invention of her own which she was using for the first time.   He was dumb and idiotic, staring into the tremor of her smile.   " Good old girl," he mumbled with a thick, uncomfortable tongue ; and then he mumbled something still more imbecile about had she enough change for all the tips ?

He heard her say, " Yes, dear.   Plenty."   And he knew that he kissed her and shut the door behind his back upon her ; and he told the man at the door, No ; he would carry his greatcoat, not wear it ; and he gave him some half-crowns and got into the cab and waited, since there was a battered pack beside his valise near the driver ; and he filled a pipe against the finishing of his cigarette.

A Sapper-Major presented a plump and cheery face at the door.   There were leather bindings to the cuffs of his tunic and patches on his elbows.   " Good morning," he said, " His Excellency there tells me there's room for a little one."

" Yes, rather," said Cartwright, " hop in ! "

The Major sat back as the car circled out of the courtyard, and took off his shapeless cap, and sighed and said :

" Dear Aunt Jane . . . ! Well, it gets no better. Lord ! " his eye had lit on Cartwright's cuff—" A one-pipper ! I expected a Colonel of the spruce young sort from your mug. First time out ? "

" Yes," said Cartwright.

" It's lucky for you I'm going your way then, instead of Folkestone-Boulogne. Stick to me ; or else you'll get let in for some dirty work on the boat or at the other end—marching a draft, or O.C. shaving-water or something grim like that. Married ? "

" Yes, rather," said Cartwright. " For some time."

" So'm I," said the Major. And they sat back and smoked.

" You look like Cavalrymen once used to look," the Major said as they neared Waterloo.

" I'm a solicitor," said Cartwright.

" A solicitor ? You'll damned soon find out that you're not, my son." The Major smiled. " I'm a Regular myself. At least I was once ; but we're all in the same hat now—catch-as-catch-cans. And there's dirty work at the cross-roads, I give you my word. I and my lot spent the winter, and then some, fixing up a little mine that *was* a mine—to be touched off instead of saying ' rabbits ' early on the 1st instant. I came home on a special leave two days before it. My older brother has just sailed out, leaving rather a hell of a mess. Poor beggar ! Wife and family rather ditched."

Cartwright saw that he had already moved into a world that was new and yet not, somehow, utterly strange.

A man dead, and a wife and family ditched had moved from the general text of life into the place of a footnote.

Out of a later meditation the sapper said, " Give all these R.T.O.s and fellas the glassy eye, and drown yourself in chat to me when you see them coming."

He stood beside him while he reported at the R.T.O.'s window and received his orders to report at the rest-camp at Harfleur, thus determining the fact that he was not on ' draft ' but a ' reinforcement.'

IT was probably at such places as the Harfleur rest-camp that the sense of a weird and peculiar libera-tion first came to men. It was there, incidentally, that reinforcements drew their identity disks from the bombardier in the Adjutant's office, together with two feet of string. A typed ' instruction' in the office advocated the use of string (as issued) rather than a metal chain as a necklace for the pendant of fibre disks, since string cannot be splintered. . . .

Meals in the officers' Mess were a cash transaction served by frail-looking gunners with the accuracy and dispatch of Lyons's waitresses. It seemed to be only the people ' on draft' that ' clicked' for duties—surprising duties like marching a detachment to the butts for musketry instruction, paying-out and a bathing parade. None of these duties fell to Cartwright or the other six or seven men from Exeter . . . and these are the only type of detail that remain with any definite shape in his memory of those days. Even as to the number of them he could not now swear ; but it was not more than two or three before he was in orders to report at the Adjutant's office.

Those who reported were grouped, as their names were called by the Regimental Sergeant-Major, into three or four lots. In Cartwright's group—the smallest of all—were four others of the Exeter men, three who had come from the H.A.C., and one of the rankers of Hut 13. All were to entrain early next morning, and the Cartwright party was told that its railhead was Tinques. " Toc-i-n-q-u-e-esses," said the R.S.M. ; ' Tanks. Valises will be collected at five, breakfast 5.15. Will gentlemen wanting dining-out passes please go to the Corporal ? " Every one, quite automatically it seemed, went. The five from Exeter went down to Havre together.

In the unending discussions that Cartwright subsequently heard between signallers cooking Quaker oats, he heard great reminiscences of evenings and nights in ' Lee ' Havre. But women of any sort seemed quite remote from the adventure of that evening so far as Cartwright's particular party was concerned. Its only real frivolity was before they had selected their restaurant, when four of them went into a small jeweller's shop and bought silver identity disks on the wristlet chain so much in vogue. They were to be engraved while they dined.

They saw batches of new prisoners from off a train. The single word " Somme " was the grim utterance of all lips as the wan herd stumbled by over the cobbles towards the oblivion of ships or camps.

" Well,—it isn't the Salient yet awhile," Cartwright remembers the old ranker saying as they sat down to dinner. " And it isn't the Somme. Here's luck ! " He drank the nearest approach to beer of which Havre was capable.

" What's left for us, then ? " asked Denney, one of the H.A.C. men. " I looked Tinques up and it seems pretty handy for anywhere up north."

" Not the Salient." Old Humphreys shook his head. " You don't wheel right at St. Pol if you're going to the Salient." The conviction had more value for him than for people who had spent the winter in England or Egypt.

" Anyhow," said Denney, " wherever it is I don't suppose it'll be for long."

" Ar—" said Humphreys. " That's right."

The conversation of new-comers into the restaurant indicated that more prisoners were passing outside.

" I wonder if we'll keep together ? " Bailey, another of the H.A.C. men said, and that amount of stability seemed desirable in the present flux, though Exeter was all they had in common from the past and Tinques in the future.

Before they left the camp in the morning there was added to their Christmas-tree furnishings of haversack, water-bottle, mess-tin, revolver, map-case, glasses, greatcoat and mackintosh, the small linen bag of dry-rations.

They had not been long in their compartment when a canny old family-man came along the footboards from one of the horse trucks and attached himself to them for the courtesy and duty of batman. He must have been an accomplished and practised traveller on those trains. At dusk he appeared with candles, at dawn with half a petrol-can of shaving-water. At intervals during the day (or days) that they were on the train he hurried to them from the engine with the petrol-can half filled with tea.

At St. Pol he announced that they were at the parting of the ways. He took the francs they gave him, counted them, saluted, assured them that the journey thence to Tinques was so short that they might accomplish it without his guidance, gave Cartwright a candle-stump because 'you never knew,' and fell in with his draft for heaven knew where. He was the first of those amazing, long-moustached gunners that Cartwright had as yet experienced who are equal to any demand in the world but the laying of a gun.

At Tinques the R.T.O. told them there was an estaminet just outside the station, where they could get something to eat.

" Tell her two eggs each for the omelette," Humphreys said as they left the station-yard. " She won't put more than two into a big one like ours even if you tell her twenty."

They ate their omelette and bread-and-butter and drank coffee at a wooden table under a tree in front of the estaminet. When the breakfast was finished the woman nodded towards the house and said " Shave. Wash and brush—one franc."

In the cool dairy there were a couple of tin basins and a large ewer of hot water. After their shave and wash Denney suggested a walk.

" There's nothing," said Humphreys. " They're all the same, these ruddy rail-heads. The only thing here is the station-yard. We'll have to shove off with the rations, I expect. Mine's a snooze in the garden."

Cartwright wondered for a moment if there would be any point in writing to Dorothy; but, clearly, there would not : he had written from Havre saying that until

ɪ

she heard from him again she would know that his address was the rest-camp.

Humphreys knew better than to waste time. He took off his boots and his putties and rested his feet in his British warm. He took the hard knobs of shaving kit out of his haversack to enhance its comfort as a pillow, faced the possibility of flies by putting his towel over his face and his hands as far as they would go into his breeches pockets. Then he went immediately to sleep.

He thus gained a good half-hour over the other four, who sprawled and smoked and chatted and fidgeted before realising that exactly these things were the only reasonable things to be done.

MEDAL WITHOUT BAR   '   CHAPTER XXVII

IN the afternoon a ration lorry took them and their five valises southwards from the railway station and then turned left along the St. Pol-Arras Road. The Quarter-master-Sergeant of the ammunition column for which they were bound unfolded his map and showed them their immediate objective, Wanquetin. He did not know how far they were from the line till one of them measured the distance from Wanquetin to Arras as about six miles and allowed another mile or two as the distance from Arras to the line.

Eight miles from the line. . . .

Looking at the map Cartwright's eye caught sight of such names as Mont St. Eloy, Neuville St. Vaast, Carency and, just where the map was folded, Souchez and Givenchy. . . .

" Pretty quiet spot, Quarter ? " Humphreys asked.

Quiet it might have been ; but Humphreys had not looked at the map to see those names.

Cartwright himself could not have told you any more about those names than that there, at any rate, you were " in it." The lorry trundled on, nearer, at the rate of about a mile in four or five minutes.

Two cavernous, veiled carcasses of sheep lying on boxes and on sacks of bread, wagged their stumps of leg over the jolts in the road as the Q.M.S. folded up his map and stuffed it back into his pocket.

"So-so," he said. (It was, in fact, about the quietest part of all the line from Verdun to the sea.) "We've only just come in ourselves." The Division, he explained, had come over from Egypt after Gallipoli. It had come complete, except for the 4·5 howitzer batteries; for there had been no howitzer batteries with them in Gallipoli. . . . "The hows. came down from the Canadians, Wipers way, to join us. Not Canadians, though; Kitchener batteries."

"Had some casualties?" was Humphreys' next question, with an eye that roamed over his four companions; for he alone, as yet, of all the five had any smattering of that lore whereby auguries are made and portents read.

"No," said the Q.M.S. "But we're a bit short of officers; and they're forming trench-mortars."

This, to Humphreys at any rate, was food for thought. To Cartwright it was a mere surprise; they had been told nothing at Exeter about trench-mortars.

At Berles they swung southwards off the broad road, through Tilloy-les-Hermaville to Habareq. By the roadside after Habareq Cartwright saw, for the first time, gun-ammunition.

It was neatly stacked in boxes, and unboxed ready for limbers and wagons under a roof of fishing-nets dotted over with tufts of raffia and rags. It was one of those early efforts at camouflage that would have been enough, eighteen months later, to cause an immediate apoplexy in any beholder. But the sight of that reserve ammunition-dump was enough to cause a jerk inside the more sensitive of the passengers in the lorry, over and above the jerking of the lorry itself. It was like looking for Wanquetin and Arras on the map and seeing such words as Carency, Neuville St. Vaast and Souchez. Truly the turnstile had been left far behind with the "Adieu, madame," and "Adieu" clicked out, dispassionately and smoothly, by the woman of the estaminet.

"Come on and have some tea," some one of the rakishly-capped D.A.C. subalterns said; "the old man will be back by then. He wants to see you before you're posted, in case any of you are *horse*men. He's a hell-fire horsemaster himself. Cavalryman. Any of you Cavalrymen ?"

He had obtained a definite answer to this question by the time they had got to the mess-billet, for he said to the half-dozen others who were already having tea, "It's all right. They're all gunners."

The cheerful Denney from the H.A.C. could never allow small matters to rest in obscurity. "You seem to have been expecting Marines, or Cyclist Corps chaps or something. What's wrong with our being gunners ? "

"Nothing's wrong with it. Come on and sit down and have tea, all of you. Chuck your haversacks and stuff anywhere." The speaker now was an older man than the man who had met them in the street and brought them in ; and obviously, somehow, an older soldier. "You see, this is a big event in our lives—sending reinforcements to the guns. We've never had to do it yet, and we don't want the happy home broken up. We've been together nah for forty years. . . . We don't mind the old man and the old man likes us ; but if any one of you knows any more about horses, or any less about guns, than any one of us—well, that one of us would have to go to the guns."

"Where are the guns ? " Cartwright asked, partly because of the interest inherent in the question and partly because there was some feeling of discomfort in talking directly about the chances that were, after all, destiny ; chances like the question whether one should stay with the ammunition column in billets or go to a battery in dug-outs. . . .

"God knows," said the other. "Plastered about somewhere out there, south of Arras. The wagon-lines are near Warlus and Bernaville. That's where we give them the stuff. Headquarters at Dainville and Wailly, where you'll probably have to be dumped with the rations this evening."

A tin of cigarettes was shoved about the table. Every one remained anonymous for the reason, apparently, that names did not matter by that roadside till you were sure that the owners of the names were not on the point of moving on.

Amiable and jocular questions were asked about things at home—the state of the crops, how the roses were doing, whether England stood where she did—for these men had been away for eighteen months in Gallipoli and Egypt. Denney assumed responsibility for the necessary back-chat and discharged it adequately.

There was something about the D.A.C. that did not make of it an attractive place to the outsider. It was the buckle, as Reynolds commented in due course, a little too obviously ' swashed,' and the swash not sufficiently buckled. The hosts, one after another, looked at wrist-watches, assumed their caps, limp and peaky, picked up their jockey's quirts and huntsman's crops and went off with "Well—mustn't forget the War. . . . Make yourselves at home till the hour strikes ; and look in for a drink any time you're down this way."

The reinforcements sat uneasily about the room, omitting to talk because, perhaps, of the batman first clearing away the tea things and then bringing in a bottle of whisky, water-jug and tumblers of thick, milky-looking glass. " If you gentlemen would like a wash, Sir," he said to Cartwright, " I can fix you up in Mr. Hart's billet through here."

A wash, it appeared, was the most natural need of the soldier on active service. It was as much from mere decency towards the batman as for any other reason that Cartwright followed him through the kitchen into a room with a canvas wash-stand and a valise spread on a camp-bed. Here was the Gamage type of war-furniture in actual use. " I say," Cartwright exclaimed, " it all seems very nice and cosy."

" It's not too bad," the batman admitted ; " once you get settled in. There's been some big stuff coming

over on the road once or twice ; but—I suppose there's
a war on.   Soap there, Sir.   And I'll get you a towel."
As a final touch in the Bohemian make-up of that D.A.C.
family Cartwright noticed a howitzer cartridge under
the cot with a burnished handle made from the copper
driving-band of a shell.

It was all too fantastic for permanence.   Cartwright
knew that the address he would ultimately send to
Dorothy would not be the D.A.C.

" The Adjutant's compliments," the batman said
when he came back with a clean towel for Cartwright,
" and will you please step round to his office with the
other new officers if you've finished tea ?   I've kept the
orderly to show you the billet."

Cartwright and Denney and Humphreys were posted
to the Brigade with Headquarters at Dainville, and the
other two to the Brigade at Wailly.   It did not require
much meditation upon the strange and devious course of
destiny to discover that it was directed by alphabetical
sequence.   The other two names were Sutherland and
Wilcox.

They saw their valises embarked upon the two cooks'
carts and rode off eastwards followed by the five horse-
holders (detailed for the job as a contribution to the
No. 2 Field Punishment which they were undergoing).

Sutherland and Wilcox said " Cheerio " and turned
southwards at Warlus—pronounced, thereafter, ' Walrus.'

Occasionally, from far right or left, or vaguely from
the direction in which they were going, there came a
sharp clang as of a large metal lid tumbling to a hard
floor.

In the instants of dead silence between the clatter
of hoofs, the squeak of saddlery, the clink of harness and
the endles chat of the drivers ahead there would come
the dull throb of spent and blended sound from the
south.   Then it would be lost again in hoofs' clatter,
the whine of saddles, and the immediate badinage of
drivers.

" Golly ! " said Denney at last.   " It seems impossible ! "
Cartwright could add nothing.

Humphreys said, " Oh, I don't know. I've seen it quiet like this before. It doesn't take many minutes for a strafe to work up. But this looks like a peace-sector all right. You can tell it by the ambulances. We haven't seen one yet, and this is the way they'd come. We passed a station a bit back."

They rode on in silence again till Denney said, " What's this chat about trench-mortars ? "

" You keep your fingers crossed," said Humphreys ; but he would go no further, for within his square, closely-cropped head was an elaborate system of observances concerned with the mystery called luck. It was upon himself and Cartwright that the chance lay. C—D—H. . . . C and H were the flanks of the formation, Denney was safe in the centre. As they rode on—Denney and Cartwright with minds innocently vacuous—Humphreys tampered with his own rules by reflecting further that either the Divisional Artillery Headquarters or the D.A.C. would have done the posting to trench-mortars if any had been imminent.

It was not with a view to going into trench-mortars that he had enlisted as a trumpeter ten years before and for seven years had devoured the counsels of Brigade Schoolmasters in Woolwich, Meerut and Ambala ; not for trench-mortars that he had raised an aching head and opened burning eyelids in a guardroom at Pindi, to find that his boots, his spurs, and his bandolier were gone, and that the tepid water in the ewer could no more quench the thirst raging in his tongue and throat than it could have slaked a bazaar on fire. . . . " Prisoner and escort, halt. Right turn. . . ." It was not for trench-mortars that Humphreys for the four years following that day had lived under a vow of sobriety and chastity ; and for a week in the northern part of the Salient had kept a gun in action—ekeing out a pittance of shells—with the battery clerk and the Major's batman. . . .

JUST as you felt, on going into the D.A.C. Mess, that you were dropping into a roadside tavern, so you felt, on going into the Brigade Headquarters at Dainville, that you were the guest of a family. Only the Adjutant was there to represent it in the cool, brick-paved little room, but he carried the responsibility with easy elegance. In answer to the three salutes he pushed back his chair and got up and held out his hand. He was obviously not much more than twenty-one, and only a full Lieutenant, so that the only thought to justify the three salutes was that they had been meant for the Headquarters and not for the smiling youth who said, " Do come in and sit down."

Next he said, " How far have you got with meals ? "

They told him and he said, " That's all right, then. You'll easily get to your batteries by dinner-time. I'll call them up and say you're coming."

He asked if they had any preferences, if they knew any one in any of the batteries, or had had anything to do with howitzers.

" That's all right, then. Cartwright can go to D, Denney to B and Humphreys to A. Which is which ? "

Cartwright indicated himself. " You're going to the hows," said the Adjutant. " They're in the quarry by Agny. And Denney ? . . . B is up near Achicourt, and A up the other side of it. I suppose those D.A.C. sparks have landed your kits up here instead of leaving them at the wagon-lines ? Well, they'll have to take them back. I'll give you some labels to tie on in a minute, so that they'll go to the right battery's lines in time for rations. I'm sorry the Colonel won't see you before you go. We've been worrying like hell, wondering what we've been going to get." He looked, collectively smiling, over the three. " He'll be relieved."

The elegance came so smoothly that only Denney could instantly cope with it. He said, " Ta ; vociferously—Ta."

This gave Cartwright time. " Well, I must say I'm relieved," he said. Then, " How do we get to the batteries ? Ride ? "

" Push-bikes," said the Adjutant. " I get the battery orders off at about half-past six and you can go up with the orderlies. The R.S.M. will fix you up with bikes and the orderlies can bring them back. It's only about three miles by road. Would you like to stroll round outside till the battery orders are ready, or will you wait here ? " He was a busy man returning to his desk.

" Oh, we'll stroll," said Cartwright. They left their haversacks and other slung kit and walked out into the cobbled street. The Brigade staff and other inhabitants of the village—detached details in charge of medical and trench stores and small-arms ammunition —expansively enjoyed the leisure conferred upon the inhabitants of any village by the crest of a knoll running between itself and the enemy.

The evening sunlight enfiladed the street and the most conspicuous mark of war was tufts of grass sprouting up between the cobbles. Here and there were roof timbers stripped of tiles ; holes in brick walls had generally been made good with sandbags ; the glass of the windows had been replaced with blankets, boards or sacking—but these were not features unexpected like the grass-tufts between the cobbles.

The throbbing in the south was a steady rumble now that there was no clatter of horses and talk of drivers to stem the weary sound. Occasionally a great shell would tumble into Arras two and a half miles away with the unmistakable clang that can be produced by nothing but a shell in a hollow city.

" Seems like a decent lot we've tumbled into," Denney ventured. The shuttered windows and darkening doors of the low houses and the clefts of walls gaping on the twilight of barns had lowered his voice till it was scarcely above a whisper.

" Yes," said Humphreys ; and he, too, almost whispered —for the figures squatting or sprawling inside the doorways formed a unity to which the three were yet strangers and outsiders. "A young regular, I should say—the Adj. And they ought to be a smartish lot if they've been training together all this time instead of taking it in the neck. Not your lot, though, Cartwright. They've been through it all right, if they've been with the Canadians."

A loyalty that Cartwright recognised instantly as absurd made him say, "Well—soldiers needn't be any the worse for a bit of fighting. Almost as good as drilling, I should think."

"Yes," Humphreys admitted. "But it doesn't smarten 'em up."

A section of Infantrymen passed the end of the street, carrying shovels and followed by a man with a wheelbarrow holding a tin of chloride of lime. "That's what I mean," said Humphreys. "A Division that turns out a sanitary party as smart as that hasn't got any flies on it. Did you notice the D.A.C. officers' field-boots? Could shave yourself in the ruddy things." (It must be remembered that the brightness of metal and the shine of leather are relative qualities, and that few standards of them in the world are higher than a trumpeter's.) His criticism of the passing fatigue-party was sound; they were smart soldiers; even the grey wheelbarrow seemed to have a steady, non-civilian movement.

It was lonely in that road, talking softly and walking quietly outside that unity which was Cartwright's new division. He felt a curious need for something, and had walked half the length of the street before he realised that the missing thing was Henderson. He was feeling that the moment and the place were a little, somehow, beyond himself; he could not rise to a full appreciation of it all—the vast blur that pressed so lightly upon the ear-drums as it flowed up from the Somme, the clang of haphazard shells in Arras, the debonair warmth of the Adjutant, the spirit of a squad that carried shovels and pushed a barrow of disinfectants with pride and gusto. Henderson, he knew, would have risen to them where he himself just failed.

The shells in Arras added to the loneliness ; for they made him shrink from the letter which he must write that night to Dorothy, giving her his address : an address within a mile or two of the bursting of shells probably as big as the umbrella-stand in the hall. . . .

It was to Henderson alone that he could really write, ever again. . . .

MEDAL WITHOUT BAR   CHAPTER XXIX

HIS valise, when it arrived at the battery with the rations and ammunition, was laid down at the end of the Mess dug-out, so that he had the table at which to write his two letters before turning in. The one to Dorothy covered half a sheet of his paper and took over an hour to write ; the one to Henderson covered four or five and took perhaps half as many minutes as Dorothy's.

In Dorothy's he said,

" Here's a ' unit ' at last, my dear, which is my full address. And it is, I ought to tell you a ' good ' address. I haven't been here more than two hours yet—the battery commander is a young beefy sort of youth who seems to get very sleepy from the fresh air. He yawned a good deal during dinner and turned in quite soon after, leaving the Mess to me, where I'm writing. This seems, by the way, to be one of the quietest spots in the world. It is really a ' rest ' sector and the nearest shelling is some miles away. The Savoy is the front line in comparison. There's no need to bother about sending me anything at all. There's a canteen to which some one goes from the wagon-lines almost every day and I can get even my own special tobacco."

Henderson's letter was cut short only by a series of yawns on his own part and a dying out of the steady hiss from the acetylene table-lamp.

" The battery commander (four guns) is a man after your own heart. Quite a youngster—about twenty-five or six—named Richards. He's an engineer of some sort —had something to do with making lift shafts on the Tubes in London and has been out here for about fourteen or fifteen months, after coming to the gunners from some territorial yeomanry. The battery is in an old chalk quarry. Being "hows." we can get into all sorts of positions where eighteen-pounders couldn't clear the crest. I don't know how far we are behind the trenches. We've got some targets just over two thousand yards and a few spent machine-gun bullets go buzzing over the position and plopping into the back of the quarry just above the right section gun-pits. Richards has put up a sort of roof of chicken wire on poles over all the paths between dug-outs and pits with grass tags and lumps of chalk thrown on top here and there, for cover against aeroplane spotting. Where his genius comes in is in having this roof made lower towards the back of the pit, so that the men have to stoop down out of the flight of the machine-gun bullets, though he says most of their skulls would be good enough to keep them out at such a range. His theory has never been tested.

" I reported to him just before dinner—a first-rate one of soup, rissoles, fried potatoes, pancakes and golden syrup, cheese and coffee. He went out to see a Sergeant about something during dinner and came back laughing. The joke was that I have started with a reputation for fire-eating. I had told him at dinner that I haven't seen a gun being fired yet. He tells me that Bombardier Day, the battery orderly who brought me from Brigade is a very tough customer and has told the men what a hell of a fellow I am. What actually happened is that we were riding our push-bikes from Brigade on a pretty bad road. It is bumpy, chalky ground and there were great ruts and only about a yard of decent surface, so that Day was ahead of me. I was glad of this because it must be a dozen years since I've done any serious biking and I was doing some good wobbling over the bumps. At one place the road turns and dips—I suppose into view, because there are fishing-nets and strips of canvas on wires between the trees on the left of the road.

Suddenly there was something like a loud sneeze and four black bursts at the edge of the road behind us. Day's bicycle shot off the road to the left and Day into the ditch on the right. But I was not up to any trick-riding. I managed to keep going, in spite of a full load of haversack and map-case and glasses and things. Day seems to have told his cronies that for sheer courage and cool, calm balance he has never seen my equal. I'm glad no one knows what I went through when I was told I had to ride a bicycle between those ruts. Richards says they were only whiz-bangs and that a salvo is dumped at that corner every hour or so. In addition to courage, by the way, I have great modesty. For, of course, I didn't mention the affair to Richards, it seemed so natural to get shelled on the way to a battery. Everything else, like the typewriter and port-glasses at Brigade and the old woman selling the Paris *Daily Mail* at the gun-pits when I arrived, was much more surprising.

" I haven't, of course, got a section since there are only two in a four-gun battery. I haven't seen either of the other two subalterns yet. Only one of them is at the guns with Richards, and he's on a forty-eight-hour Brigade liaison job with the Infantry. The other is at the wagon-lines. I'm sleeping in the Mess to-night because a ratting-campaign has put the subalterns' dug-out and bunk out of action for the moment. Richards says we'll make a new one for me to-morrow. He seems to be always on the look out for jobs like this and told me he's got a fine secret dump of what he calls ' quantities ' collected in the copse, looted from the village. We're going to put in speaking tubes from this dug-out to the gun-pits as soon as we've got a few more feet of gas-pipe from the village. Skilled men can only do their work of collecting at night because the looting rules seem to be pretty strict. I don't know whether it's due to Richards altogether, but it does seem that the War is a sort of newspaper competition here—' Ideal Homes ' almost, though not quite that. But this business of pinching gas-pipes to make speaking tubes, is much more for the

fun of it than anything else. And one of the chaps—
the air-scout on duty, as a matter of fact, when I turned
up—was knitting ; and not only mere knitting but working
out some pattern of stitches from one of those *Home Chat*
sort of books. Richards says he sells everything he makes
and does very well out of it. This battery has been in
Flanders ever since it came out—and lets you know it.
It's been doing some tough work with the Canadians and
talks Canadian quite fluently. Some of the gunners have
Canadian field-boots, the battery has two extra telephones.
I seem to know everything about the domestic side of it
after two hours with Richards.

"I dare say you're dug into some kind of job by
now where you can find out exactly where we are,
if you want to. I'm pretty sure you were never
anywhere near here yourself. I suppose the front line
is different, though even here at the battery the Verey
lights are almost bright enough to read by—and they
seem to be the only sign of real war. Of course
there's an occasional rifle-shot, or a machine gun rattles
off, and there has been some gun-fire during the evening
within a mile or so. But none of it is really important—
not like that fellow's knitting and Richards' old speaking-
tubes. But all the same, you can see that they're all fine
soldiers and Richards a fine officer according to those
specifications that were laid down at Wilverley. It all
means, I suppose, that Richards is a gentlemen and the
men good fellows, like our old Ruggles and Foskitt and
Ekins and Bighe. But I think it's the feeling of ' home '
that's the most surprising thing about it all, the hospitality and welcome. Richards was obviously glad when
I turned up, partly because he's short of an officer and it
seems to bother him ; but also for some other reason.
It's really, I think, just because I don't belong to the rest of
the Division which has been in Gallipoli and Egypt instead
of France or Flanders all the time. This feeling between
the two how. batteries now posted to the Division and the
eighteen-pounders that have come with it is the funniest
thing. ' I was afraid they'd send us one of those D.A.C.
jockeys,' Richards said, ' but I suppose they will learn ;

though Plug Street would have given them a better start than this.' He doesn't seem to be a bit bothered by my being absolutely green and it's a funny thing—but I'm not bothering about it myself now. I expect it's the gentleman in Richards coming out, making me feel so wonderfully at home, and the grand good-fellowness of his servant Browne who is also the cook. He's a pretty good humbug, I think ; already he's taken three fleeting opportunities of telling me what a wonderful fellow the Captain is, but you can't help liking him for the very blatancy of it and he's no end of a cook. He's one of those lean-faced beggars who are always solemn and yet seem to be pulling some one's leg all the time—probably your own. He's developed Canadian talk into a fine art and I can quite see that I shall soon become like Richards and want to be amused by everything the fellow does. He's made a wonderful bed for me on four ammunition boxes and the wire mattress thing from the dismantled dug-out. He's going to bring me tea and shaving-water at 6·30. . . . There seems to be every inducement to *enjoy* what all these hard nuts like Richards keep calling 'this picnic.' The shindy going on all the time in the south has already got fixed in one's head, but it seems farther away than it was in Exeter and London. One wants to enjoy it—the sheer, jolly ' rag ' of it—but those incredible damned casualty lists keep on coming out, yard after blasted yard and one's wife, I suppose, searches the damned things now. Anything, by the way, that you and Mollie might do to cheer this lady up will be most gratefully appreciated. My own plan—I think the best one—is to write very little indeed to her about movements—even within the limits of censorship. And I won't write too regularly or too often, in case a time comes when it isn't possible. . . .''

The acetylene gave out, revealing the wedge of moonlight on the chalk steps of the shallow dug-out and the wreaths of smoke curling up them from Cartwright's pipe. He fumbled in his haversack for the candle-stump handed to him by the departing squire-errant at St. Pol, lighted it, and told Henderson that his light was finished.

Richards had remarked, before going to turn in, that this was a pyjama sector ; so Cartwright undressed and laid his clothes on the end of the table. As soon as he had blown out the candle, his eyes were drawn again by the brilliance of the chalk in the moonlight at the dug-out entrance. He thrust his bare feet into his boots and walked up three or four steps till his head and shoulders were above the level of the ground. Leaning upon his elbows he looked across the few yards of tangled grass and the white trodden paths under their awnings of wire-netting at the snouts of sleeping Numbers 3 and 4 in their canvas muzzle-covers. He turned round and climbed a couple of steps higher to see over the reinforcement of chalk lumps heaped on the dug-out top. Before him now were the slits of light from the lanterns of four aiming posts, and in front of these again the shadow of pits Numbers 1 and 2. To his left in the moon-bright side of the quarry was a splash of wan candle-light in the low entrance of a little lean-to affair, and seated on the ground, with his back to the light, was a signaller, reading. The elastic of his ear-pieces shoved his hair up into a tousled crest. The buzzer at his side squeaked while Cartwright watched, and the signaller's free hand replaced the cigar-ette between his lips and reached out for the instrument to buzz back what Cartwright was fresh enough from Exeter to recognise as " O.K."

Another cigarette glowed against a face in shadow outside the signaller's hut as a figure straightened up from squatting against its side.

" Looking for me, Sir ? " its voice asked—a voice subdued a little, from consideration for sleepers.

" No," said Cartwright, and he, too, spoke softly. " I don't know yet who you are."

" I'm sentry."

" Carry on, then, sentry. I was just taking a look at my first night of the Great War." The signaller by now had lowered his magazine to his lap to include himself in the conversation.

" It's a fine night for it, Sir," he said, and stretched out his legs which were luxuriously relieved of putties.

" Yes," said Cartwright. " And a fine place."

He looked into the sky to the right of them, straight over the dug-outs at the steady play of Verey lights that seemed so absurdly near and so uncannily silent. The sentry had come half the distance from the hut towards him, and followed his gaze. A large green light came up among the pallid ones. " That bloke comes up every quarter of an hour. Don't seem to mean anything."

" Well," said Cartwright, " I think I'll turn in. Good night."

" Good night, Sir," said the sentry, and Cartwright found something touching in the absurdity of the boy's knocking his heels together in the tufts of grass and pulling his rifle into his side, while he, Cartwright, stood only breast-high out of the ground dishevelled, in pyjamas with a mauve stripe.

The signaller stirred towards a position of sitting at attention and said " Good night, Sir."

" Good night, signaller," said Cartwright.

Those fellows whose names he did not yet know, wanting to chat to him in the moonlight ! That was the vague, warm kind of thought that stirred in Cartwright as he shuffled out of his boots, and into the snug roughness of his sleeping-bag. . . . Anyhow, he was as welcome to them, it seemed, as they to him. He supposed he would have to make some howlers before he was through with it ; and howlers from a man getting on for forty were not the light affair, somehow, that they were from schoolboys. He was glad that he had not made an ass of himself over those whiz-bangs on the road from Brigade ; or that, if he had, in fact, made an ass of himself the error had been in the right direction. It had been the first practical application of Henderson's great principle of soldiering, " when surprised or in doubt, do nothing."

THE genius of Richards produced a short ceremony the next morning whereby the sense of hospitality and general *bonhomie* was carried still further. It served no practical or strictly utilitarian purpose, for the battery orders for the day already contained the announcement, " Posting. 2/Lt. C. Cartwright is posted to the battery as from to-day and will be Officer i/c Signals " ; but this was not enough for Richards.

The battery mustered for the morning parade about twenty men at the guns. They were fallen in in a single rank conforming to the shape of the path from No. 1 to No. 2 gun, at the north-eastern end of the quarry where the wire netting was high enough for all but two men to stand upright.

A sergeant called them to attention and Richards saluted.

Cartwright in doubt, did nothing.

" Mr. Cartwright," said Richards, " this is Sergeant Wright—our senior Sergeant—acting Sergeant-Major at the guns." The Sergeant saluted ; Cartwright saluted and they shook hands.

Richards said, " Stand the battery at ease, Sergeant, and fall out the Numbers One, and Corporal Hine."

Sergeant Wright gave the orders and the four Numbers One and the Corporal in charge of the signallers came up the path, stooping as their heads began to scrape along the netting.

" Our new officer is Mr. Cartwright," Richards said. " Cartwright—Sergeant Wiley. Corporal Speight. . . ."

One salute from Cartwright and five handshakes completed the ceremonial.

" Right. Fall in. Carry on, Sergeant," said Richards; and Cartwright followed him down the line in front of the men and then up again behind them. At this job, Cartwright saw, a man was inspected by one officer ; but the officer was inspected by twenty men, and he wondered whether Denney and Humphreys had been put through the same ingenious rite wherein discipline was identified with an assumption of some kind of friendship.

"What about those boots, Sergeant Wright?" Richards asked, halting thoughtfully behind a gunner.

"They came up last night, Sir. Four pair. I'm dishing them out this morning."

"Good," said Richards. "Is this man down for a pair?"

Sergeant Wright's note-book, which Cartwright soon came to look upon as an inseparable part of his left hand, flickered, and Wright said, "Yes, Sir. And pants, vest, shirt. . . ."

"Complete trousseau," said Richards. "It's a pity he'll have only the boots to show for it. And what about breeches for Doyle?"

"They're in the issue, too, Sir."

The parade was duly dismissed and Richards and Cartwright walked along one of the cuttings out of the quarry to Richards's little dug-out.

"You didn't mind the 'how-d'you-do?'" he asked. "I don't know if it's in regulations. I saw it done in a lot I once joined, and it seems to come off very nicely."

"Yes, rather," said Cartwright. He did not say that he thought it a stroke of genius.

"We'll see about this dug-out and put Browne and a couple of men on to it. We ought to do our own digging, of course, but I'd like to show you the sector from the O.P. and do a bit of a shoot. It's just up there in the village."

Richards flipped a piece of chalk out of their path with a "hop-scotch" twist of his foot.

"Lovely stuff this, for home-making," he said. "You get a wall and whitewash with one movement."

A few feet from his own shelter was the empty and dismantled one from which the wire bunk had been taken down to the Mess for Cartwright.

"We'll enlarge this one instead of starting another," Richards said. "It'll clear out the rat holes for one thing." He shouted for Browne and sketched out the plan for Cartwright's new home. The general system of houseplanning and building was a simple one. A dug-out for one bunk consisted of a hollow sliced into the chalk bank about two feet wide and six feet high. The spoil from the hollow was built, in sandbags, into a wall about two feet from the face of the bank, which gave a floor space of four feet. There was no dearth of material for roof-timbers, since the built roof was only two feet wide. These timbers, Cartwright saw, were house-doors, bed-rails, odd bits of board and corrugated iron. They were covered with all the spare chalk from the excavation—in sandbags at the edges to hold up the loose filling.

" It must trickle through a bit when it rains," Cartwright suggested.

" It never has rained since we came here," said Richards. " Sergeant Wright will detail a couple of men to help Browne. They can take out another couple of feet—enough to get a bunk along the side, at right angles to Reynolds. No need for two deckers here, where we've got plenty of space. And Browne will put up his patent ceiling to keep dust and muck from falling into your face. We got some fine sacking from the brewery. And, Browne, can you give Mr. Cartwright some lino-leum ? "

" Yes, Sir," said Browne. " There's a couple more bits in stock. D'you like it blue, Sir, or a bit of checked like they have in bathrooms ? "

" Oh, I'd better leave it to you," Cartwright said. " A contract for all the furniture and decoration."

" Very good, Sir." And Browne maintained that set-jowled seriousness that had made Cartwright suspicious. " I'll put in the checked. You'll only be using it to stand on for shaving. I see you've got a bath and basin in your valise, Sir."

" That's good news," Richards said as they moved away from Browne. " My bath is beginning to leak like hell, and Meston has got Reynolds's at the wagon-line."

They pottered about among the gun-pits and telephone

dug-out for half an hour before Richards asked for two
signallers and the telescope, and they went up to the O.P.

From there, seated in an arm-chair placed on a table in
the loft, Cartwright looked out, through a long gap in the
slates, upon the battlefield. He looked through a
telescope which was steadied on a piece of wire hung from
a rafter.

" Keep well back," Richards cautioned him casually,
" so that the sun doesn't get on the glass."

Richards, squatting on a small step-ladder behind him,
looked through his glasses and conducted him by stages
of half a degree from Telegraph Hill over the glowing,
tumbled bricks of Beaurains to the stout chimney of
Neuville Vitasse, through Mercatel and down, by changing
to another gap in the slates, to Ficheux windmill. Then,
starting from Beaurains again, they made a more detailed
tour of the foreground.

It was easy ground to study. There was sufficient
greenery to make the earthworks of support lines and
communication-trenches conspicuous, and there were
still landmarks.

" That dirty looking muck is wire," said Richards. " You
can't really see much of the line from here. Reynolds
can take you down to the dress-circle to-morrow by the
railway. He comes back to-night. We might stroll up
here again after tea, when the sun's dead behind. We
can look out of the window then and see a bit more and
it's as well to loose off a few rounds to check the night-
lines."

Cartwright felt he ought to be asking some questions,
but there did not seem to be any. It all seemed too
natural and perfectly in place for any kind of comment
—a pleasant enough landscape quite decently scarred
with white upheavals of chalk, distant houses torn in the
manner of Bairnsfather drawings, desultory puffs of
bursting shrapnel and here and there a black squirt of
high explosive and earth or pink brick dust in Beaurains.
Even the two signallers in the room below, seen through
a gap in the floor, seemed very fittingly occupied in their
endless game of noughts and crosses played on a message-

pad.   One wore the ear-piece and the other rolled a stock of cigarettes while they played.

A question did occur to Cartwright.   " What shooting do you do ? " he asked.

" Damned little," said Richards.   " As little as possible.   Sixty rounds a day for the battery is the approximate allowance for ordinary strafing purposes. We don't shoot up the trenches unless he shoots up ours. We sometimes put a few over on a minnie.   We use up the sixty rounds on hidden roads and that sort of thing, and calibration.   Sometimes, with luck, you can pick up a target from here ; but not often.   He's well covered, and keeps pretty quiet.   We'll have a few knocks at Mercatel tower to show you that the guns do work and then we'll go and see how the dug-out's getting on.   We don't have to man this O.P. while Reynolds is with the Infantry."

He tapped his heel on the floor and said, " Number Three, action."   The signaller wearing the earpiece buzzed, said " Number three, action," made a cross, recorded a win for himself, drew the four lines necessary for the next game, made a nought, and waited.

Richards gave the deflections, the charge and the range to the signaller.   " You know all about this business of charges for a how., and map range and gun range ? "

" Yes," said Cartwright.   " Pretty well."

" Good.   You can work out some targets and do some shooting yourself with Reynolds.   He'll be better than me.   He's just left school and likes converting his ranges by the range-table.   I always use a slide-rule."

They fired and observed six or eight rounds and went back to the battery.   There were just a few technicalities about which Cartwright was curious.   " I'll show you on the map in the Mess," Richards said.   " Posts are more accurate than an aiming point and besides, in our positions there never is an aiming point visible.   Reynolds will show you.   He's a nailer at all that."

I T was easy, in the Arras sector during the first month of the Somme battle, to take the Napoleonic view of war and find it a grand game.

There were no casualties—Cartwright, at any rate, saw none. One morning, walking round a traverse of the front line with a machine-gun officer at a point where the parapet had been knocked in for half an hour and some rifle grenades had snarled over the wire, his stomach seemed to give a little lurch inside him. His eye stayed fastened upon a spot on the wattle reveting of the trench. The Infantry corporal must have marked the sudden pallor that accompanied the movement of Cartwright's stomach ; he jerked his head in the direction of Cartwright's stare and his eyes, too, lighted upon the little smear of brains on the trench-side.

Cartwright must have halted, for young Reynolds, coming round the traverse behind him, bumped into his back. The Corporal stood up smartly to make room for the party to pass, his back neatly hiding the smear from his own officer.

As Cartwright passed him he said softly, " Sorry, Sir, I thought it was all cleared up." Reynolds said, " Out, damned spot," and the three of them were soon crouched whispering in an emergency post, and peering through a slit at an incredibly lovely view of half a dozen yards of the inside of a German trench.

" Point-blank ! " said the infantryman.   " And there's a hell of a great dug-out just this side of it or I'll eat my hat.   In the morning and evening you can see the beggars humping past by the dozen ; but we daren't fire a ruddy shot or he'd spot it and blow us to hell in half an hour. And the old man wants to keep it up our sleeve, just in case."

" I don't blame him," said Reynolds.   " But any time you want that bit of trench shot up, or the wire cleared away, if we could do it from here, Uncle or I. . . ."

" No. I'm damned if you will ! " said the infantryman genially.   " If this place is going to be advertised at
all, it's going to be advertised by me with a few belts of
the best.   Not by gunners joy-riding, wasting the old
country's money on expensive bangs."

They crawled down the shaft into the covered trench
again and into the front line.   " I expect there'll be a spot
of tea in the dug-out," the Infantryman said.   " Don't tell
any of the others of what I've shown you.   No one else is
allowed to go, without me or the old man."

They went down to the company dug-out.   Cartwright's
stomach had subsided into its usual acquiescence with life
as it found it.   They drank tea and discussed the usual
rumours.   Was it to be Russia ?   Italy ?   Salonika ?
Mesopotamia ? . . .   Cartwright got all that any man
could get out of that particular discussion and the countless others like it—a sense of easy and magnificent fellowship.   The little smear of brains had been cleared away
and forgotten by some excellent man under the orders of
that excellent corporal.   He did the shoot, with Reynolds
sprawling at his elbow, for which they had come, and went
back to the battery for lunch.   After lunch young
Reynolds went up to the attic in Agny to meditate on the
landscape about Beaurains, and Richards came down to
supervise the completion of the speaking-tubes from the
Mess to the gun-pits.

They were a great affair, these speaking-tubes.   Water-
pipes or gas-pipes of about an inch diameter had been
collected in the village, or else had been filched, as time
and opportunity had coincided for individual drivers
passing in the execution of some canteen or ration
errand, from the sappers' dump near Fosseux.   These
pipes had been laid a foot underground, their joints
bound with sacking and covered with cement, to converge
upon a point against the outside of the iron ' elephant '
shelter that had been let into the ground to be buried
again as the Mess dug-out.   It was in the solving of
problems such as this one of disposing neatly and
adequately of four ragged ends of gas-pipe that the light
of Richards shone most brightly.   Shining, it was most

brightly reflected by Browne. The inexhaustibility of a battery's resources was still incredible to Cartwright, so he was unable to contribute any more to the bearing of these men's burdens than the boy or mate can contribute to the work and conversation of master-plumbers.

When Richards said over his mug of coffee, " Snips are the only thing for it, Browne," and Browne said, " Yes, Sir. The tin-opener's a wash-out on stuff that thick," he could realise only that the problem was a tough one. The artificer came down to them and said his snips were not man enough to cut through the iron of the shelter ; but he thought he could do it with his drill and a cold chisel. He went and came back with the tools. The cold chisel was not of the pattern usually seen in iron-monger's shops, but a bayonet snapped or cut off six inches from the hilt and ground to the shape of a chisel.

The job was completed by lunch-time the following day. A rectangle had been cut out of the iron wall of the dug-out. Five sides of an ammunition-box were let into the space, with the open end in the dug-out. Into the other end of it projected the four pipes. When they sat down to lunch Browne came in with a tray bearing a dish of stew and also four corks, each cork tied to a length of string. After placing the stew on the table in front of Richards he fitted a cork into each tube. " I'll tie them each on a nail after lunch so they won't keep getting lost," he said ; and lest anything should be missed of the breadth of his consideration he said with his usual gloom, " It carries beautifully, Sir. You can hear every word in the pits—private and confidential items and all."

Richards and Cartwright were going to the wagon-lines that afternoon. Word had been sent down by the ammunition teams the night before for horses to meet them at Dainville at three o'clock. Cartwright was finishing a letter after lunch while Richards was changing his boots in his dug-out and Reynolds, after a night of Brigade O.P. in the attic had gone to his bunk for a sleep. Browne came down the steps and studied the corked ends of the speaking-tubes in their spacious mouthpiece with a peculiarly baleful kind of satisfaction. " Well, it's done now, Sir," he said, and Cartwright looked up.

" Yes," said Cartwright. " A great job. I've just been writing home about it." He addressed the envelope to Henderson.

" It's the sure sign," said Browne, looking, as usual, beyond mere facts to the significance that lay behind them. " As soon as it's all comfortable enough for the Captain to start putting in these flourishes and conveniences, it's pack up and shift."

" Every one's been talking of a move since before I got here," said Cartwright sceptically.

" Yes, Sir," said Browne, " but the Captain hadn't had time to put in his speaking-choobs. Well, anything *I* might do can't alter it, now that the choobs are done. The Captain and you and Mr. Reynolds might just as well be properly comfortable."

" What's the scheme now, Browne ? "

But Browne was not the resilient type of underling, who can be roused to light-hearted confidence by the mere cheeriness of the overlord.

" D'you think you'll be dining with Mr. Meston to-night, Sir ? " he asked solemnly.

" I don't know," said Cartwright, " the Captain hasn't said."

" I'd be very glad, Sir, if you could." There was that in Browne's tone which said, " I am yours to command ; insist upon it, if you will, and I will speak more ; but my carefully considered and duly weighed counsel is ' ask me no more.' I, 17982 Gunner Browne, C.C., late steward in a Union Castle liner, have this matter in hand, and the matter is no trivial one. All interests will be served best if the Captain can be encouraged unobtrusively to dine at the wagon-line. I have spoken."

He folded up the table-cloth and departed.

IT was on this ride from Dainville to the wagon-line that Richards said, " That fellow Jackman that Reynolds has produced from his section to ' bat ' for you is rather an object, isn't he ? "

" Reynolds said that he's the battery dud," Cartwright admitted cheerfully. " But I don't mind. As Reynolds says, individual attention from me might buck him up a bit, and I can quite see Reynolds's point in not wanting to detail a useful man, and lose him from the section."

" Nothing on God's earth will buck Jackman up," said Richards. " We've tried him as sanitary man and as first-mate to the vet. sergeant. But if you can get clean boots and buttons out of the blighter it'll be something. We can keep him out of sight. Browne and Reynolds's fellow, Crouch, can do all the mess-waiting. Crouch is about as big a b.f. as Jackman, as a matter of fact ; only he doesn't look it. Jackman can *dig*, by the way—if some one sits on his neck."

" I rather like the fellow," said Cartwright. " And he wouldn't look so awful if he had some decent teeth."

" Well, as long as you don't think it's a dirty trick being given a man like that. There are places," Richards went on thoughtfully, " where the best all-round man in the unit is the C.O.'s batman, the second best the second-in-command's—and so on. . . . Well, I believe in keeping a decent Mess, but I don't believe in turning all the best gun-layers into table-layers. There's too damned much of that already. Too much whisky ; too much tinned marvels and tobacco. . . ."

Cartwright was astonished. The few men he had known before who were quaint enough to disapprove of smoking had not been soldiers. He recollected what he had not before particularly noticed, that there was never a bottle of whisky on the table for him and Richards and Reynolds. These reflections started him into thoughts of Richards in civil life—but the thoughts would not move. Richards in anything but a tunic with leather patches on the elbows and leather binding at the wrists, G.S. breeches and a cracked wrinkled pair of field-boots, was Richards quite invisible. Words as smug and censorious as his from any one but a soldier who had been for fifteen months under fire would have been the impossible sounds made by a prig or hermaphrodite. From the shabby commander of Cartwright's battery they represented a reasonable point of view.

" You're strict T.T. are you, Richards ? " he asked, and it was obvious from his tone that his curiosity was of the friendliest.

" I try to be a pretty strict everything," said Richards. " It's the only way for a job like this." Priggishness again was not priggishness at all. It was touching, like the piety of a Pilgrim Father engaged in piracy ; and it was pleasant to be allowed to see the crusader's mystical devotion in the amiable fellow who himself saw something of the joke in his absorption in the job of making gas-pipes into speaking-tubes, and of lowering wire ceilings to push men's heads out of the track of spent and aimless bullets. Cartwright felt that he was a better man and not a worse one for his fantastic thoughts on whisky and tobacco.

" Well," he said, " I hope you don't object to my indulgencies. I drink whisky whenever it occurs. But I'm an old, old man, Richards ; and I've smoked pretty well all my life."

" Smoke away," said Richards. " But if you ever want drivers to spend their time scrounging for cigarettes when there's ammunition to be fetched I'd probably have something to say. By the way," and his tone changed a little in the direction of lightness, " speaking of age, if young Reynolds gets on your nerves with his rot, and calling you ' Uncle ' just tell him not to."

" Good Lord ! " said Cartwright, " I don't mind. If you work it out I'm old enough—with just a few years to spare—to be his father."

' I think the Canucks must have started it," Richards said. " And now the youngsters in every unit seem to be on the look out for some one to call 'Uncle.' I suppose it's their way of bragging that they are kids doing real men's work."

"Well," said Cartwright, "it's rather marvellous to think that my own youngster would be doing it if he had been born just a couple of years earlier. It makes my hair curl to think that he could be using Reynolds's language."

"D'you mean his Shakespeare?" asked Richards.

"No," said Cartwright. "I mean the language he uses to his section, to the signallers and to the shells that drop into Arras and Agny. I can't imagine what he will find to say if one ever comes nearer."

"Ah! that's when the Shakespeare would come out," said Richards; "but perhaps he's forgotten it by now. A year ago, when he'd just left school, it was awful."

"I've had wonderful luck in my battery," said Cartwright thoughtfully; for one did, somehow, say things on field tracks like the one from Dainville to Warlus which one wouldn't have said so freely in, for example, Chiswick High Road.

"Yes. They're a good lot."

Cartwright was to see more, in the fullness of time, of his Commanding Officer's elegance in the exercise of quick and smooth evasion. "You've got the one and only Jackman among them. It's up to you to delouse him." Again there was a glimmer of that peculiar earnestness.

He was young, Cartwright reflected; younger than Henderson . . . and yet not young enough, like Reynolds, to pretend that the white man's burden as borne by every Englishman in the field was a bag of stupendous jokes. He was right, however; they did stand in *loco parentis* to the good-for-nothing rascals like Jackman and to the solemn geniuses like Sergeants Wright and Wiley.

"'Uncle' is a jolly good style for a subaltern without a section," Cartwright observed; and it was. The best he could do for a man with boils or worn-out teeth or boots or breeches was to say, "I'll tell your officer," as who should say "I'll talk it over with your father. . . ."

" You'll get a section all right. Don't worry," said Richards. " Meston is pretty senior—just five days junior to me ; he'll get his third pip and a battery somewhere soon."

In detail it turned out that Richards was wrong. What removed Meston from the battery was not a third pip but a rifle-gun bullet at the base of the skull.

" My only reason for not liking to be a spare," Cartwright explained, " is the moves that may be going on. I may get shifted."

" You won't. You've been as near to that as you're ever likely to be—two days after you reported—when they wanted three men from the Division for trench-mortars. That's the evening I went off to dine at Brigade."

" I say," said Cartwright. " D'you mean you asked the Colonel to let me stay ? "

" Of course," said Richards. " You see, you can't go mucking about with a battery."

Already a battery was beginning to take shape in Cartwright's mind too as a mysterious and august reality, something that starts with a capital letter, like God or Truth or Empire . . . and Richards again had ducked and side-stepped from the passage of compliments. He went on : " They dug out a D.A.C. jockey in the end, and two reinforcements who had just reported from your place, Exeter."

MEDAL WITHOUT BAR   CHAPTER XXXIII

R ICHARDS, Cartwright found, had given him the key to an otherwise puzzling situation when he had told him that Meston was only five days junior to himself.

Anywhere else, Cartwright could see, Meston would have been as sound and as easy as any one ; but next to Richards he was merely a nuisance. They walked over and around the horse-lines that stretched along three sides of a field, under the poplars. Cartwright walked behind them, chatting to the Sergeant-Major whenever the Sergeant-Major was not jumping forward a pace or two to answer a question. Cartwright was out of the conversation, for it was nothing to him as yet that the grey with a docked tail was a slug now being tried in the mess-cart and her place in the lead of "A" sub's first-line wagon-team taken by a remount. He was included for a moment by the information that his second charger was the predecessor of the grey in the mess-cart.

When they got back to Meston's tent, the host a little ostentatiously said " Have a drink ? It's no use asking the skipper."

" Thanks," said Cartwright. It seemed the soundest course. It was more loyal to Richards than a refusal, for it denied any implication of priggishness in his abstinence.

And then Cartwright saw the kind of thing that a difference of five days in the dates of gazetting could produce.

" I sent Wilkins up, by the way, with Cartwright's horses," Meston said with a conspicuous absence of smile from his features.

" Yes," said Richards. " I was going to talk to you about that. Reynolds told me he had detailed Loveday as Cartwright's groom."

" I've written a chit up to Reynolds," said Meston. " I'd rather he told Wilkins off for the job. He won't mind changing. I've told him why, in the chit."

" He will mind," said Richards. " He's given Cartwright the worst gunner in Kitchener's army as a batman and he's not going to give him the worst driver as groom."

" Wilkins isn't a dud," said Meston.

" He's a little too much like one," said Richards.

" Don't put any one out for me," Cartwright suggested politely ; but neither of these strong men face to face was in need of assistance from such as he.

" We're not," said Richards bluntly, " don't worry."

" I didn't think you would be likely to mind," said

Meston to Cartwright with quiet assurance. " Not after spending a week or so with Richards, and getting to know his views about the efficiency of—THE BATTERY."

It was possible to see a good deal in the way Meston tossed the last of his whisky-and-water down his throat and put down his mug. Richards was obviously knocked, and Cartwright waited with some anxiety for the next move. It came, reassuringly enough, from Richards.

" Speaking of the efficiency of the *battery*," he said quietly, " Cartwright must have a spell at the wagon-line, while everything's quiet. He can come down with Reynolds for a bit in a day or two, and you can do a turn with me at the guns."

Meston then proceeded to spoil his own game with surprising and comforting stupidity. " I thought you wanted some days down here yourself," he said. " Why don't you come down with Cartwright and leave me in command at the guns ? "

That ' in command ' gave some pathos to the poor fellow's stupidity. Richards, too, must have seen it. It was with a kindly twinkle that he said, " Efficiency of the battery, old cock. It's a long time since Reynolds put in a spell with his horses. Well, Uncle, there's a war on. We'd better be getting back to it." This conclusion again gave an assurance of the peculiar, unconscious skill possessed by Richards. This first usage by him of the style of ' Uncle ' touched Cartwright very pleasantly ; and it showed Meston, if Meston was capable of seeing anything in his moments of resentment, that some sort of working understanding already existed between Richards and his ' reinforcement.' But the most real question before the mind of Cartwright, just then, was dinner and the anxiety for Browne for what he had called ' a nice long evening without the Captain.'

Meston's grouse was, at any rate, spoiling that. He called to his batman from the tent-flap and ordered the horses.

" I should change Wilkins and Loveday over before Reynolds comes down," Richards casually advised. " Or it might look as though he is changing your orders about."

" Right.   Tell me what night to send up my flea-bag."

Meston in his submission was a bigger man than Meston in revolt ; and Cartwright was a little awed by the mystery of Command.   It was the kind of thing that Henderson had talked of so much ; the sheer domination of some quality in one man over some quality in another without any undue throwing about of weight.

Richards could have done the thing in the Sergeant-Major manner, and his orders about Loveday and about Meston's tour in the gun-line would have stood on the broad foundation of Armies ; but they stood now, quite apart from braid on cuffs and brass knobs on shoulder-straps, on something finer.   Whatever poor Meston had had to swallow, he had swallowed ; and the War was trundling on quite peaceably as they walked and jogged eastwards towards it, with the occasional clang of Farting-Fanny's arrival in cavernous Arras.

Cartwright did ask, from some vague motive of loyalty to Browne, whether there was any possibility of getting something to eat at one or other of the trifling estaminets on their road.

"Only Gibbs's dental soap," said Richards, "and Rhone Aspirin.   We'll be home by eight.   We can ride as far as your whiz-bang bit of road."

MEDAL WITHOUT BAR   CHAPTER XXXIV

A GAP had been made in the hedge and bank behind the battery, where the mess-cart and ammunition-wagons stopped at night, and where, too, the old woman from Arras stopped each evening and blew her little coloured horn which brought Browne from his kitchen and gunners from their tremendous ablutions for their copies of the Paris *Daily Mail*, for all gunners, like Mohammedans, appeared to be drawn by the setting of the sun to great washings of hands and chests.

It was the sight of the woman seated at ease upon an ammunition-box by the gap that gave the first hint of some unusual happening. The next hint was from the voice of Browne raised above a general din of scraping and scrunching in the loose chalk, and the mumble of criticism mixed with advice and objurgation. The sounds, as Cartwright learnt in due season, were sounds quite normal to a gun in the act of being manhandled out of a close-fitting gun-pit ; so that to Richards the puzzle was immediately clear-cut and distinct.

He stopped for a moment ; a direct hit on number three gun-pit and the smashing up of number three gun could have accounted for it. But then why Browne in obvious and dramatic command instead of Sergeant Wiley, the Number One of the subsection ? . . . " Steady there, my lucky lads. A long one and she's yours. Now— together—here with your handspike, sonnie—together— heave ! " Crunching of chalk again ; scraping, and a sort of hollow boom. Sheer delight on the part of the old woman with the bag of *Daily Mails*, who rocked upon her up-ended ammunition-box.

Richard grunted something and hurried forward. Cartwright jumped after him.

Browne's back was towards the gap and Richards and Cartwright. In breeches and undervest, he was leaning on a handspike as thoughtful shepherds are pictured leaning upon their crooks. His head was done up in a towel—a precaution Browne took when digging in chalk ; for his long, wavy hair was always a matter of care and very proper pride to him. The towel was valuable at that moment as a touch in the shepherd tableau. In front of Browne was a cast-iron bath of the most noble proportions and a luxurious finish of porcelain-enamel. It was the stumpy feet of this helpless and leisurely piece of furniture that were giving all the trouble in the loose footway under the wire netting.

Upon the two drag-ropes hitched about the bath were Jackman and Reynolds's servant Crouch, with four or five volunteers from the gun-pits and signallers' shed. One man bent in front of Browne at the stern of the bath with a second handspike. In the pause of this orchestra, waiting for a further tap and gesture from its conductor, the man who first saw Richards and Cartwright said, " Be'ind yer, Charlie."

Browne turned. The fantastic clown within him produced a rigidity in the brooding shepherd ; it converted the handspike which had become the shepherd's crook into a property quite normal in the hand of a soldier, and it produced a salute with the disengaged hand as profoundly respectful as it was smart.

Richards answered the salute with a salute every bit as good. Quite seriously, as though the appearance of immense bath tubs in battery positions was an every-day occurrence, he said, " I suppose Grannie brought it with the newspaper, Browne ? "

" No, Sir," said Browne. " She wouldn't undertake to deliver it, Sir. I bought it off her. Carriage forward."

" In Arras ? " Richards's eyebrows lifted.

" No, Sir. In Ag-ony." The fact that for every gunner the indeterminate vowel between the ' g ' and the ' n ' of Agny was always an O provided Browne with the joke that only needed a slight movement of his hands from the seams of his breeches to the small of his back to reward his volunteers amply for their labour.

" So she's got a branch in Agny ? " said Richards.

" Yes, Sir. And Agincourt." (Achicourt was always curiously Agincourt to men who knew, of the two, only Achicourt.)

" Did she give you a receipt, by the way ? " asked Richards next.

" No, Sir. Only the barf, Sir. And a soap-dish. The soap-dish is already up, Sir, in the new barfroom."

Richards said, gloomily, " You've had us told off for looting once already, Browne. Those damned soup-plates."

It was an anxious moment. The volunteers relaxed upon the drag-ropes and leaned a little forward towards the confidence of Richards. It may have been solicitude for their Captain in the sadness that had come so suddenly upon him. It may have been that they visualised the rough road (uphill) from the battery back to the village with that colossal bath.

"Sir," said Browne ; and he gave Samuel Johnson's weight to the soldier's opening of a charge or a defence. "It isn't loot, Sir. *She* took us past the Infantry bloke on guard, with a paper."

"What paper ? " asked Richards.

"A paper, Sir," said Browne. "Her own paper that she's got. Season-ticket it looks like. But she signed for the barf."

Richards said, "And *now* what are you going to do with it ? "

"Scull 'er along, Sir, to the barfroom. Or would you like your dinner first, Sir ? "

"No," said Richards. "Better get this done first. Tagney, get four ammunition-boxes to stick those feet into, or you'll go on doing nothing but plough. Where's Mr. Reynolds, Browne ? "

"O.P., Sir. Been gone since five. Said he'd be back at dark."

"And where's this bathroom ? "

"I'll show you, Sir." He laid down his handspike and whisked the towel from his head and shook out from it a cloud of chalk dust. He led them till he got as far as the Mess dug-out. There he suddenly stopped. "It's— you'll find it quite easy just next door to your shack, Sir," he said hurriedly. "I better get back to those boys, or they'll start knocking her about. We've got her so far without a scratch—inside *or* out."

"Good God, yes ! " said Richards. "Whatever you do, don't let them get it scratched."

In the new bathroom Richards and Cartwright sat down in a state of some peculiar kind of collapse upon a low dais like the firestep of a trench that the hewers of the chamber had left unhewn against its inner side. That, presumably, was where the bath was going. The roof was already up, and the sandbag walls completed to the thickness of a single bag.

"How the blighters must have worked ! " said Richards, filling his chest with the material for laughter. But there was something in the fantastic genius of Browne that suddenly silenced laughter into a smile. Cartwright nodded. "We've only been gone since three," he said ; and he, too, changed laughter into a silent smile.

A new mirror was pegged against the sandbags of the wall. Beside it and above the foundation for the bath was the splendid soap-dish of which Browne had spoken.

A drain was carved in the floor at the end of the platform where Richards sat. At the entrance to the chamber the drain was bridged over, probably with a door (since the use of ammunition-boxes for such a purpose would have been more illegal even than looted doors). It ran thence openly beside the path, as a gutter.

"He's been at this little job, off and on, for days," Richards said, as they walked slowly beside the course of this gutter. "Said the path needed draining in case the weather turned."

The drain ended by the signallers' shack in a shallow, square pit. Above it was a notice-board of that beloved type, inscribed in that worst of all media for such inscriptions—'indelible' pencil so-called—in a highly decorative script :

"FOR USE IN CASE OF FIRE ONLY."

MEDAL WITHOUT BAR   CHAPTER XXXV

L ETTERS home in these circumstances were an easy enough matter. Yet there was a sense of tragedy upon him when he wrote them, a yearning to make it all simple and clear and convincing to Dorothy ; war was a fantastic game among those pleasant fellows—one of whom would poke his head into a dug-out or gun-pit and say "Shop !" to interpret the officers' more grandiose "Battery—action ! "

The tragedy, as he wrote of these simple things, was that from Dorothy they must persist in remaining secret. He could not convey to her the exact, astonishingly negligible proportion of danger and hardship. When her letters, replying, ended with ". . . my poor, dear old boy, I kiss you good night . . ." he knew that the picture at which she wistfully looked before turning out the bedroom light—and after—was a fantastic picture of her own making. It was based on the terror of tired thousands herded breathless in the din of air-raids, on those grotesque and fatuous newspaper accounts of battles that Reynolds would sometimes read aloud for the sheer, idiotic fun of it ; and on her quick glances at the casualty lists.

He could tell her not to read such rubbish ; that the War was nothing of the sort ; that he was having three hot meals a day most elegantly cooked—eggs and fresh vegetables ; a tub of sparkling spring-water every morning ; crisp toast with his afternoon tea : that he had not seen a man hurt—and she answered, referring to these things ". . . my poor, dear old boy, I kiss you good night. . . ." And John, with stammerings and gurglings that had found their way into his curt letter, had sent him a steel mirror in a pig-skin case to go in the breast-pocket of a tunic over the heart, guaranteed to deflect a rifle bullet. The package had been posted in Westminster.

If he could have managed to get home and see them—if only for an hour—he might, perhaps, have done something to ease the sadness in Dorothy's ". . . my dear, poor old boy . . ." the hurt in young John's bullet-proof, secretly posted mirror. (But when he did get home, times and facts had altered.)

This was one of the two worries that occasionally pressed upon him in the sunny leisure of the Arras sector. The other worry was himself. Somehow, and for no easily remediable reason, he felt that he was falling short. There was some knack that he did not possess. Scandalous chins had occurred among the score paraded for him by Sergeant Wright under the wire netting one morning. He had walked down the single rank of the assembled braves, frowning and coming back to his starting-point after inspecting heels and tunic backs.

He had gloomily addressed the men, talking some non-sense about the probable relationship of neglected chins to neglected guns, and neglected guns to slack gunnery.

The next morning he came into the sunshine from the Mess, lighting his pipe, at the conclusion of Reynolds's ' orderly-officer ' parade. Reynolds was making a speech. " Gunner Doyle ! " he called, and the famous Doyle who would have been conspicuous even among tramps crouched up to him from the rank, and saluted. " When I want a hedgehog inspection, I'll ask the Captain to order one. And don't talk to me about your razor being no good. I know damned well that you would get a razor—if you wanted one—out of a locked-up Jew's shop—and so does every one else in this battery. The next time you bring a thing like that chin of yours on parade there'll be trouble ; *real* trouble. And don't look at my chin when I'm talking about yours. That has nothing to do with it. My beard is *afraid* to grow. It knows what it would get if it tried. I'll mention you in dispatches to Mr. Cartwright so that he'll be on the look out for you specially, on his days, to see if he can recognise you properly shaved. Fall in. . . . Dismiss please, Sergeant."

" Every man in his humour," he said when he joined Cartwright at the dug-out steps, and saw that he had been listening. " Francis Drake to Mr. Doughty is the only line with that blasted old Doyle. Do sit on the blighter's neck for me, Uncle, on your days, so that we can get a human face out of that muck-heap above his collar."

Then Richards was telephoned for one afternoon, to report immediately at Brigade Headquarters. It was the beginning of the period of knowingness and caution in the use of the telephone further forward than Brigade ; so Richards felt safe in saying " You can start your packing, Uncle, if you're a slow packer. No more Rolls-Royce bath-tubs for a bit."

When he came back after dinner, Reynolds and Cartwright were walking in the lane behind the battery, and strolled to meet him.

" War's been declared all right," he said.

Reynolds cocked an eyebrow southward over his left shoulder as they stood facing the golden sky-line where the sun had set " Yes," said Richards, " and damn' quick. A section to-morrow night, and a section the night after. Let's go in and cook some orders."

He called to Browne for a pot of tea before they went down into the Mess. Cartwright felt that the moment was charged with something he had not known before as the three of them sat down to the table and Richards gave half a turn to the tap in the acetylene lamp and emptied one of his pocketfuls of documents on to the table.

" By God ! " said Richards slowly. " I wish you fellows could have heard the old man's yarn. He hasn't been on leave ; he's been with the French, on a liaison job, at Verdun."

He unfolded and spread a new map, and folded back the top and bottom and sides, getting it compact and negotiable, to leave room on the table for the teapot and mugs. Cartwright's eyes and Reynolds's focused themselves on the pencil-marks and notes which Richards had made on the map.

" Are we going to the French ? " asked Reynolds.

" No," said Richards. " There's going to be another big splash at our end. Look here, I'll show you. D'you know how much ground we've taken in the last month down there ? " With a push of his engineer's spatulate thumb he indicated a smear of ground on the map, and did not wait for their answer. Reynolds's reading aloud of special correspondents' dispatches had always been aimed at merely giving the English language an outing, not at the study of the War in aspects that had no bearing on themselves. " Three ruddy miles ! " said Richards. " Three miles. . . . Eight minutes' ride on a push-bike. Call it ten, if you like. Here——" He paused with his thumb blotting out a square mile of the Ancre swamp, with Beaucourt and Beaumont Hamel. " Here," he said again, reflecting some of the Colonel's dramatic bombast, " we've moved exactly damn-all."

They sat back from the map, having studied the spot. But the intense quality of the situation came from something apart from the map—which was only a trifling $\frac{1}{100,000}$ road map. " D'you know what the ammunition ration has been ? Three hundred rounds per gun."

" Per day ? " asked Cartwright.

" Yes," said Richards. " And they've been using it."

But already the effort of looking upon any aspect of the affair but the purely domestic one was becoming a strain.

" Handing over, or pulling out ? " asked Reynolds.

" Pulling out," said Richards ; " except aiming-posts. We'll take out your section to-morrow night when the other lot comes in, and leave just the left-section gun-teams at the wagon-line. That'll give you and Meston a clear day to go through things and get out some indents. Uncle can bring C and D subs. along and join us. I've got the new Brigade Headquarters and wagon-lines marked on here somewhere."

The map on the table conveyed to Browne, when he came down with the tea, the information he had been expecting since the installation of the bath.

" Any orders for the morning, Sir ? " he asked.

" No," said Richards. " Breakfast as usual. But tell Grayson I'll give him the battery-orders in my dug-out at seven, after you've brought my tea."

" Very good, Sir. Good night, Sir."

" Good night, Browne.—Oh, Browne ! Tell him in the morning. Not to-night."

" Very good, Sir."

Browne went, and Richards said : " It doesn't take much to set those damned signallers chatting to other batteries to keep themselves awake. But I don't like that old girl nosing about here with her newspapers. You must head her off to-morrow, Uncle, somehow. There's more wind up just now over reliefs being given away than anything else in the whole war."

This was the first job requiring any initiative for which Cartwright had been detailed. " Do it gently," said Richards. " It's ten millions to one that she's O.K. ; but if she isn't, it's just as well not to put thoughts in her head."

" I'd like to know how——" Cartwright began.

" How ? " said Richards, astonished. " You speak French, don't you ? " That, for Richards, seemed to settle the matter.

" Just walk up to her," said Reynolds. " Smile and say ' *Excusez moi, Madame*,' or something else courtly, and dot her one over the head with a pick-handle.   If she doesn't understand your French, dot her another."

It bade very fair to disturb Cartwright's sleep, this first commission of his, a matter not of gunnery but diplomacy.   As he and Reynolds were undressing in the dug-out he said, morosely, " I would like to know how my speaking French is going to keep that old woman away, without making her suspicious."

" Oh, that ! " said Reynolds.   " Don't worry about that.   I'll say something to the Major of C Battery on my way to the O.P. to-morrow.   He's the spy-shiest lad I've ever known.   He's been grousing about the old girl's going to the batteries ever since we came in here. I'll say what a bad show it is—particularly when there's a relief going on.   I'll just wonder—out loud—if some one's meeting her and buying up all the papers and chocolate she's got wouldn't keep her away.   He'll do it.   And 'twere meeter so, mine Uncle.   His pay is bigger pay than mine—or thine."

" Suppose she comes just the same ? " asked Cartwright.

" The soldier's hazard is the soldier's lot.   I'll stake my codpiece that she will not come—saying which, sweet lieutenant, he said good night."

" Idiot—" said Cartwright.   " Good night."

THE Captain who came next day to lunch and to look at the front from the O.P. was an old hand—a young regular with three or four years' service— who had been wounded six months before and had come out again with a new battery.   He admired the speaking-tubes and the bath and the soap-dish—and, Cartwright could see, criticised Richards and Reynolds and himself. The younger regulars were still entertaining opinions and making estimates among themselves about " Kitchener's men and Territorials." Kitchener's Army and Territorials were forming their estimate of young regulars. (Young regulars were still in evidence in and about trenches and gun-lines.)

Browne's manner in his serving of the lunch was changed not only in the direction of ' company ' manners, but of ' ceremonial.' Usually he waited at lunch in breeches, shirt and a not very dressy pair of Canadian field-boots. Cartwright had known him bring in the soup or rissoles wearing ordinary issue boots and no putties, exhibiting a fine pair of sock-suspenders worn over the ends of his breeches. On this day he appeared with putties, hair slickly plastered and a tight linen jacket acquired from God knew where. Richards moved not an eyelash at the apparition. Reynolds's gesture of *hauteur* was apparent only to Cartwright. (It transpired later that Browne had asked his wife some months before, partly to strengthen her confidence in his destiny and partly for the simple reason that you never knew, to send him a couple of the old jackets wherein he had plied his First-Class broth on the decks of the Union Castle Liner.) His dressing-up on this and other occasions was due to no particular regard for regulars—young or old—but to a principle of taking people as he found them and of letting them have as good as they gave. If it was eye-wash they looked for in the Mess, whereby to assess the value of Browne's bloke, it was eye-wash he gave them.

The incoming captain confided to Cartwright when they were alone together next day, that you could judge a battery by its Mess.

It was an important day for Cartwright. He took the Captain up to the trenches and showed him where the minnie was sometimes thought to run up on a light railway. They crept, with a new machine-gun officer, into the famous battle-position and peered along the neatly reveted back of the German trench by the suspected Company dug-out. From the attic in Agny they shot-in the two new guns, and Cartwright indicated the Tower and the Windmill with a few rounds from his own two—the gunner's handiest way of pointing out important features of a landscape. Cartwright had no antagonism for the regular, *qua* regular, since Henderson and Sinclair were regulars. This fellow, incidentally, knew Sinclair and knew all about the ' group-system ' of intensive training at Exeter. He had put the final polish on his own battery by using some of it. He allowed, indeed, that a training at Exeter was about the next best thing in the world to a training at the Shop.

" It's wonderful how men like Richards have got hold of it all and become first-class soldiers," said Cartwright, " just picking up their training—mostly out here, in action."

" He knows how to run a Mess, anyway," said the other, for he wanted his praise to be ungrudging.

Cartwright rode away from the old chalk-pit on his first command, in the best of good spirits. Sergeant Wright had handled the matter of getting out the guns and hooking them into the limbers while Cartwright dined with the new-comers. The subaltern in charge of the new battery's wagon-line was so green that he had agreed with Richards, immediately and very cordially, that his gun teams and limbers, after taking up his own two guns and the rations, should bring back the others as far as the wagon-lines. It was the kind of obvious suggestion with which Cartwright himself would have freely agreed at that innocent time. The canny Richards had saved his horses and drivers six or eight miles of road without even the tossing of a coin.

It was about an hour and a half before midnight when their own teams and limbers were hooked in to the guns at the wagon-lines and Cartwright had a drink in the senior-subalterns' tent before the section took the road to Simencourt.

The command, so far, had consisted of riding with Sergeant Wright beside him at the head of a score of men and animals of whom each one knew the road. From the wagon-line to Simencourt most of the drivers could have gone blindfolded. The by-roads to the north of the main Doullens-Arras road had been allotted to the Division's artillery for the first twenty-five miles of its circuitous march southward. They could hear the rumble and clank of lorries and wagons far to their left, and beyond that the steady tide of bombardment from Hebuterne to Verdun. Cartwright had the map in his case and had written on a slip of paper the names of the villages, as far as Couturelle, where he was to be met by a guide from the battery.

Gouy, the next village from Simencourt, by the unexpressed consent of horses and drivers and out-riders and Cartwright himself, seemed to lie straight ahead. The track was deeply rutted but sound, and the little column moved along with the shamble of a single drowsy creature.

He drew them into the side and made their second halt. Drivers pulled at the tea or whatever other concoctions their water-bottles held, lighted cigarettes and whistled the soft, low warbling notes wherewith teamsters encourage and congratulate their beasts in their normal achievements.

Cartwright gave Sergeant Wright a cigarette.

" Half-way yet, Sir ? " the Sergeant asked.

And Cartwright suddenly knew that responsibility had slowly shifted from the twenty pairs of shoulders that had carelessly carried it and now rested on his alone. He was an officer commanding. . .

" Just about," he said ; " or a mile or two over. I ought to have shown you on the map. You know," he added, a little self-consciously, " —the way it says in the book. In case of casualties." This possibility was as remote now as it had ever been in the lanes near Exeter. He flashed his torch on his map and his list of village names. " We're to meet some one at the cross-roads in Couturelle. The battery is somewhere just outside. We may stay there a couple of days. We go through Gouy, Fosseux, Barly and Saulty."

It was a quarter-past twelve.

He had, about a fortnight before, spent one night on liaison duty with the infantry. Although he had slept in his boots that night, he had turned in a little earlier than he usually did at the battery. That night of sleeping in his clothes and the two nights spent smoking and dozing in the Agny attic on Brigade O.P. duty had been his only variations from civilisations' regard for sleep since leaving the train that brought him from Havre to the War.

" Doesn't sound much like our old rest-cure down that way," said Wright, nodding southward.

" No," said Cartwright, " but it might not be so very much when you get into it. It's spread over a biggish area."

Wright mumbled something ; but he knew more than Cartwright about differences in sounds.

Sergeant Wiley and a Corporal reported their subsections correct.

" Get mounted, Sir ? " asked Wright.

" Yes, please," said Cartwright.

He himself mounted (remembering that he had not examined so much as his horse's girth, and supposing that the drivers had gone over every strap and buckle of their harness and examined every hoof) ; he looked back over his shoulder and called " Walk—march."

That softly called " Walk—march " was his first fully responsible order. (The " Mount " given before it was given by the Sergeant, and was, in fact, the Sergeant's idea.)

The note on his slip of paper said " Gouy—left—half—right." This meant a turn to the left, half a mile, and then a turn to the right.

It was easy and straightforward enough going, yet he was immensely relieved to see the outline of a great windmill by the roadside which he had noticed on the map, half a mile before Fosseux. He had noticed it only because of the more familiar mill—the ragged calibration-point in Ficheux haggard in the light of flares, resembling this sleeping village in nothing but its name. As the old stump of the Ficheux mill had received his shells and been the first sign of approval of his accuracy as a gunner, so now Fosseux mill stood dark and silent, welcoming him and approving his accuracy as a guide.

The left incline at Fosseux seemed, after half a mile, to have been very much more than an incline. Flares and the vibrating glow of gunfire seemed to be almost in front

now instead of behind. Drivers were getting sleepy—
some, perhaps, were asleep—for there were sudden depths
of silence behind him. Sergeant Wright had dropped
back from his side and stayed at the rear of the column.
Command, at a midnight that was surprisingly chilly,
ambling towards a horizon that throbbed with pallid light
and muffled sound, was turning out a lonely affair. And
his holding of it, Cartwright meditated, was a precarious
one.

It depended, at the moment, on his ability to read a
map and follow a road so simple that a boy-scout ought
to have done it. If he led them wrong the men would
smile. They were such good fellows that they might
even go so far as to pretend that he had not led them
wrong ; but they would smile—and look to old Sergeant
Wright. Wright would know what to do and would
salute and suggest the moment for doing it. Command,
he meditated further, was for him a matter of chancing
on the right course. In people like Henderson and
Reynolds—more even than in the case of Richards—it
was nothing of the sort. Reynolds could have taken that
blindfolded section down a dozen of the side-tracks that
were indistinguishable in the dark of midnight from
century-old roads. He could have ditched guns and
limbers, scrambled them out and landed them all finally
in Timbuctoo instead of Couturelle—but the men would
not have smiled secret, indulgent smiles and looked to a
Sergeant for salvation. They would still have looked to
Reynolds. . . .

On the map there are but three roads in Barly and
within a mile of it that turn roughly southward. The
road to Saulty is plainly enough the last of them. But
one could not keep a torch switched permanently on to a
map ; and half a dozen lorries driven in succession off a
road to some dump or park in a field can produce track
enough to count, in pitch darkness, as a road.

An hour's silent and lonely brooding on the emptiness
of command in a world that had a liquid quality in its
heavy darkness, a turgid ebb and flow in the pressure
of its sound, was enough to produce a doubt at every

gap in the roadside. Any walking inhabitant could have allayed that doubt. But it was astonishing how soundly and how darkly a village could sleep, so little more than half a dozen miles from where there was no sleep at all.

From Barly to Saulty was no more than three miles. For the first mile of the road a low spur ran between the crawling section and the moaning growl of the Somme and the pallor of its lights. As the road slowly climbed out of this immediate cover and bore slightly to the left it seemed that the section was drifting straight for the line. The nearest Verey light was perhaps eight miles away, but there was nothing in the sullen darkness to show that it was any more than furlongs.

The sound ought to have been reassuring enough, for there was no more individuality in it than in the mumble of a distant crowd. Occasional thuds and crashes in the shapeless murmur were distinguishable only to senses that had been whetted till the very edge of them had the keenness of pain. . . .

Then gradually another sound crept up into the night. The road swung happily to the right—away from the frontier of lights ; and then writhed slowly back towards it again.

Cartwright drew aside to see that his vehicles were keeping their interval, and halted them. Sergeant Wright trotted up from the rear.

The new sound was the sound of vehicles. To ears strained in its direction it was obviously between them and the lights and the murmur.

" Another lap will about do it, Sergeant," he said.

He felt as the weary horses must have felt now that their burdens had scrambled from them to the ground to pull again at their water-bottles.

" There's a half-feed in the nose-bags, Sir," said the Sergeant. " Will you be halting long enough for a feed ? "

" Good idea," said Cartwright. " Yes. Feed. I'll just walk on a bit and see exactly where we are."

" I could send a signaller on a bicycle," Wright suggested.

" I'd like to stretch myself," said Cartwright ; " I'll go

on his bicycle." What he felt he would like was a minute with his torch and his map at the corner where his road met the one with the other traffic.

He found the corner true to the map. A road, rough and palely dusty and deeply rutted like his own, coming from the left ; houses enough on the right, dimly blacker than the sky, to tell him that he was arrived at Saulty. In the few minutes that he leaned on the telephonist's bicycle to fill and light his pipe some lorries trundled out of the village and passed up, reassuringly, eastwards. He had nothing to do now but to turn his section to the right at that corner and avoid turning right or left off the straight road to Couturelle.

"We're a mile or two better off than I thought," he said, when he got back to the section. "Another half-hour will do it."

"We'll have made a good march of it, Sir," said Wright. "That rest-cure at Agony after the Sanctuary Wood do has got the horses up lovely. We couldn't have marched 'em four hours on end a month ago, not for love nor money. Not with limbers loaded up like we got ours. We got two extra trusses of 'ay lifted off of the other battery before leaving the wagon-line, all the gun line's kit and the signallers' stuff."

Falling in with the section of one of the eighteen-pounder batteries that had come as far as Saulty by the lower road, riding the last two miles with its subaltern Bevan, Cartwright made the discovery that it was not fear he had felt on the road, but fussiness. It would not do, however. . . .

It was the kind of thing that justified the name of "Uncle."

The thought was confirmed by the manner of the section's entry into the wagon-line by the little brook to the south-west of Couturelle. It was the very simple affair of people returning late to a house where the others had gone to bed and left the door considerately on the latch. There were spaces ready among the parked vehicles for the guns and limbers, spaces in the lines for the horses. A dixie of tea had been kept at steaming-

M

point against a fire by the stable-picket. Jackman, yawning and shuffling about with boots unlaced and breeches to his ankles said, " There's supper for you in the tent, Sir. Shall I wait up ? "

In the tent where he lighted a candle, were biscuits and cheese and jam and the Thermos flask of cocoa. Meston and his valise were on the far side of the pole. Opposite to Cartwright's valise was that of Reynolds', containing Reynolds with his features in profoundest peace a yard from the candle.

MEDAL WITHOUT BAR   CHAPTER XXXVII

A FTER two or three days under the trees by the stream-side Richards and Cartwright looked out upon their home of the next eight months with the same advantages of observation enjoyed by Moses on Pisgah.

While the guns were being sketchily dug in in a little fold of the ground between the two roads from Auchonvillers—northward to Hébuterne and eastwards to Beaumont Hamel—they ate a hurried lunch and walked a mile along the northern one.

A siege-gunner Major seated high up in the crucifix tree had wearily abandoned all hope of keeping the place to himself and his two telephonists. The upper rungs of the ladder lashed to the tree were occupied by sightseers.

Australians, Jocks, Canadians, R.A.M.C., A.S.C., and dispatch-riders roosted on the tree's sounder branches.

" One shell! " said Richards looking up into the tree. " Just one decent burst . . ."

But the shell never came.

Along the road itself just beyond the crucifix there appeared to be every man in the British Army who felt that he could be spared for a few moments from the active conduct of the War. Cartwright's eye was already trained enough to sense the " employed man " as forming the back-bone of that crowd ; batmen, grooms, cooks, store-sentries, sanitary men—they were all there. There, too, were red-tabbed A.D.C.s, Intelligence Officers, Doctors and a Padre. All were looking over the low wall at the roadside into Beaumont Hamel and beyond to Thiepval, with an expression on their faces like the interested but slightly puzzled look of spectators at a Rugby match who have only seen Soccer before.

Cartwright felt a slight sense of alienation from them all and discovered that it was only because he and Richards were wearing caps while the crowd was in steel helmets.

There was no distinguishable sound from Beaumont Hamel. Din there cancelled itself out into something not unlike silence, so that the squalid thing below them which was the two visible miles between Beaumont Hamel and St. Pierre Divion seemed to be engaged in a tense writhing.

For two days now it had been drizzling at intervals. The lifting of the drizzle was like the lifting of some of the obscuring veils before a shadowless, gloomily-lighted stage. The spectators along the ridge sat still and soddenly steaming, cloaked in whatever chance or their various " employments " had offered them—sandbags, forage-sacks, ground-sheets, rags from lorry covers, horse-blankets. The only noticeable words from them were " After you, chum," when a match was struck in the shelter of one of these cloaks.

Below them the shiny ground darkened, and slowly lightened, and darkened again as black or foully yellow clouds splashed upon it, uncurled and slowly cleared away. It wriggled and shook in the play of the lightless and shadowless gloom. It snapped fragments from itself and tossed them into the torrent of the uncurling clouds. And it seemed to lose nothing thereby—for when the cloud had gone, the jagged stump of tree or rafter under it, the twist of bricks and mortar still crazily stood ; the tossed fragments had come from nowhere and gone nowhere. . . .

Reynolds was somewhere down there with a telephone and two drums of wire and two signallers, and the Thermos flask.

This was the bombardment preliminary to an assault

on Beaumont Hamel.   The Infantry were to attack next
morning, and Reynolds—as the subaltern of ripest
experience of trench-welfare—had gone off in the morning
to join the infantry as Brigade F.O.O.

The battery—or the Brigade—as yet had no orders
beyond that it was to occupy advanced reserve positions
from which to open fire during the later stages of the
battle, in the direction of Beaucourt and Grandcourt.

(The orders never did come since there were, to that
battle no later stages.)

Richards and Cartwright, their elbows touching on the
stone parapet of the road, had nothing to say till Richards
remarked that it must be tea-time and after.

Their places were immediately taken by an R.A.M.C.
Corporal and a shoeing-smith.

" God ! " said Richards, as they moved homewards,
looking up and down the road.   " We might at least try
to get this crowd dispersed.   I'll ring up brigade.   One
salvo from over there—just one ruddy salvo ! . . . "
but the salvo, like the shell in the crucifix-tree, never
came ; and the sightseers in the tree and on the road saw
their bombardment disturbed by nought but drizzle.

" Our own stuff can't be clearing this ridge with very
much to spare," he mused on.   " What these chaps
really need, to send them home in a hurry, is a couple of
shrapnel prematures.   You should just see a footslogger
when one of his own shells burst anywhere near him.
Fritz can shoot him up to hell—as he's doing down there,
just where we couldn't see round the corner from Beaumont
Hamel—and he doesn't care a damn ; but just one of ours,
a little bit short, is enough to put the wind up him.   That's
been some of the trouble with this new barrage stunt.   You
can't get the infantry to see that it's better to chance
losing one or two men by keeping too close to it and
running into a ' short ' here and there, than losing the
whole damn lot by giving a machine-gun time to bob up
at them.   But there it is.   That's one of the reasons
they're so keen on sending a gunner over with them now,
like Reynolds.   Well—we thought we knew what shelling
was, Reynolds and I—but down there's an eye-opener."

He indicated the direction in which they had been looking.

He was chewing something as he talked ; a piece of stick or grass that he had plucked out of the wall. His beard, Cartwright noticed, seemed to have grown. Yet it was not so much that the beard had grown, as that the skin of his jaws had become more taut over the bone, thrusting the stubble into a new prominence as he chewed his piece of straw.

They passed the dump of eight hundred shells that had been made for their position a month before between the road and the guns—the dump which was transferred intact as a book debt to the charge of some one else when the battle was, once again, abandoned.

In the privacy indicated by Jackman's scrawl of " Officers Only " and acquired by his flapping erection of sacks and empty sandbags and a ground sheet, Cartwright produced from his pocket the steel mirror that John had sent him.

His own beard, too, had grown into a new prominence. His cheekbones and jaws had come closer to the skin, squeezing away the superfluous juices that had given them, a dozen hours before, a colour that was not sheer parchment.

He stroked his chin and put away his mirror.

This, then, was the war proper.

Letters to Dorothy would take some writing now. . . .

Perhaps, after tea, it would be wise to settle down for an hour and get something off to her. He had sent nothing for the last three or four days—the days of rest and trekking when there had been, theoretically, nothing in particular for him to do and when there had not, in fact, been a vacant half-hour.

Sappers, at the time that the eight hundred shells had been fused and dumped in readiness for the first battle, had made a dug-out, about a dozen steps deep, behind the gun-pits which they had also indicated by cutting out sods and setting up camouflage netting on posts. The guns were now dug in axle-deep and protected by slimy breastworks of sandbags. The position was more like a gipsy-encampment than anything else, since all digging had been concentrated about the guns. Kits were lying about on the ground, and the fires propped against the cook's dixies burned in the open.

Richards bustled about the place, Cartwright following him. The men slouched from the guns to the dixies with their mess-tins, coming back cheerfully 'four in a loaf' with ingots of margarine and cheese and cardboard cylinders of jam cut in two.

"The next job's funk-holes," said Richards. "Let's see our dug-out. Browne ought to have some tea ready."

Browne was not at his happiest. His Primus was doing its worst, squirting and flapping a dirty yellow flame about his kettle instead of the purring blue one that was his pride. (The new and stout telephone-wire which Cartwright had drawn at Authie did not yield strands fine enough for a burner probe.) He had laid out the tea-things on the fourth or fifth step down the shaft ; some folded sandbags a couple of steps lower down marked the seats for Cartwright and Richards. His work with the Primus was being carried out on the second step from the top.

"We can't have that mess of soot down here, Browne," Richards said. "Get Barnes to give you some hot water. He's got a decent fire—so decent that I wonder the smoke from it hasn't had a five-nine or two by now."

"There won't be any soot, Sir," said Barnes. "She's been burning beautiful till a minute ago." There were certain qualities in Browne that Richards missed altogether —and always would miss. The idea, for instance, that he, Charlie Browne, should go begging hot water for his bloke's tea from the battery cook. . . .

And Richards was in a mood new to Cartwright. "I'd like to know why this fresh-air craze has bitten the lot of you" ; he went on grumbling to Browne. "The whole damned battery spread over the downs. Why is every-thing—all the officers' kits—lying about outside under ground-sheets, and this spread here instead of down below ? "

" Not quite 'abitable down there, Sir," said Browne.
" Eighteen inches of water and a bit of a smell. I
assoomed it would be all right and didn't look till a bit late.
But I've sent Jackman to buy a bit of stuff to make a
bunk for Mr. Cartwright." (It was one of Browne's
solemn humours to designate all his acquisitions as deeds
of purchase. He would seldom adopt a universal idea or
word like " winning.") " And he might pick up a pump
somewhere, Sir. There's sure to be pumps here like
there always was at Plug Street."

" The sooner you chaps can get Plug Street out of your
heads, the better," said Richards morosely. " This is no
Plug Street—and you'll damned soon find it out. Mr.
Cartwright and I have been watching some shelling—
that *is* shelling."

" In the bit of a place under the hill down there, Sir ? "
asked Browne, jogging the Primus.

" Yes," said Richards. " The whole damned lot of you
ought to go and watch it. You'd dig then, instead of
hanging up ground-sheets and lighting fires in the open
and chattering about pumps and thinking of Plug Street."

" Yes, Sir," said Browne. " It looks bad. I've told
them most emphatically."

" So you've been for a walk ? " asked Richards.

" Yes, Sir. Just up to the top, Sir. To find something
for Mr. Cartwright's bunk. There's the stretcher for you ;
I can fix them along the sides where you're sitting with
boxes under the bottom ends. A door would do a treat
for Mr. Cartwright, but there's about as much chance of a
door down 'ere as a sewing machine."

But Richards was in the wrong frame of mind for gossip
with Browne. He said " Let's have that tea. And since
you've spent the day sight-seeing you can put in a few
hours digging now. You and Jackman have got to be
under some cover with your kitchen junk before you turn
in. Dinner at eight."

" Very good, Sir. Will Mr. Reynolds be back ? "

" No," said Richards. " Not till to-morrow evening."

It is the fact, now somewhat curious, that this question
was asked and the answer given with no more significance

than the bare words implied ; and the conditions of life a full mile away from Reynolds had forced out the beards on the jowls of Richards and Cartwright and Browne.

Richards went on grumbling : " If we'd had a day and a half here instead of sitting on our behinds up in those wagon-lines we could have licked this position into some kind of shape. . . . It's all right as long as they're busy pumping all the stuff they've got into the infantry. But you wait till they start some counter-battery work. . . . We'll lay out some lines for the guns after tea, Uncle. It doesn't matter a damn where we lay them. Just anywhere for a starting-point."

He pulled out his road-map and studied it, chewing away at his straw or piece of stick. " Here," he said, " what about this corner in the Beaucourt-Puissieux Road ? Should we be able to see it from somewhere up there on the road ? Reynolds would have known in a jiffy by just looking at the contours if he'd been here instead of fiddling about down there in that mess with the infantry."

Cartwright moved along the step towards him and joined him in his scrutiny of the map. " I don't know," he said, " we might—yes, we would—if we moved up the road a bit farther than we were." He shifted his finger westwards a little from the road where they had spent the afternoon. " This is higher, Richards," he said thoughtfully. " It's a hundred and sixty metres up, here. Your road corner is only a hundred and forty and we would just dodge that bit of a spur. Yes, we'd see it easily."

" By golly, Uncle ! " said Richards, " you're as good as Reynolds with a map. After tea you can take out the Director and get the aiming-posts in on that corner. We'll be lucky if we can get within three degrees of it with this blasted map ; but it will be *some*-thing. While you're doing that, I'll get the fellows started on the funk-holes. They ought at least to have given us a decent scale map by now. The blighters. . . ."

Richards, it seemed, could drink tea as hot as it came from the pot. Cartwright could not ; besides, he had the map now and was trying, with the point of a pin, to determine the exact spot of their dug-out within the circle Richards had scrawled on it—a circle enclosing some twenty vague acres on that inadequately small-scale map. " I'll have to pace out a couple of distances from the road and the two hedges to the Director. I'll set it up just on top here."

" Set it up where you darned well please," said Richards.

There was a cheeriness in his excitement now, instead of the crotchety resentment of all powers and people outside the battery—everything, in short, that could be roughly described as " they." " As long as you get the posts in by dark. You can have the Number One and a layer for one gun at a time. I want all the others for digging. Signallers and the whole lot."

He went up the steps and Cartwright set to work with his rule and protractor and message-book in the most approved Cadet-school manner, laying out his magnetic North and then going up to pace his distance along the hedge from the road.

He wrote everything down in a clear and ordered column as he made his readings over the sights of his Director to the guns—and it was then that he discovered that an ' indelible ' pencil is a snare and a delusion. The pages of his message-book were uniformly damp where they were not wet from his thumb or a drop that trickled from the peak of his cap.

It was not definitely raining. The atmosphere was a soft, warm ooziness that condensed into runnels only when something solid—like the collar of a Burberry, the peak of a cap, an ear, a nose-tip or the end of a pencil—impinged upon it. With the rich turf of the down it mingled into a softly yielding foothold. With the soil wherever the turf had been cut or worn away it mixed into a pale, clinging puttiness. . . . He took his readings and deducted them from 180—smiling at the thought of poor old Hall, who was still, probably, cursing and kicking at the formula at Lark Hill or Okehampton or wherever else he now was. . . .

When the last gun was laid he picked up the Director and went down the dug-out steps with a vague idea at the back of his mind of taking some measures or other about the general feeling of dampness. He had not been there many seconds, however, before he knew that there were no such measures. Even the dial and the varnished legs of the Director defeated him. The handkerchief in his sleeve was a moist rag—he had been holding his hands up to the Director with the cuffs of his Burberry left, stupidly, unbuckled. The spare handkerchief, dug out of his tunic pocket, was wet by the time his hands and face were wiped.

Browne darkened the shaft for a moment and came down with the teapot and a mug and a tin of milk.

" A drop of tea, Sir," he said. " I've topped her up with a bit of fresh hot."

" I believe I will," said Cartwright. " You wouldn't think a man could get thirsty in—this."

" Oh, yes, I would, Sir," said Browne. " It's the noise. You don't notice it—but it makes you thirsty, parched thirsty. Jackman's come in with a lovely hurdle for you to sleep on, and he drunk up a good gallon. Will you tell the Captain there's a drop of tea, when you go out ? "

" Yes," said Cartwright.

But he found himself quite unable to do it. It would have been like trying to take an artist from his easel on some pretext quite silly while daylight still held.

Richards had gone out and mustered the twenty-five or thirty men who had marched from dawn till breakfast-time and had been digging from breakfast-time till tea. They were damp to the bone when he had mustered them and were now sopping wet. In two hours, while Cartwright had been working out his sums and laying out the lines of fire, and drinking tea, they had dug a ten- or twelve-foot trench behind each gun, a yard wide and breast-deep. The spoil from it had gone into the bags that were built around into a wall three sandbags wide. From heaven knew where on that bare downland some of them appeared carrying boards and balks and beams and—more magnificently—a blackened sheet of corrugated iron.

" There's no need to worry about roofs to-night, Speight," said Richards. " Ground-sheets will keep out some of the rain, and nothing you can put up now will keep out a hit. Be satisfied that you're splinter-proof—in places."

" Water seems to keep on coming in," said the Corporal, gazing at the feet of the two spade-men and sandbag-holders sunk ankle-deep into the grey mud.

" And I shouldn't worry about that," said Richards. " Any man who would rather have a splinter in his eye than a drop of water on his backside can cuddle down on top, in his ground-sheet—more room for the others." This was the kind of thing at which Richards excelled—the broad, common joke that was barely even a joke, but held his workmen together when they were tired and wet enough to fall apart, morosely, into themselves. " Just get some ground-sheets across the top—it'll leave you enough for the floor—and you can knock off. Sergeant Wright, the signallers will have to doss with their subsections, except the two on duty. They can have the hole they've dug, and hope for the best. I'll give you some more orders as soon as I get them. The sentry on duty when it gets daylight can dig a latrine by the hedge."

RICHARDS and Cartwright ate their dinner as they had drunk their tea, on the dug-out steps ; but they sat now on the second or third step from the top, for the rain, such as it was, had stopped.

The table was laid on the ground level ; it was the map-board (for which as yet they had no map) covered over with Browne's square yard of oilcloth. Their valises and saddle-bags were propped up on the lower steps.

" It's this damned rain that puts the lid on everything," Richards said morosely. " It's put it on Browne all right—dishing up a Maconochie. The lout! He's too interested in the shelling."

" I suppose it's going about as strong as we're likely to get it," said Cartwright.

They could see none of the bursts from the little dip in the ground that held the dug-out and the battery. Only, for the last twelve hours, there had been that persistent feeling in the ears as though one were pressing one's thumbs into them—pressing and slowly releasing the pressure and renewing it. The more immediate sounds—talk and the shout now and again of a man from a gun-pit to the cook, the clatter of Richards's knife and fork on his plate—these were clear and distinct within the pressure. There was another sound, too, neither immediate nor yet a part of the pressure of mingled bursts. It was the sound of the traffic over their heads. There were screeches in it, and snarls and whines and whizzings, all softened and blurred together, demanding no particular heed or attention but persisting, unheeded, in their by-product of hastening the growth of beards and parching the tissues of throats.

" The only difference is," said Richards, " that we might get into it sometime instead of sitting just outside. You'll have something to write home about then, Uncle. To tell the wife and little ones, eh ? "

Cartwright smiled.

" What *do* you chaps tell them ? " Richards went on thoughtfully. " I've often wondered."

" Not very much," said Cartwright. " It'll be difficult. It hasn't been till now."

" That time you nearly got knocked ears over kettle coming up to the battery. Your first day. Did you tell her that ? "

" No," said Cartwright. " As a matter of fact I didn't. What would be the use ? She'd only think it was the kind of thing that kept on happening all the time, instead of being an unusual accident. Do you write and tell any one—everything ? "

" I tell the old man a bit," said Richards. " Just for the good of his soul. I usually write a letter to him and my mother, at the house ; but I send a bit of the rough, hairy stuff to him alone at his office. It's a proper mix up, though ; with the newspaper fellows bursting themselves to write the gory muck that Reynolds reads to us and old family birds like you tempering the wind. Will you tell your missis that we've moved into a hotter corner ? "

" I don't expect I shall," said Cartwright. " I might tell her some time or other that we've just moved. I shan't go into details."

" There are chaps who do," said Richards thoughtfully. " The men, I mean. Tagney once wrote to his wife— from that Arras position, of all places—just before you came, that he'd been crouching in a shell hole all day, without food or water. I sent for the blighter and asked him why. I swear he didn't know. There hasn't been any trouble between them, ever. He just wanted her to think of him lying in a shell-hole, just as you want your wife to think of you lying on a bed of roses to-night with dry feet and flannel next your skin."

" It's best not to say anything at all," said Cartwright, " till it's over. I write to that Adjutant fellow— Henderson—occasionally ; just because he's an old soldier. I'll tell him about the shelling down there to the south, if we get there."

" We'll get there," said Richards, " don't you worry. . . ." And then, while they were still quietly talking and drinking coffee, a little snarl tumbled sheer out of the roof of blurred moans and wheezes and growls that was holding steadily above them.

There was an instant's confusion of cracks outside, and one quick stab of light before the dug-out entrance and a spattering on the tin plates and mugs. Richards shot down the steps, Cartwright beside him. As soon as they had stopped against the valises and piled kits Cartwright scrambled to his feet. It had been so near a one that his nostrils tingled for the first time with the peppery reek of high-explosive. Browne's observation had been a sound one ; shelling did make you thirsty. . . . But the thing that suddenly made his flesh creep as he crouched in the darkness peering towards the twilight was the voice of Richards. " Uncle ! " it said in a curious whisper, " Strike a match, old thing. I've got a bit—in the head. Bleeding like the devil." The match flared up between fingers that were obviously shaking for all their tight grip upon it.

Richards was leaning over his valise with his head bowed and cocked over a little away from Cartwright. The pallor of his face caught Cartwright's breath—pallor shaded black by the cheekbones and cleft by a twist of blood across the cheek and parted lips, dripping over the point of his chin on to his chest.

Browne came bumping into the frame of the shaft entrance. " Coo-lummy ! " he panted just as the match flickered. " We could 'ave swore he'd got the both of yer."

" The Captain's hit," said Cartwright sedately. " Get a light." The bulk of Jackman squeezed into the frame behind Browne, and Cartwright saw the silhouette of the fellow's great paw fumbling into his breeches-pocket for the inevitable candle-stump. " You got the match*ies*, Charlie ? " he said. (One of the persistently annoying things about Jackman was the way he always said match-ies, box-ies, glass-ies. . . .) The candle was lighted and Richards pulled down to a seat on the step behind him by Browne. Cartwright took the cap off the still bowed head and threw it aside.

" It's dished the back of his napper," said Browne, coldly critical.

" No, it hasn't ! " Richards could speak only weakly, mumbling through the blood on his lips, and it was the weakness of his voice that frightened Cartwright most. " It just stings a bit. . . . Dizzy. . . ."

There was a second runnel of blood behind his ear and down into his collar.

" Nearer with that light, Browne," said Cartwright. His mind was at its trick of waking up accurate memories of detail. It gave him a diagram of a skull in section with brains coiled up in the cranium ; blood vessels ; the great cavities of antrum and frontal sinus and the old doctor at Exeter giving one of his chatty lectures. . . .

The blood was merely trickling down behind the ear, and not coming out of it.

He took Richards's warmly sticky chin in his hand and turned his face to the light. He wiped the blood away from the lip, drew Jackman's fist nearer with the candle-stump and peered into Richards's nostrils. There was no blood there either.

" Skull's all right," he said. " Just a knock, Richards ; and a cut."

Browne flung the surviving apricots out of the soup-plate, wiped it out with his handkerchief and said to some one's legs in front of him, " Shut up, you fool ! Give us the dressing from your tunic, mine's in the cook-house. Mr. Cartwright will come in a minute."

He filled the plate from the water-jug and came down again. It took Cartwright only a few seconds to sponge the back of Richards's head and find that the blood was coming from a wound too small to be seen under the thick hair. He ran his fingers over the head and pressed hard on the spot from which the trickle was coming.

" There's nothing there, Richards," he said.

" Good," said Richards. " I've just been thinking that it's probably more funk than anything else. The damned thing seemed to go off between my teeth."

" Driver Harris wants to see you, Sir. Urgent," Browne said to Cartwright.

" What's Harris doing here ? " asked Richards. " Is it the mess-cart ? "

" Yes, Sir," said Browne. He turned to Cartwright. " I'll put on a spot of iodine to the Captain and the bandage, if you'll go up, Sir." He was cocking his eyebrows and shifting his lantern jaws about at Cartwright from behind Richards to signify urgency and secrecy. " You start undoing Mr. Cartwright's valise, Jackman." With his free hand behind the head of Richards he gave a very good imitation of a revolver being fired—pointing with the forefinger, drawing up the thumb and letting it go suddenly down.

Cartwright hurried out to the lantern and the three or our men standing by the horse in the mess-cart on the track about twenty yards from the dug-out. The horse stood quietly on three legs. The mud-caked hoof of the near fore hung a few inches clear of the ground with an end of bone gleaming out of a hole a few inches above it.

" Does the Captain say to shoot it, Sir, please ? " Sergeant Wright asked.

" I'll ask him," said Cartwright, " and get my revolver."

He went back quietly and told Richards while Jackman fumbled in the valise for his revolver. (His revolver, thereafter, was carried where provision had been made for it in the design of his belt.) He told Browne not to put on the bandage till he came back.

" You know where to put it, I suppose ? " said Richards.

The memory for detail was at work again.   " Yes," said Cartwright, " a hand's-breadth below the poll."

" Yes—or even a bit higher," said Richards.   " They can leave it at the side there for to-night.   We'll bury it to-morrow.   Ask Brigade to send a chit over to the wagon-line for another horse to take back the cart. Don t tell them about this thing of mine."

Cartwright shot the horse and telephoned to the Adjutant and told Sergeant Wright that Richards's wound was nothing.

To Richards he said, when the bandage was fastened and Browne and Jackman had gone for the hurdle and the stretcher to bed them down, " I've been thinking.   The wound isn't anything, but it's that business of injection —tetanus, you know. You ought to have the injection— just in case."

Richards was more impressed by the wound than Cartwright.   He was dizzy still and his head was obviously aching.   He was sitting fairly limp and very pale against his valise.   There was little dash about him at the moment, but he said, " Don't worry about tetanus, Uncle. I can't go down, old thing.   They wouldn't leave you here, you know.   Meston would come up and take over." This was a new and staggering thought for Cartwright— that a mere turn of chances one way or the other could land him with the sudden command of a battery.   But he said, after a moment's thought upon these chances, "Let him. You can get the injection and a couple of days' rest at the wagon-line. . . ."

"No," said Richards. "It feels like hell, but I know it's nothing, and I can't go messing about with injections. You see, Uncle—well," he paused, and then went on slowly, "I'll tell you what happened. On the third day we were in that Arras position, I put a shell bung into our front line. It wasn't our own infantry from Gallipoli, but a crack lot put in there for a rest before ours took over. They kicked up hell. The Colonel and the General were sick as mud because they were wanting to prove that Gallipoli heroes were as good gunners as any one. You bet they made it clear that I wasn't of their party really, but just one of the Flanders lot ; and I came as near as a toucher to losing the battery. It was the Divisional General that saved me in the end. I say I put the shell in, but it was one of those damned dud charges that would have fallen short if God Himself had been shooting the battery. I got the Company Commander to watch me sitting in the hole the thing had made while I fired a dozen more rounds from the same gun at the same range. But that didn't help the poor beggar of a Corporal who was pegging out in the dug-out with his chest full of splinters. And there you are. I can't afford to take any chances with reporting sick, or hit, if I want to hang on to the battery. If I've got to go, I'll go. But I'm not *giving* it away. We'll turn in as soon as those blighters have got our valises down."

But there was another experience coming to Cartwright that night. Browne, bringing the stretcher, announced that an issue of rum had come up with the rations. "And Mr. Reynolds has got the measure, Sir, on the Thermos. Sergeant Wright says please will it be issued here or at the cook-house ? "

"Cook-house," said Richards. "Give me one of your famous little coffee-cups from Agny, Browne. That will be about right."

"Hadn't you better sit tight and let me do it ? " Cartwright suggested.

N

"No," said Richards. "They can make our beds while we are out."

To the accurate mind there is a time and a place for all things. This, as Cartwright saw, was the time and the place for a little swagger and the touch dramatic.

It made a good scene : Richards with his black hair tumbled over the white bandage and his pallid forehead ; Cartwright holding up the lantern beside him while Sergeant Wright tipped the jar; the gunners, mud-splashed and wearily ready to tumble into their sodden hovels, "*en pantoufles*" in the manner of gunners—boots unlaced with black tongues agape in the grey caked 'uppers,' breeches and socks festooning their ankles, shirts and tunics open on hairy chests and identity disks ; "—health, Sir," mumbled into thirty successive mess-tins as their blackened bottoms and the throats and upturned chins of the drinkers were presented to the lantern-light ; then the salute which was made different from mere ceremonial by the hatless, tousled head and the sucking, among the old stagers like Shaw and Doyle, of great moustaches.

"I'll have a tot myself," said Richards, when they got back to the dug-out. "Eh, Doctor ? "

"I should," said Cartwright.

"It's my second since coming out," Richards said a little coyly. "The first was after I'd been on the mat over that 'short.' And—well, one doesn't get wounded in the head every day, either—or perhaps one does, down here. I shouldn't wonder, by the sound."

They drank their tots and undressed between the bunks, to the extent of boots and collars and tunics.

"It wouldn't be a bad thing, Uncle, to keep a bottle in the Mess, if you can get it," Richards observed, momentously thoughtful as he climbed into his bag. "Whisky or something. Just in case . . ."

Cartwright said, "Yes, rather."

(A *bottle* of whisky ! . . . for the unit of whisky-reckoning in the Mess was as yet the bottle, as men once reckoned a workman's wage per day in pence.)

THE battery orderly from Brigade woke them somewhere before dawn with the ' Secret ' envelope for which they had been waiting.

The orders were simple. " Batteries will continue to hold themselves in readiness as per Brigade Orders No. HG/W172 of yesterday. Zero hour is postponed 24 hours o minutes."

There was nothing to be done all day except potter about, seeing little improvements being made, wondering whether a glint of sunshine on the edge of a cloud meant that it was going to be fine or whether a drizzle meant that it was going to turn to rain.

It was Browne who discovered that the stab of pain in Richards's head when he tried to put on his cap over the unbandaged speck of a wound was due to a splinter stuck, not in the wound, but in the band of his cap.

They strolled about and found the four holes made by the single, chance salvo. " Just one blasted pot-shot probably by some battery on the loaf like ourselves," observed Richards. " My mother could have made better holes with her trowel in ten minutes—and they bagged a decent horse and put the fear of God into me for an hour or so. One man per subsection will be enough to bury it. Will you tell Wright ? "

They pottered and talked, adding patches here and there to that interminable conversation that lasted through years.

Cartwright wrote a letter home, saying that the weather was inclined to be rainy now and that he had had his first thorough wetting without any ill-effects.

And the screeching and tearing went on in the air above and the pounding went on in the valley below.

The Adjutant demanded an officer on the telephone. He said to Cartwright, " Don't say anything. I'll do all the talking. It's only to tell you that we're not relieving your man Reynolds. He's been through to us on the telephone. He thinks it's better for him to stop where he is, and for others to stop where they are for a bit. The Colonel thinks it's a good idea. So—well, he's not being relieved. That's all. See ?— His party will be all right for rations."

Richards said, " That means they're churning up the supports and communications. It'll give young Reynolds a nice time of it—two days and nights before going over. They're probably hung up ; waiting for something to happen further down the other side along that road to what's-its-name."

(They soon came to know more of that road ; but as yet, even from Pisgah the day before, they had seen no farther than Thiepval's black and sinister ridge.)

" These blasted postponements . . ." Richards grumbled on. " You don't know what waiting like this means to the foot-sloggers, Uncle. But you'll see." In time, he did see ; and in the meantime, while the noise went on with its dull, incessant pressure and Richards grumbled and chewed his piece of stick or straw, he found himself quite actively wondering.

That shell the night before had brought things in the phrase of the time, home to him. It had not been much nearer than the one that hailed his approach to the battery but it had been different—a matter for some thought where the other had been a passing joke. The shooting of the horse and the rum-issue had been melodramatic ; but the bandage against the black hair of Richards meant that his own escape from the weight of command had been fantastically narrow ; and he could no more have ' commanded ' the battery for ten minutes than have flown. He knew it from the way he had stood merely looking at the bone sticking out above the horse's hoof till Wright said, " Shoot it, Sir ? "

He could have ' managed,' of course—with Wright in command. He could have hung on, answering the telephone when the Adjutant demanded an officer, eating alone in the dug-out shaft till Meston came to take over, or till Reynolds came back. But he would not have 'commanded.' The men, too, brought it home to him.

He had not seen them soaked with rain before, plastered with mud, blistered with digging and utterly done. He could not have hit them up at five o'clock, as Richards had, and got another three hours of digging out of them. He could have served out the rum poured by the Sergeant into the measure provided by Browne ; but he would have been one man handing rum to other men but not, somehow, dramatically and obviously, like Richards, their commander.

They went up just before the next dawn towards the Crucifix-tree and the Sucrerie.

" We'll have to beat it," Richards said, " if they begin to strafe. Don't forget it isn't our show." Two signallers went with them, to run out a mile of wire in case they were wanted on the telephone by Brigade.

But it was quiet enough up there all day. A shell a hundred yards away was already for Cartwright—as it was for Richards—quite a reasonably long way off.

They saw no other spectators.

By eight o'clock there was an uncanny and disturbing silence over the valley. It made them cower into the roadside as they peered through their glasses, it hushed their voices to a whisper.

" It's been a fizzle, Uncle," Richards said after there had been one great burst and a pink cloud of brick-dust out of Beaucourt, an isolated crash that set a seal upon the new silence. " An absolute perfect fizzle."

They stared on in silence, at the curls and drifts of stagnant smoke lurching slowly over the flayed ground. They switched their glasses in the direction of crackles and of single rifle shots to see—nothing. There were little humps and specks here and there that were neither tree-stumps nor posts nor jags of ancient brickwork. Sometimes there would be a movement in one of these specks and humps, and a consequent alteration of its shape ; but generally they were all quite still as the drifting reek licked over them.

Cracks and single rifle-shots, and the pop of a grenade pricked the dank stillness where the only movement was the slow alteration in the shape of a speck, till Richards

suddenly strained forward and hissed "Crumbs!—
There!—a degree right of that shining bit of railway
stuff . . . Under that embankment . . . See them,
Uncle? Bosche? . . . No, by God, they're not. . . ."

Cartwright found them. They were crouching into the
semblance of those other humps and specks in the open;
but they moved, and moved again and kept on slowly
moving. They straightened up, slowly, and one after
another flicked across a space and then sank again,
crouching; and some of them began to crawl in the
direction of Richards and Cartwright.

"*That's* torn it!" mumbled Richards. He was
searching, foot by foot, for a crackle that burst out
whenever one of the specks straightened out into a man
and dashed across the little space of open. Suddenly he
yelled to the signallers: "On to the Brigade. Quick.
Get the Adjutant or the Colonel. Uncle, I've got those
sods with the machine-gun. Pick them up and hold on
to them while I tell Brigade. Take that railway metal
again. About eleven o'clock, half a degree. That bit
of wall and some stuff sticking up. You can only see
them when they move."

He scuttled off down the road, snatched the telephone
from the signaller, shook the thing and smacked it in the
manner demanded by the D Mark III, and finally poured
out his tidings: he could see the whole battle-front from
where he was; he had a thousand rounds lying ready
fused at the battery; a German machine-gun was in
action, in full view—asking for it; not a shell was
dropping in Beaumont Hamel. It was obvious that not
a single one of our men was in the place. The last of them
could be seen dribbling back. The whole thing was a
washout. . . .

Then Richards was silent, listening, till he mumbled,
"Very good, Sir," and handed the instrument back to the
telephonist.

"We're in reserve," he said sardonically to Cartwright,
and sat down beside him. "And—the old blighter got
funny in the end; said he thought I would have been
more canny about wanting to shoot where there might be

an Englishman. So we'll sit and let the bloody massacre go on. Did you find those gunners ? "

" Yes," said Cartwright. " There's no movement now."

" No movement," said Richards. " No, their job is done. But we could have given them some *movement* all right. Shot them up to glory, registered our four guns on the damned place and given them one every minute or so during the night. But we're in *reserve.* . . . They'll be able to stay there and comb the embankment and slog hell out of our working parties all night. You've never been under machine-gun fire have you, Uncle ? "

" No," said Cartwright. " Not yet. Where are you off to ? " for Richards was wrapping the sling round his glasses, having selected and begun to chew a new blade of grass.

" Home," said he. " The battle is over. There'll be nothing more to see but shells presently—and shells, and more shells. And we saw all that yesterday."

The silence in the valley was absorbed, during the day, in the general din of the south till by night it was as it had been the night before.

There was a general gloom pervading the battery. The men had slept well and there was neither sunshine nor a fire except the sticks smouldering against the cook-house dixies. Shovelling slabs of mud out of the floors of the funk holes into sandbags was a dull work when there was no material to carry a roof ; and going deeper meant only more water.

Men occasionally asked Cartwright if there was any news of Reynolds and the signallers, to which the only answer was " No. Not yet. No news of anything."

IT must have been at some time during that day or evening that Whitelaw joined the battery; for there was a bottle of whisky in the Mess by evening.

The only impressive feature of his arrival was the fact that he and Cartwright, both in Burberries and Whitelaw distinguished by a steel helmet, accorded to each other a very punctilious salute. When they took off their Burberries and sat on the dug-out steps waiting for Richards to come in from some job or other, they saw the single star on their cuffs and Whitelaw said, " So you're only a fightin' man too! I thought you were the Major."

" I thought you were a General," said Cartwright.

" Colonels *have* saluted me," said Whitelaw with quiet satisfaction. " But my hair was as white as this when I was twenty-three. I'm only thirty-seven now. You ? "

" Thirty-eight—rising nine," said Cartwright. " They call me ' Uncle.' God knows what Reynolds will find for you."

" I know what he'll find for himself," said Whitelaw confidently, " if he tries to be funny. A thick ear. What sort of a show is this ? Major—or Skipper commanding ? "

" Skipper," said Cartwright. " Fellow called Richards. One of the best."

" There's hope, then," said Whitelaw. " Majors get under my skin. That's why I'm here. The old man and I—down the other side of Mametz—one of us had to go. So they shifted me. They couldn't do any worse—because of these." He smacked the ribbons on his breast, the D.C.M. and another which he explained was a Russian Order, bestowed in only rare and peculiar circumstances where the V.C. had been indisputably earned but precluded by some contemptible detail of red tape.

Mock-modesty, it was obvious in the first few minutes spent with Whitelaw, was not one of his characteristics ;

but the discovery never produced anything but a smile on the part of the discoverer.

" Was that when you lost that finger ? " asked Cartwright, for the hand with which Whitelaw was filling a squat, black pipe consisted of only three fingers and a very square thumb.

" No," said Whitelaw. " That was on a bit of bottle in the Argentine. I'm ' Occidental Fleeces, Limited,' my brother and I. A man your age must have heard of it."

" Yes," said Cartwright. " As a matter of fact I have. I'm a solicitor with a fair amount of city work."

" You would, then," said Whitelaw, satisfied. " You could do worse than put a few hundreds into it—just between ourselves. Sheepskin jerkins will be in vogue this winter. Among other things. What about a small one ? "

" A drink ? " said Cartwright. " I'm afraid there's only a little rum left from the issue last night. We might squeeze a tot out of it. Our bottle of whisky hasn't arrived from the wagon-line yet."

" I'll lend the Mess one of mine, then," said the other. " In my valise on the top. I didn't fancy leaving it in Ocean Villas for the night—or spending the night there with it. There's an expectant sort of look about Ocean Villas. I found a fellow there to hump my kit, a sapper who was loafing off duty by the dump. We brought along a couple of sheets of expanded metal, too, in case there's ·some bed-making to be done."

" I didn't know it was so easy to find outside porters about here," Cartwright ventured.

" It isn't easy," said Whitelaw, " but it's possible, with a few francs, if you pick your man. In the Cavalry I was only a trooper, but I had the best batman in the regiment. Lancers."

It was then, after Richards had joined them, that Whitelaw began telling them the life story with which they had many subsequent opportunities of becoming familiar. Whitelaw and his brother, with a banker and an oil-prospector from the Argentine had enlisted, in

September, 1914, in the Lancers.   They did this after due
deliberation among themselves—and also, Whitelaw
indicated, with the higher authorities at the War Office—
in order to be with horses and to be sure, at the same time,
of getting to the front before the War was over—for the
regiment which they elected to adorn was due for em-
barkation.

They were the best horsemen, the best riflemen and the
best beaker- and trencher-men in the world.

In due course they dismounted for the last time and
threw their lances away into a hedge at Kemmel Château.
Whitelaw always paused, grandly, before and after the
statement of this dark and magnificent ritual, the throwing
away of lances into a hedge by the finest Lancers in
creation.   (The day came when he was able to point,
with the stem of his pipe held between three fingers and a
thumb, at the very hedge.)   From that moment onwards
he had learned (and expounded) the art of war.   The
consummation of this learning and teaching came on an
early morning in 1915 in Flanders when he and six others of
those lusty Lancers " cleared " and occupied the end of a
sap.   For three hours there were seven sound men in
that garrison.   For five hours there were four.   For three
hours there were three, and for six hours there was one—
Whitelaw.   The banker had picked up a fizzing grenade
to find that he had picked it up a second too late.
The oil-prospector knelt against the side of the sap
with a bullet-hole in one eye-socket.   The brother
Whitelaw was reclining on the fire-step, holding his
entrails in approximate position with a mess-tin cover,
while the Whitelaw of Cartwright's story met the changes
and chances of life with the fairly mobile material offered
by some seven or eight corpses (the original " clearing "
of the sap had given them three or four from the enemy),
with his rifle and with their predecessors' store of
stick-bombs.

And all he got out of it was that D.C.M. and the Russian
Order.   No V.C.—for the only testimony available was
the testimony of his uncommissioned brother and the
commissioned enemy—the German Lieutenant whom he

had knocked on the head with his rifle-butt and left trussed, in a corner of the sap. . . . And, for all his fantastic bragging, there was always that rare twinkle about Whitelaw that reduced the bragging to merely a remembered feature of him, like the missing index-finger from the right hand ; the square, flat thumb ; the two perpendicular, carved furrows in his cheeks and the sack-like solidity with which he sat a horse.

He told them something of the present battle, too ; for he had been working his way up, with a succession of chance lackeys stooping under his valise and his two or three bottles of whisky, by way of Albert, Bouzincourt, Englebelmer (where he had reported to Brigade and been directed, through Auchonvillers, to the battery). Civility and scraps of information would naturally have been accorded to the white hair, terracotta visage and squat mackintoshed figure stumping through Albert in rubber boots among reliefs, walking wounded and prisoners.

The show had had a good start, he told them, up the Pozieres road, and he snorted : a million dead, a million prisoners, a million missing, and a million square inches of muck-heap captured. But northwards it was again, sheer and utter failure. When the Bosche gave up that ridge or got kicked off it, he said, it would be time to think of packing up and going home. Meanwhile . . .

Meanwhile, he too, was drawn into the suspense that was so familiar in the daily life of batteries in those days, that were not too busy for suspense—the waiting, where wires had never been laid or after they had been irreparably cut, for the F.O.O. party to return.

Brigade at dinner-time had still heard nothing from Reynolds.

THEY had turned in when the Adjutant asked for an officer. Cartwright tumbled into his boots and went over to the telephone.

" Your Reynolds has turned up," Gordon said. " He's coming up to you. He won't want anything to eat. We've given him something here and a drink. The two signallers too."

" Two ? " said Cartwright. " What about the bombardier ? "

" Yes. One is a bombardier," said the Adjutant. " A bombardier and one man. I just thought you'd like to know about Reynolds so as to be ready. His bed and all that."

" Yes," said Cartwright. " Thanks. Tell him it's all ready."

" He's gone," said Gordon. " Shoved off as soon as he had grubbed. Good night."

Reynolds had about two miles to come. Cartwright wondered whether it would be worth telling Browne, just in case the Brigade Mess had neglected some detail, when Browne came out from the hole near the signallers and said, " If it's Mr. Reynolds on his way, Sir, I've got a bit of soup he might like."

Cartwright did not yet realise that it was not pure accident that always set Browne to digging-in as close as might be to the signallers. Nor did he realise that when the Adjutant had said to a Brigade signaller " Get me an officer at D Battery," that signaller was likely to have said to the battery, " 'n officer for 'is nibs, chum. Your bloke's come 'ome." Nor that the battery signaller, on his way to the Mess, had stuck his head under Browne's ground-sheet and said, " Wake up, Charlie. Rennie 'll be 'ome in a minute."

They lighted the acetylene lamp again on the board that Browne had nailed up for it across the lower doorway, over the water for which the pump had not yet been found.

The shaft itself was now filled by Richards's stretcher, Cartwright's hurdle and Whitelaw's two sheets of expanded metal stretched on frames of ' three-by-two ' produced from somewhere. The beds were in two strata. Whitelaw and Richards, side by side, occupied the lower one and Cartwright the upper, till Reynolds's servant came in to unroll his lord's valise on the other half of it. There was just space between the beds on each level for boots, and for the careful movement of feet. Cartwright sat on his pillow, some inches above the head of Richards, and filled a pipe. The map-board was spread with the oil-cloth at his feet. Browne knew the aptitude of Reynolds for the sweeping away of a complete meal to the floor by catching his sleeve or a bulging pocket on the projecting corner of a table. He was careful to get the whole board within the limits of Cartwright's bed. He put on bread, butter and cheese. " I'll bring the soup when he comes, Sir. It'd cool and spill here."

" You can bring the mugs now," said Whitelaw. " And some water." The bottle which he had lent the Mess was beside the acetylene lamp over his feet.

Then Reynolds came.

First his legs and the skirt and breast of his Burberry appeared in the frame of the entrance, like a piece of modelling executed with frantic skill in mud. It slowly moved and doubled up, bringing in the shoulders and Reynolds's face in the unfamiliar halo of a steel helmet brim.

" Hello, Uncle ! " he said.

He blinked apathetically at the light, moved sideways and very carefully between the two bunks and sat down.

He was as old as Cartwright's father might have looked if he had suffered from some old man's disease, one of the diseases that does nothing to sharpen the intelligence of its victim. He laid down his hat, produced the Thermos flask from the Burberry pocket and drew off the Burberry, continuing to sit on the tails of it.

" Hello, Rennie," said Richards, sticking his chin in his hand for a few moments, while Whitelaw sat up and

leaned forward for the bottle.   " This is Whitelaw, our
new man ; reported to-day."

" Hello," said Reynolds.   " Browne can take that stuff
away.   I won't have any, thanks.   I grubbed down at
Brigade.   I see there's a drink, though."

" Yes," said Whitelaw, " I brought it.   We'll have one."

Browne came and took away the board and bread and
cheese.   Reynolds told him to give the soup to the
signallers if they wanted it, but Browne said he expected
they were asleep by now.   Then Reynolds said, " I'm
sorry about Peckham, Dicky."

" What's wrong with Peckham ? "   Richards propped
his head up again.

Cartwright had said nothing of the Adjutant's allusion
to two signallers instead of three for the obvious reason
that it could quite well have been a mistake.

" Probably dead," Reynolds mused.   " He got one
yesterday.   No—yes, it was yesterday, under the jaw.
Yesterday morning.   There was damned little room in
the dug-outs and they weren't up to much.   It was better
outside most of the time.   We got him down after he was
hit.   The doctor was done in, by the way.   But not till
after he had fixed Peckham up.   Peckham was still there
this morning before we went over.   They may have got
him away by now.   But I should think he's dead.   You
wouldn't have thought the young man held so much
blood.   And I'll have to go down to the Hamel road to-
morrow, for the rest of the wire."

" What wire ? "   asked Richards.

" The drum of D5," said Reynolds.   " We got fed up
with carrying the bitch about.   It's hidden in a hole.
can find it all right.   Those damned great reels weigh
about a ton."

" Did you take it over with you ? "   asked Richards.

" Yes.   Got most of it laid," said Reynolds,   " then
had to reel it in again.   Oh, yes, and the telephone is done
for.   I've brought it back to hand in, for replacement
It probably kept a few splinters out of Whittle's guts
He was carrying it.   I left Day behind at the other end
in the company dug-out while we went over."

" You didn't get any reports in ? " asked Richards.

" No," said Reynolds. " Nor gathered any black-berries. We went into a trench with the Company Commander and a sergeant and five or six other fellows. There were dead Bosches and a few wounded who didn't seem to pay much attention to anything. Whittle and I got through to Day, and the wire went down. Whittle went out to mend it but couldn't get ten yards for machine-gun fire from God knows where. I shouted him in. There didn't seem to be much point in his messing about there when there was nothing to report. The infantry blokes were chucking bombs into two or three dug-outs and the Company Commander and I tried to make out where the hell we were. The trench wasn't anywhere on our maps. We tried to get one of the Bosches to show us, but he was about as fogged himself. And no one else turned up. Nothing happened. The trench just fizzled out into nothing at both ends. All shot to hell, with some wire still standing with a few infantry stuck on it. The Company Commander and I began to get windy. We couldn't see anything anywhere. One of his chaps had got it through the head and another in the shoulder, so we decided for home. He was a thoughtful sort. We each took a Hun cap and shoulder-straps for identification and I got an automatic pistol and an iron cross ; and we beat it."

" Along the top ? " asked Whitelaw.

" It was all top," said Reynolds, and yawned. " We freed the wire as we went along. The only risk was of its being cut by machine-gun stuff. The only shell anywhere was the pip-squeak that did for the telephone. And no movement. Just those ruddy bullets. We went most of the way on our bellies like crawling over sticky fly paper. Whittle and I came in more or less together by following the wire and reeled it in—practically all of it. I don't think the infantaire lad got back. We and the Sergeant and one or two of the others ; but not the Skipper."

" What was the embankment sort of place that Uncle and I saw from the road up here ? " Richards asked. ' Business seemed pretty brisk there."

" I didn't see any embankment," said Reynolds. " I tell you I saw—nothing." He yawned again, a great, cavernous yawn in the grey, puffy and peculiarly stupid-looking face. " Nobody saw anything. Except the wire showing us the way home."

" What have you been doing since ? " asked Cartwright.

" Since ? " said Reynolds. " My dear old uncle, Caspar's work was done ; And Caspar sat by his cottage door, warming himself in the sun. . . . But it wasn't so bad in the old forward trench—till about three o'clock. And then the shelling started again. And it's still going on. There's a new lot of Infantry just coming in, too. It doesn't much look as though the correspondence has ceased yet."

Part of the haggard look of him came from " make-up " streaks of mud dried under his eyelids. His hands were gloved in a thin plaster of it, cracked and criss-crossed minutely over the knuckles.

" The Colonel tried to get Gordon to take down a kind of interview while I was feeding, but there was nothing doing. I suppose some one knows what happened ; and why."

With his petrified-looking fingers he was fumbling at his tunic ; when that was unbuttoned he began at the buckles of his Canadian boots. Then he wriggled out of his breeches, saying, " I suppose you won't need me for any more warfare to-night, Dicky ? I'll get down to it."

The breeches and tunic and Burberry he pushed down to the end of his bed, from where Cartwright quietly removed them into a bundle between the two bunks in case it should rain into the shaft. His collar and necktie he took off and allowed to drop anywhere in the valise as he worked himself into it.

" Better turn the water off and stick that lamp outside, Uncle, or it'll stink the place out," he said. " Oh, by the way—no, I did tell you about the wire we've got to pick up to-morrow, Richards ? Sorry. Good night all."

Thus ended the first battle. . . .

His batman, in cleaning the Burberry next day, found two bullet-holes in the skirt of it and one through the sleeve. He alone seemed to get any thrill from his discovery, and from his exhibition of it first to the Mess and then to any one who loafed near the signallers' hole or Browne's cook-house.

The Mess was already as people quietly aged beyond lively entertainment by such trifles.

Reynolds himself was young again by lunch-time after he had shaved and drunk a cup of tea and put on his best pair of breeches while Crouch worked away with the dandy-brush at the others.

He was young, alertly intelligent; but about the battle's details he was as dumb as he had been in his senile dullness of the night before. He went off after lunch with a couple of signallers to retrieve the drum of telephone wire where it was *cached*. In its stead, however, they acquired two from a dump just outside Auchonvillers, where there was no sentry for the moment ; and so they returned in high spirits within the hour. But high spirits already seemed applicable on some plane that was not, strictly speaking, the plane of the actual war ; for on that plane the only thing possible at the moment was silence.

The Colonel came up with his orderly officer on one of his periodic visits. Cartwright took him up to the road and indicated, as nearly as he could, now that his reference point of jagged and shining railway-metal had disappeared, the machine-gun position. The valley was writhing again in foul, tumbling smoke, black or gangrenous. The Colonel was apathetic. He indicated to Richards when they got back to the battery that he expected some orders by midnight. They would probably have to pull out next night for a move farther down. Possibly the Brigade would have to stand by for a while. If he telephoned for Richards next morning it would mean that he wanted him and other battery commanders to come mounted to Brigade, to go on a reconnaissance of new positions.

They pulled out the following night, but made no reconnaissance. The new wagon-lines were behind Bouzincourt, and there they found themselves seated in a bell-tent in a drizzle, eating an early dinner whose only

o

hot item was tea, in the same state of expectancy and silence. Poor Meston seemed to make a definite contribution to this silence.

Huddling cheek by jowl for two nights in the dug-out shaft at Auchonvillers had produced a feeling of harmony between the other four, so that Reynolds had already said to Whitelaw, " What did you do in the Great War, Daddy—besides win it ? " and Whitelaw with equal friendliness had answered, " Kicked the behinds of all the youngsters who needed it."

Meston could not accept Whitelaw's manner of looking at horses and horse-lines. There was that something in his eye which may be detected in the eye of certain middle-aged men (as indeed, in his own) when it is presented with a group of young women. Or in the eye of certain schoolmasters when it is cast upon a class. (For Cartwright horses always remained about as readily distinguishable from each other as a hundred Chinamen or Gurkhas are to the ordinary European. But for Whitelaw, two apparently similar horses or mules were as individual as an emperor and a coolie.) To Meston, that a genially sardonic man with white hair on his head and a single star on his shoulder should look at his horses with a twinkle in his eye that came from some obscurely cheerful secret in his heart, brought a chill as bleak as the chill of his Captain's five-days' seniority.

Even in the moroseness of that cold and ravenously-eaten dinner Meston sat alien and apart in a morose silence of his own.

The setting was good for a short meditation upon destinies.

They turned into their valises early on the far side of some of the pressure that had impinged dully on their ear-drums for half a dozen weeks. It was now a close din, enveloping yet remote enough for the fury that raged on the crag of Thiepval and its wood to merge with the thunderous gloom that brooded over Beaumont Hamel.

The hammer-and-tongs, ding-dong flogging of Pozieres and its tortured road was lulled and softened by the wilderness about Contalmaison and the black silence of the swamps.

The only menace to sleep was the immediate snoring of Whitelaw, the grunt and snuffle of a restless horse and the occasional clatter of a lorry.

Cartwright thought, inevitably, of the uncalled-for stab of light at the dug-out entrance, of the already forgotten knock on the back of Richards's head, of the steaming horse doubling up at the crack of his revolver, of the holes in the skirt and the sleeve of Reynolds's Burberry. He thought of the little humps and specks still lying under the pall about Beaumont Hamel; he was filled with a foreboding lest a shadow of these things should fall, somehow, across his letters to Dorothy ; for their shadow, somehow, was worse than their substance ; for in the substance was the magnificent bragging of old Whitelaw, the energy of Richards, the general lustiness of Reynolds and the peculiar savour of fellowship that distilled out of the battery.   Their shadow was only black, for in it were none of these mysteries.

There were great omelettes to be had at an estaminet in Albert, and there was gossip over decent wine that contradicted the gloom of Beaumont Hamel.   Men came down the Pozieres road with hearts lightened by scrambling for a couple of miles over ground that represented conquest.

They had yarns of the things that were happening along that road ; speculations upon the things that were about to happen.

MEDAL WITHOUT BAR   CHAPTER XLII

WITH the issue of steel helmets to the battery the new phase was symbolically entered. Whitelaw, the adept, without reading the order on the subject, was able to tell novices that the lightest of bangs on the aft brim of a rigid helmet secured by its strap to the human chin would produce, unneces-

sarily, a broken neck.   Chin-straps should, therefore, be
adjusted not tightly to the chin but loosely to the back of
the skull.

The battery in these new steel helmets was of men
made suddenly grim.   They jibed cheerfully enough at
each other, in the new get-up—foreshadowing for the
helmets uses more appropriate than the covering of human
heads ; but there was a new seriousness about them.   By
next day they had covered the helmets' provocative
shine and sharp outlines as Whitelaw's helmet was
covered, with pieces of sandbag and artistic devices of
mud.

It was thus helmeted and secretly thoughtful that the
battery rode through Albert, eastward into action again.
The march was uneventful save for the meeting and passing of four or five hundred men in a condition that
silenced the battery's greatest jokers for a space of several
minutes.

They were Australians from beyond Pozieres, relieved
and withdrawn because they were spent ; and they had
given six hours since their relief to covering five miles.
Reynolds had been surprise enough to Cartwright in the
matter of muddiness ; but this battalion was a masterpiece whereof Reynolds had been the barest sketch.

They were bearded with the beard of shipwreck-
pictures and ragged in the foul rags of beggars.   They
ambled in orderly silence, hugging the gutter for the
avoidance of whatever movement would have been
required of them to make room for traffic on the road.
For this same reason of economy they (being Australians
and above merely local traffic laws) must have elected
for their descent a road reserved for ' up ' traffic.

Few pipes or cigarettes were active among them, for
most mouths were agape in the bearded pallor of their
faces ; a pallor that was itself a shock.   Some merciful
forethought (or again the accident of their being
Australians) had relieved them of the burden of kit and
rifles.   They slouched with hands dropped into pockets,
hung on belts, thrusting unbuttoned tunics aside, or
adrift as mud-clots beside slowly moving thighs.   They

moved with the dull uniformity of men shackled together, for they were so shackled by their common weariness. At rare intervals the uniformity was broken and the pace varied by the shambling gait of a man who tottered with another upon his back, or of two shuffling with their hands joined together under the weight of a third. The feet of the carried ones stuck out of the mud of their trousers, or out of sandbag wrappings, pale and naked.

Cartwright rode at the tail of the firing battery with ' the circus '—G.S. wagons, mess-cart, water-cart and the odd bicycle-pushers. Some wag in his cortège broke the silence with song, *sotto voce*, as though a little anxious that the Australians should not be disturbed :

" Form fours, right turn. How do you spend the money you earn ?

Ow ! Ow ! Ow ! . . . It's a lov-er-ly war."

But there was no response of fooling among his fellows. Badinage was of the quiet, ironic sort. " The mice 'ave been at that lot pretty bad, chum. . . ." " What price ole ' 'Appy-go-Lucky,' there, gone bye-byes on the fat bloke's shoulder ? Jer see 'im ? " and the thoughtful answer, " Yers. I seen 'im."

Richards turned them left into the road across Usna Valley to the Aveluy Crucifix. The newly-captured ridges to the north and east had let loose a traffic undreamed of by any dawn- and twilight-prowlers in peace-sectors or on the mud-flats of the Salient.

The road had the life and movement of a bazaar. A hurried masterpiece of the sappers had replaced half a mile of tattered and lost road with a fairway of pit-props dogged together. There was occasional shelling—but none of it was immediately topical. It was chance, blind shooting that fell wide of the road in the elaborate (and elaborately vanished) trench-system to the right and left of it.

It was high noon when word drifted back to Cartwright that they were ' nearly there ' ; the noon of a great August day of blue sky and a blazing disk of sun with swirls and little eddies of dazzling cloudlets that romped serenely remote from the trivial rubbish of high shrapnel and

Black Marias and the amazing dust that rose, acrid and white, from the road. A great day for the concourse on the road ; pedlars and pilgrims they might have been, with their various burdens and their staffs—grenades and wire and duckboards ; small-arms ammunition and bundles of sandbags ; stakes and pit-props ; picks and shovels and stretchers.

By a chalk-cutting to the south of the dun mass of rubble that had been Ovillers (for a fair piece of sign-writing on a large board announced the fact) an order to halt reached Cartwright and the ' circus.'

Inside the cutting were rigged up an awning and a huxter's booth in quiet accord with the general ' bazaar ' movement. It was designated (with more sign-writing) "Dressing Station." The proprietor had doffed his tunic and replaced his tobacco-pouch in his breeches-pocket as he smiled at Cartwright and strolled across the road to him.

" Pretty slack again," he said. " Not like a fortnight ago. But I suppose you blighters with guns mean that a proper hum is going to start again. A lot of you blew in yesterday. Some the day before ; but none of you seem to come down my way—of course you haven't started loosing off yet—unless that's one of you coming now."

He indicated a stretcher that two men were bringing down the road with a blanketed bundle upon it. It was not the top of the stretcher that brought any sudden check to the beat of pulses, a catch to the breath ; it was the under-side, bulged and sagging like a strainer devised for the dripping of dark jelly from fruit cooked and mashed to a pulp. Its covering of flies broke and dispersed in tenacious pursuit of the rich, great drops that oozed and slowly fell ; but the flies massed again, abandoning the chance and the meagre for the certain and full.

" I should think they're wasting time," said the doctor. " But the beggars will bring you anything—any damned thing at all."

He strolled back to his booth and the stretcher set

down before it. Cartwright looked ahead at his ' circus '
while the doctor stooped and drew down the blanket.

When he looked again, the doctor was swinging a pair
of identity disks in the direction of his orderly and
shaking his head at the two men. They had come to
the wrong stall. His poor booth had not the wares for
customers such as they. One of them took the disks and
put them in his pocket ; and they took up the stretcher
again, to carry it farther down the road.

They were not gunners—a thrill of relief that stilled a
peculiar movement in the stomach.

They were sappers.

" You wouldn't believe," said the doctor, coming
bonhomously back, " the things they'll bring you sometimes. Trying to dodge digging, I suppose. Oh, so
you're off. So long. Look in for a drink some time
you're passing. I'm alone on this job most of the time.
No mess. It's a bit dull ; but I can usually scare up a
tot when called upon."

A certain wistfulness struck Cartwright in that invitation. The fellow could not have been much more than
just barely qualified, running that fantastic booth, eating
and sleeping in the low, untimbered burrow that gaped
behind it. . . . As a genial afterthought he skipped up
to Cartwright's stirrup and walked a pace or two beside
him. " Come and have one now. A quick one. You
look a bit tired. You'll catch 'em up round the corner."

" Not now, thanks," said Cartwright. " I'm all right.
I'll look in again."

But he never did.

Ovillers (or more properly, to give it its full style,
Ovillers-La-Boiselle) had been a redoubt in the three-deep
system of trenches from Thiepval to La-Boiselle. The
line was now swung back eastwards to Mouquet Farm, on
a pivot south of Thiepval, offering the amenity of incredible dug-outs in Ovillers, of roads under cover of
crests and of ready-made holes that needed little more
than a rough levelling out for guns whose purpose it was
to shoot northwards into Thiepval in contribution to the
coming battle.

Some more elegant sign-painting on a small board nailed to a peg said " Church. X8a93.10."

The ammunition-wagons and the circus had been left in the road just clear of the dressing-station, and the battery's movement now was a hollow bumping over trench bridges, or a scramble with gunners lurching their shoulders at every wheel in a dessicated swamp of rubble and clitter. The men sweated in little runnels through the white dust that covered and scorched them. Rubbed eyelids and moistened lips moved theatrically under the still unfamiliar and impressive tin-hats. Breast-collars and traces squeezed from the horses' coats a sticky, dirty lather.

There was not, as far as any busy man could judge in passing, a single recognisable bit of trench behind him that did not present to him its row of eighteen-pounder snouts. One hoped, in passing, that they would be quiet yet awhile ; and when they were not, the annoyance was, by way of casual surprise and satisfaction, negligible ; for the standard of every item in life's furniture was changed ; as the roar of an engine, the buzz of a dynamo, the whirl of fly-belts are reasonably accepted in a busy factory.

And so already nostrils and stomachs were at peace with the unimagined, peculiarly mawkish stench that in due course became one with the dust and the fog and the drizzle of the autumn and the winter. From the dust and the fog and the drizzle it would rise, faint and startling, in the savour of food, of drink, and of tobacco till the frost of spring smote it back again into the frozen earth.

Ovillers, till it became the brief home of gunners, had apparently been but a place for men and material in transit—not home-makers, but busy men with other fish to fry. The trenches about the church were discernible as depressions with footpaths trodden at their bottom between mounds of rubble. The guns went into one such series of depressions, indicated on the map as a well-traversed switch running east and west to the north of the church. Browne and Jackman and Crouch, with the portly mess-box, the primus-box and the frying-pan, moved from hollow to hollow between the mounds with the sad intentness of all house-hunters in an over-populated district. But the battery (by reason of the high angle of elevation of howitzers as against mere guns) was once again spared the competition and congestion that prevailed a little farther from the crest of the ridge.

Richards left the battery for a few minutes to ratify Browne's choice of a home and returned to the matter of digging-in the guns. Meston and Cartwright went off with the limbers, to bring up the firing-battery wagons and the circus. While the ammunition and the kits were unloaded and dumped between the guns, the architecture went tremendously on. Material for the purposes of Richards abounded as a mineral in that place. Even a girder could be quite reasonably sought for in one mound or another after a few minutes of scraping and delving therein. For digging, in the strict sense of the word, was impossible.

Neither spade nor shovel could be driven into the soil that was not soil at all but débris and tins and bits of equipment ; and neither could a pick do much to loosen it, for tangled wire. Artillery, it was found by those geologists, may cut wire but it cannot annihilate it. Having cut it, artillery scatters it upon the earth—and, having scattered it, buries it. Having cut and buried it, it digs it up again, mixes it with parts of a house, parts of a cemetery, parts of a helmet, a water-bottle, the twisted barrel of a rifle, a belt of machine-gun ammunition, an unused rocket, a grenade, a foot—and buries it again.

Reade, the gardener in B Subsection, saying that what was wanted on such a job was not picks and shovels but a good old prong, found that not the top-spit only, nor yet the first half-dozen spits, was heavy going by reason of those ' fancy roots,' but the subsoil also. It was sheer, slow scraping and scratching, in the manner of poultry, and a laborious rag-picking of every shovelful before it could go into a sandbag ; for of what use in a sandbag are a grenade, rifle ammunition, a boot and a broken fountain-pen ? Once or twice there was a scraping away and then a scraping back of the rubble by the scraper, with " Move on a bit with the bag, son. Just tread down the dirt . . ."

Cartwright went back to the wagon-line with Meston and the limbers and wagons.

There were already two hundred and forty rounds of ammunition at the guns, and there had to be ' not less than ' twelve hundred—'immediately.' This meant three trips with the firing battery and first-line wagons—four miles up from the refilling-point at Martinsart, and four miles back.

Cartwright took up the second lot at twilight, unloaded at the battery at dusk, and brought the teams back to the dump at Martinsart.

" Richards will want you at the guns, I suppose," said Meston. " The quarter-bloke has got the rations at the wagon-line. You can take the teams back to him and go up on the cook's cart. The fewer horses messing about up there, the better. The water-cart is going with my lot this time. What was it like ? "

" So-so," said Cartwright. " About the same." The fact was simply that the shelling of Ovillers and the road had been unsystematic. Only one or two rounds had happened to fall within the battery's claim. No one had been hit ; and this, according to the new and accepted standards, brought life within the limits of normality as represented by " So-so."

" You might leave some money for the Mess," Meston went on. " The new chap was going on about running out of whisky. I'll try to get you a couple more bottles to-morrow. Well—so long."

" So long," said Cartwright, and ambled off with the unhooked teams for the wagon-line. And Meston rode off with his three hundred and sixty ' bullets,' as Cartwright with other howitzer purists called their ammunition.

There was always a pang in reflections about Meston ; a peculiar, vague regret for something about the fellow— or for something utterly lacking from him. It was with a magnificent love and devotion that he scrawled his notes, changing over teams and drivers and arranging reliefs with moves as elaborately considered as on a chessboard ; ordering a meal for Cartwright (as Cartwright discovered at the wagon-line) ; loving the battery but tragically hating it because the chances of a five days' seniority had placed the loved thing in the arms of Richards; poaching, in the ardour of his passion that knew no quietude, on the jobs of the Sergeant-Major, interfering with the Quartermaster-Sergeant, eternally nagging the farrier. . . .

The meal he had ordered for Cartwright in his tent was porridge, bacon and eggs, bread, cheese, jam, whisky and coffee. It was Cartwright's first serious application to food since breakfast—about eighteen hours before. Bread and jam and a whisky with the ammunition-column people at about four and a mug of tea at the battery at about nine had been, with the stench of Ovillers, ample freight for his stomach and ample call upon his time.

MEDAL WITHOUT BAR   CHAPTER XLIII

OVILLERS by day and at dusk was one thing. In the black of two o'clock in the morning it was quite another.

It took Cartwright not more than half an hour of stumbling over jags of wood and metal and of tearing his boots and a hand on those endless shreds of barbed wire (while the mess-cart waited at the roadside) to be sure that they were, in fact, at Ovillers; and that he was utterly lost.

He stumbled upon gunpits enough in the darkness, but the guns were all eighteen-pounders. Of man, apart from the shadows trudging silent and loaded along the road by the mess-cart, there was amazingly not a sign.

He allayed the momentary fear of having lost the cart and driver and rations as well as the battery by hurrying back to the road and finding them again.

" Wilkins," he said, since something or other had to be said, sooner or later, and he said it facetiously : " Have you ever been lost in the Great War ? "

The bundle on the seat of the cart stirred and said " Sir ? "

The fellow had been asleep; and Cartwright could have just as well sneaked away without saying anything, and continued his search.

He repeated his question, trying to get as much lightness into it as he had achieved in the original.

" Yes, Sir," said the driver.

" Well," said Cartwright, " I haven't—till now. Come on a bit farther where you can pull out of the road into a crump-hole and wait while I have another look for the battery."

He left his coat and his haversack, belt and glasses with Wilkins and set out again. Soon he had staffed himself, like the pilgrims on the road, with some odd stick or pick-handle that had tripped him up in a drift of garbage. He came upon dug-out entrances knocked or buried out of symmetry in the banks of rubble and twisted stakes and wire. There was a distant gleam of light at the bottom of one of them, and dead silence.

The waking troglodyte on duty by the candle could not, he was sure, help him in his search; so he lurched away from the entrance.

The night, as nights went between the Ancre and the Somme, was a quiet one. Shelling, along the whole front, was general and not particular. Ovillers itself was a place of contented sleep. Not a gun was in action. As the place was happily accessible by daylight the ' establishments ' of ammunition were complete, rations (all, apparently, except Cartwright's) were ' up.' The population had retired to its suburbs down those hospitable and slumbrous holes. A sleepy prowler here and there, fulfilling the rite of sentry between the guns of batteries addressed him as " chum " or " son," amended the address to " Sir " and relapsed into his meditations.

" You're not D Battery, are you ? " elicited the only information that those good warriors were capable of giving him to wit : " No."

He thought, once, of asking one of them if he knew where the church was, but spared the joke. (The man may not have seen the elegant little notice-board.) So he trudged and scrambled on.

The things that chattered softly in the next depression of ground and scuttled, still chattering, from his path were rats; the slinking forms of jackals, the gleaming eyes of wolves would have been no great surprise; for there were no surprises now. Every feature of the night that should have had some element of novelty was only an item in a dull monotony of routine. The *whang-hump-hump* of shells was no more than the clatter of tram-cars about a slum. It was sometimes to the right, at others to the left—or in front, or behind; but it was always the same—endless and of no personal significance. The lights, too, were monotonous—the white flares of routine and the pinks, blues, greens and orange of individualities remotely fidgety. . . .

It was Cartwright's first truly leisured solitude and he could have written a long and lucid letter if he had been seated by a light instead of stumping about in the litter of eight weeks' bombardment in inky darkness. Even the stench was unnoticeable, with the impersonal shelling and the scuffle of rats. The letter would have been such that it could very well have gone to Dorothy; for he saw things in true proportion.

Death, even here in this disembowelled burying-place, with its ghoulish rats and its shadows darker than uttermost darkness, was an accident; and accident was the one thing of which living man, in order to live at all, must take no count. This truth was as applicable to Chiswick as it was to Ovillers.

This business of not being able to find the battery which he had left for the second time only half a dozen hours before was a piece of sheer idiocy. He had merely not been paying attention. He ought to have known better than to jog casually out of the place, skirting holes and dodging the more obvious snags with the teams; for even in London he had always been obliged to take particular note of landmarks and turnings for places he had wanted to remember. He ought to have counted the bends and gauged distances from the dressing-station to the church. From the church board he ought to have set the direction and paced the distance to No.1 gun-pit.

The last hour of darkness he put in at the cook's-cart, the horse mumbling at some of the hay that Wilkins always carried under the seat, and Wilkins standing at the tail of the cart in a pose something between a golfer's and a cricketer's with some bat-like weapon, waiting and hoping for more rats. He had killed three while Cartwright had been gone and was anxious, for some entirely mystic and obscure reason, to make up the half-dozen before daylight. He flashed his torch to show Cartwright his bag laid out in an orderly row against the dash-board of the cart ; grey, repulsive, fat brutes with gory snouts, " the lousiest, silliest blighters that just toddle up to the wheels sniffing at the cheese in the cart, arsting for it in the neck. . . ."

Wilkins, from some motive of politeness, began a story about a terrier at home and a rat-ridden corner of a mine-shaft, but even in the darknesss, faintly paling Cartwright could see the restlessness of the complete but interrupted angler. The sweat was chilling on his body so he took his coat and his mackintosh, muffled himself up and sat down and dozed in a hollow a dozen yards from the cart.

He was disturbed by occasional scuffles and the bang of Wilkins's club against the cartwheel, and twice by squeaks and Wilkins's quiet words of victory.

When the flares were pale and the signal-rockets had lost the splendour of their colours, he shook himself and wondered why he still waited. . . . He rubbed his eye-lids and knew that it was Wilkins he had been waiting for—he was still one down for his half-dozen.

It was an easy matter to find No. 1 gun now. The ground had risen out of the darkness into a familiar shape Hollows and mounds—widened trenches and flattened parapets—were faintly sketching a pattern. Cartwright found and woke (yes, woke) the sentry and dispatched him for the cook.

The second signaller on duty was the only available man who could find the officers' dug-out ; he did it by picking up the telephone-wire and following it to the hole where it disappeared.

It was only for the first yard or two that he had to crouch
down and scramble behind his torch, where débris had
cluttered up the shaft opening under two or three smashed
and sagging timbers. The proportions thereafter were
of the magnificence always looked for by the Somme
victors; the lining of good square timbers lately white-
washed. After descending in the disk of light from his
torch for a score of steps—ignoring a scuffle of the kind
with which his night's prowling had made him familiar—
the heads of Richards, Whitelaw and Reynolds—above
the gentility of pyjama-collars—attracted the beam of
his light by the sounds of breathing that threatened at
any moment to become a snore.

It was a quaint emotion that the heads of those sleepers
brought to him—the black locks of Richards tousled into
the form, here and there, of a rooster's tail feathers in
miniature, with the small light patch cut away about
the splinter-hole ; the fine, silvery strands on the pink
scalp of Whitelaw, delicate and dignified enough for a
dome housing the brains of a grammarian ; and Reynolds's
brown and anyhow, grown ripe for another shearing by
his groom, whitened with chalk-grit.

The emotion gave Cartwright occasion for a smile.
It was, briefly, that it was somehow good for him to be
there ; for there were no better men than these. He
searched no further with his torch than was necessary to
show him the three bunks they occupied and a fourth,
holding his valise with pyjamas duly displayed on the
pillow, above Reynolds. He lighted the aiming-post
candle in its tin holder nailed to the timber near his
pyjamas.

The nails driven into the bunk posts and the sides of
this dug-out were not just ordinary, naked nails. They
were bound and padded over with strips of sandbag,
protection for clothes deliberately hung and heads
accidentally struck upon them.

He undressed as quickly and as quietly as might be,
flattening his feet, luxuriously stretching out his toes on
the mat of dry, new sandbags by the lower bunkside.
and climbed in.

" Welcome to the old home, Uncle," Reynolds softly mumbled.

" Oh, so you're awake, are you ? " said Cartwright, blowing out the candle.

" Yes—and no," said Reynolds. " Awake enough to say that much—but not enough to listen to a lot. Don't you get up till you're called to-morrow, Richards said to tell you. Well, good night. I suppose it's hellish late."

" Good night," said Cartwright. He saw no reason for telling him that it was already day and that it had taken him till then to find the battery.

T HEY ate lunch that day in genteel and leisurely style, going down together to the dug-out. They had spent the morning pottering about among the gun-pits and little ammunition-dumps in the sunshine much in the manner of gentlemen of leisure with schemes in mind for rockery or rose-garden. Browne came to find them, bareheaded as usual, with his violinist's mane brushed magnificently off his brow.

" Where's your blasted helmet, Browne ? " asked Richards.

" In the kitchen, Sir."

" The place for it is your head. If you get anything in the head when you're not wearing your helmet, you'll probably be up for a self-inflicted wound."

" Very good, Sir," said Browne ; and it was beyond Richards to see things with such a sense of their niceness as was possessed by Browne : a covered head meant a salute, and saluting was all out of key with many of the rites he had to perform.

" Luncheon, gentlemen, is served," he said, solemn as an owl, looking straight to his front and then slightly inclining his head. He turned with his soldier's smartness and butler's dignity, and preceded them to the dug-out. Its entrance had already been improved and Jackman

and Crouch were still gently working at it, taking turns
at sandbag-holding and the novelty of the straight,
long-handled German spade.

The table was laid in the twilight at the bottom of the
shaft. Soup-powders gave them their first course, and
Browne stood over it waiting for them with a folded
newspaper flicking away the drowsy, pedestrian flies. It
was appetising enough, save for the peculiar, delicate
fungus of stench that had settled by now over palates
and the bases of tongues.

" A spot of the giant-killer," said Whitelaw.

He picked up his soup-spoon, uncorked the whisky-
bottle and offered it to the Captain. Richards shook his
head, not censoriously but merely dubiously.

Whitelaw filled his spoon with whisky. The cruet—
a Petit Beurre biscuit-tin—that held the whisky-bottle,
held among its other furniture a bottle of Worcester
sauce. Giving the whisky-bottle to Cartwright, Whitelaw
garnished his spoonful of whisky with a few drops of
sauce and down his throat it went, with the lithe grace
of an otter taking to its stream.

Cartwright and Reynolds followed him. The fungus
was gone.

Browne judged the time required for the soup, and came
back through the dormitory section of the gallery with
the " mixed-grill " announced on his menu. Its title was
justified by the presence of a kidney cut in four pieces ;
for Browne was one of those marvels at drawing rations
who could find kidneys in almost any six inches of fresh
meat.

" When you're ready, Sir," he said, placing the pie-dish
before Richards, " if you'd ring the bell——"

" Bell ? " Richards searched the table and its neighbourhood.

" Yes, Sir. I thought it would save shouting, Sir,"
said Browne. " I might not hear round the corner and
up the other stairs where the cook-house is. So we've
fixed up a kind of bell, Sir—the servants and I."

He indicated it behind Whitelaw's shoulder.

Suspended from some telephone-wire was a piece of

F

wood, carved approximately into the familiar shape of the pendant on the end of a water-closet chain.   Upon it was inscribed with Browne's indelible pencil " Pull, and let go."

" Thanks, Browne," said Richards.

It was only through the nicer, more subtle shades of conduct and humour that Richards could not always follow Browne.   In the simpler matter of sheer, bleak solemnity he met him on his own ground.

Browne withdrew with the soup-plates.

The fantastic solemnity of the Mess was only part of its tribute to Charlie Browne.   If ever genius had its due measure of appreciation in the hearts of men it was the genius of this artist, the wide stare of whose thoughtful sunken eyes, the twitch and the granite stillness of whose lean jowls could dramatise himself and a mess-tin of pancake-dough into an epic figure and a significant property.

The appreciation now took the immediate form of a reading of the inscription on the bell-pull and chuckles led by the explosive, clicking titter of Richards.

But laughter and the reading of words were not enough for so zealous a gadget-master as Richards. " You carve— Uncle or Whitelaw," he said hastily and got up to examine the device.

It was all well and truly done.   An "angle" cut by Browne (or more likely by the fitter) from the brass of a cartridge, transferred the first stress of the bell-pull from the perpendicular to the horizontal. The horizontal stretch of wire worked on a small pulley that had previously carried the elastic cord, looped at the ends as button-holes for the bracing of human trousers.

Richards sat down again and they ate their mixed grill.

When he pulled the bell, according to instruction, the only result was a faint squeak from the " angle " and the pulley, and a call through the darkness of the intervening gallery from Browne: " Was that the bell, Sir ?—she didn't quite ackle."

" We'll fix it afterwards," said Richards. " We've finished."

" If you'd just give her another try, Sir," Browne called. " A bit smarter—kind of jerk."

Richards jerked. Four breaths were immediately held; for an explosion cracked through the silence of the gallery. It was followed by " Thank you, Sir. Coming right up, Sir, *toute suite*." Browne's tone had lost a shade of its solemnity and gathered a tinge of frail human delight.

" Coming right up—my grandmother!" mumbled Richards. " Let's go and see what that ass thinks he's got there."

They sallied across between the bunks to where Browne with the " savoury " and tea-pot on his tray, and Jackman and Crouch squatting on their haunches, were looking upon part of their morning's work and seeing that it was good.

" It's a little Fritz," Browne explained. " It was laying under your bunk, Sir."

It was a small automatic pistol, its stock lashed with wire to a wooden block nailed against the side of the " kitchen " (the second shaft leading down to the gallery). The bell-pull ended in a loop around its trigger. A few inches from its muzzle was a platform rigged up on a crazy scaffolding of odd boards nailed and tied together. On the scaffolding a dish-cloth or two were hung to dry, and on the platform were four bulging sandbags, tied neck to tail and folded together like a bundle of sausages.

" All that's only temp'ry, Sir," Browne explained, the artist anxious lest the quality of his work should be judged from his roughest sketch.

" Yes," mumbled Richards sulkily. " More damned temporary than you think, Browne. Playing the ass with bullets. . . ."

" It's quite all *right*, Sir," Browne said. " The dirt in those bags has been sifted through that piece of bed-netting. Sifted *twice*, Sir. There can't be anything in them to cause a ricco'. And I'll put a guard-rail to keep heads out of the road."

" But why the hell must you have bullets at all ? " asked Richards.

" Ah ! " said Browne, and he furled his eyebrows in impressive thought. " You got to, Sir. We tried a shot or two with the bullets taken out of the cartridge. But she won't have it. She'll pop, of course, but she won't reload and recover." The relationship of Richards and Browne now was of inventors in conference. " It seems to upset the charge or the pressure or something of that. You will probably know how it is, Sir."

" Who made those brass cantilever bits for getting round the corners ? " asked Richards.

" The tiffy, Sir," said Browne. " I gave him the specification."

" Come on," said Richards, turning back into the darkness of the gallery. " Let's have the savoury."

The moment of the inventors had passed.

" Will you ring, Sir ? " asked Browne, setting down the sardines on toast and the teapot. " When you want me to clear ? "

" Yes, Browne," said Richards. " I'll—ring. You might fill the Thermos for the O.P. and tell Corporal Hine to parade with two signallers and a mile of wire— D3 will do—in half an hour."

Immediately after lunch they took a lantern and discussed the advisability of opening up, for use, the lower story of the dug-out. A low, narrow shaft led down to it from near Browne's kitchen end of the upper gallery. Richards went down first, followed by Reynolds, Cartwright and Browne. Whitelaw was too blasé to bother. He had seen two—and even three-storied dug-outs before,—the other side of Mametz. The War held no wonders for him.

It was from there, it seemed, as they descended—from that lower story—that the foul fungus came to palates. But they went on down. Richards stopped, looking at a heap in the corner and from it to a heap on one of the bunks that lined the wall.

" It's only kits," Browne said. " We've been through it all, Sir. Kits and sandbags and a few bombs and rifles and muck; but nothing to account for the—trouble. It's my belief that it's only due to stagnancy, Sir. Stink would be a bit heavier than ordinary fresh air and would roll down the stairs and no way of getting out again. Some of the boys of B. sub. found a sort of ventilating fan and a lot of zinc piping about a foot wide. Fritz must have blown 'is fresh air down, and 'is stink out, of basements. We could get this cleared out and ' cresoled,' and perhaps there'd be time to put in one of old Fritz's ventilators to give her a blow out. . . ."

" We won't bother," said Richards. " We'll shut it up and bury the trouble—whatever it is. Stick some boards and wire and stuff across the bottom of the shaft. Put plenty of chloride of lime ; take out the last two or three cross-timbers there and then knock down enough of the soil from above with a pick. Unless you can think of a better way—with a couple of electric bells and a rocket or something. Perhaps a corkscrew and a fire-escape."

MEDAL WITHOUT BAR   CHAPTER XLV

W HITELAW remained at the battery while Richards and the other two went off with the signallers. Before going they selected their targets and worked out their lines, calling them A, B, and C ; for the Ovillers batteries were intended to be a surprise for the battle and those were touchy days in the matter of stating deflections and ranges over telephone lines with an earth return.

" A " on the map, was an obvious junction of road and trench on the forward slope of Thiepval nicely visible across the dip of Blighty Valley. On the map were also houses and rectangular orchards to help in identification of the spot; but houses on the map were as likely to be hollows on the ground as shapeless lumps, and an orchard might or might not be represented now by a wan array of things like bowled and broken cricket-stumps.

The target was identified easily enough while the
signallers were running out their wire to the battery from
the little hollow in which Richards and Cartwright were
lying.   Nab Road emerged patchily below them and
again disappeared utterly in a rabble of shell-holes.   The
glare of the afternoon sun was behind them and the only
caution necessary for the signallers was that they should
' look out for the sky-line '—and get over it quickly, and
low.

But even for the signallers the work was easy
and without hazard ; in effect there was no ' sky-line.'
Birds as old as Hine and Laurence and Davis had nothing
in this bleak world if they had not eyes and knees and
bellies for cover.   Two hundred yards of stopping and
crawling and twelve of chatty strolling over firm, dry
ground was the work of forty minutes.   The return
from the battery to the O.P. when the line was laid, with
a pick and shovel and bundle of bags was the work of
another forty ; and Richards and his colleagues had
been able to decide in the interval that target " A " was
of very little use for their particular purpose.   It was
there, clearly enough—a wedge of sharp, clear shadow in
the mottled browny grey of rubbish like their own rubbish
of Ovillers.   But the chances were that even with the
most careful and accurate timing of their shell-flights
they would not be able to identify their own bursts in
the racket and jostle of fire on Thiepval.

Richards told Whitelaw cryptically to switch from the
prearranged " A " to the point where their own Nab
Road, after turning northwards, crossed the hedged track
running eastwards out of Thiepval Valley.

After registering the guns they added unobtrusively to
the din of Thiepval with a few confirming rounds—
observed and unobserved—on target " A."

It may have been the mere sunshine as against the murk
of the Beaumont Hamel affair that brought a picnic-
spirit to their outing.   They started no digging, partly
because the spot was remote enough from the wilderness
behind them, from the inferno to their front and from
the dark possibilities over the crest to their right in the

direction of Mouquet Farm; partly, also, because Richards thought that they might find a better spot farther along to their right. It was vaguely in quest of such a spot that they went down towards the road but not quite into it—for gunners knew that the glare of the sun behind them was better cover than limpid shadow.

In another hole from which they could still casually see the flailing of Thiepval they drank their nomad tea, smoked their tobacco and talked their endless nomad talk.

They touched, no doubt, on the impending battle—on the Gargantuan heaps of ammunition they were to deliver on the supports and communications after other batteries, better placed than the Ovillers group, had attended to the wire and the front lines.

Richards may have talked some politics and Reynolds probably made some speculations concerning women. But most of all, in the manner of any family at tea with one member missing, they talked of Whitelaw. He was still called ' Whitelaw,' since the obvious vacancy of ' Uncle ' had already been filled by Cartwright. In the manner of chieftains in council they admitted gravely that he was a sound addition to the clan. A fine O.C. wagon-lines he would have made . . . and this suggested the topic of Meston—which it was impossible to discuss with Richards beyond an expression of the hope and confidence that he would soon get a battery, now that ' things had begun to move.' But it was seen, too, that Whitelaw was as good at the guns as he would have been at any wagon-line. He had grasped the men and they had grasped him, as they both had shown in their brisk manhandling of A and C guns into their particularly awkward pits. . . . " If he doesn't drink too much . . ." Richards mused ; and that was as near as he ever got to priggishness in this matter.

" Drink too much ! " said Reynolds. " I believe you could fill the old blackguard with coke and sulphuric acid and he'd put on flesh. Don't worry, Dicky. His guts are of leather—I shouldn't be surprised if there's a grain of truth in some of those yarns of his. Anyhow, I'm not going to be the first to try calling him ' Dad.' "

"No," said Cartwright. "You'd better not. Incidentally, he's a year younger than I am."

"Oh, *is* he?" said Reynolds, contemptuous of the thought. "You're one of us, Nunkie; a seeker after truth and values and what not. But that old blighter knows about them all. He knows. He knows. He is the father or the illicit spouse of Lilith. . . ."

"He's a thundering good soldier," said Richards. "And I'm glad B Battery didn't get him. They've got a funny little chap from the D.A.C."

"Yes," said Reynolds. "'Thundering' is near enough to the perfect word, Dicky. I wonder if he's—*sound;* knows the job."

"He put us on to the target quick enough," suggested Cartwright.

"Yes," said Reynolds. "But I planted the aiming-posts."

"Oh, *you!*" mumbled Richards. "You're a bloody marvel, you are. A nice mess the War would be in if it wasn't for you and the sixth form at Winchester. Old Uncle and I and Whitelaw and Haig are grateful to you, my son—very, very grateful. Aren't we, Uncle?"

Reynolds made a crisp, rude retort and Cartwright said, "H'm. . . . Gunnery seems to me about the least important part of being a gunner. But I should think Whitelaw can get there all right with that chipped old protractor and piece of mandolin string of his. . . . He's a good sort, anyway. . . ."

And in the midst of this conclave of chieftains there came to Cartwright the cold, desolating thought that he was no chieftain at all. He was dressed up in a uniform like a boy-scout when—unlike a boy-scout even—he had got lost with the cook's-cart and the rations till the sun rose and lifted him out of the mess of tumbled earth. He knew that Whitelaw was now stumping about at the battery keeping an eagle eye on the screwing of No. 44 fuzes into four great stacks of shells; and that if he had been there instead of Whitelaw the quality of the work would have depended altogether on the skill and care of the individual gunners.

Little puffs of shrapnel were uncurling about their calibration point, as eighteen-pounder batteries shot themselves in.

"Day after to-morrow—" Richards mused, and looked upon Thiepval. "It's time we took that blasted place. You would think that the shelling alone would be enough to get Fritz out of it."

They looked again, silently thoughtful, at the mean, tormented crag that was already the thought most sinister in some thousand minds.

And they sat but a mile away from it in the perfect ease of gunners fulfilling the conditions of the books.

Fighting was not their function. Remote from struggle and all the base, unthinkable miseries that broke a thousand men into a wan and ragged few like the Australians dragging through Albert ; their weapons concealed in a kindly hollow ; their bodies at ease in a spacious hole ; their eyes, unseen and unsuspected, upon the enemy—theirs was the royal road in this affair. Not to fight, but to determine for others the hazards of the fight, with cool minds and accurate calculation to lighten the burden upon one champion while loading woe intolerable upon the other.

AND thus the battle began.
An hour before zero they were drinking coffee in the dug-out and checking, for the last time, the four barrage-tables for the guns.

"An orderly-officer show, I suppose, Richards ? " Whitelaw asked casually.

"What do you mean—an 'orderly-officer' show ? "

"I mean just the orderly-officer on top looking after the shoot, and the others down here—spare. Turning in again if they want to," Whitelaw explained.

The question seemed to bother Richards for a moment ; but it was obviously not a questioning of his authority.

It was the merest suggestion, made from no motive but profoundest wisdom.

" What's the idea ? " he asked.

Whitelaw shrugged his shoulders. " Conservation of energy," he said. " Fairest odds that way. Gives the old lady a chance to look after her own."

" If there's anything *in* the show," said Reynolds. " I mean, if it's going to be a gory battle we could toss for it. We always tossed, Meston and I—before. Didn't we, Richards ? You did, too."

" *Before*—" said Whitelaw cryptically, " isn't now. Before—in those little Plug Street, Dickebusch fire-work parties of yours—you hadn't arrived at the age of puberty. You haven't yet—as a gunner. I *know*. I've been a mother myself, don't forget. . . . If it's always an orderly-officer's job, there's never any argument about it. I suppose the acting Sergeant-Major or the battery clerk keeps the roster and details the O.O. every day—and there's no rot about tossing for it, or volunteering like a lot of school-kids or congenital idiots. Your number just comes up. Just follow the roster. It's—I think you'll find it a good way. Things 'll probably be worse than this at times. And if it's just a matter of routine who has the dirty work to do. Well . . . I—I'm not trying to show you how to run your battery, Richards." The apologetic hesitation came handsomely and touchingly from Whitelaw ; it was his first exhibition of anything of the kind. It seemed to embarrass him.

" Don't worry, Dad," said Richards. " I know you're not. Which of you, incidentally, is orderly bloke to-day ? I haven't noticed in the general muck up of the last two days."

" Incidentally," said Whitelaw, " I am."

Reynolds, for no particular reason, exploded.

" Laugh away, you damned young fool," said Whitelaw. " But you wait. There'll be dirtier jobs than this when some one else will be orderly bloke. Then *I*'ll laugh."

" I laughed not at your misfortune, Dad ; but at your heroism."

" Heroism ! " snorted Whitelaw. " I've done with

heroism. The secret of this whole job is to take your turn. You'll always find me lying doggo when it isn't my turn to be outside ; and that's why I'm trying to persuade our C.O. there to adopt the scheme. It saves any feeling like all the ladies in the parish thinking they're expected to do something to run the stall at the bazaar. I enjoy a decent dug-out during a fierce battle, with a spot of the giant-killer—and if I'm not orderly-officer I can have it—according to the scheme. And who the hell started calling me ' Dad ' ? "

"Our C.O. there," said Reynolds. "So it's practically in orders."

"All right," said Richards. "We'll adopt your scheme, Dad. Cartwright and Reynolds are in reserve to-day."

"And you're in command down here ? " said Whitelaw.

"I'm in command," said Richards, "where I damned well please."

Whitelaw shrugged. "Would you tell Wright to cut down the detachments ? Three men per gun will be ample crew for a round per minute. The others can take it easy in the dug-outs till they're wanted."

"I've a damned good mind to make it three and a half—or four." And Richards smiled. "Just to show who *is* commanding. Though it is a good enough idea. Yes—I'll tell him. D'you mind if Reynolds has a look at his section before you take over the War ? "

"Reynolds can do us no harm," said Whitelaw.

When the other two had gone up, he turned to Cartwright and said very anciently : "We're lucky in our youngsters, Uncle. You ought to have seen the old fool that commanded my late unit. Encouraging volunteers was his strong suit. . . . As though a machine like a typewriter could carry on for long if all the keys were allowed to volunteer to do their jumping instead of having to wait their turn to be pushed. Young Richards knows how to skipper, don't you think ? "

"Yes," said Cartwright, "he does. . . . I suppose I'd better take a look at my telephone braves before we start."

They put on their hats and went up.

"By the way," said Whitelaw at the top. "You're 'next for duty' I noticed on orders. You might come up when you've finished breakfast to let me get mine. We'll be as formal as we can—to give those two a start in the way they've got to go on. They're green—but teachable."

Green !—thought Cartwright. What about himself ?

The signallers' dug-out consisted for the most part of heavy and peaceful sleepers. The man on duty sat with his hair pushed up by the elastic band of his earpiece. A linesman was transforming himself from sleeping-order to battle-order by modelling a flattened and bent cigarette stump into a semblance of its pristine roundness and straightness before buttoning up his tunic and putting on his boots and putties. The second linesman, Cartwright found, was already on his way to the brigade end of the wire in the old Usna Redoubt.

Cartwright's portion of the army was ready.

In the gun-pits the layers' torches were winking on the dials of sights and range-drums and clinometers. Talk had fallen everywhere into tones lowered towards whispers, so that Ovillers was as silent and remote from the disturbed sheet of sky to the north and east as it had been while Cartwright prowled alone from the mess-cart in search of the sleeping battery. Only the crunching was not now the scuffle of rats, but the steps of gunners in ill-laced boots as they carried ammunition from its separate dump to the gun-pits.

Reynolds and Cartwright pottered and chatted, measuring the quiet and the din against the quiet and the din of other nights and other times of night, studying the flares and the rockets, speculating as to whether the garrison of Thiepval could see any portents and read them. . . . Cartwright tried to imagine the Infantry ; but the only material for his imaginings was as yet that memorable procession in Albert and the quiet students of bombing that he and Henderson had seen in a very remote past.

Reynolds said " Seven minutes, Uncle."

They joined Richards among the 'Numbers One' behind the pits. Whitelaw came up from his checking of the last gun and saluted with ostentation. " Would you check my time, Sir ? " he said, holding up his wrist and flashing his torch on his watch. " Five minutes to, I make it, all but twenty seconds. Fiftcen . . . ten . . . five."

" Yes. Good," said Richards.

" The spare men are all below," Whitelaw went on, still ceremonially, and jabbed his head towards Reynolds and Cartwright with some significance. The Sergeants drifted out of the group, back to their guns.

" I've told them to stand to," Whitelaw went on, " and I'll start No. 1 gun off with a whistle."

" Right," said Richards. " Quite right—except in one particular. *I* will start them off with a whistle. After the ball is opened you can take over, according to your orderly-officer scheme—with which I quite agree. Rennie and Uncle can go down now. I'll join them later."

They went, and sat down on a step near the top of the dug-out entrance.

" I'm glad Dicky sat on him just that much," said Reynolds. " Just for luck—though I do believe the old sod would say anything to any one—either in praise of himself or in blame of you without making you—and by you I mean any one—' *on*,' ' *aliquis* ' or ' *tis* '—want to kick him . . . Crikey ! . . . "

After the ' Crikey ' Cartwright dimly heard him shouting, " Some one seems to have heard the whistle all right ! "

A dust of rubble was shaking loose and falling down the entrance. The acetylene lamp on the table below them had gone out.

It is probably accurate to say that Richards's happened to be the foremost battery in that particular bombardment, and was situated approximately at the centre of the concentration of guns.

There could have been no attitude more seemly for frail man than crouching below the surface of the tottering earth, hidden in all humility from the mangled and screaming heavens of that dawn.

The homely smell of escaping acetylene came up the

steps to them, reminding them that the nose is a sensitive organ. Reynolds went down and turned off the dribble of water. He used his torch going down but not coming back.

Richards soon came and joined them ; and they sat on, listening and smoking and watching the dust and rubbish slowly silting over the edge of the topmost beam of the shaft.

Then when a golden wedge of sunshine was cleaving into the dust, the way that the smell of acetylene had come there now came the smell of frying bacon and soon after it came Browne with the roll of oilcloth under his arm and the tray in his hands.

They went down as he gave the finishing touch to his work at the table by setting down two pots of tea. He said nothing, but his simplest acts were always gestures.

" Mr. Cartwright and Mr. Reynolds will want some tea, too, Browne," Richards yelled ; and Browne smiled. For the one thing in the world that he enjoyed more than a joke of his own was a better joke from Richards.

" It's because of the shelling, Sir," he said. " It gives *me* a thirst . . . " he drew a hissing breath as of air playing upon a fire. " Any shelling, Sir ; arrivals—or departures. I'll fill one fresh for Mr. Whitelaw presently. He'll want it."

Browne's estimate had been correct. It was only the hollow need for the bacon and bread that set them to chewing and swallowing it ; but the tea was joy—after two or three hours of tobacco.

Whitelaw came down before they had finished ; Browne came and took away a teapot.

" Just about finished, Richards," Whitelaw said. " They're just loosing off the last few rounds. One a minute. Any news ? "

Richards shook his head. " No. And the brigade wire hasn't been down at all. We've been through all the time."

" Cease fire and stand to, I suppose ? "

" Yes," said Richards.

Cartwright filled his pipe and went up.

All the Ovillers batteries had settled down to a morose

silence broken by isolated snarls and puffs of white dust from one surprising emplacement after another.

There ought to have been nothing, Cartwright reflected as he strolled from pit to pit, to blacken the faces of gunners, as Nelson's stalwarts were reasonably blackened. The charges were clean and miraculously smokeless. Even the dirt and dust in the gunpits were white. Yet the crews were sooty and smeared as any " powder-monkey " of old. Only throats and foreheads and eye-sockets were pale in the clammy grime of cheeks and jowls. They had collected, apparently, from the oil that lubricated their pieces, the make-up proper to gunners in action.

Bombardier Francis, the layer of No. 2 gun, took a twist of newspaper out of his ear and looked at it and tossed it away. He shook his finger into the ear and wiped another little smear of oil and blood on to the front of his shirt.

" Number two ! " said the sergeant, pulling a great watch out of his breeches.

Francis took the stumpy thong of the trigger lanyard.

" Fire ! "

Francis ducked his head a little, pressed his left thumb into his right ear, and fired. It was possible to hear the shell spinning away now, an individual. It was No. 2's last contribution to the programme.

" All right, sonnie. Cease fire. Leave the breech open." The Sergeant saluted Cartwright.

No. 3 fired a minute later, and then No. 4. The Number one of the last gun came and asked Cartwright if he should fire one more round because of an early misfire. Cartwright said no ; he did not think the omission would amount to very much.

Whitelaw ate a leisurely breakfast and after it had a leisurely shave and wash.

Cartwright was sitting on the old parapet by the signallers' dug-out when he came up. The men were sitting about with their mugs and mess-tins, or were shaving and washing. Some were plying the eternal pencil on writing-pads—the pencil that Cartwright himself must ply at some time or other that day.

Whitelaw came across from the dug-out, with his peculiar short, stumping stride, looking over Cartwright's head in the direction, roughly, of Albert.

" Seen that, Uncle ? " he asked.

Cartwright turned and looked. " Not particularly," he said. " They're always sending over something there."

" They're not," said Whitelaw. " Where they've always sent it before has been the road. And they've not sent 5·9's before, either. That isn't the road, just there. It's a six-inch how. position. Put that in your pipe and smoke it."

It was brisk shelling ; four-round salvos that searched and swept. The two stood watching the tops of the black bursts as they drifted up from the ground into view.

" No orders yet ? " asked Cartwright.

Whitelaw said " No. About four hours, too. It's another washout I expect. Richards wants to go rushing off to that O.P. you were at the other day. But what's the use ? We haven't been detailed for any O.P. work—touch wood and thank God. And we'll get all the news we want without going to look for it. We'll spend the day waiting for orders and news, and lunch—and waiting to see what that 5·9 and his friends are going to do. I wonder if it was a fluke of Richards, pushing right forward here, out of the municipal limits of this city. Or forethought ? "

" Why ? " asked Cartwright.

" It's a good egg. We might dodge some of the dirty work—if any comes. The ratepayers will get most of it."

MEDAL WITHOUT BAR   CHAPTER XLVII

IF this were, in any sense, a history of battles it would dwell on the fact that that particular assault on Thiepval was a complete and utter failure. It might have been more than a failure—a mystery and a dismal miracle as well ; but it was a failure.

(This is no history of battles, however. It is an account only of matters social and personal.)

By noon the Ovillers batteries had been ordered to stand by, and to draw no more ammunition. This meant, to readers of portents and signs, a move.

By noon, also, the Ovillers batteries were shelled. The whole world, from Hébuterne to Verdun no doubt, was shelled. But more particularly was Ovillers shelled.

Browne duly moved his kitchen furnishings from near the top of the dug-out shaft to the bottom; and the topmost timbers were duly split by a 5·9 and the entrance loosely filled in with rubble. The rubble was duly scraped away down the stairs, for light and air and an emergency exit, if emergency should arise. The emergency, however, did not arise.

Gun-pits were hit; buffers were split open; guns destroyed. But not the pits or buffers or guns of D Battery.

Gunners were killed, but not D battery gunners. When the D battery latrine was invaded by a high-velocity shell that must have travelled a dozen miles or more on a low, snarling trajectory, the latrine was innocent of gunners. Linesmen were hit in their crawlings to and fro to tie knots in the frail threads that held batteries to brigades—but not a D Battery linesman. The gun-pit wherein the charges caught fire and blazed and crackled with a column of sinister green and white smoke that brought shrapnel upon the men scurrying, with futile buckets of water, was the gun-pit of a "D" (howitzer) Battery; but not of Richards's "D" Battery.

Neither candles nor acetylene lanterns would remain alight for long that day. One thump or another, somewhere near or far away, would jerk them out.

It was impossible for Cartwright, the complete idleness and leisure notwithstanding, to write his letter to Dorothy. He sat on the steps, however, as near the bottom as the light would allow, and wrote half a dozen pages to Henderson.

Whitelaw came down from time to time, haggard and

Q

pale ; for pallor was now the normal tint of man, as thirst was his normal appetite.

And at five o'clock or thereabouts—when Browne was taking away the tea-things by the light of a candle stuck on the corner of his tray—it was all over. The air was suddenly a vacuum and the earth was still.

Strolling at ease on top and standing at gaze, it was impossible to see that the face of Ovillers was appreciably changed. There was the charred roof-tree of the neighbouring D battery pit, but that was all. Heads and shoulders occasionally bobbed along in the connected holes and hollows of trenches, the heads and shoulders of men slightly bent in the carrying of men less smiled upon by fortune than themselves.

Sergeant Wright was shaving.

Beale was digging a new latrine.

Cartwright, uneasy under the pressure on his mind, went below where Whitelaw was franking the day's mail, to write that letter to Dorothy.

He wrote hurriedly and lucidly and withal a little tersely ; for there was now a crisp and clear conviction in his mind that he could proudly share with her. Facts and local colour did not obtrude themselves either upon his mind or upon the paper. There was an exhilaration in the stillness and the steady flame of the lamp that made of Cartwright's conviction a robust and genial urgency ; a desire for communication—and communication, moreover, with Dorothy.

The words came easily, leaving facts altogether aside ; ignoring place, weaving only the sense of his discovery that the end was near, and that the end was, of course, victory. The movements of his mind were simple and obvious enough. He had spent a day in circumstances that had been, in a word, unthinkable. That such circumstances should continue for any length of time was also, as a mere corollary, unthinkable. They must therefore end. Since anything but victory was unthinkable—for victory alone was the object of the War— victory must be the inevitable end.

This happy conclusion was the mere beginning of the

letter—quite the best and most satisfying letter he had written to her yet.

He licked the envelope and signed it and tossed it on the table before Whitelaw. He saw that Whitelaw was looking at him, smiling.

" I'd sooner have been doing my job for the last half-hour," he said, indicating the pile of letters he had franked, " than yours."

This struck a little cold on Cartwright's glowing sense of achievement. Whitelaw looked at his watch and poured out two whiskies. " That's one of the ghastliest things that's struck me about women," he said. " The women one marries, I mean. If a man is a decent, polite fellow, marriage is an undertaking to keep on talking for the rest of his life. It must be hell."

" How do you know ? " asked Cartwright. " I thought you were a bachelor ? "

" You don't have to keep cows," said Whitelaw cryptically, " in order to drink milk. These boys have got about the only way of doing the thing, though ; ' Darling girl,' or ' Dear old Dad ' . . . ' the fags were very welcome. We are now going through it good and proper ' . . . and then a touch of ' the King and Country ' stuff and ' dear old Blighty.' . . . ' Roll on my leave when we'll all be together again. We won't half have something to say ' —and then most of the paper smeared over with crosses. But it must be a tougher proposition for fellows like you."

" It isn't always easy," Cartwright admitted. He did not go on to say that this particular letter had been easy enough, because it struck him quite suddenly that it had absolutely conformed in essentials to the skeleton which Whitelaw had extracted from the pile in front of him. There was not, it is true, any of the ' king and country ' business in it, no kisses dramatically symbolised in a magnificent array of crosses ; but this was only because he had found words more adequate than crosses.

" What do the men think about to-day's strafe ? " he asked.

" Winning the War," said Whitelaw. " Winning,

hands down. ' We gave him two for every one he sent over.' . . ."

" Well," said Cartwright. " I suppose that's roughly accurate."

" Yes," said Whitelaw. " But I don't think there's much winning been going on to-day. When orders go sticky and stodgy it means, generally, that the wire wasn't cut—or at any rate that we didn't get through it. Let's go and take the air before dinner."

They strolled about on top, as on a lawn ; Cartwright and Reynolds, Whitelaw and Richards.

" I wonder if old Dad thinks we've attained puberty yet," Reynolds said. " I don't want much more than we've had to-day. Do you, Uncle ? "

" Not unless we've got as good a hole to sit in," Cartwright replied.

" Dicky was just saying what a cool cuss you are ! " Reynolds went on. " You try to make out you were weaned on five-nines. And to-day was your first proper peppering."

" I expect I'm one of those so-called insensitive people," Cartwright said thoughtfully. " It didn't seem to be anything to worry about, twenty feet or so underground. I was darned glad not to be on top."

" I suppose you didn't feel the direct hits over the dug-out ? " said Reynolds. " Come and see them. Four of the great brutes."

They went and admired the fine new holes. These differed from the countless other holes in that the material of their sides possessed, by comparison, a freshness which was surprising because it was the same dry, dusty rubbish and tattered garbage as the rest. A pair of thighs and doubled knees stuck out, colourless, from the side of one of them, intact though the explosion had ripped away and annihilated the last stitch of their breeching.

" God ! " said Reynolds quietly, but Cartwright said nothing. In a world that was all prodigy there were neither prodigies nor wonders.

" Jackman can put in half an hour on that with his spade," he said, as they turned back towards the gun-pits.

Reynolds exploded with one of his unaccountable explosions of laughter.

" Damn you, Uncle ! " he said, and stuck his hand under Cartwright's arm. " You're the stuff that the tape-worms are made of. Red tape, I mean. The lads who make the jokes of asking for a return of the number of tins of plum-and-apple jam issued when a battalion is about to attack ; about pants, under, woollen and pants, under, cotton ; about screws, cork, and screws, right-handed, galvanised, long. You're worth a guinea a box to the menagerie, though. And I pledge thee my troth ; so help me, Gawd ! "

Cartwright made no particular response.

What that prodigious world would have meant without the boisterous warmth and idiocy of young Reynolds—the world wherein it was utterly normal and proper for four holes as big as rooms to be suddenly created a few feet overhead ; for naked thighs and knees to project, naked and putrifying, skyward ; for blood and rags and tangled entrails to be carried by men smoking cigarettes, to a doctor ; for an adult man to lose his way for hours within a stone's throw of his destination and to stumble, in his wandering, upon rats corpulent beyond their furtive strength—what these things, starkly alone, would have meant it was impossible to say, or think.

" Seems to me, Rennie, the only way is to take things as they come," he suggested.

" Uncle," said Reynolds very solemnly. " You can't look me in the eye and tell me things like that, you know. Honestly, you can't. For instance, if you refer to the silver-lining . . . "

" Oh, I dare say it sounds a bit like it," said Cartwright, " but what else are you to do ? "

" Let 'em rip," suggested Reynolds. " I refer to bowels. Let 'em turn to water—soda-water if they like. Mine feel like it, soda-water full of snakes and tadpoles and all small things that move—while you sit there trying to look as solemn as a ruddy old owl, thinking of a plan to dye your whiskers green or what-not. Golly, I wish you'd been with me on that Beaumont Hamel outing the other day ! "

Cartwright did not say, " I wish I had."

What he did say with a shrug was: " Well—I expect there's lots more ahead like it."

" What do you make of our old 'Vetus de Monte's' orderly-officer scheme ? "

Reynolds asked the question as though it applied directly to the subject in hand.

" Very sound, I should think," said Cartwright. " It means that things would work smoothly, without any sort of bother."

" It means," said Reynolds, and his tone was suddenly dismal; " it means that one would have to do a hell of a lot—alone."

He paused, looking over the waste that was Ovillers ; at shrapnel bursts, and at the black coils of high explosive that could be picked up anywhere without a turn of the head. " It's all right, I dare say, for old bandits like him, with prairies and cordilleras and wide open spaces and all that sort of thing behind his roving spirit—but give me the right-hand man, or the left-hand man within hail, when my bowels start turning to water and my knee-joints to banana-skins."

This, it seemed to Cartwright, was youth. It was like his David swaggering about the house at Chiswick, waiting for chance to send some one upstairs before him at dark, or preferably with him. It differed from David only in its admission.

" It's a disappointment to me," Reynolds went on. " And it cuts both ways. I would much rather have stayed on top to-day, with 'Vetus' Whitelaw and taken you along, too—if we could be together, holding hands, when it's my turn."

" Yes," said Cartwright, " exposing three valuable officers to the same shell, instead of one."

" Three valuable grandmothers ! " said Reynolds. " That's just some more of your precious red-tape ; but don't you believe it. Three different shells in three different places are just as likely as one, to wipe out three valuable officers. You will see, even as I have seen, two brothers together at the plough of whom one is taken and the other is left. And I know of two other brothers—one at Plug Street and the other at Suvla Bay. Both were taken. It doesn't matter where you are, or how many of you are there. The only important thing is psychology. Bolster yourself up with company. If you're going to get it, you'll get it. That's my theory of survival. What's yours ?

" I don't know, Rennie," Cartwright admitted. " I haven't got one yet."

Reynolds had fallen, fairly deeply, into the ways of youth. " Let's strike a bargain then, Nunks," he said ; and there was a sudden shyness—" since it's all the same to you. You hold my hand when you can—and I'll hold yours."

" Of course," said Cartwright. " That's what I'm here for, I suppose. That's what we're all here for."

" I know. But a bit more than that." What he was striving for, of course, was to bring romance into machinery, to import something from cricket-fields or summer holidays by the sea into the bleak enigma that was to stretch for them through the winter from the Ancre to the Pozieres ridge.

Cartwright smiled.

" Right you are, laddie," he said. In using the diminutive for endearments' sake he followed, no doubt, the curious impulse that prompted the usage of ' chum ' and ' matey,' and ' son,' and ' old pal ' among those million ruffians. " I'll hold your hand."

MEDAL WITHOUT BAR   CHAPTER XLVIII

THE Thiepval garrison was now given a short but well-earned holiday. Ovillers became, for some days, the dormitory only of battery-commanders who spent their days in scuffling and bickering for battery positions where the ground was overcrowded and only a single amenity remained—the joint curse and blessing of the Albert-Bapaume road.

Shells of every size and velocity sailed and burst down its length from Pozieres to La Boisselle; yet on it alone could firm foothold be found, and wheel-hold under the grey slime.

Richards and Reynolds and Cartwright went off across country to meet the Colonel at the La Boisselle crater, taking four N.C.O.s.

They admired the crater, saluted the Colonel and moved after him eastwards.

At the extreme end of Sausage Valley he made a passing gesture and said: " This'll do for you, Richards. You know the line—up there." Another gesture indicated the black and flattened little crag on the sky-line that was smoke by day and stabs of fire by night to mark the site of Pozieres Windmill.

" Yes, Sir," said Richards.

" And don't block up any trenches," said the Colonel. " Trenches have to be left open—for movement. In case."

" Very good, Sir," said Richards.

The colonel moved on with the other battery commanders and Richards stood where he was with his prospectors, surveying their claim. A piece of trench survived where the road from La Boisselle to Contalmaison had disappeared. Two faces appeared over the rounded parapet of this, as the faces of neighbours appear at a window during any moving-in. One, it soon became clear, belonged to a Canadian Sapper Captain and the other to his batman. He was able to tell them that the only opened and habitable dug-out—the only dug-out at all, so far as he knew—in the immediate vicinity was the one occupied by his office, some of his stores and himself. They went down and had a drink with him.

He agreed that the order for keeping the trenches unobstructed by building-operations was sheer nonsense since they were, of all places, the most impassable by reason of mud and the most freely shelled by reason of their existence on maps.

But part of his own varied duties was to see the order obeyed by new-comers.

And then he slightly lowered his voice and spoke of the coming push. The War, he told them, had been till then a skirmish and mere child's play. But the coming push —he stopped, utterly defeated in his search for words. At last words came to him. It was to be, this next push, no less than a son-of-a-bitch of a push.

Going upstairs with them he promised them all the material they required—provided they told no man whence it came.

It was their common memories of the Salient, the mutual acquaintanceship of Majors MacDonald and McKie of the Canadian Artillery that moved him to this princely gesture to Richards and Reynolds. Finally he told Richards that when he himself should be moved up or down or east or west, they should have his dug-out.

In the meantime they were able to count on perhaps half an acre of open ground for the accommodation of their guns, twelve hundred rounds of ammunition, thirty men, officers, cook-houses and latrines. They wanted, too, a place for the water-cart and they needed a road. They were eight hundred yards from the solid metalling of the main highway, and the lesser road (to Contalmaison) was gone, or indeterminate.

The bombardier carrying the bundle of broken-up boxes and the bill-hook followed Richards about, sticking pegs in the ground to indicate the gun-pits and other subsection holdings.

Three N.C.O.s were left behind as a guard—for it was necessary to 'guard' even the frugal possession of twenty feet of mud in those congested times, and Richards set off with his subalterns in search of a road. He found a crazy way, fairly firm as yet, leaving the main road by the single stump that survived from a mile-long avenue.

It wound and doubled between sodden holes, and tacked between mounds of earth and mounds of wire and twisted stakes. The metals of a light railway tumbled into the puddle of a trench and twisted out again.

" Good egg," said Richards, looking upon the wet gleam of the metal. " We can do with a bit of that."

They crossed the road again, plodding north-westward in the solitary roadlessness of the short cut to Ovillers and the battery.

Reynolds and Cartwright came back to the new position with a party, not of soldiers but of workmen.   They carried their tools, a thousand sandbags, their dinner and their tea.

They dug till dark ; till dusk they were rained upon and shelled—not deliberately and personally shelled, but casually and generally, together with the road some half a mile away to their left and the rest of Sausage Valley behind them.

Interruptions in the silhouette-frieze of the road, eddies in the slow stream indicated casualties or traffic-blocks.

Heads that were at first turned in the direction of bursts, faces that were fretted into sardonic grimaces remained, by evening, steadily bowed over their work of digging, palely placid.

Cartwright and Reynolds worked together at the " Mess," an eight-foot square behind the line of gun-pits. After tea, which they drank with the Canadian Sapper, a full spade of the soft clay was more than either of them could comfortably lift into the sandbag.

By dusk they had lowered the square knee-deep whilst the sandbags were built along its edge into a parapet as high as their waists.

A glance at the rest of the valley was enough to show that any efforts at concealment would be sheer pedantry ; for the whole area was mottled with the low breastworks of sandbags that distinguished artillery architecture of that place and period.

They took up their spades and called the men together and agreed in thanking God that the rain was stopping ; for therein lay their only hope that the shallow excavations would not be ponds next morning.

The mile of going back to the battery occupied them for forty minutes at a meditative pace.

Whitelaw had returned, half an hour before them, from a bickering over an indent with the Sapper at the dump in Usna Valley, and he and Richards were dining.   Whitelaw grunted at the sight of them. " Fightin' men at last, instead of seedling Majors and Colonels."

" Do take your hats and coats off," said Richards. " And stay a while."

" If they aren't washed right into us," mumbled Reynolds. With his usual magnificent clumsiness he would have swung his sopping coat towards the diners and the table if Whitelaw hadn't said, " Here ! go and shake yourself outside, or in your kennel ! Don't apologise. I'll carve you both a spot of the giant-killer, and if you take my tip you'll get out of that puddle and into pyjamas before filling yourselves with Browne's rissoles."

Reynolds took a mug from him. " Uncle," he said, " I believe he means well. Cheerio ! "

" He doesn't shake his wet togs into gentlemen's puddings," said Whitelaw.

" Beloved," said Reynolds, handing back his empty mug ; and Whitelaw said, " Ass ! Shove off and change your blasted self so that Crouch can mop up the mess before I want to get down to it. Did you get things ready for the stuff you've got to draw to-morrow ? "

" All ready except the paper on the walls," said Reynolds.

They shouted across the gallery for candles and soap and water as they groped towards their bunks.

Then followed the simple act of getting into pyjamas and soft slippers and a Jaeger dressing-gown. The roof was beginning to leak ; but a ceiling of ground-sheets had been fastened up to it wherever it mattered, and each sheet had recently been emptied—or more technically, according to the purism of Browne, ' milked.'

An evening of cosiness as incredible as the bleakness of the day ended in yawns and a comparison of blisters on palms and an early shuffling off to bed, while Whitelaw —duly emphasising the fact that Reynolds was orderly-officer and should have been the one to go—went up to see that the world went well with the battery.

CARTWRIGHT went next morning, with a copy of the indent, to meet two G.S. wagons at the engineers' dump, while Reynolds and Whitelaw went back to the new position with the working party. Two journeys with the two wagons launched on that turgid stream of upward traffic furnished the position with its necessities ; sandbags, pit-props, corrugated iron, and expanded metal for reveting.   For the nicer things they depended upon the Canadian.

This good neighbour proved even better than his word.   Steel elephants of the smallest type were tossed from a Canadian lorry to the roadside by the tree-stump at nightfall.   These made shelters for cartridges and for a few of the eclectic sleepers like Browne and Sergeant Wright.   Two or three bundles of quartering were flung, amiably, into the mud for the manufacture of furniture ; and three rolls of wire netting in case the battery should be inspired to acts of camouflage.

He reached the extremest limit of hospitality in sparing four magnificent timbers from the end of his dug-out, to be upholstered with sandbags, as cushions for the trails of Richards's four guns.

One of the G.S. wagon-drivers guided Meston to the position and the dumping of ammunition began.

Four bunks were erected in the eight-feet-deep, splinter-proof hovel whereof Cartwright and Reynolds had cut, with their own fair hands, the first sods.   (Sods that *were* sods, as Reynolds claimed, examining his blisters.) The six steps were slime ; but boards and pegs and an abundance of wire netting maintained some shape for them.   The floor was slime ; but an unlimited supply of sandbags from the good Canadian gave some substance to it and an occasionally dry surface.   Four long pegs of quartering were driven into it and adjusted to take a table top.

It was all performed, as those works were always performed—somehow.

And the battery moved in.

There were no casualties.

From dawn each day till dark the same drab frieze marked the meeting of the leaden sky with the muffled roads; and from dark till dawn the frieze became a monotone of sounds—voices and the clatter of engines geared down to the pace of laden men, the chink of harness and whinny of horses and mules—beasts as weary as the men, but unsuspicious of the designs of man.

Neither the darkening of night nor the shadowless light of day gave let or respite in the remote torment of bombardment. The tattered earth heaved up in shards and slabs and columns—wounds insignificant where there was nought to meet the eye but wounds.

And still in the battery there were no casualties.

Neither horse nor man was hit.

Driver Wilkins (the rat-killer) came back to the Mess one night, an hour and a half after delivering the rations and leaving the battery with his empty cart. The face, that is, was the round, red face of Wilkins; the rest was mud—fresh, moist mud on mud that was lighter in colour, and dry. His request was that an officer should go with him to shoot his horse.

Richards and Cartwright went with him to the road (Whitelaw had turned in and Reynolds was dining out with B Battery).

Wilkins and his cart, it appeared, had been jostled by the traffic from the fairway of the road into a master-piece of some working party of resting (and restive) Hussars from Bouzincourt. It was a ' sump '—a device much in vogue at the time—an eight-foot cube cut out of the roadside and duly filled up again to road level by the sweeping and shovelling of mud by successive fatigues. Into this the stocky old roan had slowly subsided while Wilkins hacked the cook's cart free and out of it again.

No efforts of his, combined with those of the dozen interested volunteers he had collected from the more leisurely of the passers-by, could move the horse. It had fought, said Wilkins, like a lion; for Wilkins alone, of all the battery, believed anything but evil of his old roan.

He was right, however, in his estimate of its present condition ; right, too (as Richards and Cartwright agreed after two or three soundings taken in the disk of torchlight with a shovel offered by a road party subaltern), in his surrender. . . .

But they had forgotten the ramifications of the power wielded by the Canadian : a lorry came trundling down from Pozieres—the same lorry (now carrying only dozing men) that an hour before had tossed out two rolls of felt and a bag of nails by the tree stump whereon Browne had sat, by appointment, waiting.

It pulled up, with inches to spare, at the side of the sump. Few words were spoken, or none, beyond something about ' death or glory ' from the Sergeant at the wheel and then something about a chain. In the light of volunteer torches Wilkins wrapped his coat, like a muffler, about the throat of his spent roan and around it fixed the chain with a great knot. Richards found a steel eye at the tail of the lorry for the hook at the other end of the chain.

" Hold tight, son ! " said Wilkins to his roan as the lorry took the strain. It may be that that particular sergeant was the world's greatest artist in the matter of letting in a clutch ; it may be that there are no two forces on earth whose antagonism can tear a horse's head asunder from its body.

The fact remains that the old roan came fantastically out of that mud and was hauled in the clinging shackles of mud like a pig in a sack, for a dozen feet till onlookers' shouts informed the Sergeant that his work was done.

He saw to it that his chain was duly shipped, and went his way.

Volunteers fell to work upon the roan. The mud was scraped and flung from his trembling flanks and heaving, colossally distended belly. Shovels and the lids of mess-tins ; knives (table), pulled out of putties covering legs or out of sandbags covering putties ; the smooth edges of helmets were set to shaving and scraping the sprawling champion. This was the unskilled contribution of casual enthusiasts. The expert Wilkins worked, sombrely as in the performance of a priestly rite, at the ears that some said were the bastard ears of a mule. Prodigious deflations rewarded the impressed workers. When the roan tottered to his feet they stood aside as men well satisfied. They faded away into the night along the ways they had been going—some ' up,' some ' down.'

" We'll get the cart pulled in to the battery, Wilkins," said Richards ; since no one but a fool would have left a perfectly good mess-cart within sight of passers-by.

" You can walk back. Take it easy, there'll probably be a touch of colic on the way."

He and Cartwright dragged the cart across the road and some distance along their track by the tree-stump, for Sergeant Wright to send some men for it.

They wiped their hands first on some wet bags lying in the light by the dug-out entrance and again on the door-mat—the fresh and drier bags at the bottom of the steps. They had a drink while telling Whitelaw that the business had been getting Wilkins's old roan out of a sump-hole, and turned in. This meant putting off tunics and breeches and boots and socks and collars. For there was no great attractiveness about pyjamas now ; they were as lousy as pants and undershirts after the Ovillers dug-out.

Trenches were no more the hotel corridors of the Arras sector. They were wide, sprawling and shallow gullies where men crouched and stooped and slowly scrambled to destinations behind ironically misnamed " runners."

There was good talk of demoralisation and ' last-legs ' on the other side of the rusted, barbed tangle two hundred yards away ; of apathy and despair. But the simpler tests contributed no support to this talk : a hat slowly raised on the haft of a shovel or carelessly lifted on a head showed that a keen eye was somewhere unwinking and alert behind a meticulously adjusted sight.

Wire-cutting was observed by cringing with a periscope ; and even periscopes sometimes invited the skill of machine-gunners and riflemen. It was wiser to besmirch the slender gleam of the No. 14 with mud, to drape its clean line with a rag of sandbag, to shade the glint of its bright little eye in the hollow of an empty and battered tin.

It remained an open question whether, having got to the front line for a day's wire-cutting, it was more desirable to spend the night there than to be relieved and go back to the battery. But there seemed to be some vague convention ruling the matter, so that Whitelaw and Reynolds and Cartwright did, in fact, follow each other daily—accompanied, or visited by Richards. The enemy wire was cut and scattered ; and by night under the moan and snarl of artillery and the rattle and whine of Lewis guns, it was made solidly good again.

Whitelaw told Cartwright one night that the part of the trench where their telephone-line ended had been flattened out, all the wire in front of it cleared away and the parapet shot to glory. But by next morning he found all in order again—the breast-deep trench, a parapet no more dishevelled there than elsewhere, a new, sound belt of wire. Only the last fifty yards of telephone cable was still missing, and there was one man remaining in the near-by dug-out with a shattered pelvis whom it had been impossible, as yet, to get away.

Cartwright took a chance in issuing, for the first time, one of his morphia tablets and went up again to his wire-cutting.

And so the fifteenth of September approached, and arrived with its immediate local objective the redoubt behind the belt of wire at which the batteries had been working—the ' Wonder-Work.'

Reynolds, according to the orderly-officers' roster, was to go with the Infantry. He left the battery after lunch on the 14th and with him went the signalling Corporal and two telephonists. (The signallers strode proudly, their loins girt with a revolver apiece in the manner of officers.)

THREE days later Cartwright and fresh signallers relieved him in the new front line.

Reynolds was an aged man again, hollow-eyed, scrappily bearded, with opaque, grey skin taut over his cheekbones and loose about his jowls.

But Cartwright likewise was old. For two hours or three he had been searching for the particular company dug-out in the Wonder-Work where Reynolds was to meet him.

Men came and went, and plied their various crafts in that churn full of wrack and destruction, since details of personal stillness or movement in that impartial chaos of flying clods and metal could have no bearing on the course of destiny.

Some were dragging boxes of grenades or small-arms ammunition. Some moved with a sheaf of picks or shovels ; some with bundles of sandbags ; some blundered along with corpses on stretchers and some, with steps more carefully picked, carried listless wounded. One slunk by with a blue enamelled pot of freshly made tea.

None seemed to know about the particular dug-out that was Cartwright's destination—fully styled in the message from Reynolds as B Company's No. 3. Nor did they care. It seemed like an impertinence to try to startle them into talk with questions shouted into their pallid, grimy ears. They winced when the question penetrated to them, but the sustaining of an effort so meagre as that required for mere attention was now too much for them. They usually shook their heads, or said, " No. We're " A," or " C," or mumbled a platoon number and fell again to their trudging and weary hauling.

Officers were more responsive. " To the left," one said, squatting tight against the side while he carefully split a biscuit with a silver handled penknife. Another said " Straight on, but there's no hurry. Their bit is getting it at the moment, good and proper."

" Worse than this ? " asked Cartwright.

" They've got some dirty gaps. I'd get back a bit and move along in the support for a while if I were you. It may blow over. You'll see the Doc's dug-out there. No mistaking it. You can shoot forward again up the communication-trench just beyond. Is it true the Canadians have got Courcelette ? "

" Yes rather," said Cartwright.

" Well," said the other, " I wish they had this place too."

Cartwright took the communication-trench to the support. In the slime at its bottom where the duck-boards had been removed for the higher purpose of reveting, he trod on a back. Bubbles gurgled up from the nostrils thrust deep in the filth.

He found the dug-out at last, the broad, wooden steps modelled shapeless with the scrapings from successive boots. The Company Commander would have been a shame among the dustmen of any slum.

Reynolds said, " Good Lord, Uncle. You priceless, bloody old fool ! Why didn't you wait somewhere till things got a bit easier ? "

The Infantryman shoved a box towards him, and he sat down. " Because," he said, " I could get no under-taking that they weren't going to get tighter."

Reynolds scratched his head and his chest, and yawned.

" I'll get down to it for an hour or so and have another sleep," he said, " before starting."

" I wouldn't, old son," said the infantryman. " Two hours would do you no good at all and if you wait much longer than that you'll get mucked up in the relief. It's dirty enough, and hard enough going without a brand new battalion sculling around, and taking over. I don't believe it's going to get much lighter, either. I agree with your ' Uncle ' bird here. It'll stay dirty outside—and even dirtier—till somebody does something useful somewhere else, or until those fellows over the way get their old counter-attack out of their system. Take my tip and beat it."

" Oh, well—" said Reynolds, and he slowly stood up.
" I'll just show Uncle the beauty-spots, then."

" Don't worry," said the other. " I'll do it presently.
You toddle along." He turned to Cartwright. " Sorry
I can't offer you anything but tea—presently. We
expected to be relieved last night and finished up what we
had—what with one thing and another. It wasn't much
of a night."

" That's good," said Cartwright, and he unslung his
water-bottle and put it proudly on the table. " An old-
timer in the battery thought it might be acceptable if I
tipped a Johnnie Walker into this."

" Good old Vetus de Monte ! " said Reynolds and uncorked the bottle. " Can you spare me one, skipper,
before I git ? " He asked this very seriously, as a child
asks for another chocolate.

" Young idiot ! " said the Captain. " It's yours,
isn't it ? Or your battery's—bless it ! We'll join you.
Cheerio ! "

" Nobody hurt at home ? " Reynolds asked, lighting a
cigarette at the candle.

" No," said Cartwright. " Nobody. They say B
Battery got rather chewed up behind us, and one of C's
teams last night. I'd cross the road up by Pozieres
going back, if I were you, and get well off it into the
valley. It's been pretty thick for the last two days ; off
and on."

" Well," said Reynolds, " so long." He had buckled
on his belt with his revolver and glasses. " Still raining
like hell, I suppose ? " He distastefully eyed the extra
pounds of weight represented by his Burberry hanging
on a nail.

" So-so," said Cartwright. " Sort of drizzle. Off and
on."

" You and your blasted ' off and on ' ! " Reynolds
exclaimed. " You've reduced the English language to
nineteen words—counting ' so-so ' and ' off-and-on ' as
two ! Where are your signallers ? "

" Down with Hine, taking over the wire."

Cartwright went with him to the top of the shaft, where

Reynolds suddenly turned to him and said, " Uncle, old thing, do something for me. I'd do the same for you like a shot."

" Well ? " said Cartwright, wondering what such solemnity could mean.

" This blasted coat," said Reynolds, unbuttoning the Burberry he had just put on. " Perhaps you won't be as fagged out when old Vetus comes up to relieve. If you are, you can leave it behind for the poor of the parish. I couldn't move a dozen yards in it, and it isn't raining much. Will you take charge of it for me ? "

" You ass," said Cartwright. " Give it here."

Unshaved and haggard images of Hine and his two men came up and grinned, each with a handsome spiked helmet carried with much the same self-consciousness wherewith flowers and new-laid eggs are carried away by townsfolk from a relation's house in the country.

" Well, so long," said Reynolds. " Come on, you chaps. Gird up your loins. Good luck, Uncle."

" Good luck, Rennie."

" Good luck, Mr. Cartwright," said the helmet-carriers.

They lurched off with their souvenirs and the benison.

" Good luck ! "

Cartwright went down again to where snarls and bangs were only a thudding and a murmuring tremor.

" I hope that lusty youth of yours gets it," the Company Commander remarked, before explaining a few things on the map to Cartwright. " The old man is putting him in, hot and strong for the M.C. He and his corporal just skipped around all day and the best part of three nights, as good as the man from Cook's. I suppose you gunner-fellows have more time to think of these things—but those two seemed to know the way to everywhere as soon as we got here. The Corporal guided our carrying-parties up from the support and young Reynolds sculled around with the old man, taking messages and keeping him off the grass. You see, we'd got pretty short of officers by yesterday morning. I've got exactly one in addition to myself ; if that last strafe you came through didn't find him, too, somewhere."

He spread out his map on the table before Cartwright and got to business.

" By the way," he said, when the map was folded up again, " the gent in that bunk there was a Captain ' Von ' something or other. Rather a distinguished-looking sort of cove with ' Old Heidelberg ' carved across his mug. The sort of thing our Intelligence birds sometimes like to pass on. We've reported it and are going to leave him for the next lot to make up their minds about. He'll be O.K. for a day or two in this weather. We'll go up and have a look round before it's quite dark—while this lull is in progress."

Cartwright and a signaller followed him about the trench, peering with him into the smouldering squalor and glancing down from it to the grubby map held against the sandbags.

" That bit's *here*," was the kind of information imparted to Cartwright, with a nod from the Infantryman over the parapet and a thrust of his muddy pipe-stem on the map. Every yard of hummocked ground and wire against the dull and darkening sky looked like every other to Cartwright, but he said " Yes " and " I see " before they moved along to scramble up on the fire-step and glance over the top at another.

The machine-guns were shown to him, and Lewis guns smuggled forward along shallow saps. " They're only for an honest-to-God counter-attack," the Infantryman explained. " Only the Company Commander's orders can loose them off. Your guns get two communication-trenches in quite decent enfilade ; I showed them to you on the map downstairs. But the great thing is to lie doggo as long as there isn't real trouble."

A plump, ancient youth was sitting at the table in the dug-out when they got back. The Captain called him ' Charlie ' or ' Jimmy ' and indicated Cartwright as the relieving gunner. " I know," said the subaltern. " I met the other merchant toddling down. He told me there was a certain gift. Thanks—I've had a small one."

" We'll grub now and you can turn in for a bit," the Captain said. " It's no use hanging about again for the relief. It may be like last night over again."

" That's where my news comes in," said Charlie or Jimmy. " They're coming all right. A runner turned up a couple of hours ago and I've sent back a couple of guides, to bring them along the top if he strafes the trenches again. I've been round the stores and sent down a chit. They ought to bring some bags and stakes and a bit of wire. I don't believe the counter-attack is coming, after all."

He expressed the view with the open-mindedness of complete apathy.

" Oh ! " said the other, and shouted through a suspended ground-sheet to the effect that he was ready to dine.

" No," said Charlie, " I believe he's had enough for the moment. There have been goings-on over Mouquet Farm way much worse than this ; and as for Courcelette . . ."

Beyond that they knew nothing ; and they cared nothing.

The relief was made at about ten o'clock without undue trouble of any sort. Reynolds spoke to Cartwright from the battery, asking if any change had been made in the S O S lines for the night, and till eleven o'clock he listened to the new-comers' views about the tramps and worthless vagabonds who had captured trenches and dug-outs (and occupied them for eighty or ninety hours in a barrage) and handed them over in a condition that defied human vocabulary. . . .

They went out to attend to those small things that had not before struck Cartwright at all forcibly as specific responsibilities in the minds of individual men, as work actually performed by the hands of some particular man detailed for it. He had spent days in observing wire being shot away, assuming without any great movement of thought that men had put it there ; wire had always been just a feature.

He now saw men engaged in producing this feature. They chaffered first, and haggled with a Corporal over quantities, collected their bargains together on the fire-step, put them in sandbags, tied them together with string, or shouldered them. Then they crawled, still grumbling, over the parapet into the whine of bullets and periodic snarl of shells. There, he supposed, they squatted or crouched at twisting knots of some kind at ends of barbed wire that was brutal enough stuff to negotiate with dry tools and gloved hands in broad day. They worked their corkscrews into the soft earth, drove in the stakes with the great mallet—the most treasured article of the Corporal's wares—its head swaddled and muffled in bags.

" You'd think, Sir," said the Corporal, who got up on the fire-step beside him, " you'd think those blighters *et* wire. *Et* it ! 'Ere's another of 'em coming back. 'E wants another roll or I'm a Dutchman. That'll make seven 'undred yards—to repair seventy yards. What do they *do* with it ? "

" Well," said Cartwright, " it's been strafed all day pretty heavily."

" Yes," said the Corporal, " but the more you give 'em, the more they'll want. It's the same with everything. They'd take three socks apiece if they could get 'um. But they don't get 'um."

A figure slunk along the trench to them. " What is it, lad ? " said the Corporal. " There ain't no more bloody wire, if it's more wire you want." There were a dozen spools of it laid out along the low parapet by him.

" No, Corp.," the man said and sat down on the step. " I bin 'it."

" 'ow. J'yer tell thorficer ? "

" Yes. He sent me back."

" You'd best pop down the 'ole, sonnie," the Corporal said ; he could afford to be gentle now. " Nobby's down there ; only Smiffy with the stretcher, and some 'tillery blokes. They'll see to you. I got to watch me stores."

" I'll see to him," said Cartwright. " Come on, boy." He went along to the entrance of the dug-out next to the company Mess. The man presently got up and followed him.

" Blighty? " the Corporal asked, as an afterthought, but the man's teeth, apparently, were shut together too tightly for him to answer.

Cartwright remembers the incident as his first intimacy with a wound—apart from the jocular splinter on the back of Richards's head.   It was, too, his first close-up view of the grin of teeth jammed together and bared by the pull of muscles first wearied into utter slackness and suddenly flogged into contraction.

The man's right hand was a tight knob of mud, his left a smear, wet and almost black in the candle-light. Cartwright sat him down on the box vacated by his telephonist and fell to doing the obvious.   He ripped up the sleeves, first of the tunic and then of the shirt, as far as the shoulder.   The wound was below the elbow. It bled very slowly, in a dark, blurred trickle.   " Good," said Cartwright.   It was interesting, in a quiet way.   One bone of the forearm was broken but, Cartwright thought, one only.   It would want a splint ; a pad and a tight bandage would be enough to stop the dull bleeding. " Nobby " or " Smiffy "—for both the Infantrymen below wore the stretcher-bearer's brassard—tore open a dressing from a sandbag hanging on the wall.   There was no need of the iodine in the little tube that familiarised so many men with the word " ampoule," for with the dressing in the sandbag was a small Perrier bottle with a wooden plug containing the precious tincture in handier form. The side of a biscuit-tin, whereon the signaller off duty was toasting cheese over the brazier, folded up conveniently (after being sizzled cool on the sticky floor of the dug-out), and was duly trodden flat into a shapely splint.

The wound was anointed (bringing an instant's move-ment into the steady grin) and padded ; the forearm bound to the splint and finally slung in the man's magnificent handkerchief.   Cartwright issued the second of his tablets, telling the man to keep it on his tongue ; not to chew or swallow it.   He told him also to be sure and tell the doctor he had had it when he got to the battalion dug-out.   (But the man knew better than that ; this was his second wound.)

Standing idle again on the fire-step of the quiet trench Cartwright realised that precisely this was the kind of spacious and detached leisure wherein he ought to have been writing to Dorothy. He went down to the dug-out and stuck a new candle on the guttering stump of the old one, leaving a couple of orderlies seated asleep in the far corner.

There was nothing, nothing in the world that he could say—either to Dorothy or to any one else. Yet a letter ought to go at the next possible opportunity, for none had gone now for four days and it was wrong that Dorothy should worry. Shooting, eating, sleeping, taking in ammunition, sleeping again, shaving, shooting, trudging to the forward O.P. in the trenches or the rear one on ' the Nab '—it was the simple fact that there had been no time or else no place for writing.

Now there were both time and place, but still nothing to say. Things had happened in those days during the shooting and shaving and trudging, but what was there that could be said of them ? The happenings, taken by themselves, were of no great import or significance. They resolved themselves and crystallised into a single and simple fact.

He had aged.

They had all aged. In crossing over the Albert-Bapaume Road from Ovillers into Sausage Valley, and in the bombardment of the Wonder-Work the battery had crossed the gulf which separates that state which simply falls short of being maturity, from maturity ripe and mellow. Even the horses had aged by that crossing ; mysteriously, allowing duly for the work they were doing, for the fact that their standings were as deep in mud as the unceasing scraped road, and that it was always a question whether it was better for spent animals to go three miles for an extra water or to do without it—allowing, in short, for the passing ills that could be remedied by four days of rest and water and grazing—they were aged.

It was of no great significance in itself that Cartwright had developed a new gesture—flashing his perpendicular five-feet-eleven-inches into the flatness of a mat spread indistinguishably on the landscape.

It was of no significance that his palate was still (and always) that same fungus of elusive, mawkish stench that it became in the grilling heat of Ovillers ; that he had trodden on shoulders to send bubbles reeling through the mud in front of them ; that he had ducked and sneaked for three or four hours that day, pallid as the handsome corpse covered with a ground-sheet in the spare bunk at the end of the dug-out. These things were all as the mere passing of time.

Even to Henderson—if he had had the energy just then to write to him—these were not the things that he would particularly have mentioned.

To Dorothy he wrote the only words that it was possible to write : he was well—never better in his life. But he was busy—*really* busy—with a hundred and one things to see to, now that he was becoming familiar with the workings of a battery, and getting to know the men. It was inevitable (as she would obviously understand) that all the activity in the south with which the papers must be full, should give every one more to do, everywhere. From this masterly touch of evasiveness he moved on to cataloguing a number of alternative guesses as to what she herself was doing, to questions about the servants, about the boys, idiocies about their garden at Chiswick and about his mother's garden at Bromley.

Somehow he filled the whole sheet of paper.

Then he unfastened his collar, loosened his tie, had a drink, spread his coat on the bunk with Reynolds's drier one on top of it, slipped his feet into a couple of sandbags and went to sleep.

W HITELAW came up the next evening, explaining
the peacefulness of the day with the news that
the Quadrilateral, east of Givenchy had at
last been taken.   He had other news too ; B Subsection's
first line team had been stopped by a 4·2 just after
leaving the battery.   The wheel-driver was killed,
Bombardier Butler wounded, two of the off-horses and the
riding wheeler had had to be shot.   It was lucky, said
Whitelaw, that the other teams had all gone ; two salvos
had come over, for no reason whatever, from nowhere in
particular, aiming at God knows what.

" Take my tip, Uncle," said Whitelaw, as Cartwright
made movements towards his coat.   " Wait another hour
and then beat it along the top.   The communications are
all bunged up like a builder's yard and there are staff-
birds on the way up—young Reynolds's red-tape-worms.
As likely as not they'd grab you to guide them to the
battlefield.   These new fellows in here are building and
working and patching up as though they expected to spend
the winter here.   But they're not—now that we've got
moving on the right again, and the staff is out for a walk."

Whitelaw alone had not aged during the last four days,
since he had begun them as old as man can be.

.   .   .   .   .   .

His prognostication was followed by a period wherein the
function of Artillery, as laid down in the book, was " to
exhaust the enemy's strength by inflicting constant losses
upon him and to take part in the daily minor engagements
between the covering zones."

Gun-pits were slightly altered, to give a wider traverse to
the right—Zollern Trench, and Hessian and Regina where
" daily minor engagements " were likely to develop into
something of more consequence.

But they did not so develop.   They merely contributed
dirtily-bandaged " walkers " to the frieze on the sky-line

of the road; they contributed ambulances that were filled at the Pozieres dressing-station, and an occasional little group of prisoners.

The silhouette of the frieze was now a solid mass.

Whatever the next move was to be, if it was to be a move of any kind at all, the first and most dire necessity was roads. The weather was that first memorable deluge when it appeared that men had not, after all, moved so far from the primeval slime but that life was still supportable in oozing holes and upon a diet that contained an invariable, and tastable proportion of mud.

Surviving Canadians out of the line north-west of Courcelette, Cavalrymen leaving only stable pickets behind with their horses, and sappers plodding up the road and down it with their unending burdens of cables and tools and timber.

Ambulances crept up empty and crept back filled—for the month of September, in addition to its twenty-seven thousand unobtrusive dead was working towards its total of seventy-eight thousand wounded—a half of which number, perhaps, passed visibly in the frieze above the battery in slow ambulances or on heavy feet.

Ammunition-wagons came up by day; and they came by night.

Cartwright got a letter off every second day or so, saying that he was fitter than ever—as indeed they all were— and that some days were less busy than others now. This, too, was true—for during the days at the O.P. on the Nab ('Scottie's' was its name by reason of a giant Highlander lying on the crest) there was little to be done when once the panorama had achieved a familiarity quite sterile, and the hole had been expanded and amplified to take a framework of sticks and telephone-wire for a couple of ground-sheets.

A battle developed.

The battery had to provide an officer to go with the assaulting Infantry and Cartwright, it appeared, would be Orderly Officer on the day of zero—the 26th.

At dinner on the night of the 24th Reynolds expounded his view, based on his two recent outings, that Artillery officers should adopt the practice being adopted by the Infantry of discarding the magnificence of an officer's tunic and assuming the modest jacket of a " man "—the " bum-freezer " as issued from store. The idea struck Cartwright as a sound one, though it irked him a little that he should be the first one to set the fashion.

" And don't, for God's sake, be such a fool as to take a revolver," said Whitelaw. " It's not any more use to you than a tin-opener. I bet the only time you've fired a shot with it was to kill that horse up at Ocean Villas. Eh ?— There you are ! You couldn't hit a barrel at thirty yards ; and there was a time that the Bosche didn't like 'em— lead bullets. If you feel you want anything in your hand as time goes on you can pick up a rifle, and it might be more use to you than a revolver—or a camera."

Cartwright could not help wishing that they would suspend discussion of his programme.

He was not, he could have said quite honestly, afraid ; and he was not, obviously, excited. Yet that journey to the Wonder-Work through trenches that had been cleared and cleaned, the sight of Reynolds and the company com- mander and of " Jimmy " or " Charlie," his surviving subordinate, left him no illusions. The arithmetic of the matter left none ; of seven officers, including Reynolds, the company commander and a machine-gunner—three had remained. Whether the other four were all killed or all wounded did not alter the statistics ; the proportion of chance remained three-sevenths.

This was the night that he ought to write his letter. The next night he would be starting early for the line and he wondered if, perhaps, he ought for some vague reason to indicate something in his letter ; and by considering a disguise for him, and discussing the details of his weapon the others seemed to be getting away from the real issue.

Then Meston, from the wagon-line with the ammu- nition-teams, came floundering down the steps into the light, with thunder in his face.

" Richards," he said, " I want to talk to you. Good evening, you fellows."

Whitelaw moved the bottle and a mug towards him.

" It's to Richards," said Meston significantly, " that I want to talk."

" Oh," said Reynolds, " we'd better go out for a little walk then—Ovillers or Courcelette or somewhere."

" No," said Richards quietly, " there's no need for you to go.   Unless it is very private, Meston ? "

" If *you* don't mind," said Meston, and there was a great challenge about him, " I don't."

Richards thought for a moment or two.

Cartwright, too, thought.   There was a good deal in what Reynolds had said at Ovillers about doing things together, keeping in a little crowd instead of being detached and alone—as, for example, a gunner with his telephonists was detached and utterly alone when he was in the front line (or beyond it) with the Infantry.   He hoped Richards now would keep them all together for this business with Meston.

Richards did.   After studying Meston and the storm in his face, and studying also, presumably, his own conscience, he took the chance which Meston had indicated was a formidable one, and said, " *I* don't.   Have that bit of pudding ? "

" No, thanks," said Meston.   He sat down, leaning forward, on the edge of the lower bunk near the door and tossed his hat up on the top one.

" Here," said Cartwright, " sit here."   He pulled his legs out from between the table and the box on which he was sitting, offering the box to Meston.   It struck him as unseemly that a man so charged with impulse of some kind or other should be doubled up in semi-darkness between two bunks.   It was like asking a client to talk from under his desk while he himself sat in the arm-chair.

Meston took the seat, but not the mug which the full circle of Whitelaw's hand, once set in motion, had charged and placed in front of him.

It would be an over-statement to say that Meston was mollified.

" It's about this next show, Richards," he said.   " What about it ? "

Poor Meston !   Everything he said or thought, his

smallest gesture was always the same old rankling challenge.

" Show ? " asked Richards, puzzled.

" Yes," said Meston. " *Show*. This ' do ' day after to-morrow. I ought to be in it."

" Good God ! " said Richards. " Aren't you in it, man ? You've had the only casualties, so far. That looks as though you're *in* it all right."

" Oh ! So it's my fault that a team got knocked out ? That's the idea, is it ? " The back of the head presented to Cartwright against the light was as solid as any receptacle for brains that one could hope to see ; but the words came sputtering shakily.

" Meston," Richards said, " don't be a bloody fool."

" That doesn't tell me what I want to know," said Meston. " What I want to know is, are you going to give me a fair show—or must I take it up to the Colonel ? "

" You can take it to your grandmother," said Richards. " But so far nobody knows what the hell you're trying to get at."

" I don't ask you your reason," said Meston. " Though it's pretty clear you've got one. I'm senior to every one in this battery, except you. A subaltern was wanted for that first show at Beaumont Hamel. The Colonel chose this battery from the four in the Brigade to detail him, and you detailed—Reynolds. I let it pass. Another subaltern was wanted for the Wonder-Work and you detailed—Reynolds. I'm eight months senior to Reynolds and a dozen years older. You're told to detail another now for this Zollern Redoubt business and you detail Cartwright. I've nothing against Cartwright, but he hasn't been commissioned three months and he doesn't know the battery's ears from its elbow."

" Oh ! " said Reynolds, " doesn't he ? Speaking of elbows you ought to hear what the men say about him when it comes to patching up casualties."

" I don't spend my time coffee-housing with the men," said Meston.

" No," said Reynolds, " you spend it——"

" Shut up, Rennie," said Richards. " What do you

suggest, Meston ?   That I should hand over the battery to you ?   Or is it the brigade you want ? "

" No.   I hardly expected you to give me the battery." He had become calm enough now for sarcasm.   " Though even that has been done.   The C battery skipper, Butler, has gone to the wagon-line for a week so that Russell can have a chance at commanding the guns."   The effect produced by this piece of information was not on Richards, but on Whitelaw.

He chuckled.   " Butler has done that ! "   he said. " I'll win my bet, then.   I've laid a fiver, evens, that after the thirty-first of October till the thirtieth of April there will not be more than seven regulars in the line above the rank of full lieutenant and below the rank of brigadier. Colonels without the C.M.G. are excepted, because they've got to hold on somehow till they do get it.   The C.M.G. is as necessary to a regular Colonel as breeches."

" I dare say," snapped Meston.   Then to Richards again : " I'm not asking for the battery."

" We can go on talking, then," said Richards.   " Is it a spell with the guns you want ?   Why couldn't you have said so without heating the back of your collar ? "

" I want you to stop this passing me over," said the other.   " —First young Reynolds ; then Reynolds again. Then a new man, Cartwright.   Next, I suppose, Whitelaw. What do you think the men will begin saying ? "

" I don't know, old thing," said Richards.   " I don't spend my time coffee-housing with the men."   Laughter, however, was not to be restored as easily as that.

" Well, if you agree—" said Meston, and he moved uneasily in the direction of departure.   " That's that."

" That isn't quite that," said Richards.   " Your place in a battery, as second in command, is the wagon-line— and ammunition supply and casualties and rations, and you know it—with your length of service.   It's up to me to vary it, if I see any reason.   If I don't see any reason, and you do, it's up to you to come up any time you like and eat a bit of pudding and have some of Dad's tigers' milk and talk to me about it."

" Yes," said Meston.   " And never get the chance of

having it out with you alone, without getting my leg pulled before the whole Mess, as though I was an outsider."

"Dry up, Meston, for God's sake," said Reynolds. "Don't *behave* like an outsider. We're as happy as a bug in a rug up here till you come swashbuckling in, drinking your bath-water——"

"You seem to have plenty to say when nobody's talking to you, since distinguishing yourself and being recommended for a decoration. Well, if you're always detailed for the job I dare say you'll get it in time."

"If it's the F.O.O. business you're trying to get," said Reynolds, " you can have my turn every time."

"It isn't your turn I want," said Meston. "It's my own, and mine is the next one. That's what I want Richards to see. Unless he'd prefer us to put it up to the Colonel."

"You want to go up to-morrow, instead of Uncle?" Richards asked. "Is that it?"

"Yes," said Meston. "I'm entitled to it."

"Blow your title!" Richards snapped. "Is that your grouse?"

"It isn't a grouse," said Meston. "It's what's due to me."

"Right," said Richards. "Vetus—Dad—Whitelaw will take over the wagon-line from you in the morning. You can come up before dinner, to report to the battalion at midnight."

"Mucking up our roster," said Whitelaw. "Getting us out of our turns——"

"Don't *you* start now," said Richards.

"Not likely!" said Whitelaw. "I'm satisfied as long as I'm told what to do without having to say what I want. Battery-commander's orders are as good as any other kind of chance to me."

Meston had now drunk the whisky-and-water in the mug before him.

"Thanks, Richards," he said.

"Thank him in a couple of days' time," said Reynolds.

Meston put on his hat and lumbered out. "When do

s

you want your horses, Whitelaw ? " he asked from the top of the step.

" I'll walk, thanks," said Whitelaw.   " Or jump something.   We don't want to go adding any of our horses to the happy throng on the road to-morrow.   I'll stroll down after breakfast."

There was silence in the dug-out after Meston had pulled his legs after him into the darkness above the lintel, until there was a final jingle of harness and some man said, " Very good, Sir.   Good night, Sir."

Then Whitelaw said, " So Butler of C. has got as far as the wagon-line.   Our Meston ought to get his battery. . . .   Well, they've started earlier than I expected.   After October you'll see—only subalterns and Generals sticking it out among the regulars—and Colonels without the C.M.G.   Subalterns for promotion, Generals because they're out of the draught."

' The draught ' at the moment was a thudding quite steady but generally far enough away to make a fair certainty of continuous light from the acetylene lamp.

Cartwright could not easily accept contempt for ' regulars.'   Something about Whitelaw's attitude reminded him of the impossible South-African in the O.T.C.

" Our own Colonel," he said, " is only about five hundred yards farther back than we are."

" *Five* yards are sometimes enough to make the difference," Whitelaw explained.   " And, besides, he hasn't got the C.M.G.   You fellows who haven't listened to the drip of the world's worst Major don't realise that a regular Colonel without the C.M.G. isn't properly dressed.   You'll see."

He put on his coat and his hat and went to see to his ' orderly ' jobs.

" You fellows might make a remark or two to him," Richards said, " so that he won't talk outside the battery."

" But you did the only thing possible," said Reynolds. " God knows how you stood Meston's dither.   Prophet Job was an irritable, impatient mink compared with you, Dicky, and you bet old Dad sees it.   Taken all in all he can appraise a man."

"I dare say," said Richards. "It isn't that. It's— oh, well—I wish Butler would shove off home and give his battery to Meston. Never mind ; don't say anything to 'Dad.' I'll speak to him myself." He went off out, taking his heavy heart with him.

Reynolds said, "There's a thriver on love and goodwill for you ! Poor old Dicky. It's that short shooting up at Arras that's unmanned him, where Meston is concerned. It was the second time. Once before at Dickebusch— and Meston has always drawn attention to the faultless- ness of his own arithmetic. But there are more parts to a man than his arithmetic. What says mine uncle ? "

"Yes, Rennie," said Cartwright, his thoughts not quite concentrated on the question. "But you'll have to shove along to the end of the table and shut up for half an hour. I've got to write a letter."

"But you needn't, to-night," said Reynolds. "Not now——"

This was the very thought that had just entered Cartwright's own mind. Reynolds had turned about on his box and was looking directly at him. Cartwright was aware of a sudden eagerness out of proportion to the drift of this casual talk.

"Uncle," Reynolds said, "how I avoided embracing that clown Meston and kissing him publicly, God only knows ! "

"What for ? " asked Cartwright.

"Saving my darling from the lions."

"You ass," said Cartwright. "Besides, what difference does *once* make ? "

"Add once to once and once, once more, to once. The warp and weft of being is thus wove——" Reynolds mused.

"And he who would un-once my spouse—e'en once—

His brow hath earned my most impassioned kiss. . . .

I suppose Scottie's will have to be manned for the show. Dicky would have let me go with you if there had been any one else here—but I expect he'll want to nip up for a bit himself. It'll be possible to see something, I expect, if it's a decent day."

THE visibility on the 26th, as Cartwright noted in the O.P. log at ' Scottie's,' was fair.

In the slowly ebbing minutes before zero the nearer ridge lay twisted and still, scaly and jagged and agape like the back of a mutilated reptile. Behind it was the lighter sky-line where later in the day there would be greenery—downlands and meadows, trees as yet unslaughtered, the whiteness of roads untormented.

Behind it was a rim of ghostly, pallid light ; and above it the pall, without seam or fold, of unmoving cloud.

They stooped in the hole as the sombre air was split above them and the picture smeared and shattered and tossed to chaos—the signallers to light their cigarettes and Cartwright his pipe.

It was too dark, as yet, to see against the wall of the barrage the minute gestures of men at battle two thousand yards away.

When it was light enough it was still impossible to see ; for by then there was another wall—behind those men. Later it was possible to speculate, and to confirm speculations, whether slow and straggling groups were wearing mud and grey or mud and khaki, to distinguish specks that crawled and stopped and crawled again from specks that would crawl no more.

Infinitesimal movements occurred upon the ground's dull surface—clods of earth tossed up by shovels among the greater tossings by shells.

Zollern Redoubt was clearly taken.

At the hour when the thing most normal to man is breakfast a signaller stirred a mess-tin of Quaker oats over a candle-stump muffled in a handkerchief and a torn up sandbag. Cartwright evaded the poisonous smoke of promise from this feast and ate superior sandwiches of bread with sardines, bread with grated cheese and bread with jam ; he sipped cold tea and rum from his water

bottle (since the Thermos had gone to fulfil the greater
need of Meston).

He had little to tell the battery beyond his estimates of
the intensity of the fire and its varying targets—matters
of general interest rather than immediate import.

At about ten o'clock Richards called him to the
telephone. " No. I'm not coming up," he said. " I
can't. I want you to come back. Sharp, Uncle. Quick's
you can. You're wanted."

" Not—not Rennie ? "

Cartwright had asked it before he was aware that the
question had formed itself in his mind.

" No, you fool," said Richards. " We haven't seen a
shell here all morning. Come on back and you'll know."

He left the signallers to disconnect and pack up their
mess-tins and started back to the battery.

They had caught up to within easy distance of him
before his guesses had developed much beyond impatience
with Richards for his childish scrupulousness concerning
talk over an earth-return.

If, for instance, it had been a matter of more
ammunition, why couldn't he have said so ?

Signallers, however, took a larger and saner view of
orders concerning information imparted by telephone.
That grave spokesman created by the machinery of armies,
—the ' unpaid ' ' acting ' wearer of a single stripe (in this
particular case Bombardier Whittle) detached himself
from the other two and joined Cartwright.

" That's a bit of bad luck, Sir, that the Captain didn't
'ave time to tell you," he said.

" Who ? " asked Cartwright, for questions were becoming simpler as time went on.

" Mr. Meston."

Cartwright stopped.

He had thought of Reynolds, and also, after putting
down the instrument and telling Whittle to pack up,
of Whitelaw. He had wondered, too, fantastically and
for the merest flash, if the hurry and agitation of
Richards could have come from any fantastically conveyed news about his, Cartwright's, father, or Dorothy.

He had thought even of John and David. But about Meston crawling about in the débris and racket of the next ridge there had come to him not the vaguest ghost of a thought.

" And Austin," said Whittle. " Fetching 'im back. Sniper got 'em both at the top end of Zollern where there was a bit of a mess-up. Dead as doornails. Mr. Meston in the back of the 'ead, pore old Austin in the back. Andrews 'as pulled 'em back into a dug-out."

" You know a hell of a lot about it, Whittle," said Cartwright, since the only alternative was to say nothing at all.

" Yes, Sir," said Whittle. " It's all quite right. Brigade sent it through first and then Andrews got on to the battery, through Brigade, after he got them in."

They were hurrying on again with the shamble of men in rubber boots comfortably too large for them.

" There's another party told off instead of them," said Whittle. " Us. And another mile of wire."

.   .   .   .   .   .

Four packages of sandwiches, each tied neatly in a bit of ground-sheet, awaited him on the mess-table. With them was an iron-rations bag and a water-bottle.

" I'd of packed them in your haversack," Jackman explained, " only you'd took 'er with you. Browne 'as mixed the sandwiches in each bundle so you needn't mess up the whole lot when you want a feed. The Sergeant said to dish out iron-rations for the party so I took yours. Browne's put tea and rum in my water-bottle, as you'd got yours and Mr. Meston took the Thermos. Mr. Reynolds says you can take his flask with whisky."

In the old days up north a batman had gone forth to battle with his ' bloke ' bearing oddments of kit—shaving-tackle, socks, handkerchiefs, potted meat and a knife, fork and spoon ; but those days were gone. Jackman retired to the company of Browne and Crouch in the cook-house.

Cartwright unpacked his haversack and repacked it with the wares on the table. Reynolds came down. " I just

wanted to tell you about your boots, Nunkie," he said.
Nothing, so far, had been said by any one at the battery
about Meston.

"Those damned gum-boots—" Reynolds went on.
"Wear anything but those. They might keep your
feet dry, but they make them devilish cold. They
hold on to you like the worst kind of dream. Where
movement's everything you cannot move. No. Boots
and putties was my decision last time."

"There'll be plenty of muck and water," said Cartwright.

"I dare say," said Reynolds. "But—please, Uncle.
You can't get a decent ' take-off ' in those sloppy blasted
things. And Crouch is sticking a pip on the shoulder-
strap of Jackman's tunic for you."

"But the going-over part is finished," said Cartwright.

He had already pulled off his rubber waders and was
lacing up his boots.

"Still—coming back mightn't be," said Reynolds.
"And there's to-morrow. And don't be too proud to use
your stomach for travelling over rough places—and don't
make opportunities for heroism, Uncle."

"By God, Rennie !" said Cartwright. "You'll be
telling me to be sure and take an umbrella presently, and
am I sure I've got my ticket ? "

"No. That's all. Here's Crouch with the tunic."
He went off, passing Crouch on the steps.

Richards came down with a map. "Good man !" he
said. "The signallers are ready, with another mile of
D3—in case. Zollern Redoubt is O.K. but Stuff is still
obscure. You'll have to watch your step when you get
to Zollern. Get to the Infantry as soon as you can—the
Company Commander in the advanced post—and tell us
where you are. It's somewhere here—" He laid down
the map and indicated the top of Zollern Redoubt. "R 21,
either c. or a. They may have got into a. by the time you
get there. Instead of a.b.c.d. for the squares, use c.d.e.f.,
and add two to the co-ordinates If it's here—a. 13,22,
say c. 35,44. Got that ? "

"Yes," said Cartwright. "Add two letters to the

square and two figures to each co-ordinate." He filled his tobacco-pouch from the tin in the pocket of his valise.

" Oh—mail's in," said Richards. He began one of his famous searches through the marvellous contents of his pockets and finally produced Dorothy's letter.

Cartwright took it and quickly pocketed it. Reading it just then would have been somehow like letting Dorothy see him in the grim disguise of Jackman's tunic, festooned with a haversack of sandwiches and iron-rations, a canister of tea and rum, and a pair of glasses.

" You can take this map," said Richards. " It's new from Brigade without anything marked on it—in case anything's happened to Meston's—or you may not find him.— Well—might as well shove off, old thing, if you're ready."

" Yes. Rather," said Cartwright.

" We'll relieve you as soon as we know how things are going. Probably to-morrow. Well—so long. We've just got another shoot."

" So long," said Cartwright ; and Richards went up.

Water chlorinated to well above the safety requirements was nothing for a thirst like Cartwright's. He poured out enough whisky to make the chlorine palatable, and had a drink. Then he stuffed Dorothy's letter from his pocket into the pocket of his valise, took up his hat and went up. Jackman came over from the cook-house with Reynolds's silver flask.

" Your revolver, Sir," he said. " She's hung at your bunk. Won't you want it ? "

Whitelaw's comments came readily back to Cartwright's mind—and, besides, what he had seen of Zollern Redoubt that morning from Scottie's made him feel that if Jackman had proposed a six-inch howitzer to be used at short range he might have considered the offer.

He remembered, for the first time, that he ought to be able to handle a grenade.

" No, thanks, Jackman," he said. " Nor my Burberry. I can probably pick up a ground-sheet if I want one."

"All right then, Sir," said Jackman. With his usual aptitude in crises of every kind, he said, "Better luck than Mr. Meston."

Browne, as Cartwright passed the cook-house, insisted on pressing upon him his walking-stick—a selected pick-helve shaved to slenderness, carved to a knob and fitted with a leather thong at the thin end. "She'll give you balance when the going's sugary. Well, good luck, Sir."

Gunners looked up out of pits to say "Good luck, Sir," to him; and "Cheerio, lads," to Whittle and his under-lings, each carrying his reel of cable.

This reflected a sombre mood, the grappling of those men with the tragedy of Meston. At other times Jumbo Whittle could pass no man without pleasantry and badinage. They would have suggested that he should wait for them on the Rhine, should keep his fingers crossed, mind the step up there, send them a picture post card, be sure and keep a bit of flannel next the skin. . . . But in the griefless shadow of Meston's death they were dumb— all except the idiot Jackman.

After himself Meston had dragged the laughing Billy Austin, nought-and-crosser without peer. Towards himself he was now dragging this four, through miles of daylight and barrage which he had had the good luck to tread in darkness and quiet.

Reynolds, as though by a turn in the most casual of saunters, met them by the farthest reserve dump of ammunition. "Hello, Uncle!" he said; "just off?" and he walked a little way beside Cartwright.

"I shouldn't worry about old Meston," he said. "Getting him back, I mean, and all that. The Infantry blokes will see to it. It's their job, you know. Not yours. You'll have plenty else. Well—so long."

"So long, Rennie." Cartwright did not turn to look after him. When he did turn it was because of a call, "Jumbo—'alf a mo!"

It was Browne.

They stopped and waited for him.

"Jumbo—" he panted—"Coo—that's what ration

fags does to a man's wind. . . . Jumbo, keep an eye open for the officers' Thermos. Mr. Meston had it. Andrews may have fetched it in. Good luck, son. Don't forget."

CARTWRIGHT led his party back over the quiet and familiar mile and a half to 'Scottie's.' From the 'Nab' they saw that he had chosen wisely in accepting the reputation of Mouquet Farm and the trodden ways that wound thereby.

"No one will see us," he said, looking up first to the crag of Thiepval, a mile away, the thought for so long the blackest in the minds of men—and then down to the bare seclusion of Nab Road. "We'll chance it. There'll be something like trenches by the time we start finding trouble."

"We'll find the trenches all right, Sir," said Whittle sardonically. "He's marking them for us, I shouldn't wonder."

They got to the chalk-pit unshelled, and from there they could see Mouquet Farm and thank God that it was a quarter of a mile away. There was comfort, too, in being able for the moment to drop into the shelter of the pit, for it was obviously not far to go now before a search for cover must begin.

The rest was a matter of mechanism, of witless gestures in response to stimuli. It was a walk for a couple of hundred yards, then a scramble from one hole to another ; an exhortation to those fools with the little drums of cable to break up, and watch, and follow ; then a hell-for-leather run, a cursing of wire that stuck out of the ground and wagged from broken stakes, a flying leap over one of those fairly ineffectual bundles of barbless stuff that were flung out as a last resource to unwind themselves as they fell ; and a breathless tumble into what had been part of the jumping-off trench of the morning.

The acting unpaid Bombardier arrived, and at his heels

the other two ; and the four wriggled at the bottom of the trench, from the shelter of one side of it to the tottering shelter of the other.

They were at about the middle of a few hundred yards of what was probably the best sheltered (and best-registered and best-flattened) piece of trench on the British front.

It was hidden snugly from Thiepval. It had been dominated for eleven days by Zollern Redoubt. German Artillerymen had observed their enfilade fire upon it throughout those eleven days ; and machine-gunners, through the eleven nights, had kept fresh the work of the Artillerymen. (It was into some of that particular process that Cartwright had stumbled on his way to relieve Reynolds in the Wonder-Work a little to the south.)

As soon as it had become known that zero hour had relieved it of the domination of Zollern, there was concentrated upon it the fury of every available gun to the north of Thiepval. Cartwright's exact mind had been, sometimes, inclined to wonder whether there was quite as much in the word ' enfilade ' as the word was taken to signify.

Now he knew.

The trench was deserted, so far as he could see by looking from a few inches above its bottom, save for himself and the foreshortened figures of his henchmen, and the still bodies thrust out of the footway to the vague fire-step.

He found himself ahead of his men, mumbling, " Come on . . . must get out of this," or similar unheard words.

A board presently said " Up," and pointed an arrow towards the direction in which they, and the shells above them, were travelling.

Around a traverse was a great and marvellous sight—a steady stream crossing the trench-bottom, from right to left, of heads and shoulders, of picks and shovels, shoulder-loads of sandbags, petrol-cans, bundles of corkscrew stakes, grenade-boxes and whatever else was symbolical of men engaged in something beyond the barest survival. It was the miracle trench that had been dug, somehow,

across from the old jumping-off trench, through the old
no-man's-land for three hundred yards, into the southern
end of Zollern Redoubt.

Between the pick-blades on the shoulders of one man
and the petrol-tin of water on the breast of another,
Cartwright tumbled into the stream.

Never before had there been such reason to admire the
work of human craftsmen.   The trench was eight feet
deep, narrow as the shoulders of the broadest man, straight
as a gash in the white chalk, hard and firm and dry below
the discoloured slime near the top.   It towered two and
three feet, twilit and cool, above the slowly moving heads,
gloriously at right-angles to the bulk of the fire ; a respite
from ' enfilade.'

" Pass the word back," Cartwright presently said to
the man behind him, " is Bombardier Whittle there, with
his men ? "   And in due course the word came back,
" Three 'tillery blokes just be'ind, Sir."

A great proud board faced the end of the trench—" Up.
Zollern Redoubt," with an arrow pointing to the left—
where the work of men ended in the work of machinery
and metal.

It was a climb of some feet up a ramp of duckboards
to the level of the normal fire-trench, mutilated to
formless slush and shallow inadequacy.

The immediate difficulty for Cartwright was to stand
still in the stream and wait for the rest of his party.   He
pulled out of the current among some boxes and water-
cans till his three emerged and he scrambled down again
saying, audibly this time, " Come on.   We're there—
nearly."

Even if Stuff Redoubt on the crest to the north was
taken and held, instinct for cover kept men down in the
slum of those trenches.   It was the old switches and
supports that |were drawing most of the fire, for they were
now our front line.   Spent men were still busy reversing
the old German front line, making of it a good support.
Their numerals showed them to be men from Yorkshire
and Lancashire and their movements with a shovel showed
them to be men who could dig on the barest edge of sleep.

They could be jostled and shoved and knocked, with packs
and bundles and the stock or the muzzle of a slung rifle—
they went on digging and devoutly swearing, carving out
a new fire-step, lowering the trench bottom, filling bags,
meticulously tying them at the neck and building up a
parapet.   The old fire-step was given to corpses and the
emergency traffic of runners or loafers going against the
main stream.   The dug-outs were given to the wounded,
and their shafts to men whose only portfolio for the
moment was sleep and the rubbing away of flies from
wrists and eyes and lips.

When a board, inscribed less pretentiously than the
great direction board said " Keep down," the travellers
kept down.   Another board, also a hasty piece of writing,
said " Right Battalion."

But it was the left battalion that Cartwright was
seeking.

Following the commonest of common sense he ignored
the board and kept straight on.   A carrier of petrol-cans
some distance ahead of him was hit by something which
knocked him down, to scramble up to his knees, coughing
thickly and fumbling at his chest.   The Sergeant came
back from a couple of places ahead of him, added the
petrol-cans slung over the man's shoulders to those slung
over his own.   His loads and various pendants—bayonet,
entrenching-tool, rifle, petrol-cans—and the kneeling,
scrambling man's pack, were more than even that
broadened trench could accommodate abreast.   Cartwright
shoved past the burthens that were pausing between him
and the tableaux.   " All right, Sergeant," he said.   " I'm
empty-handed."

" Thankee, sir," said the Sergeant.   " There'll be a
dug-out a bit along."   He slipped the pack from the
man to the other refuse of the old fire-step.   " Up theer,
choom !   Lay holt on thorficer."   He distributed his
four cans evenly on both shoulders and went on.

Cartwright picked up the rifle and tossed Browne's
walking-stick back to Whittle.   With sounds like faint
snoring the man got along at the general pace of the
column's crawl, supported by Cartwright on one hand,

by the trench-side and the occasional back or shoulder of a digger on the other.

At the first dug-out entrance Cartwright beckoned to an inhabitant and released his man. " Good luck," he said, and the man gurgled . `.` . " Luck, Sir. . . . Thanks. . . ."

Cartwright found that he had kept the rifle. Whittle handed the walking-stick back to him. He wiped the blood off from his hand on the mud of the fire-step ; the mud off on his breeches ; and they ambled on.

Diggers were becoming infrequent. There was, too, less feeling of crowdedness, less sense of the sheer, dull mechanism whereby drab loads are conveyed from one place to another. Men stood on roughly excavated bits of fire-step ; not dully stooping with a shovel but alertly crouching with a rifle. There was no immediate shelling.

One of these occupants of an embrasure said to him, " Better watch your step round the next corner. Spread your fellows out a bit." Then, " Well, I'm damned ! If it isn't ' Uncle ' from the old how. battery by Arras ! " He stood down, rubbed his chin and yawned.

" Hello !" said Cartwright. It was the machine-gunner who had given him and Reynolds the proud, forbidden sight of a dozen yards of the back of a German trench from the slit of the grandly styled ' battle position ' in the sector where there were no battles.

" What a treat to knock into the gunners of one's own Division these hard times ! " he went on amiably. " Sort of home-from-home feeling. We'll go down and have one in a minute. It must be nearly tea-time."

The only difference between this young man and the bright dragoman of the Arras trenches was that this one was aged and mellow—aged and grown shabby by the space of two Somme battles and a few ' working party ' duties.

Cartwright looked at his watch. It was three hours since they had left the battery—a distance, he had calculated on the map before starting, of less than two and a half miles.

" Thanks," said he. " But I expect I ought to shove on. To the left battalion."

" You're there," said the other. " This is the left battalion. Some of it. Black has got a company and a few oddments a bit farther up, but we haven't been on speaking terms with him for hours. The old man won't risk any more runners. There's a nasty open bit with a machine-gun on it and a little bitch of a light minnie. Come on down. The old man may want you to shoot it up. I've got it pretty well taped."

They walked along, stooping a little, and halting to suit the conversational stride of the machine-gunner.

" There was a gunner bloke knocked out this morning, I believe," he said. " Sniped in the back of the head."

" I know," said Cartwright. " I've come to relieve him."

" Hard cheese," said the machine-gunner.

The Major in the dug-out studied Cartwright for some moments in answer to his salute. " Give him a drink, Teddy," he said to some one beside him. Then to Cartwright, " Sit down and get your wind. Got a fill of tobacco ? "

" Yes, thank you, Sir," said Cartwright.

The Major smiled. " I rather meant that I haven't. I'll have some with you." He blew down his pipe as Cartwright handed his pouch.

" This is our own artillery, Sir," the machine-gunner enthused. " I wondered if he could have a dip at the minnie and the machine-gun down the road ? "

" Let's have a look."

The Major considered the map and the movements upon it of the machine gunner's thumb, while Cartwright had his drink and filled his pipe and lighted it.

" What's your margin of error ? " he asked Cartwright thoughtfully, after a good deal of mumbled soliloquy and some measurements with a match-stick.

Cartwright joined them by the candle and the map.

" This is where they are." The Major indicated a vague acre or two of ground on the map where Regina

Trench, running towards Stuff Redoubt, cut the fork of two tracks. " Somewhere about here. . . ."

(Cartwright recollected : " For God's sake, Uncle," Richards had said to him, " never take an Infantryman's word for a map-reference. Even if he's a General. . . .")

" Yes, Sir," he said. " I see."

" There are Canadians God knows where along this way, and Black may have some fellows . . . No. They can't be any further along than this. . . ." The argument was entirely with himself and his own exhausted wits.

" What about northwards ? " Cartwright suggested. " If you could guarantee all clear above that road, I dare say we could pick up a target there and then work back gently. If there's anywhere to see from."

" I'll give you a place to see from, all right," the machine-gunner mumbled. " But I don't guarantee you'll go on seeing for long—if it's guarantees you're keen on."

" I've brought a number fourteen," said Cartwright.

" What the hell's a number fourteen ? " the battalion commander asked. " A number nine is about the only numbered thing we know."

" A periscope," said Cartwright. " Shelling seems pretty quiet just about here, so I ought to be able to get a decent look. If you'll give me the limits——"

" Oh, all right," said the Major. " Here." He indicated a point. " This is the block, isn't it, Sammy ? " The machine-gunner agreed ; it was the crossing of the light railway from Thiepval and a traversed trench running back from the northern apex of the Redoubt. " And here—" he moved his match stick slowly to the left, becoming hesitant again, and tired. " Oh, God, Sammy ; we mustn't risk piling anything more on to poor old Black and his lot——"

" He's over to the left, Sir," said the machine-gunner. " Well over. That is all open ground outside the trenches and he couldn't possibly be there. The trenches them—selves are practically open ground, and if the gunners can put the lid on those sods with the minnie, and give 'em a shake-up generally on Black's flank, it'll buck him up no end."

" It won't buck him up if he's got any of his own lot pushed out," said the Major.

" But look, Sir ! He can't have got any one past the cutting," the machine-gunner argued. " He was told that the cutting was his limit ; and no one could miss it. You can see the damned thing sticking out from a mile away. I'll show it to the gunner."

That, Cartwright thought as he stared at the map, was encouraging. If he could pick up the cutting with certainty to verify the infantrymen's information, the rest would be fairly easy.

" Oh, all right," said the Major. " If you can shut those beggars up for a bit it might help our rush over to Black to-night. We might even try to get a runner through while you're doing it. Go ahead."

Cartwright went to find Whittle in the signallers' dug-out next door. The wire, Whittle reported, was down ' ; but he had told Andrews and his mate to patrol it on its way back to the battery.

" Good Lord ! " said Cartwright. " The way we've come ? "

" A bit worse," said Whittle. " That new trench wasn't dug when they kicked-off with Mr. Meston this morning, so the wire goes straight down through Mookay.' But I've given them one of the reels we brought and told them to lay another along near the top of the new trench and to join on to the O.P. line at Scottie's.' Andrews can find the way. If we can't keep that line up the infantry blokes can get one to Brigade somehow and Brigade can plug us through to Battery."

Cartwright approved.

" I've got your Thermos, sir," said Whittle. " The chaps are making a bit of fresh tea and I'll get it filled. Andrews and Gullion have taken back Mr. Meston's letters and watch and things ; and Billy Austin's lot."

" Oh ? " said Cartwright. " Where are they ? Mr. Meston and Austin."

T

" In here," said Whittle. " With a lot more. But the
Infantry officer said they must all be cleared out to-night
as soon as we can get a party."

Cartwright made some sort of vague movement which
prompted Whittle to say, " It's no use, Sir, till the party
does start clearing up. It's a proper jumble. Alley-mans
and all."

" Oh, all right," said Cartwright. " I want the Captain
as soon as you can get through. And you be ready with
one of the others, and the number fourteen, and some wire
to lay out a line for a shoot."

" Very good, Sir," said Whittle.

The Major, the machine-gunner and ' Teddy ' were
sitting over a teapot and mugs when Cartwright rejoined
them. Near the teapot was the absurdity of a plate of
margarined toast. " We lunched pretty early," the
Major explained. " Hence the pyramid."

' Teddy ' poured a mug of tea for Cartwright.

" I say, I'm sorry about that chap of yours this morning," the Major went on. " It was pretty short and
sharp though, I believe." He passed the toast. " There's
no jam, I'm afraid."

" Yes," said Cartwright, shrugging first to deprecate
the apology. " Through the head, I'm told. I hope your
lot haven't done too badly ? "

" No," said the Major; and he took the edge of the table
between his finger and thumb. " We've been pretty
lucky. A company commander so far; and three
subalterns. Of course, we don't know how Black has got
on, with his youngsters. That man of yours, by the
way, who went to bring back the officer, ought not to have
been killed. He was disobeying orders. He'd have been
run in if he hadn't got shot. I don't allow any retrieving
of bodies as an individual enterprise. It isn't good
enough. You might make that clear to your fellows."

" Very good, Sir," said Cartwright. He raised no
question about Andrews who had gone out later and
dragged them both in. He took out his own map
" I'd like these limits again, if you don't mind." He was
a solicitor, sensible to the possible importance of ' onus

in all matters. " The cutting to the left—here— " He marked a little ring around it. " The junction of trench and railway—— "

" No. Better take a hundred yards along the trench," said the Major anxiously. " The junction is actually our block."

Cartwright marked the spot a hundred yards up the trench. " And on the right ? "

" H'm," said the Major. " We can't tell what those Canadians are up to, if they're still there. So you'd better keep to the continuation of the trench from the railway line."

Cartwright drew a line along the side of the railway, and executed the document by writing, " Limits indicated by O.C. Battalion."

MEDAL WITHOUT BAR   CHAPTER LIV

Y OU'LL be able to do your dirty work from the spot where you found me," the machine-gunner said when they had gone out and sent a man down for Whittle. " But you'd better get along to the block first, to see exactly where you are."

A ' block ' in a trench was an experience distinctly new —a clutter of sandbags and wire and stakes, not driven into the ground yet, but tossed over anyhow ; a sniper's plate built up on more bags ; a reserve jumble of wire lying on parapet and parados, ready to be jerked down into the trench ; and men, stripped of every superfluity of kit, like lean cats on a heap where the garbage is partly broken bottles, prowling silent and alert.

" See the lines of the trolley-way ? " the machine-gunner asked.

Cartwright agreed ; and they went back, themselves as horizontal as the trench-bottom for fifty yards of the way.

Before I'd got that block in working order," his guide explained over his shoulder when they had done about thirty yards of the fifty, " this spot was a blighter. And a hundred yards farther along, for the rest of the way to Stuff, it's as open as the palm of your hand. It's along there that your fellow got it."

Cartwright dressed the top of his periscope in a rag and blobs of mud.

The machine-gunner adjusted his eye to the eyepiece and said, " God ! What a tool ! "

There was pathos in this, the awe and wonder of this simple man for an instrument whereby it became un—necessary for him to project his fragile head against the sights of a sniper in order to get a clear and magnified view of a landscape that meant so much to him. " God ! What a tool ! " . . .

Cartwright stuck the peg as firmly as was possible in the mud, and showed him how to traverse the lens. " Just leave it laid where you think your machine-gun is," he said.

Still reverently admiring, the other did so.

Cartwright looked, and to make sure that it had not moved, the other looked again.

They agreed on the point on the map—some three hundred yards from the block—and Cartwright proceeded along mysterious ways where the other could not follow him—with protractor and scale and range-table.

Richards made some difficulty at first on the telephone assuring himself that there could be no mistake or doubt about it, that it was a direct and explicit request from the Infantry, that Cartwright knew where he was and what he was about. . . . " Yes," said Cartwright—though the anxiety of Richards made him doubt it all for a moment—it was all quite clear and proper ; it was in writing on his map ; the machine-gun officer was at his elbow.

But when he had handed back the instrument to Whittle he said, " Cancel target."

To his interested audience—a corporal and a stretcher bearer were now hanging about behind the machine gunner—he said, " I'm damned if I'm going to risk it in the first over. I'll get that cross-road on the crest first—to show you ; and switch."

It meant more research with his protractor and scale and range table.

" All right, Whittle. Fresh target. . . . All guns. . . ."

The guns soon bracketed the cross-roads, and Cartwright switched and shortened, cautiously fumbling his way to the machine-gunner's target. The machine-gunner watched a couple of rounds through the periscope ; the corporal came and looked and then the stretcher-bearer.

Cartwright, seeing that he was establishing the sense of co-operation and confidence between Infantry and Artillery spoken of in the book, saw that his work was good.

" Register," he said to Whittle, with the air of a conjurer whose finale has been achieved, to suitable applause. " Target A." To the machine-gunner he said, " We've got it, for any time you want it now."

" Register. Target A," said Whittle. " Packing up for a minute, chum."

.   .   .   .   .   .

" This is the fellow for us, Sir," the machine-gunner said to the Major, when they were down in the dug-out again. " I'd let him shoot apples off my head at five thousand yards."

The Major said " Good." To Cartwright he said, " There are gunners and gunners, you know."

" This is an *and* gunner," said the other.

" You'd better turn in for a couple of hours, Sammy," said ' Teddy,' the Adjutant. " The Major wants to have a walk round as soon as it's dark."

With the simplicity of a dog going to its kennel, the machine-gunner went to the bare wire-netting of a bunk ; with the same simplicity, and the same dispatch, his clammy Burberry folded under his head, he was immediately asleep.

" Sammy's had a day of it—and a night," said the Adjutant softly. " He spent about four hours bombing up that trench and making that block ; and he's got a gun hidden up in it somewhere, ready to shoot up the slope. You'd better turn in, too, for a bit. It might get noisy later on, and we might want a shoot.   I can't think why it's so damnably quiet now. . . ."

Cartwright left the Adjutant to his meditations, and sat down on the bunk that was a continuation of Sammy's and unpacked his first bundle of sandwiches and ate it and drank some cold tea and rum from the water-bottle.   Tea and toast and margarine had been all very well, but they had not been lunch.

Then, in less than two minutes he had proved that Sammy's feat in the matter of dog-like sleep had been no unique achievement.   For such sleep had, in fact, nothing whatever to do with volition or even compliance on the part of the sleeper.   It came upon him, enveloping like a swoon, numbing the vibrations of warmth and satisfaction at the spectacular success of that first important shoot at the generous approbation of Sammy, and the Battalion Commander's " Good " ; numbing the regret for Meston the always regrettable—indistinguishable now and inextricable among the other littered waste in the far end of the signallers' dug-out. . . .

After a sleep the night began, cosily and pleasantly omened, with Oxo in soup-plates, rashers of bully fried in the good company of a shredded onion and biscuit crumbs, welsh rabbit and tea.

Day began at the moment when men no longer stood upright to the filling of a bag or the shouldering of a burden, but stooped.

Between the beginning of the night and the coming of the day-time was a procession of men with feet enormous and soft and drearily heavy, their shapes distorted with their loads and make-shift panoplies and swaddlings against the chill and the drizzle, illumined to blackness by the light of flares and the glare and blast of detonations.

The battalion commander and the Adjutant were muffled and swaddled, and gone about some business Sammy was gone, casually, to ' look up ' his precious gun in the block, to ' see about making up ' the trench where no man had been able to pass all day, and thence ' to find out how Black was getting on.'

Cartwright's immediate contribution to the night was a

few rounds from time to time on or about their " Target A."

The Major and Adjutant came back in due course and fell to earnest talk. Sammy came back with his orderly at about two in the morning. His gun at the block was O.K. ; Cartwright's shooting had delighted him ; the trench was ' made ' ; he had seen Black, and all that Black wanted was men, ammunition, grenades, sandbags, wire and water. . . .

Fire from the direction of Regina Trench had tormented Black's garrison all day and there had been some bombing.

" You had better guide the company over, Sammy. It's standing-to in the support."

" Yes, Sir."

(Sammy was duly decorated for that evening's work. In January he was killed.)

" The gunner had better go with you."

" Yes, Sir," said Cartwright.

He proceeded to strike his first bargain of the kind whereby life was made easier for Artillerymen. " I could lay out a line for you as we go along," he said to the Adjutant, " if your signallers would give us the cable. A half-mile drum should do it."

It was a fair enough offer ; guile lay only in the fact that Cartwright particularly wanted to lay two lines, to save patrolling : and his own cable, since so much had been given to Andrews in the afternoon, would probably be insufficient for even one.

The Infantryman was innocent according to the standards of Artillerymen, or else had other and greater matters on his mind (though it was difficult for an Artilleryman to imagine any matter of graver import than a reel of telephone cable). He willingly agreed ; and Cartwright added a cubit to his stature in the eyes of his three braves when he took from the Infantry signaller and handed to them a virgin reel of D3.

" We'll peg the lines up to the sides," he said to Whittle. ' Or they'll get tripped over and kicked about, and cut and chucked out of the way." Whittle and the other two began furiously chopping up a box with those most kindly of wood-splitters—bayonets.   Cartwright filled two sand-bags with the pegs.

They followed on the tail of the company led forth in sombrely grumbling file, shoving their ' kindling '-like pegs into the soft earth and hitching to them the cable, a line on each side of the trench.

THAT day saw the end of those lusty and prodigious assaults that wrung the so-called ' heights ' from an enemy that pressure could bend but no pressure seemed able to break.

And the ' heights ' were found, as yet, to be illusion. A man standing erect on a parapet of Stuff Redoubt could, perhaps, have seen over the dun wreckage and tumble of the immediate foreground ; but a man projected cautiously upwards to the extent only of his cheekbones above the dank bags—or even adding, precariously and inch by inch, the dozen or eighteen inches of the length of his cloaked and muffled periscope —was face to face with the foreground only.   A corpse and a battered water-bottle ; a helmet and a bent rifle ; crags sculptured in miniature, knolls and hummocks and cañons, flat deserts and ranges of tiny mountains fashioned from the churning and ceaseless tossing of the drab, yielding mud ; shards of metal and jags of fractured timber.

" Can you see Grandcourt ? "   Richards had asked when croakings and squeaks had at last died away from the three frail miles of wire that connected the wheezing instruments.

" Grandcourt ? "   said Cartwright, shocked by the sudden eagerness of such expectancy.   " No, Dicky. Not yet."

For the frontier of the minutely limned foreground in his periscope was the rust and dustbin-coloured smear and tangle of enemy wire.

Conquest, as yet, had brought no breadth of vision ; and—around a twist of trench where men moved warily with lips sedately pursed and fingers alert near the safety-ring of a grenade—conquest abruptly ended. It ended in a sniper's shield built across the trench in a frame of sand-bags. A man leaned alone against the shield in the manner of a theatrical eavesdropper in some corridor scene. The men nearest to him, at the traverse, had bayonets fixed, and two grenades apiece on the parapet beside their rifles—as it were on the mantelpiece. The eavesdropper had a bomb-proof canopy above his head—timbers and boxes, expanded metal and a hump of bags.

The validity of its right to this title of ' bomb-proof ' Cartwright did not himself see tested.

He slunk forward to the plate and glanced, for some moments, through its eye. It looked into the similar eye of another plate—a dozen, or twenty, or eighty feet away. The space between was a distorted drainful of entanglements. The bodies therein were flung in the expansive postures of death from shell-fire or bombs ; and huddled—' collected,' as one would say of a horse's pose —where a bayonet-thrust had left them. Between them and about them were the bric-à-brac of stakes and tumbled knife-rests ; beds hacked out of the nearest dug-out ; a twist that might equally have been the relic of some ancient plough as the carriage of a flame-thrower ; and tangles of wire.

Carnage would have been inconspicuous in the mean squalor, the menace and wreckage that submerged that day into the gloom of evening. The cautious traversing of Cartwright's periscope was suddenly arrested once and struck still by the pale, impassive jowls of a German in the shadow of his low helmet. It was some seconds before Cartwright realised that his instrument was a magnificent telescope, that the face could not be five, but must be a hundred or two hundred yards away. Still, he wondered that no one saw that reckless, prying head, to drive it down to cover. He brought an infantry subaltern to the eyepiece of the periscope ; and some one thereafter did drive it down. The some one (a bony Corporal) in due course slithered to the fire-step again with a neat hole in his throat and a frayed tear at the back of his neck ; and Cartwright interfered no more in matters strictly concerning the Infantry.

The touchy atmosphere of the afternoon found him slipping a carefully examined grenade into the pocket of his tunic, and explaining (with academic exactness) the mechanism of grenades to Whittle.

The double telephone-line to Zollern made only this difference to the patrolling—there were two wires to be repaired from time to time instead of one. One signaller or the other was always gone upon this errand—to Zollern Redoubt, and beyond it to the Wonder-Work. (Beyond the Wonder-Work the line was being maintained by the battery.) The recurrence of this duty signified little, however, to the linesmen ; Stuff Redoubt, even in a dug-out, was no more kindly a spot than Sammy's much-hated trench or the clinging puddle of Zollern and the Wonder-Work.

Everywhere the air was rain, and metal, and haggard expectancy. Information was scarce, save that which was arrived at by inference. From this it was clear, with persistent lucidity, that whatever else might have happened in quarters more distant, the situation at Regina Trench was still unchanged. Sammy prowled about with Black and without him, placing his guns, fidgeting and worrying. The Battalion Commander went round, scrubby-faced and dirty ; assuring himself, in passing, that Cartwright's line to the battery was kept in order and repair. Alarms were given ; black din hurtled up from behind upon Stuff Trench and Regina. Sammy's guns loosed off upon their appointed lines (and saw fit, immediately thereafter, to change their places). Fresh, answering din was added to the wretchedness of the garrison of Stuff ; and—nothing happened.

Each time, whether the formation of the counter-attack was broken by the barrage, or whether, as some august and sardonic portent-readers had it, ' he ' could not be made to come over ; whether, again, as Sammy's stalwarts had it, ' he ' did indeed begin to come until caught by Sammy's guns—the incredible fact remains that nothing happened.

The unobtrusively killed and wounded went their unobtrusive ways. Every man was damp where he was not wet ; and dug-outs inhabited with such men sleeping were uninhabitable for dainty-stomached men awake.

Cartwright told Richards, after telling Brigade on one occasion to cease firing, that there was no sense in Reynolds's coming up. He was happier and more comfortable where he was than he was likely to be on the way back.

" Well," said Richards, " if you like. He's ready. And what about the signallers ? "

" They're all right, too. Honestly, I'd rather stay to-night. Let him come to-morrow. Day is no worse going than night."

" Righto," said Richards. " Good luck ! "

The feeling of relief was not altogether altruism. There was a thought in the mind of Cartwright that things could not be worse and they might get better. It might stop raining. Things might, by some miracle, dry during the night. The trenches might dry ; his boots might dry and their weight diminish from their present six or eight pounds apiece. He might get some sleep.

Of these miracles only the last was performed. Its performance was followed by Whittle's miracle of waking him and getting him up one slide of steps, helmeted, and down another, to the telephone where Brigade wanted him.

It was the Colonel.

" Hello ? Cartwright ? Are you still—er—h'm—are you still—exactly where you were, say, an hour ago ? "

" Yes," said Cartwright. What, he wondered, was he trying to imply with his ' er ' and his ' h'm ' and his pauses ? " Why ? "

" Why ? " said the Colonel. " I mean—you haven't moved or anything ? "

" I was having a little sleep when you called up." Even though it was to the Colonel that he spoke Cartwright was inclined to be testy.

" Asleep ! " The Colonel's guffaw rattled the micro-phone. " Good man. Thanks awfully. I know now. Good night. Sorry we disturbed you."

The signaller with his hair bunched up by the band of the earpiece threw some light. " There's been a bit of a strafe again. Rockets and machine-guns, and all the Lewis-blokes letting go, and the batteries loosing off again, for half an hour. I suppose the Brigade didn't like to say straight out, had we been thrown out of here ? "

" Oh ! " said Cartwright. " Most probably. You fellows getting any sleep ? "

" Yes, Sir," said the signaller. " Orf an' on. The other bloke and the Bombardier are down to it just now. You never took your Thermos, Sir."

" No," said Cartwright. " Never mind now."

" We drunk that old lot up to-day," said the signaller. " But I filled 'er up again for you. We brought along a bit of tea from the position ; and sugar. The foot-sloggers give us a look in at a tin of milk."

Beside the proud man was a mess-tin as black as a bowler hat and under it the evidence of a candle stump burnt out in a nest of rags.

" Stout fellow ! " said Cartwright. " Thanks. I'll drink some. Have you got anything to smoke ? "

Thanking him, the signaller indicated a cigarette stump over his ear.

This had become one of those tours with the Infantry where community of craft and calling were a greater bond than community of rank. Black and Sammy and the other nameless subalterns were worlds away with their particular anxieties and jaws that were too slackened now for any chattering—whether in conversation or in response to the clinging, sodden chill. It was like being a guest somewhere where the host was threatened with private disaster—for it was purely as a family matter that they seemed to regard it, and Cartwright was not of the family. They prowled, silent and anxious and meticulously polite, or they tumbled, bunkwards, for their sleep which was haunted by their private trouble and ended by the groping of an orderly.

Even Sammy had been reduced to careful politeness.

So Cartwright sat down on the step and drank some of the tea from the Thermos with his fellow-guest, the signaller.

" The position's 'ad it in the neck, Sir," the signaller remarked. " Not too bad, though. 'A' sub's pit got alight from a pip-squeak, and Corporal Digby got a Blighty in the backside. I suppose Francis will get full Corporal now. . . . In that strafe about tea-time."

" Much damage ? " asked Cartwright.

" No, Sir. Only a few cartridges went up. They hadn't many left in the pit."

Cartwright knew that it would be the merest snobbery on his part to tell the fellow that signallers must not talk so much over the wire. There might have been some means in the world for making the world's greatest sceptics believe that every word of gossip with the battery could be picked up by a marvellous instrument, taken down by a marvellous operator, translated and presented to Hindenburg himself—but Cartwright did not know of them. Signallers simply did not believe tales.

At the entrance of the other dug-out he again gave his boots their first rough shave with the spade left there for the purpose. At the bottom of the steps he gave them the final, finer touches with a German entrenching tool— scraping the laces into view again and cutting out the lumps stuck in front of the heels.

Before dawn he was roused once more. It was not Whittle who woke him this time, but the sudden, electric stir in the dug-out, and the thud and clatter of stumbling out of bunks.

Dixies of hot stew had arrived from heaven only knew what hovel of a support trench. Black hurried up the steps, cursing. " Quiet, there. Quiet, you fools ! How far away do you think ' he ' is ? You'll get us strafed to hell again with all that blasted shindy. . . . Sentries and the carriers stand-to. The others back again into the dug-outs—pass it along. The dixies are coming down. . . ."

" Well done, you chaps ! " he said to the carriers ;

and then, thoughtfully, as he counted the dixies and divided a modest figure in his mind by their number, " God— some one seems to have forgotten what's been happening up here ! They've sent *enough*."

The sentries' tins were filled, and the saucepan presented by Black's batman : " Six, chum, with the 'tilry officer and Stumpy and me."

The dixies went down to the dug-outs.

Black returned along the trench. Cartwright, waiting at the top of the dug-out, heard him calling down the shaft of the next one : " See that those gunners get a fair whack, Corporal."

The din and the roaring flicker to the right over Regina Trench and to the left beyond Schwaben Redoubt were perhaps a reassurance ; but the brooding quiet of Stuff itself added a strained ominousness to solitude.

" Let's grub," said Black, and they went down to the soup-plates on the table. Sammy came down, and after him the subaltern who was killed during the next day.

" I don't think he'll come now," Sammy said thoughtfully, when he had got to the stage of eating with some precision, trowelling thick gravy on to a piece of biscuit. " Not here. He might have a rub at the flanks where all the strafing is going on."

" We're attacking to the left," said Black. " So he mightn't. Even if he did chuck us out I don't see what good it would do him. Unless he attacked along the whole front."

Arguments were carried no further than points such as these.

" Anyhow, I won't loose off from the left until he's right up to the wire."

" That's right," said Black and turned to the subaltern. " How *is* the wire ? "

" Not bad," said he. " There's none left, by the way. It's all out. But you needn't worry. You can't move, more than a crawl, even where there isn't any blasted wire. Look here." He drew his knees up from under the table into the candle-light. " Like treacle. The trench is dry in comparison. Isn't it, Sammy ? " He yawned. " Any chance of a snooze ? "

" Yes, rather," said Black. " Snooze away."

Cartwright, too, lay down and slept through the Infantry's fantastic rite of ' standing-to ' at dawn ; and Sammy came and shook him and said there was some breakfast.

" Only ' bikkies ' again, I'm afraid," he apologised when Cartwright had joined him at the table. " And bully if you want it. What with thinking there was going to be a relief last night, and one thing and another, the groceries didn't come."

" Have a sandwich ? " said Cartwright. He went to his bunk and produced Browne's last waterproof package from his haversack.

" Gosh ! " said Sammy. " I'll tell the little ones in the years to come that gunners were strange, dark men who pulled sandwiches out of haversacks. That's the eighty-seventh you've produced. I've a good mind to write to Maskelyne and Devant for one of those haversacks myself."

BY noon—a sodden, shadowless and lightless noon—the agreement was general with Sammy's view of the night before, that ' he ' was not coming over. What he was going to do, and what was his idea in doing it, God only knew. It was as meaningless and as pointless, as wearily stupid as the ticking of some immense clock that had no hands, and so no object in the monotony of its ticking.

Bangs and bumps ; whirls and whines and snarls ; the patter of earth flung high and returning again to earth ; the hiss of metal in the air, its hot sizzle as it stabbed the cold pulp of the world. To the incredible monotony was sometimes added the monotony, more sombre, of the occasional human dissyllable, " Stret-cher. . . ."

Cartwright was 'upstairs,' squatting very close with his legs drawn up on the fire-step beside a sentry ; since upstairs there was, in some peculiar sense, air. Detonations—upstairs—crashed out their own inane destiny and did, individually, end. In the dug-out they were collected and concentrated into a prisoned power, straining the lungs of him who breathed them, pressing like great soft thumbs upon his ears, tightening the filthy collar and drawing the crumpled necktie closer about his throat. The light in the shaft came sneaking and sinister, fumbling into the darkness of the hole where no candle could now live. Its direction and its object—the dark hole itself where Cartwright had sat alone on a box—was the direction and the object of those fumbling shells ; for the shaft faced the enemy.

There was nothing to prevent a shell sailing straight down the trail of the wan light into the darkness—nothing till its blunt nose struck the floor a dozen feet from Cartwright's box. And then down also would come the top —mud and water and tangled rubbish sagging through timbers all smashed awry.

And so he had stuffed his things together—glasses and Thermos—into his haversack, and joined the sentry.

The man straightened himself up from time to time in contribution to the general routine, and looked forth. Each time he looked he saw nothing ; neither was he killed nor surprised by any wound.

As time went slowly on—hours or only fractions of hours—an anxiety began to form itself in the taut idleness of Cartwright's mind, a speculation eminently reasonable and roughly statistical. It began to appear to him that the place where he crouched should, by the general odds, at some time or other be hit by something. This had nothing to do with the fact that he, personally, was there. It depended from the larger fact that if the racket went on long enough every part of Stuff Redoubt, at some time or other, would be hit by something. If this was so, places that had not been hit yet were still, in the jargon of business, 'outstanding.' Their turn was to come. . . . Whitelaw, no doubt, had a system whereby chances such as this should be assessed and properly dealt with. But Cartwright had only an unease and an anxiety, a profound distrust in a square-yard of ooze because it persisted, from minute to minute, in remaining the same unblemished square-yard of ooze.

And he distrusted the sentry beside him. He, like the yard of ooze, kept narrowing down and focusing an open chance into a definite probability. Every time he prowled up, chewing his moustaches, and crouched down again, still chewing them, he added to the weight of the balance of probability oustanding against him.

The incident of the sniper Corporal the day before made it questionable whether Cartwright should interfere again in the affairs of Infantrymen—but suggesting to a man a move of eight or a dozen feet would scarcely be an interference. The fellow's stance was in the right-hand corner of a bay—if ' corner ' and ' bay ' are words applicable to an architecture so tumbled that there was neither an angle nor a straight line in a score of acres.

Cartwright nudged him and said, " Why don't you shift over for a bit, to the other end ? "

" Don't like it, Sir," he said. " Don't like the look of it. . . . And if you arst me, we're getting it lighter up this end because of the block round the corner. It's a bit close to Fritz for 'im to be chancing any long shots on."

So he too had been quietly reading the stars in their courses.

" Well," said Cartwright. " The other end of the step is four or five yards nearer to the block."

" Don't like it," said the man, stolidly shaking his head.

It was not a point that could be argued. Nor was the feeling that had now established itself in Cartwright's mind one could be stifled or denied. The fact was also quite clear to him (and it was a faintly startling fact), that there was no reason in the world why he should stay cowering in a given spot after he had taken a dislike to it.

" Well," he said to the sentry, " please yourself. If any one wants me, I've gone to have a look at the block."

U

The sentry, it struck him then, was right. The last fifty yards of trench leading to the block was dead quiet It was there, at the far end of it by the man who leaned his face against the sniper's shield, that Cartwright wanted to sit for a while and dry his hands and take a drink from his Thermos and smoke a cigarette. He would have done it too, but for the sentry ; for squatting and cowering and flinching beside that quiet chewer of dirty moustaches until individual flinches had been merged into a single cringing and curling away within one's self—that quiet fellowship had imposed some absurd obligation upon Cartwright. Then, too, there was no certainty about any of it. His sneaking away to the extremity would look bad to the sentry and might possibly carry no compensation for himselt.

Man's normal gait now was the gait of his ultimate ancestor—bandy-legged and heavy-footed, crouching forward and lurching, the grimy knuckles of hands within easy touch of the ground to give occasional support and restore balance to his cumbersome body. His visage, too, was ancestral ; hairy and foul and leathery, his jowls gone puffy and slack, his parched lips sagging apart from the gleam of his set teeth. With this normal gait and normal visage Cartwright grovelled along, back past the sentry in his same old corner, and along to the signallers' dug-out.

He had no illusions about his two-fold motive in going to see the signallers : they would think well of the man who strolled about the trench in a barrage, visiting his underlings ; and again, they would give him company. In the last hour (if it had been an hour), watching the moustache-chewer on the fire-step, he had realised that he was among foreigners, Lancashire- and Yorkshire-men from mines and ' works,' men with peculiar monosyllables and long vowels.

" All right, Whittle ? " he asked.

" Nicely, thank you, Sir," said the bombardier. " The wire's ' dis.' Evans went out a while ago ; but I expect he's having to go a bit steady. He's shifting the line a bit lower as he goes. I told him to mind and not get it underfoot. Mr. Reynolds should be along any minute now and the men with him will run an eye over the line as they come."

"Who told you Mr. Reynolds is coming?" asked Cartwright. It was remotely absurd to be asking, somewhere in the bowels of a fantastic machine, a vaguely human question; but Cartwright asked it.

"Simmy, wasn't it, chum?" Whittle asked his colleague. "Yes, Sir; Simpson. They tapped in and O.K.'d us from Scottie's. Mr. Reynolds told him to say not to bother you if your were busy, or under cover."

"Cover!" said Cartwright. "I suppose you blighters call this cover!" Already he had had enough of the dug-out and the fact that bangs would not dissolve, but remained solid and dense. "Since you like it, carry on. . . ." Company, after all, was a curious futility in an existence that had become a detached process like the turning of some grotesque wheel or the quivering and filthy contortions of immense viscera in the act of digestion. But another glance at Whittle gave a fresh attractiveness to company. It is a very dull man whose sense of 'audience' is so weak that he is totally unaware when another thinks well of him; and Whittle, scratching his chest, was thinking well of Cartwright for sauntering up steps when he could have sat at the bottom of them. Cartwright knew, gratefully, that Whittle would brag to the Infantrymen squatting round him, about the hazards of battery-craft and the high courage of battery-officers. Answering the friendliness of Whittle, Cartwright said, "When I'm properly frightened, Whittle—I like to be somewhere where *running* is possible."

"When *I'm* frightened, Sir," said Whittle, "give me a good 'ole."

They thought they smiled at each other in their friendliness; but the gesture of their prickly jowls and flabby cheeks resembled a smile only in that it exposed their teeth.

"Through to battery, Sir," Whittle shouted up the steps when Cartwright had got nearly to the top.

Cartwright grunted.

Solitude was more seemly than chat with signallers—
the solitude to be found among preoccupied foreigners
and a hummock here and there on the fire-step, under a
ground-sheet.

He found Black some distance down the trench,
standing by a sentry, pathetically engaged with one of
those inadequate and childish periscopes—two mirrors
held parallel to each other and a couple of feet apart by
a lattice of thin metal.

" Here," said Cartwright. And he lent him the
number fourteen.

" Golly ! " said Black, screwing his eye up to it. " I
say ! This is the tool Sammy told me about ! " But
anything he might have seen was of no particular import ;
and the whole transaction was impersonal, an imperceptible
pause or tremor in that remote and monster process of
digestion. The sentry and Black and Cartwright stood
huddled side by side on the step over a dead bundle in a
ground-sheet ; each of them solitary.

The shelling may have abated or intensified, but the
principle still held : a place unhit was the place at which
a hit was due.

Cartwright took his wonderful periscope and moved on.

Around a traverse, lurching like the rest, but conspicuous among the squalid aboriginals of Stuff Redoubt in
his pale beardlessness, came Reynolds.

" Uncle," he said and then vaguely as a mere variation
in his breathing, " God's truth ! Uncle——"

Solitude was now ended.

" Come on, Rennie—a bit farther along."

" What are _you_ coming back for, you ass ? " Reynolds
called after him as he turned. " Go on home. I'll
send Whittle and the other fellow after you. Company
dug-out, I suppose—easy enough to find. I told Evans
to go on home when I met him in Zollern."

" It's all right," said Cartwright. " We're there,
practically."

Reynolds did not appear to realise the importance
of movement.

They wasted no more breath on conversation.

At the signallers' dug-out he sent down Reynolds's three men. "Tell Whittle I'll shout down when I'm ready. The officers are next door."

He moved on again, but at the next entrance Reynolds stopped. "This is it, isn't it?"

"Yes," said Cartwright. "But it's pretty awful down there. I thought we'd go on a bit, to the block."

"No, you blooming don't," said Reynolds. "Not another yard for me. Come on."

He went down without another word, so that Cartwright followed. He struck a match at the bottom, and lighted the candle on the table and the candle continued steadily burning.

"Hello!" said Cartwright, looking at it. "We couldn't do that a while ago."

He sat down opposite to Reynolds and they took off their hats and laid them on the table.

"Don't go settling yourself down," said Reynolds. "Take my tip and beat it now while the strafe is still on. It's bad enough, but you can at least move, so far as the mud will let you. But if you wait till the shelling stops and the traffic starts—God help you!"

"There isn't likely to be much traffic till night," said Cartwright.

"Oh, isn't there!" said Reynolds. "You haven't seen the stiffs. And the wounded? Or perhaps you think there aren't any? You wait till you've gone half a mile. . . . I wish to God you'd get out, Uncle. Hanging about isn't going to help you." His tone was quarrelsome; but at this point he altered it. "Gird up your loins and git! And look here, at the sort of chap *I* am. I've brought your mail!" He wiped his hand and dug through the pocket of his Burberry to the pocket of his tunic and pulled out a map, a handkerchief and two letters. He shoved these over to Cartwright; one from Dorothy, and one from John.

"Good God!" said Cartwright slowly, staring at them. Then he said, "Thanks, Rennie."

A bang overhead lifted the flame from the candle-wick and dispersed it into the darkness. Reynolds snarled an obscenity, fumbled for a match and struck it.   He broke the candle from the grease holding it to the table, lighted it and kept it in his hand for the purpose of shock-absorbing.

"Let's get out of this blasted place, Rennie," said Cartwright, standing up and putting on his helmet.

"What the hell for ? "

"Because it's not a decent place to be in."

"I've had three hours of outside," said Reynolds ; "and you'll get a bellyful yourself before long.   Can't you—and why the hell do you keep on standing by the confounded door ?   Trying to impress me with what a stout fellow you are ? "

"Rennie," said Cartwright, "don't be a little fool ! "

"And don't you be a big one ! " snapped Reynolds. "I'm ready to go up when I've got to.   When there's anything to go for—just as ready as you or any one else. But I'm dashed if I'm going swaggering about when there isn't any reason.   You needn't either . . . like a bally D.A.C. swashbuckler showing off to the old woman at his billet."

"Good Lord, Rennie ! "

Cartwright was puzzled.   Passion, like Rennie's, was a peculiarity in a human being which he seemed to have forgotten.

"Don't Good Lord me, either.   I didn't think you'd swank at *me*."   The candle was shaking in his hand. He gulped, and blew it out and flung it down on the table.   "All right, blast you. . . .   Lead on, thou great and courageous one—lion's whelp, lead on !   I follow." He stepped into the twilight at the bottom of the shaft. The face was not the face of Reynolds in the act of banter, but a mask of melodrama.   "Come on, then, I'll show you.   I'm ready."

He was breathless.

Cartwright now struck a match and found the candle and lighted it.   "Speaking of lions' whelps," he said ; "did you bring any tigers' milk ? "

In the whisky-bottle on the table there were not more than three tots, and Cartwright looked at them.

" Yes," said Reynolds, and unslung his water-bottle. " You've got my flask. Better fill it up if it's empty. . . ."

" Let's have a spot now," said Cartwright. " The giant-killer." He uncorked the bottle, slopping candle-grease, and poured into two mugs. " Here ! Lap up and don't talk any more muck. . . ."

Reynolds drank and sat down and took off his hat again. " I—I'm not really windy, Uncle. I mean—I——" The absurd fellow's lip was shaking ; his eyes were open very wide and looking into Cartwright's—as young John's lip had once shaken and his eyes faced destiny in his first dentist's waiting-room one very remote Saturday, with John asserting that he wasn't really frightened.

" It all comes down to a matter of taste, Rennie," Cartwright said. " I don't believe I'm really windy, either. But I seem to have come to a sort of conclusion during the last two days. That's why I like to be upstairs—and damme ! Look at me, I've sneaked back to this doorway again !—the conclusion is that I'd sooner be slaughtered than choked and strangled and buried ; that's all."

" And I," said Rennie, " I'd sooner be choked or buried or damned well anythinged than slaughtered ! There's a chap not far from battalion headquarters—at least he oughtn't to be there now, because I found a Sergeant and gave him hell for leaving such a thing lying about. . . . But it might have changed your views about things." Reynolds swallowed some more whisky.

" I doubt it," said Cartwright. " It's the sort of muffling, down in these holes, that gets on my nerves."

" And it's *blood* that gets me ! " said Reynolds. " If only something like shavings or broken glass or bunches of feathers came gushing out of a fellow when he's ripped up or his head disappears, instead of—blood, I'd be a hell of a fellow, Uncle."

Rennie was himself again.

Cartwright leaned against the post in the light and the air, while Rennie sat by the table and gave him what news there was.

Schwaben Redoubt had been taken and that was the

fact behind the day's fury of shelling. When was Stuff Redoubt taken?—was what Reynolds wanted to know, as there had been an argument down the line. Was it yesterday or the day before? Cartwright could not exactly tell him. When he had come in, the block was already there. Reynolds said there were great and grisly yarns coming back about the garrison and its commander; talk of a V.C.; of right arms that could not yet move after the flinging of so many grenades; of thirst and starvation till a dozen altruists with hearts of gold and steel had carried up six armour-plated cauldrons of stew. . . .

" The stew story is based on fact," said Cartwright.

" And so are the others, judging by the looks of the natives," said Reynolds. " I wish—Auntie—could see you now, Uncle. You don't mind my calling her Auntie? She's sent a ruddy great parcel—big as a cow. God knows what's in it. I tried to get Dicky to ask you if we could open it in case it's delikatessen. Browne's a little off his balance, feeding us on husks. No oil for the primus; no coal, and every stick wet to the marrow. . . ." Suddenly he exclaimed : " I do believe the shelling's less. Hurry, Nunks, for the love of Mike ! and dodge the traffic. It'll start as soon as the strafe is over."

" The best spot of all, Rennie," said Cartwright, " is along to the left—right up as far as you can go, to the block. They daren't shell it, it's so close. Cut along there and sit tight if things get bad again."

" Yes, Auntie," laughed Reynolds. And then, seriously : " I am a swine ! I haven't given you two minutes to read your letters, after bringing them to you."

" Oh, Rennie——" the voice which Cartwright heard saying this was not only tired but fantastically peevish. " Don't bother, Rennie. I'll read them at the battery. Well, so long. And don't forget—out to the left as far as you can go."

" Good luck, Nunkie."

" Good luck, Rennie."

WHITTLE called out to him when they had turned a couple of bays homewards : " Sir—blast me if I hadn't nearly gone and forgot ! Sibley said to ask if Mr. Reynolds give you your letters. He told the signallers he got some for you—in case he stopped anything on the way."

" Yes ; thanks," said Cartwright.

There was food in this for a little thought.

The shelling had now subsided to the point where it could have been described as ' heavy,' after what Reynolds's comic journalists would have called ' drumfire.' But still—a letter unopened in a pocket and another unopened and left behind in his valise—poor, poor Dorothy. . . . This torment, he saw, of shells and blurred trenches, of mute bundles under ground-sheets, of men chattering and scratching and stinking like apes —all this torment was a tormenting of Dorothy. And for her there was no defence, no frail covering even of plastic sandbags ; no holes to hide in—and to get the letters back again— brave, proud letters—unopened. . . . He put his hand in his pocket and thumbed the envelopes open.

He saw Black, standing as usual on the fire-step beside a sentry. " So long, Black," he said ; " my relief's in the dug-out. Good luck."

" Hello ! " said Black. " Cooling down a bit, I think ; don't you ? " It was the leisureliness of the fellow that was the striking thing about him. " You haven't got your jigger on you, I suppose ? "

" No," said Cartwright, glad that the Number Fourteen need not detain him. " Reynolds has it, in the dug-out. He'll let you have it like a shot."

" Oh, well, no hurry." Black had an empty pipe between his teeth. He sat down on an ammunition-box and began to tap his pockets.

" Here," said Cartwright, and he impatiently thrust forward his nearly empty pouch. " Some of mine."

" Ta," said Black and filled his pipe with great care, first wiping his hands, finger after finger. " Thanks awfully. And thanks awfully for standing by, and all that. Well—bye-bye for just now." (That, it appeared, was an infantry phrase of the moment.)

" Bye-bye," said Cartwright.

Black could think what he pleased about his hurry to be off. . . . In a hurry he certainly was—to get to his valise and open that letter.

Hurry or no hurry, the three miles took three hours.

Stretcher-bearers were already on the move ; and even when the quality and tempo of their movement was no longer of consequence to their burden, their movement was deliberate and slow.

There was nothing particularly memorable about the journey. It was pleasant to step upwards at the point where they had tumbled into sanctuary on the way up ; and after a few yards again upwards to the full extent of a man's stature above the surface of the ground. Incessantly there was a whistle of shells from the valleys (Sausage and Mash) northward toward Schwaben Redoubt, and Stuff and Regina Trenches ; but there was nothing perceptibly coming back. Puffs in the sky and black curls, stabs in the earth, were remote and negligible.

The Fricourt Ridge stood up flat and dun, jagged here and there with trees reduced to stumps and stumps reduced to barest wreckage. Nearer was the familiar road with its endless and beginningless procession of unhurrying, burdened and shadowless men.

Cartwright's own procession cut through it by the stump and the poles that held up their cable with a festoon of others. The battery—as apparently every other battery of the valley—was in action. It was slow ' battery-fire,' Cartwright estimated ; about a minute between rounds. Homely jobs were in progress—cooking, ' humping ' of a dixie and buckets, empty cartridges being tossed into an orderly heap behind one of the pits, a man chopping up a box by the cook-house, another within conversational distance of him shaving.

A head was turned in the direction of the returning

pilgrims. Whittle and the other signaller had each a sandbag of loot—helmets, a couple of pairs of boots, bayonets, haversacks and gas-masks in their neat tin boxes, a pistol and one or two daggers. Whatever had not been technically scrounged had been acquired by peaceable deed of purchase from the lawful owners from Yorkshire and Lancashire. Whittle had an Iron Cross of the second class and a fountain-pen (of the first).

Other heads turned, at the shout and the grin of the first one. The chopper was stayed, the razor poised against the lather in the kindliness and warmth of welcome.

And there was a foul and hideous bang

Unheralded by any scream or snarl, by any distant whine shrilling to a whistle, it was a sound shocking and unfamiliar to Cartwright. The bark of guns in action was a bark friendly and known. But this thing was prodigious and stark and utterly ghastly—like the annihilation of earth from under one's feet. Cartwright found that he was sprawling in mud, gulping, crushing lumps of slime in his fists, mumbling " God Almighty." Whittle, too, was in the mud with his bag of souvenirs ; and the others behind him.

" Cripes . . ." said Whittle, and slowly collected himself. " The first. The first bloody one—since March. . . ."

" First what ? " asked Cartwright in the humility of his complete mystification.

" Premature, Sir."

(In order to get the full dramatic effect of this retort and of all it finally meant to Cartwright, it is important to pronounce it correctly and shortly—' premcher.')

A filthy reptile, black and greenish, was uncoiling and writhing in the dank air at the mouth of No 2 gun-pit.

The head and chest and shoulders of Richards bobbed up out of the Mess dug-out. He paused a moment, then dropped his towel and raced over to the pit, holding up his breeches. His naked torso was stained in patches of jaundice-yellow from the ration ' Persian powder ' and the lighter hue of Keatings'.

Cartwright got up and went after him. The men,

hushed for the moment in a haggard group behind the pit, made way. One of them took the haversack and water-bottle and Browne's walking-stick that Cartwright held out as he lurched by.

Three men were in the pit with Richards.

One, presumably from his position on the near side of the trail, the 'number three' of the crew, lay with his feet towards the muzzle of the gun, his face in a dark puddle. Cartwright raised up the head for a moment and leaned down towards the face.

" Who is he ? " he asked the man who had pressed in behind him.

The man looked down as Cartwright had looked ; and then, after looking at the other two in the pit said, " Must be Sandy Heysham."

" Take him out, two of you," Cartwright said. " It'll give more room. And cover him up."

Richards was leaning over Bombardier Austin (the unrelated namesake of the dead signaller). Austin squatted among empty cartridges gripping one knee under his chin with a force that bared his stained teeth in a grin and drove the colour from his lips and cheeks. His hands were pale and gnarled with their grip upon his ankle. Richards, the top of his breeches and underpants doubled over to hold them up, was fumbling with Austin's boot.

" I've got some scissors, Dicky. And a knife," Cartwright said. Richards moved aside, and then over to the third man who sat with his legs stretched out in a leisurely pose, his back against the off-wheel, his hands moving restlessly about his chest and shoulders, quietly moaning. On his face, also, was a vestige of a grin.

Cartwright swore at the bluntness and the softness of the little folding scissors which he took out of their case in his pocket. Austin was in the state of *négligé*—his boots were unlaced and he had no putties ; but the sticky, slippery boot was immovable from the unresisting foot. Gleams of bone were visible in the dark, gaping mouth of a hole below Austin's clutching fingers. " The boot has got to come off, Austin," Cartwright said. " It's squeezing like the devil."

Austin said nothing, or ' Yes ' ; and Cartwright dug in his pocket for his knife. " Here," he said, " suck this— on your tongue." For he had remembered the bottle in the little pocket in the belt of his tunic. (Why, he wondered, had he not remembered to hand over some of the tablets to Reynolds ? . . . And Richards ought to have some . . . and old Whitelaw. . . .)

The tip of Austin's tongue appeared between his teeth, received the tablet from Cartwright's fingers and went back again.

The plentiful lubrication of the boot made the cutting of it with the small, sharp blade surprisingly easy. It tumbled off when one slit had travelled to the heel and another down the front to the toe ; and the foot tumbled a little awry among the cartridges. Austin sat looking on, silent.

There was nothing memorable about the removal of the clout of a sock, for which the scissors were good enough ; about the dabbing on of iodine or cutting open a dressing to pull out the wadding wherewith to stanch the darkly gaping wound. Austin went off on the stretcher, the smear of a foot loosely bound (as per the first-aid book) to the sound one. They took him along the tracks towards Brigade Headquarters, for the telephonist on duty had started the doctor on his way up to the battery.

For the other man, " Ikey " Fishstein, the battery's Jew, there was nothing in particular that could be done. Richards had dabbed iodine on a dozen or so of the little holes in his chest and shoulders, one on a cheekbone and one through the shell of his left ear. They bled so little that only over two of them in his arm did Richards and Cartwright fix bandages. At Cartwright's suggestion he spat ; but the spittle was meagre and clear.

He walked off after the stretcher-carriers, helmeted against the hazard of further pepperings. Browne doubled to the cook-house and back again to lend him the walking-stick lately returned by Cartwright and to arrange for its safe restoration with the stretcher.

" Let us know when you're drafted out again, Fish-stein," Richards said. " I'll apply for you."

The men said, "So long, Ikey lad," and "Good luck, Mo." He was a pet, was Ikey Mo, and something of a distinction in a battery.

His heart was light as he went, his answers cheery, his step—balanced by Browne's fine staff—had a swing in it; for his eyes, too numbed and smarting and dazzled at first to record anything, had seen—just as he was leaving the pit—the hub of the off-wheel completely missing, a spoke chopped cleanly through, and a jagged rent as long as his hand in the upper shield of the gun.

" See to the other one, Sergeant Wright," said Richards. " His paybook and things. Give Grayson the particulars for the ' returns.' "

Browne said, " I've taken your barf things out of the way, Sir, for Mr. Cartwright's. Jackman's taken down a wash for him, and I'll bring his lunch along in a few minutes. Would you like your tea, Sir, while he has it ? It's only about half an hour before time." To Cartwright he said, " It's only a Maconochie, Sir. Touched up a bit," he added significantly. " But I expect you'll be ready for it." (Whittle and his colleagues had already given audience.)

Fantastically Cartwright was ready for it—after unearthing and unwinding putties and giving them with socks and breeches and shapeless boots to Jackman ; after putting on slacks and soft slippers and washing grime and blood from his hands and gritty squalor from his lips and eyelids.

The Incredible, by the sheer force of its incredibility, was made negligible and remote ; whereas bowels and a stomach yawning empty and chilled were real on a plane of reality quite credible. The Maconochie—' touched up ' with sauce and tomato ketchup—filled and gloriously warmed them.

Richards had put his unwashed torso back into the old vest and shirt and gone out, while Cartwright ate. He came back after Browne with the tea-things while Cartwright was filling a pipe and drinking a whisky.

" It must have been the base-plate of the shell that got Heysham's face," Richards said. " But he was done in, anyway. There was something in his chest as big as your fist. Where did you learn your doctoring, Uncle ? "

" The Great War," said Cartwright slowly. " My first operation was on the head of a fellow called Richards."

" Funny how some fellows take to some jobs," mused Richards.

" I believe I ought to have fished the splinter out of Austin's wound," Cartwright said thoughtfully. " But—I was damned tired, Dicky ; that blasted thing coming out of nowhere shook me up. . . . I expect the Doc will have taken it out, if it needed it. He'll have met them."

" It was bad luck," said Richards, " you must have had enough for a bit, according to Whittle. Thank God prematures don't happen every day. This is only the third since I've been with a battery. The eighteen-pounders seem to have a lot more ; but it doesn't matter with shrapnel. It doesn't hurt the gun or the crew, or any one—unless there's some one in front."

" *We* are in front of a good many eighteen-pounders," Cartwright suggested.

Richards shrugged. " I know. But—shrapnel——" he shrugged again. " Besides, they're all shooting pretty high from here. I suppose the stuff would only come pattering down. A hat would stop it. And there don't seem to have been many, anyway."

" It's a funny thing," said Cartwright. " But I'd never heard of prematures till to-day. Never mentioned them at Exeter. If it's something wrong with the fuse——"

" What can you expect ? " asked Richards. " It's not such a bad average when you come to think of it—one defective fuse—in millions. I don't suppose there'll be enough prematures at the gun in the whole war to wipe out one battery. If prematures were all we had to worry about it wouldn't be such a bad show. D'you know we're stuck now, Uncle ? Stuck—absolutely fast—like flies on paper—along the whole blasted front—in mud ? You *ought* to know it, though."

" Oh, yes, it's sticky enough," said Cartwright, and he yawned. The subject was not a vitally interesting one. " I think I'll have a sleep."

"And I'll have that bath," said Richards. "By the way, there's a parcel somewhere for you. Jackman must have hidden it somewhere."

"Oh, I *know*, Dicky. . . ." These people with their chatter of parcels and letters . . . why couldn't they leave him alone ?

Grotesque matters like shoulders wearing out under the tread of heavy feet in a trench bottom ; a white, delicate hand sticking out from the parapet ; the sniper corporal slithering back with his head on one side and his jaw dropped down ; the cold treachery of material that could pepper Fishstein full of little holes from his forehead to his navel, could make a bootful of pulpy meat of Austin's foot and a meaningless puddle of Heysham's inconspicuous face—these were remote enough as long as they were incredible. They were incredible as long as they were not interfered with by the officious thrusting forward of letters and parcels. Impact from them fell, curiously, upon something hard as their own hardness.

But from those letters and from the parcel that he had looked at for a moment and then thrust into his valise-pocket, the impact was a hurt. . . . Dorothy took no chances with the packing of her parcels. Three had now arrived in the same stout wrapping of waxed cloth— evidence that she must have laid in a stock of this. She must have chosen it with deliberation, assessing its merits, considering its price. . . . And then she stitched it about the things she had bought for him, ingeniously and securely. There would probably be more shaving-soap in this parcel—and could he ever tell her that a stick of shaving-soap could carry a man through a spring or a summer ? There would be tobacco—bought at a price that included a fantastic duty, whereas the wagon-line people could get it for him at the canteen, duty-free. John had sent him a pipe-lighter of flint and tinder. . . . In the new parcel was undoubtedly a cake ; some tins, too, of things that were stocked at the canteen a dozen miles away. . . .

These were the things that hurt at that time ; the

gestures of baffled, gentle wits pitted against the gentler hazards.

And Browne had been at it again during the last two incredible days, with a new contraption. On the table was his ' shock-proof ' candlestick ! It was a petrol-can with one of its sides cut away so as to form a rectangular basin which was filled with water. On the water floated a raft made from the blocks out of an ammunition-box. A short string fastened to a weight kept the raft riding at anchor clear of the tin's sides, and on the raft stood two candles. The contraption, which seemed to work, found the same tenderness in those moments that the talk of letters and parcels was threatening to find, the tenderness that had been exposed to the tremor of Reynolds's lip that had been like the tremor of John's at the dentist's. . . .

" I'm devilish tired, Dicky," Cartwright said, and turned into the bunk.

The letters from his pocket he put with the parcel and the other one among his kit behind the pillow, and went to sleep while Richards had his bath.

MEDAL WITHOUT BAR   CHAPTER LVIII

THE cyclostyled or gelatine-copied paragraphs in the daily sheaf from Brigade denied any status to autumn or winter, to rain or to sunshine ; gains had been consolidated, ' offensive spirit ' was to be fostered and the offensive unremittingly pressed.

Yet the orderly from Brigade arrived later at the battery each day ; and still a little later with strides that became shorter and heavier.

The wagons could not easily get from the main road to the batteries in the valley ; having got there, they could not easily get back. Unlimbering them and, unhooking the teams, reversing the vehicles by hand, wading and sweating about them with drag-ropes and shovels and empty sandbags stuffed under the wheels, with boards and sheets of corrugated iron, with any

w

stick of timber that an imaginative coolie could dub a
' pinch-bar ' or a ' handspike ' were a labour which
Whitelaw assessed as disproportionate to the result.

He tried panniers ; and the drivers walked from the
wagon-line to the battery—each leading his two horses
burthened ignominiously, ' packing ' in the manner of any
low-born muleteer.

But ' packing ' the ammunition was also a failure—
labour disproportionate to result. Six horses in one
journey could carry over their backs only twenty-four
rounds against the forty-eight which they could draw in
wagon and limber ; twenty-four rounds as the result of
six horses and three men's plodding through eight miles
of downpour or drizzle on immense, grotesquely shapeless
feet ; twenty-four rounds !—when the function of Artillery
was to ' exhaust the enemy's strength by inflicting
constant losses upon him, and to take part in the daily
minor engagements between the covering zones.' . . .

Whitelaw bundled up the panniers in disgust ; tossed
them into a dump somewhere, got a signature for them
and reverted to the use of his wagons.

From the indestructible tree-stump on the road he
walked to the battery and turned out the gunners—the
servants and the signallers with them. From the roadside
to the gun-pits the ammunition was carried—two rounds
in the arms of each man—seventy pounds in the shape of
cold, slippery, stumpy cylinders held to a man's breast.
One journey on the part of twenty-four men unloaded
a single wagon and limber—leaving the charges and
cartridges for a final procession with sandbags. To
deliver his two shells at the battery and present himself at the wagon for his next two a man walked half
a mile ; but it was possible, and it saved the horses.

The wagon-line was shifted nearer, to where the
swamp became a chalkiness of some promise below the
Aveluy Crucifix.

Liaison with the Infantry became a brigade duty of
twenty-four hours, falling upon the battery every eight
days and upon Reynolds and Cartwright alternately
every sixteen.

Another subaltern reported to the battery for duty, a young city man of some kind from the H.A.C., via Exeter. He was full of competence and confidence, full of good humour and good cheer, conspicuous among a population hatted in the ' issue ' for a little chocolate-coloured steel helmet bought in London. (He would have grown, in time, into the texture of the battery and the Mess ; but he never had the time. It was only a few weeks after joining that he went away again from the position in Courcelette. He had gone off after dinner to relieve Reynolds in the night O.P. ; but was brought back by the signallers, gibbering and moaning and unstrung, after a shell—before striking—had punched one corner from the tail of his British warm and thereafter flung him, with a hundredweight of dirt, into the trench whose hospitality he had rejected on the score of mud.)

The view from ' Scottie's ' was still as good as the view from anywhere, so it was to ' Scottie's ' that the daily O.P. party usually went—a mile and a quarter instead of the three miles occasionally prescribed out of restlessness by the tape-worms, or demanded reasonably by movements in the situation.

In the dismal murk that rumbled to the north-east of Courcelette, Le Sars had fallen.

Men and guns and surviving ammunition were dragged out of the old hovels of Sausage Valley, woven into the frieze of the Pozieres Road and carried to the fashioning of new hovels in the spacious waste of Zollern Trench and Fabeck and the banks of the sunken road in front of them.

It was a memorably rainless day, a day inclined to sunshine, on which battery-commanders with a subaltern apiece, a director-man and Numbers One trailed off on foot behind the Colonel to reconnoitre the new positions.

Cartwright walked and gossiped, towards the tail of the comfortably straggling column, with Branson of B Battery. As they ambled along beside the fishing-net and scrim that swung in rags from a drooping wire at the roadside beyond Pozieres windmill, a shell of terrific velocity (the fiendish, " whistling Walter " type, slim and sudden) snapped into a dirty yellow wreath, a perfect ring that hung in the still air among the scrim and fishing-nets.

One of Branson's Corporals was lying on his back at their feet, and beside him Evans, Cartwright's signaller. In the corporal's smile there was a peculiar irony that told them it was a mask and not the Corporal that gazed up at them before they had got him into the ditch and found the little hole over his heart.

In the crown of the helmet beside Evans was also a hole, as neat as though punched in the course of manufacture.

They carried them from the mud of the ditch to the mud in the entrance of the dressing-station under the windmill.

Quaker oats lost in Evans one of its most prodigious clients and the battery another of its old-timers ; a veteran of twenty-one or two with a female acrobat in pink tights tattooed on his forearm and a turn for blasphemy that was no haphazard affair of accepted *clichés* but of creative ingenuity ; a mouth-organist, too, of infinite variety, with an instrument mellowed and sweetened by being soldered into a Bath Oliver biscuit-tin.

It was Evans who had chatted to Cartwright on that first night of his, when he had come up from the dug-out in his pyjamas to look up at the moon above Arras, and at the Verey lights.

The sunken road and the neighbourhood of Zollern Trench and Fabeck were obvious from the map as a position for howitzers, so Richards and Cartwright, with the Numbers One and the remaining signaller, were detached from the Colonel's party at the track before the twisted girders and the concreted, gaping vats of the Courcelette Sugar Mill. It was a road of promise for the horses, solid to the feet under the covering scum, with timbers laid and soundly dogged together by Canadian sappers.

To the right of them they came upon that breast-deep, hurried work of the 15th or 16th of September, Maple Lane. It was shared now, mutely and peaceably, by forms of men in grey who had lost the ground and others in khaki who had taken it from them and grubbed out ' the Lane ' and held it, and painted and stuck up the sign.

" Boots," Sergeant Wright observed quietly when they had got to the trench's disappearance into village rubble, and turned away to the left. " The chaps will be able to do with Canuck boots again in this muck." (The battery, in due course, became equipped with Canadian boots.)

The guns were cut into the banks of the road, roofed over with timbers from the village, rails and bags of rubble. The signallers scraped out a place on their right flank ; the detachments made their barrows in the rear. (If there had ever been dug-outs in Fabeck Graben, the battery never found them.) The officers' Mess was sunk against the lee of the chalk mound— architecture that was bidding fair to become standardised. Chalk—viscid at first, then plastic, then hard enough for a pick—was loaded into bags to a volume of a dozen feet by six or seven, by four feet deep. The bags made a two-foot wall around the three edges of the digging, the straightened side of the mound forming the battlement towards the enemy. Wall-plates (for Richards was a pedant in the matter of wall-plates) were found in hard-won planks and excavated duck-boards, to carry the timbers spanning the roof from the bank to the outer wall. Over the timbers (with two proud steel rails among them) came the usual scrap collection of corrugated-iron, doors, a battered hurdle or two and snugly adjacent pit-props. The lot was buried by the shovelling and picking down of the mound upon it.

It was Browne's theory that the chalk would ' take up ' and, in due course, ' pack ' ; it would become, by the action of water and an occasional smacking on top with the flat of a shovel, a fine substance as impervious to water as cement. When his theory was proved to be unsound it meant a loose ceiling of ground-sheets again, and the punctual recurrence of milking them into a dixie.

The battery's bereavement of Meston (translated as it was into the immediate loss of old Whitelaw, ' Dad ' and ' Vetus,' grouser and sardonic commentator, from the Mess) was not felt for long. Another reinforcement joined. It was Oakleigh, a young regular recovered from a wound.

The first impression made by him on the firing battery was the return to it of Whitelaw.

Oakleigh was senior to every one, senior even to Richards ; inclined to swagger a little with his Horse-Artillery jacket and round buttons, but on the whole he swallowed his superiority with pleasant decency. He accepted the chances that had withheld a battery from him and given it to Richards. There was comfort, it seemed, and compensation in the distinguished globularity of his little buttons, a modestly carried pride in his memories of "the Shop." He slipped into command of the wagon-line and made a job of it.

Through the dirtiest months in the dirtiest acres upon the world's bruised and squalid face, Oakleigh's chin was always smooth and clean. Whatever of his splendid boot-tops was not immured in filth by his walk from the Sugar Mill road to the battery shone in the lamp-light of the dug-out as he drank his tot ; and his buttons always twinkled.

He stands out still among the crowded men of the time with a pleasing elegance added to man's toughness ; an aseptic, sterilised sharpness and keenness among values generally blunted. (At the end of March he went away, twinkling and meticulously shaved, to be Captain of a six-gun battery till its Major was killed ; but in the meantime he restored Whitelaw to the battery's hearth.)

Browne persisted in his faith that, given a bit of dry weather, the chalk on top of the dug-out would harden. Solidified it would easily keep out a direct hit from a whiz-bang ; but it never did harden.

One night the fore hoofs of an Infantry mule under a load of medical stores sank through as far as the corrugated iron.

Whitelaw spent his leisure in lowering the floor a foot or two. Stripped and sweating in his seclusion from the chilly drizzle sweeping the dun vale, he would roll up a sleeping-bag at a time, stack up on another sleeping-bag the German ammunition baskets from under the first one, and ply his spade. Sometimes he modelled the spoil of his excavations, sometimes carved it into bags for his man, the unobtrusive Keniston, to toss to the roof, or pile against the low wall outside.

The other batteries of the Brigade had been shelled out of Courcelette, and lay a little behind, to the left of D ; and there began a round of dinner-parties. The contemplation of Thiepval and life in the shadow of ' the Road '—the one and only road with its frieze of beasts and burdened men—these had wiped out the distinction between men who had not known ' the Landing ' and ' the Evacuation ' on the one hand, and men who had not known the Salient on the other ; between these again and the men like Cartwright who had known neither. For already a new idea was slowly asserting itself as a broader and sounder basis of division within the Brigade ; survivors and non-survivors.

The party from one battery fell in with the party from another to sneak, at dawn, to the ditch and the two untimbered burrows whence a peering slightly upwards to the north would discover the impregnable and indestructible wire of Regina stretching westwards to the festering Stuff Trench. The lunches and teas and portable dinners of these O.P. parties were combined—often over the telephone or during the symposium of the night before. It would have been silly for both men to take sardines or a pot of cod's roe or bloater paste or for both to take rum and neither whisky. . . .

A sinister apprehension was in the air.

There was a belief now in the magic whereby telephoned talk was picked up ; so that even signallers would not report shellings of the battery to the O.P. party, or mention casualties. There was a little anxiety at the O.P. each dawn, as the relief came up, to hear of any contribution that the battery may have made to the last twenty-four

hours' process of attrition.   One day it was a direct hit on
No. 4 pit—a 5·9—intended, so the signallers said, for A
Battery four hundred yards away ; since A was being shot-
up by an aeroplane.   Only Shepherd, the limber-gunner,
had been in the pit polishing his hub-caps.   The shell had
probably killed him before sticking him under the trail,
setting fire to the charges and burning him to the ribs.
Some shrapnel had caught the fire-extinguishers, giving
two men what the Canadian doctor from down the road
had guaranteed to be good blighties.

Another day it was the cook who had got one, in the
stomach.

The sentry could not be found one night by his relief.
He was found in the morning.

On another morning a Sergeant and a Corporal, whose
fastidiousness had impelled them to the joint construction
of a sleeping-place apart from their subsection were
found dead under their hovel's débris; for there was no
check or tally kept upon the casual bangs of the nights.

There were systematic treatments of the vale with gas—
(for in the vale were no less than thirty-two guns) ; hours
spent in the prickly, sticky suffocation of the old, flannel
gas-bags wherein condensation on the eyepieces gave
men the purblindness of growing cataracts, and chins
became a cretinous slobber of sweat and spittle.

Major Maguire from the Canadian battery behind,
ancient friend of Richards and Reynolds and Browne from
the Dickebusch and Plug Street days, came to dinner in
the evening of the day that a premature burst of shrapnel
from one of his guns killed Sibley and wounded Bombardier
Wagstaffe.   It was one of those little gestures to indicate
that casual friendships and regard were superior to casual
accidents.

Days smouldered out into night.   " Visibility poor "
and " nil " was the meagre burthen of the O.P. logs with
" Intermittent shelling of all calibres."

The Infantry before Regina Trench had found a secret
and subsisted barely, but plausibly, on the discovery : they
had abandoned the holding, in any force, of battered Artillery targets and held, instead, isolated posts.   Richards and

Cartwright walked off northwards from the battery one day, shrouded in the phantasmal protection of a pallid fog. They saw what lay between them and the enemy,—a bare eight hundred yards away—at nights, when they cast away their boots and socks and breeches and collars and sometimes even persisted in the inevitably disappointed hope of finding a greater peace in pyjamas. It was men in shell-holes ; little groups of three men or four, with the barest furnishing of a Lewis gun, grenades and a petrol-can of water ; canny, gaunt fellows with unwinking, bloodshot eyes and filthy faces who stooped in the bottom of the hole for the lighting of endless cigarettes and talked not at all, or in hoarse whispers.

But the times were, on the whole, leisurely ; and Cartwright kept up the writing of his letters with great punctuality.

Dorothy knew now, and he accepted her knowledge, that he was not still in a land of hedgerows and meadows and standing houses.   He had never told her, specifically, of any move—but she knew ; and he made no denial. The buoyancy in his letters came from his marvellings at the Infantry and at the miracle of their survival.   The gunner's life was, by implication, a life of dryness and warmth and dignity.

And more men in the battery, from one cause or another, mutely dead or rejuvenescently alive in the sudden fact of their going, faded from the battery.

There was talk for a while among the old-timers of ' conscripts ' now coming up the line as reinforcements. But there was found to be no appreciable difference between the earlier men who had waited for nothing and the men who had had to wait till it was made humanly possible for them to come out to the adventure.

Adventure ! . . .

THE adventure of those times was talk.   Talk with the man from another battery in the toil of the road to the O.P. that brought sweat to the body when there was a film of rime over the world's stickiness ; talk in the foul ditch or cramped burrow over sardines and cheese and Quaker oats and tots of rum ; talk on the endless mile back ; and endless talk with Richards and Reynolds and Whitelaw at home.

The world was criticised in its quaint workings ; men were examined and appraised and labelled ; facts of life were assessed.

Whitelaw freely offered rewards for the finding of any Regulars within three leagues of the firing-line between the ages of thirty and forty.

It was found that the Colonel was a hollow little thing, hanging on in attitudes (' journalistic ' attitudes, as Reynolds called them) of indomitable courage and endurance, for his C.M.G.   " The sort of beggar," said Reynolds, " who'd say something like ' pour la patrie ' for tuppence without blushing."

It was seen, in these conversations, that young Gordon was a regular, transferred from the Cavalry to the Artillery, immaculately innocent of training or experience in office-routine—or indeed of any experience at all.   His efficiency as an Adjutant was a happy fluke, whereas that same efficiency would have been a foregone certainty in Whitelaw, or Cartwright, or half a dozen others in the Brigade.   In the Brigade also were engineers—electrical mechanical and civil ; yet the orderly-officer whose only specified responsibility had once been the telephone service and communications within the Brigade was incompetent to do anything with a defective telephone but shake it, and curse the signallers.   But he had come to the army from some firm of financial tipsters ; and the Colonel spent an hour each week with him and an ' Army Book 136 ' which he had ruled into an investment ledger for the Colonel had always been obliged to live on his pay and his wits. With his Colonel's pay distended by allowances and his tipster at his elbow the Colonel made hay while the sun shone ; and he insisted on a daily feed, with his lunch, of calves' head produced from a choicely and disgustingly concocted tin ; he insisted on Perrier water to mix with the puny white wine he drank—while it was sweat (and often blood) to get a sandbag of wet bread, of Maconochies and bully with a dozen cans of chlorine richly dissolved in water, up to the batteries.

Cartwright could join in no wholesale slaughter of Regulars with his memories of Henderson and Sinclair, and with their own young Oakleigh twinkling up to them with his shining chin and buttons.

He had to nod at the mere arithmetic and the demonstrable facts of neighbours disappearing towards the coast and beyond it ; but he would say stoutly, " Anyhow, the finest fellows I've come across so far have been Regulars."

" Yes," was Whitelaw's answer ; " and the finest fellow the world has ever come across was an Arab carpenter. But does that prove that the finest fellows to-day are carpenters, or that the finest carpenters are Arabs ? "

They were a little inclined to shout in their repartee across the map-board laid for dinner on the bed laid nearest to the door, while they sat on the beds each side of it ; for in the head of each of them there was now a lilt of dead and meaningless sounds, as though a head contained not only ear-drums, taut and delicate, but also an earpiece from one of the two telephones that were on the waiting list for replacement—earpieces from which not even a night spent inside the shirt of a signaller could dry out the blur and buzz and muzziness.

" The rot has got into them," Whitelaw insisted. ' The *young* Regulars are all right. They've been properly trained—by *this*. The others *were* all right ; a year ago. Six months ago—even *three* months ago—some of them were holding out. But they're done now. . . ."

Even Whitelaw was silenced for some moments on the night that the battery orderly handed in the envelope of

'Comic Cuts' and Brigade Orders that contained the information that the Adjutant had been awarded the Military Cross.

When speech was possible for him again, and seemly, he said : " When I saw him walking by the battery in the morning—the day Meston got put out and Uncle had to foot it up to Zollern and Stuff Redoubt—I knew it. The Colonel had to say something in his recommendation about ' under fire '—and a walk up towards ' Scottie's ' with a couple of signallers was good enough. What did his signallers get, Dicky ? "

" Damn all," said Richards, studying the orders.

" And Rennie— " said Whitelaw thoughtfully. (Reynolds must have been away at the moment, in the hole before Regina Trench.)

" Rennie's recommendation by the Infantry—well, it all goes to make a ' damned good show by the Brigade don't you know ? ' . . . Rennie at the Wonder-Work Meston laid out and replaced by Uncle inside of four hours through that muck of Zollern and Stuff. All the battery telephone lines kept going for every minute of the time The guns kept going. A Battery and C with a gun apiece and detachments knocked out. B and C with a subaltern apiece blown to glory. Ourselves with a pit burned and a fellow hit in the backside . . . me bringing up the bullets to you night after blasted night. . . . Every one of us frightened so that our mothers wouldn't have known us. . . . You can have the Regulars, Uncle, when they do things like this." He smacked the sheets of orders " Here comes Oakleigh—we'll see what *he* has to say about it."

He tried to bait Oakleigh ; but Oakleigh would not be baited. He seemed to find some enjoyment in the blasphemous nonsense of Whitelaw.

" Here, you damned ' Shop-walker,' what can you say about this ? " said Whitelaw, pushing the bottle and a mug and Brigade Orders in the direction of Oakleigh's legs showing in the entrance.

" What's up with Dad ? " said Oakleigh, smiling generally, and sitting down next to Richards. " Have they passed him over again ? Given an Army Corps to another soldier ? "

He read the order when Whitelaw had taken his thumb from the emphasised paragraph.

" Well," he said, and then some such lightly good-humoured thing as—" I swear I didn't do it, Daddy. If I'd been consulted I'd have given each of you an M.C. working up to a D.S.O. ; and to myself I'd give a V.C. ; for a very good reason."

" Oh, you'd find a reason all right," said Whitelaw. ' The Colonel found a reason, didn't he ? Yes. The Adjutant walked out ' under fire,' ' in the face of the enemy '—the road was full of prisoners, wasn't it ?—— "

" ' Walked,' you said, Dad," Oakleigh observed quietly. ' And that would be my reason—walking. That's more than you ever do up here, with that great pot you're putting on from just loafing when you're not frightened, and filling it with whisky and crawling about on it when you are. There's another case of the stuff for you with the bullets to-night, by the way." He fished the ammu-nition-slip out of his pocket. " Sign, please," he said, and handed the slip to Richards. One of them went out, either Cartwright or Whitelaw, to see the horses unpacked —for Oakleigh had drawn the panniers again, to ' pack ' the ammunition across to the battery from the road.

It had to be done between dusk and dawn now, for the half-mile of road where Evans had been killed was visible from somewhere north of Regina ; and the dank mist, for all its look of solid permanence, could sneak away and vanish in an instant.

It was only at night, when night's own blackness was sufficient mantle for the work of men, that the mist was known never to move, but to sprawl, sodden and foul, from Courcelette to Albert and athwart the road from Thiepval to Contalmaison. And there was room in it, or all its burden of stench, for the keener reek of gas oozing from the purring little shells that snuggled into the soft earth and popped and squirted out the heavier wraiths to lurk in the hollows.

Blunt nostrils grew keen ; dull, furry palates were

smooth and keen to muzzle into the night's pestilences, and to savour and assess them ; for accuracy in this matter of assessment meant much in comfort for the muleteers lurching with their beasts from the Sugar Mill. The smother of a clammy flannel bag with eyepieces steamed more opaque than the night, was a matter not to be gratuitously undertaken in that crazy mile.

When there was no purring or plopping, and the burden of the air came only from the clouds and from the bootless corpses of Maple Lane, a man could spit and have done with it.   When there was purring and plopping to wind· ward, if the expert nostril and gourmet palate assessed the slow reek as ' Weeping Willie ' he could still have done with it, spitting (for Maple Lane was always with them) and smearing the spate of tears from his cheek· bones with his fist.

" 'Oo yer calling dirty-face ? " became a standardised pleasantry in the light of a lantern held to a cigarette stump, from drivers turned muleteer (' the cavalry ' as the gunners called them).

Duly unloaded, his receipt folded into his book and buttoned into his pocket, Oakleigh would say, " Well good night all. Good luck," and withdraw, twinkling into the untwinkling night and back to his bell-tent and his supper on the banks of the Ancre.

TALK flowed and snapped and gurgled endlessly on It came from nowhere, started by nothing memorable or particular, led to nowhere and nothing.

It would begin with the mug of tea and the yawn in the morning and the three of them sitting up to shave (or there would be four if there was no O.P. duty until the youth in the conspicuous little helmet went away) It went on while they washed with valises bundled out of the way ; while they cursed the dull, oily dampness on leather or the chilled clamminess of rubber as boots were pulled on ; while room was made before the wall mirror for the brushing of hair and the tying of neckties. It went through breakfast and through the group thereafter ; through lunch and lazily through the swaddled siesta ; after it through tea and dinner till the lamp burnt out or was blown out and placed outside the gas blanket.

They talked of war ; and they talked of peace, and of women.

" It's a pity," Reynolds suggested ; " that they can't all agree to draw stumps—just for an interval. Nothing is happening now. In the larger view, what does it matter if we lose a dozen men and horses in the battery, or half a million in the army ? Fritz is losing the same. And no one's enjoying it."

" In the larger view," said Whitelaw, " lots of people are enjoying it. Never heard of profiteers ? I'm making a hell of a lot of money myself, and my brother is having a whale of a time in the audience. With our influence he could get me a job in no time. A real job, I mean. Red tabs probably."

" Why don't you go and take it ? " asked Reynolds. It was always Reynolds who provided the sneer for Whitelaw's bombast.

" I'm going to," said Whitelaw, quietly ; " don't worry."

" Good," said Reynolds. " We might get a chance then. You and your brother would finish the whole thing in a week or two. Dicky and Uncle could have decent jobs, and I would be your A.D.C."

" Would you ! " said Whitelaw. " I can see myself with an A.D.C. who stinks like a badger and uses bad language ; and hasn't had a bath for a month."

" Speaking of baths," said Richards, and so the talk would branch away—" We must go down to the wagon-line. . . ."

He had said it before, and again before that ; but no one had gone. It meant, since the journey would be made by day, a walk to the top of Sausage Valley— two and a half miles. It meant thereafter a ride of three and a half, or four—if any one preferred slugging along on a horse to slugging along on foot. Values had become, like elements in the atmosphere, a matter of careful and accurate assessment ; and twelve miles—five hours' journey with the best going—was disproportionate to the result of which old experiments had made them sceptical. The suspicion was accepted that you would be lousy again by the time you got back to the battery. It was well enough, and in proper proportions, to travel that dozen miles when the object was ammunition and rations ; but not when the object was an inconclusive bath.

"We'll get our 'rest' soon," said Cartwright. "And leave." For there was always talk of these.

"In the meantime," said Reynolds, "I'm all for Browne's dodge."

Browne's dodge for meeting the problem was, like all Browne's dodges, simplicity itself. The wearing of a truss had led him, as all inventors are said to be led by accident, to his discovery. It was the coarse bandage out of a field-dressing tied loosely round the middle inside of shirt and undervest. The final office of the day was the quick and furtive removal of this band and the placing of it with its refugee-horde in the brazier.

To this remark of Reynolds's, the reply of Richards probably was : "I wonder if the fresh lot of dressings has been drawn yet ? We'll have to go easy with them use a bit of sandbag or a torn-up shirt or something My body-belt does the trick, but it's such a hell of a business getting it off ; and you can't burn the damned thing."

"I don't believe in body-belts, Dicky," Whitelaw growled. "It stands to reason that they must weaken you."

"It would weaken *you*," said Reynolds, "to believe in anything."

After a surprising pause Whitelaw said very thoughtfully, "I wonder, Rennie . . . I wonder !"

"Golly," said Reynolds. "I've depressed the old one now. Given him the hump. Started a train of thought

. . . Dad, tell us honestly, do you ever think of trying to chuck in, and sneaking off ? "

" For nearly one year," said Whitelaw, still speaking slowly, " and quite honestly, my son, I've thought of damned little else."

" And why don't you ? "

" Well—— " said Whitelaw. " I'm going to, one of these days. It'll be on the day that the Brigade Orderly Officer gets the Military Cross. . . ."

Out of gossip with other batteries came the rumour that orders had somewhere been issued for the immediate opening of leave and the withdrawal of the Artillery to join its own division in training and rest ; but that the Colonel had sent in a confidential report on the sector and volunteered to continue with his brigade in the line.

It is certain, at any rate, that an order had once got down to the batteries, enjoining battery commanders to make their own arrangements for the purchase of foot-balls and boxing-gloves for the recreation of their men during rest. The order was ironically read, forgotten and after some weeks repeated. Old Pearson, the waggish Special-Reservist in command of A Battery, wrote a memo which was said to have gone as far as Army H.Q. wherein he suggested that six months' definite notice should, if possible, be given to units before the outlay was made from battery funds, owing to the notorious perishability of rubber goods. (It was this same Pearson who received a note from the General, after an inspection of wagon-lines, expressing the General's surprise at having found grass growing in inconspicuous parts of Pearson's wagons. Pearson's answer was said to contain his own wonder that the General had been able to find grass growing anywhere at all, and surprise that he himself had not yet found it growing on his men. It was Pearson also who sometimes caused the fuse of a shrapnel shell to be set at zero in the late afternoon and fired from one of his eighteen-pounders into a covey of partridges that roosted in a pile of rubble and débris on the brow in front of his battery.)

Leave did not open ; orders for withdrawal and rest got

x

no further than rumours and the paragraph about footballs.

Battery commanders alone among the officers with the guns visited the wagon-lines ; and it was only five or six weeks that comprised that eternity of funereal loafing and sudden cringings into hollows and against banks that might equally have been roadsides or trench-sides.

October was probably a record for wetness and also for cold, rivalled jealously by the first days of November. Days perished squalidly and disappeared, unnoticed, into night. Nights writhed heavily into day. Battle had died into mean bickering ; into the shelling of trenches —alleged, suspected, probable and even remotely possible trenches : the shelling of roads and dumps and alleged Headquarters ; the shelling of batteries—for there was a minimum of sixty rounds per gun per day, to be got rid of.

The time contained also two or three special shoots of gas-shell, where the secret of success was said to lie in concentration and rapidity of fire ; and the din from the four guns in the road—the left section shooting over the right—gave fresh vibrations to the old ones that were as ghosts mustered behind the ear-drums.

The bickering meant, too, the direct and simple converse of these exercises ; shelling in the trenches and alleged trenches ; in the probable and possible trenches between them, on the roads and at the battery. There were the heavy, clumsy things that had come a great way nosing and rooting through the mist and noisily slithering earthward to burst slowly and dirtily, or to leave a vacuum of startling silence after plopping into the sludge—duds ; there were the keen, slim things that skimmed over the crest with the pace and the song of a bullet, to burst with the sting of a whip-lash. All that they had in common was their intention and the names that were spat out upon them by men who froze and thawed and shaved themselves and manned guns and carried ammunition and peaceably dug holes. . . .

The sum of their toll was the youth with the pudding-mould hat from Gamages, straight jacketed in a blanket, gibbering and knocking his teeth together and getting a lucid word here and there out of the perplexity that tormented him. It was Shepherd the limber-gunner spitted and roasted under the trail of his gun (his magpie and his ferrets taken over by his successor with the succeeding gun). It was the Sergeant and the Corporal and the sentry found dead in the morning ; Sibley and Wagstaffe with the bullets from the neighbourly Canadian; and men gone limping off, with the Brigade-orderly to show them the way, or alone ; diarrhœa, bronchitis and fever vague and morose.

Oakleigh reported the evacuation of drivers with wounds that were inconsiderable, and pneumonia. Mules were posted for duty when horses were led slowly away with heels that went on cracking and foully ' greasy,' and feet rotting with thrush.

" 'Ullo," said Browne one contemplative morning from his kitchen door. " Old ' Ludwig's ' lorst 'is way. Got orf 'is road a bit."

The reference was to a row of grey caps and squalid, weary faces rising over the bank in front of the muzzles of the right section's guns, herded by a Lance-Corporal.

The eastern end of Regina Trench had fallen—fallen by the process of decay.

It was Reynolds who most nearly expressed the general feeling with which the secret order was received at the end of the first week of November, stating that batteries would withdraw from their positions on the following night, to pass Pozieres windmill ' at the following times.'

" These fellows," he said, " these tape-worms—they have no feelings for the Sanctity of the Home."

MEDAL WITHOUT BAR   CHAPTER LXI

"THEY can only think," said Richards, " of the pip-squeaks. I dare say *they* would be able to romp out at night."

' Pip-squeaks ' in the parlance of so staunch a howitzer

man as Richards meant the somewhat lighter eighteen-pounders.

He went morosely to the telephonists' shanty and asked for the Colonel or the Adjutant.

" Gordon," he said, " the times you've given me on that chit of yours—you know the thing I mean—came up with the orderly this morning—I'm afraid . . ."

" For God's sake," said Gordon, " shut up."

" Well, what I mean to say is——"

" You can't say it over the wire," snapped Gordon ; resplendent, no doubt, in his cavalry boots and spotless breeches and his new ribbon.

" I'll have to come down and see the Colonel then," said Richards.   " It can't be done."

" You needn't," said Gordon.

" But if I can't speak over the telephone . . ."

" Don't worry."   It was flatly against the principles of the Colonel to tell batteries when he was about to visit them.   But Gordon, on this occasion, relieved his signallers of the courtesy of passing the information to batteries as soon as he and the Colonel should have left, by saying himself, " the Colonel's coming up."

" Oh," said Richards.   " Thanks."

He went back to the Mess fuming.   This childish nonsense of not talking over the telephone, even now when you could sneak along Twenty-Three Road for a mile if the light was favourable, crawl up to the right of it and look across, at last, to Grandcourt ; where the conditions of life, in short, had become stabilised.

You had begun to know, during the last week or two, where you were.   Things had become utterly simplified into the possible and impossible with no intermediate grades of desirability and undesirability.

The ' tape-worms,' the dwellers in the back-blocks, eaters of calves' head and drinkers of wishy-washy wine in Perrier-water suggested, with a most lordly suggestion, that the impossible should be undertaken and achieved within an imbecile margin of minutes.

Richards went off, mumbling, into Courcelette to see if there was any ghost of a better way out through the village.

To the delight of Whitelaw, when the Adjutant and the Colonel, with his showy Indian bamboo ' khud '-stick, came slopping up behind the men's burrows Richards had not yet returned.

" I like to see the real nobs and gentry out, doing a bit of slumming," he said to Cartwright. " I'll entertain them, Uncle."

Cartwright was willing.

" Richards ? " demanded the Colonel, in answer to their salutes.

He preferred Richards to Whitelaw ; the short-shooting at Arras had delivered Richards into his little hand whereas Whitelaw had been delivered into the hand of no man.

" He's gone reconnoitring for a road," said Whitelaw. " Through the village." He indicated the deserted rubbish-heap.

His manner was, of course, superb.

The Colonel was a small man, with a head so small that the bucket-shop tipster had had a terrible time of it fitting him out with a steel helmet that did not utterly extinguish him ; his little pointed face was always on the jump—smiling at the Adjutant and Orderly Officer and all Generals, smiling differently at lesser people in the act of patronising them, glaring, frowning, furling itself in Olympian thought. He knew, that shrewd little jockey with his shrewd Orderly-dog, all about the movements of ' Occidental Fleeces ' ; and his sharp little face was, for the moment, stuck.

Whitelaw, too, was a small man. But he was square, built solidly up in the vast sewer-man's boots planted in the ground. His face was large and square ; turned upon the natural lackey (who would have known exactly what to do and say with the simple Richards but was defeated by the square stance of ' Occidental Fleeces '), it had the impassivity of a figurehead on a balk of teak. But it said, as plainly as though its surroundings had not been dirt and wreckage but the sumptuous furniture of a magnate's inmost office : " Let us hear your business. We who live and work and move in a place like this are serious men, and busy."

The Colonel said, " Richards wanted to say something to me. Some grouse, the Adjutant thought—— " He had found the line to follow : it was the assumption that he and Whitelaw, sharing a point of view, might together contemplate the lesser one, Richards. " Perhaps you know what it is about."

Whitelaw slowly stirred his foot about in the mud. " Oh, yes," he said. " Your orders. The battery to be in action till midnight and at the Windmill at four." The stirring about with his foot had wrapped his boot with a doughy paste that made of it the foot of a paddling elephant. He pulled it slowly up with a sound like a mastiff jerking its mouth open, and indicated it with a shrug.

The Colonel had stopped delicately in his London-bought fashionable waders ; but his feet too were clubbed and shapeless and there were splashes on his cheek and chin.

" Which is the important thing, Sir ? " asked Whitelaw. " To stay in action till twelve, or to get past the windmill at four ? "

This tableau of the Company Director organising a job for a rattled clerk, of the Don sitting back in his saddle to interrogate a Gaucho or a Peon, was too much for the Colonel. ' Occidental Fleeces ' might be ' Occidental Fleeces ' ; but it was only a single and dirtily dim star above the frayed cuff of Whitelaw's tunic—Whitelaw standing short and square as an orang-outang, shaggy in a jerkin like a boarding-house hearthrug tied round his middle with a piece of string.

Cartwright and Gordon were engaged in an amiable and tactful conversation of their own a few yards away.

" The important thing," said the Colonel and he filled out his chest with the air that drifted sullenly over from Maple Lane ; " the important thing is that battery commanders and subalterns should carry out orders."

Whitelaw smiled the smile of the parent wise and deeply knowing in the way of infant tantrums. " Yes, Sir," he said, smartly and very solemnly.

" If you fellows can't get your guns out of this in four

hours, in how long do you think you *can* get them out ? "
He had managed to get quite away from the plane of
Directors and clerks and Dons and Gauchos, back to the
plane of pips and crowns and braids. He had failed,
while rapping out his question, to move one of his own
snugly shod feet in the stickiness enough to collect his
pose into something more impressive ; but he demanded,
Napoleonically, " Well ? "

" Richards could get them out in six or eight hours of
daylight, I expect," Whitelaw answered. " Any one else
would take twelve. And there might be a fog over the
open bit of road before the windmill."

" Yes," said the Colonel. " And there mightn't. What
would you do then ? "

" I'd wait, Sir," said Whitelaw. " Till it got dark.
Wait on the road this side. The only trouble will be
getting to the road. Is there another lot coming in ? "

" No," said the Colonel. " The people on our right
and left are extending their zones, to include ours." He
turned to Gordon. " We'll get that order changed,
Gordon, so that they take over the targets and we can
get out of action at midday to-morrow instead of midnight. Limbers and teams will come up, passing the
windmill before daylight, and stand by till twelve."
He turned to Whitelaw again. " Tell Richards," he
commanded.

Whitelaw said, " Yes, Sir." And then " Shall I stand
the battery to ? "

" No," said the Colonel. " I'm not inspecting this
morning. I'll go on and see the others."

" Won't you come down in our hole and have something ? " asked Whitelaw hospitably. " I believe there's
a bottle of whisky somewhere." (Pillowing the old
rascal's valise was an unopened case.)

" Thanks," said the Colonel ; " no, I never take
whisky."

Good salutes were exchanged and the Colonel and
Adjutant stumped off down the dip to C.

" I do," said Whitelaw when they were gone. " Yes,
my friend, I do. It removes nasty tastes. . . . Come

on, Uncle.   The sun's abaft the aiming-posts.   Of course,
bless your innocent heart, you don't see it."

" See what ? "

Whitelaw took out the bottle and the mugs from their
niche in the chalk.   " He's so damned particular about
timing the exit that there's something *on*."

" Well—there is," said Cartwright ;   " there's a battle.
Didn't you hear Gordon ?—the biggest push there's been
so far.   Seven Divisions ;   Beaumont Hamel."

" Battle your grandmother," said Whitelaw.   " Biggest
there's been—hell.   They've all been that, haven't
they ? "

" And immediately after it—rest," said Cartwright.
It was mostly as a joke that he said it ; but he said it
without emotion.

" God—he's a strategist ! " said Whitelaw, ignoring
the joke altogether and glowering out of the doorway
in the direction the Colonel had taken.   " He's had
the tip that there are going to be brass-hats and tabs
and tape-worms about somewhere on the road ; or
why this childish foolery of assembling the Brigade by
Usna Hill ?—We're going to knock into some nob or
other, lousy with his A.D.C.'s and G.S.O.'s and God
knows what all.   He'll see our little jockey riding at
the head of his brigade, covered with real fresh mud ;
and if the nob doesn't know our jockey's name he'll tell
a Staff-Captain or the soda-water boy to find it out.
The orderly-dog might get the V.C.   I hope they ask
me *his* name.   I'll tell 'em something.   It's a great war,
Uncle. . . . Here's how."

" Cheerio," said Cartwright.

There was nothing to worry about.

Courcelette had been getting a shell somewhere or
other every minute that Richards had been gone road-
hunting—but as Courcelette got shells in every minute
of the day and night it signified nothing except that
Richards had no prospect at all of finding a road.   He
had only gone because his nerves were always unduly
shaken by Brigade.

There was nothing to worry about. . . .

Oakleigh would bring the limbers and teams past the Windmill and the exposed half-mile of road before light and hang about till he and the drivers could see to pick a way, and sound it in places, for the limbers to the guns. The horses and mules would stand till noon, feeding or tossing up their empty nosebags, trying to stamp and succeeding only in making a sound of gurgling; nipping each other's necks and quarters. Drivers would loaf and gossip and squabble till noon with gunners, each calling witnesses that his occupation was the more arduous and hazardous of the two.

At noon they would push over and drag aside the sandbags from the backs of the gun-pits and shove out the guns, and limber up; and by dusk or midnight or later than midnight—or before—they would, somehow, get them to the road.

It would all happen somewhat more easily and quietly now that Major Maguire had pulled out his eighteen-pounders from behind them a couple of days before. Whitelaw with his dodges for jibbers and kickers and slugs, for getting tumbled animals up to their feet again; Richards with his cunning in the matter of handspikes and ropes and 'purchases'; Oakleigh as slick and as crisp as a boatswain; Reynolds skipping about and swearing, lively but a little peevish after his night out in the holes which no one would now keep aired and cosy; Cartwright himself throwing a shoulder against a vacant spoke and felloe, saying, " Steady there," or " Hold her up. Keep it . . . keep it " or " Together—now—heave ! " shoving and sweating against shield or muzzle, looking as battered and as busy and contributory to the end in view as any one; the gunners—grunting and sweating and mumbling their conversational, gloomy obscenities—dragging their kits from one floundering of the gun or limber to the next, salvaging the boards and balks and corrugated iron squashed into the ooze of one hazard to push it and kick it and squash it into the ooze of the next—between the lot of them, and somehow, it would be done.

Browne would be waiting ahead with the primus installed in one of his wigwams of ground-sheet and walking-stick and corkscrew stakes, or (if he was lucky enough to find anything of a value so dramatic), the carcass of a rifle. They would hang about at intervals on the road, waiting for the hour specified by the Colonel, thanking God that the weather was so fine.

There would be no mouth-organ, or if there was a mouth-organ there was no organist of the quality of Evans to play upon it.

.   .   .   .   .   .

Unexpended ammunition was counted and stacked under cover in the gun-pits. It was listed on lists checked and signed by the battery commander ; and abandoned.

Empties that could not be carried away on the foot-boards of the limbers were buried with the latrine. (They were said to cost a pound apiece, or forty or fifty shillings —but there are limits to the responsibility of men; and a sense of proportion is sometimes keener in an acting-unpaid but philosophic Bombardier who does a job, than in the remote economist who designs it.)

MEDAL WITHOUT BAR   CHAPTER LXII

IT was done, with three or four hours of waiting on the road. Courcelette, over the low mound to the right, howled at intervals and clattered with the ghoulish shells that still prowled into its haunted emptiness, tormenting the roads and holts and crossings on the distant gunners' maps that on the ground were a few scattered and dark memories of a past removed by seven weeks from the present.

A horse had plunged a foreleg through a submerged duckboard, and struggled and broken it above the fetlock. They had shot it in a crater and put an outrider in its place—the only variation from Cartwright's forecast.

The Colonel and the General and one or two remoter than they and more august, in a coterie of Adjutant and A.D.C.s and grooms rode upon the clouds of the morning by Usna Hill. Richards lustily sang out " D Battery—

'eyes right," to the hearties jogging and shuffling along behind him.

They were men at peace with the world and magnanimous ; so that they grudged not the panto-mime of whip handles passing snappily over the withers of the off-horse, '—elbow raised and slightly bent, back of the hand up and inclined to the front, fingers firmly closed on stock and thong. . . .' They grudged not the jerking of eyes from a contemplation of backs and bullet-heads and haunches, towards gilded might and tabbed elegance. There was pride in their gesture, as there was pride in the command from Richards ; for, with the garb and gait and scant belongings of refugees from flood and volcano, they were arrogant in their survival.

It was perhaps the most persistent and most fantastic of all the Field-Artilleryman's illusions that limbering up a gun and dragging it out of a gun-pit meant one thing and one thing only—rest and ' refitting.' It was so proper ; so reasonable . . . where was ' our ' Infantry ? . . resting ; already ' refitting.'

Until the myth was exploded of some peculiar tie as of wedlock binding together the Infantry and the Artillery of a division, the illusion persisted ; so that no impending battle or talk of battles, no jostling in the road against carriers of the furniture of battle, could convince the four batteries moving hollow towards their breakfast that they were not upon the road to ' rest ' and ' refitting ' ; thence— with new green guns and twinkling harness—probably to Palestine or Egypt, Italy or even some other theatre of operations as yet undreamed of.

The new theatre, however, was under two miles due west of Courcelette, whence the shortest cut to it with a vehicle was ten miles of road marvellously renovated by sappers and magnificently drained into those pro-digious ' sumps.'

There were two days at the wagon-line ; days of crisp autumn sunshine and endless bathing-parties trudging off to Albert. There was no technically martial feeling about those two days, no great interest in the impending battle which was to be (like the others) the greatest of all, and decisive. Orders and details for this would come in due course.

In the meantime there were keener thoughts on the matter of aircraft and the chance of a ' switch ' of a few degrees right, the addition of a few hundred yards on the range drums of a dozen hostile guns that kept tossing up sheets of puddle between the submerged Ancre and Aveluy Wood (' Aveluy ' being generally pronounced to rhyme with saveloy).

There were lists of ' deficiencies ' that led its chieftains to wonder how the battery had kept its body and soul, its breeches and its rumps, its boots and its feet, its horses and its vehicles approximately together.

But there was sunshine and a high, blue sky ; there were omelettes and red wine in a certain dim estaminet in Albert disclosed by the interpreter ; and the shelling was a fixed routine of distantly impotent plops.

In those two days some of the battery's fitments of the wire from hay and straw trusses, of telephone-cable and string, were replaced with straps and buckles and thongs and chains.

Browne went forth with an assistant and the mess-cart and an immense sheaf of money to dazzle the canteen in Warloy.

Hair was cut.

Letters—as though it was a time of holiday instead of restless clamour—were inscribed by the armful ; so that it was all four right hands and indelible pencils to the aid of the orderly-officers in franking them before the setting out for the estaminet and the omelettes and the wine.

" Victory ! Victory ! Victory ! . . ." Whitelaw kept mumbling as he quickly read, and licked and signed. . . . " Victory ! . . ."

The dead had buried their dead.

The letter-writers had forgotten their vaporous dream of rest and ' refitting '—of Palestine and Italy and Egypt. Beaumont Hamel of vague memory—(and sinister repute according to the Infantrymen loafing up-stream along the water-side with poles in case the shelling should have turned a pike or a bream belly-upwards in the water)—Beaumont Hamel was become the master-word in conversation, together with St. Pierre Divion (more usually called, because of some strategist's casual misreading of an old *Daily Mail* or a map, St. Peer Div*i*sion).

" There's one more river to cross," was a slogan catchphrase in all badinage and bickering.

The sun had so shone that there were places where a footfall was beginning to ring clear, and dust to arise from the turn of wheels.

To Dorothy, Cartwright wrote that the weather had become marvellous—a wonderful change from the last few weeks ; that he believed he had been putting on weight.

To Henderson he wrote, " It's funny how flat ' Winning the War' seems to be turning out. We are winning. The paper says so ; orders say so ; I suppose you know we are—— and we can see it all around if we look for it. You can walk about and stand up and ride a horse now where you had to travel on your tunic-buttons a month ago ; and I suppose that's something. If horses didn't get so damnably hurt and if one didn't keep on losing men (and for no apparent reason and with no particular result even for the Bosche) it would be possible to get more of the victory-spirit. The battery is full of strangers —men and mules—but they all seem to fall into everything at once. Leaves are open again (or, as we call them, in this unit, ' leafs ') but I'm not even interested. I haven't been out more than four months (God ! I must read that over a few times—four months !) and most of the Division hasn't been home for eighteen— I'm last but one on the roster. The last is the new senior subaltern. Dorothy sends a good report of you and Mollie and the boy. I'm relying on you to temper the wind for her. After all, the Artillery isn't the infantry. The individual's chance does exist with us, as a pretty good one."

" The ratio of deaths to wounds is about one to four, and of decent gentlemanly wounds to bad ones, as far as I can see, about five to one. I wonder if you can

imagine the difference sunshine makes to things ?   It is
well worth the possibility of being spotted from the
air.   There's always the pious hope that with so much
to choose from Fritz will choose some other crowd for
his attentions, and it's marvellous how generally the
hope is fulfilled ; and ballistics are, after all, only
approximate.   No ; don't bother about sending stuff out
ex-bond.   There's some talk of the whisky supply being
regulated by chits from the Staff-Captain ; but our man
at the wagon-line is a match for any Staff-Captain and
we're sure to be all right. . . ."

BEAUMONT HAMEL and St. Pierre Divion fell on
the battery's third day in the new position
After the battle and its final victory the sky
darkened again and lowered.   Drizzle slowly settled
into rain ; the snug, hard road achieved by the sappers
along the old ' Nab ' track disappeared slowly under
the familiar smear of cold lava, and there was a feeling
in the air of a suitable end to affairs ; of the time having
come for leisure.   It sank into the general consciousness
—in spite of advertisements and of talk to the contrary
—that everything attainable had been attained and that
nothing more of a lively nature was impending.   It was
admitted that there was no limbering-up imminent for
march to the Rhine, no polishing of buttons and of
dust-caps on the vehicles for the triumphant entry
into Berlin.

The battery got down, in short, to winter quarters.

The position was beside the old fire-trench from Mouquet
Farm to the Thiepval Crucifix.   There were dug-outs
and dug-outs to spare. Spaciously, Cartwright and
Reynolds occupied a whole one, with their entire kit
suspended at the end of it from a clothes-line of telephone
wire.   This was a gesture of resentment rather than
confident measure of defence on the part of Reynold

against the lice that papered the walls of every one of these 'underground palaces,' as they had once been called in the Press. Whitelaw and Richards had bunks curtained off with ground-sheets, in the Mess. In this chamber was a good stove; it was known that in due course, and when occasion arose, there would be abundant fuel.

In the way of business there was a walk every sixth day, and twenty-four hours to be spent in the squalor and scant comfort of Stuff Trench. Pride of conquest, as one peered thence along the gash of Stump Road into Boom Ravine or down the slope to Grandcourt, was dulled by tiredness and by the lack, perhaps, of novelty in the scene.

. There was the same lack of novelty in the walk up and back to the battery; in the sitting in the trench, shaving one's boots with a piece of stick or the blunt edge of a bayonet; telling an Infantry subaltern (so loudly that his men might hear) that it was not due to bad shooting on the part of the artillery that eighteen-pounder shells just barely avoided tripping up on his parapet or in his wire, but owing to the slope of the ground along the shell's angle of descent.

There was a monotony for Cartwright in having hours wherein to write letters, and having nothing that he could reasonably say. The question of his survival, he presumed, was the question that preoccupied Dorothy, as it preoccupied himself; and the answer to it lay not in words, but in mere arithmetic.

As to chances in the Infantry he could not exactly say; but even in the Infantry, as far as he could see, survival was astonishingly the rule and not the exception. Infantrymen would change in the trenches while the gunners kept on plodding up and pottering along like British workmen with their bundles of dinner and their cans of tea. They plodded and pottered on till the old Infantry came back again and one would see, approximately, the same lot in the company- or battalion dug-out.

Only, one way or the other, there was no kind of guarantee.

As for his broader, more general reflections, he could see no point in recording them ; for they were the same as Henderson's own and his father's and every one else's ; or they were futile.

They were simply that it was wrong, all this business of flinging the live entrails out of men, of smashing up their faces, of crucifying them by their sleeves and breeches to barbs on wire and perforating them with a hundred holes ; it was wrong to starve and chill and batter them, to deafen them till they were sneaking curs or demented heroes ; it was wrong to chop the eye out of a waiting horse ; wrong to blind a man in the front line at dawn, and to kill him at midnight with a shell on the dressing-station. . . .

It was so absurdly wrong, that there was not a living soul who did not know it.   It was wrong, too, obviously to require the argument of a stench so mawkish-sweet that the living stomach was weakened by it beyond any orgasm of vomiting.

They all knew that it was wrong ; and this was the only immediate remedy—the only possible start towards remedy : plugging along in the darkness with two signallers from the battery to the niche in Stuff Trench, ' taking over ' from one of the C Battery men, ' handing over ' to the man from A, and plugging back again ; bathing at times in Jackman's scoopings out from a clearer hole heated in an oil-drum (for the journeyings of the water-cart were not so light a matter that their freight could be used for bathing) ; peppering one's vest and underpants with Keatings ; writing regularly to Dorothy with an occasional, lighter sort of letter to John and David.

Richards went home on leave, with Oakleigh in command at the guns and Whitelaw at the wagon-line He returned with new breeches of a light strawberry colour inviting ridicule.   His tunic and field-boots were also new and elegant ; and over his arm was a new trench coat.

The Military Cross, in the phrase of the time and the circumstances, ' came through ' for Reynolds.   It was so said the Gazette, " In the action of the Wonder-Work. For devotion to duty and conspicuous gallantry in closely co-operating with and rendering assistance to the Infantry during his tour of liaison duty." For Corporal Hine there was a Military Medal. The information came just before dinner. From humility or pride, or from the sketchiness of sleep in Stuff Trench during the night before and a magnificence during dinner and after in dealing with the whisky bottle and mugs, Reynolds wept in his bunk over Cartwright's lack of decoration. If only Cartwright could have shared the ribbon his own cup of happiness would have been full. . . .

So tremendously was Richards invigorated by his leave that he was impressed, as soon as he returned, by the staleness of the battery. Immediately he saw a remedy; things were so slack at the guns that two officers instead of one could be at the wagon-line; detachments must be changed completely over; some of the latest reinforcements could come up from the wagon-line and do some gun-laying; the servants, all drawing the ' proficiency ' threepence a day of qualified layers, would be given an occasional turn as Number Three to keep their eye in and allow them to earn a fraction of that threepence.

For himself a turn at the wagon-line would be small potatoes after ten days in London ; so he did not want it. Oakleigh therefore went back, to keep Whitelaw with him for a week.

At the end of that week they were both to come up and Reynolds and Cartwright, with their servants and their kits, were to go down.

Browne continued experimenting and continued failing, in the department of shock-absorption for the acetylene lamp. A sixty-pounder battery with a section two or three hundred yards behind the Mess put out the lamp with every round it fired ; and most of its firing occurred with peculiar malevolence between eight and nine-thirty in the evening. This was during the eating of dinners which Browne was still preparing with particular elegance from the stock he had laid in during

x

the period which was now referred to as ' the rest.
The raft in the basin of water kept a candle or two alight
out of the four or five it carried—sometimes ; but a bunch
of candles were no fit illumination of meals such as his
There was no vessel of sufficient draught to float a
barge of the proportions which the lamp would require
or of sufficient comeliness to be an adornment on his
table.

He tried suspending the lamp by a piece of plain
telephone-wire.   He tried it on the wire from a hay-
truss, wound round a pencil in varying lengths to give
it the look, if not the resilience, of a spring.   He tried
a combination of wire and the elastic from sock-suspenders.

It was a matter, he decided, of air pressure being
mucked up by the detonation of the sixty-pounders
and not a matter of vibration simply communicated
by solids.

His work proceeded thereafter along new lines, resulting
in a brief series of experimental globes and chimneys
The substance of these was inevitably opaque—cardboard
and tin, canvas, wood and paper—bent, folded, twisted
and tied into fantastic shapes, riddled with ventilating
holes in a variety of designs and formations.   When
with one of these opaque substances, his discovery should
have been made, he had little doubt that he could
materialise it in a sheet of celluloid—or ' something '—
from the sappers.

But he gave it up at last, admitting the gloom of his
defeat and agreeing that the only thing was for Richards
to ask the commander of the Heavy section to dinner
so that he might see with his own eyes the devastation
wrought by his weapons among those who were fighting
on the same side as himself, and so postpone his shoot
till at least nine, or start it at seven.

The man, a ranker with moustaches waxed out, was
open-minded enough.   A compromise was arrived at
whereby he did not shoot, unless specifically ordered
to do so, between seven and eight-thirty ; and Brown
served his dinners at seven instead of eight.

Browne, freed from his laboratory, gave his time with more enthusiasm to hanging about the gun-pit of his subsection and keeping his eye in at the range-drum or dial sight, when there was a shoot toward.

MEDAL WITHOUT BAR   CHAPTER LXIV

O N the afternoon that Whitelaw walked up from the wagon-line Reynolds and Cartwright were ready to walk down. It was not raining, and they strolled about behind the battery, keeping not far from the signallers' dug-out because Cartwright was doing a leisurely shoot of twenty or thirty rounds on a so-called ' Brigade Target '—some spot or other on the Puissieux Road fancied by the Colonel on the latest air-photograph.

" We'll have a spot of tea before starting, if the old blighter is much longer," said Reynolds, searching the sprawled, still billows and troughs southward to the jagged horizon, "—unless Dicky gets back."

Richards had gone up with a signaller and sandwiches to take a sceptic's look at some alleged strong-point.

Suddenly, in a single gesture, they ducked and were crouched on their knees and elbows.

" God Almighty ! " exclaimed Reynolds. And Cartwright, slowly and very thoughtfully, said, " Christ ! "

He knew that sound now, that had followed the Sergeant's peaceable, " Number three, fire."

In it the report of the gun, expected by a slight tightening of muscles that raised and held the shoulders a little towards the ears, by the suspension—for an instant—of breathing and the postponement of the answer to the remark of Reynolds—the report of the gun never came.

It was swallowed and annihilated in the stark burst of the shell itself.

A premature.

Reynolds said so, raising his face slowly to look in

Cartwright's and then aside from it and beyond to the gun-pits at Cartwright's back. . . . "Premature."

Cartwright was in no great hurry to turn and follow the gaze of Reynolds upon the foul black cloud uncoiling over the stricken gun-pit and the quiet crew. . . .

"Uncle. . . . Come on . . . it's got some one . . ." he heard Reynolds entreating, through the fumes of shattering noise that lingered still somewhere inside his head. " . . . Uncle. . . ."

"All right, Rennie." And they lurched across the fifty yards to number three pit, pushing aside from its entrance the Sergeant and a Corporal and a man or two who had scrambled across from the other guns.

Browne was sitting under the dial sight, facing them, his right shoulder humped up and tightly propped against the wheel. His legs stretched out under the trail. His hands, palms upward and neither clenched nor open, but slack in complete repose, lay on his thighs.

Simpson, from his position on the right of the breech, was flung over it, anyhow. His arms hung limply down—like the arms of a shirt tossed over a clothes-line except for the wrists and hands sticking out of them— and from the broken crown of his head there dripped to Browne's knees a froth of brains and blood, and God knew what.

Sergeant McCorkindale, engine-driver from Saskat-chewan, sat huddled against the back of the pit with his hands tightly clasped upon his stomach ; half his face, gone to the colour of drying mud from the colour of good bright leather, was fringed in a dark, moving whisker from a gash under his ear. He, from whom the faintest smile had been occasion for comment and report, was smiling now—grinning with the grin of a goblin—as he stopped his breath into a ripple that was neither moan nor croon nor chuckle.

Reynolds turned upon Upton who had been loading at the gun. "Shut up, you fool ! " he snapped. "We can *see* that for ourselves. Clear out ! "

Upton shut up and cleared out. He had been standing

and looking at nothing in particular, mumbling " . . .
never touched me . . . never touched me. . . ."

Browne's eyelids never flickered to lift from their
drooping over his eyes. The pull was gone that had
stretched the two straps of muscle from beside his
nostrils to the boundaries of his meticulously shaven
chin. Gone was the little downward twist of the lips
that had framed for every triviality and every mon-
strosity a comment. The sardonic mask was melted
and reset. The eyes behind drooping lids were resting
upon an open skull that dripped into his lap ; and
Browne was silent.

Smiling a smile of utter, gentle innocence, he was
silent.

No more was there a man to shun the commonplace,
the *cliché* of ' Fritz ' for Germans in the mass and to
claim the aloofness of his own individuality by referring
to them, unsmiling, as ' old Lud-wigg.' No more
would lice, with their hundred common nicknames
be distinguished with the same individualistic touch
by the gentle names of ' twilight toddlers ' or ' prahling
Percy.'

They patched up McCorkindale, painting and stanching
the hole in his neck, padding and loosely binding the
rent in his stomach. Cartwright gave him a tablet
and they hurried him away on the stretcher, while the
other three guns finished the series.

They carried out Simpson and Browne, emptying out
their pockets, wiping the contents of Browne's ; and
they took the appropriate disk from the breast of each.
The splinter that had stabbed Browne's heart in two
was one of half a dozen that could equally have killed
him ; Simpson, too, was half a dozen times destroyed,
and a thigh was broken.

They washed in Richards's bucket and had a drink.

" I wish to God," said Reynolds, " that Dad would
hurry up ; so that we can get out before Dicky comes
back. . . ."

It never seemed to strike one," he said later,
when Cartwright had been filling his silence for some

time with gratitude that there was a letter in his pocket
to Dorothy, already written that morning; " it never
seemed to strike one that *Browne* might get done in. . . .
Somehow . . ."

Jackman, from his vigil, came down to tell them that
Mr. Whitelaw was just coming across from the road.
They went up, and at the top Reynolds said, " Half a
tick," and went over to the guns to say something to
Upton.

Then they went across to meet Whitelaw and to take
their road. Stopping for a moment they glanced back
at the two blanketed and neatly tied shapes behind
number three pit. Then they moved on, silent till
Reynolds said, " Uncle . . . we shall not look upon his
like again. . . . Dicky will give the job to old Riding,
I expect ; and we'll have to find some one else to help
the quarter-bloke. . . ."

Again they were silent till Whitelaw met them.

IT was a glum enough tramp, with the light sinking out
of the sky in front of them and Jackman with
oddments of kit prowling along behind.

" During the next fortnight," Reynolds said with a
sudden look away from Authuille Wood whose gloom he
had been studying on his right, " my turn will be along.
I've thought of a great lark, Nunks. You can give me your
address and I'll posh myself up and call on ' Auntie '
and the boys. It would be rather a joke, don't you
think ? "

" Rather, Rennie," said Cartwright, " no end of a
joke."

" I expect they'd enjoy it, too," Reynolds. " Hearing
from the eye-witness what a hell of a lad the old man is."

Cartwright was glad that Rennie had thrust this last
idea into his own suddenly warm and kindly thoughts of
Rennie, shaved and groomed and twinkling in his best

behaviour, chattering an expunged chatter to Dorothy and the boys.

" Yes," he said, " rather."

But he already knew that one day, as soon as Rennie's leave was imminent, he would ostentatiously read a letter from Dorothy, fold it up and lie, " Oh, hell, Rennie ! It's sickening ; but ' Auntie ' and the kids are going down to a place in Cornwall for a month, so you won't be able to see them after all." Cornwall would be safe enough. he supposed, because Rennie's own home was in Berkshire ; but you never really knew with Rennie. He had talked for some weeks now of keeping two or three days of his leave for his own personal and private use, so it would perhaps be as well not to specify any particular place in Cornwall.

Rennie in command of the wagon-line was a strong man conscious of the weight of the destinies that rested upon his shoulders. The plans sketched at the battery for nightly dinings at the estaminet with the long, low room were only twice followed. It was a long walk to Albert at the end of a day ; Oakleigh's tent was furnished with wire beds, a table, chairs and a fine stove. There was no brace of sixty-pounders to extinguish the light on the table and drown the snuffle of horses and the peaceful grumble of men outside. A single team per gun was enough to take all the ammunition that was wanted at the guns and Richards had said that senior N.C.O.s could take it in rotation, unless there was some special reason for an officer to go ; and during that week there was no such reason.

In the day they rode somewhere, for there was always something to be done, something to be wheedled out of some one—the I.O.M. at Meaulte, the A.S.C. at Bouzincourt, the Sappers, Remounts, the Ammunition Column, or the question to be settled once and for all as to which was the best-stocked canteen in the neighbourhood. At one of these they ran into Sammy, the machine-gunner who was not yet dead, but full of recollections of the marvel which was the Number Fourteen periscope.

They lunched with him and Black wearing the V.C.

ribbon, and two or three of his new subalterns. The progress and process of the War was meaningless and therefore of scant interest to the party lunching elegantly in the billet, with glasses to drink from, and china plates. If ever a battle had been won in all the history of strife, they—actually and individually they, Black and Sammy and Reynolds and Cartwright—had won the battle of the Somme.

Yet there was no visible victory.

Their own leaves, the hosts admitted a little evasively as though the subject were one that ought to be tactfully changed, were over. But they congratulated Reynolds on the imminence of his, condoled—again evasively—with Cartwright in that his was still ages away.

In the manner of chieftains saluting guests in departure they offered gifts; whisky, Quaker oats, sardines, cylinders of biscuits (at cost price); for their training-billet was within earshot of the best canteen in Picardy. The departing chieftains thanked them, but declined; for they had in their senior subaltern the finest scrounger in the Army.

Reynolds, warmed by nightcaps of the giant-killer on those seven nights in the tent, expanding to the point where men may take the larger view of destiny, spoke some of his deeper thoughts. Cartwright likewise warmed and expanding—resenting only the foulness of the chlorine that marred the toddy—listened to them and smiled.

A shell, bursting muffled in the swamp, only made more profound the peace and isolation, made warmer still the warmth and cheer of the tent guyed taut and laced against the patter of gentle rain.

The burden of these deeper thoughts of Reynolds's at that time was women. He was nineteen, he said; getting on for, and damned nearly, twenty. . . .

The thought, with its mysterious implications, was a sombre one. His leave was coming—any day now; they were in as quiet a place as they had ever been, but he had never, so he said, been so windy . . . and that was the worst of leave. When it had got so near that one chance, and one chance only remained to do you in the eye and diddle you out of it, you began to funk that chance and try to dodge it as never before.

"I haven't noticed it, Rennie," Cartwright said comfortingly. But this, it seemed, was an irrelevance. The central, and the overshadowing, thought was Rennie's anxiety (that had acquired a mystical force) for the adventure most proper to his years.

Thoughtfully tossing his jacket to the chair he had vacated, pulling off his boots, he snarled at the War that even in the next few days could cheat him of it; he snarled at himself for the mess he had made of his last leave—tearing straight home to his parents and some early tennis and tea-fights, dining out twice or three times—with the Rector and the old Doctor. That sort of thing. . . . Tearing straight out again to the battery. . . .

But it was different now; he knew better than to dodge through London with a kind of silly nervousness that was almost funk whenever there was turned upon him the light of a glad eye. There would be no silly grinning and bolting away this time to catch a train, real or mythical—if this time should, indeed, come to pass—which seemed impossible now that it had come so near.

"Rennie, you're distinctly tight," Cartwright said, again comfortingly.

"I dare say," said Reynolds. "But there is truth in a cup of sack—What's to prevent that lousy orderly officer of the 4·2 battery shooting from Serre or wherever the hell it is, from switching a degree left for fun and adding three or four hundred and scuppering the two of us?"

"Probability," said Cartwright. "Probability. . . . The fact that he hasn't done it for two months, but has kept on plugging away——"

"Oh, I know we can *hope!*" said Reynolds, contemptuously; "but there's damned little to be *counted* on."

"No," said Cartwright, and this time he was thoughtful.

" I think it's a good deal more than just hope. You can count—on probability."

" Yes," said Reynolds. " The way Browne counted on it ; and sat down with his chest split in two."

" Well—— " Cartwright began ; but Reynolds said : " For God's sake, Uncle, shut up. One hell-fire-eater in the battery is enough—we've got Dad. It's no use your trying that—indom-indom-r-ble pose. The colour of your gills wasn't much to write home about when that premature pulled us down, tummy-to-earth, on Tuesday. You can't tell *me* you weren't frightened. I was there, don't forget."

" Frightened ! " said Cartwright. " I should think I was frightened, Rennie. I'd run a mile from a premature."

" Very well, then. Admit it."

He became very serious. Gently cajoling, pronouncing his words very distinctly and choosing them carefully, he said, " I don't ask more of you, ol' Duncle, than that you should just frankly admit it. I've admitted, quite freely, that I've just about got sick with funk ever since my turn for leave became two places down the list ; and I ask you to admit——"

" Go on with you, you idiot," said Cartwright, and he set to work upon his own tunic and boots. " Of course I admit it. Anything you like."

" No," said Reynolds, indignant but very earnest. " Not—anything I like. Just the simple truth. You're frightened. You'll be damned glad when it's over."

" I'm frightened, Rennie," he said yawning. " And I'll be damned glad when it's over. How's that ? "

" That's A 1," said Reynolds. " Now we know there's no snobbery between us. No communion of the dauntless. . . . You can put out the light easier than me, when you've done folding up your tie and messing about generally. And when I've had my leave and a couple of days in town—off the deep end—I won't care if it snows. You'll see."

" You be careful, young fella," said Cartwright, blowing out the lantern. " You and your couple of days. . . . "

" And you start trying any paternal or avuncular pi-jaw on me—— " Reynolds began.

" It was not pi-jaw," said Cartwright quietly. " What I had in mind was hygiene."

" Don't worry," said Reynolds. Presently he said, brightly as though out of thoughts quite new, " Uncle, asleep ? . . . I suppose it makes you feel no end superior, the sort of virginal dither I've been chatting ! "

" What I do think, old chap," he answered, " is that you're attaching a good deal too much importance to such things."

And Reynolds grunted. " It's all damned well for old blighters like you to talk ! After being *married* for a quarter of a century."

Again he interrupted the patter on the tent after a few minutes with : " Uncle, asleep ? "

" Is it likely—you're about as conducive to it as those sixty-pounders behind the battery. What's up now ? "

" An apology is being tendered," said he. " I may have trodden on your dreams or finer sensibilities, or what-not with that last remark of mine. It struck a bit 'arsh even on my own simple ear. 'Twas celibacy's terse and acrid snort, flouting to nought the nullity——"

" Good night, good night, good *night*, Rennie," said Cartwright. " And once again—good night. You trod on nothing, I assure you."

" With reassurance fair he gives good night," said Reynolds.

A POET (according to his class and to the measure of his fancy) might have expressed the battery's next move as into the very belly of an ancient, perished monster.

The battery, however, being strong in no poetry beyond the occasional blank verse of Reynolds, saw the move as a trundling of the kits lashed high on the limbers and the shabby guns along half a dozen crazy miles to shift them twelve hundred yards westward from the vague neighbourhood of Thiepval to the metropolis of Thiepval's self.

The word ' parish ' had by now supplanted the more stilted title of ' position ' for the acre of rubble and scrap and charnel that succeeded acre as the battery's haunt ; and the western extremity of Thiepval remained the parish from Christmas Day till a memorable day in March.

Browne had had some scheme for Christmas Day. The move notwithstanding, something or other spectacular would have graced the board set up in the vast dug-out. Perhaps, indeed, it would not have been the board at all—the old map-board, laid unenterprisingly on ammunition-boxes and petrol-cans. The odds are that Browne in his two or three hours of evangelisation would have produced a solider and comelier table ; but old Riding had no great sense of frills.

A table for him was a horizontal plane secure enough for the holding aloft of a meal ; and a meal was food.

The officers turned out after the meal to take the rum-issue with the men, and Oakleigh walked gallantly home thereafter, setting out with sprightly elegance and flashes of his torch from sleeper to narrow steel sleeper of the Decauville tramway laid from Black Horse Bridge to the road-corner behind the guns, which were housed as yet only under tarpaulin.

No time was lost in making what Richards called " a job " of things. The fire he had brought back from leave together with his new tunic and famous ' strawberry bags ' still glowed lustily.

Reynolds now was likewise kindled, for he, too, had been on leave.

Long-headed economists among the gunners unrolled marvellous chain-saws (' Canadian wonders '). These had been seen and smoulderingly coveted at first, and then duly filched from the neighbourly Canadian engineers' store so long ago as the first days in Sausage Valley.

With them their owners set to work upon the rags and stumps of trees disinterred in Thiepval Wood. Whatever was useless for trail-ramps and wheel-stops against the fluid earth of gun-platforms, useless even for the smallest span of roof-timber, was sawn up with those precious saws, split with the axes and with the wedges produced by a word (through Oakleigh) to the farrier, and carried below to a dug-out where six men slept by night and one was on duty throughout the day as guard.

For there were Infantrymen abroad in the carcass of their old monster Thiepval; gaunt, ragged men blue with the cold that became hourly colder. Sussex men made way for Dorsets and Devons. Lancashire- and Yorkshire-men passed, and after them (or before them) came Welshmen and hairy Jocks. There was little at which these perishers would stop, in either open violence or dark treachery, for a bag or two of firewood to bear away eastwards to the château dug-outs, or up St. Martin's Lane towards their frontier-hovels.

There was an ' office ' in all that dark shambles, an ink-pad and a neat square rubber stamp carved by some distant craftsman and issued from Ordnance to its holder—" ADMINISTRATOR."

The holder of the office and the stamp was an ancient derelict youngster left behind with his batman by some dim, prehistoric battalion. How long he had been there no one (himself and his batman included) seemed to know or care. His eyelids and the wheezing of the short, quick breaths he drew meant gas in some past that to him was still present. His pallor ; the totter of his legs when he went from his table to his bunk to get the cigar-box holding the field post cards whereon were inscribed the numbers, cubic contents, and current occupants of the dug-outs in his domain ; the quick contortion of his face and shoulders when Cartwright dropped a helmet to the floor—these also told their tale.

They asked him to dine at the Rectory ; but always he was ' too busy.' Reynolds asked him to come out one day, to see if the Sappers could not be made to replace some splintered timbers in a dug-out entrance ; and to stay to lunch. But he would not come. He sent his man to see the damage.

In March, when they left, he was still there as they had found him.

Long had he abandoned the formality of collar and necktie at his throat ; but wore, instead, a red woollen muffler. Slacks always covered his thin legs, and German infantry boots, cut down to the stature of slippers, his feet. He occasionally shaved during the afternoons.

Fancy, stretched no farther than the bounds of fantastic plausibility, can see him there still, pallid and forgotten in the dark viscera of the old, leprous Thiepval buried under a new one ; tottering to his cigar-box to shuffle his index-cards and deal their destiny to men in need of shelter, secure at last against all summons that might drag him up that chute of stairway to the lowering sky and the agony of open din. The batman, justly, will be there also, relieved of the trivial, the menial as also of the august, ambassadorial errands that, in the old days, ejected him from the hole into the wan daylight ; no more will there be any need for his eyes to rove darkly evasive, or his pale lips to move in the formula, " Administrator's compliments, Sir, please ; 'e's sorry 'e couldn't come 'imself, but . . . " The lips will be at rest, pursed about a Woodbine stump as he sits in his far corner frying a slab of bully over the primus with its spurts of smoky flame, stirring the endless brew of tea in a black mess-tin. . . .

.   .   .   .   .   .

If there is any one word to distinguish that living in the Thiepval parish from the livings before it and after, the word is slum.

There was a sordid meanness in every feature of it that had been lacking from every other litter of rags and equipment, of broken limbs and faces ; from the apathy and drowsiness of all earlier rats. This particular meanness had not been in the earlier fungi on palates, of gas and discarded flesh ; of chlorine with whisky, with toothpaste and with tea. The foulness of linen had now become sheer squalor; lice had no touch of mischief any more, they were a pestilence quite sombre.

Perhaps, since the spirit of man is so much the reflection of any light that burns a little brighter,—perhaps it was only that Browne had gone from them.

No man could have tried harder than Riding—but a spade could never be anything for Riding but a spade. He had no sense of Drama. Of the Mess he made a chop-house—clean, punctual and lavish; but a chop-house. He stood manfully up to the shade of Browne; Jackman or Crouch had bragged to him of Browne's menus, so Riding produced a menu—but he headed it ' Bill of Fare.' Where Browne would have inscribed, picturesquely, the exotic italicised alternatives in the index of his Mrs. Beeton, Riding admitted—in block capitals—to such things as ' Hot-Pot ' and ' Toad-in-Hole.' The fact was that the particular genius of Riding (for all he wore Browne's linen jacket with a gusset of shirt-flannel up the back) worked in other directions. He rejoiced in cutting hair and corns and ingrowing, poisonous toe-nails. He opened boils better, it was affirmed, than the Doctor; he excelled in blood-letting and ingenious ' cupping.' For the exercise of this craft that so allured him he carried a kit in his breeches-pocket —two penknives with blades filed and ground and stropped to the bright curve of scalpels; tweezers wrapped in an oily piece of leather.

Perhaps it was the ventilation of the ' Rectory ' that was at fault. The dug-out lay to windward of the catacombs and the garbage of those unnumbered, scourged and ultimately defeated garrisons. Its two entrances, with a promontory of ' bay ' sprawling out between them, opened into the original front line. The trench, twisting northwards, was a squat and sodden gulley. Into it and along it, dank and chill, the air flowed as sewage flows in a culvert, steady and slow until it struck the promontory by the dug-out entrance. Then, checked in its sluggish drift, it tumbled down the stairway through the ' Rectory ' —the length of dripping corridor that was dormitory and dining-room and office and wash-house and kitchen—flattening down the candle flames or bringing a wheeze and sputter to the acetylene lamp.

Alternatives were considered—among them the building of a Mess set up foursquare to the winds of heaven somewhere behind the guns and on the road down to the trolley-track. But there was a phase of tightness in materials at that time—cement and timbers and bags for the gun-pits had crawled with reluctance most sullen on the tottering trucks up the shaky metals, shoved and cursed by men, pulled by a brace of mules traced with rope and wire at an outrigger angle to their vehicle so that their feet might tread clear of the sharp-edged metal sleepers.

The winds of heaven, moreover, were themselves arriving with a lash and a sting of their own in them ; and there swooped, from time to time, a tornado out of the quiet solidity of the sky—a ' hurricane shoot ' as this particular type of visitation came to be called. It was a wild foray, short and sharp ; a spurt of energy and mischief from the rag-tag and bobtail of weapons lying restless and fairly idle in the hollows about Grandcourt and Miraumont and Puissieux. Five-nines and four-twos would scream and dance and leap together with the lesser fry of whiz-bangs, with the chilling snarl of a slim naval shell, with the more brutish and lumbering hurtle of stuff still bigger from some brooding howitzer. It would last a minute—perhaps two, perhaps five—with the insanity of hell let loose and concentrated in a hundred yards of tattered earth. Then hell would subside again, leaving the dull sky at gaze upon the quiet rags.

" No offence meant," as an onlooker from a comfortably deep and distant hole once observed, " and no 'arm done."

But the project of any airy, foursquare homebuilding was abandoned. A door, instead, was put together for the top of the first entrance to the Rectory, and curtains hung at the bottom of it. The mess-stores were slung on wires from the roof in ammunition-boxes, like fern-baskets in a hanging garden ; rats, as yet, could not walk, inverted like lice, upon the ceiling timbers.

The Mess was generally three ; for one was usually up

in that sloping and unlovely gutter to the north of Schwaben, with the charred, smashed ribs of St. Pierre Division lying in the puddle to the left and the morose target of Grandcourt in the hollow in front. ('Stump Trench,' or a trench with a name cleanly forgotten.)

Cartwright found that he welcomed, on the whole, the generally ill-favoured twenty-four hours in this trench and the walk thereto. St. Martin's Lane twisted along beside the walk, a refuge seldom accepted and then in straits only the most dire.

From the strongest and the seemliest defence of a prodigious stronghold St. Martin's Lane had become a shapeless, unending sump. Wild, indeed, and near would be the 'hurricane' that could make a man abandon the duck-board track or shun the hospitality of a casual hole, to crouch in the ruins of St. Martin's Lane, deep only in puddle.

When shells ripped up the slope and into the parapet of that meagre Stump Trench, like the teeth of a great saw suddenly set whirling, tearing its already tattered shape, scattering a dust of soft filth and hot metal; when great moans broke out of the sky, sharpening to a whine and then a scream; when the trench was shaken in a stranglehold of coldly observed, deliberate fire so that pale, muddy men grew paler and muddier and fiendishly thirsty—or else ceased suddenly from their thirst and other tribulation—Cartwright still, in some peculiar way, welcomed and preferred it.

He was willing and always ready to sling his haversack with the food and the Thermos (there was a second Thermos since Reynolds had been on leave) and take the squalid road; for there, at the end of the road and along it, the onslaughts—terrific though they were, and sickening in their recurrence—were open, and openly declared.

About them there was none of the lithe treachery, the quick assassin-stealth of a premature—a shell bursting at the muzzle of its own gun to slaughter those who, full of kindliness, had set it on its way.

Then, in due course—at the beginning of February

z

or towards its middle—the troughs and billows of earth and rubble, the mounds and gullies grew black and newly terrible ; harder than granite and concrete, sharp-edged as rusty steel.   No more could you fling yourself, in an easy gesture, from duck-boards to the softness of a crater-side. The crater-side was jags and knurls and jutting spigot-ends, like a sculptured scrap-heap of some demon smithy.

The face lying at the bottom of the hole, the pale hand or green, bare shoulder had no semblance of movement now under the movement of rippling slime.

They were still, bedded in a block of ice.

This quiet device of earth's own armour against the noisy devices of men brought a new ring and clangour to the burst of shells.

There was no instant's soft nuzzling and then a spattered cone composed partly of harmless filth.   It was a crack, a sting upon the ear-drums, a stab in the air and a whirr of hurtling, clean hot steel that spun not upwards—' producing,' as a geometer would say, the sides of any crater (for there was no crater).

It whirled horizontally, skimming like the separate particles of a scythe-blade ; and even plunged sharply down.   Bursts, in short (and in the language not of geometers but of those schooled to some discrimination in these matters) were all ' on graze '—a high ideal for gunners.

St. Martin's Lane, despised a week before and rejected became the thoroughfare now for slouching nomads with their boxes and tins, their tools and stretchers.   Its bottom was hard and smooth—boxes and bundles could in fact, be towed along it in places ; and the cover here and there, was breast deep.   The only point to be regarded in its disfavour was the fact that it was, in all the wilderness bounded by the tank stuck at the top and by Stump Trench clinging to the bottom, the target of most ' hurricane ' shoots.

It was there that the O.P. party, relieved in Stump one evening, ducked and crouched and waited.   When the sky had lowered again and closed over the cackle and snarl, Cartwright and one signaller got to their feet and looked at the other signaller, who remained crouching. In the sudden vacuum of silence they heard him gurgle briefly before he tumbled forward with a clatter of his helmet on the ice.

There was nothing to do but take him home ; and Cartwright's thought was of what digging would mean in such ground. . . . Perhaps they could get him down to Headquarters on a trolley and the Padre would wheedle a fatigue party out of Brigade. . . .

" One of the 'tillery blokes copped it," said an Infantryman. " Orficer wants to borrer the stretcher. Can I give it 'im, Sergeant ? They're going our way."

The battery sentry was found squatting on the trail of a gun one dawn, his feet and legs muffled in sandbags, his hands stuffed into the pockets of his greatcoat. It was probably, the Doctor said, heart failure ; for he was one of the older men in the battery, a quiet grocer with a small business in some suburb which his wife was running. (She had, indeed, always run it ; for he was the meekest, politest of men.) Whatever it was that had killed him, carrying him from the gun-pit to the trolley was like carrying a man cast in steel ; and it was bowed and still squatting that he was buried.

The old Courcelette practice of inter-battery parties was dead and forgotten ; Eskimos are no great diners out. If there were but two shoots during the night the orderly-officer usually stayed in the Mess and muffled up, turbaning his head and covering his ears, to go out and do one of them, for Richards generally took the other. If there were three shoots or more on the night's programme the orderly-officer usually estimated the journeys (perhaps a hundred yards each way) as disproportionate to the comfort of his own bunk. He muffled himself up and dozed between shoots beside the off-duty signaller in the lean-to in the bank beside number two gun. For the lean-to was no lousier than the Mess ; and it was warmer. The shoot could usually be conducted with a head stuck out of the doorway.

For Cartwright the signallers' lean-to in the bank had

this other point ; it was something in the nature of cover from a premature.

It was dozing between the signallers one night or dawn, that he got his idea about writing to his tailor ; and he wrote to him next day for a tunic and pair of breeches. Leaves were open again, to the extent of one officer at a time per Brigade. Some time or other his turn would probably come. Either of his two current tunics would tell, to an eye like Dorothy's, some tale. Of his breeches one pair had had knee-caps and part of the seat inserted by the saddler. It was in the other pair that he had attended to Austin, also to McCorkindale and Browne. Jackman had done his best to them with a dandy-brush and soap, and petrol given to him by a South African heavy gunner ; but Jackman's best in anything fell far short of adequacy.

He ordered the new ones that he might have time to wear them, discriminately, to take the shop-bloom off them, that any tale told to Dorothy by his clothes might be a quiet one.

Sammy, the machine-gunner, the indestructible, was said to be dead ; Black, V.C., the indomitable, had been corralled with red tabs among the tape-worms somewhere at the back.

The murky afternoons grew slowly longer ; so also, in the minds of survivors, did the odds against survival.

With Browne gone, with the going of others duly labelled ' bronchitis ' and ' pneumonia,' ' rheumatism,' and ' septic chilblains ' (for it was their going that mattered, not what took them) ; with the meeting of Infantrymen in St. Martin's Lane—limping, dragging, or carried with faces pallidly blue and grinning or hidden under a ground-sheet ; with those insane ' hurricane ' shoots that a hundred times would do nothing to the once that a splinter took the chin off a driver and another splinter opened the skull of the battery sanitary-man ; with gossip in Stump Trench which recorded that Bliss of " A " was dead and Kelley wounded, that Reeves of " C " was drinking so fatuously that one more chance was all he could possibly have, that to lure a man who had just joined " B " out of the dug-out was as much as any mortal could do ; with any eight pairs of feet out of a dozen bursting, and most ears bulbous and green with chilblains—with factors such as these, dramatic or monotonously sombre, making up the life of night and every sunless day for the weeks that had become months —the outlook upon the matter of survival had altered.

The odds against it were longer than gunners had been inclined to think. They thought now—and the thought was apparent in their talk—not so much that it was a bad chance that befell you to knock you out one way or another, but that you might—considering all the possibilities, and on the whole—get through.

The hazard was not like a hazard of any adventure ; it was the cold chance of individuals in the slow working out of a pestilence. Taken all in all, it was about ' evens.'

Then suddenly, about the thirteenth or fourteenth of March, without the faintest breath of a rumour before it— for such rumours had long ceased breathing—Brigade Orders had a paragraph with the marginal heading :
WITHDRAWAL.

Batteries, it announced, would withdraw from their present positions and assemble, by Brigades, in Aveluy Wood where hutments would be allotted. Details and order of march to destinations, for a period of rest and training, would be issued to battery commanders at Brigade Headquarters. Ammunition would be handed over to incoming batteries from whom receipts (in triplicate) were to be obtained.

For so long now had ultra-violet rays been lacking from the light of day that the battery could only shrug its shoulders and grunt monosyllables at the paragraph ; getting out and down that road again would be no picnic.

Whitelaw, moreover, could remember (with their dates), three separate occasions on which such orders had been cancelled two hours before the time set for their execution.

This time, however, they were not cancelled.

IT was about three o'clock in the afternoon that breakfasts were being eaten in the Nissen hut set apart for the officers of the Brigade in Aveluy Wood. The commencement of a thaw left the moss dank and soft between the smeared duck-board tracks. Successive freezing hands had torn the lining from every hut ; numb feet had kicked it into sizes that could be thrust within the stove.

Cartwright, as orderly officer, was the last of D Battery to come in. In the course of his overseeings in the gun park and the men's huts and the lines he had found four signallers cooking their Quaker oats (with one of the four posted as a sentry), over the artificers' blow-lamp ; for the direst famine of the moment was in fire-wood or coal.

" Richards," he said, " if we don't get some fuel—— "

Branson of B Battery flamed suddenly up and screamed at him— " Fuel !—God ! don't mention fuel ! . . . When there's a *War* on—fuel ! . . . And look at the state of your buttons ! . . . And did you shave this morning ? . . ."

Senses of humour had become catholic in the last six months ; but by no stretch of imagination could Branson be considered, at the moment, a joker. Neither, in the inexplicable way that such things are self-evident and obvious, was he drunk. He was the biggest officer in the Brigade and the fiercest-looking. About twenty-six or eight years of age, he had come from Canada with the dark skin, black eyes and enormous blue-black moustache of an Albanian brigand. When, therefore, he suddenly jumped up and knocked over the rolled valise upon which he had been sitting and jerked the trestle-table with his great hands, eyes moved quite naturally from the disks of deep red flaming on his hairy cheeks to the revolver at his belt.

Forgotten, disbelieved tales came to mind of decent

men having gone grey in a night, or stark mad in
a day. It was only madness that could make a man
scream when others were morosely munching bacon and
cheese and slabs of bread, or complaining peaceably of
the lack of fuel. A batman put down a plate before
Branson. "Tomatoes, God damn and blast you!
. . . And when have you ever known me eat a filthy
mess like tomatoes with my bacon?" He picked up his
fork and dashed the offending tomatoes from the plate to
the floor.

"Here, just you shut up, Brannie," his battery commander said to him quietly—Allen, the good ranker with
the waxed points to his little moustache, and hair plastered
across the bald patch on his head. "Just you try to
remember there's all the officers of the whole bliddy
brigade in this Mess."

"They ought to be under arrest—the whole dirty,
damned lot of them," snarled Branson, and tossed a rasher
of bacon into his mouth.

"That's no reason to let them think B. haven't got any
manners—chuckin' their rashuns on the mat and God
knows where—in company."

"You'll do better to keep right out of this, Skipper,"
Branson said darkly. "It's none of your business."

"Not my business? Isn't it my business!" said
Allen. "I'm going to see the A.P.M. m'self as soon as the
battery's turned into stables, and explain."

Branson swallowed quickly, knocked over his valise
again in jumping to his feet, bumped his head on the
curved steel of the hut, cursed it and roared, "Skipper,
damn you—you leave the bastard alone." He sat down
again. After a mouthful of bread and a drink of tea, he
said very quietly: "*I* am going to see him. Before he
can say knife—I'll start quite quietly and respectful—
but before he can say knife I'll have given him a right and
a left, bashed his pink face in."

"You get outside a bit more bread an' tea," said Allen,
adjusting his belt and picking up his helmet. "Have a
cot and a sleep. You're off duty. Dolly's orderly
officer from now on—come on, Dolly, stables—'e 'asn't 'ad

as much to do as you.   An' jest you stay tight in here
till I tell you you can go out.   That's an order."

" Order your grandmother," Branson mumbled as his
battery commander went.   " I'll be sorry to disobey
you, old skipper," he said dreamily.   " But if that sod
thinks he's going on looking lovely much longer, he's in
error."   He gulped more tea.

" What the hell," said Cartwright quietly, sitting down
next to Reynolds at the other end of the table, " is
wrong ? "

" Brannie's under arrest," said Reynolds, taking the
straw off a whisky bottle and placing it, economically,
in the stove.   " For going into Albert in boots, gum,
thigh !   The A.P.M. saw him."

" Brannie ! "   said Cartwright.   " I say, is that
true ? "

" True as you're alive," said Branson, and it was clear
from the trembling of his immense lower lip that a sudden
burst of tears was not outside the range of possibility.
" God, I'll tell him something . . .   I couldn't then—
I had to get to the dump where the ration-cart was
waiting to draw the coals, or the poor bloody chaps
would have had no breakfast, no fires in the huts.   I
only had time to tell him to go to hell ; that I was a
busy man. . . ."

" That was something off your chest, anyway, old
thing," said Cartwright.   " It was a goodish start——"

" That's nothing to what I'm going to tell him ! "   His
cheeks were beginning to flush again.   " There the bitch
has been—living in a *house*—with a *fireplace*—and a
concreted cellar—hot bath every morning—girl somewhere every time he's felt like it—car and chauffeur to
take him there—while we—lousy, stinking, freezing,
shelled to glory morning, noon and blasted night.   I'll
tell him——"

Reynolds had gone round the table and was standing
beside the fantastic maniac.   He laid a hand on his
shoulder and looked down at him.   " Brannie," he
said, and every one of the ten or dozen in the hut looked
at him and listened.

" Brannie "—" Go tell the Constable :
    We are but soldiers for the working day ;
    Our gayness and our gilt are all besmirched
    With rainy marching in the painful field.
    . . . and time hath worn us into slovenry."

Branson, after some moments of dull staring ahead of him, shook the hand off his shoulder, and mumbled, " Oh, shut up ! Go to hell ! "

He quietly filled his pipe.

It is possible, even likely, that what Reynolds had averted was murder.

It was the twentieth or fiftieth—or hundredth— time that Richards and Cartwright and Whitelaw had heard him spouting those particular words ; but there was in them, this time, and in the voice of Reynolds, a peculiar magic. To any one of the dozen —utterly spent as they squatted to tug at the footgear that had been upon them, sodden and chilled, for thirty or forty hours—the indignation of Branson might have seemed fantastic, but not unreasonable. To minds, quietly without bias—now that a square hot meal had been eaten—and at peace, the absurdity of punishment for swinging a pair of fists like Branson's into the offence of a face like the one he had sketched seemed no uglier trick of destiny than, for example, sitting somewhere and doing nothing whatever for twenty-four hours or forty, and being hit on the head with something out of the sky at the end of it. They had been pottering and slipping and floundering about their battery positions all the night before, trundling along the thawing road since dawn.

" . . . soldiers for the working day . . . Our gayness gone with rainy marching in the painful field . . ."

" . . . time hath worn us into slovenry. . . ."

They pulled off their foul boots and pressed and stretched their stiffened toes ; seeing, for the first time, the magic of pride and contentment which Reynolds had been seeing in the words for a dozen months.

Branson was smiling when he told Reynolds, for the last time in this scene, to go to hell.

Then he was fired, suddenly and anew.

" By God ! " he said, " I've got it ! Look here, young Reynolds—you've got to write that bit out for me and I'll learn it. I'll get it all pat, like you have, and if there's any sort of inquiry—damn it, even if it's a court-martial—I'll let the old sods have it, every ruddy word of it. That'll show 'em. Any son of a gun with one hand in his pocket could go and beat up that bird ; but it isn't every one who can shoot off a bit of poetry. That'll show 'em if all the brains of the army are on the staff ! "

" Why, 'tis a gull," said Reynolds, encouraged by the hush and smiles of his audience, " a fool, a rogue that now and then goes to the war, to grace himself at his return into London under the form of a soldier."

" Reynolds," said some one from a sleeping-bag spread on the floor, " for God's sake, shut up ! " And Reynolds carried over to him a mug and the whisky-bottle and water-jug.

" What a kid ! " Whitelaw mumbled quietly to Cartwright, then yawned and closed his eyes. " Thank God for our boys, Uncle ! We've got the whole Brigade in here now and I don't believe you could pick out a better brace in the whole outfit. . . . And we've brought them both out with us again. . . ."

Richards and his valise were on the other side of him, asleep or near enough to it to make no difference.

Without opening his eyes Whitelaw moved a hand out of the sleeping-bag and pressed his fingers to the wood of the floor as he spoke his boast. " That's luckier than the others."

Cartwright grunted. Reynolds still pottered about near the table with the bottle and mugs, ready to catch any eye and carry a drink over. He fussed as quietly as he could with the stove. " Turn in, Rennie," Cartwright said ; and Reynolds came and sat down beside him and addressed himself to his boots.

" Oh," said Cartwright (for he was thirty-nine and

Reynolds was twenty), " for God's sake, shut up ! I'm taking stables at half-past six."

" You sots," said Reynolds, thoughtfully looking along the floor at the hummocks of sleeping-bags and greatcoats, the litter of boots and putties, waders, leggings, gas-masks and steel helmets. " You mutton-souls ! This—and none of you blighters can see it—is a ' Noccasion '—a Nevent—a moment. . . . Uncle, we've come out—of the Valley. And who are these ? " He looked about the hut. ' These, Sir ? ' a fellow like you would say, ' These are a lot of gunners.' But the proper answer, ancient Uncle of mine, is ' These are they which came out of great tribulation. . . .' What a spanking word that is, Nunks ; ' tribulation '—it was absolutely made for that plugging along from the Battery to Stump, and sitting there on your backside for a day and a night, and plugging back again. . . . And humping frozen bullets from the trolley to the pits ; and crossing your fingers and holding tight when a hate was on."

" Yes," said Cartwright. " Grand word. You can have it, Rennie. I'm not needing it just now. You keep it."

" ' They shall hunger no more.' . . ." Reynolds spoke slowly and very softly. " Neither thirst any more. . . . Neither shall the sun light on them. Nor any heat."

Cartwright thought he had finished.

Reynolds, apparently, thought so himself, for he lay down.

But suddenly he sat up and reached across to Cartwright's shoulder and shook it.

" Uncle," he said, " by God, it's true ! They *shall* hunger no more—neither shall the sun light on them, nor any heat. . . . If we get through to the end—out of the other valleys and tribulations as we've got through this lot—there won't be a damned thing left in the world to upset us, and excite us, and make us get the wind up. I dare say we'll be able to smile at things, now and again ; but it'll take a hell of a lot to get a tear out of us. . . . ' These are they which came out of great tribulation . . .' the generation of the broken-hearted. Men who have sighed all their sighs and shed their ultimate tear. I wish I could impress you as much as I've impressed myself, blast you ! But perhaps I'm late ; it sometimes seems that you have discovered all these things some time ago. Good night, brother-officer."

" Good night, fellow gentleman," said Cartwright. He, too, was a little thoughtful now. " You *have* rather impressed me, if it's any satisfaction to you," he said. " I think that's a pretty sound idea."

" Good egg ! " said Reynolds. " I just shot an arrow into the air—well—good night."

EACH man awoke to the standard mug of tea next morning and to the astonishing fact that he was one among twenty. The light about him came not meanly from the flame above a candle stump in a hairy hand, but from the sky through a door that opened above the level of the ground.

Of the twenty some sat up caressing the steaming mugs, some still slept and others worked with shaving-brushes at a lather round a cigarette.

The feeling that amounted to a numb satisfaction was the vague sense that something was at last finished and done with.

Oakleigh came in through the door, in fine boots smeared and spotted with the stamping of hoofs in the lines as he had walked along them before the Sergeant-Majors of all four batteries took the signal from him to feed. Elsewhere he was speckless and already shaved. He drew a box to the foot of Richards's claim on the floor (marked out by his brushed and folded clothes), and began to expound the Brigade programme for delousing and the issue of sterilised shirts, vests and underpants in lieu of serviceable sets handed in. He mentioned the address of officers' baths and an Ordnance store of officers' clothing.

Allen blew on his tea and bragged of the way he had set things right for Branson with the A.P.M. ; for Branson was no longer under arrest. All that the A.P.M. had demanded, when Allen had finished with him, was a written apology. " That," said Branson, " is what he won't get—unless—By Golly ! he *will*, though ! Young Reynolds can write out that piece for me ! "

" No need," said Allen. " 'E's 'ad the ruddy thing. I wrote it for you, my lad— at the place where Froggie and the vet and me had a blow-out after ; and sent it round by my groom. So that's O.K."

" Skipper," demanded Branson, " what did you say ? "

" Say ? D'you think I've been in the bliddy army for seventeen years without learning the proper way to do out a written apology to a superior officer ? I done the signature a bit like yours, too—so that you can't tell its ears from its elbow." Allen twirled his moustache. " You chaps with Commanding Officers that'll look after you in a tight corner, don't know when you're in luck. You ought to 've 'eard 'is nibs telling me off for not having better discipline in my battery ; till I told him you'd been runner-up in the Canadian tennis championship."

Branson said " Thanks," and Allen sucked in his tea ; but these things were utmost trivialities in the numbness, in the vast and vacuous sensation of being twenty rested men in a spacious hut with an open door ; of being across the swamp and the river ; of Thiepval (with the rat carelessly shot by Reynolds within the last jump of its run behind the dug-out timbers) ; of St. Martin's Lane and Stump Trench already tumbled into the past. . . . Perhaps it was rest that made the difference ; something warm placed in the stomach at each end of a dozen hours of sleep—sleep that was not a dull swoon in an atmosphere that seemed to distend some part of the head behind and above the eyes.

By tea-time bodies in new vests, shirts, pants and socks were still aglow and prickling from the scalding water, cloudy with phenyl in the vast halves of wine-barrels set in a row at the officers' baths.

No one had shown any preoccupation during the day with the question of orders. Palestine and Italy, Macedonia and Mesopotamia occurred from time to time in the talk of the drivers, and of the gunners showing them how to clean harness.

After tea Reynolds softly and seriously said, " Uncle," and made a movement towards the door, so that Cartwright knew that earnest conversation was toward.

" I'm orderly-dog to-morrow," was Reynolds's first disclosure as they wandered off the duck-boards to the moss between the huts that were like great rusty cylinders half-buried in the ground.

" Yes," said Cartwright. " And Dad the day after. Then me again."

" The point is," said Reynolds, " I'm not on duty to-night. Nor are you. I ve snaffled old Froggie for the evening."

" Oh ! " said Cartwright. " I've heard some of the people talking about some sort of binge in the hut here as the Brigade's all together for the first time, and we may be shoving on somewhere to-morrow."

" It won't come to anything," said Reynolds. " Half the fellows knew at lunch-time that it's as easy as winking to jump a lorry or a flying-corps tender into Amiens. There'll only be orderly officers dining here to-night. That's why I collared the interpreter to come with us. He knows the ropes. The really secluded spots and shady nooks of the gay city."

" Is it a gay city ? " asked Cartwright.

" Not like Bethune, I gather," said Reynolds. " But according to old Froggie, if you know where to look——"

" I thought," said Cartwright, and he smiled, " that your leave was to answer the question for you—once and for all, Rennie."

" Don't be so damned superior," said Reynolds. " Have you never heard about the appetite and what it feeds on ? And God knows what sort of a place we'll foot it off to to-morrow or the next day, where the women are all done up shapeless in great bundles like officers' kits ; wearing pinched gum boots to paddle about in their manure heaps, instead of stockings pulled up all smooth and shiny. . . ."

They ambled on in silence. The hand of Reynolds slipped under Cartwright's arm for a few moments. " You're thinking of ' Auntie,' " he said quietly.

" I'm thinking of a lot of things," said Cartwright.

" I am, too," said Reynolds. " I have been—ever since we sat down in those gorgeous baths with a few minutes in which to do nothing else, but think."

They were silent again, Reynolds tapping a cigarette on his case and Cartwright attending to his pipe.

" You don't think she'd mind, do you, Nunks ? " The hand had again slipped under his arm and then gone back to the cigarette. " I mean, if she knew— all about everything ? I mean, would *any* auntie ? Would I, if I was one ? Would you ?—Of course, just dot me one over the ear if I'm causing you any annoyance or embarrassment—denying the verities or messing up the sanctities and so on ; and I'll dry up."

" No," said Cartwright. " Help yourself."

" Well, then," said Reynolds, " I advocate a night out, my son. We'll have no end of a time. We'll keep the party small. What about Dicky, if we can get him to come, and Dad, and you and I and the Frog ? Come on, Nunks. Even if only one went instead of all four of us, that one ought to be you. We three have had leaves since we got down here to this war. You haven't had a damned thing. Eight months."

" Don't worry about me, Grandpa," said Cartwright. " I've youth on my side."

" I'm not worrying, you old idiot," said Reynolds. " You're too pig-headed to worry about. But I wish you'd come. Look here—come just for the grub and the binge if you like. I shouldn't be surprised if our old Dicky would be satisfied to spend a celibate evening chatting quietly with you about old times. Come on, Nunks, be a sportsman."

They walked on, Cartwright thinking.

At the end of one of the groups of huts he put his hand

under Reynolds's arm and left it there as they turned and strolled back.

"It isn't lack of sportsmanship, old lad," he said. "It isn't blindness to the beauty of the stocking—what was it so lyrically?—'pulled up all smooth and shiny?' Neither is it just uxoriousness out of the old, lost world. . . ." He paused, smiling at the thoughtful profile of Reynolds with his head haloed in newly and neatly cut hair (for barbers and a chiropodist had functioned as an annexe to the bath-orderlies). "No, Rennie. Perhaps —well, I'm twenty years older than you, or near as a toucher. And I think I'm most damnably tired. I can't imagine anything nicer than just sitting about here to-night, smoking and listening quietly to the stuff dropping on the other side—of your poetic 'valley'— that we've finished with for a while. I'll take Oakleigh's stables, so that he can go if he wants to. Good luck to you; and Rennie, for the Lord's sake——"

"Oh, yes, I know," said Reynolds. "Don't you worry. Froggie's no fool and I'm a man of experience."

"Uncle," was the next thing he said when they were near the officers' hut again. "If you're not needing that hundred and twenty-five francs you drew to-day, you might lend me a hundred of it till we can draw another lot. Sure you don't mind, old thing? . . ."

.   .   .   .   .   .

The five who dined in the hut that night were the orderly-officers of A and C batteries, Cartwright, the Vet, and Morgan of B (Morgan had married during his leave in February and was taking duty for Burton who was married in 1914).

Riding had cooked for them, presumably impressing the three other cooks as much as he did their officers, with his shadow of Browne's menus.

Fuel had come from somewhere, filling the scuttle that must at some time have been a dustbin—a lump or two of coal, real chunky logs with scraps, more vague and varied, of wood.

They sat, after dinner, round the stove. One of

the batteries boasted a siphon, and recent leaves had stocked it with sparklets. This gave a new quality to chlorinated whisky. The conversation was at first of the comeliness and profound satisfaction of feeding well and sitting at ease about a well-charged stove, while others rattled their bones to hell, freezing in lorries and tenders on the way to Amiens. . . . And to what end ? . . . Food nothing to write home about and devilish little else to be found. . . . Then rattling back again, again freezing ; and probably a week's anxiety. . . .

But what kept them out of their flea-bags and awake was the sheer courtesy of attention to the wrangle between Morgan and the Vet upon the subject of mules.

One of them was pro-mule, the other anti ; and out of their love and confidence, their hatred and suspicion there grew an acrimony bitter and violent. It reached a point where speech was impossible on the part of the champions beyond, " All right. We'll see . . ." and a snarled " All right. We *will* see. And I hope to God you'll be somewhere near. . . ."

And some one got to work with the siphon and another sparklet ; and the Vet went back to Brigade Headquarters and the others turned in.

MEDAL WITHOUT BAR   CHAPTER LXIX

THE door at the end of the hut was a patch of cold grey when it was opened by a gloved, fumbling hand. The enormously muffled figure—sentry or stable-picket—put down his lantern and immediately extinguished its pallid flame by thudding with his slime-muffled heel on the wooden floor beside it.

" Sir," he said ; and then again—since ' Sir ' was the only formality of collective and respectful address that he knew. " Sir—can I wake you up, Sir ? "

He bumped again on the floor.

Mugs shook on the rickety table ; the lantern's handle tinkled against its slender ribs. " Sir . . ."

A A

From the mumbled confusion of "Shut that door,"
"Get out," "Whot-the hell is it?" and "What the
devil's up now?" he selected the last for his answer.

"A bit of news just come through, Sir. A—it's Fritz,
Sir—the ole Hun—he—he's gorn, Sir. . . ."

"For God's sake," mumbled some one; "—that door!
You're freezing the place out, standing there. Shut it,
and light something—on the table there. Here's a
match!"

A match-box shot along the floor.

"It's Gawd's truth, Sir," said the man in the steam
that leaped and curled from the turbaning of his head
and face as he struck a match. "It's through to Brigade.
Official. The message will be along to you in a minute.
But I thought I'd just tell you—the brigade signaller
told me the message on 'is way to the Adjutant and I
give the tip to the sentry to tell the men; and then I
come along to you."

"Who the hell are you? What message?"

"D Battery stable-picket, Sir. Fritz 'as gorn. 'Is
front line's empty. Th' infantry's arfter 'im and 'e's
burning up villages be'ind."

"D Battery stable picket" gave a vague, ridiculous
pride that made the affair Cartwright's own.

"It's Tagney, isn't it?" he asked. And then, "Where
did this come from?"

"Division or somewhere, Sir," said the man. "The
signaller 'ad it properly wrote out on a form for the
Adjutant. . . . I *seen* the message, Sir. . . . Wide front
. . . all along . . . Fritz cleared out. . . ."

He finished in a hush of silence that is rare in audiences.
His shadow splashed across the floor and curved up the
sides of the hut, black and immensely shapeless. The
four pairs of eyes peered at him; and his own with a
tiny candle-flame in them, between his muffler and his
turban, shone back.

"Sir!" he said, for that silence was impossible. It's
truth—so help me, Gawd!"

"Listen!" said some one suddenly; and he sat
startled upright, holding up a hand and a finger, straining

his ears beyond any near and trivial sounds towards the swamp and the roads and ragged heights beyond them.

Amazement was the only sensation that came in those moments, to those straining ears.

For there was not a sound.

Their lips at last breathed out softly . . . " God . . ." and again there was that silence.

" Thought—thought I'd better just tell you. . . ."

Tagney uneasily pushed his shadow about on the floor, and swung it along the curved ceiling. " Get back to the 'orse-lines. . . ." He swung a dirty mitten at the end of its tape up to the neighbourhood of his bundled head, shuffled off to his lantern and fumbled the door open.

When he was outside Cartwright shouted to him, " Tagney, come here, you idiot."

He stood up and tossed his coat down as a stepping-stone from his sleeping-bag and valise to the table. " Come in and have a drink, man. It isn't every day that you can wake officers up to tell them the War's being won. Come on."

He poured whisky and squirted from the siphon into a mug for Tagney who had disclosed a crumpled moustache and a smile in the bundle that was his apex. " Good luck. And thanks for coming." Cartwright dashed some into a mug for himself and raised it.

" Good luck, Sir," said Tagney, and the shadow of an upturned mug described an arc on the ceiling ; " good luck—I'm sure."

" What's your idea, driver ? " said Morgan cheerily, " in waking up the batteries ? Going to start chasing the Hun before breakfast ? "

Tagney accepted the joke, as he put down his mug and turned to the door. " I—sort of thought—they might just like to know, Sir. Thank you, Sir, for the drink. It went down very well, Sir."

When he was gone and the door closed Cartwright was filling three more mugs and stepping carefully with his already chilled feet from one intervening empty bed to another, to deliver them to the hands held out for them.

Once more, slowly and hushed the syllable " . . . God . . ." came forth from the tangle of thoughts in the cavernous hut.

Then the Adjutant came in, pyjamas gleaming between his gum-boots and overcoat.

" . . . complete evacuation . . ." he said. " Colonel's been on to Division. . . . Hell-for-leather retreat. . . . God knows how far. . . . I say, I'm going to have one, too." He poured, as questions began to form themselves among his listeners. " When ? " " How did they find out ? " " Who's after them ? " " Any guns going ? "

" *Guns ?* My dear chap, the *cavalry's* out ! Infantry patrols haven't struck any one for hours. The Colonel's just dashing off up the Auchonvillers road to see if there's anything in this talk of villages burning. . . ."

" Golly ! " said Morgan. " That's an idea ! I say, Gordon—couldn't we ? The others will be back from off the tiles before long. . . ."

" I don't know," said Gordon. " The old man made me stay back in case anything turns up from Division. But I should think—if *one* of you stays to take any orders for the Brigade. I don't know—I've got to stand by the office. Cheerio. . . . Just thought you might like to know. . . . *I* can't give any leave, or any orders for sight-seeing."

He went back to his office ; and the four found that they were putting on their clothes.

" We'll toss," some one suggested, " for who stays."

" I'll stay," said Cartwright. " I wouldn't miss telling the other blighters for anything. No. Honestly. I'd rather. They'll be sneaking in at any minute now."

When he was dressed and shaved he drank a mug of tea from the men's dixie, standing in the din of badinage and song, the reek of damp wood kicked and cursed and cajoled with paraffin into flame, of bacon and horses, of manure and lately carbolised men. Thereafter he walked down the track that he knew the pilgrims would use for their return from Amiens when lorries and tenders could carry them no farther.

It was not many cigarettes before they came.

His own four were among the first six or eight. It was a proud haggardness that was upon them ; not the mean, pinched haggardness of fear.

" Uncle ! " laughed Richards. " We ought to have told you not to wait up for us ! . . . But what the devil's up ? "

" The War, Dicky," said Cartwright. " We're winning it."

" Oh, yes ! " said Reynolds and he yawned. " Nunks, we heard all about that in Amiens before dinner, and after. Fritz is about to retreat. He *is* retreating."

" My son," said Cartwright, " he *has* retreated."

The mumbling among the pilgrims mingled with the din coming through the wood from the horse-lines.

" If you damned fools would just shut up for a minute, and listen. . . ." It was he who now held up his hand against the nearer sounds and directed ears to strain through the bare wood and over the marsh, to the roads and heights.

Again it was the shock of suddenly noticed silence that revealed the truth to them, and its enormity ; and they were speechless till speech came to them, too, in the hushed monosyllable.

" God. . . ."

And then Reynolds, barging out of the pilgrim group, grabbed Cartwright's arm and swung him round towards the huts. " If breakfast is *tea !* " he said, " let's go and eat it—sharp ! Pints of it, and gallons ! "

Slowly, while Cartwright and one or two of the others ate bacon and the others shuffled with bread and margarine and drank tea, realisation began to be a glow among them. Then others drifted in, having had the news from the men in the lines and about the cook-houses as they came by.

They fell upon the latest of the half-dozen tea-pots, flung away their greatcoats and belts and caps and sticks and took the glow.

This, then, and such, was the moment of victory to those who had come out of the great tribulation . . . and Cartwright knew that the next time he turned to look at Reynolds, who sat beside him, the odds were that the idiot might be weeping.

Reynolds, for consecutive minutes, had contributed nothing to the hum ; and the effort not to turn, but to keep looking ahead and joining in the general talk accordingly became a strain on Cartwright. He did at length, furtively look.

Reynolds, apparently, had been waiting for it for he held his eye and leaned forward. " Nunks," he said excitedly, " D'you get it ? This is St. Crispin's day— near enough ; and, he that outlives the day and comes safe home,

> Will stand a-tiptoe when the day is named . . .
> He that shall live this day and see old age—
> . . . And Crispin Crispian shall ne'er go by,
> From this day to the ending of the world
> But we in it shall be remembered ;
> We few, we happy few, we band of brothers. . . .

But it hasn't got through to those other huskies yet, you know. The iron has entered too deep into their souls—and last night's drinks. Lord ! I wish I wasn't so confoundedly sleepy. . . ."

Dorothy, Cartwright was thinking—poor Dorothy ! She could get nothing of this. She would see it in the papers. Retreat. . . . Victory . . . but she would only catch her breath ; and the dullness would remain upon her ; since victory is not a word read in a newspaper, but a singing in the blood ; a quietness and a glimmer of sun where before were leaden clouds and rumbling and screeches. . . .

And there was no square yard of earth whereon a man could stand solitary and think—unless, perhaps, he was an Adjutant when the Colonel and the Brigade Orderly Officer and the marvellously superfluous understudy to the Orderly Officer had gone sightseeing.

Not even the latrine. . . .

Some one was saying that it had put the lid on rest and training, anyhow.

Whitelaw was saying that it had to be a good wind indeed that blew no ill ; for the Regulars would start coming back to take over the batteries, now that Fred Karno's lot had got them through the winter and the mud.

Some champion of Regulars was citing instances of courage and tenacity, and an anti-regular yawned " 'bout time, too. They ought to be tossed out, the blighters. There ought never to have been any irregulars in the show till all the Regulars had been killed. After all, it's their job isn't it ? Let 'em come back ! "

" No, faith, my coz, wish not a man from England " ; Reynolds pushed back his box and raised his hand and got an absurd silence. " God's peace, I would not lose so great an honour

As one man more, methinks, would share from me
For the best hope I have. Oh, do not wish one more !
Rather proclaim it, Whitelaw, through the host,
That he which hath no stomach to this fight,
Let him depart ; we would not die in that man's
    company.

That fears his fellowship to die with us . . . ? And so, sweet princes all, let's to our beds ; and brew a dish of sleep—for afternoon may brew some dirty work upon these lads, who all unheeding sang last night a song. . . ." So he dithered on.

When he was sitting in the middle of his sleeping-bag and tugging at his boots Cartwright said to him, " The underlying idea, young fellow, I suppose, is that I should take stables and your other parades for the time being ? "

" Good Lord ! " said Reynolds, and he sat suddenly upright from the shock. " Uncle, my retentive mind had lost all touch with the putrid fact that I am orderly officer. Honestly—absolute fact—I'd *forgotten* it ! " He made a movement, manfully and full of the uttermost resolution, as of a weary man hastening to replace a half-removed boot in a hurry.

" You humbug ! " said Cartwright. " You know as well as I do that I'll do it like a shot, while you sleep the sleep of a rascal. But you went through the motions superbly, Rennie."

" That's what I call a truly happy marriage ! " said Reynolds. " You're a good old solicitor, Nunks. My love for you is exceeded only by my desire for sleep at the moment."

He may have heard the next two boots that were tossed to the floor of the hut ; but certainly he heard no more.

For if there was any single human act in which Reynolds had no peer it was in going, smoothly and headlong as a diver from a great height, to sleep.

BY dusk Cartwright was riding back through Beaumont Hamel with Richards from a picnic (in the quite accurate sense of this word, defined in dictionaries as a ' pleasure party including a meal out of doors '). By ten o'clock the ' rest and training ' orders had been officially cancelled and superseded by orders that batteries were to stand-to with limbers and wagons filled.

Richards preferred, when other considerations were equal, high ground to low.

He and Cartwright studied a map, concerning themselves only with the altitudes and the directions of the contour-lines in a countryside that was fully theirs. They chose the highest road as the approximate direction of their jaunt. Richards left a note pinned to the jacket of the sleeping Oakleigh, instructing him to leave a Bombardier with a message to await him and Cartwright at Serre cross-roads if the battery should have moved before they returned. Then with a haversack of Riding's slabby sandwiches and the Thermos flask of tea, with their horse's feeds in nosebags, they rode forth with their grooms at about eleven.

Before lunch they had explored many an old target, marvelling at the domination of the bleak heights upon which they had crawled and frozen and thawed. From the belt of utter wilderness through which they picked their way, often walking ahead of their horses, they came to the belt where features still presented a resemblance to the ancient facts as recorded on a map. A field track was discernible where it joined a road ; there were rags of bushes here and there along the line which on the map was a hedge.

Beyond this belt again lay the whole unravished land, where mutilation was an occasional scar upon a fair countenance. They cursed and marvelled at the orchards laid waste, at the great trees flung down across the roads, at the frailty of buildings that could be collapsed into a heap and extinguished under their still entire roofs by some ingenuity of field-engineering.

But there were wonders about them greater than these ; the marching of Infantrymen was here no lost art that lingered only in the memory and lived in the imagination of prehistoric men-at-arms like old Ruggles at Wilverley. It was a tremendous fact—a swinging, swaying four miles an hour in full kit.

They encountered pipes and bugles and drums and songs along the roads. Revivalists led " Tipperary," modern sentimentalists overwhelmed them with the emotion of " The Long, Long Trail" ; the floods of this in turn were piled high and held aside, as the Red Sea was piled and held for the passage of the Chosen, by the cheery disillusion of the " Good-bye-ee " school.

Then also, from a party in slouch hats :

> " The bells of 'ell go ringaringaring,
>> But not for you and me.
> I hear the angels singalingaling,
>> With them we soon shall be.
> O death, where is thy stingalingaling,
>> O grave, thy victoree ?
> Sing, singalingaling, sing singalingaling,
>> Sing, singalingaling with me. . . ."

It was possible, incredibly, to turn a horse aside from the crowded road, over a shallow ditch and to canter on living turf.

There was a battery of horse-artillery drawn into a field and some cavalry half a mile ahead of it.

There was the crackle of a machine-gun vaguely in

front, and again farther away on the right, with answering rifle shots ; and last of all there was a terrifying old man who bounded out of a hedge and withered them with a shriek and roared them to hell, and set them saluting and turning their chargers about on their haunches, feeling something under two years old. " If I see your blasted idiot faces again," he screamed after them, " you or any other joy-riders and sightseers—I'll have the whole blasted lot of you under close arrest." He turned away, but had an afterthought : " When we want you messing about up here we'll *send* for you."

It was a set-back ; but to such as Richards only a temporary one.

After a hundred yards of orderly withdrawal they allowed the horses and grooms to continue the retreat without them. They themselves crossed to the other side of the road and went back towards the machine-gun and rifle fire, covered by a platoon of singing Infantry against the fierce old man with his rank concealed under a raincoat.

After a mile or so of marching they stopped with their sheltering platoon where other Infantry was already stopped. The village ahead of them was probably Bucquoy with rear-guard machine-guns still in the shells of one or two attics. Beyond the bend in the road infantry had deployed and patrols were creeping forward to the flanks—creeping on clean sward, taking cover behind bushes alive with rising sap and brave in a shimmer of leaf-buds.

Yarns and speculations occupied the Infantrymen who waited—tales of wells poisoned ; of roads and cellars mined, with triggers fixed to door-knobs and hat-pegs ; of bombs fastened to the ground with helmets lying innocently above them—the safety-ring of the bomb to be removed by the lifting of the helmet ; of attractive-looking bottles that went off in your hand two seconds after the cork was drawn.

Peace terms were discussed.

Some one had seen dead cavalrymen and horses.

The horse-battery opened fire on the village from behind.

Richards and Cartwright, sitting on the trunk of a felled lime tree with an Infantry subaltern and a sapper, took afternoon tea.

.   .   .   .   .   .

The detail that seemed to have impressed Richards most in the day's outing was the way it had been possible to sit down, anywhere you pleased, without first scraping and wiping and laying down a box or petrol-can.

For Cartwright the dominating recollection in the evening was of walking among men as Ruggles had expounded the great art—arms ' swinging natural,' shoulders back and a pace of thirty inches ; for men were men again on that untattered green of downlands, on the cambered metal of unperished road. No longer were they Saurians or shambling apes.

Of the letters flung home that night by the stimulus of these and other such wonders, Cartwright contributed two. The evasiveness that had shaped his letters to Dorothy and clipped them short for the eight months wherein he had waited upon the issue of chances and the workings of arithmetic did not now keep him morosely biting his pencil and seeking the con-committal phrase that could satisfy a lawyer.

It was only the emotion now that craved satisfaction —an emotion at last admissible to Dorothy. So far as there was any lyric in him, he was lyrical about the end of winter and desolation, of feet that had been as great a burden to men and beasts as the loads upon their backs. He had seen how these men and beasts were swift again ; for earth—soft and clean and beneficent—was no more a foul pestilence. Again he communicated no specific facts ; for he could still see ahead—and he was still lawyer enough, however much he might, for the moment, be a lyricist—and a precedent was still a precedent. He kept to the general mood, covering paper with astonishing ease, and smiling as he covered it.

He told her what Reynolds had said, to show that victory was at last and truly consummated. . . . "He that survives this day and comes safe home, Will stand a-tiptoe when the day is named." ". . . We few, we happy few, we band of brothers. . . ." This, on second thoughts, he did not quote ; partly because he did not remember exactly how it went on, and partly because he did not see how any generalised sentimentality could bring Dorothy nearer to him.

He wrote of leave. It was stopped again for the moment, automatically. It had to be, obviously, in the face of anything so stupendous as this retreat—just till every one knew where things stood. But he was next—positively the very next in the Brigade. . . .

To Henderson he did not mind drawing specific comparisons such as that between seeing and hearing no burst of shells and the festoons of these upon the landscapes of four days before—either the ploppy burst in puddles, or the clangour of bursts on ice. He touched upon the matter of walking instead of merely shifting position with the gait of wasps and flies in marmalade, or beetles on a sheet of glass.

He was going up, he said, when he had finished the letter, with young Reynolds and one or two others, to a high ridge about three miles away to see the glow of burning villages.

To Henderson also he spoke of leave, saying that there was one lunch or dinner that they must eat alone, apart from the jolly affair that was to include Dorothy and Mollie.

.　　.　　.　　.　　.　　.

For two days and nights, after taking the road next morning, the battery hung about and bivouacked by the valley-road from Beaumont Hamel, through Miraumont, the two Achiets and Ervillers to Croisilles It did not go into action.

Private enterprise (with sandwiches and glasses provided episodes of Cavalry galloping down a road and of omitting to return ; of a horse-battery with twinkling hub-caps dropping into action behind a hedge of Infantrymen creeping about like deer-stalkers ; of all five officers of D Battery dropping sandwiches and vanishing, as by a sudden magic, into a ditch by Judas Farm near St. Leger. The magic was the whine of machine-gun bullets that came from heaven knew where.

When the retreat was ended, the full extent of it from Beaumont Hamel was, according to the book, an hour and a half's trot for a field battery.

It was twice the extent of the conquest achieved by those eight months of residence and survival in the sombre neighbourhood of the Pozieres Road, of Courcelette and Thiepval.

But the battery was already reversed, trekking towards the hinterland of ' Rest and Training ' ; and Cartwright was speeding ahead of it in tenders and lorries and sometimes beside the driver of an ambulance, towards Boulogne.

MEDAL WITHOUT BAR   CHAPTER LXXI

CARTWRIGHT'S first amazement on that leave was the peculiarity of the change that was being wrought upon other people.

Coming down at once to the particular instance of his own case, he was a traveller who had been away on his travels for eight months. He was the one who, by all the rules, ought to have undergone change. Instead of this he found that he (and by ' he ' is meant some inmost verity of being) was the one factor among all the others that had suffered no apparent change whatever. Now, when there were ten days and nights ahead wherein the old normal relationships had not seemed to be an unreasonable yearning, he saw that the normal was fantastic absurdity ; for the people to whom he had looked, through his lorry-hopping and train-crawling and dossing at the officers' club in Boulogne, were people changed and shrunken to the point of utter deformity. Fear had done to them all something that it had never done to men. Or had it ? Was it not something of the same sort that happened to a man—in life or in books—who walked the pavement, drank at a bar or paced the morning-room while the destiny of others was in the hands of a midwife?

But it was not simple fear with its simple results of pallor and thirst and a vacuous, simmering belly; it was that poor and mean relation of fear, wearing the family likeness—Dread—that had unmanned the lot of them. Instead of pallor to their cheeks, thirst and quaking, it had brought a depth to their eyes, silence to their throats, or speech suddenly started out of nothing and firmly carried through to an end—and handshakes of great heartiness.

And through it all there was some puzzle and bewilderment of Love that clamoured and struggled for articulation, and was stranglingly denied.

He had managed to get two telegrams to Dorothy warning her of his coming—for he was quite sure that neither of them wanted any journalistic 'surprise business. She met him at Victoria; and he thanked God the moment he caught sight of her that she was not in her V.A.D. kit, but in the coat and jolly, open-throated blouse and tweed skirt that she had bought in Exeter. Perhaps, in the fraction of an atom of time for which their lips first met that puzzle of Love was a little solved, the bewilderment eased.

"Breakfast with Dad, old boy," she announced "We're to pick him up at the office."

"Good," he said, squeezing her arm to his side.

In the taxi he drew her to him. He, who for six months of the last eight had known flesh to savour only of clouts foul and sweaty or rags coldly putrifying, now had flesh in his arms that was warm and loved and lovely.

"Dorrie . . ." he whispered as he held her; for who ever bothered to look into those proudly-captured taxis that rattled away from Victoria with the great paunch of gas on their roof, or who ever looked out of them so soon after getting in? "Dorothy. . . ."

And she said, "Charles. . . . My dear . . . my dear . . . Oh, Charles. . . ."

The depth was skulking in her eyes when she opened them.

" God ! It's marvellous to be home ! "

He looked out now, holding her hand.

" And my dear—— " she said. " To have you——" she squeezed his hand. And then her speech became hurried, in a perfectly conclusive sentence about something or other.

At the office the Old Boy shook one hand first and then both, looking him in the eye first as though looking into the eye of a son were the most natural and easiest accomplishment of man ; and then looking quickly away as though it were a detected slyness.

" You're looking splendid, old fellow," he said.

" Rather," said Cartwright. " Never been fitter in my life. And you look blooming."

" Sixty-four—very nearly—it's the prime of life nowadays, my boy. We're running the shop, don't forget—we and the girls—while you fellows are doing the outdoor jobs. You must let me show you off to the girls here after breakfast—we're a regular harem in this old office now—and they're wonderful. And you must see old Moll for a minute or two. He insists. Poor old Moll ! "

" Why—— " asked Cartwright, looking a little anxiously at Dorothy. " What's wrong with old Moll ? "

" Oh, nothing. Nothing," said the elder Cartwright. " Nothing *wrong*. But Dot won't mind my saying that he's an older man than I am ; and the strain is telling on him. He's ageing ; that's all."

Dorothy could have told them how her father had said fortnight ago at lunch that poor old Cartwright wanted watching ; he was not the man he had been ; no reserves—no solid balance. . . . But she said, " Yes, poor dear—the strain. . . ."

" Well," said the old man, and he took his silk hat off its peg and ran the polishing-pad over it. " We've done all we can to make your time your own, Charlie. You wouldn't want to be wasting it chasing about after us old 'uns—you and Dot." He had his arm in Dorothy's—

a good sight, Cartwright thought, his wife who at thirty-
six was twenty again, and his lean and leather-faced
tough old father. " We've ridden the crest of a brain-
wave, your mother and I. Taken a room at the Carlton
where she's waiting for us with breakfast. Come along
We won't hang on to you, or Dot would have something
to say about it ; I know."

The sly, jolly implication gave a touch of buoyancy and
delight that was possible in such days from the hand of a
master. They hurried out.

Of his mother there was, for some seconds, no evasion
She held him, and kissed him, and looked at him, and felt
his shoulders and his arms and said, " My boy. My dear
boy. Oh, thank God ! "

" Yes, All there, my dear," said Cartwright smiling. " Both arms ; legs ; feet ; hands. Everything complete. . . ."

She seemed to know exactly where to draw the line,
as did the Old Boy, who touched her shoulder.

" Yes. Of course. You must be starved," she said.

" Starved ! " said Cartwright ; and found his arm
through Dorothy's and his own throat now playing about
with bright silly words and idiocies ; " I should think I am
starved ! Been living on chopped-up mattresses, boiled
putties and dried mule for the last ten years of the siege
You people don't know what the War is ! "

And at breakfast they talked to him ; and each on
looked at him while he was looking at one of the others
But they seemed to want no travellers' tales ; and he
seemed to have none for them. Beyond the statement
that the Hindenburg Retreat was true enough, un-
exaggerated in the Press because exaggeration was
impossible, there seemed to be very little for any one to
say about the War or for any one else to listen to.

.   .   .   .   .   .

The delight of the ten days and nights, and their
bewildering pain, was the delight of Dorothy.

" Charles," she said, looking into his eyes and lightly
brushing their lids with her cool finger-tips, " I wonder if

you would be very horrified, my dear, if we—if I—had another baby. . . ."

" Good God ! " he said.   " Darling—but——"

" But nothing," said she.   " I probably wouldn't, any-way—after all these ages.   People don't.   But if I did—well—I wouldn't mind."

" But Dorothy," and he drew a little away from her. " It'd be a tall order for you, just now.   I mean——"

" It wouldn't," said she.   " I'm very fit.   I've seen to that, for you.   Badminton two evenings a week with never a miss."

" But the hospital ? " he asked.   " That's pretty strenuous, surely ? "

She shrugged the shoulders that her care had kept firm and round for him, smooth with the texture of silk.

" Twelve hours on and twelve off," she said.   " It's only half one's time.   If I can get off so easily for ten days and nights—for such a frivolous reason as *this*—I'm sure they'd let me go to have a baby."   She smiled.   " And it wouldn't be any bother to you.   And if you have no views. . . ."

" Darling, you know I have.   Always have had."   He, too, smiled.

They reminded each other thereafter that one of them was nearly thirty-seven and the other nearly forty ; that for nearly eighteen years they had been married.

They laughed ; and they loved.

But the delight of Dorothy (with the depth in her eyes and her sudden silences) was as the delight and the yearning sorrow in the hearts of eleven out of the twelve at the last supper.

It was a gulf for which there was no crossing.   Always, if it was light, he would see and if it was dark he would know that she was gone away from his hunger and his thirst and hers, to her lonely sacrament ; to cower in the bleak shadow of dread.

John, approaching seventeen and solemn as an owl, got him apart once and asked some leading questions. How near to him had people been killed ?   Had any part

D B

of his clothing or equipment been hit ? Had a horse been shot under him ? Had he ever been buried ? . . .

People were killed in all sorts of places, Cartwright told him ; John himself had been in a taxi whose driver had had his neck broken by a skidding bus. The answers to the other questions were in the negative. John shrugged. " Well, I feel it's up to me to say *something* to her at times, you know. I thought you might give a chap something to work on."

" There isn't much, old fellow," Cartwright admitted. " It's all just a chance. All life is, really. Something might get one or other or all of us any day if our luck is out. The chances against must be a good deal heavier out there, but we're pretty comfortable on the whole ; and generally a pretty long way off—except from chances. You can all see how fit I am. All I can tell you about it is not facts, but philosophy. It's no use worrying. The majority of people—even in the Infantry, John—don't get killed ; and there you are ! It's no use worrying. I suppose I'd worry a good deal more myself if it wasn't for old grandad and for you. I'm always very grateful to you, old son," and he took John's loosely hanging arm. " It means a tremendous lot to know, all the time, that you're here with Mother and Davy. . . ."

" Oh, yes." John sniffed and removed his arm. " I know. You mean the hand that rocks the cradle, and they also serve, etcetera. But it's about time that we swopped over, and you did a bit of cradle-rocking and standing and waiting and I did a bit of your dirty work. I could, in less than another year, you know. . . ."

" Another year ! " said Cartwright, and he laughed. " My dear chap, you haven't seen what's been happening since last September. You haven't seen the riff-raff of prisoners that came in at the tail-end of the offensive."

Then he was stopped short in his tale by a sudden jerk in his consciousness that was altogether too lacking in direction to be a thought.

It was an overwhelming seriousness.

" Good God, Johnnie," was all he could say, " don't talk of—*another year*."

" No," said John. " But it's only a year since you sloped off to Exeter, isn't it ? When I wasn't sixteen."

.   .   .   .   .   .

Upon Henderson, too, the shadow of change seemed to have descended. He wore a light tweed suit of mufti, and to Cartwright's " Hello ?—why ? " he said, " Oh well . . . the other was only fancy-dress, wasn't it ? I ought really to be togged up as a sexton or a grave-digger for my present job."

" Still on casualties ? " asked Cartwright.

" Yes," said Henderson. " Our off-season just now. Rough luck getting your leave during a general holiday. It is a holiday, I suppose, after the winter ? You've been down in it all the time ? "

" Yes," said Cartwright. And he went on to tell him of the Retreat.

" No casualties . . ." Henderson stopped him lazily, without seeming to interrupt. " A hundred and twenty thousand killed. . . . Three hundred and sixty thousand wounded—so the fair maids in my department tell me—is the score from July to December. Isn't that figure about one and a half times the number of the whole old army ? Half a year's fighting. . . . No casualties in the Retreat, though ! " He was talking out of a mood of depression that seemed unintelligent.

" I shouldn't imagine," said Cartwright, " that you're in quite the cheeriest department of the War House. You were better at Wilverley, Jim ; with me and those old ruffians. It was a great work that, you know. I've realised it more and more, as I've seen the difference between one lot and another—depending on the sheer quality of their officers. A great work." He drank with gusto ; remembering Sammy, now so regrettably dead, and Black.

The thought of Richards and Whitelaw and Reynolds, too, was a merry one. But it seemed that to Henderson his drink was bitter, and bitter the thought of fine young men.

"Mufti doesn't seem to agree with you, either," Cartwright suggested next.

"It agrees with me better than fancy-dress," said Henderson shortly. "You're not by way of thinking that the War is over, are you ? "

"No," said Cartwright. "But I think we've been making a damned sight better job of it than you give us credit for. You ought to have seen that advance, you know, from Beaumont Hamel and knee-deep muck, on good roads and turf again. *Every one* ought to have seen it."

"Yes," said Henderson. "Any little rooster will crow on a bit of high, dry dung-hill, you know."

"Jim," said Cartwright ; for a Henderson who even drank morosely was a peculiar phenomenon. "Jim— you haven't got something really foul up your sleeve, have you ? I mean, some dreadful official secret of disaster ? You know, there was all sorts of wind up about this Retreat being a colossal ' trap ' and all that. It isn't anything of that sort giving you the hump, is it ? "

"No," said Henderson, still without any gleam or glimmer in the eye that used to twinkle. "I don't know of any ' trap '—except a brand new war against a brand new line."

"How's Mollie ? " asked Cartwright, grasping at another possible explanation of the inexplicable.

"Mollie ? " said Henderson. "You'll be seeing her for yourself to-morrow evening, won't you ? Aren't we dining with you ? What the hell's Mollie got to do with it ? "

The eye did gleam a little now ; with anger. "Can't you see, you ass ?—those names coming in ! Reams, sheaves, stacks of the bloody things. . . . Killed ; wounded ; missing ; missing believed killed ; wounded and missing ; died of wounds ; died. . . . Oh, God ! On and on and on. And it's going to start again with the fine weather. And you ask, ' How's Mollie ? '—trying to sleuth out some tuppeny-ha'penny domestic depression. Mollie's all right. Thank you.'

Then Cartwright had a wildly impossible, but happy, thought. "Look here ! " he said, "what you want is a change, and a few days' rest from the War. I expect you can still wangle things—you and Mollie! Jim, pull up your socks and put on your old kit and get sent out to my battery for a fortnight. Instructional purposes—or inspectional—or any damned thing you like ; just to give you a change from your ghoulish flappers and their casualty lists. We're out at rest at the moment, and we're sure to get a quiet bit of the line after our last eight months. You'd like our lot and they'd buck you up. . . ."

But Henderson slowly shook his head. " My dear fellow," he said. " This war isn't what it was. It couldn't be done."

And Cartwright, even while he had been speaking, knew that the thing was an impossibility.

Henderson was stale and sick ; and Cartwright was not surprised. Could any man spend his life doing nothing but compile casualty lists without getting the hump ? (There had been a story current of a suicide in a Salvage Company.)

Henderson was sick ; and there Cartwright had to leave the matter.

Between Dorothy and Mollie Henderson there seemed next evening to be a deeper intimacy. They both, apparently, loved their husbands in the old, lost-world way ; and in the eyes of both was the same shadow of their several dreads.

Mollie once caught Cartwright's eye in a private signal, just as their party was breaking up. His own eye had just caught the emptiness of the glasses on their table and was shifting thence to catch a waiter. It was caught, instead, by Mollie's, shadowy and alert as a sniper's. It smiled upon him and quickly questioned and made a statement.

He sought no further for a waiter, and very soon declined Henderson's suggestion of another drink.

Hatreds appeared to flourish in Henderson's present mood. His eye glowered once across the room to a distant table. " And you ask me," he mumbled, " why I don't wear fancy-dress ? Look at that fella grubbing there. Look at the colour of him from dodging about under a flower-pot for the last year. And their name is Legion—Legion of Honour, often enough—while chaps like you . . ."

" But dash it ! " said Cartwright, " I've only had eight months of it, though it does seem like eighty. However, there's a kid in the battery who's had eighteen or twenty and an old scoundrel who's been out for more than thirty."

" I didn't say *you*," said Henderson peevishly. " I said chaps *like* you. Thousands of them."

A childish squabble could have developed out of this on the ' You did '—' I didn't '—' You did ' basis. But Cartwright contented himself with the absurd pride that filled him ; the private satisfaction in that ' resting ' battery that numbered Richards and Reynolds and Whitelaw among its living, and Charlie Browne foremost among its dead.

But it had to remain a secret, that pride in a gang of blasphemers and that curious love for its verminous individuals. Even Henderson, now peevish and disgruntled as he was by his ghoulish snuffling in the records of battle's garbage, could not share it. Even Henderson could not come out from mud, to gallop over turf or march on a hard road with a singing platoon. . . .

It was secrets, Cartwright decided as he looked ruefully at the empty glasses ; at Henderson smouldering through his solitary eye at his red-tabbed, twinkling and pallid *bête noire* drinking chartreuse with a fairy in the corner ; at Dorothy and Mollie, bright and silent—it was secrets that played hell with moments of leave ; for the others, too, had secrets, and their secrets were darker than his.

He wondered, smiling, whether Dorothy—with the old estimate in her mind of man's alcoholic index—watched his drinks as Mollie watched Henderson's ; whether some of the darkness came to her eyes from the fact that his cigarettes had acquired a way of lighting themselves, one off the stump of another ; that three whiskies occurred during one evening with a possible fourth ; and that in ordering he specified, quietly, ' double.' He wondered, looking into her eyes, whether any of their darkness could come from such absurdities as that 'God' and 'hell' and 'damn' figured in his smoothest talk. . . . And he wondered that he had never noticed (or else forgotten) the loveliness that is immediately below a woman's clavicles, a little towards the shoulder from the throat, where flesh is only a faintest ripple beneath the skin, a shallow dimple, white and peculiarly luminous. . . .

On the last night of his leave, Dorothy at last wept in his arms ; and he accepted it, kindly and gently. He knew that it was inevitable ; since she was not—as he and Reynolds and the others were—of the generation of the broken-hearted that could weep no more.

" My dear . . . my dear . . . my dear . . ." she said in her tears. " Truly, my dear, it's for you that I feel it. It isn't for me. So many women—hundreds and thousands—it's just pure selfishness—it's themselves they're worried about. They don't want to lose the man who keeps them and lackeys for them and lets them scold. But you, Charles—I—dear one, I swear I don't want you saved for any of these things. I want you saved for you. I don't want you to suffer—this dear, dear body to be hurt. . . . Charles . . . Charles. . . ."

It was a lucky thing for him, thought Cartwright, holding her to him and kissing her tears that he did, in fact, belong to that famous, tearless generation, whose heart was already broken.

" Dear girl," he said softly, " you're being a little journalistic, you know. Matter of fact, I *don't* suffer."

" Charles," she said piteously. " *Don't !* "

" But, Dot," said he, " do poor, suffering creatures get fitter than they've ever been in all their lives, and stay fitter ? Admit it, dear ; I'm a good stone heavier, and hefty as a bruiser. This has been the first winter I've ever got through without coughing—even once. My ' smoker's cough ' you used to call it—on perhaps eight cigarettes and half a dozen little pipes a day. Admit it." He gently kissed her.

She said, collectedly though she still wept : " If you wouldn't try to keep *that* up, perhaps it would be easier."

" What, sweetheart ? " he asked.

" That *bluff*," said she ; " that *nonsense*. It hurts a little. It *itself* hurts. Don't do it, please."

" But dash it ! " said he. " You can't get away from facts. A stone added to one's weight is something that can be weighed."

" Oh, Charles, Charles," she besought him as she pressed his face between her hands. " Dear, silly, hopeless old boy—*I know*."

She meant something by that " I know " ; something that was intended to carry far ; and Cartwright's eyebrows twisted together in the darkness.

" You know a hell of a lot ! " he mumbled, but was uneasy. " As much as all these journalists and other idiots fill you up with. Now, the Infantry——"

" Dear boy," she said quietly, " I know you're not in the Infantry. You've told me so yourself—more than once, I think. But was there no one but Infantry at— at Stuff Redoubt ? "

He thought only " Hell ! " but he said guardedly : " There are all sorts of odd ' details ' knocking about in every show."

She was lightly caressing his cheeks and his ears, and the chin he had shaved very closely before going to bed so that the dawn might be, to that extent, unhurried.

" I swore," she said, " by all that is holy, I swore that I would never tell you. But I must ; I simply must, to make you straight with me, Charles. I know. About everything, I know."

" What, in God's name," he said, " is it that you know so much about ? " It might have been true that he could not weep ; but he could still be uneasy.

" Your very devoted friend and admirer made me go out to dinner with him. He came and dragged me off from the hospital."

" Rennie ! " said Cartwright. " Curse and blast the little fool. . . ."

" No, no, no," said Dorothy. " He is a perfect dear, Charles. And you mustn't—you won't be angry with him ? He'd never forgive me if he knew I'd told you. The dear boy——"

" Dear grandmother's ducks ! " snorted Cartwright.
" Carrying through that ' dear boy ' pose with you !
Hard-drinking, hard-swearing little rascal ! He's old
enough to mind his own damned business. I told him
you were in Cornwall."

" Yes," she said. " And he didn't believe you. But
he didn't bother, because he knew there was such a thing
as a telephone-directory."

" And what the blazes did he want ? "

" I'm not quite sure," said Dorothy. " It was all
very funny and childish and sweet. It wasn't to make
love to me. He seemed to have other fish to fry, because
he took me back to the hospital quite early and trotted
off. He just spent the time adoring you ; and me,
because of you."

" The little fool ! " was all that Cartwright could
say.

" All I really got out of it in the end," said Dorothy,
" was that—if anything happened—to you—he will
devote the rest of his life to taking care of me." There
was quiet amusement in the way she spoke.

There was a pause which Cartwright had no means of
filling.

" You won't be angry with him, dear ? " she asked him
presently.

" Angry ! " again he snorted instead of speaking.
" One isn't angry—somehow—with that blighter. People
go on allowing him to live."

" I've been happier since he came," she said ; " knowing that he was with you, loving you as he does."

" Loving me ! "

" You're the greatest friend he's ever had," said
Dorothy quietly. " And he spoke as though he'd had a
hundred years of great friendships."

" He treated you to some Shakespeare, I suppose ? "
Cartwright suggested.

" No," said Dorothy. " —Oh, yes, perhaps he did. He
said that you're the noblest Roman of them all."

" Yes," said Cartwright. " There are a lot of noblest
Romans of them all for young Rennie. But it does.

somehow, make a difference having a spark like him about."

" That's what he says of you, Charles. He says they'd be lost without you and what he called your ' long-visaged ' way of doing up men who've been wounded ; and carefully emptying out their pockets when they're dead."

" Dot ! " said Cartwright. " The little idiot didn't tell you that ? "

" He did," said she. " And he told me of your three days up in that ghastly place without any meals and only three Infantry officers left out of I don't know how many ; and you just as steady and as solemn as ever when he came to relieve you ; reading him a lecture as soon as he arrived ; and pulling him together."

" Anyhow, Dot," said Cartwright, " you must at least have seen that you must take everything Rennie says with a grain of salt. You know—a kid who romps off into Shakespeare every now and then. . . . He's mostly a joke with us, is Rennie—though he's about as sound an officer as you'd find anywhere."

" A good joke, my poor Charles," said she wearily and almost as though dreaming. " A very good joke indeed to have any one so fond of you, ready to do anything in the world for you. Even to break faith with you so as to come and kiss Auntie's hand and tell her, so tactfully, that she need not worry. As the widow of Rennie's greatest friend, of the noblest Roman of them all—she need not worry. . . ." Then suddenly she broke off as though startled from her dream. A piteous sobbing tore at her breath. She collapsed, spent, in his arms.

" Charles, Charles, Charles," she whispered wearily. " Don't again, ever, my dear one. It hurts dreadfully that you should be forced to be so lonely. . . ."

And he, not clearly knowing what it was she asked or what he promised, kissed the poor exhausted creature, and said " Darling, very well. I won't."

HE knew where to look for the battery—if it was still there—for the marching orders to the place of rest had been issued before he left.

He was boat-wise and train-wise now and got to Auxi-le-Château without hunger or undue thirst or any casual roadside duty. At Auxi he found that the Brigade was indeed still there, three or four miles away at Maizicourt, the battery a mile and a half beyond, at Montigny-les-Jongleurs.

Diplomatic and cheery, he called straightway for a drink and gossip at the Army Service Corps billet to find out how the ration-lorries ran. One took him to Maizicourt, whence he walked, in a late afternoon aglow with sunset and crisp with the crackle of a surprising frost, to Montigny which was, every moment of the five or six days for which he knew it, a remembrance of ancient Wilverley where Henderson had dreamed his dream of Samurai and wrought his work in the fashioning of them.

There was still a civilian letter-box in Montigny-les-Jongleurs, stuck upon a short post in the village street. The battery was the first body of troops to be billeted there.

The Sergeant-Major was in the horse-lines on the left of the road, with Whitelaw and Richards. But Cartwright, instead of calling to them, paused to stare and wonder. For the lines were larger than he had ever seen them. With breech and muzzle in their canvas covers, and hub to shining hub there stood, instead of four guns, six.

" Glad to see you back, Sir."

It was Whittle, saluting him over the hedge. " Been a bit of an increase in the family while you were gone. A section, and a Major. And Mr. Hoakleigh's gone off, on promotion. Two new guns. New pattern gas-bags. One new telephone and the old duds sent away for tuning up. All the D3 wire handed in and changed for

D5. Dirty-work blowing up somewhere, if you arst me, Sir. Dirtier than the Somme lot, going by the stuff being dished out. Boots and everything, and no trouble. Have a good leaf, Sir ? "

" Yes," said Cartwright. " Splendid, thanks."

He was looking across the field, gloomily, at Richards.

" Two of the other Captains in the Brigade," the chatty Whittle continued, " A and C, have kep' command of their lots and been made Major. Captain Richards could of got promoted Major to another Division but he went up before the General and asked to stay on with the old lot as Captain."

And why the hell, thought Cartwright as he walked away from Whittle, could they not have given his own battery to Richards ?

It was Richards himself who told him. " Once a short-shooter, always a short-shooter, Uncle. That shell—damned nearly a year ago now—the Colonel tells me is on record."

" It's a blasted shame," said Cartwright.

" The War's a shame, Uncle," said Whitelaw. " Didn't you find that out on leave—and here, in a place like this ? But you can't expect a regular gunner Colonel and a regular gunner General to let regular Infantry Generals think they believe an irregular skipper innocent of having carried the short round to the spot purposely in his pocket ? "

" And you wouldn't go, Dicky ? " asked Cartwright.

" Who the devil told you ? " said Richards startled. " Go where ? "

" To command another battery, in another Division."

Richards appeared to be relieved. " I'd like to know who told you, all the same," he said.

" Oh, one of the signallers," said Cartwright with a shrug. " I didn't know it was a secret."

" It doesn't seem to be," said Richards, smiling again. " But it wasn't to command a battery, Uncle. It was a transfer they suggested, if I was dissatisfied at being passed over. To the Anti-Aircraft—where a thousand yards one way or the other doesn't make any odds. But come on, meet the—commanding officer."

Cartwright wondered if that pause before ' commanding officer ' meant that Richards was going the way of Meston ; but his next remark did something towards answering the doubt. " Anyhow, you've got a section at last, Uncle. A decent lot of chaps too. Mostly Londoners ; newish guns and not bad horses. Rennie's sharing your billet. Dad and I are next door and the old man in the Mairie, with the Mess. I suppose you'd like a wash. You've had a long journey, now I come to think of it. How d'you leave Missis and the little 'uns ? "

" Fit as anything," said Cartwright.

He found, when his two new Sergeants came to see him within half an hour of his return, that the ' dear boy who adored ' him and would ' do anything in the world ' for him had used his absence for jockeying his section out of the superior barns allotted to it, so that he might filch them for his own. He had, so the Sergeants told him, disposed of the drainage from his horse-standings, by directing it subtly into Cartwright's. They had complained to the Captain on neither point, they said, since they were new and wished to make no bad feeling ; they had decided to leave it to their officer.

Cartwright recognised in the older of the two Sergeants, the spokesman of the plaints, the sea-lawyer type who was likely to be a nuisance. He said to him, fixing upon him the glassy eye whose occasional use Henderson had advocated in lectures to the Samurai : " Sergeant, Captain Richards is as likely to deal fairly with a grouse as I am." Then he climbed down from his high horse. " Where 've you fellows come from ? Is the section a tough old lot like you two seem to be, or reinforcements ? " The sea-lawyer was about Cartwright's own age, the younger thirty-four or five.

" Bin properly through it, Sir, most of us," said the younger, Brice. " Like your lot. Only a bit more south, Combles way."

" And you, Sergeant Stevens ? " Cartwright said, turning to the other. " It's no use your telling me you've

never been a trumpeter.   Half an eye can see that what
you don't know about soldiering isn't worth knowing.
And that's a bit of luck for us ; because I know nothing
about it."   Then, wiseacre that he had become, he smiled
a designedly genial and knowing smile and said, " But I
am a lawyer.   We'll get these wangles straightened out
to-morrow.   You can parade the section for me sometime, so that we can have a look at each other."

He entered his billet.

Jackman, after the formula of " Hope you had a
good leaf, Sir," pointed out that Mr. Reynolds had
taken the best bed in the billet—the only bed, in fact,
that was a bed—lending his own folding camp-cot to
Cartwright.

Cartwright smiled and thought of some of the things
he would have said to the dear boy who would do anything
in the world for him, if the dear boy had not been on his
way to dinner and a game of poker with C battery in St.
Acheul.

" Of course he used the bed while I was away," said
Cartwright to Jackman.   He drew a franc or a shilling
from his pocket.   " I won't wait till he comes back to toss
for it, so that you can make up the beds."   He spun the
coin and called heads.

Heads it was.

" All right.   Get Crouch to change them over."

He had washed and changed into slacks, and was
thinking about going over to Richards's and Whitelaw's
billet again, on the way to the Mess and the new Major,
when Reynolds, also elegant in slacks and twinkling
buttons, carrying a new cane with a leather thong and
gaudy brown gloves, came in.   ˙

The dear boy, Cartwright grinned to himself, was
obviously uneasy.

He said, " Nunks, you dirty old thing, why didn't you
let us know somehow ?   I was on my way out for a quiet
evening—but heard on the road just in time to cancel,
and come back to spend the evening in reunion with our
ancient.   How did you find—your people ?   All in the
pink, as it leaves me at present ? "

" Yes, rather," said Cartwright. " They came up from Cornwall."

Reynolds never turned a hair. " Better than if you had had to waste the time going down to them," he suggested.

" Quite," said Cartwright. " My wife—' Auntie,' you know—was very sorry to have missed you by being away, when you were home."

" Better luck next time, perhaps." His relief was obvious. " You don't happen to have brought any decent cigarettes ? D'you know, the canteens in the back-blocks here are a scandal."

Cartwright handed over his case. " Rennie," he said, solemnly, " I've saved you from some embarrassment."

Reynolds paused in the lighting of his cigarette. The announcement shook him, but while there was life there was always, for Reynolds, hope.

" You are my father and my mother," he said. " Prince and benefactor."

" Yes," said Cartwright, " I knew you'd appreciate it."

" That's why you pinched my bed, I suppose ? " Rennie asked. Jackman and Crouch were making the change.

" Didn't pinch it," said Cartwright. " Won it. Tossed you for it. I was afraid—so terribly afraid, Rennie— that you'd come back and try to insist on my having it ; and I of course would refuse and you would go on insisting and there we'd be—two strong men face to face, neither willing to concede to the other in such a matter of courtesy. So I thought I'd . . ."

" It has done you good," said Reynolds, and his relief was now final and conclusive. " You dirty old thing, it wouldn't surprise me if you burst into song at any moment—so damned jocular and perky we've all become. Have you been drinking, Charles ?—or not yet, dear ? But it's no use ; when we of the lighter touch are dealing with the likes of you, the cannon-fodder of emotion who have no *nuance* of or for the more delicate offices of friendship, we have to label a thing and rub it in and then hit what's left with a sledge-hammer to get it home. Confound you and blast you, and spare my blushes, but

that old bed is infested with *things*, Uncle! They are not
any reptile familiar to us, but whacking great chaps like
oysters with feet of velvet and snouts of flame. That's
why I took it. I thought I might draw them forth,
sacrificing my own fair flesh that another's might be saved,
and so hand the bed to you—clarified and worthy. But,
thank God, I've only nurtured them instead, and inspired
them to courage and feats of enterprise. They'll cheerfully bite an officer's teeth now and croon aloud as they
carry home a sheaf of his whiskers for nesting purposes—
and from to-night that officer will be you."

" I suppose," said Cartwright, " that in the barns which
you filched from my section and gave to yours, you had
found a nest of alligators ? "

" Oh, that's one of the things I really came back to fix
up with you." He now spoke quite solemnly. " You
see, by making that little change in Dicky's arrangements
I kept the sections in their proper order—right, centre
and left—instead of right, then a subsection of left, then
a sub. of centre, then right again—all messed up and
confused. . . ."

" To-morrow," said Cartwright, " Dicky will come
around the billets with you and me. A fatigue-party
from Mr. Reynolds's left section will do most of the
moving, after that it can do a bit of digging—to divert
certain drains from the centre section's horse-lines into the
ditch."

Reynolds shrugged his shoulders. " Oh, well," said he.
" Friendship will have been served ; for the essence of
friendship is sacrifice. I shall have established you with
your new section as a hell-of-a-fellow. A father and
mother, which is important." He became still more
serious, and after a pause said : " But as to your new
section, Nunks, God help you ! "

" What's wrong with my new section ? "

" Just not quite the same stuff as our old lot," Reynolds
said. " You'll see. They might take the colour of the
rest in time ; but they look a bit like ammunition-
column just now ; saucy swashbucklers—and then a
little mixture of base-details. A perfect home foɪ

Jackman. By the way, we've transferred him to you from mine—subject, of course, to your wanting to hold on to him, and not wishing to toss for it some time when no one else is about."

The servants had gone from the room.

" No," said Cartwright, " I'll keep him."

Jackman, he had long realised, was the Albatross about his neck. The War, without the incessant burden of Jackman was not undesirable; it was unthinkable. " Come on. You might witness my shaking hands with the Major."

" The Major," said Reynolds, " is dining at Brigade. He shoved off just as I came in. Pity they've taken our Oakleigh from us ; but we'll have the Mess to ourselves to-night, like the old days. Thank God."

" Oh ? " said Cartwright darkly ; for the one thing in the world about which these fantastic men could be nothing but dead serious was " the Battery." " Oh— it's like that, is it ? The old man——"

Reynolds sat down and lowered his voice. " Of course," he said, " he isn't Dicky ; and I believe that's about the worst you can say of him so far. He's been on the Reserve for some years, doing Boy Scouting and that sort of thing—one of the lads of the vestry. Had a four-gun battery after Loos and then went home to a training depot till he came out with a six-gun lot in October or November. I don't think he's a bad old stick, really. Writes too much."

" Writes ? " asked Cartwright.

" Yes," said Reynolds. " Notes. Minutes. Memos. Likes to ' put ' things ' on record.' Writes to us all the footling little piffles that Dicky and most ordinary humans sing out from the fullness of their hearts with a cheery ' damn your sowl.' Touches of Poonah in his background which get old Dad's goat."

" By Jove, yes," said Cartwright ; " Dad will take it pretty hard. Is he behaving ? "

" Just by the skin of his teeth," said Reynolds frowning. " You can see the old devil grinding them and sitting on the valves to keep quiet when the old man lets off some

c c

tape-worm chat, or writes a note about the gun-park sentry not having any rifle-ammunition in his bandolier."

" And how does he take to Dad ? " asked Cartwright anxiously.

" Respectfully," said Reynolds. " And it's pretty sticky going, in Mess. I suppose, from Poonah onwards, all the sojers the old boy has seen with hair as white and mugs as red as Dad's have been God Almighty ; and Dad keeps rubbing in his one pip and bragging about his ribbons. I don't mind telling you, old Nunks, Dicky and I have been counting a hell of a lot on you."

" On me ? " asked Cartwright. " What for ? "

" Oh—tact and one thing and another," said Reynolds. " To knock your section, somehow, into the battery so that the joins don't show ; and to do something diplomatic and large about getting those two to swallow each other. Perhaps things will be easier when we get into the line again. Dad's at his best then and the Major might un-tape a bit : and write less."

THE Major made it clear that the government was the small table by his bunk in the dug-out where the Mess found itself ten days after Cartwright's return from leave.

The dug-out was a good one in chalk, timbered here and there, in a cutting to the east of Arras.

The Artillery were " Army " troops now. Their own Infantry were heaven knew where, and their neighbours were the gunners of every Division under the sun.

The quiet hub and centre of the incessant din was the gaunt black skeleton of the railway station, where the ' permanent ways ' (so called) were swept at odd moments by swarms of drowsy machine-gun bullets, so that Allen, now a major, of B Battery, was shot through the knees and Humphreys of C through the head while chatting about old times in Pindi or Ambala, on their first evening in the new position.

Cartwright had intended to let Dorothy know that the rest was over. The surprise of this information would, he thought, convince her that he was fulfilling his promise. But at the disappearance of Allen and Humphreys he felt that the information would keep for a day or two.

In that two days the Major had indicated the positions of the flank guns and then, in the dug-out, handed to Reynolds—as senior subaltern and Battery-leader— a message form inscribed with the lines of fire to be laid out. When it was done, he said, he would come and check it. The detachments had dug themselves in between the guns and roofed themselves over with the material lavishly dumped from the G.S. wagons by Richards. Reynolds, Cartwright and Whitelaw had dug, with two of the servants, bunk space for themselves away from the Mess dug-out and the Major. Richards had supplied them with quartering for the bunk-frames, wire netting and canvas for the bottoms.

Two million shells, perhaps, of the nearly three of the battle's preliminary bombardment had been expended, and replies thereto duly received.

While the heart of the battery was beating beside a succession of candles in the dug-out, the three section commanders lorded it over the movements above ground.

The best emotion that Cartwright's section could display, apart from a quite genuine affection concerning the Major it had brought to the battery, was humility ; and this humility made of them an adaptable lot. There were two boxers among them, who had set a great pace in the finals of the Brigade tournament on the last afternoon at Montigny. There was one fellow who could fold a strip of paper so that half a dozen notches made with scissors produced something like a yard of elaborate lace. Another, with two spoons rattled or scraped or rolled together, could produce a Lewis gun, trains shunting, ducks feeding in a puddle, a Brigade clerk using a type-writer, a team at the trot and other such homely and familiar sounds. There was a tailor who would make any tunic fit any man snugly under the chin and elegantly waisted, for two francs ; and there was a circus acrobat who, at the word " Shun " from his accomplice would cross his ankles behind his neck and at " Stand at ease " would flash them, again crossed, under his haunches ; he could also climb endlessly through his arms with his thumbs tied together and give a very fine imitation of a fat man running upstairs, two at a time, with a hand on the banisters when there were neither stairs nor banisters within a mile of him. " Just 'old my 'at an' stick " was the gag that always preluded this, and became the best-used phrase in the battery.

Of material such as this, with C subsection ruled by the memorised King's Regulations and ' F.A.T.' pedantry of Sergeant Stevens and D under the truculent good-humour of Sergeant Brice, with the tailor busy upon the tunics of the right and left sections, the new centre section was in no time undistinguishable from the rest of the battery.

It looked in its retouched jackets, as a critic put it, like a battery of quarter-blokes.

The life of it was the life of Reynolds and Cartwright and Whitelaw at the guns, and of Richards at the wagon-lines on the Dainville-Duisans road.

" There's one thing about an old man like ours," said Reynolds. " He doesn't try to be the cook and the captain bold and the crew of the Nancy Brig. Not like poor old ' Bliddy ' Allen. Our sections are *ours*."

" Yes," said Whitelaw. " He does realise that it's our war ; just as a decent company-director realises that the guts of commerce are commercial travellers. We'll allow him that."

.   .   .   .   .   .

The next official document of any import from the Major delivered to Reynolds as senior subaltern was an order to detail a subaltern to accompany the Infantry in the morning of the 9th, reporting to Battalion Head-quarters at midnight of the 8th-9th."

"Oh, hell," said Reynolds, "I wish he'd do at least *that* much himself. Why should I——"

"No need for any one," said Whitelaw coldly. "I'm orderly officer. Uncle to-day; you to-morrow; then me."

"But, Dad," said Reynolds, "oh, Lord—sending a chap an order like that looks like giving him a chance to volunteer." He looked at the wooden face of Cartwright and then the wooden face of Whitelaw. His own became graven of a similar material. "Well—I *do* volunteer. There!" he added, after the time required for the lighting of a cigarette. "I don't a bit mind going. Honestly I don't."

"As a matter of fact," said Cartwright. "And it's God's truth—*I* don't mind going."

He stared at the fact, for a fact it was.

They had their maps with tracings on them from the Major's—the 'Black,' the 'Blue,' the 'Brown' and the 'Green' Lines of the successive objectives. They had thoughtfully studied the maps and, as thoughtfully, the ground itself, tattered and cobbled with sprawls of wire, rising away to Tilloy.

Beyond the immediate and visible crest imagination found no great task in filling in the picture with the details which the eye had not yet actually seen. There was a feature suspected here, in the hard chalk country, that had not figured with quite the same menace in the plastic field of the Somme : machine-gun posts of a particular soundness and permanence. There were sharper-looking irregularities of ground, and there was a weight and violence of shells unprecedented, falling upon wire unprecedented—and unimaginable even by wits so schooled as those that had seen Thiepval and its shabby bastards, Stuff and Schwaben. . . .

And yet what Cartwright stated was the bare fact and neither more nor less. And it was not heroism, even in any of its most fantastic disguises, that hastened him to the statement ; but fear with no disguise at all.

He preferred tangles of wire in front of him, underfoot or curling about his ankle or his sleeve like brambles in a copse; he preferred the curdling yap of bullets; he preferred slinking round a traverse or past the sagging shaft of a dug-out where bombs and bayonet might have done their work—or again, might not—he preferred them all to hanging about by the breach of a gun whence a shell might speed upon its way, clean and swift and harmless to the stooping crew—or again, might not; he preferred to see Infantrymen going quietly down under their packs or ripped asunder from them by the arrival of a shell, to seeing gunners butchered by the departure of one. . . .

" I swear to God, Dad," he said very slowly, " I don't mind going."

Whitelaw, as slowly and as thoughtfully, answered: " You can go to hell. Both of you. It's time you learnt to leave me alone."

He went, sulking, out of their euphemism of dug-out. He stuck his head in again before either Reynolds or Cartwright had said anything. " That's the end of it," he said and stumped off, smoking his pipe.

" Well," Reynolds presently said, " there was no need for you to follow suit like that. I wouldn't have waltzed in with that heroic offer, except that it somehow seemed to be up to me, since the old man had stuck the responsibility on to me, instead of tackling it himself. . . ."

He spoke again, after another pause, " it'll be you to relieve Dad—if we go on following the orderly officer roster."

" Yes," said Cartwright. " Unless one F.O.O. per brigade is going to do the job. In that case another battery—A, I expect—will have to do it. Will you tell Corporal Hine to detail the signallers, Rennie? Dad will object to volunteers even there, you know. I wonder if he's right."

" *He* doesn't wonder," said Reynolds. " The old sod's opinions are heavier than holy writ to him. I always thought my father was the cocksurest blighter in the world—till Dad settled on us. Anyhow, it's an ill wind, *etcetera*. His cocksureness about volunteers has saved me from a sleepless, uncomfortable night. Saved you,

too, Nunks, though you're too good a prig to admit it—
and saved ' Auntie,' too, if she but knew ! "

Reynolds smiled in a most friendly and confiding
manner now, and Cartwright had a feeling that either of
them could allude to his absurd visit to Dorothy without
any necessity for either ragging the subject or treating it
warily. A stage of emotion had somehow been reached
where that enterprise could have been accepted without
comment.

But Cartwright was forbidden from drawing Dorothy,
mysteriously, any nearer to that grotesque hovel in
the earth with the guns plunging back and sliding up
behind it, and the haggard men who waited in front—
waited to scramble over the crumbling bags and scattered
jags of wire towards the lines traced on maps and scrawled
in the chalk ; or to amble back with their loads, against
some future time, leaving the present scrambling forward
to some others—with Dad Whitelaw among them chewing
a pipe-stem and fingering the bolt of an adopted rifle.

It was revealed to him, suddenly and completely, that
that was why some obstacle always came into his throat
and a paralysis into fingers that held a pencil. Saying
things, or writing them down, made the things from
phantasmal, real ; it dragged in the remote persons to
whom the saying or the writing was addressed, leaving
them remote no more but making them one with the thing
made real.

So, to Reynolds he said nought of either Dorothy,
or the possibility of prematures ; to Dorothy he wrote
no word of the battle.

He told her only that the battery—six guns now
commanded by a Major—was on the move and busy.
Thus he kept phantasmal the dullness that was again
blurring the clarity of sounds upon ear-drums, phantasmal the brave, remote, fine love of Dorothy,
phantasmal the shrinkage of his stomach within the
barrel of his ribs when the Number One in a gun-pit
said ' Fire,' so that the shell might speed, clean and
harmless, on its way—or else might not.

IT was just before dinner, when the three were washing at the door of their hovel, that a signaller presented the compliments of the Major to Mr. Cartwright and asked him to go to the dug-out as soon as possible.

In a life where the unexpected and unseemly were the only routine, any presage of the unexpected was particularly disturbing. Cartwright said hurriedly, trying to mass all improbable possibilities into a group for examination,

" Oh, hell. . . ."

Whitelaw said, " What the devil now—unless it's something to do with the Mess—" and Reynolds said, " He only wants legal advice, Nunks—or he'd have put it on record. He hasn't run out of writing-kit. He's got a dump of message-forms and pencils as big as a canteen."

" It's bad news, I'm afraid, Cartwright," the Major said, when Cartwright went in to him. " At least, *I* look upon it as bad news." And it was the gentleness of him, Cartwright saw, that was this man's offset against his love of dug-outs. " Very bad news for me, Cartwright."

That, at any rate, was a comfort ; and Cartwright said " I'm sorry."

" It may be a matter for congratulation," said the Major. " I've got to let you go to Brigade. Assistant Orderly Officer. At once."

Immediately and automatically, Cartwright again said " Oh, hell ! "

The Major shrugged his shoulders. " I've protested," he said. " I've put my protest on record. I'm only just up to establishment in subalterns. Other batteries, I believe, have supernumeraries at the moment. If it must be from my battery, I've suggested an alternative." Cartwright knew well enough who the alternative would have been. " But it's you the Colonel wants. Because of your knowledge of office-routine."

Cartwright took it all in as though it were a stream

flowing into a fairly empty receptacle. " Oh, hell . . ."
kept on reverberating in his mind, a mere tinkle of the
stream and the receptacle, and not the product of any
active thought.

" To-night ? " he asked, when the Major had finished.

" After dinner," said the Major.

" Jackman ? " asked Cartwright, " do I take him ? "

" You might as well. I expect they've got some dud
they'll be glad enough to palm off in exchange for
him."

" I'll tell him to pack up," said Cartwright, and he
moved towards the door. . . .

Yes, the Major's love for his dug-out and his pencil for
the placing of trivialities ' on record ' was distinctly
outbalanced by his gentleness. " Good luck, Cartwright,"
he said. " I *ought* to congratulate you more lustily—the
Staff's the Staff, you know—but one doesn't get used to
losing the officers one likes. . . . And I suppose you'll
miss the battery. You strike me as pretty good cronies,
the four of you. . . . Anyway, good luck. . . ."

" Thank you, Sir," said Cartwright, and went up the
shaft.

It was cold outside, and Cartwright had no coat. But
he found himself walking farther away from the slit of
light in the bank where Whitelaw and Reynolds were
probably sitting like two birds, on the edge of a bunk,
probably squabbling. Possibly he was tired beyond
consecutive and conclusive thought, as most men along
the line from Souchez to Croisilles and the dozen miles
east and west of it were tired during that April and May ;
for there was no particular thought in his mind, only the
gesture of impatience and resentment that shaped into a
mumbling of the same two syllables—" Oh, hell ! "

If he walked slowly enough, and far enough away
beyond the gun-pits, he knew that Whitelaw and Reynolds
would go down to the dug-out, as they quite decently
could since it was dinner-time, to find out what was
happening. Thus they would find out without his having
to tell them.

When the slit of light from the hovel was enlarged by

the raising of the blanket and then extinguished, he knew that they were on their way.

He was taking another quiet step farther away from them when he suddenly visualised himself facing them after the Major had given them the news.

" Reynolds," he shouted across the hundred yards of broken ruts and smooth foot-tracks between them ; " Dad ! "

They said, " Hello ! " and came towards him.

" Well," said Cartwright, " I've been given my ticket. I'm posted to Brigade. Assistant orderly-dog."

Reynolds said, " Uncle—" and then, a moment after, " You *haven't* ! "

Whitelaw said, " The hell you have ! "

" All the same," said Cartwright, " I have."

And he took the beginning of a pace towards the Mess. For the conversation was obviously ended.

But Reynolds stood in his way and grabbed his arm. " God Almighty ! " he exclaimed. " What is that putrefying old man down in the hole thinking of ? We're only just up to strength. The other three batteries have got spares—C. has *two*. And what's the D.A.C. for— stiff, positively *lousy* with subalterns ! Damn all for any of them to do, too, with all the supply being done just now in ' Army ' lorries ! "

" He's told Brigade all that, Rennie," said Cartwright. " He's put it on record."

" He's put it—oh, God ! Dad, blast you, can't *you* say anything ? "

" Yes, young feller," said Whitelaw. " It's been said before, though. In the first paragraph of that immortal letter to Aunt Jane."

Themselves more minute than the metal pellets that plunged in a quivering canopy across the sky above them, unsubstantial save for the crunching of their boots in the flashes that thinned and shook the air without shaking its darkness, they went slowly down the shaft to where the Major's face smiled gently to them through the steam above a soup-plate.

" I say, Sir ! " said Reynolds. " Oh—sorry we're a

bit late—but this news about Uncle. It's—it's bowled us over."

"No one is sorrier than I am, Reynolds," said the Major quietly.

"But—I mean to say—you see, Cartwright doesn't *want* to go, Sir. There are fellows who'd jump at it; champion cork-pullers. Surely, Sir, the D.A.C. is the place reinforcements ought to come from?"

"This isn't a reinforcement," said the Major. "It's an appointment."

"If——." Reynolds considered for a moment and then plunged, "It—it isn't that you want him to go, is it, Sir? I'm sorry—I don't mean to be impertinent, though it sounds pretty like it; but honestly I don't. What I mean to say is, if Uncle applied definitely to the Colonel —even the General—to let him come back—you'd have him back, Sir, wouldn't you?"

The Major barely had time to say "Yes. Of course I'd——" when Whitelaw's fist crashed down on the table. "Damn you, be quiet! Talking—" He stopped suddenly. His outburst had been a snarl of rage. But the word 'talking,' and then the sudden cessation, had been like a moan.

The furrows were gouged deep and blackly shadowed in his cheeks, thrusting forward the tightly set lips. The shaggy brows were pulled low over the eyes that flashed with fury upon Reynolds and then darkened with the pain as he turned them towards the blinking Major. "Major," he said, with surprising softness, "For God's sake, shut that youngster up!"

The Major played his trump again—gentleness.

"What's he done, Whitelaw?" he asked, mild as a vicar at a bedside. "I'm sure we all want to keep Cartwright."

"So *you* don't know, either . . ." Whitelaw said, as though he were lying stricken in the bed where the vicar sought to bring comfort, and finding no comfort wearily turned his face to the wall and his own dark thoughts.

Reynolds winked at Cartwright but it was unsuccessful, a merely silly grimace. He, too, knew that they had all arrived somewhere beyond the scope of winking, with old Whitelaw like a spring, taut and strained.

A section of the battery was on duty, firing off its round or so per minute, to ' keep open ' some wound in the chalk and concrete of the earth and in the nerves of men that the last few days had made.

Two hundred other guns on the Corps front were engaged in the same leisurely exercise, and perhaps a hundred others were replying. Arras itself was pandemonium ; but nobody cared, since the city's life was now lived and its pedestrian traffic plied in the cellars, in the arched sewers and immense grottoes under its deepest foundations. The roads behind it were picked out with stabs and thumps ; the railway station was a clank and a roar like a prodigious shunting of its departed rolling-stock. The candle-flames in the airless dug-out were set in the fantastic shapes of their incessant wriggling.

" I don't appear to know, Whitelaw," the Major said. " But I'm always ready to learn. I'm sure Reynolds is, too."

" He isn't ! " snarled Whitelaw. " That's the hell of it. He isn't. You'd think he'd have seen it for himself by now. God knows he's had enough chances. But he doesn't. This is the second time in the last two hours that he's come brassing in with an attempt to *upset* everything."

" Dad ! " said Reynolds. He was wistful enough now, a mere twenty to Whitelaw's venerable forty or fifty or sixty—whichever accorded best with the whiteness of his hair and the furrowed leather of his cheeks. " Dad— *honestly*—Dad——"

" You *did*," said Whitelaw. " This job of F.O.O. day after to-morrow——" And he turned to the Major. " Reynolds knew as well as I do—and I've known it for the last week, I give you my word—that I would be on duty and it would be my show if we had to send a man. But what did he do as soon as he got your chit ? *Volunteered*, the damned little fool ! And then, of course, old Uncle had to volunteer just to hold up the fair name of the British Empire and the undying spirit of our Public

Schools. And that let *me* in for *seeming* to volunteer—but only *seeming*, let me tell you, because all I really did was stick to my place, and prevent any one from butting in."

" All you're accusing me of—and losing your wool over —is a bit of self-sacrifice and heroism, then," said Reynolds. He had a hope that the position had been manœuvred back to where he could deal with it lightly.

But Whitelaw was grave and disconcertingly grim in his earnestness. " What I'm accusing you of, Rennie, is attempted murder. Attempted suicide, too, but that isn't so important. Can't you see ?—oh, God, can't you see, without my having to tell you ?—that the only system worth a damn in all this nonsense, is to let orders and things take their course ? Have you forgotten Meston ?—It was Uncle's turn to go over the top with the feet, but Meston, the damned fool, came butting in and made Richards give him Uncle's place. But it wasn't Uncle's place he took—because one man *can't* take another's. You remember what happened to him for trying, though—and that wasn't enough. His blasted interference wasn't only suicide, it was murder. Meston's corpse dragged that boy Austin out to get it in the neck."

He paused, drawn away from speech by the darkness of his thoughts. A grunt brought him back to speech again. " And Browne ; Richards's orders were that batmen should lay for twenty rounds each week, just for practice. Browne had done his twenty—he'd done over thirty that week as a matter of fact—but the damned rascal had to go interfering, and exceeding orders. Instead of sitting in the cook-house and going on with his job—cleaning Dicky's buttons and making tea—he had to dash off *volunteering*—just because the layer had a bit of a sore ear. The result was—well, you know the result. . . ."

He stopped to pour some whisky into his mug and from his mug into his throat. What he was saying was obviously a matter not of opinion, but of religion ; and the three men were intent in their listening—as Balaam was intent ; for earnestness that came from religious brooding and not irascibility was as impressive from Whitelaw as the quiet human talk instead of a bray from Balaam's ass.

"Then my brother . . . I was the senior trooper in that sap of which I may have told you. I'd told the chaps off in a proper order of duty, and rest. I was on for an hour ; my brother next. But the fool got up a good twenty minutes before it was his turn and started mucking about, telling me he was awake, and that I ought to take a spell off. In came a grenade and out came a yard of his guts. The grenade damned nearly did for me, and *did* do for one of the others. . . ."

Then he turned quite definitely to Reynolds. "Now," he snapped, "you've got it ! I wish to God you had found the system for yourself instead of my having had to tell you. It sometimes breaks the luck to give a system away. . . . But I couldn't very well help it this time. Even the Major was inclined to listen to you. . . ."

He was explaining now, not to the three who flickered before their shadows in the candle-light, but to the demons of destiny and chance that lurked behind them.

"But, Dad," said Reynolds, with the wistful humility of a convert questioning the priest who had given him a glimpse of revelation ; "Dad—if we all try to kick up a hell of a dust at Brigade—if Uncle sticks his toes in, and bites and kicks and screams—so as to prevent their taking the old thing from us—surely we're not butting in anywhere ? It's only because it's so damned unfair and out of turn, that we resist it. We're only just up to strength. All the other batteries——"

But the subject was, indeed the subject of a man's deepest and most precious belief. Heresy and doubt upon it were intolerable pain to the dully humming ears of Whitelaw. "Rennie !" he said. "No ! You can't dodge it that way. You've got to draw the line somewhere —and the only line you can draw, is *orders*. Even if they're unfair and idiotic—as they generally are—they're *orders ;* and if you've got any sense, and want to save your skin, the only thing to do is to follow them."

The clash went slowly on, surrounding them, metal

upon earth, metal upon air, metal upon metal ; and the vibration of ear-drums, tremulous and delicate, had steadied into a grosser, duller movement like the panting of blown lungs.

"There's nothing else left," the liturgist concluded. "Nothing ! There's nothing bullet-proof, bomb-proof, shell-proof, gas-proof and louse-proof—but routine and *orders*. Even if they come from a fool or a rascal, they stand. . . . So we've got to let old Uncle go. Better to lose him that way, sonnie. . . . Luck, Uncle."

His face disappeared into the shadow of his chin and his mug, only the knobs of his cheek bones standing above it into the light.

Whitelaw's eyes came back into the light again, to see Reynolds playing with his soup-spoon and staring at it. Cartwright played with nothing. The Major was trying to model a pellet of bread between his right finger and thumb which should be the exact duplicate of the one he had modelled with his left.

"Here ! " and Whitelaw impatiently snapped the cork out of the bottle and dashed some whisky into the four mugs. "If we're not damned careful we'll make it like a funeral. Lap it up, Rennie—a bit of Shakespeare——"

Cartwright leaned over the corner of the board and laid his hand on Reynolds's elbow. "Not ' The noblest Roman of them all,' Rennie ; ' we shall not——' " then he very suddenly stopped.

Reynolds, looking as though he would never smile again, slowly took his mug and raised it. "Good luck, Uncle," he said into it ; and gulped.

"Good luck, Rennie." And Cartwright drank.

The Major lifted his mug. "Best of luck, Cartwright."

"Good luck, Sir."

.   .   .   .   .   .

Reynolds followed him up the shaft when he had shaken hands with the Major and Whitelaw.

At the top, when he had shouted to Jackman and turned towards the hovel, Reynolds said, " Uncle, is it—I mean, do you *want* to go ? "

" Rennie," he answered, " to tell you the honest truth I don't feel anything. Absolutely nothing at all. I suppose—well, Rennie, how would *you* feel ? I suppose that's about the best answer possible. . . ." And then he thought, quite suddenly, that he would be able to tell Dorothy in his next letter that he had been given a Staff appointment—the most menial in the world but, nevertheless, ' Staff.'

" I can't imagine it," was the mumbled answer of Reynolds.

" And I can't, either," said Cartwright, thoughtfully. " I've just been thinking ' Oh—hell ' for the last hour and can't get any further. . . . Arras, by the way, doesn't seem to be the most tranquil spot in the world at the moment."

" Arras ! " Reynolds snorted westwards. " I'm sick of the whole shooting-match, Nunks. And this has put the lid on it. This is the dirtiest, bloodiest, lousiest battle we've touched yet. I've felt uneasy about the damned thing from the start. It's a marvellous idea, really ; with the Canucks banging at Vimy on the left, slogging at the flank of the Hindenburg line—those Somme efforts were childish mucking about in comparison. But I hate it—every damned silly detail of it. I don't care——"

" Now, Rennie——" Cartwright began.

" ' Now ' your grandmother," said Reynolds. " You needn't start self-helping me. I don't want it. And you know it's all a swindle as well as I do. You're going now and it's no use bluffing any more. Who's there to bluff ? Dad ?—The Major ?—Only the men ; and even they are beginning to get as wise as Dad. I wish to God he hadn't done that sermon to-night. Did you see what it did to the Major ? Uncle, he was white and shaking while Dad growled on. . . . And Dad has smashed something with that blasted talk of his. He's made it all—*sinister*. It was only shells before, and muck floating about that you could hear and dodge with a reasonable, belly-to-earth fear of God. But that old sod was like a witch-doctor. He's filled in the spaces between the shells and the stiffs, with claws that have got hold of you—shoving, tugging to God knows where. It isn't safe to duck any more ; and that's why he walks straight ahead, steady as a chap showing off on a tight-rope. I thought it was swashbuckle ; but it isn't. It's funk—is bad as mine, and yours."

" He's got a system," said Cartwright. " And he's got the guts to follow it."

" He's got *something*," said Reynolds, " that's put the fear of God into all of us to-night. You won't dare now to move a finger to get back to the battery. And you're the only one who might do it."

" Nothing's permanent, Rennie," Cartwright said. "Nothing's definite and final, you know."

" Nothing *was*—till Dad brought out his black Ju-ju's to fill in the empty spaces and show that *they* are definite and final and permanent."

" Dad be damned ! " said Cartwright uncomfortably.

You know you've got to let him talk. You know he's Probably telling the Major now, how the War could be won in a week, with half a dozen subalterns running H.Q. It's no use minding what Dad says. It's what he does that matters."

" Uncle ! " said Reynolds ; and he suddenly stopped Cartwright at the door of the hovel, pulling him back to the path from the blanket over the door. " Uncle—d'you mean you will have a shot—you *would* have a shot at aiming back—if—if——"

" If what, Rennie ? "

" I don't know. If you wanted to, I think. Or, Perhaps, if Brigade isn't any safer than the battery." they went in and lighted the candle.

"Of course," Reynolds went on thoughtfully. "There's no going over and mucking about with the Infantry, when you're on Brigade staff. There's sometimes a cellar, and generally a decent dug-out to sleep in—but it isn't often in bed that stiffs are made. It's tootling about somewhere—I don't suppose there's very much in The odds, really. My God—he's changing his boots ! does that mean your new tunic, too ? You won't cut

D D

any ice that way, Nunks ! They prefer the war-worn garb in Headquarter Messes—so if you want to make quite sure of your job——"

" You fool," said Cartwright. " I'm just going to change into gum-boots. They're looser. My ankle's still sore where I kicked it into that piece of wire or something yesterday. Jackman can lug just my sleeping-bag and stuff for the night and we'll see about my other kit—later."

" You'd better wait for the orderly, before shoving off," Reynolds suggested. " No one's allowed above ground in Arras at night. Sentries at most of the man holes to direct people into the sewers and keep 'em down. And you know what sentries are—you'd never find the Rue des Capucines in a month by asking *them*."

" Oh, well—" said Cartwright. " Might as well go and try. The orderly may be late." He felt an uneasiness like the futility of hanging about a railway platform. " Jackman's own kit won't take him long to pack. He's probably lost most of it again."

He was stuffing whatever he could into his haversack to lighten Jackman's load and to be sure, too, that I would not be left behind. " Oh—the night's targets he said, and tore out and handed Reynolds a page from his book. " The centre section is on till two, and then the left. I've got about thirty francs of Mess funds I'll keep it if you like and get some stuff for the Men after the show. There's a canteen——"

" Nero fiddles—" said Reynolds. " Well—might as well wait in the Mess while Jackman packs up. Or are you going round to bid farewell to your section ? Most of them are in the pits, I suppose ? "

Cartwright felt an impact of some sort ; but the only sound it made was its echo, coming out very slowly and faintly through his lips. " Oh—hell——"

Then he said, " I'm not, Rennie. I'm just going to slope off quietly. . . . We'll roll the valise ourselves and then shout for Jackman and you can tell Crouch to take care of my other stuff. I'll see about getting it. . .

They rolled and strapped the valise and shouted for Jackman.

. . . . . .

" Good luck, Rennie," Cartwright said when Jackman, now the loaded coolie, stepped into the night.

" Good luck, Nunks," said Reynolds. " Don't forget the blow and the harsh word waiting for you here, whenever you're passing—and a spot of the giant-killer. . . ."

Gunners, for a fraction of an instant, stood bowed and black in the wraith of pallid orange light about number four's opened breech ; then they were gone again into the blackness of the night.

MEDAL WITHOUT BAR   CHAPTER LXXV

THE days of his appointment to Brigade Head-quarters will remain till the end of time for Cartwright one of those crowning idiocies among the considered actions of man that have no explanation.

If it be granted that Brigade Headquarters needed a man, D Battery was the one battery in the Brigade that ought not to have supplied him. The ammunition-column, as Reynolds had observed, was verminous with subalterns, and it was—through a change in the organisation of ammunition supply to the batteries by ' Army ' lorries, practically idle.

The other batteries had at least one surplus sub-altern apiece. D Battery had no surplus subaltern and was, moreover, about to detach one as the Brigade's F.O.O. with the infantry.

But the postulate that Brigade needed another officer was one that no man, sane or insane, could grant. It could be admitted that the Adjutant had work to do. It could be argued that the Colonel was not superfluous. but not the subtlest sophistry in the world could mate-rialise a burden for the shoulders of the Brigade Orderly

Officer, Taffy Dolbey.   There had been a time, vaguely
before the Somme, when the orderly officer of an
Artillery Brigade, besides being an understudy to the
Adjutant, was the officer responsible for the communications between the Brigade office and batteries.   Sometimes, for reasons of some spectacular nature or because
times were slack and the O.O. a vague enthusiast, he
had a wire laid from the Brigade Mess to some spot
whither the Colonel could invite a visiting General to
walk, after lunch or before it, to see the front.   Since
the Somme days, however, this burden had been taken
from the O.O.'s shoulders ; for the 'establishment' of
Brigade H.Q. staffs had suddenly been expanded by the
' attachment for discipline and rations ' of a subaltern
of Royal Engineers who brought a sapper batman and
an N.C.O., a roll of adhesive insulating tape obscured
by tobacco-crumbs and pocket-fluff, and an immense
pair of pliers in a leathern holster pendent to a button on
his breeches.   (There are no cases on record of the advent
of one of these youths to a Brigade Headquarters being
followed by very many minutes wherein it did not grow
clear that the Colonel himself in the whole Brigade was
the only Artilleryman who might address any comment
on his craft to this august technician and his henchman.
   All that was left then to the orderly officer—all, that
is to say, of work in the term's broadest interpretations-
was understudying the Adjutant.   Men of intelligence
and ingenuity, men imbued with something of the spirit
of humility, might have made something of this job
but it must have taken some doing.   As for Taffy
Dolbey, Nature had endowed him with all the vacuum
she had abhorred and set aside from her more serious
works.   There seemed to be no subject in the world
upon which he had a spark of sense—either horse, common
or technical ; yet he had received a salary before the
War in that Midland bucket-shop and looked forward to
receiving it again after.   The only function of his mind
was feats of memory.   His brain was a more accurate
record of the Colonel's little gymnastics on the Stock
Exchange than the fortnightly transcript sent out from

the jobbers' ledger. Dolbey's foulness and meanness in the art of bullying batmen and cook, signallers, grooms and even the Regimental-Sergeant-Major was, since he had neither wit nor sense, stark genius. He was, in short, a Grotesque—defying all description, incredible and insufferable. It is a further mystery beyond human understanding that at a time when death was unexciting and unobtrusive, this individual and any others like him continued to survive.

At Suvla, for example, when he was still with a battery, there must have been a hundred opportunities for a signaller, writhing in some petty humiliation, to close his finger over a rifle-trigger behind sight's coldly laid on Taffy's ape-like cranium. Any one of a hundred fatigue-men, in those days of soft caps, could no doubt have laid him one over the head with a pick or the flat of a spade. Neither would have met with comment, or else the only comment would have been congratulation. Yet such is human charity that Taffy Dolbey and his kindred lived. He lives to this day. (Such is the blank and glorious insensitiveness of the man that he sends, fortnightly, to Cartwright's office a circular from the bucket-shop arm of which he is now a senior partner.)

It followed that Gordon the Adjutant, who was a fine soldier, a fine adjutant and a decent man—one, roughly, of the old Henderson Samurai-specification—it followed that such a youngster as Gordon left mighty little of his work for such an idiot as Taffy. There was a touch of pathos in the way Taffy would hang about while Gordon was away—at the wagon-lines for an outing with the Colonel, bathing, or even at the latrine—on the off-chance of being able to issue an obvious order to the batteries or sign an already dictated one as 'acting adjutant.'

Gordon stomached him, as he would have stomached anything, in the doing of his job ; but Dolbey's relationship to the Colonel was a very different matter for the Colonel was a sociable creature condemned to isolation and loneliness.

The astonishing fact that he had weighed, for a

dozen years, seven-stone-six, had made him a famous subaltern and Captain in India among senior officers with good horses but generally large frames and a distrust of Eurasian jockeys. Among leisurely men, amiable and fairly dull-witted, the bright little jockey gave out distinct sparkle and shine. Meanwhile the date of his gazetting receded slowly but surely into the past, and it was not long before casualties and recruiting made of the senior Captain a smart little Major, and of the Major a acting Colonel. He carried his bounce and his sharp gamin-wit upwards with him ; but his patrons had become dispersed and there was something in his new subordinates that just prevented their being impressed— all of them, that is, except the insignificant, goggle-eyed subaltern Dolbey, in one of the batteries at Suvla.

Dolbey was arraigned, through the proper channels, by an indignant and dignified old Sergeant for cursing him on parade and in the presence of his subordinates with the two words that no good soldier may use, save in jest or to a peer. Something passed between the Colonel and the quaking Dolbey which revealed to the staring eyes of one the God among men, and to the crafty narrowed eyes of the other the lackey and the insatiable bootlicker.

There was something disgusting in the stare of adoration and wonder in Taffy's eyes at some pigmy-posturing of his deity, something that positively turned the stomach when he smiled his flaccid, cretin smile and snickered at some very ordinary joke.

The Doctor and Vet and the Interpreter had long since abdicated from a Mess run by Taffy Dolbey, and farmed themselves out to a battery and the wagon-lines. The signal-sapper was generally out on his business or on visit to his host of friends. Gordon, as often as not, had his meals taken through the passage cut from the Mess cellar to the office ; so that the table was manned by the Colonel, Dolbey and Cartwright.

The daily calves' head and the white wine Cartwright found to be not malicious libel but solid fact.

The way Dolbey sprang up to open a bottle of soda water for the Colonel was as nauseous as his smile ; and precisely one day of loafing about in that cellar had passed, and it was at the beginning of Cartwright's first dinner in the Mess that Dolbey, instead of leaping to this service, said " Cartwright—the Colonel's Perrier."

Cartwright looked, until they were shifted from himself to the Colonel, at the bulging china orbs of the man whom he had come from the battery to assist. A warlike touch of Dolbey's was a polished eighteen-pounder cartridge standing on the table. Cartwright struck it with the handle of his knife. When the batman came in, Cartwright said, " A bottle of Perrier for the Colonel, please."

The innocent batman produced a bottle from the box in the corner of the cellar, opened it, placed it before the Colonel and withdrew. The silence was terrific, a small cavity in the solidity of the bombardment's din. In about nine hours it would be zero. . . . The three of them sat munching their dinner in it ; the small thing that was the Colonel ; the worm that was Dolbey, and Cartwright.

There was no getting away from the fact that he was afraid of the Colonel ; Colonels did inspire people with simple, inexplicable, undeniable fear. Whether they were giants or pygmies, boys or patriarchs, pious, profane or waggish, bounders or the salt of the earth—by dint of some weird mystery they inspired it ; so Cartwright fished for some remark in his mind that quaked and shook with anger and hate, something to ease the strain and advertise to the Colonel that in putting the idiot Dolbey in his place he had no intention of slighting the commander of his Brigade. But he stoutly rejected the possibilities that presented themselves. They—Dolbey and the Colonel— had made the ridiculous strain, he told himself ; let one of them, if they wanted it ended, end it.

They could, in short—both of them—go to hell.

Then inspiration came to him while he studied the bubbles wriggling and bursting in the neck of the bottle beside the Colonel's glass.

He poured some whisky into his own tumbler with a magnificently steady hand and said, " Is the Perrier yours, sir ? Or Mess ? "

It came off absolutely ; as smooth as though he had said to an acquaintance, concerning roses, " Are they from cuttings of your own or did you buy the plants? "

" Mess," said the Colonel.

His curiosity as to what was to follow was satisfied by Cartwright's strolling over to the box and producing another bottle. There was a flange on the stud of the tin-opener in his pocket-knife that had served, very conveniently, for pulling the stoppers of Perrier bottles whenever the battery had been able to come by them. This saved Cartwright from the necessity of asking Dolbey for the racquet-shaped key which he carried in his pocket.

Gordon came in towards the end of the meal to bolt his share of it and tell the Colonel of some talk he had been having with the Brigade-Major at Divisional Headquarters Cartwright heard the Colonel and Dolbey pouring forth precisely the same acrimonious contempt for Division's remoteness from the forefront of battles that battery Messes expressed for Brigades. In company dug-outs in the front line he had seen the same fine score for ' Battalion.' In the battalion headquarters' dug-out it existed, flourishing, for ' Brigade.' It was at Brigades for Division. (At ' Army ' it is said to have existed for G.H.Q.). . . .

The three or four stories of the house over the cellars and of the houses opposite made the ground-floor as reasonably safe as the cellars themselves. Cartwright had a room above the office, furnished with his sleeping-bag and valise on a box-mattress.

He had done, in the last twenty-four hours, absolutely nothing beyond censoring five letters.

At about half-past nine he said to the Colonel, " Is there anything for me to do to-night, Sir ? I think I'll turn in if there isn't."

This was the Colonel's opportunity to get back any point that he might have lost, and he took it. " Taffy," he said, " is there anything for Cartwright ? "

" No, Sir," said Dolbey promptly. Then the idiot

added, solemnly and Napoleonically, " I've done every-thing, Sir."

"Ask Gord," said the Colonel. His nickname for Gordon tickled Dolbey every time he used it. Cartwright, sulkily unsmiling, went through the doorway. Gordon, obviously as a sheer courtesy, allowed him to read out the co-ordinates of sixteen barrage-targets which the short-hand typist Bombardier had been doing quite adequately.

On his way up the steps he summoned Jackman. " Bring a bucket of hot water, as hot as you can get it, and some cold. We'll give my foot another doing."

He had nothing to read. His letter to Dorothy, telling her of his ' appointment to the staff ' had been written after lunch.

He had written to Henderson and to his father.

He took off the boots which he had put on for dinner—having taken them off and put on slippers after breakfast, lunch and tea. The left one required unlacing more completely than the right, and a more careful removal. Then he lay down, untired and utterly bored, with his left ankle, to relieve the pressure and throbbing in it, cocked up on his bent right knee.

Jackman, ministering with kettle, bucket and basin said, " That little bit of green never come from the iodine, Sir. She's going black and blue. You'd best to have the doctor take a look, Sir, now that Riding ain't here."

" Yes," said Cartwright, " I will, if it isn't better to-morrow."

On the morrow, however, the doctor stayed at the batteries and did not pass on his way to wagon-lines. At night he was moving in the advance, with the Mess that housed him, to a fresh position.

TWO or three days later Cartwright found Gordon alone in his office and took him into his confidence. He began the conversation by not taking him in, saying only, " Gordon, is it quite impossible to work a move back to the battery ? "

Gordon was worried by the question. After a little thought he said, " The Colonel personally appoints his staff, you know."

" Yes," said Cartwright. " That's the devil of it. If I say anything to the Colonel about it, it might—er— look as though—— "

" Quite," said Gordon. Then he added, casually, " I shouldn't let Taffy bother you—we all know our Taffy."

" It isn't Taffy," said Cartwright. " I think I've settled with Taffy."

" What is it, then ? " asked Gordon. " I think you'd settle down to the job after a bit."

" The *job* ? " Cartwright laughed. " You know you have got the only job here—a job for the likes of us, I mean," for he knew that he must not involve a good Adjutant in any slighting of the Colonel ;—" you and the Sapper bloke—and I wouldn't like his job, I assure you."

" If it's idleness you're objecting to—— "

" It's a lot of things," Cartwright interrupted him, for he saw by now that Gordon, in the isolation of his job and his temperament, even through the barrier of the grudge borne him by a score of the undecorated for his Military Cross, was approachable and companionable. " It's a lot of things, Gordon. I—I've somehow got to like the battery and—well, I'm a little bit afraid I might lose touch with it. I might lose the Brigade altogether— if something isn't done."

" You won't lose the Brigade by staying at Brigade Headquarters," Gordon suggested. " What the devil are you driving at ? "

Cartwright was removing the slipper from his left foot. Then he took off the sock.

"Good Lord!" said Gordon. "What's that? Chilblains?"

"No," said Cartwright. "I ran a spike of wire or something into it and it's got poisoned. But I'm damned nearly immobile. It's beginning to stiffen up behind the knee. And it might become pretty awkward if we had to move suddenly and I had to put on any sort of a boot. I'd like to get back to the battery." He was putting on his sock again.

"Very handy addition you'd be to a battery, I should think!" said Gordon, "—particularly at the moment when everything's stuck in the snow. Don't be an ass, Cartwright. The only thing for you to do is to go sick."

"Yes," said Cartwright gloomily. "Go sick. I might get evacuated and lose the Brigade altogether and then have to start with some new lot—all over again."

At the battery he knew he could lie up for a day or two—or three if necessary—with his foot cocked up on a bundle of some sort to relieve the throbbing. Riding, restrained from opening it and ' cupping ' it, could poultice it while Dad and Rennie carried on. As for getting back to the battery, he had the waders designed for some giant of a man, and the slush of ice and snow would be a comfort. He had Browne's walking-stick ; and he knew that Jackman was capable of producing an arm from somewhere out of the bundle of greatcoat, ground-sheet and muffler under the load of a valise and his own generous kit. Careful timing of the journey, moreover, might produce a lift in the cook's-cart or on a G.S. wagon or Infantry limber. . . .

"Has the Doc seen it ? " asked Gordon.

"No. It's only really got moving the last two days and he hasn't been by. I didn't want to make a song by asking you to get him to look in. I'd be all right with the battery, Gordon."

"I'll explain to the Doc about striking you off, and all that," said Gordon. "You needn't be afraid of losing the unit, unless the foot's going bad and has to be amputated." His smile was most friendly. "And about going back to the battery—better let that rest for the moment. We'll see what the Doc says."

The doctor came late in the afternoon on his way to the wagon-lines, kicking snow off his boots and shaking it out of the collar of his coat.

What he had to say he said in three letters on a casualty label, " I.C.T." (Variant information translated the diagnosis to be 'infected condition of the tissues,' and 'infected contusion of the tendons.') He said, in postcript, " I don't think you need worry about being sent far down the line. I expect they've got all they want at the Clearing Stations and the hospitals ; and it's still going on like the very devil. You'll get stuck at a field ambulance and laid up for a week or two. It probably won't take any longer than that. There doesn't seem to be any sympathetic inflammation in the groin—yet. You'll want your kit, by the way, at a field ambulance."

The Colonel saw him before he went. For reasons as obscurely mysterious as those for which he had summoned him, he said : " If you're not evacuated, Cartwright, you'll report to the battery when you're fit."

They shuffled off, Jackman and he, to the dressing-station in some sort of arched subway beside the Doullens road.

Jackman had spun for himself a fair dream. " I suppose, Sir," he said with one hand under Cartwright's elbow, the other lifted up and sprawled over the strap to steady the valise on his shoulder, " I suppose I'll mark time at Brigade while you're at orspill ? "

" No, you won't," Cartwright chuckled. " You're going back to the battery with the orderly to-night."

The dream was shattered.

" And give my compliments to Mr. Reynolds the minute you get there—wake him up if he's asleep—or Mr. Whitelaw if Mr. Reynolds is away—and tell him I'm coming back. Don't leave it till the morning ; there's another officer being posted to the battery to-night and there's no need for my section to be given to him—for such a short time. Keep my glasses and compass in your own kit. Tell Mr. Reynolds I've taken them with me."

They stumped on. The battle was gone five miles away at their backs. The Canadians, carrying eyes and telescopes to the ancient heights of Vimy, had spread a mantle of scatheless quiet over Arras. To men on foot the boarded and lighted sewers and peopled quarries underground were ways more familiar than the upper surface of the cobbles; so the only traffic was the endless string of wagons and limbers in the next street, the chatter and clatter of lorries and ambulances in the broader street beyond.

They swished from the grey of snow on shadow to druggets of snow in moonlight where a wall was cleft or roof timbers bereft of tiles.

" Got any money, Sir ? " said Jackman.

" A few francs," said Cartwright. " But what the hell do you want money for ?—at the battery—or even here ? "

" I don't," said Jackman. " But there may be a canteen handy to your 'orspill. I could lend you thirty-four francs till you get back."

When he had conducted him to a seat on a box in the dressing-station and placed the valise under his foot, Jackman handed over the thirty-four francs and took his leave. " Well, Sir, good luck, Sir, I'm sure. I'll tell the chaps at the battery it's all right."

The substantial thermometer which an orderly had stuck under his tongue relieved Cartwright of the onus of replying. He moved the knob of Browne's walking-stick from his right hand to his left. They shook hands and Jackman saluted like a buffalo performing a difficult trick, shoved his hands back into the mittens that hung on a tape from his neck and went back, eastwards.

A TWENTY or thirty-mile drive in an ambulance brought Cartwright to the château which had been given over to the sheltering of men with peculiar woes. Through a medical Major the château was ruled by the twin demons, Suspicion and Fear. His life's Practice had been in a suburb where it mattered little whether men were ill or merely fancied themselves ill, so long as they called him in and in due course paid their seven-and-sixpence. Here it mattered greatly, for there was another whilom practitioner, younger and more fortunate, with a star added to the crown on his shoulder, a coloured band on his cap with gilt on its black peak, and coloured gorgets on his collar.

The sole function of this younger, luckier individual was to arrive in a car during the peace of high noon, the dishevellment of morning or the lull of evening, to find pale men packed up and girt ready to depart again for battle who ought to have been in pyjamas, ready for evacuation to the Base. He found men reading magazines in bed, dozing, sitting in the garden and staring at nothing, whom any idiot ought to have recognised as fit as fiddles. . . . And he made things hot for the Major.

The peculiarity of the patients' woes lay in their dark secretness and privacy ; for the sick men, unlike soldiers, had little to say and scant curiosity for the sayings of others. All that seemed to transpire from their talk was their units and the exact points of the front from which they had come. (There were no Majors among them— perhaps Majors and Colonels were not similarly afflicted ; or else, similarly afflicted, went elsewhere.)

There were noticeably few youngsters. They were subalterns and a few Captains, for the most part of ages neighbouring, from one side to the other, on thirty. The present difficulty of some was in the finding of sleep ; of others in waking up from it. Some gibbered and shook and cursed when a door was banged; one or two suddenly choked over their food. A giant fusilier wandered about the place cursing monosyllabically, laying proud claim to fitness and a becoming thirst; it was clear that he was liked by his Colonel and others, and that he wanted to get back to a Mess from which they had contrived to exclude him for a while—a Mess where there was whisky. This man occupied one of the four or five beds in Cartwright's room, and knelt beside it for some minutes each night, in pyjamas of striped flannel, praying. There was one who went about corridors mumbling an acrimonious plaint that there should be no nurses in such a place out of the thousands upon thousands of V.A.D.s wasting for jobs—instead of those swine of orderlies. Three of these he placed under arrest for insolence and insubordination. There was a Highlander who was for ever sneaking into the conservatory with the gramophone and an armful of selected records. He would sit there playing them from one meal to the next, noting in a small pocket-book the number and the manufacturer of the records that were new and specially delightful to him. There was one man who had come down in the ambulance with Cartwright and had been heard to utter only one word—" Piles."

It was the unhappiest place that Cartwright saw in all the War, where men tottered about, solitary and anxious, hoping for they knew not what or not daring to say; expecting nothing in particular.

His own case was different. For a day or two, and a couple of nights while the orderly's blobs were high on the temperature-chart, his wits itched with an absurd discomfort that a foot like his would sooner or later have to come off, somewhere below the lump behind his knee, or else above it. Then the hot discomfort would cool a little with the thought that that, at any rate, would be that. . . . Dorothy, on the whole, would have little to complain of. . . .

As the blobs moved down and steadied, he realised that what he might still lose was not his foot but his friends. He wrote to them, now counting among them the Major. Men were "evacuated" from that place, in spite of the Brigade doctor's assurance ; and for the gunner, evacuation was sheer annihilation with fresh beginnings in emptiness.

With great cunning Cartwright dissociated himself from the universal and hearty loathing of the peevish and bullying medical Major. He wooed him with fair words, saying little of his malady and nought of his anxieties or hopes. He congratulated him on the Mess (which was atrocious), on the smartness of his orderlies (who were louts). He spoke of the fortitude and stamina that must be required for the maintenance of equilibrium in a job (a 'command' he called it) conducted practically single-handed in such a God-forsaken spot.

Nature took its course.

The Major did the obvious and the reasonable thing : when Cartwright's foot was nearly well he discharged him from the ambulance with instructions to rejoin his unit, by way of Amiens. It happened on a day that the Colonel did not come to reverse any of the Major's orders.

HANNIBAL and Alexander, Cæsar and Napoleon had been cheated of the glory of conquest such as Cartwright knew on the journey from Amiens to the battery.

None of them had crawled, pressed to a freezing or sullenly thawing earth, to the scrutiny of amphibian movements in a swamp ; and then sat, three months later, in a railway train behind an engine that boldly roared its solid progress over the way of the old foul swamp.

Beaucourt, of old the meanest of jests, was now a comely hamlet, bright with the amenity of biscuit-boxes nailed over the chinks or shanties and kraals, proud in its possession of the symbol that was as the symbol of pump and village-green in those days and climes—its incinerator.

Miraumont was now a place of emporia—ordnance, engineers' junk, ammunition, rations and forage with appropriate sidings for unloading them, and a busy governor, the Railway Transport Officer. The alternative and more usual translation of his initials into " Rude to Officers," did not particularly apply to this individual ; he was as new as his domain. He was eating breakfast in the two enormous packing-cases that were his office when Cartwright got down from his truck and went to him.

" Oh, yes," he said, giving Cartwright a mug of tea. " They're a bit farther on. Came in three or four days ago. There's going to be a show, you know. Nothing much to write home about, just another local shot at that Bullecourt place. . . ."

Cartwright suppressed this information when he got back to the truck. The company in it was mixed ; for the resources of rolling-stock beyond Albert could not run to the delicacy of a third-class carriage for officers. An Infantry subaltern sat on his pack beside Cartwright's valise and it was for him that Cartwright suppressed the word of imminent battle. To the twenty or thirty men, huddled and sardonically grousing, the word would have meant nothing ; for they were a wise lot, returning from leave or hospital. The subaltern, with his authoritative talk of billeting-areas, railheads and dumps was a recent transfer from the A.S.C. to the Infantry. Cartwright, wise as the men and as cold, felt that a passable craftsman would emerge in time from this jocular fellow-traveller but it was early—early in the day, for he alone had as yet poured anything hot into his vitals, and early in the Infantryman's service—for communication of battle. They talked instead of the Officers' Club in Albert where an excellent dinner had been eaten the night before, where a French girl had whisked a pudding-plate away and answered " Cheese—two kinds " in answer to the suggestion, " Fromage ? " The interior decoration of the club—so said the Infantryman—clean, pale washes of distemper, and panelling in blue and white linen had

E E

been done under the direction of a German Sergeant,
a painter by profession.   The furniture had been made
in a ' shop ' run by a Bavarian joiner.

Bully-tins were opened and breakfasts eaten.   Tea
was brewed in mess-tins with bangs of steam released
by the sapper Corporal in charge of the engine ; and they
waited till noon for the reading of mysterious portents
by the R.T.O. before he released his daily half-dozen
trucks behind the samovar of engine from Miraumont to
Achiet. . . .

The reward of conquest for Cartwright was again,
as its foretaste had been in March, simply and almost
entirely the clean and comely fact of turf under foot
instead of foul ooze.

When the greenery was growing golden in the afternoon
sun he had walked the three miles into the now tidied
and orderly rubble of Ervillers to find that the wagon-line
was half a mile farther along the road to Boyelles.

There he found Richards, drinking tea in a bell-tent
beside a stream.

When first a Corporal came and stuck his head into
the tent and saluted with some trivial pretext, then the
Saddler-Corporal who had made the case for Cartwright's
scissors, razor and the Thermos and last of all the Sergeant-Major, he knew that their object was only to
confirm the report of the stable-picket that he had come
back to them.

And Richards kept saying that it was the same old
battery still, with their two selves and Dad and Rennie
—for the old man was no bother and the centre section
had become one with the old lot.   The new spare
subaltern, Dowland, was a good enough fellow, an
Infantryman really, but happy in the battery to which he
had drifted through the devious way of trench-mortars,
a wound, evacuation, coast defence at home and base
details.   He knew nothing about horses, but sat any one
of them by the grace of God.   Reynolds was having the
time of his life coaching him in the mysteries of a range-
table.

They exhausted the gossip over their tea.   The Major

was to "bloke" permanently for Riding. Jackman had been assisting the wagon-line cook who would therefore be the most grateful man in the army for Cartwright's return to duty. Richards had taken a reinforcement as his new batman ; cooking even for one had been too much for his groom. Reinforcement ? —Yes, three of the old lot had fallen out during the Arras show—a signaller killed, one wounded and a driver gone sick.

"I can take up the bullets, Dicky," Cartwright suggested at about six o'clock when his groom had returned from Achiet with his valise. "You can have a night off."

"No fear," said Richards. "It's a good war in these parts. I'll come up to dine in the Mess to-night and foot it back after. We'll go soon, so that Riding can put in a touch of fatted calf for you. It's only a brigade O.P. after dark so they might all be there—Dad and Rennie and Dowland. We guarantee that the old man won't be out anywhere. Rum old stick. I was afraid Dad would be uppish over his love of shelter—but he's swallowed him whole and seems to like him."

He told him of the little show impending ; some sort of factory or other that bristled with machine-guns and kept Bullecourt an annoying little salient.

A local thrust, it seemed, was all that was needed. Some heavies had been peppering the factory, and a sixty-pounder battery had given a hand with wire-cutting. The infantry of the attacking division was in the line already. Ammunition supply, over good roads and hard tracks, was easy. . . . And the battery-position said Richards, was a beauty ; a long sunken road with the whole brigade in a line—their battery on the right where the banks were highest ; no dug-outs ; the guns scratched into the banks and lean-to's scooped out between them and to their flank ; half-timbered and the other half canvas and corrugated iron and string —Heath-Robinson specification. Then Richards said the compound word that was the apotheosis of ancient dramas—" Open warfare, Uncle. . . ."

And they went out to their horses and the waiting column of wagons.

.   .   .   .   .   .

" Uncle ! " Reynolds shouted, from some preoccupation with a couple of men at the door of an outlying shanty. On the shanty roof were the canvas buckets, grey towels and here and there a shaving-brush of the battery's evening toilet. Reynolds left the men and came romping up like a puppy. " Uncle, you dirty old dog ! We swore you'd have the sense to stay away till the show was over."

Then Whitelaw appeared, grinning and looking ostentatiously at his watch ; for it was true that he never uncorked the bottle without first seeing what time it was. And then, when they had dismounted and were walking behind the guns to the Mess, some man whom they did not see but whose voice Cartwright suspected of being Whittle's, forgot his sense of the fitness of things to the extent of being overheard saying to another man, whom also they did not see : " Uncle's come back, Scrubby ! Take a look-see ! " And Scrubby, whoever he was—some one of the new section probably—thinking, no doubt, that a curtain of suspended, empty sandbags, was impervious to sound, said complacently, " Oo-bloody-ray ! Give the drum a one."

Even about the Major, now that there was no eternal twilight of dug-outs, there was a hint of sprightliness.

" I hope, Uncle," Whitelaw said quite playfully during dinner, " that it's act of God that's brought you back among fightin' men, and not mutiny ? "

" It's I.C.T., Dad," said Cartwright. " You see, Brigade couldn't possibly be hampered by a man who isn't absolutely fit and *mobile.*" He knew that he was evasive ; for he knew that Whitelaw's earnest dissertation before he had limped off through subterranean Arras with Jackman, was one of the things he would never forget.

" No," said Reynolds, " you've got to be road-worthy and full of steam to keep up with Brigade. But if you're going to start another lecture, Dad, I'm going to have three quick drinks and then slip out for a walk. I always lose sleep after your magic-lantern slides with moral."

" I'm not," said Whitelaw. " But—" and he turned suddenly to the Major. " Could you give Richards a definite order, Sir, to dine at the battery when he comes up ? It's quite a pleasant walk to the wagon-line in the cool of the evening."

The Major smiled, yet he was serious when he said, " Richards, the O.C. wagon-line will dine at the battery whenever he wants to. The wagons will be divided up to return under N.C.O.s. It's an order."

" Thank you, Sir," said Richards ; and to him alone, who had not heard the talk of Whitelaw, it was mere pleasantry and foolery without a hint of ritual.

The O.P. to which Cartwright went with Dowland next morning was again an affair of lordly spring sunshine. From it nothing whatever could be seen till the sun had lifted from its blaze, point-blank, into the eyes of the observer or the object-glass of his periscope. It was manned, therefore, at the comely hour of nine-thirty or thereabouts, after breakfast. Till then the responsibility of the Brigade was carried by the liaison-officer in the trenches. It could be approached, moreover, perpendicularly for every yard of the way, instead of crouching. It was in a deeply sunk road running along the crest from Croisilles to Ecoust. Narrow cuts had been slashed into this through the rear bank, a spacious cubicle sunk into the forward one twenty or thirty feet from the road, on the forward slope, and connected with the road by a twist of good trench. From this cubicle and others like it, or by scrambling up the roadside while engaged in gossip with a man from another battery, the observer could look down upon the trenches and Bullecourt and the gnarled skeleton of the factory a mile to the left. Never before had there been such a place for gunners ; such visibility and such targets—unless, perhaps, for German gunners looking towards and over Ypres, or from the old Schwaben Redoubt into slimy Hamel.

Along the slightly lower crest between the O.P. and the battery were memorials to the " open-warfare " which the bated breath of Richards had celebrated at the wagon-lines : broken chains of earthworks scooped quickly with entrenching-tools by eagerly grubbing men ; a scatter of the empty cartridges that had leapt from the breach of a hot rifle ; the belts of a machine-gun ; expended drums of Lewis guns.   And there were no corpses, smashed and sprawling.   The scent in the air was the scent of spring.

.   .   .   .   .   .

The battle was a dead and miserable failure.   Second-rate Infantry, second-rate management or second-rate luck made of it the dismal massacre of which only those knew who saw it, and the few others who heard of it from these while they were still eager to talk.

The survivors of the Infantry were withdrawn for rest and training.   Others came in, storm-troops of repute who had encountered such things as ' strong-points ' and sugar factories and redoubts before.   They took the place in due course, and held it.

But between the failure and the success the atmosphere changed.

Malevolence came into the air again ; signallers at the O.P. mumbled and suddenly spat and shifted a woodbine stump from ear to lips and quickly lighted it when a breeze stirred over the slope in front of Bullecourt. Such breezes no longer wafted to them the message of sap rising in greenery, of daisies unfolding tight little buds into bloom.

Shells, instead of occasionally dropping just anywhere, began to come from new quarters and in systematic groups, sweeping the road and the railway, stirring up the trenches with steady, observed fire ; hurtling over the O.P. towards the batteries behind.   Among the old familiar bursts of high explosive on soft ground were bursts with the newness of those in the ice-age north of Thiepval.   The new ' graze ' fuse was coming over in a certain small proportion with the blunt and solid old

'Dopp Z' (or whatever it was that had formed the familiar snouts of old duds). Whether fitted to a whiz-bang or a five-nine they made a hole scarcely more than a rabbit-scrape, and a burst, suspended a few inches above the turf, with a clang like the gates of hell.

It was one of these that got Richards.

The Major and Reynolds and Whitelaw and Cartwright were in the Mess, waiting for him to get the last of his teams away and join them at dinner. Dowland had not yet come back from the O.P. There had been some shelling earlier, to the right and left of the batteries in the road, in front of them and behind. The exact times of it, its extent, its calibre and its supposed objects had been gauged and silently noted by the Major who found material in such things for endless meditation. He was at peace as they waited, savouring a watered drink and smiling at the bicker between Whitelaw and Reynolds when there was a screech and the racket of three bursts or four ; a patter of splinters and then the clatter of Riding's boots and his bald head stuck in at the door.

" It's the Captain, sir," he said. " They've got 'im. Pretty bad."

He was gone again, down the road.

The square figure of Whitelaw blocked the door against the movements of the others. " Orderly officer," he said quietly.

" Yes," said Cartwright, for he was orderly officer. " I'll get him into the nearest dug-out. There may be more about."

Whitelaw too had jammed on his hat. " Next-for-duty," he mumbled. " I bet Dicky won't be the only one. . . . You keep still, Rennie, you little fool. Stay with the Major. There's crowd enough already—till we break it up."

And there it was, a hundred yards down the road, a crowd as when some one has fainted in the street ; and above it the heads and ears of horses that might have been cab-horses.

Richards was against the wagon-wheel, teeth jammed together and exposed in a haggard grin at the men who knelt and fumbled about him. A bony, white hand pushed back the helmet knocked forward over his eyes ; the fingers flickered and plucked at the drawn lips which struggled into the formation of words—" Uncle " —" Dad," and then stiffened back to the inhuman grin.

" Two of you," said Whitelaw, giving Riding and another man a jab on the shoulder, " You—and you. The rest clear out. Get the team away."

" Can't, Sir," said some one. " The riding centre's done in. And Brightman."

" Unhook the centres, then. Where's Brightman ? "

A Sergeant looked up from the end of the crowd which was, in fact, another crowd about another space on the ground. " I'll mind 'im, Sir," he said, shaking his head confidentially above the surrounding shoulders, and pushing out his lip and raising his eyebrows.

One leg of Richards's breeches was ripped open to show a whiteness of thigh, and below it a knee trivially split.

The gorgeous and polished field-boot on the other leg lost its shape and its shine some inches above the ankle.

They got him quickly against the side of the road while the centre horses were taken out of the team for the near one to be shot by the Sergeant, and the wagon taken away.

Riding was ready, kneeling by the boot, eager with his knives and scissors. Cartwright snatched a knife and opened the boot downwards from the knee till it became lost in the wet and shapeless muddle. Whitelaw had tied a ligature of something with a pad behind the knee. " Cut off that muck of breeches, Riding," he said. " Iodine and bandage the other knee. I must hang on to this strap for a bit."

Richards grinned on, his eyelids taut over his eyes. His breathing was jerky hisses and occasionally his teeth ground together.

The Major and Reynolds stood behind the group. Cartwright stood up and glanced at his hands. " In my ticket-pocket, Rennie. My tablets. Get one between his teeth."

Reynolds took the bottle. Cartwright knelt again and peered down. "What about that foot, Dad? I'm afraid I'll take it off if I mess about with the boot any more." He hesitated. "*Shall* I take it off?"

"Not in this light," said Whitelaw thoughtfully. "We'd never find the arteries and things to tie up in that mess. He'll be all right if we can keep the blood in him till he gets to the dressing-station. Have another go at the boot, Uncle. I expect it's that that's giving him gyp as much as anything. Wants room to swell. Rennie, get a light."

Reynolds answered with a grunt and the torch from his pocket, leaning over Cartwright.

Cartwright's hands were slippery. He wrapped his handkerchief over the flat, slender handle of one of Riding's knives. "Here, Sir," said Riding, holding out his hand. "You take holt the foot, Sir. I'll nip off the boot."

With a sense of proportion keener than Cartwright's, for he realised that a small knife-cut one way or the other would count for little, he deftly inserted his blade between the sole and the 'upper' and ran it round the welt, slick as his opening of a tin of beans. Then, with another single movement he opened the 'upper' from the toe to where it was lost in sock and flesh.

There was something, they found by gentle, careful testings, more than the boot-leather holding the foot to the leg. "Leave it alone, Ridin'," Whitelaw said. "It isn't bleeding."

Then Richards spoke.

Leaning down they saw that he had opened his eyes. "Uncle," he said, and the contortion of a smile trying to wriggle through his grin struck a chill upon them. The next salvo snarled over, bursting on the left in the direction of C Battery. The next, in ten minutes or so, would be still further left, on B . . . or else to the right where there was nothing. "Uncle . . . 'bout 'nother— your old pills?"

"Another pill, hell!" said Whitelaw. Then he stooped closer and said, "Those morphia things are all right when a fellow's bleeding, Dicky. But we've fixed you so that you can't bleed ; and what you want is *ginger*. You've got lots, old son, but a spot more won't hurt you. We're going to cut out that first dressin'-station, run by a man and a boy and get you straight to Bapaume. It's a longish way. A bit of the giant-killer, Rennie—" And Reynolds was scampering towards the Mess.

The Major, who had disappeared some time before, came slowly up the road out of the gloom. "The driver," he said softly to Cartwright. "He's finished, poor kid. One of your old lot."

"Yes," said Cartwright. "Brightman. I had a look at him. Hopeless."

"And—Richards ?" asked the Major, looking in every direction but that of Richards.

"If his pecker can be kept up for the next day or two," said Whitelaw, jerking the cork from the bottle and slopping whisky into the mug.

He knelt by Richards's head. "Dicky, you semi-teetotalling old sod, get outside of this as if you meant it." There was a minute clatter of teeth against the mug. The three-fingered hand of Whitelaw was dark against the forehead of Richards, white against his black hair. "Don't choke, laddie," said Whitelaw—a mother now. "Don't try to swallow, sonnie. It'll go down itself if you let it."

Riding and Cartwright had swaddled the ankle in shell-dressings and bandages and tied it to the other foot. A couple of men had materialised with the stretcher, their putties on, tunics buttoned, and tin-hats on their heads. Cartwright's incessantly grousing Sergeant Stevens came bustling up with a blanket. "Two more men, Sergeant," said the Major, "and a Bombardier to take charge."

Richards cursed as they got him on to the stretcher. They tucked him into the blanket and the Major pressed his forehead and said, "Good luck, my boy, good luck, good luck!" Reynolds said, "So long, Dicky, write. . . ."

Cartwright and Whitelaw walked along beside the stretcher for a few yards. "Take the track here, Bombardier," said Whitelaw, "to the wagon-line as hard as you can lick, without tossing the stretcher about too much. The wagon-line, mind—and don't hand over to any one ; not even an ambulance. Mr. Cartwright or I will catch you up—or join you. Wait at the wagon-line if we don't. Hold on, Dicky. See you presently. Come on, Uncle. . . ."

Richards hiccoughed more frequently than he moaned. "G' luck," he said.

They went to the adjacent sleeping holes—Cartwright's and Reynolds's, Whitelaw's and Dowland's. At the doors were Jackman and Keniston with a bucket, soap-dish and towel. In the further one was Dowland changing from breeches and puttees into slacks and shoes. Reynolds sat on the bunk beside him. "But, damn it," Dowland was saying, "I came here for safety. It's a dirty swindle. D'you think I started learning to call a Lance-Corporal 'Bombardier' at my time of life, for this ? "

Keniston, outside the door, was working Whitelaw's sleeves up his arms, Jackman Cartwright's.

"I think I'd better be the one to go, Uncle," said Whitelaw, thoughtfully. "I've got a better face than you for the job. The medical bloke at Bapaume is a Major and he may need talking to. He may want to send Dicky straight along ; but that foot ought to come off quick. God knows what's in the wound. Bits of boot——"

"I'm orderly officer," said Cartwright.

"I know," said Whitelaw, very seriously. "I'd thought of that, too. So your job is really to stick with the guns. I'll go."

He sent Keniston to tell Riding to get the Major's British-warm from the Mess as soon as he had taken it off ; if it looked as though the Major intended to dine in it, to get it from him with some yarn of blood on the back ; having got it, to hang it outside the Mess and to get on with serving the dinner.

"Major will talk to Major —— or to Captain if he can

find one," he said when Keniston, proud in his ' bloke,' had gone upon his errand. " I'll bag an ambulance on the Ervillers road and get Dicky there in no time. . . . Well, *he's* done with the War. The old baby, he would have liked to get one of those bits of ribbon out of it. . . ."

He hurried off to the Mess. Reynolds had drifted out of Dowland's dug-out and was waiting on the road for Cartwright, filling his loneliness with loosening and kicking up little bits of chalk. He looked towards the moon creeping up through a smear of jagged cloud.

" . . . The sods with our bayonets turning," he said. Farther down the road half a dozen cigarettes glowed where a grave was being carved out for Brightman, a crater widened and deepened for the horse. Reynolds sighed : " Christ——"

" Not a bad finish for him, Rennie," said Cartwright, also looking at the moon and the cigarettes, listening to the quiet scuffle of the gravediggers—" considering. He'll have a wooden leg——"

" No. Not a bad kind of finish. . . ." He was sulky with foreboding and slowed Cartwright's pace with the slowness of his, still kicking little bits of chalk. " Not bad so long as there's some one like Dad—" his arm slipped under Cartwright's—" or you, Nunks, to do any odd carving that's left. I hope mine comes before yours— if any more are on the way for us. God knows what other batteries do, who haven't got either of you."

In the Mess Whitelaw was explaining to the Major that he was going to the wagon-line to see Richards comfortably disposed of ; the Major was suggesting that he might as well stay there for the night. Riding, with the British-warm over his arm was helping the Major into his Burberry, for the night was chilly.

Riding went out with the Major's coat. Whitelaw emptied his mug, cut off a slab of bread and followed him.

IT was a quiet, thoughtful dinner ; a quiet, sombre passing of Cartwright among the men assembled in the pits to lay the guns on a new set of S O S lines for the night.

Forty rounds had to be fired on these, in bursts, between ten o'clock and five.

It did not take a great deal to make Cartwright uneasy now, while standing behind the battery in action. Even at the guns here there was no cover except against a drizzle of rain. The only protection against the sort of deluge that would come snarling back from a shell bursting at the gun's muzzle was in the lean-to's under the bank ; the sleeping-holes and the Mess. He sat casually in the Mess while the first salvo was fired ; took off his collar and tie beside his bunk when the next was due, put on a woollen muffler, brushed his hair, started a fresh pipe.

For the third one and the fourth, to demonstrate to himself the sheer nothingness of a nothing, he suggested a stroll ; and he and Reynolds and Dowland walked about behind the guns.

They speculated as to what they should get in the shape of a new Captain. " Is there no chance at all for you, Rennie ? " Dowland asked. " You're as senior as hell, aren't you ? "

" None," said Reynolds. " I'm senior enough in the battery ; but it doesn't go much by batteries now. The old man—funny old spud—said a few words to me while you and Nunks were out an hour or so ago. Said what a pity it is I look my age. The old thing was really apologising for not thinking I was suitable for his recommendation. Then he mumbled what a pity it is Dad is such a putrid gunner. Before he could say any more I butted in with what a pity it is Uncle is so junior. rubbed it in that he hasn't been commissioned a year yet. Knocked any scheme of *that* sort right on the head.''

" Pause, during which Uncle thanks you heartily for your timely help," said Dowland.

" Yes," said Cartwright.   " If there'd been a ghost of a chance——."

" Chance or no chance, I wasn't taking any risks We don't want Uncle shoved away at the wagon-lines," said Reynolds.   " But I shouldn't be surprised if the Old Thing does it all the same.   He doesn't mind what he says to Brigade—on paper."

" Suppose *you* get shoved away to the wagon-line, your youthful countenance notwithstanding ? " Cartwright suggested.

Reynolds did not answer with his usual speed. " Well," he said, " even if by some rum chance—— No, I don't believe I'd take it.   I don't mind for a week or so, till the new skipper shows up.   But I don't believe I'd shine in a lonely command.   Not like old Dicky.   There'd be plenty of *men* about, of course.   But it's showing off among my peers that raises up my wavering spirit. Pulling old Dad's leg and posturing before Uncle is worth a guinea a box to me.   That's what beats me in those flying blokes.   I believe I'd die—no, I wouldn't even have the guts to die ;   I'd just absolutely vanish with funk ;   I'd just cease being there if there was no one looking.   Heroism, as I see it, is just pulling a certain kind of face, quipping a timely crank—and what's the use of pulling faces and quipping cranks if no one's looking ? "

" Salvo—" the Senior Number One cautioned the battery.   " Salvo—*Fire !* "

Cartwright's shoulders imperceptibly stiffened ;   his fingers tightly closed upon money in one pocket and his knife in the other.   He shut his eyes and for an instant held his breath.

When the shells were purring on their way, one with the rusty-hinge-like squeak of some minute projection on the driving-band or a piece of dirt on its body, Cartwright said, " For myself I find a good wheeze is to pull no face at all."

" And for me," said the cheery Dowland, since the

general mood was philosophical and confessional, " for me the best line is to go about telling the chaps that I'm as frightened as hell, challenging any man to prove that he's in more of a funk than I am. D'you know—they think it is leg-pulling ? "

In the dug-out, when Reynolds was taking off his tunic, Cartwright said, " Give me Brightman's next-of-kin, Rennie. I'll write a couple of letters in the Mess and send off his watch and photographs and stuff. It's not worth turning in before the next shoot."

" Oh, Lord, don't fidget ! " said Reynolds. " Can't you stop and chat a bit ? I'm not sleepy. You seem to have a blasted mania for disposing of the dead."

" My training in probate-work, Rennie," said Cartwright. " The Old Boy and I are pretty heavy on trustee and executor stuff. And some of Brightman's pictures probably won't do to send to his legatees."

" You might as well touch in the ' right-hand man ' business then, since you're writing," said Reynolds, " and spare me the job." He yawned.

" You're a cynical little sod, Rennie," Cartwright observed.

" Cynical ? Just shove my pyjamas over. Ta ! " He pulled off his breeches and flung them on Cartwright's bunk. " Cynical ? Uncle—take a look through the battery roll and through the roll of officers. See who's left of the old lot—and see whose turn is coming. Cynical ? God——"

" You little ass," said Cartwright, "—and look at my bunk !—as soon as you're in bed I'm going to dump every damned stitch of your confounded kit on you. How the hell d'you think I'm going to turn in under it ? "

" Oh, sorry, Nunks. Sling it anywhere, old thing. I really am sorry. But do take a glance through the roll if you want something cheery to bite on. It doesn't seem to work out according to length of time out here, you know ; but according to length of service with a unit. I wonder if your having been posted to brigade and then coming back to the battery—sort of *new*—

will have given you a fresh lead ? What d'you think ? "

" Rennie," said Cartwright, very earnestly, " you know as well as I do that one just doesn't, and can't, think. One talks—sometimes—but one doesn't think. Losing old Dicky has shaken you up——"

" Shaken me up ! " Reynolds mumbled, " hasn't it you ? "

" You forget," said Cartwright. " —You forget the truth revealed to me by a babe and suckling two or three months ago. Rennie—we're the generation of the broken-hearted. We have no tears. The only enemy we've got left—for the rest of our lives is—nerves. A week at the wagon-line will buck you up."

" Uncle ! " said Reynolds, started into sitting up by his tremendous idea. " I wonder if the old man would let you come too. I'll think of some yarn to tell him. Golly, yes ! That boil on your side ! I'll tell him about it, and that it might mean there's still some of the old foot poison lurking in your carcass. I'll tell him you ought to go and rest up a bit while things are quiet. You can tell him that *I* ought to be the one to go ; and the old thing might have a brain-wave and send us both down. There's really nothing doing here, is there ? "

" No," said Cartwright. " But thanks to Riding the boil's gone. I can't feel it, even under a belt."

" Anyhow, I'm second in command till the new skipper blows in," said Reynolds proudly. " I can confer with my chief in conclave. My suggestion is the resting of officers at the wagon-line, starting with you and me. He *might* agree, you know. . . . I think he's fairly strong in what the bard calls the bowels of compassion. While you fellows were cobbling Dicky he kept saying quietly, as though no one was there, ' Poor boy. Poor boy. Poor, poor boy. . . .' I wonder how he'd take a smack like Dicky's."

" I shouldn't think he'd take it much better," said Cartwright.

And Reynolds said, " Lord, the perfect solicitor ! But what I meant was—very few chaps kick up much fuss. Whenever I see a mess like Dicky, and the fellow just sitting tight in it and biting like hell and grinning like a dog, I wonder if it's because he's a man of iron and a will of steel and all that, or if it doesn't really hurt such a hell of a lot. D'you think it does ? "

" Dicky's was hurting pretty fierce," said Cartwright ; " but there's a lot of your iron and steel business in Dicky."

" Yes," said Reynolds. " ' We shall not —'and be damned to you—' we shall not look upon his like again.' " He got into his flea-bag. " Don't shoot for at least half an hour, there's a good lad. Let a fellow get properly to sleep before you loose off."

" Righto." Saying this Cartwright wondered if Reynolds, too, consciously made the exciting attempt on the noisier nights—an attempt rather like hurrying out of one door before some unwelcome visitor comes in at another—to tumble off to sleep immediately after one ' arrival ' and before the moment of suspense that would accompany the next.

When he had packed up Brightman's watch and domestic photographs, a little pen-knife, a gun-metal cigarette-case, a couple of pocket puzzles and some francs and sous and had written to Brightman's next-of-kin (an aunt), he kept the book open, to begin a letter to Dorothy.

He smoked, and thought, till it was time—even giving Rennie an ample margin for getting to sleep—for the next shoot. He called to the sentry to wake the detachments and strolled about waiting for them. For all of three or four salvos he pottered about behind the guns, remembering the wisdom of his words to Rennie—that for the broken-hearted the only enemy is nerves. An act of will was all that was required to keep one of that generation slinking about upright behind firing howitzers when an absurd yearning drew him towards the lee of an overhanging bank.

But the writing of a letter by one of the broken-hearted to one whose heart was as yet unbroken was a different matter altogether.

He stared long at his blank sheet before his pencil

F F

began to move across it.   In the staring, and during the shooting, an ingenious scheme had come to him.   It was all very well to let Dorothy know that he had gone from Brigade to a kind of hospital and from the hospital, at his own specific request, back to the battery.   It was all very well for her to know that the battery was quietly in action.   All these things, strictly according to contract, he had told her.   From wondering first whether he ought to tell her, newsily, about Richards, he began to wonder whether she did or did not, daily—and thoroughly—study the casualty lists.   He had, like a fool, talked to her of Richards.   The odds were that he had mentioned his initials and that they had stuck in her mind.

Even if he had not mentioned the initials, 'Richards,' and ' R.F.A.' would be enough to jar her, to bring a poignant and ugly exaggeration and an immediacy to her imaginings.   Richards would be in the casualty lists in, perhaps, a week.   His letter she would get in three days or four.   And then the simple plan came to him.

The device was trivial ; but so also—after all was said and done—was the hazard.

In the course of a letter containing no particular news he mentioned how they were missing Richards, since he had left the battery a fortnight ago, to go to another one.

At breakfast next morning the Major handed an order to Reynolds for circulation round the table to the effect that field-boots, in future, would not be worn by officers when the battery was in action.

IT was immediately after this that the battery fell on evil times.   Disaster came upon it out of clear skies, seeking it out when not only the Brigade but the whole division was assembled near St. Omer (*en route* for the Messines battle) and the bombs that fell from an aeroplane, fell among the tents and the horses of no other battery than D.

Any one of twenty or thirty subalterns could have stepped out from a bridge- or poker-table into the small garden of a roadside-billet for a minute and not come back again to take up his hand. But the one who did so step out to come back no more was the cheery Dowland. The bucket in the billet-well next morning struck something and would not fill. It was a narrow well and the obviously named " Tich," the battery's smallest driver was lowered on the winch with a candle, perched on the stock of his whip with a thigh each side of the rope knotted to its middle. He called up from the depths, " Crikey ! Woa !" He was a West Country lad. " 'Tis an officer."

Getting Dowland up was a business that took the whole morning. Only " Tich " could move comfortably in the space of the shaft, and " Tich " lacked deftness in the nice adjustment required for drag-ropes under shoulders in such a way as to avoid jamming and shaking loose the ancient bricks in the well's sides.

There was the damage to the well to be haggled over with Gordon and the interpreter, the farmer and the Maire.

Rest, when the only rest known to gunners was trekking like ragged showmen from one show to another, was no longer a respite from Chance.

The new Captain, in that he had captained two batteries before and had been accustomed by wounds and evacuations to knocking about from one battery to another and taking hold where some one else had left off, was a success. He had no illusions ; but he had a sense of cover and also the road-sense whereby men divined whether hoofs would sink and wheels go down and stick in the twisting tracks between crater-lips or whether they would hold.

After the mean fiasco of Bullecourt, and memories of those meanly bickered-over successes of the Ancre, Messines gave to disillusioned and unexpectant men new expectations and a fresh illusion.

The battery, limbering up and bundling out of its position in a hedge at the foot of Kemmel behind the main Kemmel-Ypres road, was in action in half a dozen craters of Wytschaete before the last of the wounded or the first of the dead had been cleared from the spacious pill-box at the edge of the wood that became the battery Mess. Prisoners of the shier sort were still joining the little groups shepherded by an Ulsterman or Sinn Feiner. It was still the barest possibility that a hump of khaki or of grey was not dead, but living.

A walk of three minutes from the battery showed you Houthem and the distant bright verdure of the Canal. To the right, and beyond, were straight, clean chimneys about Wervick. Menin itself nestled somewhere to the left in the kindly turf ; and beyond, Courtrai. . . .

There was talk of Cavalry.

The battery was in action ; but in the battery, of the gunners and N.C.O.s and drivers not fifty remained of the old lot whom Cartwright had joined in the receding days when an old woman used to come to the guns with a daily paper and Browne, solemn as an owl, would say, " Dinner, gentlemen, is served."

Of the old Sergeants only Wiley was left. Francis, the fresh and chatty Bombardier then, acting and unpaid, had climbed to the command (paid and confirmed) of E subsection ; and he had been lowered in his ground-sheet into a grave with Cartwright's Brice at the foot of Kemmel a week before.

Whittle was a Sergeant now, and Day.

The Sergeant-Major still hung on, and the ' Quarter.' About them and Wiley and half a dozen of the long-moustached, illiterate dumb philosophers who smoked stemless clay-pipes as they had smoked them in Pindi and Peshawar, Meerut and Ambala in the days when a battery was designated and known by a simple number and by the name of its Major—about these men, as about their threadbare kits there was something indestructible and immovable. They were the timbers of a wreck that remain, shabby but stuck, when all the looser, lighter stuff has floated away on tides, or sunk.

Cartwright's old groom—one, incidentally, of the ancient clay-pipists, and featherweight champion of the Indian Army in his day—was gone. His successor had been killed in the St. Omer air raid. Now Cartwright had—it did not much matter whom. The puzzling and irritating, the wearily disgusting aspect of it all was that it was all peculiarly unnecessary. The killing of Infantrymen and airmen had a difference. They went forth with their teeth set, for a specific battle with specific hazards. Death, in a certain ratio to survival,was just and seemly. It was, moreover, important to the immediate issue. The killing of a driver or a gunner, on the other hand, mattered nothing ; and it seemed never to be the result of humanly deliberate design. The Artilleryman had no specific objective and could seldom visualise a specific chance. He moved under a sky that was not so much baleful as erratic, in an atmosphere that was not malignant, but secretly foul with pestilence.

Only the most fantastic of exaggerations could suggest that the enemy was one whit better off for the fact that those hundred men had slowly, imperceptibly faded from the battery ; that Dowland had stepped into the well instead of to the dung-heap ; that a mule had smashed the face of the farrier ; that the saddler whose insatiable passion had been the cobbling of neat cases, wallets, purses and gloves for every enclosable article possessed by his officers should have gone with his old malaria, after St. Omer.

Among the officers it was impossible to consider Whitelaw of the flesh and bone of the old battery any more than Moses could be reckoned strictly among the corporate Israelites. . . . Besides, he had not joined them till the Somme. Of the others, who were one with the old lot of the Arras, daily-newspaper days, Cartwright and Reynolds remained. A fifty per cent survival.

After the settling down into the Wytschaete pill-boxes, after the realisation that this again was a stopping-place, that the Cavalry talk was the invention of romantics for the fooling of men more solemn or of some staff-bird for the exercising of horses and troopers, a peculiar spirit of seriousness settled upon the battery. It became as a man worn by cares not so much of the present as of the past ; a man in a small way of business who has attained middle-age or passed it, and can see only that the business has not yet failed. A stocktaking and audit can offer him none of his old illusions. The resultant spirit is the spirit of bourgeosie—the spirit whereby ends, without much margin, are barely made to meet.

The pits were duly roofed, concreted with an air-space, veiled with netting and tufts of scrim. Some colossal shell from a siege-gun had knocked the signallers' pill-box a shade out of the horizontal and perpendicular during its German tenancy, so that its fine steel door would not fully swing. This was rectified.

Ammunition was securely housed ; neat trenches were cut from it to the guns, and from one gun to another.

A turning-place for the teams was beaten and metalled with chunks of concrete, tree splinters and barrow-loads or rubble—for the little, ageing shopkeeper was taking the wise man's care of his stock.

The officers' pill-box was fumigated with cordite and with creosote burnt on a spade ; it was washed and painted with chloride of lime.

If lice were killed thereby, lice also survived.

A signaller was killed on the line to the O.P. on a day when it seemed that the only shell between the horizons was the whiz-bang that got him. The teams behind the Captain got mixed up one night on the Kemmel road in a tornado of bursts from those fiendish new ' graze ' fuses. He piloted them out of it ; but he was two horses and a mule to the bad, and two drivers.

Cartwright—for it was Cartwright who did most of the talking with the Major on the glum matter of ways and means—had persuaded him to cut down the numbers in the pits to three men per gun. His arguments were that the time was slack, that it was at the wagon-line that hands were wanted. There could be a weekly change, beneficial to all—arguments plausible and specious to the old man, concealing the hideous blackness of the monster that was known to Cartwright and no other—the beast that lurked at the muzzle of every gun, to spring and devour the crew at its breach and the officer standing behind it. A Premature.

He found now that the most memorable incident in the whole lyrical episode of that rest at Montigny-les-Jongleurs had been a particularly uninspiring lecture of the General's to the officers and senior N.C.O.s of the Division. It had been in the sleepiest period of the afternoon, in the perishing coldest barn in Christendom. At the end of the barn, at a long farm table, had sat the General flanked by the Colonels, the Brigade-Major, the Staff-Captain and the soda-water boy (more officially the Divisional Artillery Reconnaissance Officer, little Doggett who had passed from the 'Shop' at Woolwich to Head-quarters, putting in a criticism-disarming fortnight or three weeks with C Battery on the way, plump and smiling). The General had done his best with his subject— " The Spirit of the Regiment," or something of the kind. It was as good a best as could be expected of any man after the best lunch that a Brigade Mess could put up for its Divisional Staff—a man who was neither poet, orator, wit nor total abstainer. It was, taken by and large, drivel.

The Majors and Captains in the foremost benches sat upright and solemn. Yawns were stifled among the subalterns by the heavy leaning of chins on the knobs of walking-sticks. The Sergeants behind them, chins on fists, slept for the most part like the dead.

" Ginger ! " the General had said. " The game's half played now "—or some other words to the same effect. " What we want at this stage is—*ginger!* You can't beat ginger. No, by God, you can't beat ginger. I mean to say, in a brigade—in a battery or a section—or a sub-section—what I mean is you've got to look out for the kind of thing I mean—*slackness!* It's—that's the thing that lets a unit down. A fool in a subsection can be turned into something useful at some other job. The rogue—the out-and-out wrong 'un can be kept straight by jumping on him. The chap who isn't quite the thing can be kept up to the scratch with—*ginger*.   What you've got to look out for is the *dud*.   Now what I want in my division is no *duds*.   There've been none so far, and it's up to you—to my brigade commanders, to the battery commanders, to the section commanders and to the Numbers One, to beware of the dud.   Don't let's have any duds in this division.   We know what gunners think of a dud shell.   A dud man is worse."   He paused.   He grasped what he took to be a new thought and hastened to express it.   " Yes, a dud man is a damned sight worse than a dud shell."   His lecture was ended ; all it lacked was peroration.   " Dud ? " said he indignantly, picking up his cap and smacking it upon his head.   " I'd *sooner have a premature.*"

It was then that Cartwright was extremely wide awake, with a feeling of disgust so profound that he felt it as a wriggling somewhere inside him.   The General wore a starched and glazed collar of so light a khaki as to be a very pale yellow.   His face was pink and plump ; his hands white and very hairy—and for these little things he was utterly hateful.   " I'd sooner have a premature. . . ."   No fanatic believer was ever more horrified by foul blasphemy than was Cartwright by the innocuous burbling of his General.   It was as though the silly old creature had spat in the face of Browne startled into death against the gun-wheel ; and it fixed the thought " premature " in Cartwright's mind as war's direst and most secret terror.

So when he saw three men and heard them growling in a pit as they did the work of five there was a little thrill in him of secret triumph, since two men—the two kept from the crew at the wagon-line—had been saved.

The little trenches behind the guns were a pride so great that he could share it with no other.

Not even with Reynolds ; for there was now a dull morosity about Reynolds that fitted him very ill.   He did his job better, perhaps, than he had done it before.   But instead of the old, keen flame of a spoilt boy's anger that had once flickered in his eye at finding some petty rascality on his parades—such as a respirator-satchel stuffed out with an under-vest and pair of socks instead of a respirator—there was now a smoky glow of baleful wrath.

"I'm trying to get a leave for Reynolds," the Major remarked to Cartwright one day out of a clear sky. "It's what ?—seven months ?—since he had one."

"Yes, Sir," said Cartwright. "It must be all of that . . ." and he fell to calculating, applying fantastic measurements to the immeasurable. "Six months and a bit."

"He is a highly-strung youngster," said the Major.

"Perhaps this is too quiet for him," suggested Cartwright. "It's the softest we've struck for ages." For the Major himself now spent some hours of every day outside the pill-box.

"Has he ever said so ? " he asked.

And Cartwright said "No. He's done very little confessing of late."

"It's no easy matter getting a leave," said the Major. "Naturally I don't want to say anything that's likely to give people *ideas* about Reynolds."

"No," said Cartwright. "Rather not. He's a great baby you know. Sir ; I shouldn't be surprised if this birthday-party of his cheers him up like anything."

Some very special parcels had arrived for Reynolds that his twentieth birthday might be celebrated in some style. Cartwright, as Mess secretary, had been in conference with Riding. There were to be eight at the dinner. The Captain was staying from the wagon-line, for there was no reason in the world why his horse should not be kept for a couple of hours at a battery position so quiet and comfortable. Dowland's successor, a ranker of the unpleasing and unwelcome sort named Clarkson, made the one fine and graceful gesture of his sojourn among them by insisting that he should take the O.P. duty that night. "That's quite all right," he insisted. "It wouldn't do for one of you old crowd to be out of it. Quite all right. Riding can save me a bit of the stuff and warm it up next day and keep back a drop of the drinks." There were to be three guests from the other batteries.

Bevan of A brought his roulette ; but the party was flat. Reynolds drank and talked, but it seemed to be a lightless smouldering in him that produced his thirst. His talk came only from the drink and produced no laughter. "' Jealous in honour,'" he mumbled at some time or other ; "' Sudden and quick in quarrel;

Seeking the bubble reputation

Even in the cannon's mouth. . . . Last scene of all

That ends this strange eventful history

Is second childishness and mere oblivion——'" his pause was sheer discomfort for the other seven, for there was no rift of light in his sombre mood which could be taken as a loophole for a joke.

People did not plod a mile over the crumpholes and bits of wire between Messines and Wytschaete to share the burden of ill-humour.

The discomfort did not disturb Reynolds, however. His lower lip gaped a little from the drink, but his eyes were darkly alert, staring in the manner of a crystal-gazer at his glass—for the Mess's two surviving tumblers had been given to him and the Major. Staring and musing he concluded, "' sans teeth, sans eyes, sans taste—sans everything.'"

Whitelaw was fairly quiet, beaten utterly at his own game of croaking.

It was some time after the middle of that quiet night when Cartwright discovered that Reynolds, for some time, and systematically, had been stealing his morphia tablets.

Their two bunks, of which Cartwright had the upper, were at right angles to the Major's and Whitelaw's, with the corner of two concrete walls between them. Half an hour after they had turned in Reynolds said, " Uncle, awake ? " and out of his mood of sheer heaviness, a little fogged by the dull carousing of the evening, Cartwright did not answer. Anything that Reynolds had to say could be said just as well in the morning.

Then Reynolds's ever-handy torch was flicked on and focused on Cartwright's tunic where it hung on the outer post of the bunk at his feet. Reynolds's free hand appeared in the light. The wire-netting of his bed squeaked as he strained forward, to slip his finger and thumb into the ticket-pocket. They emerged again with the bottle of tablets and disappeared under Cartwright with the light of the torch. To close the incident the light focused again on the tunic, the hand reappeared to slip the bottle back ; and the light clicked off.

Reynolds bumped his head on the post or his elbow against the wall and whispered out some slow, elaborate curse ; it was not one of his old, bouncing and meaning-less obscenities but something thoughtfully foul or blasphemous. Wits dulled and utterly weary were coping with an inevitable detail in a dreary situation.

Cartwright studied his bottle next day. It was a neat, stout little screw-capped phial that had contained, apparently, a hundred or more of the minute tablets. It now contained perhaps a dozen ; and he had given away, at most, twenty.

In the leisure of the O.P. after relieving Clarkson he sucked one and sat in the twilight to study its effect. He could not be sure that he detected any at all. At about nine o'clock he was dully sleepy ; but at about nine o'clock, if there was nothing in particular happening about him after a normally busy day, he was always dully sleepy. He decided, however, upon four things : since the effect of one tablet was imperceptible or negligible, two would not be too many to give, in future, to a man badly hit (in the event of handing them out to himself he would risk three) ; he would transfer the remaining dozen in their bottle to the pocket of his pyjamas or his breeches each night according to whether he was on duty or off. He would himself write to the old fellow in Harley Street for another bottle, since only six wounded men were required to use up all he had left ; and he would say nothing to the young idiot Reynolds in his present mood of bumptious sulk.

R EYNOLDS relieved him next evening.
      Cartwright, looking down upon him from his
      Olympian height could see no kind of change in
him. The beggar, he realised, might well have set in a
stock on his last visit to the pocket. . . .

Day after day, either his stock was still holding out,
or else Reynolds doped and Reynolds without dope were
the same ill-natured, peevish and unlovely hobbledehoy.

" Come on, Uncle ! " he snapped one evening after
dinner, when the June sky was golden over the warm,
torn earth of the old no-man's-land and the shadowed
work of patient sappers.

" Come ? " said Cartwright. " Where ? "

" Oh, anywhere," snapped Reynolds. " Any blasted
where at all." This was more like the old Reynolds ;
and Cartwright was inclined to chuckle within himself
that the stock was now probably exhausted. Perhaps
the little blighter was going to have the impudence to ask
him outright for some, now that he must have drawn a
blank in the ticket-pocket. . . . " Away from this
God-forsaken—*everything*."

From the top of the pill-box where they were standing
he indicated the snug acre of holes and humps that held
the six guns with their dozen tons of projectile and the
men loafing and gossiping in the low, kraal-like dwellings
of the period and the place.

" Constitutional ? " asked Cartwright. " Good idea."
He moved towards the steps down to the Mess.

" No ! " said Reynolds. " Don't go down. One of the
servants can get our gas-bags and hats—and your stick,
since you never seem to budge without it, as though
it was a solicitor's umbrella in the City of London."

" I thought I'd put it to the old man that he might
join us," said Cartwright casually, as they strolled down
off the other end of the roof and called into the kitchen
for a servant.

" Oh, did you ! " said Reynolds, " You'd have had his company to yourself, then—if you could have got him out—which you couldn't."

" Has he been strafing you for something ? " asked Cartwright amiably.

" No," said Reynolds. " You know as well as I do he never strafes any one for anything. He just *looks* at you."

" Looks at you ? "

" Yes. That's what I said," Reynolds growled, and snatched his hat and respirator from Crouch or Jackman. They walked towards the track to Kemmel. " *Looks* at you with the helpless, sorrowing-father eye. And I'd like to know why the hell he always keeps those glasses clipped on his snout. He never looks through the damned things except to file his nails—always over the top of them ; and he stares and stares and stares. I think it's that that's got me, Nunks."

" *Got* you ? "

" Lord, yes. Got me. Once more you seem to have heard aright. Your brightness to-day, my dear Watson——"

" Look here, young fellow," said Cartwright, " if you're going to be *funny*, you can just go to hell and take the air by yourself—and choke on it. I've got letters to write. You can spend the evening snorting at the men. They've got to put up with it, poor devils, instead of being able to give you a thick ear or a boot across the backside when you deserve it."

Very humbly and quietly Reynolds said : " Sorry, Nunks. Thanks for the soft answer which turneth away wrath." But there was a great sadness, and a weariness profound.

Above the dun tumble of earth, pocked and heavy with shadows, towered the luscious green of Kemmel purpling in silhouette against the sky.

They walked on in silence. The daily ' hates ' were mild in those days, leisurely and regular as meals. Occasional whistlings and clatters in the air, more immediate than the steady rumble beyond the flanking

horizons, were far to right or left ; or they stopped in
a crash far behind, in the hollow between the battery and
Oostaverne.

" Uncle, aren't you sick of it ? " Reynolds asked at
last.

" Sick, Rennie ? " said Cartwright.   " Sick as mud."

They were silent again, and then Reynolds woefully,
speaking to himself, mumbled, " and that seems to finish
it.   As though there was nothing more to be said. . . ."

" Well—" said Cartwright thoughtfully.   " Is there ? "

Reynolds shrugged his shoulders.   " I suppose it's
different," he said.   " You chaps who've lived a long
time and had a cut at everything.   It doesn't seem to
matter so much.   You don't seem to get an itch in all
this blasted boredom and muck, with your number
coming slowly up all the time—well, I suppose it doesn't
matter so much to you whether it comes up in forty days
with a crump or forty years with senile decay.   You've
had your whack.   Women——"

" My dear fellow," said Cartwright, " you don't kid
yourself that one is ever finished with women ?   Even
if one was, you silly young idiot, he wouldn't feel any
better for it.   It's no consolation to a man who's run
through a fortune, to be told ' That's all right.   You've
spent it.' "

" Anyhow," said Reynolds, " it's *different !* "

Cartwright was again thoughtful.   " Yes, Rennie,"
was the product of his thoughts.   " It *is* different.
But the difference is that you're a highly-strung beggar
and I'm not, thank God.   You're run down and jumpy
—you'd be the same after a year in an office.   Peevish
and ready for a holiday."

" That's all *you* know about it," said Reynolds.   " I'm
not as run down as you are.   *I* haven't got any silly
boils like yours on my side for Riding to mess about with.
No.   You're a damned sight more run down than I am ;
yet you're as happy as a sand-boy."

" I say, Rennie ! "   Cartwright was truly shocked by
this fantastic accusation.   " Happy as a sand-boy. . . .
Good God ! "

" Well. You're not frightened."

" Not frightened ? " mused Cartwright, and again, " Good God ! . . ."

" But damn it ! " Reynolds exclaimed, and grabbed and shook his arm with exasperation. " You don't *do* anything about it."

" No," said Cartwright, " thank the Lord one doesn't have to worry about that. There's always some one to tell you what to do. And you just go ahead and do it."

" Yes," said Reynolds, and his thoughts seemed to sink into himself again. " You mean that up to date we *have* done it. But suppose the time came when we didn't do it ? "

" Suppose your grandmother ! " said Cartwright. He was beginning to feel a thoroughly middle-aged annoyance at the way Reynolds spoke so glibly thoughts that might quite well, under unfavourable conditions, become real thoughts in the mind of a man. " You know damned well that you always *will* do it. And that's that."

" Listen ! " said Reynolds. " The last time I went to the O.P. to relieve you, you may remember there was a bit of a strafe going on behind it."

" Yes, I should think I do," smiled Cartwright. " It seemed a good deal more than a ' bit of a strafe ' to us, though. The damned things were just scraping over the roof, by inches."

" Yes, but there weren't many of them," said Reynolds. " And it was all small stuff. But I just sat down, Uncle, and made Crouch and the signallers get down to it, too ; and there we stuck till it was all over."

" And I should jolly well think so," said Cartwright, indignant. " What else should any one have done ? Walked into it ? Rennie, what the hell's the matter with you ? Haven't we, dozens of times, had quick and high-diving competitions up by Thiepval and Schwaben, and sat there shivering and hoping for the best—without any of this sentimental, morbid, journalistic dither——"

" Oh, God ! " said Reynolds, perplexed and exasperated. " You don't *see*, Nunks. You won't understand. . . .

Of course it was all right to sit down and hide till the strafe was over; but that's not the point. Before, I would have done it because I knew it was the best thing to do. This time I did it—because I—*couldn't—go—on.*"

" That's a bit subtle, Rennie," said Cartwright, very placidly. " Bit too subtle. It's good soldiering to give the cross-roads a miss when there's dirty work on them—and no hurry. Whether you enjoy doing it, or don't, is a matter for journalists. We're good heavy soldiers, you and I—let's be satisfied with that, till we're out of the wood."

" And not try to be good, heavy fathers," suggested Reynolds. Then he slipped his hand under Cartwright's arm and said, " Uncle, don't try to bluff me any more, old thing. I—you can't, you know. So, for God's sake, don't try. I've seen you like it—once. The time the premature got old Browne. That wasn't like all the other times we've crawled and sneaked about, belly to earth and quaking. You were different that time. Your face and eyes were hollow; a disembowelled look about your old mug that I shan't forget in a hurry." He paused for a moment, and then tore suddenly on, breathless and headlong: " Uncle—oh, God—I'm like that all the time now—and there isn't any reason for it either—quietest spot we've had since Arras—but I'm dished and dithered—morning noon and night—and I do every damned thing under the sun and it gets no better and the men will spot it sooner or later and the blasted old man with his eyes stuck out, steady as lanterns, over his glasses—and nothing alters it—I've been praying, Uncle, praying like hell at night and——" His rush had spent itself. Brokenly he asked, " What's the use ? "

"Rennie, old boy——" Cartwright began, but there he stopped. He could not, for the life of him, find anything to say. The hand was still under his arm, clutching at his sleeve and shaking. Any talk of the ridiculous business of the morphia was unthinkable in such a crisis. " Rennie—" and then fatuously and idiotically—" Buck up, Rennie. . . . Someday it'll be over. And we'll laugh like anything then."

"Yes," said Reynolds and the hand dropped from Cartwright's arm to his side. "It'll be over. . . . And as long as nothing *happens*——"

They trudged on. And then, fantastically, something did happen.

Out of the open sky behind them, innocent and benign, there came a sudden ugly snarl, actually preceding—so nearly were they in the direct line of the shell's flight—the shrill wheeze of its travelling. Simultaneously with it there was a hot spatter of bullets about them ; but simultaneously, also, with both of these, was a gesture from Reynolds. In a flash so immediate that thought itself could not have moved so smoothly or so fast, he had sprung backwards from beside Cartwright to behind him, spreading his arms in the manner of a hen spreading wings against the swoop of a hawk—flinging his body between that of Cartwright and the greenish white puff that was already curling away in the sky.

Other quick gestures followed, as quick and as unprompted by any process of calculation ; so that the next tableau was Reynolds and Cartwright seated close together with breeches pressed firmly into the loose, powdery bottom of the good hole nearest to the road, their backs braced into its eastern side.

No more shells came ; and the work of that one was well and truly done.

Cartwright was still aghast at Rennie's quixotic gesture that had in it something of the Don's own peculiar pathos. He was breathless, too, from the start and the spring and the dive to the shell-hole.

"Rennie," he said, "you're a marvel. A marvel and a blithering fool."

Reynolds looked up at him, unhunching out of the contortion whereby man contrived, in a hole, to occupy a cubic space considerably less than was demanded by his stature. His back straightened out ; his shoulders broadened ; his arms and legs seemed to come, like a tortoise's, from somewhere out of his trunk ; his throat, also like a tortoise's, lengthened out of his collar and held up his face. His eyes were aglow ; the slightly pendulous

G G

sag of his lower lip that had given him a look of spent
dissipation or sulkiness, was utterly vanished. The
fellow's eyes glowed and he flung back his head, to roar
with laughter. Then he jumped up. " Uncle ! " he
demanded, breathless and eager. " You old blighter
—you saw it ? "

" Yes," said Cartwright. " I saw it. While I, the
man of indomitable courage, was diving hell for leather,
for a hole, you—the craven-spirited—were offering your
sweet young life for mine."

He smiled.

" Oh, don't rot, Uncle ! " Reynolds said. " Don't you
see it's serious." He himself was very serious now.
" By God—it's—it's *fine !* "

" Your opinion of yourself," said Cartwright, " would
appear to be regaining its old robust health."

" Oh, you can be as funny as you like ! . . . Come on ;
he won't send any more of those in a hurry—it was one
of the twenty-guinea efforts from Timbuctoo, and he
only dishes them out about once a week."

He scrambled out of the hole. " But what it *means*,
all ye who have eyes and see not—is that the boy's all
full of guts and sinew still. Lead me—said he, setting
his fine square jaw doggedly athwart the binnacle—to
the white man's burden. . . ." He fooled on, for a
hundred yards or so of road, fairly prancing. Even when
he had steadied down his eyes still glowed, and a grin
of surprised, enormous satisfaction kept ante-dating his
face by ten or a dozen years. " No. Honestly, Uncle,
don't you see ? I mean to say, if the feet had really
gone absolutely mutton-cold, I wouldn't have come over
all heroism like that. I mean—I think it's pretty sound,
don't you—honestly ? " For an instant the smile
vanished and his eyes darkened as he pondered the weighty
question on whose answer so much hung.

Cartwright took his arm and felt the great biceps rising
in the quick caress that squeezed his hand against ribs
He smiled. " Rennie," he said, and chuckled, " have
a spot of morphia with me ? "

" You dirty, low-down, nameless *thing*," said Reynolds,

keeping the hand still jammed to his side. " You worm and consort of worms ! If you had been anything but the foulest, meanest, sneakingest sod that crawls this foul and shameful globe, you would have let that pass —now, at any rate, in my hour of proud triumph. But you can put your morphia in the safest of safety as far as I'm concerned. The damn stuff's dud, if you ask me ; only mildly emetic, and I think it's a dirty trick stuffing it into poor wounded blokes, as though they haven't got troubles enough of their own without being made sick at the tummy."

Then he said : " However, taken all in all, you're not a bad old stick, Nunks. We could turn a bit southward here and have one or two with A and C before turning homeward."

When they had, in the phrase of Reynolds, ' duly hospitalitied ' with bridge-players and a gramophonist in the Messes of A and C Batteries and were walking home under a paring of moon, meeting the Captain going back with his teams, Cartwright said, " So you're all bold and breezy again, Rennie ? "

" You talk," said Reynolds, " like a hell of a hard-boiled egg. But I believe you see, in spots, what a fellow means. You know," and he was serious, "— I've been at it a bit longer than you, and I expect that makes a difference. You've had ten or eleven months. I've had damned nearly two years. You've seen the rotten worst of it—but the other wasn't all picnic, you know. We lost chaps here and there, and horses. And there was dirty—hellish dirty work with the Infantry. The winter in the Salient was on the grubby side ; Plug Street and Sanctuary Wood. . . ."

Cartwright, in all humility, rapidly imagining his own ten months stretched into two years, said slowly, " I know, Rennie."

" Oh, it's nothing to sob about ; but a chap gets tired, I suppose," Reynolds said. " He ought to get theories and highfalutin bits of stuff out of it all. The pen is mightier than the sword and all that. Peace is better than war—but he doesn't. At least, I haven't. . . .

All I've got out of it is, ' Surely, surely slumber is more sweet than labour in the deep mid O-shun.' . . . Ever hear that thing, Nunks ? "

" No," said Cartwright. " What thing ? "

" ' Lotus Eaters ' ! Fine, hairy-chested bass chorus in it with that bit about slumber in the deep mid O-shun, and a wallop of big drum like a brace of five-nines dropping in the next parish. Ought to hear it some time."

(Cartwright has made a point, since, of hearing it.)

" You, I suppose," Reynolds said presently, " *have* got some theories out of it all. For instance, you know whether you'd stick your toes in and go to jail rather than encourage another war by taking a hand in the mess again. D'you believe in War any more, Uncle ? "

" Good Lord ! " said Cartwright. " I suppose one will think of that sort of thing some day."

" But you'd think that *our* sort of chap, with a modicum of brains and time to burn, with food and lodging found, would be thinking about it—for instance, now when things are quiet."

" Yes," said Cartwright. " But you must admit we don't. The people who really think about the War, and about War, are our wives, Rennie."

" Wives——" said Reynolds thoughtfully. " It's all right for those that's got 'em. I've a good mind to assume one on my next leave, Uncle."

Cartwright said, " What the devil for ? "

" Bit of ballast," said Reynolds. " Touch of seriousness that makes the whole world kin. I think a good deal of the trouble with me lately is that I haven't known where I stand. Whether I'm a kid or a solid member. Marriage seems to solidify a bloke in some way. Even out here. I think I wouldn't have got the wind up so badly and gone wool-gathering if I could have fastened my wayward thoughts on the little woman waiting for me with arms outstretched——"

" *That's* what we think about, Rennie," said Cartwright. " All the time now."

" What ? " said Reynolds. " Women ? "

" No. Ourselves," said Cartwright. " We've lost

sight of the War. We don't even wonder when it's going to end ; or who's going to win ; or what winning will mean. Each one of us is wondering—when we're not actually doing a definite job—if he is really anything at all and whether he's going to keep on being it. You had carried the thought a little further, suspecting that you had stopped being it and had become something else."

" And the fact is," said Reynolds, obviously rejoicing in the thought which he burlesqued with a thump of his fist on his chest thrown out towards the moon, " that the great spirit of the heaven-born like us just *can't* be broken ! You think you've got me cold-footed and beat—and I, being of somewhat hysterical and much finer clay, think so myself. Then you set the dragon on me, tooth and nail, straight out of the blue, and up comes ye parfait knight all bright and smiling. Nunks, the old man can ponder me as sadly as he pleases over his glasses now. He can stare till his orbs roll into his soup-plate. I'm just going to knock off thinking about inwardnesses. I'm serious about that marriage idea, though. *You're* married."

" What the hell's that got to do with it ? "

" Mysticism," said Reynolds. " There's some inwardness about it, but not morbid. It started with Whittle, I think, on your famous tour in Stuff. He told the chaps at the battery that the only thing that pulled his party through that show was keeping within a yard of you and stepping in your footprints. One of the signallers told me the other day that you always go round to the left of that scuppered old gun-pit on the way to the O.P. instead of to the right ; and always touch the broken post in passing. The blighters all do it themselves now. So do I. You're married ; argal, I get married too."

" I was twenty-two before I married," suggested Cartwright.

" Twenty-two pre-war would be about fifteen now," said Reynolds. " That's called parthenogenesis in cultured circles."

" And how long," said Cartwright, a little uneasy, but withal a little proud, " have I been a mascot ? "

" Since you were in the fourth form, I suppose," said Reynolds, " because even then you must have looked as solemn as a whiting—but you don't mind my using your footprints if it gives me any comfort in this sad vale ?   I prefer that to Dad's theory of just not speaking out of your turn.   Seems matier.   I suppose, secretly, every one of us has got a special ju-ju.   What's yours, Nunks ? "

" I don't believe I've got one," said Cartwright. " Not a real ju-ju.   I've got an idea that it's a good thing to behave as though you're frightened when you're not and to behave as though you're not when you're frightened as the devil.   It's pretty vague——"

" So *that* is why you make inventories of the stuff in fellows' pockets the very second they're knocked out ! " said Reynolds ; and Cartwright made some appropriate answer.

Since the only possible end to talk in those days was an end to the circumstances wherein it was conducted, they talked on till they had said good night to the sentry seated on the roof of the signallers' place, and stumbled round the corner of the pill-box into its open door.

MEDAL WITHOUT BAR   CHAPTER LXXXII

CARTWRIGHT himself was impressed and a little startled by the efficacy and the range of the Major's staring over his glasses when, so soon as after lunch next day when they were alone in the Mess, he said : " I think, so as to satisfy the superstition of our dad, I shall issue a definite order for my officers to go out for after-dinner walks.   What have you done to the boy, Cartwright ? "

" Nothing, Sir," said he.   " It was a phase of depression, you know—" he wanted to tell him of Reynolds's glorious gesture ; but it flashed into his head that an occasional brisk walk would do the Major himself no harm and so he decided to tell him nothing of the shell. " He was very depressed and—and the depression seemed to pass. We had a drink with A and C. Every one was very cheery. Would you—I mean, perhaps you would care to come with us sometimes ? "

The Major looked at him. His gaze betrayed no sort of emotion at all—neither surprise nor resentment nor pleasure, till there flickered into it that ray of gentleness.

" Don't worry about me, Cartwright," he said. " I'm better. We've got to adopt our own means, haven't we ? It's different with youngsters like Reynolds. But with us—we know ; and we're best left alone. I'd like to tell *you*, though," and his voice fell a little lower ; " there's generally a touch of lumbago in addition to the —other."

He did not specify ' the other ' ; and Cartwright did not question him. He knew.

" I'll manage, Cartwright," the Major added with the quietest of confidence ; and then, rather disconcertingly : " thanks."

" Oh—it's just as you like, Sir, of course," was the only possible answer. " And about Reynolds—the beggar explains it himself better than any one else could. A touch of hump and sheer hysteria. Of course, leave would set him up—but even without it he'll be all right now. He's cheered himself up thoroughly. He's not likely to get ' down ' again."

The accuracy of this guess was never tested, for within two days of it Reynolds was a problem no more.

Cartwright went in the morning, followed by his signallers and Jackman with his sleeping-bag and shaving-kit and rations, to relieve Whitelaw at the O.P.

The O.P. itself was a spacious and comfortable ' chesterfield ' of sandbags and boxes and ammunition-baskets heaped against the front of a captured gun-emplacement by the Oostaverne-Warneton road, to the left of whatever ' beek ' it is that flows there.

In quieter times elbows were leaned upon the pit's

flat concrete roof and targets sought and examined
through glasses.   At others, elbows were removed from
the roof, lowered to the side of the stout ' chesterfield '
and observation carried on through the number fourteen
periscope.   When even the ' chesterfield ' was a spot wild
beyond reasonable comfort the O.P. party slid into the
gun-pit and the officer dislodged an Infantry clerk in
order to stand on his seat and peer through a slit above
him ; or else, leaving the Infantrymen to their curious
occupations, to sit unobtrusively on a box till the
' chesterfield ' and the roof were again tenable.

The gun-pit was one of those lowland masterpieces of
' pill-box ' work, for it had once housed a solitary and
precious gun on naval mountings.   It had housed, also,
its crew, its officers and its ammunition with appropriate
space, differentiation of ranks, hygiene, sanitation and
shelter.   The battle had found it in a state of some
dishevelment and chaos—occupied for a while by a field-
gun and then by a rear-guard machine-gun, a medical
squad, by rallying and ultimately surrendered bombers,
by wounded and corpses.

It had been adapted thereafter to its obvious purpose—
the Headquarters Mess, orderly-room and dressing-station
of a company of Irishmen.   It was as the guests of this
company that the Artillery party spread its sleeping-
bag and blankets at night on some bunk, and in cosy
corners.   By day the party cadged hot water, shared
the cook's brazier or took a turn with a mess-tin over
the primus in the old ammunition-store ; it often accepted
the hospitality of a complete meal.

The company was being relieved on this particular
night, so Cartwright spent most of it—a warm night of
moonlight and extraordinary quiet—dozing on the
' chesterfield,' away from the bicker of Infantrymen
bitter with the acrimony of every tenant for his
predecessor.

In the morning Jackman stooped and melted the fringe
of his bacon in his mess-tin over sandbag-rags and a
candle-stump ; and then, in despair, took it inside and
cremated it over the company primus or brazier.   The

Company Commander, however, in due course presented his compliments to the Artillery officer and would he join him at breakfast, please. . . .

There was business to be done during the morning, in which Cartwright, with his gunner's smattering of local knowledge acquired through a succession of Infantry occupations and reliefs, was able to give a hand. It was not till about tea-time that the company staff could give itself up to various branches of pure criticism. Cartwright sat above the signallers and drowsily swept the front with his glasses, an ear on the incessant grouse of orderlies and batmen who came out with an armful or a sandbag of tins or paper, ashes or ragged equipment —the garbage wherein their contemptible predecessors had been content to pig it.

Jackman's souvenir lust and his friendliness for ' muck ' in any shape or form lent his ape-like arms and his raking finger to the task. He got a few inches of German tinder out of the job that would fit no British lighter ; and a German shoulder-strap. The signallers made quiet comments on Irish idioms.

When Reynolds arrived at sunset with his two signallers and his sleeping-bag on Crouch's shoulder, the work was practically done. Cartwright stretched out his legs and yawned and grumbled of the sleepless night. Reynolds went in to see the Company Commander and to see also that the bunk on which Crouch laid his valise should be a lordly one.

He must have been standing by the doorway, just inside it, when the house-proud Corporal clerk of the company saw that the work of sweeping and garniture was not, in fact, accomplished. In some dark corner was a jumble of signal-rockets, a broken pistol and some stick-bombs. He loaded them into the arms of an orderly.

That much is known, for the Corporal himself was able to tell it afterwards. He himself went, after loading the man and telling him to get out with the rubbish, along the narrow corridor to the old ammunition-store to get a mug of tea. The details thereafter are partly

conjecture. The armful of rubbish must have been a
little too much for the orderly—clumsy stuff to carry
haphazard, long sticks overbalanced by a cone of rocket
at the end, the stumpier grenades and the elusive loops
of a machine-gun belt. Another man helped him but
some hitch must have impeded the transaction—a difficulty in dividing the load without spilling a mess on the
cleared and scoured part of the floor ; friendly or angry
badinage. In snatching away a grenade among rockets
the helper left behind, over the belt-hook of the orderly's
open tunic, the little ring at the end of the grenade's
trigger-lanyard.

The explosion that shook Cartwright's glasses out of his
hand flung Reynolds out of the doorway. A signaller
turned him over to his back as Cartwright stooped over
him.

" Rennie ! " he said, " Oh, Christ. . . ."

It was no casual blasphemy.

Moans came from the inside of the pit, with a scuffle of
curses and of feet on the cement floor ; the hot stink
of the explosive.

And Cartwright found that there was no mist at all
where everything, for a moment, had seemed to be
enveloped and obscured ; but that he saw things crystal
clear and was doing things, quick as flashes.

Already the sling, unhooked from his haversack, was
looped once round Rennie's thigh over his tobacco-pouch
pressed to the artery in Rennie's groin.

Cartwright knelt back, pulling upon one end of the
haversack-sling, the signaller leaning back to pull upon
the other—for the white bone of the thigh had been
drenched in gusts of blood—the thigh of Rennie who so
particularly hated blood in a sticky, smeary state.

" Steady, Rennie," he was saying, " steady, old son.
He'll be along in a minute. The Doc. Good old fellow ;
met him at breakfast this morning." And the fact that
he had met the doctor at breakfast that morning and
judged him to be a good fellow did seem to alter the
situation.

The tip of Rennie's tongue flickered about his lips,

pink and strangely clean in the squalor of a chimney-sweep's make-up.

In the face, here and there, were dull little holes, darker than the squalor. A small splinter, like the point broken from a pencil, stuck out of one ball of his open eyes. And the eyes were obviously working, for in them was a light of comprehension and intelligence, and slow assessment.

The tongue again moved at the lips, and again.

Cartwright nodded. With his end of the haversack-sling transferred to one hand from both, he took out the little old bottle of tablets from his ticket-pocket and handed it to the other of the signallers, who had been wiping a little spot under the hair on Reynolds's forehead with his handkerchief.

" Two," said Cartwright.

The signaller nodded and unscrewed the cap.

Rennie's tongue disappeared with the two little white disks on it, and something flickered and passed—on his lips or in the darkly unwinking eyes—though it were idiotic to write any such word as ' smile.'

When a sound came into the bleak silence—the dry grinding together of Reynolds's teeth—the second signaller bowed again over his gentle dabbing at the spot on his forehead. " 'Old up, chum," he said softly, the driver trained into a signaller. " 'Old up, laddie . . ." and he mumbled something encouraging about ' Blighty'; hanging his head, however, for shame at such spurious cheer.

Rennie's collar and necktie were a miracle in their undishevelled order upon his throat where no rag of shirt or vest or tunic-front was to be seen. Of breeches there remained a tattered sporran in front, and flaps with crumbling, perished edges. Putties had held them secure and sound below the split and shattered knees. White chest and stomach were peppered over, like his face, with tiny, sluggishly growing spots. Low down the side was one great, darkly-gaping hole—like the hole from a spear-thrust.

There was not much that the doctor could do.

To him Reynolds did say something, clicking and

hissing the words into the ear lowered to him. But the old Irishman only snapped, "Don't talk such blasted nonsense! A nice officer to say such wicked things! Lay still, then——"

While Cartwright and the signaller still held their tourniquet he fixed another above it, a good pad of shell-dressings under a strap.

The strap he wound tight by a couple of turns of the haft of an entrenching tool slipped under it, which he secured with a piece of string round Rennie's waist. He bound up the knee of the other leg, for above it there was flesh, shapely in the semblance of a thigh. He padded and bound the hole in the side and gave him two injections. With his finger and thumb he picked the splinter from his eye and said, "Away with you now to the dressing-station. D'you want boys to carry him?"

"No," said Cartwright. "Thanks. They're six of us, or seven."

They put him on a stretcher (Cartwright promising to return it), a rolled blanket under his head, a blanket over him.

He seemed, uneasily, to sleep. Cartwright was going, but the doctor jerked his elbow.

Cartwright turned.

"Go on, you chaps," he said to the four quiet signallers and the servants with the rolls of bedding, "—slowly. I'll catch you up in a minute."

He followed the doctor through the pit and the corridor to the Mess. "Two dead," the doctor said in answer to Cartwright's inquiry as he poured a drink. "Dead before I'd got from here to there. . . . That boy of yours, poor fellow, was lucky."

The sound made by Cartwright's throat must have been construed as some comment.

"Yes," said the doctor. "If that ligature holds. Divilish smart of you to slap it on at once, the way you did, with the femoral artery severed. He'd have been gone inside of minutes. You saved him, I'd not be surprised. The thing in his side may be into the boy's liver; but maybe not, and he'll get well of it. He'll lose his legs, with the knees of him shot to glory and his left sartorius lifted clean away. He'll be blinded of his one eye and they'll have to take away the left hand with the works of his watch shot into the wrist of him. But if you can see to the tourniquet, that it doesn't slip, going alongside of him to the dressing-station——"

It was then that Cartwright noticed young French, the new subaltern of B Battery, sitting in the Mess.

"Hello," he said, mildly curious, "what are you doing here?"

"It's been made into a Brigade, instead of a battery job," French explained. "Reynolds had left when the Adj. rang up. I got here as soon as I could find the blessed place. You were with Reynolds outside." It had been his first acquaintance with casualties. He hesitated a moment and said " . . . awful luck."

Cartwright nodded. Then he said, "Doc—there won't be any one coming up from the battery to-night. Will some time to-morrow do for the stretcher and blankets?" He was at his old trick of niggling about with details—like collecting the things from a man's pockets and making an inventory. . . .

"Yes," said the doctor. "So long as it *is* to-morrow; but you know what divils the boys are with the chance of winning a stretcher to sleep on. . . ."

.   .   .   .   .   .

The signallers and the servants were halted for a moment when Cartwright caught up with them.

"He's—kind of woke up a bit, Sir," one of them said. "Swore a bit—asking——"

Cartwright hurried and bent towards the slightly moving lips where the point of tongue was again moving. "A drink," said Cartwright and uncorked his bottle of tea and whisky. Some went between the lips and teeth, some down the dirty, peppered chin and neatly collared throat. The clicks and hisses formed words against Cartwright's ear. " . . . did the dirty on you, Nunks— Dug up Auntie on leave; dined with her . . . chatted. . . ."

" Rennie . . ." he said and smiled. " Yes. All right, old boy. I know. I'm glad. Damned glad." He stroked the forehead till he knew that he was stroking an open wound. " Get on, you fellows," he said to the men. " You four spare ones. Don't stand there. Get back to the battery, sharp. . . ." The two servants and spare signallers moved off.

The lips moved again. The words this time were "—Uncle—*must* I ? "

Cartwright looked at the other two signallers.

" You two go back to the doctor hell for leather and get more blankets. No—not one of you ; both. . . . Give him my compliments. . . . Another blanket. . . ."

They went and he was left kneeling alone beside the stretcher.

Reynolds, too, apparently, was thinking of an endless journey with its starting- and countless stopping-places, its jolts and jerks and groaning men—with a rent in his side and some jagged thing stuck in his liver, his knees smashed and most of a watch's mechanism buried in his wrist. He, too, must still have had wits to wonder what would be left of Rennie when two legs had gone, one hand and an eye—for he said again, " Uncle—oh, God—*must* I. . . . Old doctor *had* to talk big . . ."

Fingers tightened upon Cartwright's hand. The pressure of one of them was the hard pressure of a naked bone.

" Rennie—Rennie," said Cartwright. " God bless you. . . ." The words were from an old ritual of leaving John and David to the peace of their slumber in earlier years ; fairly meaningless on the whole, except as a vague endearment.

Reynolds spoke again : " You'll have to make up some damned lie or other for Auntie. . . . I've been writing to her . . . she asked me to. . . ." Then he closed his eyes.

" God bless you, Rennie."

Kneeling, Cartwright also closed his eyes, and fumbled— ' seeing to ' the tourniquet. . . .

When the signaller came panting back over the little rise of ground that hid the stretcher from the pill-box Reynolds had sunk again into the stupor of his stertorous sleep.

Mechanically they took, Cartwright noticed, the track at the side of the humped gun-pit which Reynolds had mentioned as their superstition. Then they turned away sharply left from the battery track, towards the dressing-station in an old pill-box.

"Take him in, you chaps," said Cartwright. "I won't come. I'll wait here for you." He sat down on a soft hump of earth, tapping his pockets for his tobacco-pouch.

He looked, not at the signallers with their burden, hobbling away towards a glow still bright in the sky, but at the dun expanse of wilderness; earth flayed and torn and scattered and then abandoned and forgotten by pursuers and pursued as though it were not there that the object of their seeking lay. There was not a man in it nor a movement, except the signallers at whom he did not look. Yet in the utter emptiness something still remained—it was wan and haggard, tatterdemalion beyond recognition and beyond belief, but it still lived. It was the battery.

He got up to his feet that he might go back to it ; then sat slowly down again to wait for the signallers.

About half an hour later they found him sitting there. The blanket on the stretcher extended now from the wrists of one to the wrists of the other.

"It's no good, Sir," said one of them. "'E was gorn when we got there. Lorse of blood. The doctor's corporal said the thing round his leg wasn't tied up proper. We thought you'd like him took back to the position, Sir."

"Yes . . ." said Cartwright, "good lads. . . ." Then, "Has either of you got a cigarette ? My case is empty and Jackman took my tobacco-pouch. . . ." A couple of bent and flat Woodbines were held out to him, and a packet of Bees' Wing or Flag. Cartwright took one and lighted it. "Thanks. I'll take an end from one of you in a minute, when I've had a smoke. There's a drink in here. Rest a bit——"

He handed them his water-bottle.

" Good luck, Sir," they said when the removal of the cork and the raising of the bottle made it clear that it contained not only tea.

They corked the bottle and returned it.

" It's only you, Sir, now of the old lot," said one of them.

" And you," said Cartwright. The other man, the converted driver, was fairly new. " And a few others.. . ."

" I meant the orficers."

" Ah, yes," Cartwright admitted, "—the officers. There's Mr. Whitelaw, of course."

" 'E wasn't in the old chalk-pit," said the man jealously. " Not when old Charlie Browne pinched the barf from Agincourt and the Captain put in the speaking-choobs from the dug-out. That's when the old lot reckons from ; before the bloody Somme turnout started to make a nole in it. Is it official the Captin's lost both 'is legs, Sir ? "

" No," said Cartwright. " One, when he wrote last. Come on—one of you. . . ." He took an end of the stretcher and they started for home.

JACKMAN must have bragged at the battery, about the state of Cartwright's breeches and tunic ; for it was at them that eyes peered as he walked past the cook-house and the guns and the signallers' place.

The men pulled up in front of him with the stretcher. " Where, Sir ? " they asked.

" Oh . . ." said Cartwright. " I'll ask Mr. Whitelaw." Whitelaw came flapping across from the Mess in his waders unsecured to his thighs. Looking at the stretcher he began, " But—Jackman—those fools—said——"

" No," said Cartwright, and shook his head, and looked away. " No go, Dad. . . . Dad, there are a couple of pockets left——"

" Ridin's got your dinner," said Whitelaw. " Go on down."

. . . . . .

He was in his shirt and slacks and slippers when Whitelaw came down, eating a piece of bread, smoking a pipe and drinking a whisky while Riding took away his dinner.

The Major, peering over his glasses at Cartwright's mug, had one hand beside the bottle, ready to move it forward. Clarkson was talking.

Whitelaw flung his hat to a bunk and with it a meagre bundle in a handkerchief.

" He'd never believe ! " he snarled. " Never. Pig-headed. . . . Nothing on God's earth could make him see. . . . And yet there he was—where he shouldn't have been at all. It wasn't his turn. Just like all the rest of them. . . . And now . . ." In his throat he growled . . . " Jesus wept."

" Oh, Lord, Dad," said Cartwright. " He didn't know. When he left——"

" Yes ! *When he left !* " Whitelaw exclaimed, and poured into Cartwright's mug and into his own. " If he had waited till it was the proper time to leave, instead of dashing off to play the ass and get an hour's gossip with you he would have got the order. . . ."

" Never mind," said Cartwright, and then, as though great thought were required for the new pronouncement, " Good Lord . . . never mind. . . ."

The next remark, from Whitelaw, was : " And it would have turned the kid up. . . . Still—even after two and a half years of it—it would have turned him up to see such a job as himself. Funny. Funny kid ! "

Cartwright got up and moved towards his bunk. " Yes," he said. " And it's just about now that he would

have remarked, ' We shall not look · upon his like
again.' "

One function of the Major's eyes, poised above the
rimless edge of his glasses, had always been to register
for some silent contemplation the number and the size
of the whiskies poured and swallowed by his crew.   But
as Cartwright lurched heavily away from the table he
nodded suggestively to Whitelaw, indicating the bottle.

" A spot, Uncle ! " Whitelaw said casually, pouring
another for himself.   " Nightcap.   I expect you were
on the tiles with the new company coming in last night.
Quiet though, wasn't it ? "

Cartwright yawned and said, " Yes," and emptied
the mug.   He discarded his boots and undid his collar
and his buttons ; and he slept.

.   .   .   .   .   .

He saw next day all the shifts they made to lighter
the weight at which they assessed the burden of his
grief.

The Captain's kit came up at night, and Cartwright's
went down with Jackman, Cartwright following on the
Captain's horse for a turn at the wagon-line.

The Sergeant-Major, detailing teams for · a night's
work would say,   " Only N.C.O.'s parties, Sir.   We
can break the lot into three.   No need for you to turn
out, Sir.   Not really. . . ."

After a day or two Cartwright suggested to Gordon and
the Colonel that since things had become stabilised again
five or six miles could be saved on every journey to the
guns by moving the wagon-lines nearer.   They did
the necessary telephoning to D.A. and gave him an area
against the wood of Kemmel Château.

Flanking the new horse-lines was the deep trench of
some old defensive scheme, with a good entanglement.
But between the trench and the château moat were
half a dozen acres of wasting, knee-deep hay.   Means
appeared for bridging the trench and making a lane
through the wire.   Head-roped together, four horses to
a driver, the right section went first over the bridge to a

stealthy grazing of such a sort that horses perhaps but certainly no driver had ever dreamed of.

Cartwright pottered about the lines.

After about an hour of it two shells tore harmlessly into the wood ; and two into the midst of the grazing section. In the stampede the drivers were magnificent, hanging on like demons each man to his four horses. Some broke away, however, and were a little torn and spiked by the belt of wire hidden in the hay by the trench.

Tetley was brought in dead, and Anderson with a shattered hand. While Cartwright and the farrier were tying up the hand some one standing by the hay-truss against which Anderson leaned his back made some exclamation which caused them all to turn and look.

It was Helmesley walking towards them, slowly, over the bridge. The stumps of his famously rotten teeth were bared in a grin. A cigarette-stump hung upon his lower lip. His face, save where beard had become suddenly conspicuous, was the familiar loathsome colour of drying clay.

In his right hand he carried, as though it were a bottle or a cucumber, his tattooed left forearm. The whole upper arm—deltoid, biceps, bone and shirt-sleeve—was gone. Looking again, more closely, one saw that two smooth cords connected the fantastic elbow to the cavity at the top of the shirt-side ; one was like rubies, the other a stick of macaroni. Not a splinter had touched the man. The explosion had flung away the shirt sleeve, the bone and the muscle, leaving only the tough nerve and elastic artery to the forearm.

He sat down on the hay-truss ; then slipped to the ground beside Anderson and sat, silent and grinning.

The vet of another Brigade was brought over from a neighbouring tent or shanty to fish splinters out of some of the horses, to put in odd stitches here and there, and to ' certify ' the seven that had to be shot—for reinforcements in horses were now a tighter business than reinforcements in men.

The Medical Officer of some Sapper unit in the château cellars came over and gave injections to Anderson and

Helmesley and filled out labels for them. For neatness and convenience he severed Helmesley's nerve and artery, first tying the artery with a piece of string as though it were the mouthpiece of a balloon or football bladder.

A new subaltern was posted to the battery, *vice* Reynolds.

The Captain came back to the wagon-line and Cartwright was suddenly instructed to report, with his kit, and his servant, to Divisional Artillery H.Q.

The Reconnaissance Officer had gone, for a fortnight, on a course; and so Cartwright was given the luxury and rest of a fortnight's ' acting ' soda-water-boy to the General.

If there had been nothing to do at Brigade, during a great battle, as assistant orderly officer, there was even less to do at Division—when there was no battle at all —as acting soda-water-boy.

It was a little surprising to find that the General and his staff were not unfamiliar with the names of subalterns at the batteries. It was touching to find that the pink individual who had expounded, dithering, the drivel about preferring prematures to duds, was a kind and pleasant old man with an anxiety for Cartwright's health and happiness, a gentle solicitude.

" That man of yours, Cartwright," he said to him one day. " Awful-looking fellow. . . ."

" Jackman ? " said Cartwright. " Oh, he isn't a bad sort, really, Sir, when once you're used to him."

" My dear Cartwright ! " said the General. " But think what it must have taken out of you to *get* used to him. *Awful*-looking fellow."

" He's a pretty *stout* fellow," Cartwright insisted.

" He's an awful *looking* fellow," said the General.

" It isn't that he's particularly dirty, Sir," Cartwright explained. " He looks just the same after two shaves, in a brand new kit. It's——"

" I *know* what it is," said the General. " I'm *telling* you. It's that he's an—*awful—looking—fellow*." This time, for variation, he emphasised all three words equally.

" Well, Sir," said Cartwright, " there's nothing we can do about it."

" Oh ! " said the General. " Isn't there ? You wait, my lad. We're going to send him to the base and get a man for you—from the column or somewhere—who *is* an officer's batman. Not a gaping orang. I've spoken to Barney." (Barney was the Staff-Captain.)

There was much that Cartwright wanted to say. But as men were frightened (quite accurately speaking, frightened) of Majors and Colonels, they were more frightened still of Generals. All he said was, " I say, Sir— it seems—I don't quite see how——"

" Oh, don't you ! " said the General. " You will, though. Positively gives me the creeps. Awful-looking fellow. I can't imagine what that Major of yours was thinking of, allowing you to bring a thing like him to appear at D.A. Awful-looking fellow."

If he mumbled " Awful-looking fellow " again, Cartwright felt that something, from somewhere, would surely have to hit him. And then the inane absurdity of being frightened—literally frightened into silence—by another man, pink and softly plump and unarmed, was clear to him.

" Look here, Sir ! " he said. His tone was friendly and perfectly civil, but firm. " Jackman's been with the battery since it came out. And if—I mean, for nothing, absolutely nothing——"

" Nothing ? " said the General. " D'you call it nothing that there should be a chap like that in my Division ? I don't believe he could close his mouth if you paid him——"

" He's got adenoids," said Cartwright.

" A man's got no business having adenoids in my Division. The base is the place for adenoids."

" Well," said Cartwright, " I'd like to speak to him first."

" You can go to hell," said the General. " Speak to any one you like and be damned to you, but the fellow's got to go." And then, as he left Cartwright, he did mumble it again : " *Awful*-looking fellow. . . ."

When Cartwright told Jackman that probably he could,

now that they were at the Division, get him away to
the base, Jackman expressed no grief. On the contrary
his lips sagged farther away from his long, yellow teeth
into a grin and all he said was, " Before we go back to
the position ? "

" Yes," said Cartwright. " Pretty well at once."

" Oh," said Jackman. " Good."

" So you've had enough of the battery ? " asked
Cartwright.

" What *is* the battery now ? " asked Jackman. Even
when making a joke he was about as dismal an object as
could be imagined. Asking a question of rhetorical
sadness such as this one he was misery itself. " It's
only you, Sir, now. And—" he hesitated—" and you're
a married, family-man and everything, Sir."

" Well ? " said Cartwright, " what's that got to do
with it ? "

Jackman stirred his shoulders into a shrug. " You'll
go—some time," he said.

Cartwright smiled. " Because I'm a married man ? "

" Because it'll be your turn," said Jackman slowly.
" Mr. Meston, the Captain, Mr. Reynolds—killed,
wound-eed, killed. It's the order in which they come out,
Sir. Then you joined at Arras. . . ."

" What about the others who've come and gone in
between ? " Cartwright asked. " Mr. Dowland——"

" Yes," Jackman interrupted. " There have been
others in between. But we only count the old lot. . . .
And in the old lot you're next."

So Jackman was cheerful in the thought of going ;
another of the old lot. In the Mess it would leave only
Riding ; for Crouch, now that Reynolds was gone, would
go back from ' employment ' to ' duty ' unless the new
subaltern took him. Even Jackman's going added to the
bleakness.

The General again got Cartwright by himself and
said, with no preamble, " Cartwright, about leave——"

" Oh, God," said Cartwright under his breath ; and
aloud, " Leave, Sir ? I wasn't—I'm not worrying about
leave particularly."

" And unfortunately you're not going to get it," said the General. " That's what I was going to tell you. You *can't* get it. A special leave would have to come out of the Division allotment, and you'd have to take some one else's turn . . . can't very well do that ; but I think we might be able to get you a week in Paris."

" Paris ? " said Cartwright, amazed at the thought.

" It's a new idea," said the General. " A special stunt—at the discretion of Divisional Commanders—to meet special cases. I think you could do with it, Cartwright, what ?—gay Paree——" His eyes twinkled, playful and merry and sly. But they quickly became serious again. " Unfortunately, though, there may be a catch in it," he added sadly. " A special Paris leave might put you back on the ordinary leave roster. I don't know. But I gather your name is a hell of a long way down."

" Yes," said Cartwright. " But I don't mind. I'm not very keen on going home just now. . . ."

And that was the truth of it. A fine figure he would have cut at home just then. There had been ghastliness enough in the leave before with the gloom of the last supper overshadowing the merry sacrament of love. He had gone home then bouncing with some of the bounce of the battery trekking on unbroken roads and solid turf, Richards and old Whitelaw somewhere at its head, himself and Reynolds gossiping along at its middle. Oakleigh sparkling in the frosty sunshine at its tail. Fellows had been singing then. . . .

The battery from which he would go to Dorothy now— (or in two months or three, if one still applied to time the measurement of days and nights and weeks)—was the tottering and haggard wreck of the one that had sent him home before with a spring in his stride, with the oxygen of hope and victory distending his lungs. Instead of stepping light and sprightly he was secretly cringing now from the snarl of a premature, from the one snarl which, according to theorists, was the one he would not hear—the one that got him.

By Jackman's theory; by the pure arithmetic of

averages; in the light of common sense unaided by emotional theory or cold calculation, he was doomed— as all of the old lot were doomed.

Whether it should be wounds like those of Richards's or death like Browne's or Reynolds's ; whether it came in a week or a month—or three months—was no great matter.

He was doomed.

Since even before the sealing of his doom, Dorothy's silence and the dark glow in her eyes had been a sore discomfort, he said to the General : " It's jolly good of you, Sir.   I think I'd like the week in Paris."

And away from the sadness of Dorothy and the last supper gloom—to Paris, for a week, he went.

MEDAL WITHOUT BAR   CHAPTER LXXXIV

THERE was something childishly proud and mis-chievous and touching in the way the General said to him, immediately on his return, " Seen your new man, Cartwright ? "

[Jackman had gone, leaving a sealed envelope for Cartwright containing an exhaustive inventory of his kit (down to such details as button-stick, polish brown $\frac{1}{2}$, Brasso $1\frac{1}{2}$), duly signed by the new man, Stonehouse. Jackman's personal postscript to this was " Good luck, Sir, and thanks and Ile wright a letter when i get there and ile swing it O.K. with my varicose vans not to come up the line again without the old lot, and the best of health to you and hope you go on dodging them as before Sir.   A Jackman Gnr."   And his regimental number.]

" I *have*, Sir," said Cartwright.   " And to think that he was a grocer's assistant !   What would he have done to my kit if he'd been a professional valet, instead of an amateur ? "

For it is the fact that Cartwright had failed to recognise most of his belongings.   The cases of his revolver, compass and glasses he had thought to be the General's.

The tin-hat hanging above his bed was newly cased, not in ordinary sandbag, but canvas of some rare and superior quality. On the front of it was drawn large, in duly moistened indelible pencil, the badge of their Royal Regiment, complete with its scroll and motto; " *Ubique* " above ; and below, " *Quo fas et gloria ducunt.*" Everything that was capable of bearing a mark was marked with his initials ; scratched, carved, branded (as on Browne's walking-stick), cut, pencilled or punched with a nail.

Stonehouse's salute was the click of heels and rigor of forearm associated with guardsmen. He wore a canvas belt as wide as ' athletic ' corsets, studded with every badge and button of the British Army ; and every badge and button twinkled like the morning star. . . . Such was Stonehouse.

Cartwright gathered from the General that there was soon to be a move, and a battle. The Reconnaissance Officer was back from his course and ordered a horse for Cartwright and the mess-cart for his kit to be paraded after tea for Cartwright's return to the battery.

At the wagon-line the Captain congratulated him, enviously, on the Paris affair. Clarkson was gone from the guns. The Captain lowered an eye-lid over an eye for a second or two, saying, " Gas . . . and debility. . . ." There was a new subaltern, first-rate fellow, called Dawson ; not a youngster, but not a family-bloke like Clarkson.

Cartwright had a drink, left his kit to be sent up with the rations, took his refurbished helmet, his gas-mask and Browne's walking-stick and started off with Stonehouse to walk up to the guns.

He reported to Gordon at the Brigade office in the farm on the way. Between the farm and the road they walked through the position occupied by the battery for the Messines–Wytschaete business five weeks before. The bridge which they had made over the stream for the wagons in front of the guns still bore the inscription of authorship punched on a piece of tin and stuck up on a willow by some proud signaller. The sleeping cubicle that Whitelaw and Rennie and Cartwright had dug and roofed over contained a foot or two of water. The pits were tumbled in—their timbers gone the way of fire-wood. The shack where Francis and Brice had been killed was as the shell had left it—except that its floor, too, was under a foot or so of soupy water.

Cartwright noticed a peculiar package strapped to Stonehouse's haversack. It was a neat, obviously saddler-made wallet of canvas and leather.

" It isn't a camera that you take into battle with you, is it, Stonehouse ? " he asked.

" No, Sir," said Stonehouse, requiring no more than these two monosyllables to link him with Lambeth, S.E. " It's me squiffer."

" Squiffer ? " asked Cartwright.

" Yes, Sir. Accordion."

Cartwright wondered whether Stonehouse and his accordion would bring back to the cook-house that which had left it when Evans fell down on the Courcelette road to ply his lips no more over the keys of the mouth-organ against the resonance of the Bath-Oliver biscuit-box. No piping in the world would bring back the comments of Rennie, or the voice of Rennie, atrocious as it was shameless when applied to song. . . . But the squiffer might do something at the cook-house and at the side of roads on their trek to the new battle. . . .

They crossed the high road near the husks of Kemmel village to the track that branched, a mile eastwards, to Messines with its crater and to Wytschaete with its home. Cartwright questioned Stonehouse upon the craft of assisting grocers; upon his career in an eighteen-pounder battery, in hospital with a punctured thigh, in the Mess at a Base Officers' Club and in the D.A.C. In turn he answered questions about the battery and the mystery of 4·5 hows.

Passing the track that forked to Messines, Cartwright saw approaching them a slow procession—two stretchers, four bearers and three or four loafing ' spares.' Within himself he cursed—the morose, ill-humoured and apathetic curse of a dozing or busy man disturbed by some casual fatuity.

" Coo . . ." said Stonehouse, " Dirty work, Sir. See it ? "

" Yes, I see it," said Cartwright.

By that strange sense whereby men can recognise groups before they can identify individuals he knew that the party was from the battery; and he cursed again with profound disgust.

He soon saw that the twisted face above the blanket on the first stretcher, green and ugly below the hanging forelock of ginger hair, was Corporal Gibson's. The bearers and spares stopped, saluting Cartwright and greeting. The wounded men twitched in their grinning (the second was one of C. Subsection's gunners with a bandage tight round his throat).

" Just these two, Sir," the Bombardier at one end of the Corporal's stretcher said, then, for an instant Cartwright froze beyond speech or movement, as the Bombardier spat on his hands to take up the stretcher-handles again and said, " Prem-cher."

Cartwright moistened his lips. " Is—is this—*all ?* " he asked.

" Yes, Sir," said the bombardier. " Best bit of luck we've 'ad with prem-chers. Best bit on record, I wouldn't wonder. Nobody put out, and the other bloke in the pit not touched. Just the Corp with one in the guts and a little one in the shoulder ; and 'Ardy in the neck. Both blighties."

" Why are you going this way ? " asked Cartwright.

" I thought we'd try the Crater dressing-station," said the bombardier. " The other's the one where Mr. Reynolds went. This isn't much further, Sir."

" No," said Cartwright, " carry on. Oh—they haven't had an injection, I suppose ? The doctor not about ? "

" No," said the bombardier, " Mr. Whitelaw give 'Ardy a spot of whisky, but not the Corp because of the 'ole. He said just to get them 'ome to the station quick."

Cartwright had unstoppered his bottle. He put two tablets between the teeth of each. " Well—good luck, chaps," he said.

They twisted words up to him with their green, thin lips. "Good luck, Sir."

.   .   .   .   .   .

"Wot causes these premmichewers?" Stonehouse profoundly asked as they walked along.

Cartwright, as profoundly, said: "Good God. . . . If any one knew that, Stonehouse! . . . There are about four or five things that *could* go wrong in a fuse—but somehow don't—except once in about ten thousand times. . . ."

"Looks a bit like just luck, then," Stonehouse mused.

Cartwright did not challenge the suggestion. For his own part he was a little impressed by the possibility that a premature need not, inevitably, kill.

"Give me the old eighteen-pahnder," was Stonehouse's next philosophy. "She can premmichewer 'er 'ead orf, and no 'arm done. Not to 'er own lot. Not wiv shrapnel, any'ow; and as most of 'er game is done wiv shrapnel you know where y'are. . . ."

"But, Stonehouse—" Cartwright said, and he was arguing a point of extreme importance, "there have been only three in the battery. Three in a whole year, you know. . . . That isn't anything to worry about, is it?"

"No, Sir, not as you might say *worry* abaht," Stonehouse admitted. "But gimme the ole eighteen-pahnder."

MEDAL WITHOUT BAR   CHAPTER LXXXV

IT had occurred to men, thinking and talking matters over in the quieter intervals of March and May and June that the wild months and roaring skies of the Somme represented something like the maximum of hazard and of human effort.

The Passchendaele phase of "Third Wipers" (as it began to be called when it was settling down from a matter of surprise into a matter of routine) altered their estimate of these matters.

Cover, on the Somme, had been a possibility. Guns had aspired to it and generally achieved something in the direction of their aspiration. Men had dug holes. They had evaded disaster by nimbleness of foot—trivially by leaping aside from a beaten track and more largely by diverting the track itself and beating a new one.

In the Salient, north of the cowering garbage that was the city, there was neither cover, nor possibility of cover. Any hole for man or gun, deeper than a single spit, was a water-hole. Dodging to right or left of the established, authorised, recognised, registered and duly punished road meant abandoning the deck of a raft for what was with equal probability water or slime, six inches deep or with a depth sufficient for drowning.

The ruling mind of man, adaptable to circumstance, had devised a new method in his new world. He knew that the dominating factor—though not the ultimately decisive one—was gunnery ; and that gunnery is a science only approximate. It postulates with all due modesty that of a hundred shells projected at a given point fifty should fall within a rectangle of a certain magnitude about that point, and the other fifty—wider and woolier—within a rectangle four times the area of the lesser one. It follows from this that if one battery is placed in a given field and all the possible batteries of hostile Christendom trained upon it for a space, that battery will probably in the end be silenced. But it follows also that if twenty batteries are placed in the same field and the field treated in the same manner, some of the twenty—fragmentary or complete—may survive, articulate.

This same logic was applicable to men—singly and in groups ; whether they slept or waked, sat or lay or walked. It was applicable to the shelters which some-times housed them—shelters that now aspired to with-stand no greater inclemencies than rain and wind. If a single Nissen hut in a distant field was doomed, twenty other huts—or fifty—in the same wide field shared and therefore lessened the doom of the solitary one.

Twenty (or fifty) there therefore were. Squads of

chattering workmen, attending vestally the while upon the glow of fag-stumps, kept them in repair.

In the nakedness of that open plain, a-jostle with men and beasts and vehicles as the greatest bazaar in history, hazardous and clangerous and foul, man's only thought of safety lay in the doom of his neighbour.

It was not so much a matter of opinion or conviction that one should be taken and the other left as a matter of looking about, of listening, and of counting.

What would now be called a ' complex ' concerning prematures had a prodigious opportunity for growth in a series of fields where guns stood up unashamed with their wheels sunk only as deep as the shock of discharge drove them ; with as little space between hubs as in an ancient gun-park, and naked except for the fishing-nets and poles and tufts of painted rag coaxed out of the genial artists in charge of ' Camouflage ' at Vlamertinghe— painters, architects and sculptors, famous and not yet famous.

It is merely accurate to say that Cartwright welcomed the hum of the 'planes that came now in insolent gangs by night, heavy with bombs and gibbering with machine-guns ; for they perhaps would, for a few minutes, quiet the din of batteries.

Through a wrangle with Whitelaw he secured for himself the job of going with the Infantry on the 31st of July.

The tour is only a heavy, muddled memory now, clear as to neither time nor place nor particular men. Times were pretty much alike under the lightless sky, places were the same in their drab, utter featurelessness, distinguished one from another only by the direction from which the bullets whipped over them. Men became as one man—laden and irked only by the shapeless tentacles at the end of him that had once been mobile feet. There was a bent, brown fag in the dirt and stubble of his face ; a gobbet of beef sticking half-way out of the broken tin in his hand, or a piece of biscuit.

From the days spent among the holes and ditches and shabby breastworks above Pilkem he went back to the battery in its new position by the Canal. Half a dozen of the men had gone, their identity of no particular significance. The Mess was a bell-tent in a ring of sandbags. Whitelaw was in it, with Dawson and the Major.

The guns were blazing away. Runnels of water ran down the tent seams and trickled down the pole into the coats that hung on it.

Cartwright slept.

Concerning rain also, ideas liberally formed on the Somme were now readjusted. That which had been accepted then as the limit was found to be limitless.

Days and weeks smeared into a month.

His premature-complex could be faced no more with denial. To himself he admitted it to be his only adversary now in the whole grotesque affair ; his only preoccupation.

The rise and fall, with their itch and throbbing, of little boils under his belt was an annoyance only trivial.

The ache in a tooth that began to answer the jar of the nearer " arrivals " and the howl of every " departure " from the battery was finally tackled, after a suitable whisky, by the reluctant doctor and a pair of forceps.

The haunting foulness of pyorrhœa could be laid, from time to time, by the sting of iodine. The other presences on tongue and palate—phosgene and mustard-gas, lost and forgotten men, mules that fringed the planking of roadways, horses distended and burst—even these were not quite unamenable to whisky (without the chlorine of water) and tobacco.

But the haggard terror of destruction by the treachery of a fuse was amenable to no power on earth. It was the only thing that he sought now to keep out of his letters to Dorothy. As to the rest, she probably knew or could guess . . . and he could only shrug his shoulders.

Every ' Fire ! ' from the Number One of a gun-detachment, when Cartwright was among the guns, meant a wriggle of the close-cropped bristles on his scalp. It meant a vacuum inside his ribs, a nauseous flapping of his stomach, and the boom of heartbeats against his ears.

*   *   *   *   *   *

And then, when the lily was being painted by intense bombardment in preparation for a further battle along the Streenbeek Cartwright took Whitelaw and walked him away from the battery, and they had their famous talk.

"Look here, Dad!" he began, "you don't *like* the Infantry ; and you might as well admit it."

"You did Pilkem," said Whitelaw tersely. "Dawson had Langemarck. This time it's me."

"But it'll be my turn for orderly officer," said Cartwright.

"That rule's altered," said Whitelaw. "Major's orders. If it hadn't been you would have got all three shows."

"And I wish to God I had," said Cartwright.

"Uncle," said Whitelaw, twisting a magnificent sneer, "pot-hunting?"

"Pot-hunting?" Cartwright repeated.

"Well——" said Whitelaw. "The man who insists on going over with the Infantry every time, allowing none to say him nay—eating fire and swallowing swords—sooner or later the Military Cross at least."

"You fool," said Cartwright. "Dad, you damned, blind fool. . . . Can't you see, man—I *want* to go with the Infantry?"

"Yes," said Whitelaw. "I can. That's why I've been telling you all is vanity."

"All is—funk, you idiot," Cartwright snapped. Whitelaw's stupidity had stripped him bare. "You just don't know what it means to me, staying at the guns. It's—God, Dad, it's torture! I know as well as you do that it's probably got to come some time or other. But, oh, hell, I don't want it to be from a premature. I—I think somehow—away from the guns it's a fair chance. *That* is why I'm going again with the fut."

"Oh, *are* you!" said Whitelaw. He, too, spoke fiercely now. "Let me tell you you're damned well not. It's my turn, and I'm going to stick to it."

Cartwright thought for a few moments. He knew that in all ordinary cases the battery was probably the safer and more comfortable job of the two. " Dad," he asked, " are you scared of the battery, too ? "

" I'm more scared of the other," said Whitelaw quietly. " Machine-guns. Scared stiff."

" Then——" Cartwright began, but he saw that Whitelaw was smiling at him.

" Who would foment your boils for you ? " he asked quietly. " The Infantry Colonel—or the Adjutant ?—or a company commander ? Who'd poultice your jaw ? Who would cook your porridge now that your blasted teeth can't chew anything harder ? "

For a week now Stonehouse had been feeding Cartwright on thin Quaker oats and fomenting two particularly noxious boils.

In the last two days his right cheek had swollen up, peeling from frequent paintings of iodine but relieving the throb above the teeth. Poultices on this swelling soothed a dull pain in the ear.

" I can take Stonehouse, can't I ? " he said.

" They'd be delighted," said Whitelaw. " Charmed ! There's nothing Infantrymen like so much as an invalid gunner and his nurse ; one who ought to be on his way down the line. . . . Uncle, you fool, why don't you go ? The Doc told the old man a week ago. . . ."

" Look here ! " Cartwright snapped. The only emotion of which he was aware was dark anger. " You can just shut up ! When you leave this damned battery I will. See ? So—so you can just shut up." But this was not enough to appease the anger. " You and your blasted talk ! One would think, to hear it, that you and your brother, with your sheep-skins and money-bags, ruled the whole bally War Office. From the day you blew in at Auchonvillers you've gassed about nothing but being fed up and wanting to go home ; and you've bragged about being able to wangle something soft. That was more than a year ago. And here you still are. Still grousing. Still bragging. I'm sick of it." He turned away.

" I'm sicker," said Whitelaw, not particularly ruffled
by the outburst, " of the grousing *and* the bragging."

" Then why the hell don't you work it ? " asked
Cartwright. " You could do it without any special
pull now—with this ' war-weary ' scheme. You've had
more service out here than any one in the Division—in the
Corps, I should think. If half your yarns are true."

" True ? " said Whitelaw. " You've seen my trooper's
pay-book, haven't you ? "

" Yes," said Cartwright. " I've seen it. Why don't
you go ? "

" Because, you ass," he answered quietly, " I just
can't. There ! You have got to finish this ruddy picnic
out frightened of prematures, and I've got to finish it out
frightened of—of *moving*—out of my turn. That's why
I can't—and damned well won't—let you take my show
next week with the feet. It'd be heroism beyond my
poor powers. Young Rennie, I dare say, would have done
it. But I won't—I'm not a suicidal gent. I've as good
a right to come out of all this nonsense with my skin on
as you or any one. So I'll stick to my turn. And I've
got to stick with what's left of this blasted battery——"
he glowered over his shoulder at the guns whose wheels
tossed up a whorl of puddle every time the hair shifted
on Cartwright's head. " I've got to stick with the
filthy, God-forsaken, damned thing till I'm *carried* away
from it. A decent Major, Uncle, would have sent us both
out of it months ago. That would have been all right.
It would have been our turn if he had *made* us go. But
that poor old blighter can't. He's trying, God help him ;
but without us he'd be dished and he knows it. And
when you're gone, it'll stick another rivet in me. . . ."

" Dad," said Cartwright, and heaven only knew what
gave him the emotion that made him say it, " I won't go,
old thing. I'm hanged if I do. . . . If——I mean I'll get
these damned teeth taken out somewhere—it'll be a lot
better. Honestly——"

Whitelaw mumbled some kind of thanks and the talk
petered out ; but Cartwright knew that he had formulated
a compact with Whitelaw and those six shabby, amphib-

ious guns and the men and beasts that served them. He would in time forget that gibbering, ghastly and completely idiotic fear of the least of all war's dangers— prematures.

MEDAL WITHOUT BAR   CHAPTER LXXXVI

HE forgot it sooner, and more completely than he would have thought likely. There came to him in its place, and quite suddenly three or four nights later, some vague but terrifically forceful ideas about the possibility of a formula for the prognostication of prematures. At best it could be only approximate—within a hundred rounds or so—but it would be something. He sat up in his flea-bag and said, " You awake, Sir ? "

The Major answered, " Yes, Uncle, near enough." He had been calling him " Uncle " for some time now, a final embellishment upon his unfailing gentleness.

Cartwright began to expound his theory. After some quiet word from the Major who had turned his torch on him, he knew that his talk was sheer and utter nonsense. But he went on talking it.

He was aware that the Major must be thinking of some soothing word to say. The Major said it. " I see, Uncle. I—I dare say there's something in it. Tell me in the morning, though. Better in the morning. Always better after sleeping on a thing, you know. Go to sleep now, there's a good fellow. Sleep now. . . ."

Cartwright was mildly amused by the fact of a timid, gentle Major who had been running boy-scouts for some years, chatting to soothe the delirium of a subaltern, both of them sheltered by canvas against projectiles varying in weight from a dozen pounds to vulgar fractions of a ton.

He lay down again, mumbling " all right . . ." and " good night."

But it was impossible to leave the matter thus ; for
some weeks now he had been, in his rare moments of
solitude, turning over ancient battery records.   One
of the old indestructibles of the gang, loose-jowled and
hairy, was Corporal Grayson, the battery clerk.   With
the genius of an antiquary Grayson had preserved the
carbon copies of the battery's paper-war.   He had the
ammunition returns and indents from the times that
the battery's ration had been fifteen and twenty rounds
per day to those when its allotment had been three
hundred per gun.   He had the indents for dial-sights,
buffer-springs, packing-gland rings, breech-blocks and
for guns complete. . . .   From this evidence—massed
and collated in Grayson's hovel of box-tops and bottoms
tacked together under an old tarpaulin and breasted
with the malleable clay of sandbags—one problem had
crystallised out for Cartwright's decision : was it in the
age and the wear of the *gun* that the clue to prognostication lay, or was it rather in the mystery of some recondite
system of numbers of shells ?   Must the individual layer
also be taken into the sum of calculations ?   Could it
be stated, for example (when investigations should have
been completed), that it was about the seven thousand
and eightieth round loosed off by an individual layer
that would detonate at the muzzle ? . . .   And was the
fact of the new graze fuse, the 106, going to upset all
earlier research ? . . .

He was sitting up again in his flea-bag, very lucidly
stating these considerations through the dishevelled
flannel of the poultice on his cheek.   Again he was
aware that he was mumbling the most fantastic nonsense,
disturbing and alarming the harmless Major, making a
fool of himself. . . .   And he went on for a few moments
mumbling it.

The Major lighted the candle and woke Dawson.
Whitelaw was among the guns, getting rid of some of
their allotment for the night.

" Dawson, a drink for Cartwright," the Major said.
Cartwright was quiet, his sheepish smile lost in the rags
of pants and undervest festooning his jaws.   Dawson

came over with a mug, also his sponge picked out of a bucket.

Cartwright shrank away from these offerings. " Golly —not *cold*, Dawson ! " he said, in horror. " It'll touch it up again like hell—if it's cold."

Dawson dropped the sponge and wiped his fingers. He felt Cartwright's hand and forehead, and pulled a face at the Major. " He's bust his fan-belt ; " he said. " Radiator's boiling."

Whitelaw scraped his helmet in under the tent-flap and looked at the three of them. Avoiding bed-corners with his great rubber boots and flapping coat he went across and pinched out the candle.

" Couple of buses going over," he said. " God knows whose. I'd knocked off for a minute or two, and saw your light."

" Could we, d'you think," the Major asked, " give him some more aspirin ? He's rather inclined to be delirious."

Whitelaw said, " No. Aspirin's half his trouble, I think. Lowering stuff." He always used quaint old-fashioned words like ' lowering ' in connection with drugs. He spoke, for instance, of ' a physic ' or a ' purge.' " He's had about six or eight a day for weeks. . . . I'll get through to the Doc at A as soon as the Brigade wire is mended. Chaps are out on it now."

He stuck his head out of the flap and listened. The 'planes had gone. " All right," he said. " Give us a dry match, Dawson," and lighted the candle again. He felt Cartwright's forehead and made some vague movement of adjusting his poultice wrappings. " Better let him rip till the Doc's seen him in the morning. I don't hold with all that aspirin ; and a tot might set him going again. . . ."

When the little Welsh doctor and the Major told him next day that he was going to the Casualty Clearing Station Cartwright believed them. If they had told him, in the same matter-of-fact tones, that they were going to make of him a Field-Marshal or that he must start on an apprenticeship to a plumber he would have accepted either fact equably.

With Browne's walking-stick in his hand and his haversack braced up high under his arm-pit to swing it clear of the beginning of the boil-area, he slunk away from the battery. The doctor's label marking him "Debility. P.U.O." (which was said to stand for 'Pyrexia of unknown origin') and "Abscess antrum (?)" he tucked out of sight, into his tunic. Stonehouse—respirator on chest, haversack on one hip, accordion-case on the other and Cartwright's valise-roll on his shoulder—followed.

He did not take the stretcher because he was able to walk, and because the jolting of a stretcher would have got an answer from the throbbing in his cheek. He did not ride because there would now have been a new boil between him and the saddle.

He shook hands with the Major and cleared out of the tent. Nimbleness of movement, if he had had it, might have made it possible to elude Whitelaw. (Dawson had gone up at dawn to the holes and breast-works to put a hundred rounds as nearly as possible on a visible stronghold said at last to be tied down to a spot on the map.)

But he had no nimbleness ; and it is perhaps worth noting that the official estimate of the speed of advancing (or, journalistically, "charging") Infantry was, at that time and place, something under nine hundred yards per hour—a minute for fifteen yards ; and the 'going' at the flank of the battery was much the same as the 'going' of no-man's-land.

He glanced towards the battery and began to plug away towards the track that was high and a little drier, towards the road ; but Whitelaw came out from the sandbags around the nearest gun, paddling after him. "Here, you old deserter," he called, "Steady ! "

Cartwright stopped and Whitelaw took his shoulder. "Come on and see the chaps," he said. "What's the idea in sneaking——"

"I'm not sneaking," said Cartwright, "and I don't particularly want to see the chaps. I—well, so long, Dad."

" You old fool ! " said Whitelaw. " You've damned well got to see them—trying to shove off like a blasted burglar. You ass—come on ! Let them see that confounded mug of yours with your eye gone black and mouldy. Every confounded one of the blighters will want to *carry* you. Come and wish them a spot of luck. Damn you, you owe it to them. . . ."

It was absurd, like being badgered, at the age of seven, to go through a recitation.

He turned and retraced some steps towards the guns. Then he stopped resolutely, indicating to Whitelaw that he might go to hell. " Good-bye, you fellows," he called to a couple of loafers behind number six gun. " Good luck all."

" Good luck, Sir."

Their call was lustier than his, and a score of other men tumbled into view.

" Good luck, Sir . . . Best of luck, Sir . . . Good-bye, Sir . . . Good luck. . . ." It was everything that he had preferred to avoid ; and then a few—some half-dozen—detached themselves and hesitated, and then came on, shuffling towards him. First was Sergeant Stevens, the grousing lawyer ; then Whittle and hopeless, shiftless old Shawl of B. sub. ; then fantastically-named young Turtle, the present layer of number four. He had always had a particular liking for this youngster from the earliest Arras days and had got him into his section by exchanging for him, with Reynolds, the performer on spoons (who had since died of a wound in the jaw). Turtle's ears had been a great bother to him of late ; twists of newspaper stuck out of them as he stood saying " Good luck, Sir . . . Good luck."

They all shook his hand ; and Stevens, who could not reasonably be expected to get through a minute without connected speech, said : " When they send you out again, Sir, fit and well, the boys will be glad to see you back, Sir. . . . I'm sure, Sir. . . ."

The ' boys,' for whom he spoke, thoughtfully scratched their chests and stomachs, thinking their thoughts and finding in them a smile.

" Good luck, Sir," they said again, softly and finally ; and slouched back to the guns.

" If *I* was being sent away out of this," Whitelaw said, walking alongside for a few yards, " there would be a song and dance in progress.   My heels, moreover, would be invisible for dust."

" H'm," grunted Cartwright.   " That's all you know about it."

Bitterly he resented such a thing as a battery that could make a man feel like the meanest and the lowest worm on earth. . . .   There were, however, the ordinary signs of a black-eye above his puffed-up left cheek and the pale stripe where the skin had peeled off under iodine ' fort ' and poultices.

For these small mercies he was thankful.

" Well—bye-bye for just now," said Whitelaw, holding out the three fingers and thumb of his right hand.   " You might write. . . .   Well, good luck ! "

Cartwright said, " Good luck."

And so, he thought, as he wiped his boots a little on the edge of the boarded road, he had finished with them.

A meeting with old Ruggles was a chance not likely to occur twice in a war ; and he was glad he had got that over three or four weeks before, for he would not have liked to meet old Ruggles, loaded up with spare kit and rifles, now.   It was vastly different at the time when they had met—Ruggles and his platoon coming down, himself going up to the line. . . .

At St. Jean they got an empty lorry ; for they were still eight or nine miles from Poperinghe, and in an ambulance he would have had to sit or lie ; whereas in the empty lorry he could stand.

" You've done me very well, Stonehouse," he said as they went along.   " You're a fine nurse, you know, with your gruel and poultices and things."

" My muvver," said Stonehouse, in modest explanation, " she'd a cancer of the stummick when I was a nipper, so we all knew 'ow to knock up a poultice and a bit of grool."

Cartwright noticed the accordion. " Can't you trust the battery with that ? " he asked.

" It's for coming back," Stonehouse explained. " You won't be there to get me on to a bus, and some of these A.S.C. blokes are a bit above themselves when it's just another bloke wanting a lift and not a norficer. But if they can get a bit of a chune for the uvver blokes on the lorry to sing . . ."

Cartwright thought of Stonehouse's accompaniments, making *bel canto* of the battery's plaintive song around the dixie that grew blacker against the meagrely sputtering fire :

" And the roses rahnd the do-o-er
Makes me love mother mo-o-er
I see my sweetheart Flo and the friends I used to know
I am thinking to-night of the fields of snowy white :
Banjoes ring-ging-a, darkies sing-ging-a
All the world seems-a gay——

And the roses rahnd "—and so on, and on, and on. . . .

" . . . All the world seems gay. . . ." Between twenty and thirty such men as he had left behind in the filth where a fire could be coaxed into no more than smouldering, would sing those words even though the music itself was a dirge and a wail most dismal.

But they would.

As soon as Stonehouse was among them again and the cook had hammered his dixie-lid and shouted " tea-yup ! " they would be at it. . . . Whitelaw, meanwhile, would be attending to the packing of his haversack with the waterproof bundles of sandwiches for this battle that was coming, filling his flask, rubbing up a supply of tobacco, folding some ' Bromo.' The Major would check the barrage ranges and the times of ' lifts '—for the twentieth time. Dawson would carry out his pet scheme of numerous little dumps of ammunition ready for every gun, each dump containing the number of shells for every ' lift.' Stevens would devise a question for every order.

There would be ' area shoots '; the inhabitants of every area would trust, with an open and bonhomous mind, that the ' area ' thus shot would continue to be a neighbouring one. . . .

" . . . All the world seems gay. . . ."

" Bit of tea, Sir ? " Stonehouse asked, uncorking his water-bottle.

" In a minute," said Cartwright. " If this thing slows down. I don't want to knock my teeth about, over these bumps."

" Pity you couldn't sit a while," said Stonehouse. " Narsty little walk that, to the bus. Must of took it out of you, Sir. . . . But I suppose it's non-stop for Blighty from the Casu-ality Clearing Station ? "

" I suppose so," said Cartwright. Then, thoughtfully, " I think I will sit down." And he did, beside Stonehouse on the valise.

For two or three nights he stayed at the Casualty Clearing Station. Stonehouse, to his surprise, stayed too, scrubbing a piece of floor by his bed at dawn, bringing him thin porridge for breakfast and soup at other times.

In the eye of one of the doctors who paused by his bed was a glimmer of that rare quality that prompted Binding, meditating on the other side of no-man's land, to say, " Fine men are encountered by the way, but they are lost in the dust of the road before one has been able to take a good look at them."

" H'm," said this doctor, reading Cartwright's label, " thirty-nine and eleven-twelfths. . . . I'm forty-one— and *two*-twelfths. Not much in it." He looked down, smiling and exposing that glimmer. " It's a boy's game, this. Not unto us ancients, O Lord—not unto us. . . . I don't believe that's antrum, though. Not for a moment. They'll X-ray it at the base." He lowered his voice a little. " It's really quite incredible how different you'll feel in a fortnight when you've got rid of some of those teeth for one thing, and had some decent sleep for another."

That night the settlement was historically bombed.

Stonehouse, scrubbing his allotment of floor in the morning, had yarns of nurses killed and wounded.

The memorable doctor was killed among them; or else he went on leave, or off duty for a couple of days—for Cartwright did not see him again.

Stonehouse carried his valise to the hospital-train, and handed him his haversack at the carriage door. They shook hands there, the master and the flunkey.

" Good luck, Stonehouse."

" Good luck, Sir."

Then he snapped and quivered his guardsman's salute and hastened out to the yard on his troubadour's errand of earning the hospitality of a battle-ward vehicle with the cunning of his lute.

Cartwright made one joke on the journey to Wimereux. A Sister, seeing him prowling about a corridor, said " Are you a sitter ? "

" Off and on," said he.

Perhaps it was not much of a joke; but it was as near as he got to jocularity for some days. There was still a dull ache, ready to stab out a cold sweat on his temples at a careless shutting together of teeth or the knock of a pipe-stem upon one of them. There was the taste of pyorrhœa indistinguishable from gas and mules and burst horses; and there was, over everything, the sense of failure dismal and utterly futile.

In sneaking away from the battery with boils, on his stern (ignobly humorous), with sore teeth and a faintly black eye, he had not even paid the toll. He was, therefore, taking a mere rest with the toll still ahead of him for payment. With a wound he would have felt differently about it; the debt would have been paid; and he would, if he started again, have started afresh.

Whenever he started again now he knew that the old unpaid score would be lurking against him. " His," in the language of the mystics who pondered these matters, was still to come to him before Whitelaw's should come to Whitelaw; and the softest ' blighty ' would, mystically, have altered this.

With a ribbon on his breast he might also have felt

differently. All that could be said now was that he had been overworked ; not as a man is overworked and strained and temporarily broken by a great and triumphant effort that makes his fortune ; but as the little petty tradesman is broken down by the sweating whereby he has striven to keep himself solvent.

To Dorothy he wrote that he was having a rest cure ; the odds were a hundred to one that he would come home since, for some peculiar reason, there was a limit placed upon the dental treatment to which an officer was entitled in the field.

MEDAL WITHOUT BAR   CHAPTER LXXXVII

FOR ten days, when he had been some days at home, he saw in Dorothy's eyes the light which kindles the eye of gamblers. For ten days there was in his own talk—his new denture being a great success—a strain of robustiousness ; and during ten days he hunted up all sorts of people with whom such talk was possible. Even the still flourishing secretary of the Belgian Home he did not avoid on the station platform.

He told yarns to John and David.

The days were the ten that followed the bell-ringings and rejoicings at the first reports of Cambrai.

Dorothy, after a year of handling laundry in a West End hospital and tours of other menial duty, had ample material for forecasts and guesses. She had picked up the meanings and significances of a Medical Board's pronouncements. She knew how long such pronouncements were likely to hold.

The Cambrai cheering and bell-ringing sent her thoughts along channels which Cartwright knew she had not adventured before ; and for ten days and nights there was gaiety in her venturesomeness. So far was constraint gone from between them in the high hopes of those ten days that they talked of Rennie.

Cartwright let her see the forlorn and ragged thing in his mind that stood now for the battery.

He calculated, hopefully, that Whitelaw's leave would soon be due and that there would be a dinner for him. He talked of somehow digging up Richards, with his wooden leg.

The ringing of the bells for the Cambrai victory was a fresh beginning. It was better than the Exeter high-spirits because those had depended largely on his own bluff.

To him, a man of business, it had been hard to believe that so much investment as he had seen on the Somme, at Arras and towards Passchendaele could bring no dividend at all. Cambrai looked (and felt) like the ship coming home.

The ten days ended. People again said little as they looked, alone, at maps. Again it was only Henderson to whom he could talk; and to Henderson there was freezingly little to say.

They sat drinking in his club.

" One would think," said Henderson, as he looked at Cartwright's cuffs, "one would think from the gunners we're always chalking up in my department, that promotions would have been a bit swifter."

Cartwright shrugged his shoulders. " The old man did put me up for Captaincy," he said. " But I was about the most junior subaltern in the brigade. A lot of repaints were sent out and posted to the Division after last winter. I dare say—now——"

" *Now*," said Henderson, " if you've got a ha'porth of sense you'll sit quiet where you're put, and not worry about Captaincies. There's still a long way to go."

They fell silent.

" Another winter . . ." was Cartwright's answering thought. He spoke it aloud.

" That's none of your business," said Henderson. He beckoned a waiter with a wooden foot. The waiter went and returned. Henderson morosely lifted his replenished glass. " Your ticket ought to hold for the winter all right. Here's to it."

They drank.

" By the way," he said a little later, " I had a visit from your boy the other day.　Wanted to know if I'd help him into the Flying Corps with a perjury about his age."

Cartwright said, "Good God ! . . . Jimmy. . . ." Then he mused : " By Jove, he *is* seventeen. . . ."

" Seventeen's no good," said Henderson.　" Anyhow, I told him to go to hell.　I wouldn't do it."

Cartwright, after a little while, said " Thanks."

" You needn't mention the incident," Henderson suggested casually.　" Fact is, I rather like the young to think well of me ; and I told him I'd keep it to myself."

" Rather not," said Cartwright.　" I won't."

" Speaking of family visits," Henderson went on, " your venerable parent also dug me up not long ago. He took me out, and we lunched."

" Oh," said Cartwright listlessly.　" Did you tell him to go to hell, too ? "

" No," said Henderson.　" We talked eye to eye. Fact is, I felt you yourself would be taking a rather different view of matters *now ;* for the time being at any rate."

Cartwright could do no more than shrug his shoulders again.　It may have been that the fervent mysticism of Whitelaw had made its impression on him with its dread of movement outside of the machine's rotation.　This new, fantastic rôle of John's had startled him. . . .　" Another winter . . ."　That, too, was a numbing thought.

And there was the bleakness once more of Dorothy's quiet defeat.　She had said to him, " Dear . . . don't ever worry about that old question of another baby. There probably won't be one.　If there is—well——" All that could be said now was that they took much the same view of the ultimate facts.　It was all a chance unbiased by the faintest probability of anything one way or the other—a chance completely open.

.　　.　　.　　.　　.　　.

He was posted to a coast defence battery at Becton in time to get three days' leave for Christmas.

THE holiday entailed, of course, a party with the Hendersons.

It was again on the two women and on Henderson that the year had made its mark. For Cartwright its result had been abscesses and boils and a pet, peculiar funk. The abscesses were gone already; a dermatologist in Harley Street had scribbled for him the prescription for a vaccine to be injected weekly by any doctor at Becton, so that the boils also could be said to be done with ; and as to the condition of the premature-complex Cartwright himself had an open mind. His knowing that it was of all fears the most unreasonable was no great assurance that it would not again be the one most dire. He tried to picture himself standing again behind a gun, seeing the shell rammed home, the cartridge winking in and the Number Four's hand flicking out of the breech as the great block snapped across. . . . ' Set ! ' . . . ' Ready.' . . . The layer's right ear cringing down to his left thumb over the crouching piece, his right fist tight over the trigger-thong ; the Number One's ' Fire ! ' . . . and then, inside himself, either the old innocence and lightness of heart—or the foul wriggle of hair under his helmet and the instant's utter blackness. . . . He could not tell which it would be. That, too, was an open chance ; so it was little use wondering.

There was time yet. . . .

The boils and the abscesses had both gone and it had seemed that both were endless as well as immemorial.

The change in the others was that they were engaged in some effort or preoccupation ; they bore some burden which had never been a concern of his.

In Henderson's opinions there was now a cocksureness that was a little reminiscent of Whitelaw, except that Whitelaw always, sooner or later, discredited everything he had said with some fantastic touch of brag. About

Henderson there was no brag.   He talked with a secretive glum air and a bitterness that had no spark of indignation.

"We're *out*," he said, and the heaviness of his gloom would have been sufficient to gain the ears of listeners far less attentive than the three he had.

The heads were drawn close together over the table, for conversations in public places just then were more furtive than ever.   "Down, and absolutely out. . . .   There isn't another kick in us—and that's God's truth."   There was a little—just a very little—of the young War Office-official telling secrets, of the 'straight-from-the-horse's-mouth' unctiousness in his pronouncement.   Then his one eye darkly challenged Cartwright.   "And, by Jove!" he said, "you ought to know it.   You would know it, too, if you had kept any sort of account.   You alone, hanging about three or four areas from July of last year to November of this must have seen or heard of every confounded Division we've got, going in and over—and coming out.   You've gone yourself with some of them—and you've seen them coming out.   How many could you name that will be of any use as fighting units for the next six months ?   And you're just one solitary gunner—and you don't know what happened at Cambrai."

He allowed that to sink in.

'Cambrai,' as he said it, was a word dark and sinister.

"Those other shows that you do know about—Thiepval and all that Ancre business ; Bullecourt and Passchendaele—they were bad enough, God knows.   But Cambrai——" he drank a little, and Mollie watched him drinking.   "Cambrai was one in the eye for us, old Charles," he said slowly, "and in the wind.   For the time being we're done.   The next knock is coming from the other side.   The most we can hope to do is hold on.   Hold on against fresh Divisions from Russia and Italy, with our ragged, winded lot of repaints as you call them.   Hold on till the Americans can throw a bit of weight and ginger into it, because there's none left in us.   And——" he paused, a little awkwardly, sipping at his drink again, and again closely watched by Mollie.   This time Dorothy, too, seemed to observe him closely.

" And what I mean to say is," he went on as though refreshed, re-focused by his drink, " what I mean to say is —in a job of sheer holding on like that, one man more or less makes no odds. Particularly one gunner-subaltern. . . ."

The women sat back at last, looking at Cartwright ; and Cartwright laughed. " You old idiot ! " he said. " All that eloquence wasted ! " He smiled at Dorothy and touched her hand. " Jim, you needn't have bothered. I'm not the fellow to champ at the bit. Becton-on-Sea is good enough for me as long as it lasts—and I won't be the one to cut it short, I assure you. I'm among the very wise ones now." He looked knowingly upon the three with an ancient knowingness.

The fact was that he felt sorry for the effort of persuasion that had been forced on Henderson ; for Henderson, obviously, would have been happier just quietly drinking with only a remark here and there, morose and bitter. He was sorry for the women—Mollie anxious for the way Jim would acquit himself in eloquence, Dorothy waiting for its effect. Eloquence and persuasion were now unnecessary to make Cartwright ready to play some golf again at Becton as an alternative inanity to loafing and sitting about in ice and water, and sleeping in some fantastic hovel.

MEDAL WITHOUT BAR   CHAPTER LXXXIX

THERE was no detail at Becton-on-Sea (in either personnel or *matériel*) that was not of the kind that had to be seen in order to be believed.

The unit to which Cartwright was posted was an alleged battery of six guns ; but he found enough subalterns already there to people a Brigade. It was all too weird to bear any close analysis. There was a young Territorial Major who had been in command since the winter of 1914, neither proud nor ashamed of never having been overseas, but merely satisfied—and most amiable and likeable in his satisfaction—that the state of affairs

K K

at Becton was normal and proper warfare.   For some reason or other connected with his heart-valves or his toes he was classified as 'Permanent Home Service.' He had a Captain, also 'Permanent Home Service,' and two subalterns of the same category—one a ranker from one of the famous horse-batteries broken up in the Mons Retreat, and the other a very superior youth who had been a bank-clerk before the war in Becton itself.

There was, it transpired after some days, a so-called 'Brigade Ammunition Column' in a village three or four miles inland, with a fantastic full Lieutenant under the command of the battery commander.

Five miles from Becton, but on the coast, was the battery's flank gun, commanded by a Captain—with another Captain in his Mess and two subalterns.

The amazing thing about it all was that the crowd itself seemed to know exactly who was who and what was what in the organisation.   A sardonic full Lieutenant, for example, was negligibly small potatoes compared with the ranker and the bank-clerk who were second Lieutenants.

The Lieutenant commanding the ammunition column was undisputed lord over the Captain commanding the flank-gun and the Captain accompanying him.

Cartwright took his place among the dozen hangers-on in the Mess who were not acknowledged and proclaimed 'Permanent Home Service' and who were not, therefore, of the inner councils of this unit of home-defence.

The Major and the Captain—lords, it seemed, of equal might—appeared to take a passing fancy to him. When they found he was a solicitor they allowed him to draw the lease of a furnished house on behalf of the Mess with one of the Becton residents on the sea-front.   They did not interfere with the drafting of the document beyond instructing him that it was to be in two parts— the first for the house alone at four guineas a week—so that they should all be entitled to field-allowances as occupying unfurnished billets; and the second for the furniture and effects at two guineas a week.

They all moved, on the fifteenth of January, from huts into this house.

A striking peculiarity of the daily nine o'clock parade was that about half the host appearing on it were obvious Infantrymen with their short cylinders of putties showing below slacks. These, it was explained, were lent by the Infantry battalion to assist some three hundred men in grooming a handful of horses.

The duties of the surplus dozen officers were light enough. They appeared on parade at nine o'clock, saluted the Major and drifted into a knot behind him. When he and the Captain had drawn away to the stables, smacking their field-boots and discussing in undertones the cares that weighed so solemnly upon them and the ranker and the banker, the supers melted away to the Mess. Only the orderly officer for the day strolled about behind the Major and the Captain, out of range of their secret conversation.

The orderly officer spent the night in the battery office. (The ranker and the banker subalterns, as ' permanent staff ' of the battery, were exempt from orderly duties.)

One day the Major had horses saddled for his whole establishment of officers and led the cavalcade forth to look at the guns in their emplacements, at intervals of half a mile or a mile, along the cliffs. The guns were ancient fifteen-pounder breech-loaders with great arc sights, more like derelict farm implements than pieces of Ordnance. The Major very solemnly, starting with ' This is Number one gun,' impressed upon them the number of each successive one. In the event of guns being required to get into action, it appeared, ammunition would be brought to each in a wagon from the column.

But the crowning idiocy of all was the ' Stand-to ' following air-raid alarms, when gun-detachments and officers turned out of their beds if they had yet got into them, and marched and doubled to the guns. Infantry-men followed, equipped and fully girt for battle with packs, entrenching tools, rifle-ammunition, prehistoric heliograph apparatus, steel-helmets and iron rations. Smoking was not allowed.

Bombs and anti-aircraft fire could sometimes be caught by ears strained towards the distant play of searchlights.

The most grotesque part of the foolery was the excited seriousness with which the Major and the Captain and some of the Sergeants took it all, and the breathless saluting of one another that went on in the darkness.   But since Cartwright and his fellow-supers were wise enough to know a good thing when they saw it, they saluted and prowled about in the darkness with the rest and kept their sneers and their jokes among themselves.

They were, on the whole, these supers, a fairly worn and battered lot in much the same frame of mind as Cartwright himself.   Of the dozen, eight, perhaps, or ten, had wintered abroad at least once.   Two or three tunics among them had the stripes and spots at the cuffs where the braids and pips of acting Captains had kept them unfaded.   Others had wound-stripes with here and there the Mons or 1915 ribbon, so they were well content with the magnificent house on the sea-front as shelter in the winter's dirtiest months.

They were a friendly, sociable lot ; the Mess, run by the ranker, made good money out of their preference for dining and drinking afternoon tea with the hostesses of Becton.

When the subaltern who had struck Cartwright from the first as very senior saw Cartwright's golf clubs he said, " God ! what an idea ! "

" Why ? " demanded Cartwright, a little nettled. " What's wrong with it ?   We're supposed to be taking steps to get ourselves fit, aren't we ? "

" My dear chap," said the other, drawing Cartwright's mashie out of the bag, squinting along the shaft and then addressing a bud in the bedroom carpet's pattern of roses. " My dear chap ! Here I've been for two blasted months and it never occurred to me ! " He played a neat chip, shifted his stance and addressed another rosebud.   " I'm sending for mine this very day.   Telegraphing for the blighters. . . .   What's your handicap ? "

" Oh—just solicitor's golf," said Cartwright modestly, " Sixteen ! "

" Well—it's the real thing, anyway," said Sparling— for that was his name.   " I can see you're a player of the game, not just one of those chaps who go out for fresh air with a bag of walking-sticks."

Cartwright watched his second chip shot, the club just skimming the pile of the carpet.

" I should say you're scratch," he said.

" Good Lord, no ! " said Sparling. " Seven. At least, I was seven three and a half years ago. But we were a hell of a lot of things three and a half years ago that we aren't any more."

The reflection seemed to undo everything that the twiddling of the mashie had done for him. He pushed it slowly into the bag again. " I don't believe I'll do it, Cartwright," he said. " No. I'm damned if I will. It would be tempting Providence. I want to stay here for a bit. Don't you ? "

Cartwright, with equal frankness, said : " You bet I do. But I don't think Providence acts that way. Send for your clubs, old thing. We'll kill these afternoons in great style. . . . Yes ! I *do* want to stay here for a bit."

This sentiment was in no way abated by three good weeks at Becton ; golf every afternoon with the amazing Sparling who played to his old handicap as though his clubs had never shown a spot of rust, and a perfunctory Medical Board at Pelchester which found them both still unfit for service overseas.

Cartwright began to wonder whether a change from London would not be a good thing for Dorothy ; whether a furnished house or rooms could not be found ; whether arrangements could not again be made with Dorothy's sister.

And then came the letter from John.

" . . . There's no need for me to try to explain much," he said towards the end of it. " You'll understand, Dad, because you went through it yourself and had to join up. I'm pretty well trained too. I've stuck to the O.T.C. and got Certificate A, and I don't look any younger than heaps of the chaps you see swanking about in uniform. If you'd give your consent in writing I could get a commission in the Infantry like a bird, and I hope you'll do this, Dad, as you've had your turn at it and are out of it now so that Mother will be all right and there won't be that to worry about any more, otherwise, honestly, I'd have joined up ages ago and could have done it easily, in the ranks, I mean, but I didn't want to do that as long as you were out there, but now that you're not it's different and a Commission would be better with your written consent.   An 'old boy' with a D.S.O. came and gave us a pi-jaw the other day and said every one ought to try to become a good officer first instead of enlisting straight off, as good officers are harder to replace than good men, so I thought I'd write to you, Dad, about your written consent, and besides, in addition, it's getting on one's nerves just looking on all this time.   I know that you've been having a toughish time of it and that it's my turn now and this 'old boy' D.S.O. chap (with red tabs) said those fellows who can go now ought not to delay in getting ready as there's a lot going to happen in the spring, so I hope you'll pull up your socks, Dad, and answer by return and you'll see what I mean about it all.

" With love from

" Your affect. son,

" John."

Cartwright, folding up the letter, was conscious of a savour of frying meat.

It was not in the splendid bedroom of the house on the Becton sea-front, for that house had been designed for a successful cutler (now making bayonets or jack-knives or something of the sort for the Ministry of Munitions) by a prize-winning domestic architect ; and no reek of frying meats could leave the kitchen.   It was up a cellar stairway in Bapaume that the savour floated, nearly a year before. The incident had seemed, at the time, a transient one, occurring on one of those Hindenburg Retreat joy-rides quite unconnected with the life of the battery.   He and Reynolds were strolling among the ragged sights of Bapaume and chatting with some leisurely Australians while Richards and Whitelaw strolled and chatted elsewhere.   Suddenly they felt a thud and heard a boom and the crumble of masonry.

"It's the 'Quarter' store," said an Australian, and pocketed his knife and the tobacco-plug he had been slicing. They trotted, with others, after him, stopping where two or three men were already at work with picks and shovels in a rubble heap and smoulder and dust. More tools materialised, and all were soon shovelling. When they had found the cellar stairway the work became easier, two men at a time flinging up the soil. When they were at the bottom it was found that the arched brick-work of the cellar-roof had caved in— whether as the result of a shell or a booby-trap was not then decided.

More stifling shovel-work produced for those on the stairway that savour as of fresh cutlets on a frying-pan. After the reek, in a moment while the diggers were hushed and listening, there came a string of slow, thoughtful blasphemies.

"God," said one of the diggers, "it's the Quarter," and he fell to shovelling again, fiendishly.

Thigh-boots were pulled out of the rubble, bundles of shirts, new tunics and unissued underpants. The place became like an oven, and the frantic digging and scraping went on, those at the bottom getting the rubbish on to the stairs quicker than Cartwright, Reynolds and others on the stairs could get it up and away.

"Come on!" one shouted from the bottom. "We're through to 'em."

Three or four, with Reynolds and Cartwright among them, raced down and scrambled over the rubble into the farthest part of the cellar.

There was plenty of light through the hole above which had supplied the débris for blocking the stairs. The curses had been coming from a face bent over the stove, a face dark with anger and bristling with immense moustaches.

"Hell's bells!" it snarled. "You've started the draught again. Tell some fool to go and block up the chimney. The pipe's still standing. . . ."

They scraped away and dug and shovelled towards him, at the ton of rubble and timber that held his thighs jammed against the cylindrical stove of iron that had glowed a transparent red when the collapsing arch had stuck him against it.   It would glow red again if they did not soon get at the top of the pipe to block it.   Soon, however, some one did find it in the rubble-heap above ; there was a sound of shouting and scurrying ; water came sizzling down into the stove ; but the inner sides of the now inert Quartermaster's thighs were fried to the bone with a charred fringe around the frying.

It was found, too, when they had smashed the stove away and pulled him out, that his back was broken at the waist. . . .

Sparling at the other end of their bedroom was spinning a mashie in a rag of emery-cloth, saying, " The moral effect of clean clubs is something I've never been able to understand.   Ready ? "

" Yes," said Cartwright.   " I left mine for the deputy-pro-fellow to change those grips and touch up a couple of lappings."

" Of course," he said thoughtfully, as they lowered their heads and butted through the North Sea wind and walked along the front towards the club-house, " of course—you haven't got any kids ? . . ."

" No," said Sparling.   " Touch wood. . . .   Why ? What's up ? "

" That youngster of mine," said Cartwright.   " The elder fellow.   Wanting to join up.   Says he's old enough.   . ."

" Well," said Sparling.   " Is he ? "

" No.   Not quite.   At least, I can forbid him—legally. He's as old as some, though. . . .   But it doesn't seem right."

" D'you think *we* are old enough ? " asked Sparling. " Is any one ? . . .   It doesn't seem to me that it matters very much.   Stark, utter, drivelling lunacy is just about as indecent, however old or young you happen to be.   But I suppose it's a tall order to expect others—particularly youngsters—to believe that it *is* lunacy.   I became a convinced pacifist fairly early on, when a gun-team was shot up and a couple of the horses strolled about among their innards with a funny, old-fashioned sort of look, rather disapproving. . . . But still, I suppose you'd take it worse if this kid of yours told you he preferred to go to Dartmoor and make nose-bags with the conscientious objectors. . . ."

" I suppose I would," said Cartwright.

John himself, curiously, had not actually entered into the picture of the Bapaume cellar that his letter had spirited up, or into the aroma of meat being fried. He had not taken upon himself the personality of Reynolds, digging like a fiend, quaking and shrinking away from the Quartermaster's glowering eyes. Yet it was quite simply and quite obviously to keep John out of the cellar that something had stirred in Cartwright ; to keep his thighs from getting jammed against a red-hot stove, to keep his nostrils from the stench of living flesh being grilled, to shut his eyes away from looking into eyes like those of the Australian Quartermaster ; absurdly, too, to keep his ears from words like those that writhed out through the great moustaches.

Then later—after the overgrown caddy who kept the pro's shop going had mixed gin and vermouth for them in the club-house and Cartwright had paid over to Sparling the customary ninepence or shilling that he had lost to him ; when lights were beginning to wink upon women and pink, fat, bald and gullible men behind windows as blinds were drawn down, and the dank fog curled up over the land from the sea, John did get himself into pictures.

He moved in the pictures as Rennie had moved, and the Australian Quartermaster ; or he was still as Charlie Browne or Evans the signaller. His eyes were the kind of question asked by a rabbit smashed in a trap. More trivially—and, absurdly, it was not quite trivial—he drank and cursed ; and he lurched out of the billets to where a narrow well lurked open beside the dung-heap.

" Dear old son," he wrote to John that night, " This has got to be a secret between you and me ; so I'm sending it to my friend Henderson to get to you somehow at school. I don't want Mother to know yet. I can't do as you ask, because I'm fit now and may be sent out again *any day*. As you say, if I was staying at home it would have been different. The way you've relieved my mind over Mother all this time has been great. I'm very thankful to you, old man, and very proud. I know you wouldn't let her down now. She's been splendid : but she can't spare you. You must hold on, old fellow.''

One had, Cartwright felt, to be careful with John. There was that long-headed something about the fellow that was not easily bluffed or gulled. It would not do, for example, to say—as Cartwright had first thought of saying—'' What you're doing is just as fine and straight as being in the trenches. . . .'' That kind of thing simply would not wash with John. Instead he wrote, after ' You must hold on, old fellow ' :

'' I've come to certain hazy conclusions about luck in the last year or so. It's no use trying to hurry into things, or to dodge them. Just wait, old Johnnie. If this business goes on long enough, you'll be old enough to come into it in the ordinary course of events without our worrying or hustling over it. If I were not fit and on the point of going out again myself I think I would have done as you ask. But I'm awfully glad you see that it wouldn't do, as things are.''

THE Medical Board, held four or five days after the writing of this letter, found the entire personnel of the battery still fit for home-service only. The '' Board '' itself was affable enough, looking at tongues and eyelids and twirling stethoscopes and handing signed forms to a very smart Sergeant. It was only in half a dozen encounters with the greater and lesser lights of the Divisional Staff that Cartwright and Sparling exchanged glances, but held their tongues. Going back to Becton in the train Sparling said, " It's a pity those fellows there bring such discredit on the art of taking cover. This is my third time among them, and each time they've made me feel worse. We ought to be proud, Cartwright, of having dug ourselves in so snugly here, next door to a quite decent golf-course. But I bet you're as ashamed of yourself as I am, like a fool. . . ."

" How many of them do you think there are in that place ? " asked Cartwright.

" God knows," said Sparling, " mere decency would prevent there being more than one General—unless it's eight hour shifts. But it's the slighter lads that get me. The Brigade Majors and G.S.O.-threes and soda-water boys, and all their red facings. And the ribbons—my God, Cartwright !—the ribbons ! "

" Expensive noses, too," said Cartwright.

" I begrudge no man a red nose," said Sparling. " Tastes differ. We like golf ; others like gin ; good luck to us both. But red tabs I cannot stand—not when they're worn like a birth-mark, with self-conscious shame distorted into pride, and permanence. . . . And those ribbons—My hat ! those ribbons ! French ; Italian ; Serbian ; Roumanian ; Russian ; Papuan ; Mons, 1915 wound-stripes—enough of them to carpet the staircase of a town-hall and enough bar-pips to tack it down. . . . Cartwright, those blighters will drive us out of this. You mark my words. Honest, simple souls like you and me will have to get out of it to save the honour of the good old name. Damn them ! They do nastily what you and I would do honourably and well ; to wit, hide. . . . By the way, what did you do about that youngster of yours who was worrying you about joining up ? "

" Oh—withheld my consent," said Cartwright.

" H'm," said Sparling very seriously. " I do honestly think it's up to every one to save himself and his own now, as long as he can. It isn't like the beginning any more. It was a gamble then ; its driving a slow, damned stiff bargain now."

" Yes," said Cartwright, " . . . our gayness gone. . . ."

" Eh ? "

" But I suppose kids going into it now," said Cartwright; " like my youngster—would go with some of the old dash."

"' I doubt it, said the Carpenter,' " Sparling mused; " ' and shed a bitter tear.' "

" You're a rum card," said Cartwright. " I wonder what sort of view we'd be taking now if those birds had marked us ' G.S.' instead of Home Service."

" View ? " said Sparling. " That's the whole point, my dear old chap. We don't have views any more. Our only eye is the eye for cover. When those old vets had finished with us we said, ' Thank you. Good morning.' If they'd marked us fit and bursting to go out again, we'd have said—' Thank you. Good morning.' We wouldn't have argued. We'd have just gone on in the fresh place, looking for fresh cover. And we'll do it yet."

They filled their pipes and pulled down the blind of the railway carriage.

" You wait," said Sparling ominously when they had settled down. " We'll keep on talking pretty big among ourselves ; swearing that this is where we're going to make our home for the rest of the show. But we'll go like lambs. Wanglers are born, not made."

Sparling had returned from two Medical Boards before this one without finding any particular attention on his return from the old-established home-servers—the Major, the Captain, the ranker and the banker. They had been no more interested in the results of them than an American would have been in a cricket score.

This evening, however, the Major and the Captain seemed to have been waiting for them. As they opened the front door the Major called from the dining-room, " Coming in for a drink, you fellows ? "

" Just having a wash first," Sparling answered, pulling a face at Cartwright and tossing his cap to a peg.

" Oh, have a drink," the Major said very amiably. " Wash after. It's—I want to say something before the others start coming in."

" They won't get in till late—our lot, I mean," Sparling said morosely. It was quite unconsciously that his mind and Cartwright's, and the minds of the other dozen supers distinguished themselves from the permanently home-defending four. " They've stayed on to go to the pictures and see a bit of high-life among the red-tabbed gents."

" Oh—well—anyhow—*do* come in." The Major had come to the door ; he smiled and beckoned. When they were in the dining-room he said : " Well—what luck ? Home-service still ? "

" Yes," said Sparling. " Both of us. All of us, in fact."

" Good," said the Major. " Look here, there are going to be some changes. A couple of the Staff were over here this morning."

" Impossible ! " said Sparling. " We saw and saluted the Staff of the whole British Army this morning. Every mother's son of it."

" The Brigade Major was here," said the Major, eschewing frivolity but maintaining his *bonhomie*. " It's quite official. I'm giving up this unit to some one else. I'm going with the Captain and four subalterns to take over a battery on the Plain. We've got two of the subalterns already. The Captain and I have been talking it over. We'd like you two to come."

The Captain stirred in his chair. " Probably," he said, " there wouldn't be any more Medical Boards."

There was something preposterous about it all. First of all there was the lugubrious gravity of the two and their condescension ; their references to each other as ' the C.O.' and ' the Captain ' ; the general ' high-hatting ' that went on ; the creation, quite imperceptibly, of a feeling that they and their two acolytes were the cream of the earth whereas those others who had come to them from nowhere on their way back to nowhere were its dregs ; the fact that they had never worn any but starched and glazed collars—these details somehow made of their present advances something a trifle indelicate.

" We're taking the Sergeant-Major, of course," the Captain said in an easy and lordly manner.

" That's something, anyway," Sparling mumbled, but was immediately sorry. Cartwright, too, was sorry ; for neither of them had illusions any more, and the Major's suggestion was not to be sneezed at. Sparling hurried on—" It's pretty bad luck though, Sir. This was a decent command. All on your own. Not much interference."

The Major shrugged his shoulders. " Mustn't grouse." He was obviously being an example in the matter of sacrifice and fineness of feeling to men of feelings less fine.

They could have guffawed at the idiotic complacency of him whose rest had never been disturbed by a rat or a louse or the collapsing of the roof above him—and never would be ; but they merely looked furtively and quickly one at the other, and held their peace.

Yet, whatever other implications there might be from the broad fact of some men staying permanently at home and other men doing so not at all (or else pre-cariously), one thought came clear. Cartwright, while Sparling fumbled with his many thoughts, handsomely spoke it. " It's thundering decent of you to think of taking *us*, Sir. Isn't it, Sparling ? "

" Rather," said Sparling ; and it was clear that this was the one thought for which he had been rummaging among the others. " I should think it is. I—You said ' the Plain,' didn't you ? "

" Yes," said the Major ; and of that, too, he seemed a little proud.

" Well," said Sparling thoughtfully. " Of course— the fact is—well, the fact is it's all damned difficult. Isn't it, Cartwright ? "

" Yes," said Cartwright. " It is." Hoping that Sparling had something more to say, he waited.

Sparling went on, not very fluently. " I know well enough it's so decent of you to think of us that we ought to jump at it straight off ; but there's more in it than meets the eye. I'd like to think it over myself—talk it over with old Cartwright. We—we've rather clicked, you know. And—well, we've taken rather a fancy to the golf course. Haven't we, Cartwright ? "

" Yes," said Cartwright, speaking more responses, " we have." He wondered how much of this was solemn truth and how much a mere shift of courtesy.

The Captain was the kind of man who would have made a gesture of lofty pride at this point and said that they need not bother further since there were ten or a dozen others who would not hesitate. But the Major said, " Of course. I was a bit staggered myself when the Brigade Major told me of the move. Of course. Think it over till dinner-time. . . . In fact you'll have all evening if the others are not coming back."

When Cartwright and Sparling opened the door into the hall the other two subalterns came out of the morning-room. It was obvious that they had been kept there by complicity and discretion.

" Hello," they said, " how d'you get on ? "

It was a pleasant enough question, pleasantly enough asked ; but it was a flat impossibility in those days for any permanent home-defender to avoid offensiveness and patronage in dealing with the hand-to-mouth, Board-to-Medical Board lot. These two now showed that they were bone of the Major's bone, flesh of the same flesh as the Captain sprawling by the fire—and of the transparent old humbug and lead-swinger of a Sergeant-Major whom they were taking with them. Suppose, Cartwright mused, that it had been old Whitelaw and Reynolds and Richards who had been plotting this piece of jobbery. There would have been some kind of a lilt in it—probably the lilt, from Reynolds, of iambics ; a jolliness among confessed and admitted rascals. . . . None of this priestly pomposity. . . .

They answered the question and went up to their room.

Because of the complications in the psychology of the time, discussion of the question was not an easy one. There was, behind all thinking, the blurred, dark background which was a concern with the delicately balanced organism—Luck ; destiny could be determined by the most casual choice of a road to the right or slightly to the left ; dooms were averted through postponements of a minute, through hastening by a minute, through the casual reversing of a decision most casually made. Likings and personal dislikes were lusty ; it went against the stomach of him who had vomited with fear, to dip in the same dish with him who had not, nor ever would ; the contempt between virgin and debauched was mutual as it was high. And there was the fear—no other word will indicate the feeling with any accuracy—the fear in the heart of him who wore but one star on his cuff for the nincompoop, the bully or the good fellow with a crown among his embellishments. . . . And for Cartwright there was also the question of John, against whom his only weapon was the lie he had told him.

" Damn their eyes," mumbled Sparling, as they shut the bedroom door ; and thereafter they were silent as they washed and changed from breeches into the slacks laid out on their beds.

" A point to consider," said Cartwright, when they were changed and sitting on their beds, smoking, " is what we would have done if his nibs had just told us we had been detailed to go with him. Would we have kicked ? "

" Suppose," answered Sparling, " that those old lads had seen to-day that we were fit as fiddles and we had been detailed to report at once to our old friend and benefactor, the R.T.O. at Victoria. Would we have kicked ? "

Cartwright attended to his pipe.

" So that's no way of looking at it," said Sparling. " It doesn't help. But I say, old thing, it's all rather different for you, you know. You go ahead and suit yourself. I'm not married and all that."

Cartwright said nothing. The technique of family-defence had become a little complicated and paradoxical now that the best means of protecting John's interests lay in pretending to chance his own. He was impelled a little towards telling old Sparling of this, because of its value as a joke ; but refrained. . . .

And then Stonehouse, the world's greatest batman and marvellous nurse, bucklered and girt with gas-mask and accordion came into the dim concourse of thoughts that stirred in front of the dark background of feelings about Luck. Whitelaw prowled in, accoutring himself for the battle of Passchendaele with sandwiches and a primed water-bottle, tobacco and ' Bromo.' The wan old Major peered at him over his glasses; and the ragged old indestructibles around the cook-house dixie said " Good luck, Sir. . . . Come back, Sir. . . . Back to the old lot . . ." and Cartwright cursed and damned that sandy-haired, foxy-faced jackass of a so-called Major downstairs who had put upon him the onus of decision on points where decision was impossible. He tried to picture Samurai in his shoes now and Sparling's—young Rennie, or the Henderson who had kidnapped him at Wilverley.

But Samurai were no more.

The spirit of Reynolds had slunk out of a gibbering mess through the slipping of a ligature and Henderson was white and puffy about the gills, acrimonious and bitter.

Samurai were gone, leaving only such as Cartwright and Sparling to face tough posers.

All that could come out of the position for them was discomfort.

" Of course, if we *liked* the blighters it would be different," Cartwright suggested. He was thinking of those others again, Richards and Whitelaw and Rennie. But what was the use ? They belonged already to the past.

" And on the Plain," said Sparling, " there won't be any golf."

They thought on, secretly and in solitude. Cartwright wondered how, if now suddenly tested again with the clipped words, ' Set ! ' ' Ready ! ' and ' Fire ! ' his funk of prematures would prove. Sparling, staring out of the window at the North Sea, said, " And this is the one blasted thing that's always stuck in my gizzard as the dirtiest deal a fellow could get. I've never known how chaps have done it—coming home and being patched up, and then getting sent out again. And perhaps again . . . and again. . . . It's a pity every decent hiding-place is lousy with things like those downstairs, and those we saw

L L

at Division to-day. And the way the women fairly *eat* them."

Cartwright grunted.

"It's fine to have become a brace of moralists!" Sparling observed.

Cartwright knocked ashes from his pipe into his bedside ash-tray. "It has become that now, Sparling," he said, very thoughtfully. "Nothing is left of the War but some sort of argument with one's self."

"Let's be damned superior, then," said the contemplator of the North Sea. "It won't hurt the happy warriors downstairs and it'll set us up a bit. We'll get tight among them to-night, just to show there's no ill-feeling." Whether he was serious or otherwise did not seem to affect the question.

"That remark of yours about golf is rather a point," said Cartwright solemnly.

They knew now that each of them was waiting for the other to say it. So Cartwright, when the munition-factor's brass gong was sounded for dinner, said : "Well, we'll try not to hurt the feelings of his nibs."

"We'll put it on to golf," said Sparling, "but I'm damned if you're going to do me out of a bit of superiority. Let's—if we can—make them feel a shade like mud. Face to face with sterner stuff, you know. . . . Damn the lot of them."

They went down ; and in due course announced their decision.

IN the course of a day or two a Captain arrived to take over the unit from the departing Major. He had commanded a section of one of the old famous horse-batteries, since when, as Cartwright and Sparling put it, he had used no other. But he was distinguished from other home-defenders by a twinkle of friendliness. For he was not a mysterious 'unfit' but a youth for whom four hours of sleep in a night were a stroke of great luck. He owned, it transpired in the course of a few hours, a set of golf-clubs ; and for these he sent out a servant with a telegram to his mother in London.

As soon as the sententious home-defenders had gone with their Sergeant-Major and their valets—the valets kidnapped after a two-years' process of jealous selection from the Infantry—the Mess entered the category of 'cheery.' The first dinner without them disclosed the fact that there was still in the heart of man a capacity for friendship and badinage. Only two, or perhaps three of the surviving dozen found that they had what was described generally as 'anything better to do' among Becton hostesses that evening. A bridge-table came into operation and enough pennies were raised to provide the chips necessary for a school of poker.

There was a warmth about the evening ; and Cartwright thought of the bleakness wherein Dorothy lived, where there was no ribald jolliness of poker-playing and hot toddies and bottles of beer warmed by the fire ; no prospect of a round of golf next day against Sparling's wonderful chip shots if the North Sea should be yielding anything less than a gale.

A Major reported a very few days after the Captain, a tough, quiet old stick from India by way of Egypt. This was about the only information concerning himself that he gave, saying also that there was no point in his taking over from the Captain as he had been told at the War Office that a Colonel was following him who would, of course, take command.

The Colonel came ; a substantive Major with acting rank of Colonel and a back painful at the end of each day, with wounds.

It is likely that there is still a 'Langridge file' in the archives of the War Office; for Langridge was this Colonel's name, and the writing of 'minutes,' 'memos,' 'reports' and 'replies' was to him the meat and drink of convalescence ; and though he spent but three weeks at Becton he convalesced furiously for every second of it.

The Captain said to him, " These fellows can tell you

more about it all, I expect," and indicated Cartwright and Sparling.

In five minutes of conversation with the three of them in the battery-office (the ' orderly-room ' rechristened) he was mystified by his command.

He read through his roll of officers and looked at the morning's dispatch from Division.

" Battery ! " he said, " My God ! " He had been looking, the while, at Cartwright.

He ordered horses, and the four of them went for a ride along the cliffs. For a while he rode quietly ahead with Hartwell, the Captain. Then he took Sparling for half a mile, giving Hartwell time enough, and opportunity, to say to Cartwright : " I thought his sort were all gone. . . . Spit, polish *and* mustard. But he's a good egg."

Then it was Cartwright's turn ; and within a hundred yards Cartwright knew that another of those fantastic friendships had been formed. " Cartwright," he said, " I ought to have a Chief-of-Staff, a couple of cars and chauffeurs, a private bodyguard and a hundred clerks. But all I can decently seize is an Adjutant. I'm told you're a man of affairs and office-routine. I'm going to institute you as my Adjutant. You'll be excused all parades and you can get your game of golf every day. But if we don't make an office that *is* an office I'll eat my hat."

Cartwright, as from an immense distance, beheld himself stirring peculiarly as out of a coma.

" Yes, Sir," he said, like a boy scout.

The Colonel said, " It'll help, you know, Cartwright. I mean it'll help *you*."

Cartwright thought " What the devil can the old fellow mean ? " and he said, " Oh, I'm all right, Sir. Don't worry——"

" Yes," said the Colonel. " You're all right. That's why I want you to Adj. for me, dear fellow."

It was the first of the many occasions on which Cartwright thought him, vaguely, ' not quite right ' ; for perfectly sane people did not ride about calling other people, dreamily, " Dear fellow."

Between him and the Major restraint, after a long talk in the Major's bedroom, took the form of an understanding which the Colonel, slipping his arm through Cartwright's on the way back from Cartwright's new office explained.

" It's a ridiculous and absurd position for any one of his seniority, Cartwright. I've put it to him. He's going to be supernumerary. He's done for, poor chap. *Genuinely* done. Spent. Smashed. So Hartwell will be active second-in-command. He'll lick the battery into some kind of shape on parade and so on, while you and I look after the other side of it. We'll make a *unit* of it."

It was not quite as it had been when Henderson said such things ; Henderson, for one thing, had been twenty six whereas the Colonel was about fifty. For another, Henderson did not call people " Dear fellow," or beam upon them and say, in a room that contained half a dozen others, " you are a treasure, Sparling (or Cartwright). I'd do anything, anything in the world for you. . . ." Henderson, in a word, had been conspicuously sane.

In four days under Colonel Langridge the new game was generally accepted and its rules universally observed, though no one could have described accurately what the game or the rules were.

" Hartwell," the Colonel said at dinner, " surely among all your millions you've got a trumpeter ? One must be discovered and equipped, to sound ' Mess ' for us in front here. We'll impress the fairies in these houses along the front. If there isn't a trumpeter and a trumpet on the roll, Cartwright will write a note to Division."

This was part of the new game, and for some days it was very cheerfully played.

Then one morning the Divisional dispatch contained an order that all officers, excepting the Colonel, the Major and the Captain would parade at Division in two days' time for a Medical Board, special and extra-ordinary.

With the order was a list of seven new subalterns who were under orders to report to the battery.

Cartwright rang up Division saying that the Colonel thought this last information must be an error. He was told that it was no error at all. The Colonel himself took the telephone. Already, he said, he had more officers than he knew what to do with. Cartwright observed an ugly twist developing in the Colonel's lip. . . . " Oh," he said. " Indeed. I thought for a moment it must be the G.O.C. Division. Will you please go, at once, and ask the Staff-Captain to come to the telephone ? At once, I said. Before you go, tell me your name. How d'you spell it ?—Thank you."

With a very red face while he waited for the Staff-Captain to come to the telephone, he said, " One thing we've got to put an end to, Cartwright, is acting A.D.C.s commanding this Division."

Talking to the Staff-Captain made his face redder and the twist of his lip uglier.

" There was a Medical Board ten days ago," he said testily. " If they were all unfit for overseas duty then, it's unlikely that they're fit now. . . . " Not much later he said, " Go to hell. Please ask the General at what hour it would be convenient for him to see me. It's urgent. I have certain statements and some personal complaints to make. This afternoon, if I can get there, or to-morrow morning."

Within half an hour he had written a confidential " minute " upon the acting A.D.C.'s impertinence and another upon the ineptitude of the Staff-Captain, who had, among other things, at least twice and very distinctly called him simply " Langridge " in the course of their conversation. He recorded a protest against the constitution of any Medical Board which could make pronouncements that were likely to be invalid ten days later.

Then he said to Cartwright : " I'd like to see some of these new men who are reporting, before we carry things any further. . . . Oh, Cartwright, my dear, you don't know how rotten things are. By rotten, I mean *rotten*. I want you to come with me to Division. We can talk in the train."

They waited, at Divisional Headquarters, in an office-room while the Divisional Mess finished having tea. Their own tea-time had been spent in walking up from the station.

A Sergeant, in due course, came in and asked the Colonel to ' step this way.'

Cartwright, waiting for his return, was joined by a red-tabbed Lieutenant. No allusions were made to tea. " He'll be a bit better after the old man has done with him," said the youth. " Of course he'll be a bit sore on the way home, because it won't be pleasant—in there."

" Oh ? " said Cartwright. " I thought it was the other way on. I thought it was he who had the grouse ? "

" He ? " said the A.D.C. " You mean Langton, or whatever his name is."

" I mean *Colonel* Langridge," Cartwright snapped.

" Colonel ! " said the A.D.C., " we're seeing about that. It's only an acting pip under his crown. He's not really entitled to it till he gets another brigade. If he does get one. We're seeing about that now."

" Oh," said Cartwright, " are you ? " Then he added, " Lucky you're not understaffed here, with so much on your minds."

The A.D.C. was startled into a profound study of the solitary pip on Cartwright's sleeve. Cartwright's remark was a triumph in a field which he had seldom explored, and it warmed him pleasurably. It reassured him that he was a score of years older than the puppy with the red tabs.

" Tell me," he said, " what *is* this Division ? It seems to keep on filling up pretty freely ; but there's no outlet.

" Oh, yes, there is," said the A.D.C. " You'll find that there's quite an outlet." Significantly he added, " when it's needed."

" Anyhow," said Cartwright, trying only to make time while he thought out something masterly to say about their having waited—tealess like a pair of touts—while the Division had tea, " anyhow, we all seem to be agreed that it's a dreadful war."

The Sergeant who had summoned the Colonel came in at that point and said to the A.D.C., " The General's compliments, Sir, and will you go in, please." Without any but the most casual of attempts to hide it from Cartwright he pulled a sly grimace at the A.D.C. and said " Apology. . . ."

The Colonel presently came out and Cartwright joined him in the corridor. Faces, like the faces of a bad type of schoolboy, looked at them through doors left ajar for no other purpose ; and they walked out into a drizzle.

" If there's any tea to be had in this miserable place," said the Colonel, " let's drink it, Cartwright, my dear."

It was the time of day at which his back was inclined to hurt him.

" Let's," said Cartwright, and they found a tea-shop after five minutes of walking.

The Colonel was a broken and sad man now. He was not old, as Cartwright on the verge of forty considered age, but he was worn and haggard, having leaned on Cartwright's arm heavily, and sighed like a child.

" What a place . . ." he said miserably with his face between his hands over the tea-table. " What a place. . . . And, God ! what ideas. . . ."

" They're a nasty lot in there," said Cartwright consolingly. " Sergeants and A.D.C.'s winking at each other and brushing their hair down flat. . . . Sparling and I spotted it in about two minutes."

" Sparling and you would," said the Colonel.

This was working in the impossible ' my dear ' direction, so Cartwright said : " Sparling and I are no fire-eaters, you know, Sir. We're glad enough to be here."

" And so," said the Colonel, " am I. I mean I was. But damn it, Cartwright ! we'll *work* at it. We'll clean the place up. We'll get the muck cleared out and given a turn-out on the other side. We'll bring the spirit into the place ; pride and confidence and—*Love*. . . . Cartwright, you ought to have known my old Brigade."

" I did know my old battery," said Cartwright. " There's a difference, isn't there ?—between that sort of thing and—this ? "

" The difference," said the Colonel, " is just *love*."

This, in a fantastic kind of way, was interesting.

" Or is it funk ? " Cartwright suggested.

The Colonel shook his head. "Love casteth out fear," he said, "and what's more, it's the only thing that does. Whisky doesn't ; not always."

Cartwright wondered. Owing to the peculiar manner in which his mind worked the only answer to his wondering was a picture of Reynolds suddenly behind him with arms outstretched, materialised there by the snap of a shell and the snarl of bullets.

"We'll fight these sneaking haters !" the Colonel announced when he had drunk a cup of tea and straightened his back. "Fight 'em every minute, and clear them out to where they've got to love. . . . We'll fight 'em, Cartwright ! They think they can pull strings. And so, by God, can I ! If they can out-pull the Duchess, I'll eat my hat. We'll make a place of this where a decent man needn't be ashamed to rest his spirit and heal his wounds."

What imp was it, Cartwright wondered, that always made a mess of the things the old man said ? Any ordinary person, smarting and indignant, could have followed him and backed him up—until his pose became a posture and his speech became elocution as it had done in his saying " rest his spirit and heal his wounds."

Cartwright mumbled something, thinking of the fun that Reynolds would have got out of the old fellow ; and, getting his fun, Reynolds would have loved him. But to Cartwright, somehow, the fun would not come.

MEDAL WITHOUT BAR   CHAPTER XCII

FOUR of the seven new officers arrived next day. Three of them were full Lieutenants, the fourth a boy from school. One had not been abroad since the beginning of the Somme, and he spoke ostentatiously of the 'aftermath of gas.' Another mentioned Loos. The third spoke casually of 'my feet.' But all three spoke with the same peculiar assurance as the departed Major and those gunners and drafted Infantrymen in the battery whose path was straightened before them and made clear by the classification of " Home Service." Their safety depended on something more dignified than the condition of ancient wounds.

The boy's uniform was not a week old ; he had the final distinction of never having been to a cadet school.

There was a letter at the battery-office from each of the other three, asking if their urgent private affairs might detain them a couple of days longer, and enclosing stamped telegraph forms for the reply.

" Tell 'em yes, Cartwright, tell 'em yes," said the Colonel. And then, " No ! Tell 'em to report to-day. I'm beginning to get the depth of these waters, Cartwright. Tell 'em to report to-day. We'll put 'em all up before the Medical Board to-morrow."

" The order said, ' The subaltern officers at present on the strength,' Sir," said Cartwright.

" The sooner my challenge is issued, the better for all of us," said the Colonel, twinkling. He was in the highest of spirits ; for he intended, as soon as he had gone through the dispatch with Cartwright, to write an intimate and humorous letter to the Duchess. The Duchess was not an old friend of his but new, as she was to all the many men who passed so happily through her hospital. " There are no flies on the Duchess, Cartwright. She's white, and Spartan. I'll take you to lunch with her one day. She'll help us clean up this lot."

He fell to writing, saying at one time that ' ritual ' did not look comfortable with a ' c ' before the ' t ' and at another that ' incertitude ' seemed to cut a bit more ice than ' uncertainty.'

" I don't want to let you read this, Cartwright, old Adj.," he said when the letter was finished and folded together into the envelope. " Only because it's my heart speaking to the heart of the Duchess."

" Good Lord," said Cartwright. " Of course not, Sir."

" I love her," he continued, trivially serious, as though he were stating the time of day or that his watch had stopped. " —as I love you. And I've told her it's just between us two. So it wouldn't be quite fair——"

" Of course not," said Cartwright.

" But the fighting we'll do shoulder to shoulder, you and I, blade to blade. Starting with the Medical Board. I'm going to write a chit now, asking the General's permission to be present at the Medical Board myself."

" I say— " said Cartwright. " Can you ? "

" I can *ask*," said the Colonel. " My reason is that I am naturally anxious to know all there is to be known about the officers in my command, and to answer any questions that the Board may wish to ask me." There was a glimmer of mischief in him now that would have made any declarations of sentiment possible.

" Am I to ask if these new men are required to attend ? " suggested Cartwright.

" No," said the Colonel, " I know they're not. But we might succeed in embarrassing the enemy by just taking them along."

He had licked and sealed the letter to the Duchess, and endorsed it PERSONAL. He put it in his pocket and then came beside Cartwright's chair and laid his hand on his shoulder.

" You are to go before the Board to-morrow," he said, sorrowfully. " How is it, Cartwright ? Are you *fit ?* As man to man—are you ? "

Cartwright shrugged the one shoulder on which the caressing hand did not rest.

" I'm a long sight fitter than I was for some months before I came away," he said.

" You don't feel—up to it ? "

It was a sad question and Cartwright's answer came sadly. " No, and I never shall. Will you ? "

The Colonel paced the room. " If," he said, " you were to ask a man half-way through life whether he would like to be born again, for another shot at life, he would probably say ' No.' Yet the number of men who give up life half-way through is surprisingly small." He spoke quite untheatrically now, forgetting the game he was playing and his various poses. But Cartwright reflected that the daily life of a Colonel at the front differed considerably from the life of a subaltern. . . . Yet Colonels were killed, daily ; and this particular one's back had been torn by splinters whereas his own skin was whole.

"Have you any family, Sir ? " he asked him out of the blue.

"A legal," said the Colonel, "and two daughters ; twelve and ten."

"What do they think about your going out again ? "

"You mean do we love each other ? " asked the Colonel, and smiled. "Yes. We do. But they want me to be admirable though they don't always know it. It's a good guide to conduct that, Cartwright—being admirable in the eyes of your own legal fairy and offspring. You've a family too, haven't you ? "

"Yes," said Cartwright. "I've beaten you there. My eldest boy is worrying to join up. He's seventeen."

"Admirable ! " said the Colonel. "Admirable ! "

"Admirable hell ! " mumbled Cartwright. "It's sheer idiocy, at his age."

"It may be," said the Colonel. "And you must do all you can to stop him. But it's admirable all the same.

Cartwright grunted something.

.   .   .   .   .   .

Only 'acting' and 'assistant' officers of the Staff seemed to be present at Headquarters at the time of the board. They were able to tell the Colonel, after referring to documents, only that the seven new officers were not required to attend. The doctors told him that they were unable to Board any man without his history-sheet ; so the seven new men sauntered back to the town for coffee and the next train to Becton.

He was admitted to the session and sat at the end of the table, to smile upon his subalterns as they came in.

On identifying Cartwright the three doctors bent their heads over a paper. Cartwright unbuckled his belt and began to unfasten his tunic.

" Oh, you needn't undress," the presiding Major said. " Are you getting better ? "

" Oh, yes," said Cartwright. " Rather. A lot better." " Sleeping—eating well ?—all that sort of thing ? "

" Oh, yes," said Cartwright, " Very well."

The Colonel had put on his glasses and was reading a newspaper.

" Thanks," the Major said. " I think that'll do."

Cartwright buckled his belt again, put on his cap, saluted and went out.

Instead of going back to the Mess from the station at Becton the Colonel went to the battery-office, taking Cartwright with him. In the office he shut the door.

" I'm going, to-morrow morning, to see the Duchess," he said. " I'll stop at Pelchester on the way back to see the General. I'm going to write a minute to-night, of protest, to hand to him immediately after our interview."

He paced about the room, and it was only the consciously dramatic quality in his movements that produced in Cartwright a tendency to be amused.

" The findings of the Board will be in orders to-morrow," said the Colonel. Then, pausing for emphasis and greater drama than he could convey in his pacing, he said : " Cartwright—man to man, dear fellow—what did you think of the Board ? "

" Oh—the usual eye-wash." Cartwright could not rise to any intensity over it.

" The result," said the Colonel, " is seven men passed fit—to make room for these new ones they've sent down. Sparling is among the fit——"

" Oh, Lord ! " said Cartwright, " Poor old Sparling ! " It meant another friendship snapped in a bleakness where friendships were scarce.

" I—I suppose——" he began, and saw that the Colonel was subjecting him to a peculiarly close scrutiny. " What's up, Sir ? " he said.

" You don't know, then ? You really don't know ? "

" How should I ? " asked Cartwright. " I supposed, from the casual, cheery way the beggars passed me through."

" They were just as casual with Sparling," said the Colonel. " But——" and now he was on the stage again ; " Sparling's papers weren't marked like yours, Cartwright. You are home-service. I'm glad, Cartwright ——" he laid his hand on Cartwright's shoulder again. " I'm more glad than I can say—but I wish it hadn't been such a dirty swindle ! "

" How were my papers marked ? " asked Cartwright.

The Colonel shrugged. " I couldn't read it. Just a little slip pinned on, with a note, and some one's initials. It was like magic. You have nothing more to fear."

The taunt in the Colonel's words was exactly and marvellously the taunt that came from any ordinary, normal conscience of the time. It was friendly, and a little jocular. It was a little ridiculous ; a trifle bizarre ; it was melodramatic but—there it was. It was possible to laugh at it, to sneer at it, loftily to scorn it, but—there it still was ; and there it stayed.

Indignation stirred in Cartwright. " Look here, Sir ! " he said ; and he was gone, in one headlong plunge, from among the Bectonian and the Pelchestrian soldiers with their ribbons from the remotest allies of hues defying the rainbow. He was gone to become kin once more with the old mud-eaters again, in the noble company of Reynolds and Whitelaw and Richards, exchanging salutes once more with the dreary old indestructibles grousing round the battery dixie, bickering for another gobbet of stew while destruction moaned above them in the dirty sky. . . . Again it was possible to laugh at such heroics and to sneer, but—there it was. Perhaps it was the sheerest snobbery, but—there it was.

" Look here, Sir . . . ! "

The Colonel stopped him, seeming to relax his pose.

" Dear fellow—I know." His hand was on Cartwright's shoulder again. " I know. We'll stay and fight 'em together. We'll stink them out of their dug-outs——"

But things moved too rapidly for the Colonel's method of campaign.

Minutes, memos, records and protests ; **personal**

letters to one Major or Colonel or another at the War Office ; the visit to the Duchess and a cryptic telephone conversation with her niece were set at nought by a special Medical Board.

It was convened two weeks after the inception of the Colonel's campaign and found both the Colonel and Cartwright ' A1 '—fit for immediate service abroad.

Sparling was still on the strength with the other ' A1's, hanging about, waiting for orders.

" Never mind, Cartwright," he said. " We can thank God for these cheese-mites we've seen hanging about there. They do make us feel proud. Hero's grave and all that."

" Yes," said Cartwright, " they do. . . ."

The Colonel called him into his bedroom that night. " I want to show you something, my dear," he said, and slowly pulled off his shirt. He worked his lean torso out of his woollen vest and turned his back to Cartwright. Below the neck which was red and wrinkled it was smooth and white against eight or a dozen raw and angry slashes. One of these, low and long across the kidneys was not yet properly healed. A loose dressing had come away with the undervest, leaving some fluff sticking to the edges of the wound.

" Good Lord ! " said Cartwright, shocked and noticing that something strange must have happened to him that he should be in any way disturbed by a spectacle of wounds ; " Good Lord, Sir ! D'you mean to say those blighters passed a back like that ? "

" No," said the Colonel. " Of course they didn't. The President of the Board just said he believed I was dissatisfied with home-service and wanted to get out again ; and that with an officer of my seniority and distinctions a Medical Board was only a formality, and a close examination would be an impertinence. Pretty smart that ! "

" The dirty dogs ! " said Cartwright. And then, thoughtfully : " they've beaten you, Sir."

" Yes," said the Colonel. " Damn them ! They've beaten the Duchess—which is rather surprising ; and

they've beaten whatever power it was that got your other
Medical Board papers marked."

" Oh, *that!*" said Cartwright with a sullen shrug.
" That was beaten long ago."

He sat down on the Colonel's bed, thinking of Henderson
while the Colonel assumed the jacket of his pyjamas.

" Damn them ! " said the Colonel again, more savagely
than he had ever spoken before. Then suddenly he
smiled. "We've never hated the old Bosche like this,
Cartwright ! "

Cartwright, a little listlessly, said, " No."

" And it isn't that we're cowards—you and I." The
old man concluded in such a way that Cartwright's eye
slunk away from the pride that blazed in the Colonel's.
For the simple fact of the matter was that he, Cartwright,
was a coward. Within him, as he sat upon his Colonel's
bed and filled a pipe, there was no stomach at all for battle
—the Artilleryman's shabby battle, not of man against
man ; but against mud and vermin and metal, wherein man
was already doomed.

Time was the ultimate and only arbiter in that conflict,
since the moment of execution depended only upon the
individual's position on a roster. Survivors were, like
Whitelaw and half a dozen others, sheer exceptions—
and even they were not yet out of the wood. . . . He
reflected again that if he had come home with a wound
instead of boils and toothache, his mystic obligation
towards that roster would—perhaps—and to some extent
—have been fulfilled.

Now, however, he saw that he had only evaded it.
He would return to his place on the roster, his old
place where his number, in the phrase of the battery's
chat, was already 'up' when he had sneaked away. It
was February now—ice again like the dark embattlements
of Thiepval whence shells bounded in the air to snarl
and snap into a scatter of sickles and razors. . . . And
he had no stomach for it ; no stomach for horses that
looked with dull, inquiring eyes as they shuffled their
great mud-burdened feet among their entrails, into the
eyes of men ; no stomach for the men who waited, startled

and expectant, for the obvious word or gesture from him (or any other like him) to set their stiff fingers to work on the buckles of harness or the snicking of a round into the breech of a rifle. . . . He had no stomach at all; and the Colonel could brag, with a light in his eye, of courage. . . .

"Cartwright," he said, with the light undimmed, and came suddenly to Cartwright. "Look here—these dirty Thugs and barn-shoots might be strong *here*, you know! Lots of defensive strength—properly dug in. But they're nothing out there. I'll be given a new Brigade. Will you come as my Adjutant ? "

Cartwright knew that he could say nothing to this but " no." Yet it was not easy to say it.

He fumbled for excuses but could find none, since the real reason was merely that he could not answer the light in the Colonel's eye with any light in his own ; that the Colonel's pose and posture were something far beyond his own power of drama.

"Why not ? " asked the Colonel. "Tell me, old fellow." There was something so wistful in the question that it had to have an answer and a gentle one.

"I couldn't go back to France and not to the old lot." The answer came to him out of a void, and he gave it thoughtfully, startled and impressed by the truth in it. "I'd—I'd just have to go back to *them*, Sir," he said. "I've promised. They're great fellows. . . ."

The hand on his shoulder tightened into a squeeze.

"I'm sorry," said the Colonel. "I'd have liked you with me in a new Brigade. But I understand. One loves a battery."

What, Cartwright wondered, was the dear old fool highfalutin about now ?

Loves a battery indeed !

WHEN he lunched with Henderson two days later he was able to present his case in a nutshell ; for he had spent the greater part of two nights thinking about it.

" I—it isn't exactly that I'm trying to dodge the column, you know," he began.

Henderson, from the depths of his disillusion, smiled a wan, twisted smile and said, " my dear old fellow——"

" But hang it ! " Cartwright insisted hotly, for one of the few things that still seemed to retain some importance was that Henderson should understand. " Honestly, Jim—you'll see."

Then he explained.

All he wanted was a clean, unbiased chance. If he was sent back to France he would go, inevitably, to the wreckage surviving from the old battery. Henderson might have questioned this, but the answer would have been conclusive : it would, perhaps, have been no more than a shrug indicating that which could not be argued. For how, in argument, could any statement be made of the bond forged by the shaking of half a dozen dirty hands, by " Good luck, Mr. Cartwright. . . ." " Good luck, Sir. . . ." " Come back, Sir. . . ." " Don't forget the old lot, Sir, . . ." by the grip old Whitelaw's three stumpy fingers and spatulate thumb before they went back to fumbling his dark tobacco ?

The other points of argument Henderson seemed quite readily to see. He nodded with understanding of the cycle and the sequence among those men, the roster of names whence had been smeared away the names of Meston and Richards and Rennie and half a hundred of the men in a rotation almost strict. Others, too, had gone : Dowland and the youth at Courcelette and one or two scarcely memorable others and a score or fifty gunners and drivers and N.C.O.s, coming up out of their turn. Their names and numbers had come up to meet the doom that mere postponement and evasion could not avert from those whose turn remained ' next ' and ' next ' and always ' next.' . . .

Henderson saw that going back to France would be going back to the old place in the old queue that had in five months moved slowly but inevitably towards the sinister portals that were either Mutilation or Destruction ; and that a man can lose his heart and his stomach for these alternative adventures. . . .

Henderson seemed to see, too, that the Adjutant job with Colonel Langridge would have been even of itself, impossible. " He's fine," Cartwright admitted. " He really is, you know. There couldn't be a better soldier anywhere. But—I don't know. Somehow I just couldn't stand it, Jim. Not now. A year or two ago, perhaps ; but not now. He's one of the sword-swallowers and fire-eaters. You know—*says* things with his chest thrown out and head up. And—oh, you know, one gets too tired for that sort of thing."

Henderson, stroking the stem of his glass, said thoughtfully : " I wonder who it is, organising and running the wangle up there at Becton. Must be a pretty big noise to swamp the Duchess—and the hint I got through to them about you."

" Oh ! " said Cartwright, impatiently. " Damn Becton ! That's finished with. The sooner I get out now, the better. I'm down and out—with the Colonel, as his Adjutant. As I've told you, there's John. I've got to shut him up—somehow. I don't want to be done in— which is what France would mean : but I don't mind another chance. It's as Sparling says : those things at Becton and Pelchester have been an emetic tonic, like the drunk making a beast of himself for the benefit of the doubtful Spartans."

Henderson was thinking deeply. He was familiar with procedures. He knew that an officer on leave could report sick at a hospital. In London, for example, he could report at Millbank where Henderson himself had a staunch and familiar friend in a Major. He was thinking that if it had not been for this new, nonsensical development of young John it might have been worth while to say something along these lines to Cartwright. On the whole he doubted it ; but there might have been the barest possibility.

But this was the beginning of February.   Grounds had come to Henderson from things said in corridors and numbered rooms, from information and ideas darkly exchanged over lunches and dinners—grounds for the suspicion that France would yet be something to surprise even such as Cartwright.

" What about Palestine ? " he said.   " Egypt ? "

" Egypt's just a garrison, isn't it ? " Cartwright asked.

" So your old Colonel *has* taught you a bit of his fire-eating ? "   Henderson smiled.   " But   Palestine's   no garrison.   It's a proper war.   About the best war there is at the moment."

It was a long time since Cartwright had seen such a glimmer in the solitary eye of Henderson.   It was long, indeed, since he had seen aught but dull shadow in the eye of any man who was not drunk or ' permanent home service ' or addressing a golf-ball, or yet was not a fanatic like the Colonel at Becton.

He responded to the light in the eye of Henderson, saying, " I say, Jim, could you ? "

Henderson nodded.   " I think so," he said.   " Those budmashes passing you fit so soon has shaken me.   Shaken me to the core ; but Palestine might be done.   It's normal, you see."

Again Cartwright said, " I say ! If only you can. And Jim—could you wangle old Sparling, too ?   E. G. Sparling ;   Egerton   Graham   S-P-A-R-L-I-N-G,   M.C. I'll write it down so that you won't go and get it wasted on some other blighter.   Jim, you are a good fellow."

" Yes," said Henderson.   " But it isn't done yet."

" But there's a chance ? "

" Oh, it's as good as done.   I know the A.G. Sixers pretty well at the moment.   I think you can get busy ordering a pair of Jodhpurs and a mosquito-net and a topee, and all that."

DELIGHT is perhaps a strong word to apply to the emotion of a man of forty when he receives a telegram which only his greatest possible effort of will has prevented him from expecting for three or four consecutive days.

Yet in the reading of that telegram, which instructed him to proceed on leave and to hold himself in readiness to join the Egyptian Expeditionary Force, he felt that he could breathe deep again and lift up his head, smiling, and spread his shoulders on which there no longer rode the prodigious weight of doom.

All he had craved in the later days was what was generally called a run for his money, somewhere where Destiny was not already written—in mud. The telegram gave it to him.

He was not as one utterly reprieved, but neither was he any longer doomed. His belief in Chance, where chance existed, was still unshaken. Honour (the dim joke among those who were not on the Divisional Staff at Pelchester or guarded by that Staff among the personnel of that fantastic battery and Infantry battalion) was satisfied.

Sparling, too, had such a telegram.

The Colonel had already gone, protesting his love and assuring Cartwright that there would be a welcome for him in his Brigade if there was no room for him in his own.

Cartwright had not told him of the Palestine scheme. Nor, from mystic reasons connected with the operations of luck, had he told Sparling—till the telegrams had come.

Though the War had become to Cartwright a private affair, there was about this new turn which he knew to be so nearly a reprieve, one difficulty : Dorothy must be made to see the full brightness and splendour of its bright side, and John the darkest depths of its dark one ; for no such luck as unknown and unimaginable Palestine would be likely to come John's way if John should persist and succeed in his smouldering, preposterous desire.

But one look at John was enough to make the idea of John as a soldier unthinkable. No man in his senses could see in the fellow anything but a schoolboy ; lanky, nothing but wrist, ankle and Adam's apple ; prodigiously dignified for the two days immediately following his bi-weekly shave, fluffy and diffident and gawky for the other five. Flatly and absolutely it was unthinkable.

Remarks were dropped, significantly and furtively out of the hearing of his mother, that should sink slowly into the taciturn and apparently sulky youngster, showing him that they were by no means out of the wood.

With Dorothy restraint was not necessary. In her mind also France has assumed a peculiarly sinister ugli- ness. She, for a year or more in the basement of the little hospital, had studied a few of the ' returns ' of which Henderson had been studying the bulk on paper. So Cartwright found a quick response in her to the new exuberance in himself.

There was a point (backwards) beyond which any imagining was impossible ; for it was there that existed the old battery—that of it which was dead and scattered and that which still hung together and survived. Thought upon it was merely impossible, to be substituted imme- diately by the thought that the last office of friendship to Rennie had been well and truly performed, and the further thought that his own glum presence among them could in no way brighten the squalor among those ragged mumblers of " Good luck, Sir. . . ." " Come back to the old lot, Sir. . . ." It could not divert by a hairs- breadth the course of their destiny and old Whitelaw's. They must, in fine, shift for themselves. . . .

It was in high satisfaction, therefore, that Cartwright left, with Sparling and their new kits, for Palestine.

Into his new mood, into this new private world of his, cut cleanly off from the old one, where there were no gaunt memories of the dead and no utter doom over- shadowing the living, he seemed to have borne with him Dorothy and also his father and mother.

Dorothy ' wangled ' light-heartedly, exchanging night- duties for day-shifts ; cutting duties altogether ; helping decisions between one light gabardine for tunics and another, expressing views in the choice of a valise and sleeping-bag.

His father was hale and robustiously lively.

His mother, in her silences, was assumed to be thanking God and not only beseeching him.

Material reward also for his travail had come to him ; the passage of time from the date of his Commission had produced upon the cuffs of his new tunics two pips instead of one, and added a daily shilling to the scale of his remuneration.

MEDAL WITHOUT BAR   CHAPTER XCV

NO greater change or finer holiday could have been devised for any man than the march, in crisp spring weather up the Judean hills from Lydda through the Pass of Beth-Horon to Bethel where Jacob had slept to dream his dream.

There also slept Cartwright and Sparling in a tent shared with a Sapper and a couple of Infantrymen and two other gunners, fresh from school.

The Division was beginning to reorganise its Artillery from the snug little batteries of four guns into units of six. But as yet Cartwright and Sparling knew nothing of this, and therefore read no portent.

They found the Division's transport cheek by jowl with the batteries' and ammunition columns' wagon-lines hard by a lake of opaque, red water. The horses were strangely gaunt and largely hairless, their tails still bare and scabby from having been eaten by neighbours in the hard days and nights of Beersheba and Jerusalem.

Cartwright went, naturally, to the howitzer battery and Sparling to an eighteen-pounder.

Even so far back as Divisional Artillery Headquarters, they found some enthusiasm and curiosity at their coming. The complete staff came into the tent to

see them, and the General shook their hands.   They
found the astonishing fact that men were individuals
here—that even they, two subalterns reporting at
Divisional Headquarters with two others—four in all—
had identities larger than the records punched upon their
disks.   The formal and friendly introduction of them to
the Brigade-Major by the General was like a touch of
fantasy.

At Brigade Headquarters the friendliness was warmer,
the curiosity keener.   The Colonel was quite frank in
his delight that his Brigade had got both the veterans,
and that Cartwright's craft had been plied with howitzers.
He said they must dine with him one night after they
had settled in, and tell them at Brigade some of their
yarns of France and Flanders.

After tea they departed—each followed by a camel-
boy and camel bearing their kits, Sparling along a rocky
track a little northward of Cartwright's—to their respective batteries.

Cartwright followed the telephone wire for a couple of
miles and found his battery commander, a man two or
three years younger than himself, wearing large round
spectacles, seated outside his tent engaged in the very
careful darning of a sock.

The tent, on a great slab of rock, its guy-ropes secured
to a ring of boulders where no pegs could be driven, was
in the shadow of the eastern slope of the hill over which
Cartwright and his camel had climbed.

Beyond the tent and lower down in the valley, in clefts
between the great grey and brown slabs, were the four
guns.   The low ' bivvies ' of the men were scattered about
between and around them in the groups determined by
fancy and friendships.

Cartwright saluted, and the Captain smiled and
waved his sock.   He looked like a great and profound
scholar with his six feet and few odd inches of bony
frame, his sunken cheeks, and his pale eyes reduced to the
size of peas by his enormous glasses.   Scholar he might
have been, but he had ' lumbered ' in Canada, and done
something or other in the Argentine so that the name of

Whitelaw was not unfamiliar to him. He could correct casual mistakes about the geography of Cape Town and Singapore.

"Come along," he said. "Awfully glad you've turned up. Have a pew—something to drink——" It was already obvious that nothing would ever cure this individual of shyness. "Oh—my name's Potter. But I expect you gathered that at Brigade. They told me yours is Cartwright. Dickinson will be back from the O.P. in time for dinner." He looked up towards the jagged crest of the hill, obviously wishing that Dickinson were there to help him over the enormous difficulty of expressing his welcome.

"How senior are you?" he said next, when they were seated and the darning of the sock was again in progress.

"Only July, '16," said Cartwright.

"Well," said Potter, "I was hoping, when I saw you, that you had saved us."

"From what?" asked Cartwright.

"The most senior subaltern in the Division . . in the British Army, probably," said Potter sadly. "A fellow called Parley; known to the rank and file as 'Voo-voo.' God! he's a horror, and I'm afraid he's destined for this battery. He's a scandal. His seniority itself is a scandal. He's a Special Reserve—senior to the Colonel, as a matter of fact, who's only a territorial. He's not only a drunken swab, but he's equally a swab when sober. At present he's dozing at the 'Column.' He's been there for two months, and two months is more than his limit anywhere. Thank God, anyhow, that— that you're the sort that's likely to sit on him!" This expression of an estimate and opinion seemed to embarrass him. He hastened to explain. "A *solid* fellow, I mean. Not a schoolboy. Don't, for the Lord's sake, tell him the date of your commission. There—I'm already taking it for granted that he'll come to us. That shows you what a bugbear he is."

"You bet I won't," said Cartwright. "Unless he asks me."

"And if he asks you," said Potter, "tell him to go to

hell. It's the best, and only, way with Voo-voo. The really poisonous feature about the fellow is that no battery commander can go on leave—there are leaves going occasionally, in Cairo and Alex—because friend Voo-voo has to be put in temporary command of the battery."

It soon appeared to Cartwright that the only serious trouble on the mind of the whole Division was this individual, the contemptible Parley. To a younger soldier than Cartwright it would have been incredible that such a man, in such circumstances, could exist. But in circumstances worse than these Cartwright had known Taffy Dolbey, the orderly officer of his old Brigade. He knew, therefore, that nothing was impossible.

Viewed in proportion to this overwhelming and over-powering and unique menace of Parley, the fact that no cut, large or small, upon the skin of horse or man or officer would ever heal, was of no importance. Two-month-old scratches from razors were as raw and as fresh —sometimes a little septic though often quite clean—as the cuts of yesterday or to-day.

Cartwright's eye measured, and his mind pondered the distance from the tent to the nearest gun ; and he smiled. Standing in front of the tent on his second day he fired the battery ; just one round of battery-fire—four rounds in all. . . . A few more quiet, peaceable shoots like that, he felt, and he would not turn a hair.

But he did not fire them.

The next evening he went up to the O.P. to relieve Dickinson, who was going on leave to Cairo. The subaltern from the wagon-line, Hardy, went off at the same time to Alexandria on some course or other. This left the Captain alone at the battery and Cartwright at the O.P.

Potter was a fine economist of energy. Wherever there was no reason for its expenditure, he allowed it to be saved. There was no reason in the world why Cartwright should trudge and scramble for two miles each dawn and dusk over rocks and thorn from the battery to the O.P., and back again to the battery.

Within half a mile of the hill-top and the Sage's tomb

whereon the battery telescope reposed there was ample room for Cartwright's and his signallers' bivouacs among the crevices where bivouacked the company of Infantry. Six signallers were accordingly detailed instead of two for O.P. duty. Cartwright's new batman, with a bag of such thoughtfulnesses as Quaker oats, self-raising flour, salmon, sardines and peaches, was added to the party; and it settled permanently away from the battery. The arrangement was that Macdonald, the batman, and a signaller should go to the guns every second afternoon for rations and mail, and that Cartwright, whenever he felt like it, should stroll down for a meal and a bath.

The Infantry battalion was a marvel; after three years and more it consisted still of men as God had made them and as they had romped into the War. For the most part they were small farmers and ploughmen, carters, woodmen, labourers, gamekeepers and poachers from Somerset, Dorset and Devon. They had started as Yeomanry with aspirations for galloping to victory. At Salonika they parted from their horses; but, moving from Salonika to Egypt and the capture of Jerusalem, they still kept some of their illusions. Their war had remained largely a matter of personal skill and sprightliness, of caution and timely dash, of reasonable humour, and some chivalry. . . . " Ar . . . Johnnie's a clean fighter . . . " was still said of the Turk—whatever it might have meant and whatever it might have been worth as human sentiment. They had fought, murderously enough, but simply—man to cunning man, rifle against rifle, and eye against unwinking eye. They had not laboured belly-deep, cringing in carrion mud beneath a burden of metal beyond man's humour and endurance, and so perished.

Kipling would have recognised them as soldiers; and to Cartwright and his signaller-gang (which turned out to be a passable troupe of ribald glee-singers) they gave a lusty welcome.

He and the Company Commander prowled about sangars and outposts in the starlight, followed by Macdonald and the Company Commander's servant.

Sometimes there would be the sneeze of a bullet (*one* sneeze ; *one* bullet—not the festering scourge of a thousand) ; it would tell that somewhere in the dusk an ear was cocked and an eye straining—an eye and ear whose sole preoccupation was your good self.   But it would be, somehow—for all that your pulses had missed a beat and you found that you were suddenly not on the soles of your feet but on the flat of your stomach behind a rock—it would be more like a plunge into ice-cold water than a miserable drowning in it.

One night they planned and the next afternoon carried out a great shoot from the Sage's tomb.

The distressing news had been brought back by a platoon commander from one of his posts that a man had been killed.

A heap of stones was thought to hold a machine-gun ; but one heap of stones, seen from the distance of the Sage's tomb, was utterly like another.   Cartwright and his glee-singers, with the detached and superior wits of Artillerymen, overcame this difficulty.   Creeping forth behind the platoon commander, laden with bundles of sticks as like cricket-stumps as a bayonet could make them from a door brought out of the empty and forbidden hamlet between the O.P. and the front line sangar, they planted two stumps (like aiming posts) in alignment upon the machine-gun emplacement.   From another point a hundred yards to the right they planted another two. They extended these two lines with the remainder of their stumps for a quarter of a mile down the homeward slope of the hill ; and to each stump they fastened a small pennon from a field-dressing.

It was easy enough to pick up the flutter of these rags in his telescope on the tomb next day ; to see where the two lines intersected and thus to distinguish from all others the one heap of stones that was his target.

The battalion doctor, the sniping-officer, and the signal-officer had got wind of these doings.   They crept to the tomb with the Company Commander and an odd orderly or two to see the shoot.

Cartwright had succeeded in cajoling twenty rounds out of Potter.

The switch was a narrow one and the drop in range a short one from a familiar and registered target. This was a point where a small splash of green indicated a well or a water hole whereon Cartwright dropped at least one round at ten o'clock in the morning, on the appearance of a smartly-moving man proclaimed by his scarlet breeches to be an officer.

The seventh or eighth round was near enough to the emplacement to cause some anxiety to its occupants. The next dozen did everything but hit it. Further argument and persuasion got five more out of Potter. The third of these struck and shook the target. Five men tumbled out of it and ran like demons—not backwards, towards Kefr-Malik and home, but forwards into the valley between them and their enemies from Dorset and Devon. Among the rocks they suddenly disappeared ; but at earliest dark that evening five men crept up to the front-line sangar with their hands held high above their heads.

Battalion Headquarters, Brigade and Division discussed the affair that evening. Division spoke to the C.R.A. The O.P. signallers talked to the signallers at the battery. The C.R.A. rang up the Colonel, the Colonel called up Potter. In due course—at about ten o'clock the next morning Potter called up Cartwright.

He had added a laurel to the wreath of the Royal Regiment and strengthened that confidence which the book laid down as so essential between Infantry and Artillery.

Baths and an occasional meal at the battery produced a peculiar fellowship between Cartwright and Potter wherein Cartwright never discovered, for example, whether Potter was married, an only son, or an orphan. He never, till the end of that fellowship, could form any idea of Potter's attitude to women. What seemed to interest Potter most was the Division's problem of Parley and the ' possibilities ' and ' openings,' after the War, in West Africa as against those in Mesopotamia.

It began to dawn on them all, a little irksomely, at about the end of March, that the War, somehow, was not being won. They themselves—Infantry and Artillery—had sat fast from snow through sleet and rain and thunder into sultry heat, some miles short of Kefr-Malik and El Mughier on the road to the valley of Shechem. Tales were told of doings across Jordan; but there was no movement to be seen. The blue, dark slab of the Dead Sea lay still as ever behind the right shoulder of a man looking through the telescope from the Sage's tomb to the height of El Mughier, or in front of a man looking out of the battery tent.

Then, when the old Somme and Ancre battle-grounds were a thoroughfare for the armies roaring down on Amiens, that blue slab was plucked from Cartwright's vision as suddenly as it had comfortably come into it.

The Division was snatched out of the line, giving place to Sikhs and Gurkhas; and it was hurried down the hills again, for France.

Cartwright, because Potter had a sense of proportion, got a day's leave in Jerusalem. Because of his famous shoot on the Turk machine-gun he had five days in Cairo. Sparling, because his battery commander also was a good fellow, went with him.

They rejoined the Brigade when it was encamped in lines miraculously straight on the sands of Kantara.

Batteries had six guns now. Captains (Potter among them) were Majors; subalterns had become Captains.

Cartwright was introduced, miserably, to the Captain of his own battery—Parley.

When this individual had gone out of the tent Potter said, " Let's vomit and get it over. You know the worst now."

" Cheer up, Major," said Cartwright. . " We'll manage. Four of us to only one of him."

" As long as there's no leavening of the whole loaf by him," said Potter. " And if only the man would *show* his drink we might be able to do something. But he's just as wet and fatuous when he's dead sober—if a man could ever be dead sober after a dozen years of sozzling in his blasted ' Kel-cutta.' ''

And that was the evil of Parley in a nutshell. Any less drink would have meant his immediate and pitable collapse as surely as any more meant D.T.s.

He had money ; albeit it was incredible that he could, by means of his wits, do anything with money but lose it, even on the Calcutta Stock Exchange. His adornment of this institution was his chiefest boast. He seemed to get some kind of " Old Blue " feeling out of his pointless reminiscences, rivalled in depth of sentiment only by his memories of the Calcutta Turf Club. Touts of one sort or another had apparently nursed him well over a period of years, and it was through a sheer miracle of human apathy and kindliness that he had gone on in the Division, year after year, whining and strutting and staggering, doing no particular harm in spacious theatres of war beyond making an idiot of himself and a squabbling gang of every Mess that for the time being harboured him.

" Well, you've each got your sections," Potter said. " You've got the centre, Hardy the left, and Dickinson the right. It's up to you to keep his nose out of your affairs. I'll not miss a parade from now on, so help me, God ; so that you poor blighters need never salute him."

Cartwright had not lived as long as these others with a threat and the horror like that of Parley. He was able to laugh.

" Well," he said, " what does being a Major feel like ? "

" In this Voo-voo situation," said Potter, with his shy, scholarly smile, " it's a fine thing. I can be nastier and nastier and nastier to him without the necessity of assault and battery. And it does seem to add a weight and pull to the words of one's mouth. Even with the General who's known me from a boy in the Division. I stuck my toes in yesterday, about *you*, as a matter of fact. Hope you don't mind, Cartwright—but there's been some shuffling and shifting of officers. The Division's got to leave a couple of men here, for the Desert Mounted Corps or something."

" Oh ? " said Cartwright.   " Who's gone ? "

" No one yet, as far as I know," said Potter.   " You—I mean, if you really wanted to go and—and sort of *insisted*—I'd recommend it, of course.   But——"

" But what ? " said Cartwright, irritated and disgusted at being pushed again into a position where a decision was required of him.

" But I'd—I mean, I personally would rather you didn't." The confession had been a big effort to a man so shy as Potter.   He twitched, and twisted a pull at his pipe. " There was a fellow turned up last night with a draft from Alex," he went on.   " A Sapper who was in school with me.   He's just straight, non-stop from home, after a couple of years, like you, in France. . . . Cartwright, it's a filthy show over there just now.   Touch and go. This beggar thinks it's ' go ' ; but anyhow, it's pretty bad. There's wind up at home as it's never been before. They're combing out, conscripting and recruiting hell-for-leather. . . ."

A single thought stabbed cleanly into Cartwright's confused resentment of being involved in decisions. In the leisurely adventure of the past two months he had been inclined to overlook the fact that a spot still existed in the world where crises and puzzles were possible.

" John ! " was the single, sudden thought.

John was not of the excitable kind, to be carried away by a general ' wind-up.'   But was he, Cartwright ? And had he not been excited and carried away, he who had been getting on for forty and now was for ever past it, by this same business and same large fact of war ?   And in the fact and the business there was now a shadow that there had never been before—the possibility of defeat.

There was only one thing that seemed to matter now ; he must somehow get word to John that the Palestine adventure was over and he was on his way back to France. But how ?   He could not cable it, or even write it.   His only hope was to find some one going homewards who could post a letter in England.   There was a chance of finding such a man in the officers' canteen the other side of the prisoners' cage, or in a bar when they got to

Alexandria. . . . The greater the menace and the more dire the straits were thought to be for those in France, the greater would be the pressure on young John to stick to his trust. For Cartwright thought with some satisfaction of the way he had rubbed it into the boy that his mother was a trust. . . . Poor Dorothy. . . .

" Oh, I'll come, Major. . . ."

He said it a little listlessly, for he was thinking again of some of those things of which this happy and amiable battery as yet knew nothing. . . .

" Thank God ! " said Potter. " I—I'm awfully glad, Cartwright. You see, Parley . . ."

" Oh, to hell with Parley ! " he snapped. " Parley hasn't anything to do with it. Damn him ! " He could afford to talk like that, having squashed the Brigade Orderly Officer in Arras under the Colonel's very nose. Short work would be made, if and when necessary, of the simpering, dithering, incredible Parley.

Sparling hurried over to see him that evening when Brigade Orders had been delivered to his battery for circulation among the others. They strolled out of the mess-tent across the sand to the wire-road.

" I'm detailed to stay behind," said Sparling. " I and a chap from C."

" Good," said Cartwright.

" Good ? " said Sparling. " But what's wrong ? Why aren't you the other one ? This other chap's been here all the time. It ought to have been you."

" Well," said Cartwright, " as a matter of fact it would have been. But the Major protested and put it up to me. I said I'd go with them."

" Good Lord ! What the hell for ? " demanded Sparling. He went on, disgusted : " I suppose I've got to do the fine, hero business now and do the same. ' It's a far, far better thing——' ' Major—boys—no I cannot leave you——' Cartwright, what *is* up ? "

" Nothing's up," said Cartwright. " Honestly, I wish I could stay, old fellow. I'm not keen on France, as you know. But there you are."

" There I'm where ? Confound it, the whole idea of

N N

coming out here was yours ; the whole wangle. And now you calmly go and let a fellow down by dodging back again. Only yesterday we were having a good grouse together at the foul luck of being sent back to that muck-heap."

" I know," said Cartwright. " And it *is* foul luck. I'd have gladly put in some years here."

" Well, I suppose I must ask to go too. Be thankful for small mercies, eh ? We've had two months of sunshine. But I wish I knew what's bitten you all of a sudden. . . ."

There was a touch of impossibility about telling a man anything so fantastic as Cartwright's only reason for going back to France. He said, " I've got a family, you see. There are all sorts of reasons. It's a good deal nearer——"

Sparling interrupted him with a monosyllable. Then, " It's a good deal nearer to lots of other things, too. Things that can shift you a good way off from your family in pretty quick time. . . ."

" I like the battery, too," Cartwright said. It was as well to tell whatever of the truth could easily be told. " They're an awfully good lot. You know Hardy and Dickinson ; and you couldn't find a better fellow than the Major anywhere."

" H'm," said Sparling. " And what about that famous Voo-voo thing that's been stuck on to you ? Would you share your last crust with him, too ? "

" If I could be sure that it would choke him," said Cartwright, " I would."

Sparling gloomily said, " Well, it beats me, but there you are ! I didn't really think it could last."

" But it *is* lasting for you all right," said Cartwright cheerily. " Lucky beggar ! Let's go in to the bar and have a drink."

" No," said Sparling, " it isn't lasting for me. I can't do it either. I don't know what gets into us fools, but I'm going back to the Major to ask him to work it. I think he'll be pleased."

Cartwright adjured him not to be such an idiot. " I've got reasons that simply don't apply to you," he said.

· " If I hadn't them I'd raise the devil to be allowed to stay."

" H'm," said Sparling. " And if you hadn't them you'd find some footling others. I don't know why it is. I tell you it beats me. There must be something about a blasted battery that gets under your ruddy skin. You and I don't really know our sections by sight yet, beyond a dozen or so of the dirty rascals who were up at the guns, —and yet we want to hang on to them. Fellows seem to be willing to leave their wives, and their girls—for a battery. Can you beat it ? "

" I don't believe that," said Cartwright. " It's too picturesque. I'd stay here like a shot if I could ; and you're only being sucked in by a mistaken sense of loyalty—or something—to me. You'll be nothing but a fool if you go trying to mess the orders about now."

He did try, however, immediately after they had had their drink. His Major was obviously pleased by the suggestion and went, forthwith, to the Colonel.

The Colonel, however, was only human. He had already been persuaded out of a nomination by one of his newly-made Majors and he was not to be persuaded out of another. What he had written he had, like Pilate before him, written.

So Sparling stayed while the others entrained for Alexandria and took ship for Marseilles.

CHAPTER XCVI

CARTWRIGHT found that there was a new sense in him with this new battery. He felt it so soon as the first commotion arose at the railway siding over the entraining of Ginger, his section's famous, freebooting mule. Where two years before he would have loitered busily apart, allowing the competence of the Number One and the farrier, of Bombardiers and drivers to cheat and cajole Ginger up the ramp, he now saw at a glance the mess and the useless hullaballoo they were making. (He had not been a year with Whitelaw for nothing.)   To dispatch the spare loafers to hell out of the way was the first item of the job, and it took no more than seconds to accomplish it—with the absurd Voo-voo among the dismissed.

With his gallery gone and his own driver at his head, with neither whips nor shouts of advice at his stern and his mate already in the truck sneezing into an armful of hay, Ginger strolled up the ramp as peaceable as an undertaker's mute.

Thus easily is born the fame and prestige of officers.

Cartwright was, in short, a soldier now, fully grown. His section was commanded not by the subsection's Numbers One and the casual goodwill of seventy men, but—in fact and in detail—by its officer.   He was up to the tricks of every one of the seventy men.   He knew the kind of thing that R.T.O.s were likely to try on. He knew the dodges of Camp Commandants and Town Majors, of ' Ordnance ' and of the A.S.C.   He knew when a fatigue could be legitimately foisted on his battery or his section, and when it could not ; and he could talk, as man to man with the foisters.

Through May there was ample time for thought of Dorothy and of John ; but of such thought itself there was very little.   North of St. Pol, in Amettes, where trout jumped at evening in the stream beside the cobbled street, with the men in barns and the officers and Mess in miners' cottages with trim gardens of runner beans, cabbages and gooseberries, the battery was lodged for training ; and God knew it wanted training.   It was not in gun-drill that it fell short, or in mounted manœuvres over the meadows outside the village.   It was something more subtle than mere efficiency in which Cartwright found it lacking.   It had a peculiar, baffling innocence.

The Infantry were near by, route-marching, skirmishing by night and by day, shouting and snarling at their bayonet practice, bombing and rattling away with their Lewis guns.   There were lectures by visiting pundits on spies, on pigeons, on hygiene, on camouflage, on demolition in retreat, on cookery and sanitation.

The lectures were attended and most attentively absorbed ; but that disturbing, ghastly innocence remained in the battery.

Parley was skilfully disposed of for most of that month, detailed for a succession of courses—gas, horse-management, cookery and anti-aircraft defence with Lewis guns.

The Major himself went on a battery commander's course while Parley was away, so that Hardy was in command.

Cartwright made a miniature-range of garden-mould and sticks and broken flower-pots near his billet's manure heap, and allowed the N.C.O.s and gun-layers to play at ranging a battery. And still that confounded innocence remained, the kind of persistent innocence that nought but rape would cure.

The battery had never had a casualty other than his own predecessor, a famous fast-bowler, who was killed —the only Artilleryman in the Division to be so served —at Samuel's tomb in December or January.

He had other preoccupations too, unspoken wonderings as to what the line was like in these new days of defeat and retirement. Were roads like open, filthy sores again festering with distended horses and pallid men ? Were guns still herded and huddled together into the seething congestions wherein prematures were a natural outburst of their frenzy ?

Little could be gathered in answer to these questions. No travellers passed by way of peaceful Amettes. Within ride of it was no market-place and barber's-shop-gossip such as had abounded in the old days in Albert and Bailleul and Poperinghe. Sounds themselves told nothing ; for they were distant and blurred. On the immediate front—no more than a dozen miles away —there was, for the most part, silence. But that, too, told nothing—for there had once been silence at Arras.

Meanwhile the innocents played House and Nap and Crown-and-Anchor. There were cricket-matches, boxing tournaments and a prodigious horse-show entailing rides abroad and chafferings with Sappers for paint, with dames in" little shops for ' Brasso ' and ' Zebra ' and emery-cloth wherewith the hubs of vehicles and harness-links might be caressed into the semblance of gold and platinum.

.   .   .   .   .   .

The first position taken up was on the Lys—a re-entrant of the sketchy line, good and comfortable for gunners. Quiet as it was, the atmosphere of the time was touchy.

Things were in the air.

There was, sooner or later, going to be movement over these ripening fields and undamaged roads. That much was clear to all—but whether the movement would be forwards or backwards no man as yet could say.

Batteries, as a matter of simple routine now, were broken up. Two sections were dug properly in, in a solid position of reserve; while one was thrust forward for purposes of daily sniping, and in readiness for tanks, for assembling and advancing Infantry.

" Will you take the sniping-section, Cartwright ? " Potter asked him as they jogged the last lap of the trek into action. " You've been there before, you see. Just as well to have an old hand on the job till they—we—others——"

And Cartwright said, " Yes, rather. . . . It's as flat as a confounded pancake, all this ground. I'll go on presently and try to find a hedge or something—it'll be the only cover."

A shell dropped periodically into St. Venant some miles ahead of them with the metallic, hollow clang that solitary shells used to make two years before in Arras.

The Sergeant-Major trotted up. " All right for the men to go on smoking, Sir ? " he asked, and his voice was dropped towards a whisper.

" Yes, I suppose so," said the Major. And then, " Eh, Cartwright ? "

" Yes, rather," said Cartwright. " Those flares are still a good four miles away."

Singing, however, had stopped of itself among the drivers, and the battery's conversation was being carried on in tones as low as the Sergeant-Major's.

"How about somewhere here, Major, for your lot?" Cartwright suggested when they had turned aside, half an hour later, from the beginnings of some old suburb and were moving along the road into St. Venant. "The men could dig in quite decently inside those barns, and it looks as though the guns could be fairly decently covered. There probably won't be anything better farther on, when the buildings stop."

They halted, and the right and left sections pulled off the road. "I shouldn't let them cut up the ground too much, Sir," was Cartwright's next suggestion. "There might be 'planes over first thing in the morning, and fresh tracks would show up like the devil."

"And even that," laughed Potter, "isn't as fine an inspiration as our leaving friend Voo-voo behind to get his blasted wagon-line ready, and go to bed. I'll tell Dickinson and Hardy to see to it and we'll go on and find your doss."

They left the centre section to wait extended along the road, and went on with their grooms and Cartwright's two Sergeants.

About a mile in front of the battery's main position, at the end of a good cart-track between two cornfields, they found a small farm and Cartwright said, "I think we've got it."

Between a small square orchard and the lights of the line some three thousand yards ahead, was the farmyard with its high brick wall, its barn and empty byres and pigsties. The forward wall with its great gate gaping open had some crazy holes of the Bairnsfather 'Mice' joke type. The roof of the barn was blobs of slates still holding together on a skeleton of rafters against the pallor of Verey lights. The main wall of the yard was still good.

They dismounted and walked across the half acre of orchard and yard. Then, standing under an apple tree in the middle of the orchard and looking at the mass of the farmyard in front Cartwright said, "Well, it's flash-cover, anyway. A hedge wouldn't give us even that. Can I stay here?"

"It's your funeral, old son," said the Major. "Your

pigeon. Stay where you like. What about the ' un-impeded view of the country in front ' that the orders chatted about ? Those walls are scarcely transparent."

" The front one is," said Cartwright. " If necessary we could run the guns by hand into the yard, and up to a couple of those holes. I'll keep the bullets there, anyway, in the pigsties—most of them. The signallers can dig into the floor of that place, *there*." He indicated a small brick room on the orchard side of the wall. " We can all doss along the ditch for the rest of the night, and start digging to-morrow."

" You prefer the guns under the trees ? " asked Potter. " I should have thought in the ditch, behind the bank—" he looked at the backward boundary of the orchard that divided it from the cornfield.

" A little *too* obvious, don't you think ? " suggested Cartwright. " A good solid bank like that is just what he'd be likely to go for."

" You know the lad a little better than I do," said Potter. " If you're happy you might as well sit down. The Numbers One can bring up the guns and wagons."

" Oh ! " said Cartwright, " I think I'll come. . . ." The fact of the matter was that the stillness about the road and the track were disturbing.

The one thing about shelling in progress was that it did tell you roughly where you were and what to expect. Silence, and the waxing and waning pallor of Verey lights, told you nothing at all. The first shell to break a silence was as likely to land on an innocent section as anywhere else, since there was in either case no precedent.

" I think I'd better come."

They rode back to the battery. " If—if you're not in a great hurry," Potter said, " you could come and have a drink. Hardy 'll have found somewhere for the Mess to get going. And—well, I'd just like you to have a look over our place. You might make a suggestion or two about our town-planning before you shove off back to your own estate. . . . It won't take you long."

It was handsome speaking. Many a Major, if he had recognised doubt and hesitation in himself, would have discovered also some anxiety about the wagon-line or some necessity for a visit to Brigade. He would have hurried off to one place or the other, leaving Cartwright with Hardy and Dickinson to get the battery in.

" Rather," said Cartwright. " But giving the show away is about the only thing to worry about. Do every bit of digging and building inside those barns. Don't make any wheel tracks and make the men walk dead up against the walls. That's the trouble I'm most afraid of with the blighters—making fresh tracks all over the place for aeroplanes to spot and worry about. And there's only one way of worrying about a thing in this ruddy country, that's to strafe it to hell."

" Wise words," said Potter. " I'll rub it into them."

After a drink and a walk over the position with the Major, Cartwright mounted at the head of his command and led it to its home.

There was a good feeling abroad that night in the dry, grassy ditch behind the bank while Macdonald unstrapped Cartwright's sleeping-bag and the section unrolled its ground-sheets and blankets. The men, the youngest of whom was twenty and the oldest perhaps fifty, had arrived—with the moment of unlimbering the guns in a French orchard—at an important point in the career they had followed for three and a half years.

Cartwright was their patriarch and their familiar friend.

Patriarchally he addressed them.

" Any man," he said, " taking short-cuts over the grass will be put under arrest. You've got to walk under the hedges and keep to the tracks. There's to be no going in front of the yard during daylight, and no smoke from fires. The country is as flat as a board; I'll probably be able to see the front line from the loft of that barn—and he can see us just as well; better, if the Calonne church-tower is still standing. If we give this position away we're for it. And mind, no rushing out to look up at aeroplanes. You'll see all the aeroplanes you want without that. We've got to shoot in by nine o'clock. Reveille as soon as it begins to get light, to give us time

to get things tidy and under cover. The sentry can wake
me if there's any shelling near ; it may be gas."

He paused, and the cook said, " What about breakfast,
Sir, if there's to be no fires ? "

" Oh, there'll be fires all right," said Cartwright.
"—in the ditch here before it's properly light. And
there'll be plenty of wood dry enough to get the dinner
and tea without any smoke. Well—good night all."

" Good night, Sir," said the Sergeant.

" Good night, Sir," said the men.

A signaller came along the hedge from the little brick
building. " Through to battery, Sir," he said. " The
Major's compliments and would you speak to him ? "

All the Major had to say was : " Everything O.K.,
Cartwright ? "

Cartwright said : " Yes, rather. I'd like some stuff
to-morrow if Parley can get it. Sandbags and some
pit-props and netting to begin with ; and corrugated
iron."

" Righto," said Potter. " You'll have it. Good night,
Cartwright. Good luck ! "

" Good night," said Cartwright.

Instead of going straight back to the ditch he went
through the little yard.

There was a gloomy grandeur in the night as he stood
for a minute outside the gaping gateway. The ' line '
slept in front of him, breathing with the heave and sub-
sidence of pale lights. The rattle and tap from a restless
machine-gun crew or nervy Lewis-gunner were only as
movements of the sleeper. The solitude in front of the
farmyard was as complete as it had ever been on a hill-top
of Judea. And of the gloomy grandeur of the whole
business Dorothy, he reflected, could know only the gloom
and the menace. Whatever there was for him of grandeur
in it was an infidelity to herself. It was, in the wild
words of Colonel Langridge of Becton—who was now
' my dear-ing ' an Adjutant somewhere behind similar
lights—love ; love of something other than Dorothy, a
fantastic love of some sort for the already snoring
innocents who would give the devil's own trouble before

they learned to walk along two sides of a rectangle, covered by a hedge, instead of cutting across its diagonal. . . .

Standing alone in the road he had a cunning thought concerning the matter of prematures and the possibility of his own attitude thereto. He would live, not closely behind the guns, but a hundred yards in front of them. The old hay-loft would be his O.P. and he would excavate through the barn's brick floor for a sleeping place.

MEDAL WITHOUT BAR   CHAPTER XCVII

FOR three weeks they stayed in that position, behind which mines were ready laid and fused under the road, and in front of which the little timber bridges over the stream were each provided with two cans of petrol and largely printed instructions for the bridge's demolition.

The calibration of newly arriving guns wore the tower of Calonne church into a toppling jag ; from a jag into a mound that yielded up pink, bellying clouds to satisfy observers that their lines were true and their guns good.

The innocence of the section in those three weeks was a little ravished.

First a team was caught one night as it left the road for the track to the guns. Then, during a night shoot there fell upon the whole area a deluge of gas-shells. The shoot in which the section was engaged was not a casual ' harassing ' shoot of the kind that could be suspended till the clouds rolled by ; it was part of the programme for the systematic blocking of a road. It was clear now—clearer than ever—that one side or the other was surely going to move, and still no man at a battery could say which that side would be. The rate of fire had to be kept up ; the very fury of the gas arrivals indicated that it must be kept up. And so, till morning, they kept it up. Sweating, gurgling and snorting into their masks, occasionally vomiting as they went from the guns to the pigsties for ammunition, they kept it up till dawn— in much the same spirit that Cartwright had dealt with his first shell, the whiz-bang that came near to disturbing his balance on the bicycle from Brigade Headquarters at Dainville to Richards in the chalk-pits.

A pepper-shell burst on another dawn at the base of a tree in the bank, collapsing the roof of a rickety shack in the ditch. Among the sleepers in the shack the young Bombardier's right cheek was stove in by a splinter and his eye-ball annihilated so that he died of a hæmorr-hage into the antrum before the old doctor had arrived on his bicycle from Brigade. Stupid, placid Hooker, the limber-gunner, was buried in the rubbish with an ear pinched and caught fast in a crumple of corrugated iron so that Cartwright had to slice through the gristle of ear-rim with his knife before they could get him out. Wilson, the bald-headed miner who had made good money for some years as a cellar-digger for commuters to New York, lost his denture till the plates were found with more naked little gold pegs upon them than teeth.

Cartwright, knowing the value of a man who could dig, set about getting a stripe for Wilson *vice* the boy whom they buried in the orchard.

Then, one midnight, while the section was sending over a few rounds on to some cross-roads or suspected dump and Cartwright sat in the little dug-out which Wilson had made for him under the barn floor, he tried to think of some conclusive answer to a letter from John. The only thoughts that would come to oppose themselves to John's letter, came ponderously. They were too slow, too nebulous and too vast for any jotting down of them upon a page of his 'book 152': War was wrong; the dis-covery by it of the things that were right in life did not make it itself right. These things were only man's persistence in good humour and in the poise of something within himself; they were the fellowship of women and the love and comradeship of men. Those who had started the grotesque and bloody picnic, those who were in it and had grown old in it—they alone were the ones

who ought to go on with the dismal business and finish
it—if they could. He knew that there would always be
a lure in the thing which no verbal argument would
ever expose as an empty mockery—for what was it
but mockery that demanded of a friend what had been
demanded of Cartwright for Rennie?—what might be
demanded, God knew, of some one for John. . . .

A signaller presented him with the Major's compliments.

Number Three gun blared in their faces as they went
from the yard into the orchard, bunching up their
shoulders and fanning them with a warm rush of air as
the shell hurtled upwards and away. The Sergeant
apologised ; but it was Cartwright's fault, for he had
omitted the flash of his torch with which he usually spared
himself the discomfort of a blazing muzzle in front of
him.

" Can you toddle down, Cartwright ? " the Major
asked. " Pretty quick—at once, in fact ? "

" Yes," said Cartwright. " Shall I dress ? I'm in
pyjamas."

" Oh—yes. Better dress,' said Potter. " In fact, better
bring your shaving kit—and a change. And——" He
mumbled, " Oh, hell——" and stopped altogether.

" What's up ? " demanded Cartwright, for in spite of
his tendency to stammer Potter did usually manage to
get out what was in his mind. It was only thoughts on
the subject of Parley that stumped him altogether, so
Cartwright knew a moment's hope.

" Is it—er—wagon-line, Sir ? " he asked.

" No," said Potter. " It's—but why don't you come
down ? You'd be here in ten minutes. Hardy's coming
up to relieve you. I've sent a chit down for your
horses."

That last knocked on the head a theory that had
quickly suggested itself, of a sudden need for some one to
report to the Infantry—some impending stunt. . . . And
it couldn't have been anything to do with an officer
having to go on some footling ' course ' or other. . . .
It couldn't have been a transfer—old Langridge, for
instance . . . but Cartwright didn't try any more to

fathom it as he went back to his hutch to dress ; he could learn from the signallers what he had failed to learn over the wire from the Major.

This time he flashed his torch and waited a few seconds before rounding the wall in front of the guns. He stuck his head into the signallers' door and said, " What's up at the battery ? "

They looked up, startled, and then turned and stared at each other. Then, looking still at each other and not at him, one of them mumbled, " Don't know, Sir. 'Ave —'aven't 'eard anything."

That, Cartwright knew, was a lie. But he could be at the battery in ten minutes, so he only said : " Tell Macdonald to bring my haversack and shaving and washing-kit, and a change, and a pair of slacks. I've got my glasses and revolver."

Ahead of him, when he was near the corner where the track joined the road, he saw the outline of an officer followed by a man with a valise on his shoulder. He called out, " Hardy ! " for there were some millions of chances to one that it was no other. But the couple stopped and appeared to confer for an instant and then went deliberately and unanswering past the track, towards St. Venant.

He knew then that it was Hardy and his man, as surely as he had known that the signallers had lied to him and that the men had lurked with some secret as he passed the guns.

Steadying the bulging pockets of his tunic and the loose money that jingled in his breeches he ran till he was pumped, and arrived at the battery sweating and breathless.

" Major—" he began—having, for once, omitted a salute where a salute was due.

" Sit down, old son," said Potter. " Sit——"

" But what the devil's up ? " If it turned out to be some novice's panic over nothing, he felt that he would have something to tell Potter.

" Old chap," said Potter, and he got up from the table and took Cartwright's hand, " it's a perfect sod, I'm afraid. Awful bad news has come through for you. Your father——"

" Oh, God ! " said Cartwright.

He sat down ; and then, because thought had been schooled to clarity and precision on such a point, he asked " Ill, Major ?—or dead ? "

Potter sat down and drew the two mugs and bottle towards him. He nodded. " I'm afraid—dead. I'm—you know—you don't know how sorry. Quick work it must have been. The telegram saying he was down with pneumonia came after I spoke to you—an hour after the other one ; handed in twelve hours before." He had poured out drinks. " You're to go, on special leave. Division's had a wire from further back instructing them. Sorry, old Cartwright. Thundering sorry. Good luck." He sipped his drink.

" Thanks . . ." said Cartwright, his mind moving again back among the clouds of hazy thought that the Major's message had disturbed concerning the love of men, and some inward balance. . . . " Thanks, old thing. Thanks awfully."

That, for the moment, seemed to be all there was to say. They heard some one outside telling Cartwright's servant with the haversack that Cartwright was within.

" It's not going to mean any unusual distress—financial bother and all that—I hope ? " Potter said. " He was getting on, I suppose ? "

" Sixty-five," said Cartwright ; " —no, sixty-six now. I'm getting on for forty-one—but we expected the old boy to last another dozen years. He seemed pretty fit four months ago."

" I suppose the strain has lowered the condition of all of them," said Potter. " There's been a lot of them last winter, conking out quite suddenly."

They heard horses in the yard, and Potter wearily said, " Well——"

They stepped out of the little " elephant " shelter into the rest of the room that held it like a piece of furniture, loaded up with sandbags ; and Potter said, " It's poisonous luck. Poisonous ! " His moment of peevishness

passed and when he spoke next it was apprehensively :
" Cartwright, I hope to the Lord you get back before any
dirty work begins. It's—I know it's a rotten thing to say
just now—but what d'you think ?—will a week——? "

Cartwright said, " Yes—I dare say—I should think
a week."

" It's—you do see what I mean ? " asked Potter, shy
again. " You're—the Colonel said so himself yesterday
after he and the General had been to look at your place
with that damned silly Heath-Robinson shower-bath
your chaps have made in the cowshed—he said you're
the only real old tough in the Division."

" I'll get back," he said, " as soon as I can."

It struck him that the section, too, must think well
of him ; and with the thought came the desire to see them
again and hear them say some word. " Well, I'd better
get moving," he said, and held out his hand. " It might
make the difference between catching a train somewhere,
and missing it. I've got to get back to the section
for a moment first."

" The section ? " said Potter. " What for ? "

" Oh——" Cartwright shrugged away, seeing that no
reasonable answer was possible, so he offered trivial
lies—" just one or two things. Letters I may need.
Field-Cashier's book. And my cap ; can't very well
go home in a tin-hat—sprinting in the blasted thing
for a quarter of a mile on the way here showed me that.
Well—good luck, Sir."

" *Sir* your grandmother ! " and Potter shook his hand.
" *I*'m the one to do any hat-raising there might be at
the moment. *We* all know—the Colonel and General
too—who has been the life and soul of the party for the
last three weeks. The old man said—just between
ourselves, you know—he touched wood and said it was
as neat a piece of soldiering as he'd ever seen, to get
away with a job like that show of yours with only two
casualties—and a shower-bath for the men. I hope to
God something comes of it. My own ribbon was awarded
for inventing a fly-proof latrine in Salonika. Very neat
gajit weighted with a couple of horseshoes. . . . Don't

pull my leg any more by saying ' Sir ' when we're quiet, by ourselves, like this. A good journey and good luck ! " He went back to the inner shelter over the bunks and table and bottle and mugs.

At the section they had finished their series and the men had turned in. The nights were hot, so that the gas-blankets were flung back from the doors in the bank. It was only in the farthest shack that there was a light, and in it Cartwright could see the two Sergeants sitting up in their blankets, with the solemnity of men engaged in one of those endless arguments.

Hearing the horses, old Crozier stuck his head out of the door.

" All right, Sergeant," Cartwright called. " I've had to come back to get some things."

Through the gap in the hedge he came upon the sentry and said, " All right. I expect you all thought I'd gone ? "

" Yes, Sir," said he. " It's come through that special leaf orders had come for you to go at once. I'm sorry about your bad news, Sir."

They were silent for a few moments under an apple-tree that had a ragged fishing-net flung over it, tufted with painted canvas for the reason that its leaves had withered and fallen from the blast of the gun it sheltered. Cartwright saw in the tableau a man whose father had just died, trying to impress with a suitable touch of philosophy a lad who already thought well enough of him. " He was a good soldier, my father," he said. " He stuck to his job. I never heard of his letting any one down."

The sentry said, " Yes, Sir."

" Well," Cartwright went on, stepping back to the path under the hedge that led past the signallers to the yard and his hutch, " I hope you chaps will let Mr. Hardy see what the centre section is made of while I'm gone." This, he knew, was the stuff to give them ; for already the centre-section drivers were developing a swagger of their own at the wagon-line. Parley had sent a couple of them up to the Major for conduct contrary to good order and military discipline.

" Coo ! " the sentry chortled. " You are coming back

o o

then, Sir ? The chaps said it's good-bye when special-leaf orders come through from on top without an application."

" No," said Cartwright, " I'm coming back."

Hardy sat up in his valise spread luxuriously on Cartwright's, and struck a match to light the candle behind his head.

" I only want my cap," said Cartwright. " It ought to be in the hole above the pillow ; not the one with the candle and whisky."

Hardy handed the cap towards the little shaft " Awful hard cheese about your governor," he mumbled. " I thought I might run into you on the way up——"

" Yes," said Cartwright, and he sat down on the bottom step. " I saw you thinking it."

Hardy smiled and looked silly. " Oh, well—I hate giving rotten news. I knew you'd get it in a minute, anyway. But I am sorry ; you know that ? "

" Yes," said Cartwright, " I know. Can I do anything for you, by the way ?—In town, a message, or anything ? Lord, I forgot to ask the Major."

" I don't think so, thanks," said Hardy. " My people hang out in Lincolnshire."

There was a shuffle of footsteps and a throat-clearing. In answer to Cartwright's " Yes ? " the voice of old Sergeant Crozier said, " I've brought up Bombardier Wilson, Sir. He wants to have a word with you before you go."

Cartwright shook hands with Hardy and said " Good luck ! " in answer to Hardy's " Good luck ! "

On the floor level, as Hardy blew out the candle in the hole, Wilson made a jerky sound of saluting and said, " I'd like to have just a word, Sir, since you've come back."

They stepped into the moonless light of the yard. Wilson still hesitated, indicating the Sergeant by a movement of his head haloed in the blackness of his tin-hat. " All right, Sergeant, thank you," said Cartwright, " I'll look in and see you on the way out. By the way, you want to look out for lights in those shacks when there's any flying going on."

"I thought you mightn't want him to hear," Wilson said when the Sergeant had gone. They stood by the relics of the farm's old dung-heap. Wilson was in the normal *négligé*—under pants, shirt, unlaced boots, helmet and box-respirator. "It was in case you don't come back. I thought there'd be no harm in asking."

"Asking what, Wilson?"

"If you're fixed up," said Wilson. "Fixed up for afterwards."

His meaning was obviously as clear to himself as it was obscure for Cartwright.

"After what, Wilson?" he asked. He was aware that Wilson liked him well enough; but he had taken Saunders's stripe too willingly for a man who was now soliciting for the job of groom or batman.

"After the whole lot," said Wilson. "After the War."

"But you've got a business of your own, haven't you?" said Cartwright, able now to see what the man was driving at.

"Yes," said Wilson. "That's just the trouble. I want a partner." The gaps and pegs in his shaken denture now introduced quaint clicks and slurs into his old mixture of Lancashire talk with New York. "'Strong i' th' arm; weak i' the head,' we used to say at home. It's the miners' motto. But no man can do work and get it at the same time. I can do the work all right; and I can do the pricing and that, to a T. I just thought that—afterwards—if you weren't fixed up——"

Cartwright held out his hand.

"Wilson," he said, grasping and shaking part of an implement that needed for its completion a short-handled pick or a shovel. "Wilson—honestly I don't know what to say. . . ." There was no hope of posturing here, as there had been with the sentry.

"Think it over," said Wilson. "No *need* to say anything yet. Fair do's, of course. Fifty-fifty. You've got my address in the section roll."

"I don't mean that," said Cartwright. "I've got a business of my own, you see. It's a hundred years old, and more. Solicitors. Its—it's—I mean, it's so——"

" Well——" said Wilson, " No harm in me asking, I suppose ? "

The handshaking was completed. They walked through the gap in the wall, into the orchard where the gun-snouts gleamed as two cold rings in the darkness of the scorched apple trees.

" The boys are sorry at your news, Sir," said Wilson. " They wisht you wern't going off like this."

" But I'll be back," said Cartwright. " You can tell them that."

" Gee—they'll thank me for waking them up to tell them a thing like *that !* " said Wilson.

Crozier's face in the candle-light did not wear its usual expression of ancient gravity. " Sir," he said, and jumped up standing among three sleepers, " did you tell the chap on duty that you're coming back ? "

" You people ! " said Cartwright. " You seem to think one can just pack up and clear out of this business —without even packing up, in fact."

" Oh, no, Sir. Not just like that, Sir. But your bit of trouble, Sir. And when special orders come down from up top—and an officer——"

" Well——" said Cartwright. " I think you're all wrong."

On that they shook hands and Crozier said, " Good luck, Sir."

MEDAL WITHOUT BAR   CHAPTER XCVIII

HE found in himself no impulse to send telegrams on this journey. Dorothy would know that he must be coming ; for whatever force— Henderson or Dorothy's father—had succeeded in having him detailed for special leave on ' Urgent private affairs ' would also have informed her of it.

He had a shave and a bath and breakfast at Victoria and went to the office to face the new fact before telephoning to Dorothy, and before old Mollison should arrive to start fussing.

Turnbull, surviving as the one male clerk in the office by reason of his sixty years, welcomed him drearily and gave him a packet of papers.

At the will he did not even look, beyond seeing that it was the one he himself had drafted five years before. There was a year-old codicil, placing the trusteeship of the estate in the hands of the testator's bank, for he could no longer put faith in the stability of such individuals as Cartwright himself, old Mollison who had developed asthma, and the Harley Street crony who was at the moment doing some research in Malta.

". . . To my son Charles . . ." Cartwright read, and then could read no more, for it did not particularly matter what followed. All that would be, as Turnbull said, "in order." ". . . my son, Charles. . . . " The words were the fleeting pressure of the Old Boy's bony fingers on his arm above the elbow when they had gone to Harley Street to get the chit for the morphia tablets. . . .

It was only its speed and its precision, Cartwright reflected, that distinguished this firm from other solicitors in the City of London. . . . It was characteristic of the Old Boy that he should have packed up and gone inside of three days, leaving a clear desk; that the announcement of his death should have reached the battery before any word of his illness ; and it was only the smile of Rennie that could soften the poignancy of Rennie's formula, ". . . We shall not look upon his like again."

He glanced through the schedule of securities, at the balance-sheet roughly drawn by Turnbull and old Mollison.

A memorandum on the small sheet of a telephone-pad written, presumably, by one of the girls, said "Captain Henderson (or Henson) is anxious to get in touch with Mr. Charles at the earliest opportunity. Very important. Preferably lunch." There was a note of Henderson's telephone number.

He pressed the buzzer on the desk and Turnbull told

him, in answer to his question, that the funeral was already over—yesterday.

He telephoned to Chiswick and found that Dorothy was at the hospital till three in the afternoon—where, of course, he could ring her up. The maid told him also that his mother was there, but that she was not yet down. Was there any message ?

" Tell her I'm very well," he said. " I'll be home to tea, with Mrs. Cartwright. I'll meet her at the hospital."

He was glad his mother was there—glad, too, that she was still in bed, for he knew that he did not yet possess the technique for talking to her.

He rang up Henderson's number ; but Henderson, of course, was not yet there. He left a message saying that he would call for him at 12.30.

Old Mollison arrived and saw the papers on the desk.

" It's all in apple-pie order, my boy," he said. " You'll have nothing to worry about there. Just one or two signatures." But it was not the question of probate, obviously, that was on the old man's mind. The thing that startled him was the threat to himself in this sudden destruction of his adjacent file. He told Cartwright the details of the attack and the quick illness, of the pig-headed carelessness that alone could have made such a thing possible—sweating in the office on a day that had been as close as Hades, leaving off a waistcoat to stroll towards lunch along the shady side of the Strand in a freshly-risen breeze.

Then the old man said, " You ? What about *you* ? How long have you got ? "

" Five days," said Cartwright.

" Is that all they'd give you,—under the circumstances ? " He was indignant.

Cartwright grunted.

Dorothy's father seemed to accept the situation and said casually, " Seen anything of your friend ?—the one-armed, one-eyed young fellow at the War Office ? I met him at lunch with your father a week or ten days ago."

" Not yet," said Cartwright, without bothering to

remind him that he had only been in the country about five hours. " We're lunching together to-day."

" Um . . . " said old Mollison. " Five days doesn't seem much time ; under the circumstances. Now that the boy's gone, too."

" What boy ? " asked Cartwright. " Gone where ? "

Old Mollison looked at him for a moment as though he had said—" Gladstone ?—who was Gladstone ? "

" *Your* boy," he said. " My grandson, John—this flying pilot business."

" John ? " said Cartwright. " Pilot ? "

" Last week—Monday it must have been. Yes, it was Wednesday that the old man took to his bed." Old Mollison soon settled the matter of which day it was. " Yes, Monday. He got your father's consent, as his guardian on the spot. He's at Calshot. There's enough boasting about our postal service at the front for you to have heard before leaving."

" I hadn't," said Cartwright. " The last from him was some argument about joining up, in the Infantry. I—I'm afraid I didn't answer at once."

Again Mollison said " Um. . . " And then, " I don't see that you had much to answer. Your father and I talked to him. But the facts seemed to be on the boy's side. Well—it leaves poor Dot fairly high and dry."

.   .   .   .   .

Henderson took his hat and stick from a peg and came down a long room rather like a railway goods-office. " God ! " he said, shaking Cartwright's hand. " The fellow must be made of brass. . . . Unwounded and unhung. We'll go to the club. I can do better there than anywhere else on ration-tickets." But his levity soon passed.

He was grave as they walked down Whitehall talking of the old man, of whom, it appeared, Henderson had seen quite a lot.

His gravity seemed to lead towards the peevishness that Cartwright had begun to associate with him. They talked a little of the sudden move from Palestine, of the retreat, and of the touch-and-go position now. "Oh, well," said Henderson wearily. "We'll win now, I suppose. Every one seems to think so. We've only got to go on not losing for a bit longer, and it'll come out all right, with the Americans. . . . Yes, we can't help winning—whatever's left to win."

When they had swallowed gin-and-bitters Henderson reverted to his first mood of robustiousness. When the lunch, with gin and tonic and lemon was ordered, he said, "The flying corps for your youngster, by the way, was my idea. I hope you approve."

"I don't," said Cartwright. "I think the whole thing's damned nonsense. He's only seventeen. I want to talk to you about that, Jim. I never gave my consent. Suppose I were to put my foot down; withhold my consent——"

"Suppose," said Henderson, "some one were to withhold their consent from you."

"Rot," said Cartwright. "He's seventeen."

"He's a damned sight nearer to one limit of subalterns' age than you are to the other."

"It's not altogether my fault that I'm still a subaltern," said Cartwright. "I spent a year at home as a Sergeant, instructing, don't forget. I'd have had a battery by now. Possibly a Brigade."

"Possibly," sneered Henderson. "Possibly, too, you'd have been among our countless glorious dead. Fat lot of good that would have done you. About as much as a battery or Brigade. Since when, by the way, has this thirst for advancement been upon you?"

"It isn't upon me," said Cartwright. "It's only reasonable though that—that—oh, Lord! You know well enough what I mean."

"Yes," said Henderson. "I do know what you mean. Honestly I do. You've come to the dead end, old Charles. Even if there are more massacres ahead, like the Somme and Passchendaele and last March, the supply of Captains and Majors will exceed the demand. Hosts of them have been found and dug out of secret places— places like I got you sent up there on the coast. Lots more are beginning to creep out and give themselves up, from a lot of cushy jobs. Lusty lads whose service has been years of health-giving rest or rest-giving employments. There's terrific talk among these fire-eaters now. 'In at the death. . . .' That sort of emetic. I know it must be pretty sickening to have just those two pips still. But the way to advancement, my dear Charles, is blocked. Only a flanking movement can serve you now." He paused, with a look of great cunning. "My object," he said, "in convening this meeting, is that you should become a Captain to-morrow or the next day, and a Major in the course of weeks. *Guaranteed*, Charles."

"Just *any* Major ? " asked Cartwright. " Because there's one subaltern senior to me in the battery. It's true the Captain ought to be in cold storage somewhere—but there's still a first-rate Major."

" No. Not *any* Major," said Henderson. " And I wasn't thinking of a battery. A Major of a very special and particular brand. On the lines of your own job. It's the very thing for you, old fellow, and I hope to God you'll take it. It's a new job—newish. It's ' Court Adviser.' . . . You buzz about, seeing that Courts-Martial are conducted according to the rules." He paused and fidgeted ; and then went on, " You see, look at it coldly, without any nonsense. You can't afford—it's not as though your old governor was still going strong, and young John hadn't joined up. You've done a fairish whack, too, and got nothing out of it—you're still only a full ' loot '——"

He went on talking thus ; and on . . .

When he had finished, and had sat for some moments looking at Cartwright, the sneer that had come to live about his lips was supplanted for a little time by a smile.

Cartwright said, in a voice that was toneless, " Jimmy, you know that if I could do it, I would. There's nothing to prevent any one from jumping at such a chance—things like ideals and patriotism and highfalutin stuff of that sort. We've done with all that. I know only one man—old Colonel Langridge—who still talks through ribbons and the Union Jack.   I see everything, old fellow, almost exactly as you've put it ; and I'd do it like a shot. Only—I can't. I've got to go back to that damned battery."

" *Got* to ? " said Henderson. " Of all the damned nonsense—why have you *got* to ? "

Cartwright only shrugged his shoulders. " For one thing," he said sardonically, " the beggars are expecting me."

" Pity to disappoint them ! " said Henderson ; and the sneer was back again. " Altogether too bad, I'm sure. Of course you're quite irreplaceable, too—! It must be that that makes it so difficult for you. . . . Oh, you ass, d'you think it's going to make a ha'porth of difference to any one in the world except yourself whether a subaltern in a certain battery is C. Cartwright or one of the thousands of Smiths or Browns or Joneses at the base, and the depôts ? "

" It was you," said Cartwright thoughtfully, " who once said to some cadets——"

" If you don't mind——" said Henderson, and the urgency of his disgust had to be observed and respected. " We'll leave anything I *used to say* out of this argument. And any other arguments we might have.   God Almighty ! I'm not talking to cadets now."

" No," said Cartwright. " It's just a conversation between full-fledged Samurai . . . I say, though, Jim "— and he became more eager over a thought than he had been for many a day—" what *has* happened to it, everywhere ? We were honest enough then, in those talks about the ' Officer Spirit ' and that sort of thing ; endurance and all that.   We believed in it all ; and so did every one else, and there was a certain amount of unblushing talk about it.   Quite decent man-to-man stuff.   When you come across it now, it's always in a soldier-story or else in the talk of a peculiar old fellow like the Becton Colonel, who's not quite of our generation.   Where's it gone, Jim, all that thundering unbreakableness of the spirit of man ? "

Henderson ordered two more gins and tonics.

" Search me," he said glumly. " I haven't got it. You seem to be the fella who saw it last."

" Yes," said Cartwright, and for an instant he was face to face with a jumble of objects, visual and dire. They were his father, now utterly gone ; John in an aeroplane beset by greenish little puffs ; Dorothy in black solitude— and a battery that did not yet know, and would not believe, that half a dozen men walking in file over turf had a tale to tell as a sharp line, black or dazzling white, on an aeroplane photograph. The fools would not see, left to themselves, that the difference between a walk of wagon-teams and a trot was the difference of a cloud of dust in an observer's telescope a yard or two from a telephone to his waiting battery ; they knew not that ' cease-fire ' could at one time be a word honourably wise, and at another fatally stupid. They still had the scepticism of the fools they were, upon such matters as tetanus and gas, and unchlorinated water. They had said, " Good luck, Sir," and " Come back, Sir. . . ." Just as those old others had said, " Come back " ; imposing upon him the old tryst wherein once he had ultimately failed. And he saw Rennie who had never failed a tryst. Whether pink and sprightly from a night of prodigious sleep, smooth from one of his famous half-minute shaves or haggard and foully daubed with grime and beard-fluff when the spirit in him was utterly fore-done, the spirit had always functioned to the extent of placing his body at the place of tryst. So it had been with Rennie, till the slipped ligature had set the fantastic spirit loose from the broken body.

And so he said to Henderson, " Yes. I saw it last. But it's gone now." For he could not delude himself into thinking that any spirit survived within himself to scrape kinship with Rennie's and whatever it was that had departed from Henderson to leave behind the nervy, jeering and cunning pot-hunter lunching with him. There might, perhaps, have been a glimmer of it in the old days—the days of Stuff Redoubt with Black and Sammy ; of Thiepval and its darkly frozen battlements of Bullecourt. But there was not a glimmer now.

Henderson could jeer and sneer his utmost—but unfairly ; for there was no motive from within that drew him back to that confounded battery. He would go to it only because he could do nought else. Whatever thrust and drew and bound him was not the force of any passion, but the drift of mere necessity.

. . . . . .

And thus, also, he let John go. There was not in him the power to stop the boy. The next day he went to Calshot to see him. He acknowledged his salute, shook hands with him and they went to lunch together.

" Not seen Henderson yet, I suppose ? " John said casually, when they had made some allusion to the death of his grandfather.

" Oh, yes. We lunched together yesterday," said Cartwright.

John, in the trappings of a man, was taking with his victuals the man's drink, beer.

" Well ? " he said.

" Well, what ? " said Cartwright.

" Anything doing ?—He told me there was a job for you."

" No, old man," said Cartwright. " There's nothing doing. I can't go scrounging after jobs—now."

" I should have thought," said John, " that now—after you've had about two years of it, with old Grandad gone—I should have thought that now would have been the time." Nothing came out of the pause to help him. He munched quietly and drank his beer. " I suppose it'll be a bit thin for Mother—not that I was much of a mainstay. But it leaves her a bit on the high and dry side, with both of us gone—and the Old Boy. That is, if I do ever get out."

" When," asked Cartwright, " do you expect to be through here ? "

" About the beginning of October," said John.

That left a bare three months.

TO Dorothy herself there was nothing, absolutely nothing, that he could find to say. He could only look at her, and marvel. He knew that she had been in touch with Henderson, because of the instructions that had come to the Division for his special leave and because of the elasticity of that leave. He knew also that Henderson nowadays had few restraints upon the things he said to women. He would have told her of that fantastic court-adviser job and of his ability to wangle it. She and his mother must have talked. Yet they treated him handsomely ; they boasted nothing, hinted nothing of the middle-aged orphan man's duty to his women.

Dorothy changed her immediate night duties to day ones.

In the nights thus salved for his delectation and his company there should have been some words wherewith he could have told her that the necessity which held him was no infidelity to herself. It was just a fact, like the fact that the hair on his head was a very dark brown, quite straight and beginning to go grey, whereas she could reasonably have preferred it to be sandy, or ginger—and wavy. There was no disloyalty or infidelity either way about that. It was her bad luck and his.

After three nights, lying in the dawn beside Dorothy who slept—or feigned sleep as he was feigning it—he knew that a fourth was as much as he could stand.

There had been, so the papers said, " some activity in the Lys sector."

Dorothy, alert to his lightest caress, but silent and dead beyond the torment of her woe, was more than any man could be expected to cope with. For there was nothing to be said or done. The wistfulness of her little gestures was unendurable. Her unpacking of a parcel on the second night, and the drawing forth from it of a night-dress that could have been folded into his cigarette-case was like a blow that smashed him. And her saying,

as she kissed him, " Dear boy—what would it matter ?—
a death one way or the other, or a birth, nowadays——"
And a man had to keep some sort of balance with things
like that going on about him. . . . One of the generation
of the broken-hearted, who have no tears. . . . And now
there was this business of John, with only three months
ahead. . . .

She had to be early at the hospital so he got quietly
out of bed when it was time, and lighted the spirit-lamp
under the kettle.   When she had wakened or abandoned
her pretence of sleeping, he brought the biscuits and the
tea and raised the window-blind to give them light enough
for the meal that would carry her till breakfast at the
hospital.   Any words, he supposed, would be good enough
to set the ball rolling, for all were equally grotesque.
With his arm under her white shoulders he said, " Darling
—my dear, to-morrow will make the fifth day—and the
Old Boy's business will all be done to-day—as far as I can
do it——"

" Do you want to go," she asked, " to-morrow ? "

Did he *want* to go ?—But what was the use, even now
when she had given him an opening, of talking ?   He
knew that there was none.   Very gently he said, holding
her closer to him, " To-morrow, or in two days or three—
sooner or later.   The beggars have left it up to me.
I've to go as soon as I can."

" I suppose so," she said.   " Might as well."

She finished the biscuit she was eating and drank her
cup of tea.   When he had finished his and lighted a
cigarette and disposed of the match, the cool, still strength
went out of her shoulders and they were shaken with sobs.

" Dot," he said, " not now, little girl.   Not now
—when——"

" I know," she said.   " I know, dear . . . yes.   To-
morrow.   This is awful.   Awful . . . Charles, dear boy.
If—when—Charles, will you ever come back ? "

With the hand holding his cigarette he sought for the
wood of the bedrail, and pressed upon it.

" Of course I'll come back, you silly," he said robustiously.   He pressed her shoulder with his other hand.

"Come back ? My dear—everything is different now. It's a different war altogether. You don't know, old girl. You wouldn't understand. But, honestly, it *is*. Chances are different. And every one knows it's only a question of time."

He did not expound his theory in full ; for—albeit his one hand was touching wood—any theory was better left unexposed, a challenge unvaunted to whatever Furies lurked about the path of man ; and his doom—so went the private theory—was the doom of a large proportion of a whole Division. Numbers must still come up— as they had done in the old lot—pretty much in rotation. There was just one dire possibility against him ; his number, to wit, might be still on the old roster and not on a new one. That, however, was an annihilating thought, and unthinkable. The alternative was the thought he adopted : even allowing for vagaries in the routine of Luck's workings, two or three of the battery's officers would have to go before him, and thirty, perhaps —or fifty—of the battery's men.

So everything was resolved into a matter of pace.

Time was the only element now. It governed, in- exorably, the destiny of John also ; for in three months he, too, would be in the race with doom. His turn also would be set in its proper place and in due succession to the turn of those ahead of him. Survival, his and John's, depended only on which should move the faster—the War itself, or the names above their own on the rosters.

"But let it be to-morrow, dear one," he said, knowing that it was impossible to sit still any longer while the race went on. "You can carry on with your old hospital better—without me butting in like this."

"Oh, yes," she said. "Better to-morrow, I suppose." And with that the strength went out of her again.

WHEN he was back at the battery he found that his name was " Uncle " again. Dickinson or the Major had tumbled to the obvious classification of him, probably from casual contact with some neighbouring battery of the older, time-worn sort wherein uncles were part of ' establishment.' At any rate, the Major's first words on his return were, " Uncle ! Hooray ! Jove, you've been quick, though ! "

" I thought you'd have moved," said Cartwright. " It looked, from the papers, as though——"

The Major shook his head. " Just a bit of sparring," he said. " They're coming to conclusions that the line is thinly held. It may be a blind, of course. But they don't think it is. Jerry isn't expected to do any more advancing ; not here, anyway. But your old section has to blaze away all night just the same, in case."

" Every one—all right ? " Cartwright asked.

" Yes," said the Major.

" Voo-voo ? He was out when I landed at the wagon-line."

" He's all right," said the Major thoughtfully. " Damn him. Uncle, is there nothing to be done ? A fellow like that makes one feel uneasy and rotten every time one has a drink. If he wasn't so far gone all the time he'd see himself that he oughtn't to be here. And he's got some kind of pull and backing behind him. He could get away if he wanted to."

Cartwright shrugged his shoulders. He did not, from his new understanding of the cycle of chance, want any one to leave the battery—not even Parley.

But Parley went.

.   .   .   .   .   .

The Major was sent away for four or five days—on some urgent course or for some instructional tour north or south. Parley was in command and came up to the main position, sending Hardy down to the wagon-lines and commanding Cartwright's presence from his section, at dinner. Dinner scarcely interrupted his sozzling ; and he talked some nonsense or other of what he could bring about for those officers in his ' command ' who should be loyal to him and for those who should not. He did not, he said, insist on being called ' Sir ' off parade by his officers.

" Don't worry, Voo-voo," said Dickinson. " You won't, till you get a crown up."

A squabble could have developed out of this, but somehow did not.

Orders arrived from Brigade, outlining a move to be carried out the next night. Parley saw some pretext in them for dictating a letter to the Adjutant. He demanded that the table should be cleared immediately of everything but bottle and mugs, and sent for the battery-clerk.

The clerk arrived with his book and pencil. His salute was a masterpiece of impudent burlesque.

Parley dictated his letter. ". . . Presumably, I take it, I am to withdraw my battery . . ." and he went on for a sentence or two, making difficulty where there was absolutely none in the original orders. " Read it, Metcalf," he said, when he had lost the thread.

Bombardier Metcalf cleared his throat and read : " Presumably I am to withdraw my battery——"

" Presumably, *I take it*, is what I said," snarled the commanding officer. " Why the hell can't you take down what I tell you ? "

Young Metcalf glanced, with a tendency to wink, at Cartwright and Dickinson who were carefully studying the curved ceiling of the steel shelter. His heels were together, his arms stiffly down—thumbs an inch behind the seams of his trousers. He was a railway booking-clerk at other times.

" ' Presumably,' Sir," he said, " means ' I take it.' "

Parley fixed his eyes on the Bombardier and the Bombardier stared twinkling back, knowing that for all their gaze upon the ceiling Cartwright and Dickinson were

P P

watching every flicker. The youth must have taken on some fantastic and maddening shape in the weird, muddled mind of Parley. Abuse in words foul and specially forbidden trickled from his loose lips. Metcalf actually smiled.

" Damn you ! " Parley screamed at last. " How dare you ? I'm commanding this battery—you're under arrest ! "

Metcalf saluted with a snap. " Very good, Sir. I'll bring the fair copy for your signature in a minute, Sir."

He withdrew ; and Parley's lips foamed more abuse. " I'll show him ! " he mumbled, " I'll show him ! I'll teach him to grin at me. I'll teach the whole damned lot of you. You'll see ! I'll give him—I'll give him———"

" I shouldn't worry," said Dickinson. " You won't give him anything, Voo-voo. Metcalf knows his King's Regulations, don't forget, a damned sight better than you do. He'll refuse to take your award and elect for trial by the Colonel."

" This is a *plot !* " Parley suddenly howled. " Witness that, Cartwright ! A dirty plot between an N.C.O. and his section officer to make a fool of me before the Colonel. . . . But d'you think it'll come off ? Haven't I been up against the whole damned lot of you all the time ? Me —senior to the Colonel, Cartwright. What d'you think of that ? "

" I think it's bed-time," said Cartwright. " At any rate it's time for me to be getting back, to begin a shoot."

He tied on his respirator and took his helmet and stick.

Dickinson got up to follow him out.

" You stay where you are ! " said Parley. " I won't have that—whispering behind my back. Turning even old Cartwright against me. You sit down."

" Oh, go to hell," Dickinson mumbled darkly and went out.

" Now," he said when they were outside and strolling leisurely in the road. " Now we've got him ! He'll make a wonderful ass of himself before the Colonel. He might even break down and weep, if we can get the Colonel to do it to-morrow. I'll stay out a bit longer and he can have one or two more, to send him over the edge. Blast him ! "

Metcalf wrote out the charge against himself next morning.

" Conduct contrary to good order and military discipline."

Bareheaded, with hair marvellously brushed, he stood between his ' escorts ' and heard it read to him. Then, calmly smiling, in answer to the statutory question, he said " No, Sir, I'll go before the Colonel, Sir."

It was impossible, however, for the Colonel to be bothered with a prisoner that day.

The battery moved at night to the neighbourhood of Lestrem. There was, according to the map, just one fold of ground that could possibly have afforded cover. Parley rode off during the day with the other battery commanders and the Colonel to walk the last bit, and reconnoitre positions. Cartwright tried to go with him ; Hardy tried to go, on the pretext of making some wagon-line arrangements. But these efforts impinged on the sore touchiness of Parley ; Cartwright and Hardy shrugged at each other and abandoned the impossibility of persuading him.

During the move at night Cartwright came upon the old doctor and the Adjutant. He asked one or two questions and the Adjutant said : " Don't worry, Cartwright. The Colonel showed him exactly where to put the guns, and marked his map. There's actually a little crest in front of the position."

In getting the guns in there were some absurd moments of bickering, for Parley screamed out the ridiculous order, " Limber supply."

" I say, you know, Parley," Cartwright remonstrated quietly. " Why ?—Dash it, we mustn't keep limbers lying about up here. It's absurd. It's *never* done."

" Are you commanding this unit ? " asked Parley, " or am I ? You're not even second-in-command. Hardy's second-in-command."

" I'm not commanding any battery," said Cartwright. " I'm just trying to prevent your making a damned fool of yourself—and of the whole lot of us. Limbers stuck about a battery position!—" He went off sullenly, reflecting that it was scarcely worth squabbling about ; and started the men putting up some nets before they began any digging.

An hour or two later, when the detachments were in shallow, narrow earthworks by the guns, he found the Mess installed in a cellar by the roadside, three or four hundred yards behind. Parley was seated at the table, pompous as Ludendorff ; maps, papers, revolver and glasses, the whisky-bottle and a mug were before him.

Cartwright looked about for another mug and sat down. From outside he heard the stamping and shuffle of horses without any chink or clink of harness.

" What the devil's that ? " he asked, with casual curiosity.

" That," said Parley bombastically, " is the emergency wagon-line gun teams. In the orchard."

" Good God ! " said Cartwright. " Horses ? Up here ? "

" Yes," said Parley, and he gave the inconclusive hiccough of the man whose machinery for hiccoughing has grown weary and listless. " Ec-exactly. Horses up here ; and I don't want any more insubordination from my subordinate officers. You men don't try to treat the Major like this, do you ? "

The fellow, Cartwright realised, had to be swallowed somehow. And something had to be done about the horses.

" Parley," he said, " you know what you remarked about fellows who support you and are loyal and obedient to you. Well, old thing, I'm one of them. I want you to make a success of commanding the battery."

" Well—why don't you let me command it, then ? " he said childishly.

" About these horses," Cartwright went on. " I suppose you must have about fifty of them here—away from the wagon-line. And all those men. Just think what that means in the way of humping rations and forage unnecessarily—in addition to bullets—and fifty horses less for them to do it with. And then there's the possibility of being shelled, up close like this. If you lost a lot of horses unnecessarily you'd get into an awful scrape."

" This is where they're going to stay, all the same." And Parley performed a rather insecure little strut. " This is open warfare, don't forget. The battery under my command is going to be ready to move—at a moment's notice."

Well, thought Cartwright, it could not seriously matter —just for a night. Next day something would have to be done. Brigade was not far away, farther down the road.

As orderly officer he was at the guns before dawn, assembling the director on its tripod, so as to be ready for the first glimmer of light for planting the aiming posts. As the sky lightened he pottered about a hundred yards or so in front of the guns where there was, he knew from the map, a meagre rise in the ground from which he could pick up some point in Merville.

As it grew lighter still he thought, peering through his glasses, that he had found the rise, for there was the smear of shadows and crazy patterns of standing brick-work that must be Merville. He waited for something that might be an identifiable spire or tower to detach itself from the heap.

Then, lowering his glasses as soon as he thought he had found what he was waiting for, he glanced back towards the battery.

He saw that the only rise of ground within the limits of the whole waking horizon was not in front of the guns but just behind them.

There was a sudden feeling of clamminess on his fore-head and at the back of his neck. He folded up the dazzling white square yard of map in his hands, stuffed it into his pocket and ran back to the guns. From them the view of Merville was as fine as from the paltry hundred yards in front where his director-tripod stood.

" Limber up ! " he shouted to the senior Sergeant who

had come to meet him for orders. " Limber up as quick
as you damned well can. And don't let the blighters
make any more movement than they must. . . . Put that
fire out ! " he yelled to the cook, who was on his knees
blowing lustily on the sticks he had kindled—for Cartwright
himself had rubbed it well into him that the more flame
he made the better, since more flame meant less smoke.
The flame leapt merrily. " Jump on it, man ! Quick !
Water—anything to put it out ! "

Then softly he said to the Sergeant : " Every blasted
gun is in full view, Sergeant. Get that director in and
get down into the holes as soon as you've limbered up.
I'm going to get the teams. We've got to get out of
here ! "

The ghastly light grew against the darkness as though
by the steady turning up of a wick. He saw the men,
with bands of underpants and sloppy socks between
unlaced breeches and unlaced boots, tugging at the
limbers and lifting the gun trails ; and he ran, for all he
was worth, for the Mess billet and for the horses in Voo-
voo's crazy ' emergency ' wagon-line.

This was an emergency good and proper.

The light came impartially from the flank of both
Jerry and the battery.

He could have sat on a trail and shot the battery
in on its target with one half-shut, naked eye.

" Turn out the drivers ! " he shouted from the road.
" D Battery drivers ! double ! "

The stable-picket, clattering the lantern that he had
blown out some minutes before, answered something.

" Yes. Turn them all out, sharp. Harness up like
hell." And then he rested, fairly puffed ; for sprinting
had no place among an Artilleryman's accomplishments.

The Corporal in charge of this invention of Parley's, a
lean and serious individual named Lawrence, who had
travelled in cretonnes (but was destined to travel in
cretonnes no more), ran up to him buttoning his
tunic. " The men will be dressed in a minute, Sir,"
he said.

" Dressed ! Good God, man ! " said Cartwright.

"Dressed! Corporal, for the love of God get the teams harnessed and into the road—by Golly, come on—*I'll* get 'em out."

In a few moments he was among the men. "Harness and saddle up, you fellows," he shouted. "Come on. Blow that titivating. To hell with your breeches there——" they were struggling with saddlery now, some of them bare-footed, dragging traces across the turf to their horses.

There was just one hope : any Artillery observer—Teuton or Anglo-Saxon, sober or drunk—would find a six-gun battery laid out to twinkle at him, bang in the open and less than two thousand yards away, sheerly incredible ; a delusion of optics.

But distant objects far down the road towards Hinges, the ragged poplars of the Canal three miles away were growing up—positively, it seemed, *squirting* up—out of darkness into the light.

A team jingled out of the lines, ready. The centre driver had underpants and no breeches ; the lead had breeches but neither tunic nor helmet. "Off you go ! Hell for leather. To the guns," said Cartwright. Then, "No. As you were. Stand fast." He was making a fool of himself. . . . Cat on hot bricks . . . hysterical. "Corporal Lawrence," he shouted. "No. Dismount, Corporal. *You* won't want a horse."

Lawrence came up to him. "Go to Sergeant Crozier at the guns and tell him to wait for the teams. Keep dead still, not a single movement till the teams come. Then hook them straight in and let them go—starting with number one gun nearest the road—at about twenty yards' interval. The gunners to stand fast. Don't worry about the kits till I come and tell you. All right —oh, keep as low as you can when you're fifty yards from here. Jerry can see you. I'll tell the drivers."

The six teams were in a line, with the first one on the road. "Listen, you fellows," he said. "You've got to pull the guns out. I'm going up the road a bit. Wait here till I stop ; then come up to me, slowly. As soon as you're up square with me—gallop. You go to number six gun, the next team to number five, the last to number one. As soon as you've hooked in come back, hell for leather as far as here. Then *walk*. Pull off the road after you've passed here—anywhere you damned well like, as long as it's *off the road*—on either side—pull clear about fifty yards. And mind—*walk*. No dust or you'll get it in the neck. There won't be any more orders ; so don't wait for any. Just get there, hook in and get back— number one first, then two—so as not to get tied up. It ought to be done in two minutes."

He walked off ; and as he stopped and retreated a few yards when Merville began to come into view, a shell whizzed over and burst somewhere on the ground well short of the battery. . . . " Walk, march " he heard the leading driver say, not in the tone of a command but of mere information to those behind him. Another shell burst—also short, though not as short as the first one. " You'll do it," he shouted as the teams came up. " Only whiz-bangs so far——"

The teams were past him, galloping in a wild cloud of dust beside the *pave* of the road. . . . But dust didn't matter now.

He doubled after them and left the road, cutting straight across to the guns. Shrapnel came, sneezing and sizzling, short and bursting very high. Then some burst over—not so high. Two batteries were flinging it over, or three. . . . Number one gun and limber lurched up on to the road, swerved and were away as the next team plunged into its gallop with number two. " Off you go ! " he shouted to number three, as two got near the road. Then " Go on, four." The shrapnel had begun to puff at the road ; a burst cracked over number three as it disappeared over the little crest.

The odds were that number four would pass before another came.

" Five and six ! " he yelled through the din, grabbing the bridle of five's off-leader to signal his change of orders. " Five and six, go back straight. Not the road—he's waiting there for you. There's nothing in your way till the stream. Then turn left towards the road, out of B

Battery's way." He stood away from the horse, then yelled, " Go on."

It was done quickly and well. While only twenty or thirty shells had been able to come, confused and a little wild, from the presumably mystified individuals a mile away, the teams were away out of sight.

Two or three men knelt and stooped between two of the gun-nets over Lawrence.

It was the same dirty, monotonous mess, thought Cartwright wearily. The same as ever—on and on. . . .

There was one little hole in the back of the Corporal's neck where he had for so long worn a stud to hold down a spotless collar, and then for years had worn no stud at all.

" He's dead," he said to the men. " We'll cover him up and leave him till dark. We've got to get away from here. Break up and sneak off separately. Shooting might begin on this place—*properly*—any minute now."

One of the gunners suddenly felt a stiffness and a pain in his leg ; and the reason was found to be a bullet that had gone cleanly through his thigh. It was the novelty of his condition that seemed most to appeal to the man. *"* Straight froo, chum ! " he kept saying to any one who listened. " Straight bloody well froo ; and I never so much as knew it."

Cartwright saw an easy opportunity for cutting something of a dash with these shaken fellows.

His own excitement had gone. At the bottom of his mind was the immense relief in the fact that the Major was on leave, Hardy at the wagon-line and Parley and Dickinson probably still asleep in the cellar. The shells were bursting at random over the crest (roughly in B Battery's direction). It was harmless so far as they—and because of their protection, he himself—were concerned.

" Come on, laddie,' he said to the wounded man, most fatherly, " you come with me. We'll tie you up at the Mess, all ready to go home. You other fellows keep down in the holes and pick up some of your kit. Report at the Mess—and mind, no bunching. One at a time, and don't all take the same track till you're over the crest."

With an arm around the proudly punctured one he set off. No shells bothered them on the way. It must have been that the observers opposite were trying to puzzle out the inexplicable performance, assuming also that when a battery galloped away the gunners went with it. Isolated loafers were no fair target in those days for an enemy battery's allowance of ammunition.

Before leaving the road for the orchard he saw three or four of the teams in the distance standing with their vehicles wide of the road. The others, presumably, were hidden by odd bits of hedge or brickwork. He ordered a horse to be saddled for him, tied up the gunner's leg with dressings over spots of iodine and sent him off down the road with Dickinson's batman. Then he went down into the cellar.

He had had a vague plan of lighting the candle, shaking Parley up and talking to him very quietly. The ultimate result of the talk was clear enough in his mind—it had been clear from the moment that he had held his breath, folded up his map and doubled back from the director to Sergeant Crozier : Parley, bag and baggage was to be clear of the battery by lunch-time, on his way to the D.A.C., to the base, to Becton or to Timbuctoo.

But Parley was already awake, talking to his batman when Cartwright got down the steps ; and quietness became at once an impossibility. There was an obscene, startling loathsomeness about Parley sitting up in his sleeping-bag in costly pyjamas open at his pink, softly pneumatic throat. As he blinked in the candlelight, the dirty sleep that had just departed from him gave a Mongolian ugliness to his eyes. He whined at his man, foully abusing him, dithering some complaint or other about the mug of tea before he had tasted it. To Cartwright he said, ceremonially, " Well, Mr. Cartwright— what have you to report ? "

" Well, *Mr. Cartwright!* " snapped Cartwright ; but he gulped down his suddenly wild hatred of the small round head of Parley with its cluster of silky black curls, of the idiot's little moustache over the fat, pink and wet lips, of the peculiar smell of him and his flea-bag in the close little cellar. To the man he said, " Leave that tea on the table and shut both doors as you go out. I'll call when you're wanted."

Then he shook Dickinson. " Wake up, Chubby."

" You're under arrest, Cartwright," Parley said. " I won't have familiarity from my officers on duty—you're orderly officer, aren't you ?—in the presence of the men——"

Cartwright stared some moments at the miracle of Voo-voo. The incredibility of it—pyjamas and sickly, sickening smell and all—brought quietness upon him again.

" You hopeless, bloody fool," he said. " Shut up."

Voo-voo gave some indication of speech or movement, but Cartwright said " No. . . . Shut up ! "

He drank Voo-voo's rejected tea and then said, " Let's have your map."

" You've got a map," said Voo-voo. " You signed for one yesterday."

" It's your map I want," said Cartwright. " With the battery position marked by the Colonel." Then he saw Voo-voo's lovely map-case—since where should Voo-voo carry a map but in a lovely map-case ?—and took it from near Voo-voo's feet. He took also his revolver, and put it on the table—for Voo-voo was, after all, incalculable.

" You're under arrest," said Voo-voo. " Don't forget that—I place you under arrest."

" For the love of God," said Cartwright, " shut up, or I'll hit you. Come here a minute, Chubby."

Dickinson slipped his feet into his boots and came over to the map spread on the table.

" There ! " said Cartwright, indicating the Colonel's pencil mark on the map. " Not *there*." He indicated another spot on the map, five hundred yards or more in front of the mark. " That's where the battery was——"

" Why aren't you reporting the situation to *me* ? " demanded Voo-voo, and Cartwright swung round on him.

" You ? " he said. " Because you're a congenital idiot, a doddering, slobbering swine——" his further descriptive touches served their purpose of the moment, which was to disperse a dark cloud that was obscuring his vision, to break up a mob of words that was engaged in a stampede for exit, and to give young Chubby Dickinson something to bite on. " You've planted a battery down in the open when all you had to do was either to give your map to one of us, or else measure fifty paces from the stream—instead of five or six hundred. You've killed a man. Your Corporal Lawrence, Chubby ; this bagful of tripe has killed him getting the guns out of that mess. God damn him ! "

" I'm going to the Colonel," said Voo-voo.

" Put those blasted feet of yours back in your flea-bag or I'll jump on them," snorted Cartwright, and the nails of his boots made a noise on the bricks of the floor. " Understand ! " he said, as the feet disappeared again into the Jaeger. " You'll go to the Colonel when he sends for you. Not before. I'm going to see him now. If you try to shove that beastly face of yours outside the door Chubby will smash it. Won't you, Chubby ? "

Chubby came from Liverpool, from some Insurance business or other and in Liverpool, apparently, it was no great drain upon a man's resources that he should smash a sufficiently displeasing face.

" Nicely, thank you," he said.

Cartwright folded up and pocketed the map and picked up Voo-voo's revolver, for he was going to see how the horses were in the teams, on his way to the Colonel ; and his own revolver was heaven knew where in his kit. Then he hesitated—thinking for a moment on the ways of Luck. Finally he took the revolver on the principle of carrying an umbrella on a cloudy day to prevent rain from actually falling.

No horses had been hit. Only a dial-sight had been broken ; and two or three drivers were anxious to get back to their cellars for their breeches.

He unlimbered the guns in their proper positions and sent the horses back to the orchard, since there was visible ground behind again, and they could not get to the wagon-line till dark.

By noon Voo-voo had gone from them—map-case, sword and all.

By night Hardy was in command at the guns and Cartwright at the wagon-line.

MEDAL WITHOUT BAR   CHAPTER CI

THE Major came back. Though he had reported at no Headquarters or dropped in to no Mess on his two-mile walk to the wagon-line, the first words he said to Cartwright, beaming on him through his glasses and wringing his hand, were—" Uncle ! Stout fellow ! Well done ! I mean Voo-voo."

" Yes," said Cartwright, " He's gone. We shall not——" but he stopped.

There was a peculiar ghastliness about the whole Voo-voo affair. The man seemed, too, in the manner of his going, to have abused an opportunity, to have missed a turn which must now fall upon another.

" The account I've heard," said the Major, grinning, " is too good, I think, to be true. You gave him one hour to clear right out or you'd shoot him in return for Corporal Lawrence. You called him twenty-six nasty things without repeating yourself, and you disarmed him. You've still got his revolver."

" Good Lord ! " said Cartwright, " so I have ! I picked up the darned thing in case there were horses to be put out."

(Cartwright collected neither helmets nor fuses, neither pieces of driving bands nor bits of aeroplane propellers. He has a few odd pieces of leather-work done by the saddlers—of the old battery and of the new—a case for nail-scissors somewhere, a sort of folding scabbard for two razors, a divided wallet for bottles of aspirin, cascara, thymol, iodine and permanganate of potash. . . . Voo-voo's revolver ironically remains his only strictly martial souvenir.)

"Those hairy things are looking pretty good," said the Major, looking towards the horses.

"Plenty of grazing," said Cartwright. "And damn all to do."

For the War, it seemed to him, had got stuck. Things—a lot of things—were still in the air ; but from day to day they stayed there. He had been at the wagon-line two days or three—but they were days that seemed like the beginning of an age. One product only of the slow machine continued to be ground slowly forth—casualties—Voo-voo and Lawrence and the youth shot through the thigh. A driver had taken a splinter in the stomach coming back from the guns on Cartwright's first night with them, when the morning's performance had kept the whiz-bangers opposite a little livelier than usual. B Battery had lost a couple of men. The other product of the machine—the end of it all—was still, it seemed, in complete abeyance.

On the 19th of July Rudolf Binding had written, "I know that we are finished."

But Binding was a cool, balanced philosopher, a long-sighted observer—and in a Staff billet where worsts and bests were seen both sooner and clearer than in rubble-heaps and barrows and hutches.

Victory, ultimate and final, was never doubted among the rubble-heaps and hutches any more than Binding now doubted ultimate defeat. Survivors on the Somme of 1916 and about the Salient in 1917 had never doubted it—arguing that ground gained was conquest. Survivors at the retreats and routs of the 1918 Spring had never doubted it—arguing that ground lost was conquest ; for the enemy was outrunning his guns and supplies, scattering his strength, using up his reserves.

And now the Americans were giving an account of them-selves, unlimited in their numbers, incalculable. . . . The point in question was not whether we should win or lose. The only question was—"When ? "

At that pace—the pace of July and earliest August—there was no indication of an answer. It could have gone on and on, till John had come out to a fighting squadron, and after ; till the battery, without necessarily moving its position, was thinned slowly out of its old horses and hands in the course of daily routine and from causes that now were perfectly natural—till it was the ' old battery ' no longer, but ragged survivors again, like the other battery, wreckage hanging on to wreckage, outliving any normal, decent span. . . .

Then the pace altered so that memories thereafter lack the orderliness of any chronological sequence, the crescendo and cadence of dramatic development or climax. They merge into the single vividness and into the chaos of a detonation—and the wild, directionless scamper for safety.

By the end of August the battery had entrained at Aire, in a blurred past, for the Somme. It had trekked through Corbie, through the colossal emporium of ammunition at Bray and northwards, along with the course of battles, through Ham to St. Quentin. It had seen prisoners passing till it had ceased, from boredom, in its bitter arguments as to their probable number. It had seen wounded men and dead till it no longer turned its head away from them, nor widened its eyes to stare.

It was grown tough ; and it was growing wise and canny. It could scratch up shelter out of nothing against the sun, against rain and against splinters. It could dig and scrounge with the oldest stagers and exchange sardonic back-chat with the best of them. Some, of course, had gone ; a dozen, perhaps—wounded, slightly and cleanly or so that only luck and hob-nailed insides could carry them as far as the base. A few were dead and others tired into worthless apathy of dysentery or boils and tonsilitis.

It was no longer a question whether the horses were fit according to any standard of fitness. The only questions were whether another journey from wagon-line to guns could be got out of them, whether two miles to water—water—and two miles back was better for them three times a day or worse than only two waterings. The Colonel had fought against senior immigrants coming to

the Brigade—his last successful fight in that respect—
and Hardy was Captain instead of Voo-voo.

.   .   .   .   .   .

By mid-September the old wheel was again visibly
turning.

The Infantry that had come with them from Palestine
was a thing of the past.   The subaltern who had reported
the machine-gun below Kefr-Malik now commanded
perhaps sixty of the old company of poachers and ploughmen among the host of reinforcements ; for the Company
Commander was dead, his second-in-command dead and
another subaltern wounded.   They were training behind
the lines.

Eight or ten or another dozen of the battery had
gone.

Big things were ahead up to the north-east of Peronne.

Letters stated that John would be coming out any day
now ; and Hardy was dead.

A third star was sown on one of Cartwright's tunics, and
fresh braid.   He wore them for some weeks, commanding
the wagon-line and beholding the wonder that even to
him was new—the routine of night bombing by aeroplanes.
Two Sergeants came back from a Lewis-gun course, and
the battery's Lewis guns were drawn from Ordnance.

At odd, fantastic hours of twilights and dawns
Cartwright himself took the gun, with a Sergeant standing
by, to form some estimate of the flier's chances against the
weapon, but he could form none ; whether the tracers
seemed to go through the machine and through the
pilot himself, or whether they missed him by miles, the
flier plodded steadily on and appeared to get safely home
again.   Neither did any detached study of machines,
floating among Archie bursts or mixed up in a dog-fight,
give any clue as to their margin of risk or the magnitude of
their hazards.   Shells could burst under them, over them,
apparently inside them and they would go on till suddenly
—and once in a great while—when no shell seemed to
have burst even neighbouringly, a flame and a trail of soot
would come spinning to earth.

Fights were the same in their baffling unpredictability. At one time there would be a mix-up wherein it seemed that wings themselves and tails must become entangled— and nothing would happen. At another a single dive to the attack, a rip of sudden fire and there would be the spinning flame and trail of soot.

And then John was said to be out.

This marked, to Cartwright's mind in its workings at that time, the end of the last lap in the race; and the War had won it.

The immigrant Captain came with an arm and a foot wounded and healed as ragged as his tunic and his ribbons.

Cartwright went back to the guns. All that remained of the exaltation of his rank was the darker line around his cuff and the darker spot between the two stars whereon for a matter of weeks the rain and fiendish sun had had no play.

He had many things to learn in the next days and weeks. He slowly learned them : to watch those incredible fights in the air and at the same time to believe the obvious truth that there was no reason in the world why one of the frail contraptions should be John's ; to hear a machine flying eastwards at bedtime and not to lie awake like a fool to hear if it ever came back ; to count six in a lot going over and to realise that it signified little to him, personally, if only five—or four—came back ; to yearn for a comforting of Dorothy with some comfort that he knew he could not give.

He could not, now, write even to Henderson.

He was sick enough of it—dead and utterly sick. There were stretches of unhurt country and standing harvests ; reaping machines clean and untwisted into any of the familiar mockeries ; but a turn in the road, a crawling forward to some little knob of ground would discover the mockery again—rubble and charred, jagged timbers ; a face with unwinking eyes and chest turned upwards to the sky while the heels of the same carcass pointed skyward with the toes to the ground ; a fly creeping out of the nostril—and the stench that came to the beholder not from without, but seemed to revive, slowly from within, where it had been only waiting, smothered.

Men crumpled up, unloading the wagons at night, reeling up wire that had been laid out before the order had come to move on, cooking, cleaning their boots or loafing to look at American engineers laying a trolley-line. . . . They would crumple up and groan, and grin the old hideous grin ; or else just gurgle and be still. . . .

It was all over, too. That was the meanly exasperating part of it—all, as every one said, bar the shouting. They were still a prodigy on the other side, the old soldiers as hard as flint, and the haggard boys. With their backs to a crumbling wall and the world against them they were a prodigy of valour and idiocy ; for only massacre remained. They believed still in the solidity and the brave colours of a bubble that was already burst. . . . And still men could not leave it.

Chance, incidentally, was working smoothly along the lines of the scheme that was immutable in Cartwright's mind. Only the aboriginals had so far gone. Voo-voo and Hardy among the officers ; none of the post-Palestine reinforcements among the men. Whether men and officers were picked off on different rosters, or roughly the same one, he could not be sure with any confidence. Safety for him, in either case, meant safety for the others first. A concern, therefore, in the conservation of the battery became his surviving passion. The horses began to be a factor in the cycle of Chance.

Horses and mules ; gunners, drivers, N.C.O.s, Dickinson and the Major merged into a single, precious thing for his jealous guarding. He lied freely about ammunition when he knew (as any half-wit would have known) that orders for a move would come before a dozen rounds could be fired. Thus he saved horses from dragging another load and drivers from the hazard of a journey. Once, when the Captain for some reason or other could not do it, he had to take twelve wagon-loads from an abandoned position to a new one after twelve had already been delivered. He suspected that they could not be
ded there. He took his second dozen loads a mile

beyond the battery while the roads were still quiet on the heels of the Infantry, and dumped them by the roadside, ready for the next advance. He reported to the Major (with empty wagons) that the ammunition was ' correct.'

What looked like altruism and a fund of energy quite inexhaustible was, in fact, the strictest economy. In dashing out of whatever hole or cranny that sheltered them in their sore and utter weariness to see what any near and sudden din might mean, he saved himself by keeping Dickinson and the Major, his predecessors, underground.

He studied air-casualties to see only how rapid was the movement on John's roster.

Then, under a clear enough sky early in October the Major took his turn and was wiped away. The walk to the O.P. of the moment and back to the battery made a pleasant stroll after tea.

The Major spent an hour with Cartwright, chatting and looking towards the promise of Lille, and then set off on the walk back with the signaller who had come up with him. They had been gone about ten minutes when Cartwright's signaller picked up his instrument saying, " ' Ooray, Sir, that bit of a strafe didn't get the wire. . . . Yes. Yes. . . . Oo? . . . Cripes! All right, chum." To Cartwright he said : " The Major's took it, Sir. In the foot. About half a mile down, Sir. Along the wire. The bloke with him has T'd into the line. Shall I come, too, Sir ? '

" Yes," said Cartwright. " Might as well pack up. Tell the battery first to send up the stretcher."

It was not a bad wound ; but bad enough to produce the old cheese-like pallor and to twist the shy smile into the old, haunting grin.

The going of the Major was disturbing enough, but more disturbing still was the going, next, of the subaltern who had come after the departure of Voo-voo.

He had gone off, with a Sergeant and his groom to meet a Staff-officer from Corps who was to show him and other subalterns where there was to be a forward Corps dump of ammunition. The Sergeant and the groom came back in the evening to say that he and the Staff-officer were killed.

He had not been out three months.

This showed that in the ways of Chance there was, after all, no system whatever ; and the discovery was a staggering one.

The next shell for the battery could be Cartwright's, though there was still Dickinson and possibly a hundred men (with the somewhat vaguer possibility of horses and mules) ahead of him.

There was neither fairness nor design.

Any tumble of flame and filthy smoke could be John— though John had not been in the running for more than the waxing and the waning of a single moon, while others were still at it who had seen the circle of years.

Brooding in sudden and strange silences, or flinching as all men now flinched—openly when there was any din— for rest was now scarce and consecutive hours of sleep rare—he knew that he still could have written to Henderson. A wangle would be easy ; for there was a host of desperadoes clamouring to be in it now that it was all over—bar the shouting and a few more buryings. They were chafing at last for a sight of France, agog for their gallop to the Rhine and vengeance on the Kaiser. The risk in their way was small now against their just meed of glory. . . . Henderson would work something, thinking none the less of him.

But he did not write except to say, as all were saying, that the end was very near.

There is neither pride nor shame for him in the statement that he could not write that tout's letter. It was no peculiarity of Cartwright's own. There were thousands and tens of thousands such as he, hanging on for the simple and only reason that they could do no otherwise ; that is, for no reason at all, since all reason was coldly ranged against such futile hanging on.

He was not particularly Cartwright—with John buzzing about frailly in the sky and Dorothy waiting more ghastly than a starveling at home. He was not particularly Cartwright any more than the hundred thousand surviving others were particularly Smith or Harrison or Williams or Robinson. He was something of the blood and the bone, the haunch and the hoof and the guts of —the battery. He was only a link, a mere buckle in the ultimate perfection of its harness, a man of its still unbroken men. Wheresoever the section (the battery, the company or the platoon) should go there must he (and those others) go also. There was no nonsense about it, either; no illusion; none of the " Far, far better thing " business.

It simply was so.

At the head of the battery (before the Captain of B was given a crown and the command of it, and while the Captain was away on some detached detail) ; somewhere in the middle of it when the Captain and the new Major were both there ; with ' the Circus ' at its tail when the Major was present and the Captain away— somewhere or other, with the battery's movements he also had to move.

It was at the tail of the battery, as its second-in-command, that he rode through Lille ; for the new Major had not yet come and the Captain was in command, and it was already like the first wildness of peace.

Then, in three or four days it was war again with a snarl in the air and a stampede by the new canvas water-troughs, with a man brained and tumbled down still wearing on his head the brim only of his steel helmet and in the buttonhole of his pocket the flowers tossed down to him from a window in Lille.

The Major was on the point of joining them so the Captain stayed with the horses and left Cartwright in command of the guns.

The Colonel called him to the telephone on the second evening of this new war and said, " A young puppy has been inquiring here who we are. I've sent him along to you with another of the same kidney, as he claims to be your son, in search of the 'plane that crashed somewhere in front of you this morning. The battery orderly is showing them the way."

Cartwright thought, with a glow of relief, of the hours

of safety behind the youths and before them while they visited brigades and batteries on foot. . . .

The orderly in due course lifted the blanket from the cellar doorway and John's face came into the light and out of it again. " Come on, Jumbo ! " he shouted. " It's quiet as anything down here—not a stronghold of Fritz's—only my guv'nor."

" John, you young scoundrel ! " said Cartwright, and shook the fellow's hand. " Come in and—have a drink." This, the only current formula of welcome was one which he had not applied to a son before.

" I should think so ! " said John. " So'll Jumbo— after what we've been through."

Dickinson was introduced, and Jumbo was accepted as Jumbo, a twice decorated swashbuckler whose years added to John's fell short of Cartwright's by five or six.

" God ! " said Jumbo, when the drinks had been allotted, " how you fellows don't go stark, staring, beats me. Here have the Duchess and I been crawling on our bellies for about forty miles in a barrage and that Colonel of yours had the sauce to ask ' *What* shelling ? ' Whew ! What a life ! Come on, Duchess, drink up and we'll crawl forth to have a look at poor old Carnie's bus and then back again, sharp."

" Bus ? " asked Cartwright. " There's devilish little to see of any bus. Some of my chaps bolted out as soon as it crashed ; but the clock had gone before they got there ; so had the compass, the gun and most of the prop. A working party of Jocks was nearer than us. They'd taken the pilot, too, dead."

" No," said John. " We've heard. He'll be all right. Mostly concussion. I thought he'd be dead, right enough, the way he came down."

" Oh ! " said Cartwright.

And John said, " Yes. I was in the other bus. I got old Fritz, by the way, over on his side. He went down just like Carnie ; though these blighters won't give him to me."

" Oh, I'll get the old man to let you have him all right," Jumbo said with great superiority, " if you can lead me to Carnie's bus and we can hand in some sort of a report." He turned to Cartwright and explained, wisely: "It's this 'salvage' bug that's bitten the lot of them."

"I'll lead you to the spot," said Cartwright, "and then we'll find a dinner for you."

"Oh, no, you *won't*," said John. "Thanking you and all that—but you won't. We're off back, hell for leather and lickety-scoot as soon as the shelling stops."

"Shelling?" said Cartwright, and then in the Colonel's words, "What shelling?"

"Holy Moses!" said Jumbo. "There they go again —'what shelling' when the terrain is *lousy* with shells. And if the Duchess and I get back alive——" It was banter, but they were uncomfortable enough on that evening which was as quiet as any that Cartwright had known.

On the way to the sticks and rags and scrap-iron whereon they would make, in due course, a 'report' they ducked when a shell burst a quarter of a mile away, and paused in their walking when a whine tore the air, so distant that it would end somewhere near Lille.

"Any shooting for you to-night?" John asked casually as they were coming back from their lightning post-mortem.

"Oh, yes," said Cartwright, "any amount—later on. We'll get started as soon as you've gone—if you really won't stay to dinner."

"Well—we really won't," said John. Presently he said, "I say, Dad? D'you think you could persuade your commander to let Jumbo and me touch off a shell or two?"

"I am the commander for the moment," said Cartwright.

"Golly!" said John. "Hear that, Jumbo? My dad *commands* this battery."

"Let him," said Jumbo sardonically. "He's welcome!"

"Jumbo, let's touch off a couple of shells, just to give the Mess something to write home about."

" Touch off as many as you like," said Jumbo. " I'll
go below and wait for you."

He did actually go below, while Cartwright called the
battery into action and gave it a target.

" Jumbo's no end of a chap, really," John said, and
he whispered with bated breath, " he's brought down
twenty-three. But this shelling isn't much in our line,
you know."

" And you ? " asked Cartwright, morbidly. " How
many have you——"

" Oh—if they give me to-day's," said John, " and I
believe they will—three and a couple of shares in two-
seaters the gang has brought down."

The guns were reported ready and Cartwright took
John to number six, and said to the layer, " This flying-
officer wants to tell his Mess when he gets back that he's
fired a real gun. He brought down a Bosche to-day, but
that isn't enough. . . . You take hold of that trigger-
lanyard, Johnnie, and give it all the wallop you can when
the Sergeant says " Fire ! Steady a minute. Have a
trial one first."

The number two took out the cartridge and four
slammed the breech home, grinning.

" Keep your legs out of the way, Sir," said the number
three, and handed John the lanyard. " Jerk it good and
proper."

John jerked successfully ; and the charge was replaced.

Cartwright ordered a round of battery fire.

John pulled the flaps of his cap down over his ears,
fired his round in great style and then bolted out of the
pit to the delight of the gunners.

Jumbo came dancing out of the cellar. " I say,
Cartwright *père*," he said, " let's have one, too. That
is, if the Duchess is still all right. It struck me down
there something like the William Tell effort—shooting
buns off the boy's head business—it must be safe enough."

" Come on," said Cartwright, " you can have a
duet."

He took him to number five and deposed the layer for
him, and instructed him in the jerking of a lanyard.

" We'll give you a section salvo," he said. " Wait for the word ' fire ' when I shout ' Left section—salvo—salvo—*fire*.' "

" Right you are," said Jumbo. " All aboard."

" Mind yer knee, Sir," said the number two of Jumbo's crew, and pushed the knee clear of the breech's recoil.

Cartwright saw the two of them standing there beside the shining breech-blocks among the grubby gunners ; and for an instant his pulses froze.

There had not been a premature in this battery since he had known it ; and a premature, by all the odds, was approximately due. A premature, again by all the usual odds, would lay out three or four of the six or eight grouped about the unsheltered guns. . . . But then he realised—though for an instant he had forgotten it—there were no odds in the whole affair, one way or the other ; no ghost of a system anywhere. Six shells were as likely to premature in succession or in mad unison, as an isolated one in a million. A man was as likely, or as grotesquely unlikely, to be shot in his first ten minutes in the line as during the last ten seconds of the whole war.

" You dirty little funk, Duchess," Jumbo called, " what have you got your lugs muffled up for ? Look at me standing up to it. And I bet I'll keep my eyes open all the time, too."

" Section—salvo—salvo—*fire*," said Cartwright and the shells sailed off—Jumbo's, as he at once bragged, making the better row of the two, whistling like a top, with some little jaggedness of grit or a burred edge on the driving-band.

They went off, after another drink, thinking well of themselves and their evening's work.

But they were afraid.

In that fact was surprising comfort ; since, for all their robustious, Rennie-like foolery, their fear was obvious. It was a night of all nights when Cartwright or Dickinson would have gone very far towards guaranteeing universal safety ; and so, that they should fear on such a night gave proportion to the scale of their daily hazard. . . .

He and Dickinson walked along with them towards the tender that was waiting for them near Brigade, to take them thirty or forty miles to their aerodrome.

" Look after yourself, old chap," Cartwright said in an undertone when they had dropped a little behind the other two.

" Me ! " said John.   And then, " Good God !   You're a nice one to talk I   Don't forget, there's no going over the top for us like there is for you poor blokes."

" We don't go over any tops now, John," said Cartwright.   " But you—I should have put it that you go over the top, more or less, twice a day.   It is twice a day, isn't it ? "

" Oh, yes, it's a brace of flips—most days," John admitted.   " But it's not like yours, and I'm used to it now. . . .   And if you call this *quiet* "—he had winced at a burst that was no more than a little flash in a meadow five hundred yards away—" if you call this *quiet*——" He gave it up, leaving the condition of his clause unfulfilled.   " Golly, Dad," he said.   " You're a rum old stick."

" Well—take care of yourself all the same," said Cartwright, since comparision and assessment of chances were a futility.

" That," said John, " is exactly what the ratepayers' twenty-five bob a day is invested in.   Don't worry. ' Value for money ' is the motto of the Service."

" What sort of machine are you flying ? " Cartwright asked, when they came up with Dickinson and Jumbo who had stopped for them.

" Oh—well," said John, " 's matter of fact, you never know, you know.   Do you, Jumbo ?   We've all sorts at the 'drome.   Might be this or that or anything.   Mightn't it, Jumbo ? "

Any batman would have known that he was lying, but Jumbo mumbled something appropriate for assent.

" Come and look us up some time," said Jumbo, as they shook hands.   " There's always a blow and a harsh word for honest soldiery."   He gave the number of their squadron.

Cartwright, in the phrase of honest soldiery, said, " Some 'opes—I don't think. Forty miles——"

" By the Lord!'' said John with sudden inspiration, " come now ! There'll never be such a chance again. We've got the tender and you'd be back by midnight.''

" You forget,'' said Cartwright, " that I'm commanding the battery.''

" And *I* was led to believe,'' said Jumbo thoughtfully, " that individuals who commanded batteries had bald, pink heads with wrinkles and little blobs on them, and guts full of chutney and Poonah ; blokes all plastered up with notices, ' Do not spit. Penalty, forty shillings,' and braids and ribbons and crowns and what not.''

Cartwright said, " That was usual, once.''

The handshaking was done.

" Wish you could have come, Sir, all the same,'' said Jumbo.

" Wish I could,'' said Cartwright. " Well . . . so long, John. Good luck ! ''

" Good luck, Dad ! I'll take pen in hand and indite a few kind words to Mother when I get back. I'll leave out the shelling—except the bit Jumbo and I did for you. Well—good luck ! ''

MEDAL WITHOUT BAR   CHAPTER CII

ONE fact appeared quite clearly during the next weeks : conditions were variable for the batteries. There were days of action and menace, and days that even Jumbo and John would have admitted were quiet ; but for the flying-men there were no such variations. The act of flying at all involved them, as far as one could see, in the same invariable circumstances. . You could, if you still believed in odds, say that as the end was neared the odds against the Artilleryman lengthened ; against the airman they would remain the same till the last minute.

November mornings trundled into November nights and dawns and noons, and nights again. . . .

And there was still a chance. The battery might be asleep at last, in a barn or a ditch, mute and muffled in heavy quiet, at dawn or midnight or at noon. But there would still be 'planes in the air, the popping of Archies, the rattle and rap of duellists.

On the very last night of all the inanity, when even in the horse-lines hard by the guns, talk was utterly spent, the air was still taut with chance ; for 'planes were still up.

It was not a sleepless night for any in the battery, that night of November the tenth ; not a night of suspense, for even if some circumstance had kept the battery standing all night—standing, it would have slept.

Philosophy and every last anxiety, weary and intolerable, were sunk in the depths of emptiness enveloping the consciousness of men.

The Quartermaster-Sergeant had no rum ; the Mess no whisky.

'Planes flew ; but the battery, with Cartwright, slept.

At as many minutes past eleven next morning as it took an inexpert man to cycle from the battery to Brigade, Cartwright was with the Adjutant, persuading him to wangle an inquiry through Division and Corps and wherever else it might be necessary to John's squadron, after the state of John's health.

.   .   .   .   .   .

It was three o'clock in the afternoon, when Cartwright was again sleeping on the floor of an outhouse, that the apparition of John woke him by shaking his foot. With him were the battery orderly again, from Brigade ; and again Jumbo.

John was very neat and spruce, very much shaved, smoking a cigarette in an elegant long holder, and carrying a large attaché-case.

" Hello ! " said Cartwright when he had blinked himself into an acceptance of them and a new acceptance of the strange vacuum that was only the startling silence of guns. " Hello—so the message did get through to you ? "

" Message ? " said John. " It wasn't a proper message. It was just a general sort of rumour, Dad—that batteries and that sort of thing had run quite dry. So Jumbo and I thought—well, we collared a tender—Jumbo's promotion came through last week—we collared a tender and got your pin-point from a cheery bloke at Corps. And look here—— " He snapped the natty, initialled attaché-case open and disclosed the golden necks of three bottles of Johnnie Walker sticking out of the towel that nested them.

" John, old fellow," said Cartwright ; " Jumbo—— " then he stuck.

But they stayed there, suspended in the void of the new silence that was peace. Men moved and shouted outside, horses chuffed and stamped and snorted ; but they, too, were within the deathly quiet and did not serve to break it. . . .

And that was the way of its ending.

The tide had simply washed them up with bones and breath and blood still in them.

.   .   .   .   .   .

Women—good and happy, sound and sensible and great as Dorothy herself—such women can now be heard to say, " No. Things haven't changed at all. It hasn't done a bit of good. There was something about it all that men must have *liked*—and would like—*again*—or you wouldn't think about it the way you do ; and read those books ; and *talk* about it—— "

The sons and daughters begotten of these survivors— wise and wideawake as Cartwright's David with his deadly approach shots and his six handicap ; shingled and serene and nimble as his David's new spouse, unshaken and unshakable even by the bearing of a baby—they say, these sons and daughters, and they say rightly— " After all, ten—twelve years—it's a long time, you know. And what I mean to say is, it's not a good soldier we're looking for ; is it ?—it's a chauffeur. . . ."

These are the things they say, and rightly, for they have seen only the badness of that execrable job. Those who saw not only the job's badness but the best, also, that was made of it, pause. They have no answer. For they are the generation of the broken-hearted.

Pausing, they behold the ghosts that rise from the tide's inscrutable blackness ; and they look upon the shadows of them whose mighty fellowship made misery tolerable.

So it is not for War they yearn in their pausing. Their eyes have seen and their ears have heard arguments for Peace incontrovertible by any wit of man.

Their yearning is for man's brotherhood, revealed to them only through the chaos of his imbecility—the brotherhood whose tokens are the simplicities of courage and faith ; and laughter.

THE END

Lightning Source UK Ltd.
Milton Keynes UK
UKHW021818080822
407006UK00010B/2784